Second Language Writing Systems

SECOND LANGUAGE ACQUISITION 11

Series Editor: David Singleton, *Trinity College, Dublin, Ireland*

Second Language Writing Systems

Edited by

Vivian Cook and Benedetta Bassetti

Viva Books

New Delhi | Mumbai | Chennai | Kolkata

Bangalore | Hyderabad | Kochi | Guwahati

First Indian Edition 2010

VIVA BOOKS PRIVATE LIMITED

- 4737/23 Ansari Road, Daryaganj, New Delhi 110 002
  E-mail: vivadelhi@vivagroupindia.net, Tel. 42242200
- Plot No. 76, Service Industries, Shirvane, Sector 1, Nerul, Navi Mumbai 400 706
  E-mail: vivamumbai@vivagroupindia.net, Tel. 27721273, 27721274
- Jamals Fazal Chambers, 26 Greams Road, Chennai 600 006
  E-mail: vivachennai@vivagroupindia.net, Tel. 28290304, 28294241
- B-103, Jindal Towers, 21/1A/3 Darga Road, Kolkata 700 017
  E-mail: vivakolkata@vivagroupindia.net, Tel. 22836381, 22816713
- 7, Sovereign Park Apartments, 56-58, K. R. Road, Basavanagudi, Bangalore 560 004
  E-mail: vivabangalore@vivagroupindia.net, Tel. 26607409, 26607410
- 101-102 Mughal Marc Aptt., 3-4-637 to 641, Narayanguda, Hyderabad 500 029
  E-mail: vivahyderabad@vivagroupindia.net, Tel. 27564481, 27564482
- First Floor, Beevi Towers, SRM Road, Kaloor, Kochi 682 018, Kerala
  E-mail: vivakochi@vivagroupindia.net, Tel: 0484-2403055, 2403056
- 232, GNB Road, Beside UCO Bank, Silpukhuri, Guwahati 781 003
  E-mail: vivaguwahati@vivagroupindia.net, Tel: 0361-2666386

Published by arrangement with

Multilingual Matters Ltd.
Frankfurt Lodge, Clevedon Hall
Victoria Road, Clevedon BS21 7HH
England

ISBN 978-81-309-0514-3

Published by Vinod Vasishtha for Viva Books Private Limited, 4737/23, Ansari Road, New Delhi - 110 002. Printed and bound by Jaina Offset Printers, Delhi.

Contents

Acknowledgements

We are grateful to the authors who gave their time and support to this project and produced such interesting and diverse contributions. We hope they will be as pleased with the result as we are. We are also grateful to David Block and Iggy Roca for comments on various parts of this book, and to Charmian Kenner for permission to reproduce a figure from 'Biliteracy in a monolingual school system? English and Gujarati in South London', in *Language, Culture and Curriculum*, 13. The editors would also like to thank each other as this project could never have emerged from one of us alone.

Benedetta would like to thank her parents, Dr Francesco and Mrs Orietta Bassetti, for their constant psychological support and for sending tons of Italian chocolate from across the Channel.

Finally the editors would not have managed without the musical works of Miles Davis, Enrico Pieranunzi, Domenico Scarlatti, Padre Antonio Soler, Antonio Vivaldi and Cassandra Wilson. Fortunately the editors' views on writing systems were more harmonious than their musical tastes.

Contributors

Nobuhiko Akamatsu is a psycholinguist teaching at Doshisha University, Japan. He holds a Ph.D. in Education from the Ontario Institute for Studies in Education (OISE), Canada. His current academic interests include first language effects on second/foreign language reading, automatisation of word-recognition processing, and the bilingual lexicon.

Department of English, Doshisha University, Imadegawa-Karasuma Kamigyo-ku, Kyoto 602-8580, Japan: nakamats@mail.doshisha.ac.jp

Benedetta Bassetti is completing her Ph.D. in Applied Linguistics at the University of Essex, UK, on reading processes in learners of Chinese as L2. She has presented her research at various international conferences. Her interests are: second language acquisition, second language writing systems and bilingual cognition.

benedetta@onetel.net.uk

Nobuko Chikamatsu teaches Japanese and Applied Linguistics in the Department of Modern Languages, DePaul University, USA. She holds a Ph.D. in Linguistics from the University of Illinois at Urbana-Champaign. Her research interests include second language word recognition, reading and writing.

DePaul University, Department of Modern Languages, 802 West Belden Ave., Chicago, IL 60614, USA: nchikama@condor.depaul.edu

Gloria Shu-Mei Chwo is currently completing her Ph.D. in Applied Linguistics at the University of Essex, UK. She worked at different levels in the education system of Taiwan. Her main interests are in word recognition in Chinese and English and the teaching of reading, especially in her home country, Taiwan.

Department of Language and Linguistics, University of Essex, Wivenhoe Park, Colchester, CO4 3SQ, UK: cho2.cheng@msa.hinet.net

Vivian Cook works at Essex University, UK. He is chiefly known for developing the multi-competence view of second language learning. He was founder and first President of the European Second Language Association. He has been involved in researching the English writing system for some time.

Department of Language and Linguistics, University of Essex, Wivenhoe Park, Colchester, CO4 3SQ, UK: vcook@essex.ac.uk

Therese Dufresne, Ph.D., has a research affiliation with the University of Ottawa. She is currently a school principal and educational researcher in the Sir Wilfrid Laurier School Board, Rosemère, QC, Canada. Her broad research areas are language, learning and second language education, specifically language and literacy research and the sustainability of early interventions in promoting literacy.

Principal, Terry Fox School, 900 Des Lacasse, Laval, QC, Canada, H7K 3V9; 615 du Côte du Rhône, Rosemère, QC, Canada, J7A 4N6, tdufresne@swlauriersb.qc.ca

Tina Hickey is a researcher in the Psycholinguistics Department at ITÉ, the Linguistics Institute of Ireland. Her current research interests are in L2 reading, first and second language acquisition, immersion education, and bilingualism.

Department of Psychology, Belfield, University College Dublin, Dublin 4, Ireland: tina.hickey@ucd.ie

Keiko Koda is Associate Professor in the Department of Modern Languages at Carnegie Mellon University. Her research interests include cross-language transfer of reading skills, second-language lexical learning and processing, and biliteracy development. She recently completed a monograph, *Insights into Second Language Reading,* exploring ways to apply cross-linguistic analyses to current, research-based, conceptions of monolingual reading. She also is involved in on-going projects on cross-linguistic variations in reading acquisition, which will be published in a volume, *Learning to Read across Language* (2006).

kkoda@andrew.cmu.edu

Lily Lau, recently graduated with a Masters in Applied Psychology from the National University of Singapore. She now works at Kids in Discovery, a centre which specialises in intervention programmes for children with mild-to-moderate learning difficulties. Her main research interest is on optimising the acquisition of bilingual literacy skills.

Kids in Discovery, 6 Fort Canning Road, YWCA 8th Floor, Singapore 179494: hsll23@hotmail.com

Diana Masny, Ph.D., works in the Faculty of Education at the University of Ottawa, broadly in the areas of language, literacy, culture and second language education. Her current interests include language and literacy research and minority language education.

145, JJ Lussier, Ottawa, ON, K1N 6N5, Canada: Diana.Masny@uottawa.ca; website: http://aix1.uottawa.ca/~dmasny/

Takeshi Okada works at Tohoku University, Japan. After studying conjugational patterns of verbs across text categories in large corpora, he worked at Birkbeck College, University of London, on the corpus analysis of spelling errors generated by Japanese EFL learners. His current interest is using corpus-based research to improve the performance of vocabulary acquisition in computer-assisted language learning (CALL) systems.

2-10-18 Sakurada-higashi, Yamagata City, Yamagata, Japan 990-2323: ty-okada@ma.catvy.ne.jp

Mick Randall is currently a visiting Senior Fellow at the National Institute of Education in Singapore. In addition to working with Malaysian and Chinese teachers, he has worked extensively in the Middle East and completed his doctoral research into Word Recognition in English and Arabic.

Institute of Education, British University of Dubai, P.O. Box 502216, Knowledge Village, Dubai, United Arab Emirates: mick.randall@buid.ac.ae

Susan Rickard Liow is an Associate Professor of psychology at the National University of Singapore. Her research interests include the development of reading and spelling skills in bilingual children, and models of skilled reading in English, Malay, and Mandarin.

Department of Social Work and Psychology, National University of Singapore, 10 Kent Ridge Crescent, Singapore 119260: swksusan@nus.edu.sg

Miho Sasaki is completing her Ph.D. in second language acquisition at the University of Essex, UK, and now working at Ibaraki University, Japan. Her current interests are L1 and L2 reading processes, acquisition of writing systems, and bilingual cognition, focusing on English and Japanese. Her research has been presented at various international conferences.

mihosasaki@yahoo.co.uk

Stephan Schmid works at the Phonetics Laboratory of the University of Zurich, Switzerland. He obtained a Ph.D. in Italian linguistics and spent two years as a research fellow at the University of Padua, Italy. His current interests deal with sociolinguistics, second language acquisition, and the phonetics and phonology of Italian (and Italian dialects).

Phonetisches Laboratorium der Universität Zürich, Freiestrasse 36, CH-0832 Zürich, Switzerland: schmidst@pholab.unizh.ch

Phil Scholfield is a senior lecturer in applied linguistics at the University of Essex, UK. His main research interest is vocabulary in English as a foreign language, including learners' dictionaries, vocabulary teaching methods and the strategies learners use when learning vocabulary and handling it in the process of speaking, writing and reading.

Department of Language and Linguistics, University of Essex, Wivenhoe Park, Colchester, CO4 3SQ, UK: scholp@essex.ac.uk

Harold Somers is Professor of Language Engineering at the University of Manchester, UK. Although his main field of research has been Machine Translation, he is also interested in corpus linguistics and its application to various areas of Computational Linguistics including CALL and SLA, as well as resources for minority languages, and in language engineering applications to assistive computing.

Manchester School of Informatics, University of Manchester, P.O. Box 88, M60 1QD, UK: harold.somers@manchester.ac.uk

Ans Van Berkel is an applied linguist working at Free University Amsterdam, the Netherlands. After studying French and Applied Linguistics she worked in a teacher training college. Her current interests are dyslexia and L2 learning, and Writing Systems.

Vrije Universiteit, Faculteit der Letteren, De Boelelaan 1105, NL 1081 HV Amsterdam, Holland: aj.van.berkel@let.vu.nl

Walter Van Heuven is a postdoctoral researcher working at the Radbond University of Nijmegen, the Netherlands, where he obtained his Ph.D. on visual word recognition in monolingual and bilingual readers. His current research project focuses on the wiring of the language network in the bilingual brain.

Nijmegen Institute for Cognition and Information (NICI), Radbond University Nijmegen, PO Box 9104, 6500 HE Nijmegen, the Netherlands: w.vanheuven@nici.ru.nl

Chapter 1

An Introduction to Researching Second Language Writing Systems

VIVIAN COOK and BENEDETTA BASSETTI

Over the past 10 years, literacy in the second language has emerged as a significant topic of enquiry in research into language processes and educational policy. This book provides an overview of the emerging field of Second Language Writing Systems (L2WS) research, written by researchers with a wide range of interests, languages and backgrounds, who give a varied picture of how second language reading and writing relates to characteristics of writing systems (WSs), and who address fundamental questions about the relationships between bilingualism, biliteracy and writing systems. It brings together different disciplines with their own theoretical and methodological insights – cognitive, linguistic, educational and social factors of reading – and it contains both research reports and theoretical papers. It will interest a variety of readers in different areas of psychology, education, linguistics and second language acquisition research.

What this Book is About

Vast numbers of people all over the world are using or learning a second language writing system. According to the British Council (1999), a billion people are learning English as a Second Language (ESL), and perhaps as many are using it for science, business and travel. Yet English is only one of the second languages in widespread use, although undoubtedly the largest. For many of these people – whether students, scientists or computer users browsing the internet – the ability to read and write the second language is the most important skill.

The learning of a L2 writing system is in a sense distinct from learning the language and is by no means an easy task in itself, say for Chinese people learning to read and write English, or for the reverse case of English people learning to read and write Chinese. Italian learners of English still face the problem to some extent since, even if both English and Italian are written with the Roman alphabet, they are read and spelled in different ways. When L2 learners become fully-fledged L2WS users, they still differ from native users of the target writing system. From one perspective, they are less efficient than first language writing system (L1WS) users; they are slower at reading the second language than people who read only one writing system and often have problems with comprehension and memorising due to inefficient decoding. From a more positive perspective, they are simply different from L1WS reader-writers of the target writing system, with different reading and writing processes that result from the interaction of previously developed reading and writing processes with the characteristics of the new writing system. Not only do L2 researchers and teachers need to bear in mind these differences between L1 and L2 users of writing systems but so do those working in the psycholinguistics and neurolinguistics of reading and writing.

Research on L2 writing systems is at present scattered across different research areas within applied linguistics, psycholinguistics and other disciplines. This book aims to present this interdisciplinary research area to students, teachers and researchers in different fields of second language acquisition or writing system research. This introduction sketches the common background and terminology of writing systems research in general, concentrating on the cross-linguistic aspects, as a basis for outlining some of the previous achievements of L2WS research. It provides an introduction to the whole of this field, for those who are unaware of its scope and achievements, as well as to the papers in this volume. It is intended partly as a reference source that readers can go back to while reading the following chapters.

The Nature of Writing Systems

Before looking at how L2WSs work, we first need to establish the basis for the concept of writing system itself. This section provides an overall view of writing systems, together with some of the crucial terms. First we outline the major types of writing system in terms of the meaning-based versus sound-based division, then the variations in sound-based systems, particularly in terms of phonological 'transparency'. Next we outline some other variable characteristics of writing systems relevant to their acquisition and use. More detailed accounts of writing systems can be found in Coulmas (1989, 2003), Cook (2004a) and Sampson (1985).

What is a writing system?

The term 'writing system' has two distinct meanings, one attached to general ideas of writing, one to specific languages. In the first sense, a writing system is 'a set of visible or tactile signs used to represent units of language in a systematic way' (Coulmas, 1999: 560). The various types of writing system are primarily distinguished by the type of linguistic unit represented, whether consonants (consonantal WSs), morphemes (morphemic WSs), phonemes (alphabetic WSs) or syllables (syllabic writing systems).

In this general sense 'writing system' is related to the terms 'script' and 'orthography'. A 'script' is 'the graphic form of the units of a writing system' (Coulmas, 2003: 35), that is to say, its actual physical form – letters, characters, or whatever. For instance, the Roman alphabet is a script, it is one of the actual physical forms of alphabetic writing systems. A particular type of writing system may in fact employ very different scripts. Alphabetic writing systems take many forms, say, the scripts used in Devanagari, Greek, Cyrillic or Roman alphabets. 'Orthography' on the other hand is the set of rules for using a script in a particular language (e.g. the English or Italian orthography for the Roman alphabet), such as symbol–sound correspondences, capitalisation, hyphenation, punctuation, etc. For instance, the Roman alphabet letter <j> is read as /dʒ/ in the English orthography and as /j/ in the Italian orthography (for native words). The same script may instantiate orthographic rules of different languages: the Roman alphabet is used in different ways in the English and Italian orthographies.

The second sense of 'writing system' overlaps with orthography by referring to the set of rules employed in a particular language for spelling, punctuation etc, namely 'the English writing system', 'the Japanese writing system', and so on. 'In this sense a writing system is language specific' (Coulmas, 1999: 560). The writing system for a language may include more than one script or general writing system type, as in the Japanese combination of kanji characters, kana syllabic symbols and Roman alphabet script. While Japanese is often considered the classic example of a mixed writing system, writing systems of other languages also have elements of other types nestling within them. For instance, English, which is primarily alphabetic, contains syllabic symbols, as in <c u l8er> ('see you later') and morphemic symbols, such as <£ & ed> (representing the meanings 'pound', 'and' and 'past'). We also feel it is important to distinguish a 'language' from a 'writing system' used to represent a particular language; 'Japanese' is not the same as the 'Japanese writing system'; the English language could logically be written in the roman alphabet or in Braille or in the Shavian alphabet and was indeed for a time taught to children through the initial teaching alphabet (ita) (Pitman, 1961).

Writing system researchers rarely agree on how these terms should be used, in particular shifting between the two meanings of 'writing system'. We will try to adopt a few standard terms here, mostly following Coulmas (1989, 2003). These are intended as a rough working guide rather than representing a theoretical position. We will also adopt the convention of presenting examples where the actual written form is important between angled brackets, as in <cough>, with the exception of non-Roman alphabet symbols where it becomes awkward; examples of spoken forms will be presented in International Phonetic Alphabet (IPA) transcriptions between slashes, as in /kɒf/ (suprasegmentals such as tone will not usually be shown); the word itself as a lexical item neutral between speech and writing will be in single quotation marks 'cough'; it is, however, hard to be consistent in observing this three-way distinction in practice. Contributors to this book who are using different terms and conventions will explain their own usage in their chapters.

Overall Terms

Writing system:

either

(i) the overall term for the ways in which written symbols connect to the language (e.g. alphabetic, syllabic writing system)

or

(ii) the specific rules for writing used in a particular language (the English writing system, the Chinese writing system . . .)

Script: the physical implementation of the writing system (e.g. the Roman and Cyrillic alphabets for alphabetic writing systems)

Orthography: the rules for using a script in a particular language (e.g. the English or Italian orthography for the Roman alphabet).

Types of writing system

The smallest units in a writing system are its *graphemes*, or written symbols. Following Sproat (2000), this introduction uses 'grapheme' as a convenient term for the smallest unit of a writing system, regardless of any relationships between the words 'grapheme' and 'phoneme' – essentially as a synonym for 'written symbol'. The major divide between the writing systems of the world has been seen as whether their graphemes connect with meanings, as in Chinese – 中文 means 'Chinese', regardless of how it is said – or connect with sounds, as in Italian – 'italiano' is read aloud as /italjano/, regardless of what it means. This fundamental division is central to many of the issues in writing system research, generating massive amounts of research and controversy. A major topic in L2 research concerns people who have acquired a meaning-based L1 writing system, such as that used in Chinese, switching to a sound-based L2WS, as used in English, and vice versa. This overall division is illustrated in Figure 1.1.

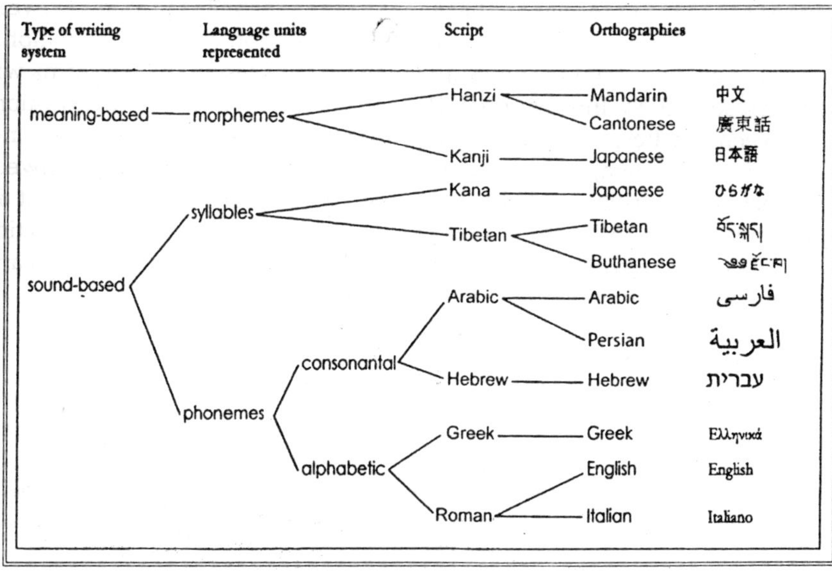

Figure 1.1 Major types of writing system (examples are the names of the language given in the script)

Meaning-based writing systems

Meaning-based writing systems connect graphemes (written symbols) and meaning directly. The main examples are the Chinese characters called hanzi and the Japanese equivalent kanji, which represent morphemes, i.e. units of meaning. For instance, the hanzi 文 represents the morpheme 'written language', whose spoken form is /wən/. Many morphemes share the same pronunciation /wən/, but each has a different written form: when /wən/ means 'to hear' it is written as 闻; when it means 'mosquito' as 蚊; when it means 'line' as 纹. These characters have been called ideographic, logographic, morpho-syllabic, etc., drawing attention to alternative concepts of the script as being based on ideas, words, morphemes or syllables. The term preferred here is morphemic, that is to say the representation of morphemes as graphemes (written symbols), distancing the term from the spoken language.

Meaning-based systems can be read by people who do not know the phonology of the language or who indeed speak different languages: 文 means 'written language' regardless of whether it is said /wən/, as in Standard Chinese, or /mɐń/, as in Cantonese. Indeed a Japanese who would read 文 as /bun/ would still understand it as 'writing, literature', as would a Korean who would say it as /mun/.

Nevertheless some elements in meaning-based system may be associated with phonology. For example hanzi contain *phonetic radicals*, components of a character that correspond to some aspects of pronunciation, such as the 隹 /tʂuei/, seen on the right-hand side of 椎 and 锥, both pronounced /tʂuei/. This is not fully reliable since it is also used in 谁 /ʂuei/, 堆 /tuei/, 推 /tʰuei/, 睢 /suei/, etc., where it only indicates part of the pronunciation. Chinese readers can then use this information for guessing the pronunciation of the 80% or so hanzi that contain a phonetic radical. Take the hanzi 刎 /wən/; relying on the pronunciation of its phonetic radical 勿 /wu/ provides the correct first phoneme; analogy with 吻 /wən/ yields the correct pronunciation minus the tone; analogy with 物 /wu/ only provides the first phoneme; etc.

Sound-based writing systems

'Sound-based' ('phonographic') writing systems connect graphemes with the sounds of speech. The unit of speech that the symbol links to varies in different writing systems. In syllabic writing systems each grapheme links to a syllable of the spoken language: for example Japanese kana represent the morae of speech (mostly equivalent to a syllable, but syllables containing geminate consonants, nasals and long vowels are counted as having an extra mora); the word すべての 'subeteno', meaning 'all' consists of four kana – す /su/, べ /be/, て /te/, の /no/. In other writing systems the graphemes links to phonemes: Arabic and Hebrew writing systems represent primarily spoken consonants; the English, Greek and Nepali writing systems represent all the segmental phonemes including vowels. Sometimes a script may combine symbols for individual sounds into a symbol for a syllable, as in Korean han'gul.

Hence we reserve the term 'alphabet' for scripts that represent *all* the phonemes of speech: 'a writing system characterised by a systematic mapping relation between its signs (graphemes) and the minimal units of speech (phonemes)' (Coulmas, 1999: 9); Arabic is an example of a consonantal, not an alphabetic system. This definition then relates to the so-called alphabetic principle: 'one consistent symbol per phoneme' (Carney, 1994: 474), divided into two sub-principles: the one-to-one principle that letters correspond consistently to phonemes and vice versa; and the linearity principle that the linear order of letters corresponds to the order of phonemes (Cook, 2004a: 12–13). It should also be noted that alphabetic scripts themselves do not usually represent tones, even when phonemic, with some exceptions such as romanised Chinese.

Rules for linking sounds and letters and vice versa are called *correspondence rules*, for instance in English the letter <a> corresponds *inter alia* to the phoneme /æ/, in Japanese the kana か corresponds to the mora /ka/. These are *grapheme–phoneme correspondence rules* (GPC rules) when they indicate how the written symbols represent phonemes – <b> written as /b/; in the opposite direction, they are called *phoneme–grapheme correspondence rules* (PGC rules), when they indicate how phonemes are represented by written symbols – /b/ is said as <b>. When the written symbols represent phonological units other than phonemes, they are called *grapheme–sound* (or symbol-to-sound) *correspondence rules*. The notion of correspondence is sometimes shown by the symbol ≡, i.e. <a>≡/æ/ in English <fat>.

The phonological transparency of writing systems

Within the same type of writing system and script, different orthographies vary in the regularity of the correspondences between the phonological and written forms, even for the same unit of language. The writing systems of both Italian and English are alphabetic, since they are both based on the phoneme, and both use the same script, that is to say the Roman alphabet. They differ, however, in the regularity of their correspondence rules. The Italian system is 'phonologically transparent' because letter-to-sound and sound-to-letter correspondences are almost always one-to-one (although less so for varieties other than standard Italian); for instance, <pace> corresponds to /patʃe/ letter by letter. Hence Italian is popularly called a 'phonetic' writing system. English is an example of a 'phonologically opaque' writing system in which the correspondences between sounds and letters are far from regular. This variation is captured by a notion called by researchers variously 'transparency', 'orthographic depth' or 'regularity', the term 'phonological transparency' being preferred here.

English has multiple links between sounds and letters and so needs a complex set of correspondence rules. For example the letter <o> corresponds to at least 10 phonemes: /ʌ/ 'love', /ʊ/ 'good', /ɒ/ 'cough', /ɔɪ/ 'oil', /ə/ 'actor', /uː/ 'moon', /ɔː/ 'floor', /əʊ/ 'dough', /aʊ/ 'cow', /wɑː/ 'memoir'. The phoneme /əʊ/ on the other hand corresponds to at least 8 spellings: <o> 'cone', <ow> 'glow', <ou> 'soul', <au> 'chauffeur', <eo> 'yeoman', <oh> 'ohm', <oo> 'brooch', <eau> 'Beaufort'. English also has non-linear correspondence rules where the order of the information presented in the letters does not correspond to the order in which the sounds are said: the <e> in <dime> shows the preceding <i> corresponds to the 'free' vowel /ai/ rather than to the 'checked' vowel /ɪ/ in <dim>. In addition many English correspondence rules rely on a knowledge of grammar. For instance, the distinction between function and content words separates the voiced correspondence for <th> /ð/ in function words such as <this> from the unvoiced correspondence /θ/ in content words such as <thesis>; the single spelling <ed> is used for the three different spoken forms of the past tense morpheme 'ed' /ɪd/ 'started', /t/ 'liked' and /d/ 'stayed'.

The Italian system on the other hand has almost exclusively one-to-one grapheme–phoneme and phoneme–grapheme correspondences, with some exceptions such as the grapheme <o> which corresponds to both /o/ and /ɔ/. It nevertheless has a few context-determined variants in which the correspondence is based on the presence of other phonemes. /k/ corresponds to <c> before <a> and <o> ('caldo', 'cosa'), but to <ch> before <i> and <e> ('Chianti', 'Marche'), because <ci> and <ce> already represent /tʃi/ and /tʃe/. Since these correspondences are predictable from the following vowel, they are regular despite departing from the strict one-to-one alphabetic principle. Italian has some exception words, in many cases homophonous words distinguished by different spellings (for instance, an extra <i> distinguishes <cielo/celo> 'sky/I hide', both pronounced /tʃelo/). Where Italian uses orthographic rules to determine these variant correspondences, other phonologically transparent writing systems use morphology. In Greek the vowel /i/ can correspond to six different graphemes <ι η υ ει οι υι>; in most cases these variants depend on morphology (Harris & Giannuoli, 1999); when /i/ represents the inflectional ending of a female noun, it is always spelled with <η>. Even an almost totally phonologically transparent system such as Japanese kana has two different symbols for the same sounds /o/ (を/お) and /wa/ (は/わ), depending on whether they are syllables or case particles. The Greek writing system and kana are therefore transparent since, even though their symbol-to-sound correspondences are not one-to-one, they are predictable.

The distinction between phonologically transparent and non-transparent writing systems is not then a matter of either/or but a continuum: English is less phonologically transparent than Italian in that more effort is required to make the connections between letters and sounds in terms both of correspondence rules and orthographic regularities. No writing system is 100% phonologically transparent or 100% opaque, save for phonetic alphabets devised to record spoken language, such as IPA. There is also the issue of dialects: the same writing system usually represents the standard variety more transparently than the various dialects, e.g. RP English <th> corresponds to /ð/ in 'bath', to the surprise of English-speaking children in Essex who pronounce it as /ba:f/.

The concept of phonological transparency applies to different types of writing system as well as within the same type of writing system; for instance morphemic writing systems can be considered less phonologically transparent than alphabetic writing systems. Both Chinese and Japanese are morphemic in that hanzi and kanji characters correspond to morphemes in their respective languages. Chinese is, however, more phonologically transparent than Japanese since each hanzi has a single reading, whereas kanji have multiple readings that depend on the context. For instance, though 文 corresponds only to /wən/ in Chinese, in Japanese it can be read with four distinct pronunciations /mon/, /bun/, /aja/ or /humi/ depending on the context. The pronunciation of a

Chinese hanzi can be determined without knowing the context, whereas reading a Japanese kanji often requires the use of context; in this sense Chinese is more phonologically transparent than Japanese. While it is possible to compare overall writing systems by saying that a morphemic writing system is less phonologically transparent than a phonological writing system, within the morphemic type of writing system itself, Chinese is more phonologically transparent than Japanese, and, within the phonemic type, Italian is more phonologically transparent than English, as illustrated in Figure 1.2 (which inevitably distorts the relationship between kana and alphabets).

The same writing system may also vary in phonological transparency according to the kind of activity being performed. While orthography-to-phonology and phonology-to-orthography conversion rules are equally transparent in Japanese kana or in the Italian writing system, French is more transparent in reading than in writing, because the rules relating letters to sounds are more reliable than those relating sounds to letters, and the same applies to Greek (Harris & Giannuoli, 1999). Even a consonantal writing system like Hebrew, which is not very phonologically transparent as it does not normally represent vowels, is less transparent for writing than reading, because the phoneme-to-grapheme correspondence rules are complex with many graphemes representing the same

	type of writing system	**phonological unit**	**examples**	**transparency level**
more transparent ▲	alphabetic	phoneme	Finnish, Italian English, French	more ▲ less ▼
	syllabic	syllable/mora	Japanese kana Tibetan	more ▲ less ▼
	consonantal	consonant	Arabic, Hebrew	
▼ **less transparent**	morphemic	1 syllable 1	Chinese hanzi Japanese kanji	more ▲ less ▼

Figure 1.2 The phonological transparency continuum

phoneme (Share & Levin, 1999). In general, when there is a difference, the phoneme-to-grapheme correspondences tend to be less transparent than the grapheme-to-phoneme correspondences.

So far, as in most research, we have used 'transparency' in general as a synonym for 'phonological transparency' – the correspondence between the symbols and the corresponding sounds (grapheme–phoneme correspondences). But writing systems also vary along a continuum of morphological transparency. Morphemic writing systems represent morphemes with only slight clues to pronunciation; consonantal writing systems focus more on representing the consonantal roots of morphemes and leave out vowels; mixed systems like English sometimes represent underlying morphemes rather than sounds; even one of the most phonologically transparent systems, such as kana, represents morphology to a certain extent, as seen above. For this reason, 'phonological transparency' is here preferred to 'transparency' to refer to symbol–sound correspondences.

Other aspects of writing systems

As well as the actual letters or characters (graphemes) and the spelling, writing systems also make use of a number of other conventions or devices, which can only be sketched here.

Direction

The orientation of writing on the page varies. English is normally written in rows from left-to-right and from top-to-bottom of the page. Other alphabetic scripts such as Burmese and Greek are also left-to-right. The two consonantal writing systems, Hebrew and Arabic, are, however, right-to-left. The two morphemic writing systems, Chinese and Japanese, were both traditionally written from top-to-bottom in columns from right-to-left across the page; Chinese has chiefly changed to a left-to-right top-to-bottom arrangement. Direction also applies to the orientation of symbols – in the Roman alphabet <d> and <b> are distinguished by the direction in which they face – and to the sequence of pages: in English and Italian books pages are numbered from left-to-right and are turned from right-to-left; the pages of Hebrew or Japanese books are turned from left-to-right.

Punctuation

Most writing systems have added a set of punctuation marks to the letters or characters. According to Nunberg (1990: 10), Western alphabetic writing systems have 'only one system of punctuation ... subject to the fixing of a few parameters'. Full stops <.>, commas <,>, exclamation marks <!> etc. are recognisably similar in many orthographies. Double quotation marks vary noticeably in form, say <“ ”> in England, <" "> in Germany, and <“ ”> or goosefeet <« »> in Italy (but <» «> in Switzerland)

(Bringhurst, 1992; Tschichold, 1928). Spanish introduced sentence-initial <¿> and <¡>. Japanese and Chinese imported punctuation marks over the past 150 years using such distinctive forms as the hollow full stop <。> and the listing comma <、>; Chinese distinguishes between <“ ”> (for quoting) and <« »> (for titles).

Punctuation has two main, often parallel, uses (Cook, 2004a):

(1) to indicate grammatical features of the text (grammatical punctuation), such as the apostrophe which indicates the grammatical relationship of 'John' and 'wife' in 'John's wife'; or the comma that introduces the non-defining relative clause in 'John's wife, who lives in New York, is called Sally'. In particular the full stop <.> is used to signal the end of a written 'text-sentence', which may differ in many ways from a spoken 'lexical sentence' (Cook, 2004a; Nunberg, 1990);

(2) to indicate phonological features of the text (correspondence punctuation), such as commas that indicate pausing and intonation patterns.

Even if the symbols are similar, punctuation is not used in the same way across writing systems, though few accounts of the punctuation of different writing systems exist as yet.

An aspect of writing systems that can be included here is the use of spaces between written symbols. Chinese and Japanese have an even space between the characters; English has a space between words. Hence English and other writing systems that use word-spaces present the reader with a text pre-analysed into words; Chinese and Japanese do not. Word spaces are not necessarily found in sound-based writing systems: they are not used in some syllabic writing systems such as Thai and Tibetan, nor is their use well-established in some alphabetic writing systems such as Vietnamese. Indeed in some writing systems, such as Thai and Burmese, spacing has the function of separating phrases, breath groups etc., rather than dividing words.

Orthographic constraints

Writing systems constrain the position and co-occurrence of symbols: not all graphemes can occur in every position; many are limited in how they may be combined with other graphemes. Alphabetic writing systems may restrict where letters can occur in the word or syllable and what combinations they may take, unrelated to the occurrence of phonemes in the spoken language. English <tch> must be a word-final correspondence as in 'match'; <ch> is its word-initial equivalent 'charm'; English <o> can double as in 'boo', but <a> cannot, with a few exceptions such as 'baa'. In Chinese, the radical ⺮ ('bamboo') can only occur at the top of a hanzi, whereas 心 ('hearth') can only occur at the bottom: 箱/想; 答/念.

These 'orthographic regularities' concern purely written conventions of writing systems based on arbitrary restrictions on the occurrence of symbols in particular positions or combinations. They are neither meaning-based nor sound-based but concern properties of the written form alone.

Letter alphabets

Many alphabetic systems make a distinction between three distinct alphabets (Gill, 1931): lower-case <a b c>, upper-case (capitals) <A B C> and italics <*a b c*>, each with distinct letter forms. In Japanese a similar distinction is made between different kana syllabaries, hiragana shows that a word is Japanese in origin for example きれいな /kiɾeːna/ ('beautiful'), katakana that it is of foreign origin セックスアピール /sekkusuapiːɾu/ ('sex appeal'). In English capitals are used partly to indicate proper nouns <Bill/bill>, partly for emphasis <BILL>, partly for a few special words such as <I> and <Monday> (Cook, 2004a). Italic letters have a similar range of functions for emphasis <on *Mon*day>, and for particular text types such as stage directions <*Exit pursued by a bear.*>. In Italian capitals are used in much the same way as in English, with some differences: for instance they are not used for the word <io> ('I') but are used for <Lei> (formal 'you') – an interesting difference in the pragmatic use of writing systems. Italics are used in Italian for unusual foreign or technical terms, and for titles of books, magazines, music pieces, theatre pieces and paintings, but not for titles of TV programmes (Lesina, 1986). Upper-case letters are not however found in sound-based writing systems other than those using the Roman alphabet or in character-based systems.

Symbol formation

The users of a writing system have to master the conventional ways in which the symbols are formed in handwriting; Chinese hanzi for example are written with a predetermined sequence of strokes, which also serve as a method of organising dictionaries: one method to look up a hanzi is to search under its first stroke and then under the number of strokes it contains. Hanzi are written from top to bottom and from left to right, generally starting with a top horizontal stroke or a left or central vertical stroke; angled lines are drawn clockwise. The hanzi has to be inscribed within a square area in order to look right. English letters are written top to bottom, and loops are drawn both clockwise and counterclockwise; they have descenders and ascenders that go below and above the line – <tdb> versus <pyg>; only capitals are square <TGHLVO>. Modern media are exerting pressure on writing systems, for example by imposing word-spaces on character-based scripts in which they have not previously been used or by making writers of character-based scripts less aware of strokes, since they are all produced simultaneously on the computer keyboard. Similar adjustments have followed earlier changes in the methods of writing, whether chisels, quill pens, metal nibs, typeface or typewriters.

> **Terms for Types of Writing System**
>
> *Alphabetic:* graphemes (letters or letter clusters) represent all the segmental phonemes
>
> *Syllabic:* graphemes represent syllables or morae
>
> *Consonantal:* graphemes represent primarily consonants
>
> *Morphemic:* graphemes such as Japanese kanji and Chinese hanzi represent morphemes; these are also known as characters, logographs and ideograms
>
> *Phonological transparency* (also known as 'orthographic depth' and 'regularity'): a writing system is phonologically transparent to the extent that its graphemes correspond to the spoken sounds of the language
>
> *Direction:* variously used for the left-to-right direction on the page versus right-to-left, for the direction in which individual letters face, and for the sequence of pages in reading, whether left-to-right or right-to-left

Cross-writing-system Differences in Reading, Writing and Metalinguistic Awareness

The characteristics of writing systems described above result in differences in the reading, writing and awareness of different writing systems, as L1 users of different writing systems decode, encode and are aware of different units of language with different degrees of phonological and morphological transparency. This is not to deny that some aspects in the use of writing systems are universal. Dealing with L2WSs, however, necessarily highlights the differences across writing systems and their consequences for L2WS users.

This section describes the cross-writing-system differences in reading, writing and awareness (with a short mention of non-linguistic activities); their consequences for L2WS users will be presented later.

Cross-writing system differences in reading

Psychologists and psycholinguists have most commonly conceptualised the process of reading English words aloud in terms of a *dual-route model*, given in Figure 1.3, sometimes known as the 'standard' model (Patterson & Morton, 1985) (a 'route' is a sequence of processing

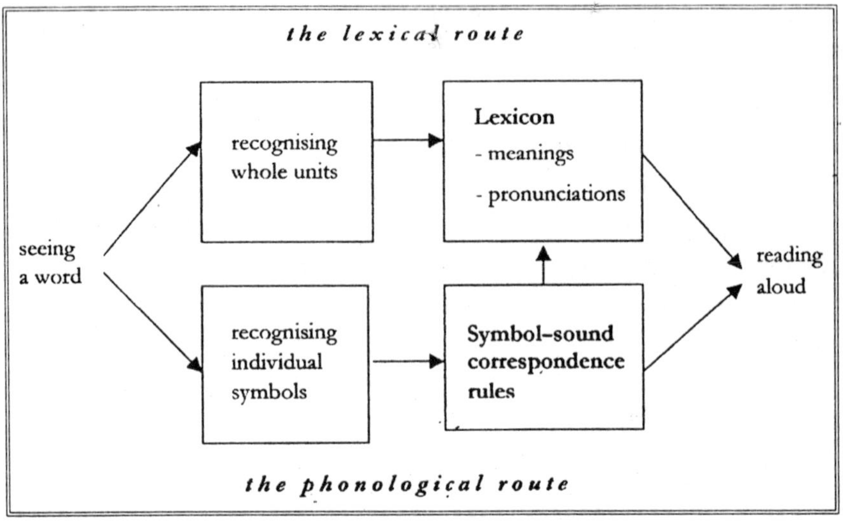

Figure 1.3 The dual-route model of reading aloud

components). One route relies on rules for finding sounds to correspond to letters, the other on whole words held in a mental lexicon – another version of the perennial discussion of language as rules or as instances, found for example in Pinker (1995).

Following the *lexical route* the string of letters is recognised as a whole and then looked up in a mental lexicon in order to retrieve the pronunciation and meaning of the whole unit. The word <yacht> for instance is recognised as a whole word and then checked in the mental lexicon for its pronunciation /jɒt/ and its meaning 'boat'; finally it may be said aloud, though this final step is often superfluous, say in silent reading.

Following the *phonological route*, the word is turned letter-by-letter into the spoken form: <tree> becomes /triː/ by transforming the letter <t> to the phoneme /t/, <r> to /r/ and <ee> to /iː/. Finally either the word can be read aloud, without necessarily knowing its meaning, or the meaning can be consulted in the mental lexicon. The lexical route treats the written symbol as having meaning, which may be connected to sounds; the phonological route treats it as having sounds, which may be connected to meanings.

This basic two route architecture has been verbalised in several different ways. A pair of terms derived from computing is 'addressed phonology' versus 'assembled phonology' (Coltheart *et al.*, 1993): the pronunciation of the whole item is retrieved from its address in the lexicon, or the pronunciation of the item is assembled bit by bit. Other formulations distinguish the 'lexical route' from the 'sub-lexical route', stressing the involvement of the lexicon, or the 'direct route' from the indirect route (see Van Heuven, this volume). The differences in phonological transparency of writing systems led to the Orthographic Depth Hypothesis (Frost *et al.*, 1987), according to which 'deep' writing systems have least connection between symbols and sounds, 'shallow' systems have most.

There are obvious parallels between the two routes and the two main types of writing system. Meaning-based systems exploit the lexical route, connecting Chinese 大 with the meaning 'big' and the pronunciation /ta/ without any intermediate stages. Sound-based systems can use the phonological route connecting the four letters in the Italian <pace> with the sounds /patʃe/. In cross-writing-system comparisons, different writing systems can be seen to rely to a greater or a lesser extent on these two routes.

The dual-route model has provided a useful peg for much research. It demonstrates how it is possible in sound-based writing systems to read words aloud without knowing what they mean, hence allowing nonsense words such as 'varg' or invented words such as 'Accenture' to be rendered in speech. In meaning-based writing systems, this option is not available as a new or unknown symbol carries no clue to its pronunciation: a Japanese place name such as 札幌 (Sapporo) has no obvious pronunciation even for a Japanese news-reader unless they happen to know the characters involved – a common problem with proper nouns. Instead, an Italian place name such as 'Marche' can be read aloud by an English-speaking news-reader as /mɑːkə/ at least recognisably to other English speakers, even if they have never seen or heard it before.

However, the two routes are not restricted exclusively to users of one or the other of the two main types of writing system but can be employed to some extent by users of either system. Frequent English words are probably read as whole items via the lexical route (Seidenberg, 1992); the <e> in <the> is often not noticed by English people as they are processing <the> as a whole by the phonological route (Cook, 2004a). Chinese people similarly have some access to the phonological route, as shown by their use of phonetic radicals.

Even deaf people have been shown to use a phonological route in that they have problems with written tongue-twisters (Hanson *et al.*, 1991). The process of reading probably involves both routes simultaneously. Controversy nevertheless reigns over how the two routes interact, some feeling that the phonological route is primary, even in meaning-based writing systems (Perfetti *et al.*, 1992) – called the 'Universal Phonological Principle' by some – others seeing the routes as a 'horse-race' where one route produces the word quicker than the other (Paap *et al.*, 1992). In general, a distinction should be drawn between reading and recognition: it is commonly agreed that reading texts requires phonological recoding regardless of the writing system, but it is not clear whether single word or morpheme recognition requires phonological recoding and, if so, at what stage.

As well as linking to the two routes, phonological transparency also results in other differences such as:

- The timing of phonological activation: in reading a meaning-based writing system, phonology may be activated after the hanzi or kanji is recognised rather than from the start.
- The effects of word familiarity and frequency: these are greater in less transparent systems than in more transparent systems because whole-word recognition is affected by frequency but the phonological route is unaffected; hence there will be more effects in reading Japanese kanji or English words than Italian words.
- The skills that correlate with learning different writing systems: these are not the same for various writing systems. In alphabetic writing systems, reading skills correlate with phonemic awareness, in meaning-based writing systems with visual skills. Huang & Hanley (1995) found that Chinese children's reading ability correlates with visual skills tests, not with phonological awareness tests as in English-speaking children.
- The use of letter names: English children find letter-names a convenient way into spelling (Treiman, 1993); letter-names are also used by Hebrew children, but in a different way (Levin *et al.*, 2002).
- The grain size: readers of more phonologically transparent writing systems are likely to decode words using letter–phoneme conversion; readers of phonologically deeper writing systems rely on strings longer than a letter, such as word body, rime or whole word; this is called the *grain size,* i.e. the amount of orthographic information necessary for phonological recoding, which varies across orthographies depending on their phonological transparency (Goswami *et al.*, 1998, 2003).
- Furthermore, spelling of less phonologically transparent writing systems requires morphemic awareness (Muter & Snowling, 1997), which may not be necessary in transparent writing systems.
- Neighbourhood effect: cross-linguistic comparisons also showed differences in the neighbourhood effect, that is the fact that a pseudoword is read faster if it has many similar neighbour words differing from it minimally in spelling (e.g. differing in a single letter, say <man> and <mat>) (see Van Heuven, this volume). Cross-linguistic comparison of neighbourhood effects show higher effects in English than in French and in French than in Spanish (Gombert *et al.*, 1997). More phonologically irregular writing systems require greater use of analogy, more phonologically regular ones require less, because grapheme–phoneme correspondence rules are used instead.

- More phonologically transparent writing systems are acquired faster: German and Italian children learn to spell their writing systems faster than English children: Italian children reach 97% accuracy in word reading by the middle of their first year of school (Cossu, 1999).

Cross-writing-system differences in writing

Several aspects of writing vary across writing systems. One is spelling, that is to say converting language into writing. Another aspect is the use of punctuation, orthographic conventions, etc. Finally there is the actual production of the written signs: directionality, stroke order etc; this is non-linguistic in nature and will be dealt with under the Other cross-writing-system differences section (p. 23).

The most studied aspect of writing is spelling. There has been much less research on the relationship between writing systems and spelling than on that between writing systems and reading, and the amount of cross-orthographic studies of writing is much smaller than for reading. Spelling is affected by the type of writing system and its phonological and morphological transparency. Research on English spelling, like research on reading, proposed a dual-route model: the assembled or non-lexical route uses phoneme–grapheme conversion; the addressed ('lexical', 'direct') route uses direct retrieval of a word form from the orthographic lexicon (Barry, 1994) (the orthographic lexicon is the mental repository of the written form of words). This route is necessary because it is not possible to spell a word like /jɒt/ using sound–symbol correspondence rules, as this would be more likely to result in <yot> than in <yacht>. There must therefore be an orthographic lexicon that contains orthographic information about the whole word. But, on the other hand, it is possible to make up a spelling for an unknown word or a nonword (or indeed to misspell a known word because of its sound, as in writing <surfdom> for <serfdom> because of the higher frequency of 'surf' these days). The two routes must therefore coexist in English spelling. Figure 1.4 presents the dual-route model of English spelling. According to this model, irregular and/or frequent English words are spelled using the lexical route, but regular and/or infrequent words are spelled using the phonological route. In more recent approaches, the two routes are seen as simultaneously activated and interacting, with one or the other taking over.

Given the different nature of the linguistic units represented, different writing systems may require increased reliance on one or other of these routes. Writers of Chinese, a morphemic writing system, must retrieve the whole hanzi from memory in order to write it. An unknown hanzi cannot be written down using sound–symbol correspondence rules

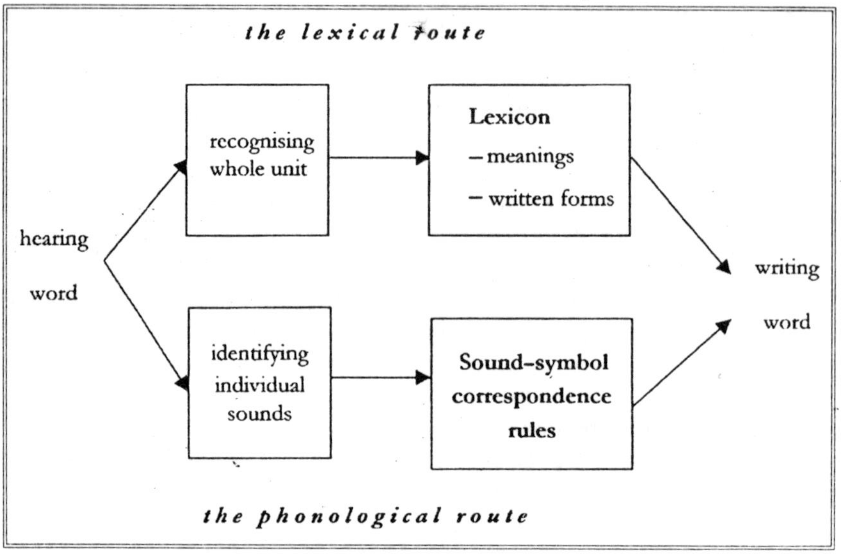

Figure 1.4 The dual-route model of spelling

(apart from experiments in which children are asked to create a hanzi for a new morpheme combining a semantic and a phonetic radical). In consonantal writing systems, Hebrew children, who learn to write Hebrew with diacritics representing vowels, learn to write consonants earlier than vowels, either because of the consonant's central role as the carrier of meaning in the language or because of their centrality in written Hebrew (Share & Levin, 1999).

The skills necessary to learn to write different writing systems may differ. While both phonological and morphological awareness are important in most writing systems, their relative importance may vary according to the type of writing system. For instance, phonological awareness is highly correlated with spelling skills in English children (Goswami, 1999), but not to the same extent in Hebrew or Chinese children (Hanley *et al.*, 1999); while morphological awareness correlates with spelling skills in Hebrew children (Share & Levin, 1999), it would be almost useless to Italian children since very few aspects of their writing system represent morphemes. The stage when these skills are needed could also differ: English children acquire morphemic awareness later than phonemic awareness, for instance misspelling <ed> until the third year of primary school (Bryant *et al.*, 1997).

Within each type of writing system, spelling is also affected by the level of phonological transparency of the orthographies for different languages. For instance:

- German beginner spellers spell differently from English beginners because of the relatively more transparent phonology–orthography correspondence in German: a comparison of German and English first-year schoolchildren spelling cognate words in their respective languages revealed that the English children made more, and more varied, errors, including as many as 22 different spellings for the word <friend> (Wimmer & Landerl, 1997).
- Phonological transparency affects the type of phonological awareness required: for instance, in English children word reading skills correlate with rime awareness, but in Greek children there is no correlation (Goswami *et al.*, 1997), because Greek is read at the grapheme level, English at the level of longer units.
- A less phonologically transparent writing system like English requires not simply the use of sound–symbol correspondence rules but also the use of analogy: for instance, if the English pseudo-word /preɪn/ is presented after /breɪn/ <brain>, it is spelled as <prain>; if it is presented after /kreɪn/ <crane>, it is spelled as <prane> (Campbell, 1983). As Ohala (1992) argues, morphological knowledge helps English spellers: they would not write 'definate' or 'defenite' for <definite> if they realised the connection with <finite>, or 'radience' for <radiance> if they realised the connection with <radiate>.
- Phonological transparency similarly affects the learning process: German children can spell correctly after nine months of schooling (Wimmer & Landerl, 1997). Some L1WSs will therefore be easier to learn than others, other things being equal.

Sometimes learning to spell requires the acquisition of linguistic sub-systems that are not present in the spoken language. For instance, spoken Chinese does not mark gender and it has only one third person singular pronoun /t^{h}a/, but children learning written Chinese must acquire the gender distinction between three different written forms of /t^{h}a/ – 他 (masculine), 她 (feminine) and 它 (neuter). The Taiwanese variety of the Chinese writing system has five written forms for the same spoken pronoun: 他 for male humans, 她 for female humans, 牠 for animals, 它 for inanimate entities and 祂 for divine entities. In the same way, French children learn to mark the singular–plural distinction for the written form of nouns, verbs and adjectives, which has no correspondence in the spoken language: for instance, /pɔm/ corresponds to <pomme> or <pommes> ('apple/apples'), and /vɔl/ to <vole> and <volent> ('[it] flies; [they] fly') (Fayol *et al.*, 1999). They take some time to acquire the distinctions that are not present in the French spoken language (Totereau *et al.*, 1997); experienced adult spellers make mistakes in writing from dictation if they are performing a concurrent task

(Fayol *et al.*, 1994). In the reverse direction, English children have to learn that /t/, /d/ and /ɪd/ all correspond to one written form, the morpheme <ed> (Beers & Beers, 1992). Bryant *et al.* (1997) found that eight-year-olds still get only 57% of regular past tenses correct; the same difficulty appears with plural and third-person <s>s, both written morphemes that represent different spoken sounds (Treiman, 1993).

Cross-orthographic comparisons of 'slips of the pen' also demonstrate systematic differences of spelling: Moser (1991) describes slips of the pen by Chinese writers that could never happen with English writers, such as substituting one hanzi for another with similar meaning but totally unrelated sound or inverting the two hanzi inside a lexical item. He also discusses how similar types of spelling mistake take different forms in the two writing systems. For example 'capture errors' in English involve replacing a part of an unusual word with a similar-sounding part from a more frequently used word, as in writing <enought> for <enough> because the sequence <ought> is more frequent ('thought', 'fought', etc); in Chinese this leads to writing 生 /ʂəŋ/ (be born) instead of 气 /tɕʰi/(anger) because the two hanzi share the same first three strokes but the former hanzi is more frequent (Moser, 1991).

The main alternative to the dual-route model has been the general connectionism model applied to writing. This sees the mind as a unified overall system (Brown & Loosemore, 1994) that cannot be divided into separate modules. Learning spelling means weighting connections between the input letters and the nodes of the system; the more often the reader sees <t> linked to /t/ the stronger the connection becomes. The main argument for a connectionist approach to spelling is provided by the computer simulation by Seidenberg and McClelland (1989), which 'learnt' English spelling from input in this manner, making only a small number of mistakes. An account of a connectionist model is given by Van Heuven in this volume.

Cross-writing-system differences in awareness

In the context of reading and writing research, research on *metalinguistic awareness*, that is to say conscious awareness of language, has focussed on *phonological awareness*. In this context, phonological awareness refers to the awareness of those sound units of the spoken language that are represented in the writing system. Since writing systems differ in the units of phonology they represent, readers of different writing systems need to be aware of diverse linguistic units in order to learn and use their writing system. Given the English-oriented nature of much reading research, researchers have mainly been concerned with *phonemic awareness*, that is to say the conscious knowledge of the phoneme – the minimal segmental unit of phonology – represented by one or more letters in alphabetic writing systems. Only occasionally is phonological awareness extended to the allophonic level, as done in the chapter by Lau and Rickard Liow (this volume) which tests allophonic variation of flapped plosives in English.

A preliminary issue is the chicken and egg problem about whether phonological awareness is necessary for reading or reading creates awareness. Nation and Hulme (1997) suggest that the ability to segment speech into phonemes is a strong predictor of early success at reading and writing. In this volume Koda states that metalinguistic awareness makes an 'irrefutable' contribution to reading (p. 320). In a recent extensive review of studies, Castles and Coltheart (2004), however, found no evidence that phonological awareness precedes and influences reading acquisition. Some phonological categories are created by children when they learn to read, say final nasal consonants in English-speaking primary school children (Treiman *et al.*, 1995): Goswami and Bryant (1990: 19) claim 'explicit knowledge about syllables precedes reading while an awareness of phonemes follows it'.

Non-alphabetic writing systems require other forms of metalinguistic awareness. Learners and users of the Chinese morphemic writing system clearly need to be aware of morphemes rather than phonological units (Li *et al.*, 2002). In Chinese readers, *morphemic awareness* is the ability to match spoken syllables with the written representation of the correct morpheme. Since the same Chinese syllable corresponds to many hanzi with different meanings, children must be aware that the same spoken syllable corresponds to different units of meaning, each represented by a different hanzi. For instance, the spoken syllable /nan/ meaning 'male' is written 男. But there is also a spoken syllable /nan/ that means 'South' and is written 南; for instance, /nan faŋ/ meaning 'the bridegroom's side' is written 男方, /nan faŋ/ meaning 'Southern' is written 南方. A similar issue is seen in English with homophonic words, rather than morphemes, as in /weilz/ corresponding to three words with different spellings, 'Wales', 'whales' and 'wails'. This remains important beyond the beginning stage: if Japanese children are asked to match the definition of an unknown lexical item against lexical items written in kanji or kana, they perform much better with kanji: given the definition of 'leukaemia', they have more difficulty matching it with はっけつびょう /hakket^{s}ubjo:/ than with 白血病 ('white-blood-disease') (Hatano *et al.*, 1981 cited in Nagy & Anderson, 1999). Readers of meaning-based writing systems also need to be aware of semantic radicals at the sub-hanzi level: the ability to identify them correlates with reading ability.

Readers of a syllabic writing system need to be aware of syllables rather than phonemes or morphemes. For instance, Japanese kana represent morae (essentially consonant-vowel (CV) syllables with some exceptions), and so literate Japanese children are necessarily aware of morae (Akita & Hatano, 1999). Hebrew readers, with a consonantal

L1WS, are aware of CV phonological units rather than phonemes; when Hebrew adults were asked to delete 'the first sound' in a CVC Hebrew word, in 27% of cases they deleted the initial CV sequence (Ben-Dror *et al.*, 1995).

Language awareness is thus related to the specific units used in the user's writing system: whether you think of speech as phonemes or as morphemes depends on how you read and write. (And at another level undoubtedly affects the judgement of linguists who have to guard against the trap of seeing other languages through the lens of the phonological categories of their first language, as argued by Faber (1992) and Aronoff (1992).) Nobody needs to be aware of linguistic units that are not represented in their writing system: Brazilian illiterate adults are not aware of phonemes, so that they cannot perform initial consonant deletion tasks (Bertelson *et al.*, 1989), just as Portuguese illiterates cannot segment sentences into words (Morais *et al.*, 1986); English adults are not aware of syllables, so that they disagree with each other on where to place syllable boundaries in English sentences (Miller *et al.*, in preparation); Chinese readers are not aware of phonemes, so that they cannot segment words into phonemes (Perfetti & Zhang, 1991). Interestingly, Japanese children who are literate in syllabic kana can perform a phoneme deletion task with a high level of accuracy, albeit lower than children literate in English (Mann, 1986a); however the children's self-reports revealed that they were operating with morae rather than phonemes: when asked to delete the first consonant in a pseudoword, almost 75% of them either substituted the CV sequence (corresponding to one kana symbol) with a V (corresponding to one kana, i.e. replaced *ki-ru* with *i-ru*), or added a V (one kana) at the end of the syllable and then deleted the initial CV sequence (i.e. added *i* after *ki*, then deleted *ki*: *kiru* → *ki-i-ru* → *i-ru*). Speakers of the same language need to be aware of different linguistic units if they use another writing system with the language. For instance, there are differences in phonemic awareness between Chinese adults who had or had not learnt *pinyin* – a supplementary writing system used to represent hanzi with Roman alphabet letters (Read *et al.*, 1987): Chinese children showed an increase from 35% to 60% accuracy in a phoneme deletion task just 10 weeks after learning *zhuyin fuhao*, another supplementary writing system used in Taiwan (Huang & Hanley, 1997), and similar results were obtained with adults (Ko & Lee, 1997). Equally, Kannada-speaking children, who are literate in a semi-syllabary, perform some phoneme inversion and deletion tasks worse than blind Kannada-speaking children, whose *braille* is alphabetic (Prakash, 2000). The terms normally used to talk about units of language vary; Hebrew speakers only use the names for consonants and names of vowels are specialised knowledge (Tolchinsky & Teberosky, 1997); interestingly the games intended to promote language awareness are writing-system-specific: both American and Japanese children play a game where they have to create a new word with the last sounds of the previous word, but the 'last sound' in the American game is the last phoneme, in the Japanese game the last mora (Akita & Hatano, 1999).

While users of different types of writing system (such as syllabic versus alphabetic) show different levels of awareness of different phonological units (for instance, higher syllabic versus phonemic awareness), within the same type of writing system, users of different orthographies also show different levels of phonemic awareness. For example, although both Italian and English are alphabetical writing systems, Italian children outperform US children on phonological segmentation (Cossu *et al.*, 1988). Furthermore, phonemic awareness is affected by instruction and is higher when symbol–sound correspondences are explicitly taught; Belgian children who were instructed in the phonics method performed phoneme segmentation tasks better than those instructed with the whole-word approach (Alegria *et al.*, 1982).

Other cross-writing-system differences

The type and phonological transparency of writing systems affect other aspects of linguistic activities apart from reading, writing and awareness, for instance, the methods used to recall the written form of a partially unavailable lexical item or to communicate it to others. When English speakers are unsure about the spelling of a word, they can write the word down to see whether it 'looks right', i.e. use the visual form of the word to check it; this is not done by users of a phonologically transparent writing system like Italian. Also, if English speakers need to communicate the written form of a word to others (for instance when the interlocutor did not understand it), they will spell it letter by letter; Italian speakers do not use oral spelling unless there are communication problems, for instance with foreign words or on the telephone. When a Chinese or Japanese speaker cannot recall how to write a hanzi/kanji, they use 'finger-tracing', that is drawing the character in the air according to its stroke sequence, and will also use it to communicate the written form of a word to others.

Apart from the linguistic units represented and the level of phonological transparency, other aspects of writing systems that affect reading and writing are orthographic conventions or physical properties, such as direction, letter formation, etc. For example, because of the left-to-right directionality of their script, English readers are better at identifying letters in horizontal rows than in vertical columns (Freeman, 1980). In addition the orthographic convention of using spacing to separate orthographic words in English text affects English readers' eye movements; their eyes tend to fixate the centre of the word, but due to the lack of interword spacing in Chinese, Chinese readers' eye movements show no preference for word-central positions (Yang & McConkie, 1999); Japanese readers show another pattern of eye movements because their eye movements are guided by the alternation between kana and kanji (Kajii *et al.*, 2001). English readers also have a wide horizontal perceptual span suited to their horizontal writing system; Japanese readers have no differences in horizontal versus vertical perceptual span because they can also read vertically (Osaka & Oda, 1991).

Although this book concentrates on linguistic activities in the L2WS, it is important to note that different writing systems also have an impact on nonlinguistic aspects of cognition. For instance, there are effects of a morphemic writing system on visual memory: the importance of visual memory for using the Chinese and Japanese writing systems results in better memory for geometrical patterns in Japanese children than in English children (Mann, 1986b, but see Flaherty & Connolly, 1995, for counter-evidence). There are also cross-orthographic differences in how writers of different writing systems draw. When Chinese children draw geometric patterns comprising horizontal and vertical lines, they tend to start with the horizontal line, whereas English children start with the vertical line, in accordance with the writing principles for the graphemes in their writing systems (Wong & Kao, 1991). The directionality of the writing system also affects how people perceive movement: when shown small drawings that appear to rotate, English adults perceive the rotation as being right-to-left, but Japanese adults perceive it as being left-to-right (Morikawa & McBeath, 1992).

Directionality also affects the representation of temporal sequences. When asked to put images of events in order (such as having breakfast, going to school, going to bed), English children put images in a left-to-right order, while Hebrew and Arabic children, whose writing system is written right-to-left, choose the opposite direction (Tversky *et al.*, 1991). Also, when asked to name pictures of objects on a sheet of paper, Hebrew children name objects starting from the right and moving to the left and English children start from left and move to the right (Kugelmass & Lieblich, 1979). To take a mundane example, before and after pictures in English advertisements go from left-to-right (for instance, a pile of dirty laundry on the left, then the detergent, then a pile of clean laundry on the right); in Hebrew such advertisements are read from right-to-left. Chinese temporal metaphors refer to 'before' as 'up' (as in 'the week above' meaning 'last week'), whereas English temporal metaphors refer to 'before' as 'left'; time's winged arrow probably goes from left-to-right in all classroom explanations of English tenses. This mirrors the directionality of the two writing systems, where what is written before is above (in Chinese) or on the left (in English). These metaphors in turn influence behaviours such as thinking of 'before' as up or left

(Gentner *et al.*, 2002). Linguists' representations in phrase structure trees clearly also express direction in a left-to-right direction.

Some Cross-writing-system Differences

Reading

- the balance between the two routes (lexical/phonological)
- timing of phonological activation (before/after word recognition)
- correlates of reading acquisition (phonological/morphological awareness, etc.)
- size of unit used for decoding (grapheme, rime)
- size of neighbourhood effects
- use of analogy between words
- speed of learning to read

Writing

- reliance on the two routes (lexical/phonological)
- correlates of spelling acquisition, e.g. phonological/morphological awareness
- size of unit used for encoding (grapheme, rime, etc.)
- use of analogy between words
- time required for learning to spell
- types of spelling error

Awareness

- language units that people are aware of (phoneme/syllable/morpheme, etc.)
- levels of phonological awareness

Other

- methods for recalling partly unavailable written forms
- eye movements in reading, perceptual span, etc.
- preference for direction
- visual memory
- sequences in drawing
- mental representation of temporal sequences

Introduction to Second Language Writing System Research

What is a second language writing system?

The term 'Second Language Writing System' (L2WS) can be applied to any writing system other than the system that the person learnt to read and write for their first language. For instance, the English writing system is a L2WS for a first language writing system (L1WS) reader of Chinese who learns English at school or in the UK; s/he is a L2WS learner. Many L2 speakers can read and write their second language and in this sense are L2WS users; a bilingual secretary in a Japanese company in the US uses Japanese as a L2WS, English as a L1WS (in the literature, L2WS users are often called 'biscriptals' or 'biliterates'). Like 'second language acquisition', Second Language Writing System serves as an umbrella term for a third language writing system, a fourth and so on (although this does not mean that learning or using a L3WS is the same as learning or using a L2WS).

There is therefore a crucial difference between a Second Language Writing System (L2WS) and a Second Writing System – any additional writing system for representing the same language. Children in China learn to read not only Chinese but also the Roman-alphabet-based *pinyin*, which acts as a supplementary second writing system, mostly for pedagogical purposes. On the other hand there are minority or immigrant children who are native speakers of a language, but learn to read in a second language, say Bengali-speaking children in Tower Hamlets in London acquiring literacy in L2 English. In this case they are learning neither a L2WS nor a L1WS, but a *first* writing system that happens to be in their second language. These children are users of *two* languages but *one* writing system. The concepts of language and writing system need to be kept logically separate, even if in most situations they overlap. Indeed there are also children acquiring two writing systems simultaneously, one for the L1WS and one for the L2WS, for example Arabic-speaking immigrant children in the UK learning the English writing system during school hours and the Arabic writing system after school. Some of the chapters to follow will demonstrate the sheer diversity of combinations of language and writing system in, say, children in Singapore (Rickard Liow) or in Switzerland (Schmid).

It is also necessary to make the obvious point that writing system research across languages (cross-writing-systems research) is not the same as L2WS research. Huang and Hanley (1995) compared the use of L1WS Chinese in Hong Kong and Taiwan with the use of L1WS English in England; this does not necessarily tell us anything about the acquisition of Chinese and English as L2WSs. In general, it is important to separate what is cross-linguistic and what is cross-orthographic, i.e. what is L1 transfer of aspects of the first *language* (phonology, syntax, morphology, etc.) and what is L1WS transfer of aspects of the first *writing system* (orthographic conventions, phonological transparency, written morphology etc.).

Terms

L1WS: a writing system that represents the first language.

L2WS: a writing system that represents the second language.

L2WS learners/users: people who are learning/using a second language writing system.

The first writing system: the writing system that the person learns first, regardless of whether it is in their first or second language.

The second writing system: the writing system that the person learns second, regardless of whether it is in their first or second language.

Issues and methods in Second Language Writing System research

The concern of Second Language Writing System research is the reading, writing, learning and awareness of L2WSs by L1WS-literate children and adults, as well as any other consequences of using a L2WS for linguistic and nonlinguistic activities. Like children acquiring their first writing system, L2WS learners are affected by universal aspects of writing system use, by the characteristics of the specific writing systems they are learning and by the limited capacity for decoding and encoding initially available in a second writing system.

Some characteristics of the writing system being learnt may be consistent across L2WS learners as well as across L1WS learners. For instance, a highly transparent phonological writing system is learnt faster than a less transparent one by both L1 and L2 learners. Just as Italian children learn to read Italian faster than English-speaking children learn to read English (Cossu, 1999), so English–Hebrew bilingual children learning to read Hebrew decode L2WS Hebrew words faster than L1WS English words because Hebrew, when it is written with added diacritics to represent vowels, is more phonologically transparent than English (Geva, 1999). Another similarity between L1WS and L2WS learners is that neither are initially proficient in decoding and encoding the writing system. Huge differences in reading speed are normally found between L1WS and L2WS readers; Jackson *et al.* (1994) found that the English reading speed of Chinese students at American universities was more than four standard deviations below the American students' reading speed.

Beyond these shared features with L1WS acquisition, a L2WS learner may have to learn *inter alia*:

- at the most global, a new writing system that represents different linguistic units from his/her L1WS (for instance, consonantal versus phonemic, or syllabic versus morphemic);

- a new script for the same writing system (for instance, both writing systems are phonemic but one is written with the Roman alphabet and the other with the Cyrillic alphabet, say Spanish versus Russian);
- a new level of phonological transparency for the same script (for instance, more or less phonologically transparent orthographies both written with the Roman alphabet, such as Italian versus English, or both written with a morphemic script, such as Chinese and Japanese).

When the learners have essentially finished acquiring the L2WS, they still may read, write, and analyse the L2WS in different ways from the L1WS user of the same system. L2WS learners, however, differ from children acquiring their L1WS because they have already had experience of another writing system. On the one hand, L2WS learners are facilitated because they do not have to learn some basic facts about writing systems, for instance that there is a direction to the sequence of symbols and their orientation. On the other hand they are handicapped because what they already know does not necessarily apply to their new writing system. For instance, English L1WS learners learn that the length of the spoken word in phonemes roughly corresponds to the length of the written word in letters, but English learners of L2WS Japanese cannot apply this knowledge because spoken word length is not reflected in the number of kanji in writing: for instance /ko/ and /mizuːmi/ are both written as 湖.

Main issues in current L2WS research

The bulk of L2WS research to date deals with the effects of the L1WS on the L2WS, particularly the transfer between the two major types of writing system, the sound-based and the meaning-based, and between the two routes for processing, the phonological and the lexical. Research into such effects on L2WS reading began in the early eighties (e.g. Adams, 1982; Barnitz, 1982), but only became widely known through the efforts of Keiko Koda in numerous publications (e.g. Koda, 1988, 1994, 1996, etc.). Within the field of Second Language Acquisition (SLA) research, the transfer of diverse aspects of language from the first to the second language (*language transfer*, see Odlin (1989), which also contains a short section on writing systems) was a major early preoccupation. Recently transfer has been seen as a process that also goes from the second language to the first (Cook, 2003). What makes second language acquisition distinctive is indeed the first language already present in the learner's mind. The major task of SLA research must be to map out the complex relationships between these two languages in the same mind – whether they stay separate, interact or merge.

Because of the distinction between language and writing system, it is not so much aspects of the language itself that may be carried over as the attributes of a particular writing system. It is not Chinese *per se* that is transferred by Chinese learners to the English writing so much as features of the Chinese morphemic writing system. A parallel in other areas of second language acquisition is intonation: speakers of 'tone' languages have a particular set of difficulties acquiring an 'intonation' language and vice versa (Ke, 1992); it is the move from one type of linguistic system to another that is important, not from one language to another. In principle, it is important to separate *language transfer* from *writing system transfer*, say rather than the conventional directions. It is also important to separate *language transfer* from *writing system transfer*. A specific feature of the Italian language may be carried over to English, say writing <*termometer> for <thermometer> because Italian lacks a phoneme /θ/; this is an example of cross-linguistic influence (asterisks indicate impossible spellings). Or a specific feature of Italian orthography may be transferred, say writing <*ingiury> for <injury> because in Italian <gi> corresponds to /dʒ/ before <u>; this is cross-orthographic influence. Transfer shades over into the question of which route is used in processing (reading and spelling) (Hayes, 1988).

Research methods in L2WS research

The different research disciplines involved bring their own diverse methods to the study of L2WSs. Much research consists of quasi-experimental studies, comparing different groups of users of the same writing system (seen in this book for instance in the chapters by Lau & Rickard Liow and by Sasaki). Other quantitative approaches include observational research (seen here in the chapters by Van Berkel and by Somers) and simulations as in connectionist models (seen here in the chapter by Van Heuven). Finally, qualitative approaches can also be used (as in the chapter by Hickey). Tables 1.1 and 1.2 display some of the typical methods employed. This section cites a representative sample of the important papers in this area so that readers can follow up particular approaches or writing systems they are interested in. Table 1.4 organises these in terms of the types of writing system.

Experimental methods

In a sense fully experimental research is not possible when the variable is the L1WS as participants cannot be randomly assigned to groups, unless, say, an artificial writing system were used. Much L2WS research is thus quasi-experimental, involving groups selected by their L1WS and L2WS.

Figure 1.5 gives some of the standard research designs. Most studies employ the same task in the same writing system performed by one or

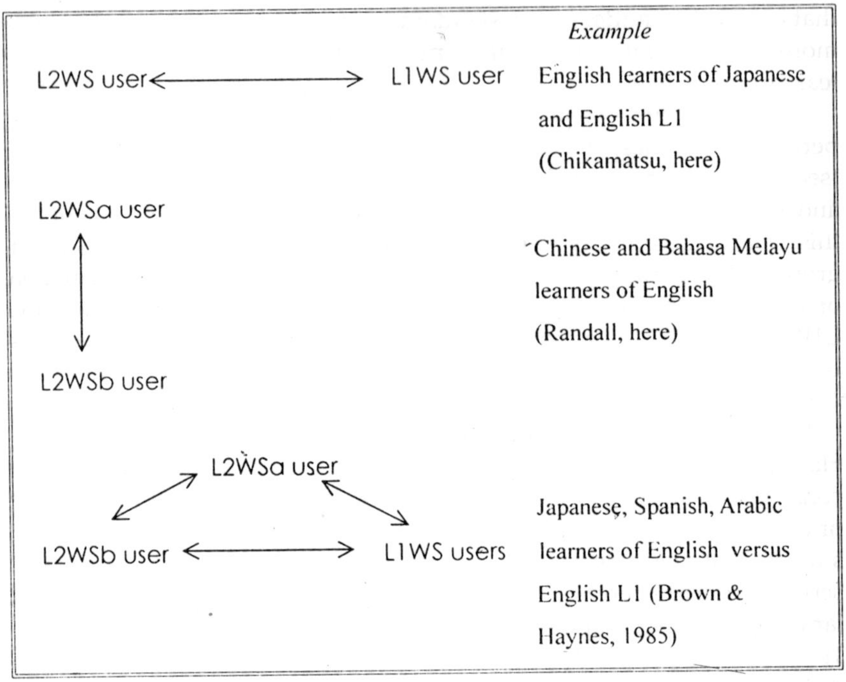

Figure 1.5 Experimental designs

more groups of L2WS users and L1WS users of the target writing system; for instance, English learners of L2WS Japanese compared with Japanese L1WS readers (e.g. Chikamatsu, this book) or by two or more groups of users of the same L2WS with different L1WSs, say, Chinese and Malay learners of English as a L2WS (e.g. Randall, this book). The two designs are combined in studies comparing groups of L2WS users with different L1WSs compared with L1 users of the target writing system, say Japanese, Spanish and Arabic learners of L2WS English with English L1WS users (e.g. Brown & Haynes, 1985; Koda, 1988); the L1WS users can be adults or learners, i.e. children (e.g. Jackson *et al.*, 1999).

Differences in performance are then explained as the consequences of the participants' L1 writing systems, i.e. as transfer from the L1WS to the L2WS. For instance, L1WS readers of alphabetic and morphemic writing systems are compared in a task involving phonological recoding of materials in an alphabetic L2WS; differences are attributed to transfer of reading strategies from their alphabetic or morphemic L1WS (e.g. Wang *et al.*, 2003). Comparing groups of learners of the same L2WS may be less likely to involve an implicit judgment in terms of deficiency than comparing learners with L1WS users (as in one study which declares that the English readers 'set a standard' for word processing), and may be more likely to show the creative processes and strategies in the L2WS learners/users rather than their failure to conform to those of L1WS users.

Other approaches that have been used include predictions about the performance of L2WS learners/users, based on a contrastive analysis (see Lado, 1957, which contains a section on writing systems) of the L1WS and L2WS, which are tested against their actual performance (Schmid, this book). When the variable investigated is not the L1WS, other groups can be used: studies looking at the effects of L1WS instruction or of L2WS proficiency on L2WS use compare groups with the same L1WS and L2WS (chapters by Akamatsu and Scholfield & Chwo, this book), sometimes with L1WS users as controls (Bernhardt & Everson, 1988). The most popular paradigm is participants with a morphemic L1WS combined with an alphabetic L2WS, say Chinese > English (e.g. Haynes & Carr, 1990; Leong & Hsia, 1996; Jackson *et al.*, 1994), but also consonantal L1WSs and phonemic L2WSs (e.g. Randall & Meara, 1988) or alphabetic L1WS and morphemic L2WS (e.g. Hayes, 1988), etc. Some studies also use participants whose writing systems have the same script but with different degrees of phonological transparency, in particular combinations of alphabetic L1WS and L2WS (e.g. Chitiri & Willows, 1997; James *et al.*, 1993). Research usually concerns the reading, writing and awareness of single orthographic units (mostly words, but also kanji or letters), sometimes presented in context (compounds, sentences, etc.) (e.g. Chikamatsu, this book; Randall, this book), sometimes following experimental manipulation, for instance degradation of the word's visual shape (Akamatsu, this book).

In all these methods, researchers measure the time taken to perform the task (response time, reading time, etc.) and the accuracy (number of correct answers), or only one of these two. Standard reading tests can be used (Nassaji & Geva, 1999; Wade-Woolley, 1999). Table 1.1 illustrates a range of the methods that have been employed, including all those represented in this book. This is intended as a nonexclusive list rather than a logical categorisation. (References in brackets are examples of studies that adopted the task.)

The methods used to test awareness of the linguistic units represented in writing systems include a variety of metalinguistic awareness tasks involving recognition or manipulation of linguistic units, some of which are displayed in Table 1.2. These tasks can involve words or nonwords (as in 'poor teddy' → 'toor peddy'). They measure accuracy, but can be used in conjunction with measures of response times, as in the phoneme deletion task in Ben-Dror *et al.* (1995). They can be used for other linguistic units besides phonemes, for instance Bassetti's word segmentation task (this book). Awareness can also be investigated with the same methods used in spelling research, such as spelling (Holm &

Table 1.1 Some experimental tasks for researching reading and writing

Task	*Description*
Word naming (reading/recognition)	Reading aloud the target (word, pseudoword, etc.) as quickly as possible; accuracy or reaction times or both are measured (Akamatsu; Schmid; Scholfield & Chwo, this book).
Oral reading	Reading a text aloud (Jackson *et al.*, 1999).
Silent reading	Reading in silence; reading time is measured in words per minute, seconds per word, hanzi per minute, etc. (Nassaji & Geva, 1999).
Silent reading with comprehension measures	Reading in silence, followed by multiple-choice questions, recall, etc. (Koda, 1995).
Silent reading with eye-tracking	Participants' eye movements are recorded during silent reading, revealing what parts of the text they are reading and for how long (Bernhardt & Everson, 1988).
Item recall	A series of items (words, nonwords, pseudokanji, etc.) are presented, followed by a second series: the participant decides whether s/he has seen the item in the previous series (Sasaki, this book), or which item preceded or followed the one just seen in the previous series (Koda, 1988; Mori, 1998).
Lexical judgment/ decision	Words and nonwords are presented, the participant decides whether each item is a genuine word or a nonword (Chikamatsu, 1996; Muljani *et al.*, 1998).
Similarity judgement	Participants decide whether two items (e.g. words, pseudowords) are the same or different. Items can be presented simultaneously or with Stimulus Onset Asynchrony (SOA) (Brown & Haynes, 1985; Haynes & Carr, 1990).
Auditory/visual word matching	Participants listen to a spoken item (word/ nonword) and choose the one that matches it from a set of written items (Holm & Dodd, 1996).

(*continued*)

Table 1.1 *Continued*

Task	*Description*
Visual search	Subjects check whether a previously presented symbol is present in a list of symbols. For instance, in 'letter cancellation' they have to find a letter in a series of words (Chitiri & Willows, 1997; Green & Meara, 1987).
Sentence acceptability judgment	Deciding whether a sentence is correct or incorrect; the sentence may contain phonological or visual foils, i.e. items (words, hanzi, etc.) that sound or look like the correct item, as in 'a pair is a fruit' (Hayes, 1988).
Spelling test	Timed or untimed test of spelling words from dictation (Brown, 1970; Okada, 2002; van Berkel, this book).

Table 1.2 Some experimental methods for researching phonological awareness

Task	*Description*
Phoneme addition	Adding one phoneme, 'tool' → 'stool' (Leong, 1997).
Phoneme counting	Counting the 'sounds' in words (Holm & Dodd, 1996).
Phoneme deletion	Deleting one phoneme, 'smeck' → 'meck' (Wade-Woolley, 1999).
Phoneme odd-one-out	Finding the odd-one-out in a set of items (words, pseudowords) which all but one contain the same phoneme, e.g. 'fan' from 'fan/cat/hat/mat' (Prakash *et al.*, 1993).
Phoneme reversal	Transposing two phonemes, 'lip' → 'pil' (Holm & Dodd, 1996).
Phoneme segmentation	Separating the initial or final phoneme (Leong & Hsia, 1996) or each single phoneme
Rhyme judgment	Judging if pairs such as 'rang/sang' rhyme (Holm & Dodd, 1996).
Spoonerism	Inverting the initial phonemes of two words, 'big dog' → 'dig bog' (Holm & Dodd, 1996).

Dodd, 1996), dictation (Leong & Hsia, 1996), word or pseudoword naming (Holm & Dodd, 1996; Koda, 1989; Lau & Rickard Liow, this book). Orthographic awareness of the L2WS can also be measured: for instance, awareness of legal letter sequences in the L2WS can be tested with a decision task where two words are shown and the participant decides which one looks like a L2 word (Wade-Woolley, 1999).

Descriptive methods

Another broad approach is to collect and describe L2 learners' writing. As in other areas of SLA research, a starting point is the technique of Error Analysis (Corder, 1974), in which the learners' writings are scrutinised for mistakes, i.e. forms that are not correct in the target writing system (even if L1 writers may also make them), which are then analysed in terms of preset categories.

Errors can be collected from different sources, such as free compositions or dictations. As with experimental research, L1WS users or learners (children) can be compared with L2WS learners (Bebout, 1985; Brown, 1970) or groups of L2WS learners/users with different L1WS backgrounds (Cook, 1997), but most studies look at a single group of L2WS users, sometimes to test predictions deriving from contrastive analysis (Oller & Ziahosseiny, 1970). The same learners/users can be retested over time (as in Van Berkel, this book), providing longitudinal information by showing which errors are persistent and what is or is not a temporary compensatory strategy; it is indeed possible to collect all the misspellings produced by a single L2WS user (e.g. Luelsdorff, 1990).

After errors are collected, they are categorised. Cook (1997) used the simplistic categories taken from the L1 English studies conducted by the National Foundation for Educational Research (Brooks *et al.*, 1993): letter insertion, omission, transposition and grapheme substitution. Bebout (1985) analysed Spanish learners' errors with English using categories such as consonant doubling, other consonant errors, errors with schwa /ə/, errors with silent <e>, other vowel errors, letter misordering and homophones. Errors can also be categorised according to the spelling processes or strategies they reflect: Luelsdorff (1990) used categories such as overgeneralisation (of L2 spelling rules) and transfer (including 'orthographic cognatisation'); James *et al.* (1993) began by performing a Contrastive Analysis of the similarities and differences between the English and Welsh writing systems and classified errors into categories such as mispronunciation (L1 phonological interference), misrepresentations (writing a L2 phoneme using a L1WS correspondence rule), lexical cognate misspelling, etc. Some studies also use miscue analysis (see Pumfrey, 1985) to analyse errors in reading aloud (e.g. Sergent, 1990).

Table 1.3 Some types of normal language material

Collection of naturally occurring material	Student essays etc. (Somers, this book); dictations produced as part of normal homework (Luelsdorff, 1990).
Specially elicited full texts	Compositions, for instance games instructions. Used by James *et al.* (1993).
Collection of mistakes	Mistakes collected from sources, rather than treated as part of a text. Used by Terrebone (1973) and Cook (1997).

The difficulty with many of the above error collection techniques is that only unusual forms may strike the analyst's eye (see Van Berkel, this book). A more balanced approach uses a large corpus of materials from which errors can be drawn and their frequency established against a larger mass of material (Table 1.3 provides examples of such materials). The possibilities of a computer-based corpus approach are described in the chapter by Okada in this book. At the moment these are limited by the lack, or limited availability, of corpora of L2 learners' writings that accurately reflect the spelling and other writing system properties of the original texts. The difficulties involved in creating such corpora are discussed by Somers (this book).

Computer simulations

Computer modelling of some aspects of the L2WS has often occurred in connectionist work on the first language writing system (Seidenberg & McClelland, 1989). Connectionist spelling networks 'learn' to transform a representation of spoken input into written spellings; they learn to produce correct or acceptable spellings for regular and irregular words, including previously unseen ones. Computer simulations have been mentioned occasionally in SLA research, e.g. Sokolik and Smith (1992) and Blackwell and Broeder (1992). The issues are:

(1) Whether the simulations are based on the crucial SLA assumption that there is a pre-existing L1 system in the person's mind. A connectionist model of SLA has to demonstrate that there is already a functioning system to which a second system is added, rather than, say, make a cross-language comparison of two writing systems.

(2) Whether the simulations remain purely in the computer or connect to real-world evidence of writing system use.

The paper by van Heuven in this book shows some of the future possibilities of modelling that takes these points into account.

Qualitative research

While most research in second language writing systems is quantitative, L2WSs are also studied by means of qualitative research methods. For instance, the think-aloud technique, whereby L2WS users perform a task while reporting the processes they are using, was used to study hanzi and word recognition strategies in US learners of Chinese (Everson & Ke, 1997). Interesting insights into low-level processes of L2WS reading and writing can also be found in narratives, such as the personal account of using Hebrew as a low-proficiency L2WS user by Andrew Cohen (2001). De Courcy (2002) used a variety of qualitative methods to investigate how a group of immersion students learn and use the Chinese writing system, including learner diaries, interviews, think-aloud protocols, etc.

Examples of L2WS research

Table 1.4 presents some of the studies that have been done. While this list is far from exhaustive, it can help the reader trace the L1WS and L2WS combinations they are interested in. Some of these studies are widely cited, others were included to show the variety of possible writing system combinations; the list is exemplificatory rather than comprehensive.

Main Findings of Second Language Writing System Research

Research has consistently shown that L2WS users differ from L1WS users because of the other writing system they already know. Most research has concentrated on reading processes, especially word recognition, but it has also touched on writing and metalinguistic awareness. The characteristics of the L2WS and the L1WS experience interact in many different ways, as shown below.

L2WS reading

When the L1 and L2 writing systems encode the same linguistic units, L1 reading experience facilitates L2 reading. L2 readers are better equipped to read a L2WS that uses the same script or at least encodes the same linguistic units as their L1WS, and they read it faster than readers with a different L1WS background. For instance, L1 readers of Japanese (a partially morphemic writing system) are faster than L1 readers of an alphabetic writing system at word naming in Chinese, a morphemic L2 writing system (Yang, 2000). The same is true when both writing systems encode syllables: Chinese learners of Japanese as a L2WS read syllabic kana faster than romanised texts (Tamaoka & Menzel, 1994, reported in Kess & Miyamoto, 1999). It is also true when

Table 1.4 Summary of some L1 and L2 writing systems relationships that have been studied

L1WS type	*L2WS type*	*L1WS(s)*	*L2WS*	*Source*
Morphemic	Alphabetic	Chinese	English	(R) Haynes & Carr (1990); (R) Leong & Hsia (1996); (R, A) Jackson *et al.* (1994); (A) Wang & Geva (2003); (O) Freeman (1980)
		Japanese	English	(W) Okada (2002)
Syllabic	Alphabetic	Kannada	English	(A) Prakash *et al.* (1993)
Consonantal	Alphabetic	Arabic	English	(R) Green & Meara (1987); (R) Ryan & Meara (1991); (R) Randall & Meara (1988); (W) Ibrahim (1978); (W) Haggan (1991); (O) Morikawa and McBeath (1992)
		Hebrew	English	(A) Ben-Dror *et al.* (1995); (O) Kugelmass & Lieblich (1979)
		Persian	English	(R) Nassaji & Geva (1999)
Morphemic vs. alphabetic	Alphabetic	Chinese, Vietnamese	English	(A) Holm & Dodd (1996)
		Japanese, Russian	English	(A) Wade-Woolley (1999)
		Chinese, Indonesian	English	(R) Muljani *et al.* (1998)
Morphemic vs. consonantal	Alphabetic	Japanese, Chinese, Persian	English	(R) Akamatsu (1999)
		Japanese, Arabic	English	(R) Fender (2003)

(continued)

Table 1.4 *Continued*

L1WS type	*L2WS type*	*L1WS(s)*	*L2WS*	*Source*
Morphemic vs. consonantal vs. alphabetic	Alphabetic	Japanese, Arabic, Spanish	English	(R) Brown & Haynes (1985); (R) Koda (1988, 1995)
		Japanese, Greek, etc.	English	(W) Cook (1997)
		Chinese, Arabic, Spanish	English	(W) Oller & Ziahosseiny (1970)
Alphabetic	Morphemic	English	Chinese	(R) Hayes (1988); (R) Jackson *et al.* (1994); (R) Sun (1994)
	Consonantal	English	Hebrew	(A) Ben-Dror *et al.* (1995)
		English, Russian	Hebrew	(A) Wade-Woolley & Geva (1998)
	Alphabetic	Greek	English	(R) Chitiri & Willows (1997); (A) Loizou & Stuart (2003)
		German	English	(W) Luelsdorff (1986)
		Welsh	English	(W) James *et al.* (1993)
		Spanish	English	(W) Bebout (1985); (W) Terrebone (1973); Staczek and Aid (1981)
Alphabetic vs. morphemic	Morphemic	English, Chinese, Korean	Japanese kanji	(R) Mori (1998)
Alphabetic vs. syllabic	Syllabic	English, Chinese	Japanese kana	(R) Chikamatsu (1996); (R) Tamaoka and Menzel (1994)

R: reading; W: writing; A: awareness; O: other activities

both writing systems represent phonemes: Spanish L2WS readers of English are facilitated compared with Chinese readers, even when matched for reading comprehension (Haynes & Carr, 1990). Thus, reading is facilitated when the L2WS represents the same linguistic units as the L1WS, even when the L2WS user has to learn a new script, as in the case of Chinese learners of Japanese reading kana (Tamaoka & Menzel, 1994).

L1WS reading processes also affect L2WS reading when the two writing systems encode different linguistic units. While it might be supposed that L1WS reading processes would not be used when the two writing systems are different, the evidence suggests the opposite, mostly based on morphemic and consonantal L1WS readers reading L2WS English, but with some other writing system combinations. For example the effects of a morphemic L1WS (Chinese, Japanese) on the reading of an alphabetic L2WS have been repeatedly demonstrated. Comparisons of different readers of L2WS English revealed that morphemic L1WS readers rely more on sight-word knowledge in reading English in that they:

(1) are less affected by the unpronounceability of English words than Spanish readers (Koda, 1987);
(2) are less efficient at reading pseudowords than Spanish readers (Brown & Haynes, 1985; Haynes & Carr, 1990);
(3) are more affected by word familiarity than Spanish readers (Brown & Haynes, 1985; Haynes & Carr, 1990);
(4) are faster at recognising words than Arabic readers, who use the more time-consuming phonological recoding (Fender, 2003);
(5) are more disrupted by alterations to word shape than Persian readers, whose L1WS is semi-alphabetic (Akamatsu, 1998).

This means that L1 readers of morphemic writing systems recognise English words in the same way as they recognise hanzi and kanji. In general, they use the visual route for reading *all* sound-based L2WSs, whether alphabetic or syllabic. For instance, Chinese learners of L2WS Japanese rely more on visual information for reading kana than do US learners of Japanese; when a Japanese word normally written in hiragana is presented in katakana (or vice versa), Chinese readers of L2WS Japanese are more disrupted (Chikamatsu, 1996).

There is also evidence of effects of a consonantal L1 writing system on an alphabetic L2WS. For instance, L1 readers of consonantal Arabic rely more on consonants than vowels in L2WS English word recognition. Arabic readers of English, when asked whether two English words were the same or not, tended to ignore differences in vowels; Arabic readers, who are used to reading by consonants only, when reading English are faced with 'what seems to be far too much information' (Ryan & Meara, 1991: 533). Effects of a phonemic L1WS on morphemic and syllabic L2WSs have also been found. For instance, US learners of Japanese recall a novel kanji more easily when it contains a pronounceable phonetic radical than when it cannot be pronounced (Mori, 1998), showing that they are searching for phonological clues in the morphemic characters. They also rely on phonological decoding to read kana words more than Chinese learners (Chikamatsu, 1996), and are less disrupted than L1 readers when morphemic information is removed but phonological information remains, as in reading romanised Chinese (Bassetti, 2004) or Japanese texts solely written in kana with no kanji (study reported in Everson, 1993). The reliance on phonological information also affects their learning strategies, so that English learners of L2WS Chinese rely on phonetic radicals to learn hanzi more than Japanese ones (Shi & Wan, 1998).

Even when both writing systems represent the same linguistic units (or even use the same script), L2WS reading is affected by differences of phonological transparency in the two writing systems, as evidenced by several chapters in this book: Hickey's account of English L1 children learning Irish L2WS and Van Berkel's account of Dutch L1WS children learning English L2WS. L1 readers of a phonologically transparent L1WS use grapheme–phoneme recoding to read an opaque L2WS; in reverse, L1 readers of an opaque L1WS use a whole-word approach to read a phonologically transparent alphabetic L2WS. Over-reliance on phoneme–grapheme recoding frequently occurs in L1 readers of more phonologically transparent writing systems reading L2WS English (Birch, 2002). For example, Spanish L2WS English learners are slower at word recognition in English than Japanese learners, even though Spanish and English use the same script, since they are using grapheme–phoneme conversion via the phonological route, which is more time-consuming than the whole-word recognition used by Japanese learners (Akamatsu, 1999). On the other hand, readers of a less transparent system may fail to use the phonological route to read a more transparent L2WS: English children reading French as a L2WS without instruction in French grapheme–phoneme conversion rules use a whole-word approach, although the French GPC rules are more reliable than the English ones and a phonological decoding approach would be more successful (Erler, 2003).

Experience of any previous writing system can affect L2WS use: Japanese ESL readers with better knowledge of *romaji*, the Japanese romanisation system, have better English word recognition skills (Yamada *et al.*, 1988, cited in Buck-Gengler *et al.*, 1998), and Chinese readers who know *pinyin* are better at reading English pseudowords (Holm & Dodd, 1996). In this case, knowing a second writing system helps the person to use a second language writing system (but it can also have negative effects – see Okada, this book).

Apart from the linguistic units represented and phonological transparency, other aspects of L2WS reading have also been studied, such as orthographic conventions. For instance, adding interword spacing affects eye movements in English readers of L2WS Chinese but not Chinese L1WS readers (Everson, 1986); marking the boundary between prepositions and nouns in Hebrew facilitates English and Russia L2WS readers but not Hebrew L1 readers (Wade-Woolley & Geva, 1998).

There is also some neurolinguistic evidence from L2WS users. L2WS users with disabilities have different impairment in their two writing systems, showing the writing-system-specific nature of the impairment: Rickard Liow (1999) describes the case of a Chinese user of English who is dyslexic in English but not in Chinese; Wydell and Butterworth (1999) report the case of a Japanese user of English who is only dyslexic in English. While it is true that readers with some disabilities have difficulties in reading both languages, the nature of the difficulties is different in the two writing systems (Geva & Siegel, 2000).

To generalise, the main finding of L2WS research is that the greater the similarity between the L1WS and the L2WS (i.e. representing the same linguistic units, using the same script, having the same levels of phonological transparency or using similar correspondence rules or orthographic regularities), the more L2 reading is facilitated. But, even when the two writing systems differ, L2WS reading is still affected by L1WS reading processes.

L2WS writing

The writing component of L2 writing systems has received rather less attention than reading, for various reasons. On the one hand, L2WS spelling, like reading, is affected by characteristics of the target writing system: in one study English learners of L2WS Hebrew were asked to write down previously learnt Hebrew words including diacritics for vowels; most of their spelling errors consisted of incorrect vowels, consistent with the fact that Hebrew only represents consonants (Cowan, 1992). And spelling is an area of second language acquisition where L2WS users reach fairly high levels of performance (Cook, 1997).

On the other hand, L2WS spellers do not necessarily behave in the same way as L1WS spellers or as L2WS spellers from other L1WS backgrounds. A fairly sparse scattering of research into spelling mistakes in L2WS English suggests effects of both the L1 phonological system and the L1 writing system. L2WS users with different L1s or writing systems have characteristic mistakes; for instance Japanese spellers of English show the Japanese /l~r/ confusion in the spelling of <recentry>, or the use of epenthetic vowels in <yesuterday>. L2WS spelling research has found that specific groups differ in their performance in ways that are consistent with their L1 writing system and phonology.

Turning back to the effects of the L1WS, L2WS spelling accuracy is affected by the *type* of L1WS: Oller and Ziahosseiny (1970) found that L1WS readers of various writing systems that use the Roman alphabet produced more spelling deviations than L1WS users of other writing systems (Chinese, Japanese, Arabic). The L1WS affects L2WS spelling processes and strategies. Luelsdorff (1990) describes the spelling strategies of a German high-school learner of L2WS English. Some of these involve the use of the L1WS: for instance, using L1 letter names to spell L2 words, or L1 phoneme–grapheme correspondence (PGC) rules in spelling <station> as <*steschen>. James *et al.* (1993) also found effects of L1WS Welsh PGC correspondences on L2WS English spelling, using <c> instead of <k> because the L1WS does not have <k>, or spelling <ship> as <sip> because in Welsh /ʃ/ is spelled as <s>, or spelling <nephew> as <neffew> because in Welsh <ph> for /f/ is only used in word-initial position.

Differences between L1 and L2WS spellers were also found outside the phoneme–grapheme conversion rules, for instance in morphological spelling. Adopting the same method used by Bryant *et al.* (1997) for English children, Cook (2004b) found that L2WS learners of English are quicker to get the uniform morphological spelling for the written morpheme <ed> than L1WS children. The reasons for this might be various, including the difference in age and the effects of literacy in a L1WS, but are most probably the consequence of instruction, with L2 learners being specifically taught that the English past tense is spelled <ed>.

There are still limitations to L2WS spelling research. First, the sparse research available sometimes did not aim at finding effects of the L1 writing system; some researchers denied the possibility of there being any (e.g. Wyatt, 1973). Second, often the same L2WS spelling error can be explained as a consequence of either L1 phonology or L1 writing system. For example, the confusion between <l> and <r> in Japanese ESL spellers is explained as a consequence of either L1 phonology (Cook, 1997) or the Japanese *romaji* transcription system (see Okada, this book) – indeed both probably play their part. Finally research looks at the product of spelling, i.e. the spelling errors, rather than at the process of spelling. The techniques developed in L1WS spelling research are rarely used in L2WS spelling research; such as misspelling tasks where spellers are requested to spell a word incorrectly, or studies of spelling production time using keyboarded responses, etc.

There is even less L2WS research on the effects of orthographic conventions than on spelling. A bibliography of ESL writing (Tannacito, 1995) lists 19 papers about 'spelling', but only one for 'punctuation' and two for 'orthography'. Although this bibliography is now quite old, the situation has not changed much in the interval.

L2WS awareness

As seen above, using different writing systems requires awareness of different linguistic units (morphemes and syllables in Chinese, phonemes and words in English and Italian, consonants in Arabic, etc.). Researchers working on language awareness in readers of a second language writing system have largely focused on phonemic awareness, probably because

English is the most studied L2WS. A common finding is that the metalinguistic awareness of the linguistic units represented in the L1WS affects phonemic awareness in L2WS English learners and users.

Firstly, users of a phonemic L1WS outperform users of a syllabic L1WS in phoneme awareness tasks with L2WS English: L1 readers of the alphabetic Russian writing system perform better than Japanese L1 readers at phoneme deletion in L2WS English even though matched in word recognition and pseudoword decoding (Wade-Woolley, 1999).

Secondly, readers with different L1WSs have different awareness of the phonological units represented by the L2WS. English users of L2WS Hebrew are faster than Hebrew L1 readers in deleting the first phoneme in Hebrew words and, unlike Hebrew readers, are unaffected by whether words are written with or without vowels (Ben-Dror *et al.*, 1995).

Apart from the differences in the linguistic units represented, there are also effects from the phonological transparency of the two writing systems. While both Greek and English are alphabetic, Greek-English bilingual children outperform English monolingual children in phoneme awareness tasks, probably because the Greek writing system is more phonologically transparent (Loizou & Stuart, 2003).

Other aspects of L2WS awareness have also been studied, such as orthographic awareness, i.e. knowledge of the possible combinations of symbols in the L2WS. Wade-Woolley (1999) found differences in the orthographic awareness of Japanese and Russian users of L2WS English: the Japanese learners were faster than the Russians in deciding whether a sequence of letters could be an English word. He explained this as a consequence of the Japanese learners relying more on orthographic information for reading English than the Russian learners, who rely more on phonology. Jackson *et al.* (1994) also found that Chinese readers had better orthographic awareness than phonological awareness of L2WS English. Regarding orthographic awareness of writing systems other than L2WS English, western learners of Chinese learn to use the phonetic radicals of hanzi in just six months, compared with two years in Chinese children (Chen & Wang, 2001).

Other aspects of L2WS use – linguistic and nonlinguistic processes

Other aspects of writing systems, i.e. their physical properties, also affect L2WS use. Anecdotes are sometimes found: Ball (1986) reports that Arabic ESL learners turn to page 62 instead of page 26, reading the number in the wrong direction. But there is also experimental evidence, for example that L2WS reading is affected by L1WS directionality: unlike English L1 readers, Chinese readers of L2WS English, whose L1WS may be written vertically, are not negatively affected in letter recognition when reading English letters vertically (Freeman, 1980). Arabic readers, whose L1WS is read from right-to-left, locate letters in English words faster when the letter is on the right-hand side of the word rather than on the left-hand side, whereas English L1WS readers are faster at locating letters on the left (Randall & Meara, 1988). Physical properties of the L1WS also affect L2WS writing: Sassoon (1995) reported that L2WS users are affected by their L1WS experience in terms of how they form letter shapes, how they join letters, how they hold the pen, etc. Anecdotal evidence is found in the literature, for instance that Chinese native speakers who learnt *pinyin* in school write Italian with all letters separated as in print writing, i.e. not joined up (Banfi, 2003). Other examples are presented in Cook (2001), for instance the fact that Chinese writers of L2WS English start writing the letter <t> with the horizontal line, following the order they use when writing hanzi.

L2WS users are also affected by both their writing systems when performing some nonlinguistic activities. For instance, after learning the English writing system, Hebrew children showed an increase in left-to-right directionality in the way they arrange pictures of temporal events (getting up, going to school, going to bed, etc.) (Tversky *et al.*, 1991); they also name objects from left-to-right rather than from right-to-left as they did when they were literate only in Hebrew (Kugelmass & Lieblich, 1979). When shown drawings that seem to be rotating, English readers perceive an illusory right-to-left rotation and Arabic readers an illusory left-to-right rotation, but Arabic L2WS English users perceive rotations as being equally left-to-right and right-to-left (Morikawa & McBeath, 1992). In other words the directionality of both writing systems affects nonlinguistic activities in L2WS users.

The Multi-competent L2WS User

Most of the research findings reported above deal in one way or another with the issue of transfer from the L1WS to the L2WS. Indeed the term 'transfer' often figures in the titles of articles (e.g. Verhoeven, 1994), book chapters (Gesi Blanchard, 1998), conference papers (Durgunoglu & Öney, 2000) and books (Carlo & Royer, 1994). Even when it is not explicitly mentioned, transfer is still generally the framework for researchers working in this field, as in Koda (1995; this volume). The review of findings above shows that most research concentrated on transfer from the L1WS to the L2WS. In other areas of SLA research, the transfer of some aspect of the first language to the second is now so well-established that people have turned to other research questions. Indeed if the first language had *no* effect on the second language in the learner's mind, there might not be a discipline of SLA research since L2 acquisition would be effectively covered by L1 acquisition research. While the new area of L2 writing system research initially needed to make this point about transfer, it is not clear that much mileage can be gained from continuing to make L1-to-L2 transfer a main theme of research: once transfer has been shown to apply in general, is it necessary to demonstrate it over and over for all possible pairs of writing systems in all possible ways? L2WS learning and use are more complex and involve many other factors apart from L1WS transfer. The findings reported above show that it is not simply a matter of transferring L1WS habits to the L2WS, but that there is an interaction between the characteristics of the two writing systems and the processes associated with them in the L2WS user's mind. In general, L2WS users use their writing systems differently from L1 users with one writing system. The L2WS user is not simply failing to use the L2WS in the same way as a L1 user, or trying to use a L2WS in the same way as his/her L1WS; L2WS users read, write, learn and analyse their L2WS *differently* from L1WS users, because they have more than one writing system in their minds.

We can therefore extend the notion of multi-competence, first proposed in Cook (1991), to writing systems. Multi-competence was defined as the knowledge of two or more grammars in one mind (Cook, 1991), expanded later to the 'integration continuum' which deals with the various relationships that may obtain between the two or more languages in one mind (Cook, 2002), in particular to the effects of the second language on the first, sometimes known as 'reverse transfer' (Cook, 2003). A multi-competent L2 user is not two monolinguals in one person, but has an integrated knowledge of the two languages, which interact and affect each other. Applied to L2WS research, this suggests that the multi-competent L2 reader, as well as knowing two or more languages, also knows two or more writing systems. This means that L2WS users:

(1) have different uses for their L2WS, compared with L1WS users of their L2WS, and for their L1WS compared to L1WS users of their L1WS;
(2) have different knowledge of their L2WS compared with L1WS users of their L2WS, and of their L1WS compared with L1WS users of their L1WS;
(3) have an integrated system in which both writing systems coexist.

These points are explained in more detail below.

Uses of writing systems in multi-competent L2WS users

The multi-competence theory predicts that L2 users use their L2WS in ways that differ from L1WS users with only a single writing system. For instance, a L2WS reader can use the L1WS to represent the pronunciation of L2 written words, as in the case of Japanese learners of L2WS English who use *furigana* – raised kana symbols used to show the pronunciation of difficult or infrequent kanji – to note down the pronunciation of

English written words (Okada, this book). The L1WS can also be used to develop L2-reader-specific reading and writing strategies for the L2WS, as when a L2 reader sounds out unknown L2 words using L1WS rules, to encode them in working memory and to keep reading, or a L2WS writer uses L1WS orthographic patterns to spell unknown L2 words, as in Italian-German children acquiring literacy in Italian, who borrow graphemes from German to represent Italian phonemes (Schmid, this book).

The L2WS user is not just a monocompetent user reading and writing another writing system as if it were their first one but with lesser proficiency, but is a new type of reader-writer who, consciously or unconsciously, adapts the processes and strategies developed for using one writing system to the particular cognitive needs of using another. A L2 user can use his/her specific strategies to perform tasks more efficiently than monocompetent L1WS readers:

(1) Japanese readers of L2WS English are less disrupted by the presence of unpronounceable symbols in English texts than English L1WS readers (Koda, 1995);
(2) L2WS readers of English are better at detecting word-final silent <e>s in text than English L1WS readers (Cook, 2004a);
(3) Italian readers of L2WS English are less affected by phonological foils than English L1WS readers in English word recognition tasks (Sasaki, this book);
(4) English readers of L2WS Chinese and Japanese read faster than L1WS readers when only phonological information is available, without morphemic information, as in reading romanised Chinese (Bassetti, 2004) or Japanese written in kana without kanji (study reported in Everson, 1993).

L2WS users also perform differently in their L1WS from monocompetent users of the same L1WS. They develop specific reading and writing strategies for the L1 writing system, which differ from the strategies of monocompetent users. For a start, L2WS users can perform better than monocompetent L1 users of the same L1WS: children who are skilled English readers and are also literate in the more transparent Italian L2 writing system perform English word recognition and spelling better than children who are skilled English readers but are only literate in English (D'Angiulli *et al.*, 2001). Secondly, even when performance is apparently the same, processes and strategies may still be different from those of monocompetent users of their L1WS. For instance, letter search patterns of Greek users of L2WS English in their L1WS Greek differ from those of monocompetent Greek WS users, showing different effects of stress patterns, word length and content/function word distinction (Chitiri & Willows, 1997). L2WS users' reading and writing practices become a mix of the reading/writing practices of their two writing systems, as in Arabic readers of L2WS English, whose L2WS letter search patterns differ from those of both English and Arabic L1 readers (Randall & Meara, 1988). L2WS users can invent new meanings for L2WS symbols, as the Chinese writer of L2WS Italian who uses full-stops to separate 'information units' within the sentence (Banfi, 2003). L2 readers can also use codeswitching in writing, take notes in one writing system while reading another, and in general take advantage of all the writing systems they know.

Knowledge of writing systems in multi-competent L2WS users

The multi-competence theory applied to L2 writing systems predicts that the L2WS user has a knowledge of his/her two writing systems that differs from the knowledge of L1WS readers of either writing system. The research reviewed above suggests that the L1WS affects phonological awareness in L2WS users: English users of L2WS Hebrew are better than Hebrew monocompetent readers in phoneme deletion (Ben-Dror *et al.*, 1995); Greek child users of L2WS English outperform English monocompetent children in phoneme awareness (Loizou & Stuart, 2003). But researchers also found effects of a L2WS on awareness of L1 phonological units that are not represented in the L1 writing system. For instance, Kannada-speaking adults, who are literate in a syllabic writing system, perform phonemic awareness tasks in their L1 better if they learned L2WS English: on a phoneme deletion task performed in Kannada, Kannada-English biliterates obtained 99% accuracy, but Kannada monoliterates only achieved 46% accuracy (Prakash *et al.*, 1993). This confirms the multi-competence hypothesis: a L2WS user has different knowledge of their L2WS from L1WS users of that writing system and different knowledge of the L1WS from monocompetent L1WS users.

Co-existence of writing systems in the multi-competent L2WS user's mind

Finally, when L2WS users are using one of their two writing systems, both WSs are simultaneously activated in their minds at some level: readers are slower at recognising L2 words whose orthographic patterns are legal in both their writing systems than those that are legal in only one of their writing systems (Altenberg & Cairns, 1983; Beauvillain & Segui, 1992). This may happen because, when a word's orthographic pattern is legal in both writing systems, bilingual readers have to check more entries in their orthographic lexicon(s). L2WS users are also faster at recognising L2 words whose orthographic patterns are legal in their L1WS than those that are illegal, showing that the effects of the legality of a word in one writing system carry over to the other (Muljani *et al.*, 1998). When L2WS users read, both the meanings of interlingual homographs (words spelled in the same way but having different meanings and pronunciations in the two WSs) become activated (Van Heuven, this book). For example, in English <pain> /peɪn/ means 'suffering'; in French <pain> /pɛ̃/ means 'bread': French users of L2WS English are facilitated by <pain> more for the French <beurre> 'butter' than the English <ache>. In English <four> /fɔː/ means '4', in French <four> /fur/ means 'oven': French users of L2WS English have the <five> facilitated (Beauvillain & Grainger, 1987). In both cases, the most frequent lexical item is activated, regardless of the language being read. So the orthographic lexicon of the writing system that is off-line is always available, resulting in activation of lexical items in the other language. On the other hand, the amount of activation of words from the other writing system may depend on which of the two writing systems has been previously activated (Chitiri & Willows, 1994; Jared & Kroll, 2001). When people write in their L2WS, orthographic conventions are also activated from their L1WS. This includes using L1 punctuation marks when writing in the L2WS, as in Arabic writers of L2WS English who use spacing before full stops or treat quotation marks as brackets (Somers, this book); and using L2 orthographic conventions when writing in the L1WS, such as Italian users of L2WS English who write the names of the days of the week in capitals when writing in Italian, where it is not necessary.

In conclusion, the presence of a L2WS in the mind affects the use and knowledge of the L1WS, and all the writing systems of the L2 user are present and interact during reading and writing. An approach based on unidirectional transfer from L1WS to L2WS cannot handle such evidence.

If this argument is correct, it also raises a question about the methodology of L2WS research. Research that compares monolingual L1WS users with L2WS users often takes the results for monolinguals as being those shown by the subjects in their L1 rather than those shown by 'pure' monolinguals (e.g. Chitiri & Willows, 1994). Even when (rarely) a supposedly monolingual group is used for comparison, the subjects often turn out on closer inspection to be people who are living in a country where the other writing system is used, especially when the L2WS under investigation is not English and native controls are drawn from the English-speaking country where the research is performed (e.g. in a study comparing Chinese natives and English L2 readers of Chinese, the Chinese controls were students in US universities (Hayes, 1988)). The same applies to research comparing L2WS learners or users with different L1WS backgrounds, who often turn out to be all studying the L2WS in the US (and therefore to be literate in L2WS English): for instance, comparisons of American, Chinese and Korean learners of Japanese all studying at a US university (Mori, 1998). The problem is that all these learners and users are in a sense 'contaminated' in that their use and knowledge of their L1 writing system may have been affected in some way by the L2WS they have acquired. While such effects may only arise at advanced levels of L2 reading and writing, this would need to be established: D'Angiulli *et al.* (2001) showed benefits in the L1WS (English) for English-Italian children with just some exposure to the Italian writing system. This methodological point is not of course peculiar to L2WS research but affects any research that tries to establish native performance; Kato (2004) showed that the Voice Onset Times established for plosive consonants for monolingual Japanese in their L1 had been distorted by the fact that the subjects measured had been living in the United States. In syntax too, if linguistics insists on accepting the monolingual native speaker as the gold standard, those who know another language may be suspect in the first language: Cook (2002) warned 'The judgements about English of Bloomfield, Halliday or Chomsky are not trustworthy, except where they are supported by evidence from 'pure' monolinguals' (p. 23). In L2WS research as well it is important to control the whole linguistic and orthographic background of participants.

Research Questions in L2WS Research

The most common research questions in research into L2 writing systems has undoubtedly been the effects of the L1WS on a L2WS which represents different linguistic units and/or has different levels of phonological transparency, as we have seen. We should nevertheless point out that the ability of people to use a L2WS raises a number of other interesting questions for SLA research and psychology.

Even with transfer from L1 to L2 writing system, there are unanswered questions such as:

- *ultimate attainment:* do L2WS learners from different L1WS backgrounds differ in their ultimate attainment in terms of speed and accuracy in reading and writing the target WS?
- *rate of development:* do learners from different L1WSs develop L2WSs at different rates compared to each other or compared with native learners?
- *learning strategies:* are L2WS learning strategies affected by L1WS learning strategies (say rote repetition of written symbols as in Japanese children)?
- *orthographic conventions:* are L2WS users affected by differences in orthographic conventions, such as the absence or presence of capital letters, or the use of spacing to represent pauses rather than word boundaries?
- *physical properties:* are L2WS users affected by L1WS directionality, ways of producing actual written symbols, etc.?

But a number of research questions go beyond the question of transfer from L1WS to L2WS. Some of the questions that can be asked are:

- *reverse transfer:* does learning a L2WS affect how people read, write and analyse their L1WS (for instance, does learning a more phonologically transparent L2WS affect the reading and spelling processes used for the L1WS)?
- *awareness of other units not utilised in speech:* are L2WS facilitated for instance in learning that -ed is one written morpheme?
- *L1WS attrition:* do L2WS users lose L1WS writing automaticity, say Chinese students using L2WS English?
- *integration of the L1WS and the L2WS:* to what extent are the two writing systems distinct in the mind of the L2 user or do they form a merged system?
- *multiple language writing systems:* how does each subsequently learnt writing system (including supplementary writing systems such as romanisation) affect the others, say second on third and so on?
- *effects of teaching:* what are the effects of teaching method on L2WS acquisition, say the differences between phonics and whole-word methods? What are appropriate L2WS teaching methods?
- *learning setting:* are there differences, say, between the English spelling of an Italian waiter and a student in a language school in London?
- *individual differences:* are there effects of age of L2WS onset, number of L2WSs known, motivation, cognitive style, working memory, visual and phonological skills, etc.?
- *sociolinguistic factors:* how do sociocultural practices in the two societies, and particularly the status and attitudes towards the writing system, affect L2WS reading and writing?
- *neurolinguistic research:* which parts of the brain are activated when reading or writing a L2 writing system, compared with native readers of both the L1 and the L2 writing systems?
- *nonlinguistic consequences of learning a L2WS:* does learning a new WS's directionality affect how people represent temporality, arrange images, etc.?
- *the effects of new technologies:* how does L2WS interface with computer-mediated communication such as e-mail in learning and using L2WS?

Organisation of the Book

This book contains 16 chapters, organised roughly into four sections on the reading, writing, awareness and teaching of a Second Language Writing System.

Writing a Second Language Writing System

The chapters in this section look at two aspects of writing a Second Language Writing System: spelling and handwriting.

Nobuko Chikamatsu looks at whether kanji are stored and accessed by English-speaking learners of L2WS Japanese as units or decomposed into radicals (semantic or phonetic components of kanji), through an experiment with the 'tip-of-the-pen' technique. When participants were in 'tip-of-the-pen' state, i.e. remembered some information about the missing kanji but not the complete kanji, they had to indicate the likely internal structure and likely number of strokes of the unknown kanji. The results show how the Japanese mental lexicon of L2 learners is organised and how an alphabetic L1 writing system affects the writing of a morphemic L2 writing system through the role of phonological, morphological and orthographic information for character recall. Apart from the results themselves, the most striking part of this chapter is perhaps the innovatory use of the 'tip-of-the-pen' research technique.

Ans van Berkel investigates how Dutch high school students learn to spell English, aiming to find out whether they rely on L1 spelling strategies, which are mainly phonological given the transparent L1WS, or orthographic strategies (i.e. discovering rules). An error analysis of data from dictation of familiar words concentrated on two types of error: L1 errors (due to transfer of L1 phonological knowledge) and L2 errors (due to inadequate L2 spelling knowledge). An analysis of correct answers looked at the role of phonological and orthographic strategies. Dutch learners of English clearly rely on phonological strategies in the early stages of learning English as a L2WS but start using orthographic strategies at later stages. The strengths of this paper are its clear contrastive descriptions of the spelling system in two languages and the use of large amounts of elicited spelling data.

Mick Randall looks at the effects of a meaning-based L1WS (Chinese) and a phonologically transparent alphabetic L1WS (Bahasa Malayu, or BM) on L2WS English, with a view to disentangling the relative contributions of the L1 phonology and of the L1WS to L2WS word knowledge, using experiments that compare first English L2WS learners with different first languages (Chinese and BM) and same first writing system, and then learners with different L1s and L1WSs. The patterns of spelling errors reveal that the L1 phonology plays an important role in determining L2WS spelling errors, as speakers of different languages showing the same spelling errors for consonant clusters that do not exist in their first languages. The main difference between the Chinese and BM groups was the treatment of the inflectional morpheme <ed>, which could not be explained in terms of orthographic distance. The chapter provides a new insight into the complex relationships of meaning-based and phonologically based writing systems.

The chapter by Harold Somers looks at the creation of learner corpora, i.e. computerised collections of language produced by L2 learners, and argues that the handwriting of L2 learners of English contains features that should be represented in corpora. The author discusses the features that should be made available for researchers and teachers and how they can be marked up with reference to spelling, punctuation, letter shape etc., using examples taken from a small corpus of hand-written texts produced by Arabic ESL learners. The chapter is valuable in providing a background in corpus linguistics for L2WS research and for discussion of the implications of corpora for writing system research.

The chapter by Takeshi Okada investigates the role of a previously learnt supplementary writing system, Japanese *romaji*, on the mental representation of written words in English as L2WS. This results in spelling errors that are specific to Japanese EFL writers, never occurring in native English writers. Okada compares two corpora of elicited spelling errors produced by Japanese and English spellers of English, explaining a range of error types and relating the data to a description of the spelling and word learning processes of Japanese learners of English. The chapter provides further insight into the complex Japanese writing system situation, reminding us of the importance of the roman alphabet *romaji* as well as the more studied kana and kanji scripts.

Stephan Schmid looks at how the L1 phonology and the L1WS affect the L2WS spelling and reading, taking the situation of Italian-German bilingual children learning Italian as a second writing system in Switzerland, based on a contrastive analysis of the Italian and German phonologies and orthographies. He describes the effects of the L1 phonology (both the standard and the regional variety) and the L1WS orthography in qualitative and quantitative terms based on classroom experiments. The chapter is important on the one hand because of its use of rigorous phonetic analysis, on the other because it shows the complexity of the real world situation once one goes beyond the stereotype of a standard speaker of a language.

Reading a Second Language Writing System

The next four chapters look mostly at L2WS reading, mainly using experimental approaches to investigate word recognition.

Phil Scholfield and Gloria Shu-Mei Chwo look at the effects of different L1 and L2 reading instruction methods on word recognition in English as a L2WS for Chinese primary school students in Hong Kong, where they had learnt to read both the L1 and L2 writing systems with the whole-word approach, and in Taiwan, where they had learnt by means of phonological recoding. A similarity judgment task was used, involving a decision whether two words presented simultaneously had the same meaning or not; the pair were either phonologically similar, visually similar or neither. The significant differences between the two groups in response times and accuracy confirmed that reading instruction methods result in different L2 word recognition processes even in readers with the same L1WS. The interest of the chapter is its insistence that initial teaching method as well as writing system may be crucial.

The chapter by Nobuhiko Akamatsu investigates whether increased L2 reading proficiency reduces the effects of the L1 writing systems on L2 word recognition, looking at how the ability of Japanese learners of L2WS English to read via the lexical route can hinder their reading via the phonological route. The task involves English words in their normal word shape or with alternating case (alternating lower and upper case within the word), a manipulation that forces readers to use the phonological route as it disrupts the word shape. The results showed that increased levels of proficiency in Japanese readers of L2WS English do not change the preferred reading route. This chapter is interesting in reminding us of the role of proficiency in research on the effects of the L1WS on L2WS reading.

Walter Van Heuven describes the BIA+ (Bilingual Interactive Activation) model, a recent model of bilingual visual word recognition. He argues that previous evidence from experiments into visual recognition of cognates and 'interlingual homographs' can only be explained by language nonselective access to an integrated lexicon. The BIA+ model implements such nonselective access and simulates the visual word recognition processes of a (balanced or nonbalanced) bilingual. An implementation of the BIA+ model is the SOPHIA (Semantic, Orthographic and PHonological Interactive Activation) model which can replicate bilingual readers' performance with interlingual homographs and pseudohomophones and account for some experimental findings not covered by the previous model. Van Heuven's chapter is a good example of the integration of careful experimentation and a computer-based psycholinguistic approach in L2WS research.

Miho Sasaki looks at the effects of a phonologically transparent alphabetic L1WS (Italian) and a morphemic L1WS (Japanese) on reading a less phonologically transparent alphabetic L2WS (English). She compared Italian and Japanese users of L2WS English as well as English native readers using an item-recognition paradigm. The results revealed differences among the Japanese, English and Italian groups in accuracy (number of errors) and speed (response time). This chapter broadens the database of research into the effects of L1WS transparency on L2WSs.

Awareness of Language and Second Language Writing System

The three chapters in this section look at L2WS users' awareness of the linguistic units represented in their L2 writing system.

Keiko Koda presents the Transfer Facilitation Model, which describes how metalinguistic awareness developed for the first language is transferred and facilitates second language reading. Taking a functionalist approach, the model predicts that: (1) aspects of metalinguistic awareness that apply to both L1 and L2 writing systems facilitate L2 reading at the initial stages; (2) awareness of how language elements are represented in the L1WS affects the rate of development of such L2WS awareness; (3) the orthographic distance between the L1WS and L2WS determines differential rates of L2 reading development; and (4) L2WS decoding skills vary systematically across readers with different L1WS backgrounds. Tested against a range of empirical studies, the Transfer Facilitation Model provides a useful framework for future research. This chapter is useful in adding to the few general models that are available for L2WSs and showing the latest progression in Koda's thinking.

Benedetta Bassetti looks at how awareness of the L1 linguistic units represented in the L1WS interacts with characteristics of the L2WS in affecting awareness of the linguistic units of the second language, by looking at word awareness in English-speaking learners of L2WS Chinese and Chinese L1WS users. Using two word segmentation tasks, she compared the L1 and L2 groups' mean word lengths, levels of agreement on segmentation and word segmentation strategies. Results showed differences between the concepts of Chinese word in Chinese and English users of Chinese. These results are explained within the multi-competence framework in terms of the interaction between the L2 learners' first language word awareness and characteristics of their L2 writing system. This chapter contributes to the academic discussion of second language awareness extended to units larger than phonemes.

The chapter by Lily Lau and Susan Rickard Liow looks at the reliance on phonological awareness in spelling English as a L2WS by kindergarten children with different L1 and L1WS backgrounds (English, Chinese and BM) by means of a Flaps Spelling Test which shows processing skills in spelling words that are spelled with <t> but pronounced with a flapped voiced /d/. BM-speaking children showed poorer performance in the spelling of t-flaps, i.e. more reliance on phonological coding, than English children. Both exposure to the first language and exposure to the L1WS affect phonological processing in the L2WS. This chapter is interesting because of the complexity of the situation it deals with and because of its neat use of the flaps technique.

Teaching a Second Language Writing System

The last section of the book examines the L2WS in educational contexts.

Therese Dufresne and Diana Masny propose that, from a post-structuralist perspective, learning a new writing system involves destabilisation of the system and a quest to seek and maintain stability of that system. They use two case studies: one concerns how an English-speaking child interacts with a new concept through learning French, the other how a Gujarati-English child, literate in English, interacts with the Gujarati writing system. The post-structuralist approach can provide an alternative based on the acquisitional processes rather than products, and on the restructuring of previous knowledge to accommodate new. The paradigms of teaching and learning (constructivism) that have replaced the traditional ones, both in the context of the teaching of language and writing in Canadian immersion programmes and worldwide, affect language and writing research as well. This is related to Dufresne's theory of the Telling Maps and Masny's Multiple Literacies Theory. This chapter takes the discussion of L2WSs to a different plane by reminding us of their status within general contemporary theories.

Tina Hickey looks at the difficulties of children learning to read Irish as a L2WS in Ireland, and reports the results of a successful experimentation with Taped Book Flooding. English L1WS children learning Irish as a L2WS have a number of difficulties – poor decoding skills, interference from English orthography, lack of motivation and lack of reading resources. The problem of preparing Irish reading materials for these readers is illustrated with an Irish-language storybook translated from English. The author then describe their own successful trials of 'Taped Book Flooding' as a means of encouraging extensive L2 reading. The interest of the paper comes from its highly contextualised focus on one situation of contact between two alphabetic writing systems and its practical discussion of actual reading texts and new teaching techniques.

Vivian Cook looks broadly at how L2 writing is taught in foreign language teaching by analysing how various coursebooks present the written target language. The author first discusses the neglected role of written language in language teaching and lists what learners have to know to use a L2WS. An analysis of written language in coursebooks for English, Italian and French shows that their use of written language is not representative of actual written texts or actual activities. The same level of neglect of the writing system is also present in modern language curricula, both in England and in the rest of Europe. This contribution tries to situate L2WSs in the broader educational context of foreign language teaching.

References

Adams, S.J. (1982) Scripts and the recognition of unfamiliar vocabulary: Enhancing second language reading skills. *Modern Language Journal* 66, 155–9.

Akamatsu, N. (1998) L1 and L2 reading: The orthographic effects of Japanese on reading in English. *Language, Culture and Curriculum* 11 (1), 9–27.

Akamatsu, N. (1999) The effects of first language orthographic features on word recognition processing in English as a Second Language. *Reading and Writing* 11 (4), 381–403.

Akita, K. and Hatano, G. (1999) Learning to read and write in Japanese. In M. Harris and G. Hatano (eds) *Learning to Read and Write: A Cross-Linguistic Perspective* (pp. 214–34). Cambridge: Cambridge University Press.

Alegria, J., Pignot, E. and Morais, J. (1982) Phonetic analysis of speech and memory codes in beginning readers. *Memory and Cognition* 10, 451–556.

Altenberg, E.P. and Cairns, H.S. (1983) The effects of phonotactic constraints in lexical processing in bilingual and monolingual subjects. *Journal of Verbal Learning and Verbal Behavior* 22, 174–88.

Aronoff, M. (1992) Segmentalism in linguistics: The alphabetic basis of phonological theory. In P. Downing, S.D. Lima and M. Noonan (eds) *The Linguistics of Literacy* (pp. 71–82). Amsterdam: John Benjamins.

Ball, W.E. (1986) Writing English script: An overlooked skill. *English Language Teaching Journal* 40 (4), 291–8.

Banfi, E. (2003) Dagli ideogrammi all'alfabeto latino: osservazioni sull'italiano scritto di un apprendente cinese. In E. Banfi (ed.) *Italiano/ L2 di cinesi. Percorsi acquisizionali.* (pp. 181–211). Milan: Franco Angeli.

Barnitz, J.G. (1982) Orthographies, bilingualism, and learning to read English as a second language. *The Reading Teacher* 35 (5), 560–7.

Barry, C. (1994) Spelling routes (or roots or rutes). In G.D.A. Brown and N.C. Ellis (eds) *Handbook of Spelling: Theory, Process and Intervention* (pp. 27–49). Chichester, UK: John Wiley & Sons.

Bassetti, B. (2004) Second language reading and second language awareness in English-speaking learners of Chinese as a Foreign Language. PhD thesis, University of Essex.

Beauvillain, C. and Grainger, J. (1987) Accessing interlexical homographs: Some limitations of a language-selective access. *Journal of Memory and Language* 26, 658–72.

Beauvillain, C. and Segui, J. (1992) Representation and processing of morphological information. In R. Frost and L. Katz (eds) *Orthography, Phonology, Morphology, and Meaning* (pp. 377–88). Amsterdam: North Holland.

Bebout, L. (1985) An error analysis of misspellings made by learners of English as a first and as a second language. *Journal of Psycholinguistic Research* 14, 569–93.

Beers, C.S. and Beers, J.W. (1992) Children's spelling of English inflectional morphology. In S. Templeton and D.R. Bear (eds) *Development of Orthographic Knowledge and the Foundations of Literacy* (pp. 231–51). Hillsdale, NJ: Lawrence Erlbaum Associates.

Ben-Dror, I., Frost, R. and Bentin, S. (1995) Orthographic representation and phonemic segmentation in skilled readers: A cross-language comparison. *Psychological Science* 6 (3), 176–81.

Bergh, G., Herriman, J. and Mobarg, M. (eds) An international master of syntax and semantics: Papers presented to Aimo Seppänen. Acta Universitatis Gothoburgensis No 88, Goteborg.

Bernhardt, E.B. and Everson, M.E. (1988) Second Language Reading: A Cognitive Perspective. Paper presented at the National Reading Conference, Tucson, AZ.

Bertelson, P., deGelder, B., Tfouni, L.V. and Morais, J. (1989) Metaphonological abilities of adult illiterates: New evidence of heterogeneity. *European Journal of Cognitive Psychology* 1 (3), 239–50.

Birch, B.M. (2002) *English L2 Reading: Getting to the Bottom*. Mahwah, NJ: Lawrence-Erlbaum Associates.

Blackwell, A. and Broeder, P. (1992). Interference and facilitation in SLA: A connectionist perspective. Seminar on Parallel Distributed Processing and Natural Language Processing, San Diego, UCSD, May 1992.

Bringhurst, R. (1992) *The Elements of Typographic Style*. Vancouver: Hartley and Marks.

British Council (1999) Frequently asked questions. Online document: http://www.britishcouncil.org/english/engfaqs.htm#hmlearn1.

Brooks, G., Gorman, T.P. and Kendal, L. (1993) *Spelling It Out: The Spelling Abilities of 11- and 15-year-olds*. Slough, UK: NFER.

Brown, G.D.A. and Loosemore, R.P.W. (1994) Computational approaches to normal and impaired spelling. In G.D.A. Brown and N.C. Ellis (eds) *Handbook of Spelling: Theory, Process and Intervention* (pp. 319–35). Chichester, UK: John Wiley & Sons.

Brown, H.D. (1970) Categories of spelling difficulty in speakers of English as a first and second language. *Journal of Verbal Learning and Verbal Behavior* 9, 232–6.

Brown, T. and Haynes, M. (1985) Literacy background and reading development in a second language. In T.H. Carr (ed.) *The Development of Reading Skills* (pp. 19–34). San Francisco: Tossey-Bass.

Bryant, P., Nunes, T. and Bindman, M. (1997) Children's understanding of the connection between grammar and spelling. In B. Blachman (ed.) *Linguistic Underpinnings of Reading* (pp. 219–40). Hillsdale, NJ: Erlbaum.

Buck-Gengler, C.J., Romero, S.G., Healy, A.F. and Bourne, L.E. (1998) The effect of alphabet and fluency on unitization processes in reading. In A.F. Healy and L.E. Bourne (eds) *Foreign Language Learning: Psycholinguistic Studies on Training and Retention* (pp. 273–90). Mahwah, NJ: Lawrence-Erlbaum Associates.

Campbell, R. (1983) Writing nonwords to dictation. *Brain and Language* 19, 153–78.

Carlo, M.S. and Royer, J.M. (1994) *The Cross-Language Transfer of Component Reading Skills*. Amherst: University of Massachusetts.

Carney, E. (1994) *A Survey of English Spelling*. London: Routledge.

Castles, A. and Coltheart, M. (2004) Is there a causal link from phonological awareness to success in learning to read? *Cognition* 91, 77–111.

Chen, H. and Wang, K. (2001) Wai guo xue sheng shi bie xing sheng zi de shi yan yan jiu [Experimental research on the recognition of semantic-phonetic compound *hanzi* by foreign students]. *Shijie hanyu jiaoxue* 56 (2), 75–80.

Chikamatsu, N. (1996) The effects of L1 orthography on L2 word recognition: A study of American and Chinese learners of Japanese. *Studies in Second Language Acquisition* 18, 403–32.

Chitiri, H.-F. and Willows, D. (1994) Word recognition in two languages and orthographies: English and Greek. *Memory and Cognition* 22, 313–25.

Chitiri, H.-F. and Willows, D.M. (1997) Bilingual word recognition in English and Greek. *Applied Psycholinguistics* 18, 139–56.

Cohen, A.D. (2001) From L1 to L12: The confessions of a sometimes frustrated multiliterate. In D. Belcher and U. Connor (eds) *Reflections on Multiliterate Lives* (pp. 79–95). Clevedon, UK: Multilingual Matters.

Coltheart, M., Curtis, B., Atkins, P. and Haller, M. (1993) Models of reading aloud: Dual-route and parallel-distributed-processing approaches. *Psychological Review* 100, 589–608.

Cook, V.J. (1991) The poverty of the stimulus argument and multicompetence. *Second Language Research* 7 (2), 103–17.

Cook, V.J. (1997) L2 users and English spelling. *Journal of Multilingual and Multicultural Development* 18 (6), 474–88.

Cook, V.J. (2001) Knowledge of writing. *International Review of Applied Linguistics* 39, 1–18.

Cook, V.J. (2002) Background to the second language user perspective. In V.J. Cook (ed.) *Portraits of the Second Language User*. Clevedon: Multilingual Matters.

Cook, V.J. (2003) The changing L1 in the L2 user's mind. In V.J. Cook (ed.) *Effects of the Second Language on the First* (pp. 1–18). Clevedon, UK: Multilingual Matters.

Cook, V.J. (2004a) *The English Writing System*. London: Arnold.

Cook, V.J. (2004b) The spelling of the regular past tense in English: Implications for lexical spelling and dual process models.

Corder, S.P. (1974) Error analysis. In J. Allen and S.P. Corder (eds) *The Edinburgh Course in Applied Linguistics, Vol. 3. Techniques in Applied Linguistics* (pp. 122–54). London: Oxford University Press.

Cossu, G. (1999) The acquisition of Italian orthography. In M. Harris and G. Hatano (eds) *Learning to Read and Write: A Cross-Linguistic Perspective* (pp. 10–33). Cambridge: Cambridge University Press.

Cossu, G., Shankweiler, D., Liberman, I.Y., Katz, L. and Tola, G. (1988) Awareness of phonological segments and reading ability in Italian children. *Applied Psycholinguistics*, 177–95.

Coulmas, F. (1989) *The Writing Systems of the World*. Oxford: Blackwell Publishers.

Coulmas, F. (1999) *The Blackwell Encyclopedia of Writing Systems*. Oxford: Blackwell Publishers.

Coulmas, F. (2003) *Writing Systems: An Introduction to their Linguistic Analysis*. Cambridge: Cambridge University Press.

Cowan, R.J. (1992) A model of lexical storage: Evidence from second language learners' orthographic errors. In P. Downing, S.D. Lima and M. Noonan (eds) *The Linguistics of Literacy* (pp. 275–87). Amsterdam: John Benjamins.

D'Angiulli, A., Siegel, L.S. and Sierra, E. (2001) The development of reading in English and Italian in bilingual children. *Applied Psycholinguistics* 22, 479–507.

de Courcy, M. (2002) *Learners' Experiences of Immersion Education: Case Studies of French and Chinese*. Clevedon, UK: Multilingual Matters.

Durgunoglu, A.Y. and Öney, B. (2000) Literacy development in two languages: Cognitive and sociocultural dimensions of cross-language transfer. Paper presented at the Research Symposium on High Standards in Reading for Students from Diverse Language Groups: Research, Practice and Policy, Washington, DC. Available online: www.ncela.gwu.edu/pubs/symposia/reading/4oney.pdf.

Erler, L. (2003) Reading in a foreign language: Near-beginner adolescents' experiences of French in English secondary schools. PhD thesis, University of Oxford.

Everson, M.E. (1986) The effect of word-unit spacing upon the reading strategies of native and non-native readers of Chinese: An eye-tracking study. PhD thesis, Ohio State University.

Everson, M.E. (1993) Research in the less commonly taught languages. In A. Hadley Omaggio (ed.) *Research in Language Learning: Principles, Processes, and Prospects* (pp. 198–228). Lincolnwood, IL: National Textbook Company.

Everson, M.E. and Ke, C. (1997) An inquiry into the reading strategies of intermediate and advanced learners of Chinese as a Foreign Language. *Journal of the Chinese Language Teachers Association* 32 (1), 1–20.

Faber, A. (1992) Phonemic segmentation as epiphenomenon: Evidence from the history of alphabetic writing. In P. Downing, S.D. Lima and M. Noonan (eds) *The Linguistics of Literacy* (pp. 111–34). Amsterdam: John Benjamins.

Fayol, M., Largy, P. and Lemaire, P. (1994) When cognitive overload enhances subject-verb agreement errors. A study in French written language. *Quarterly Journal of Experimental Psychology* 47, 437–64.

Fayol, M., Thevenin, M.G., Jarousse, J.P. and Totereau, C. (1999) From learning to teaching to learning French written morphology. In T. Nunes (ed.) *Learning to Read: An Integrated View from Research and Practice* (pp. 43–63). Dordrecht, The Netherlands: Kluwer.

Fender, M. (2003) English word recognition and word integration skills of native Arabic- and Japanese-speaking learners of English as a second language. *Applied Psycholinguistics* 24, 289–315.

Flaherty, M. and Connolly, M. (1995) Space perception, co-ordination and a knowledge of kanji in Japanese and non-Japanese. *Psychologia* 38, 130–42.

Freeman, R.D. (1980) Visual acuity is better for letters in rows than in columns. *Nature* 286, 62–4.

Frost, R., Katz, L. and Bentin, S. (1987) Strategies for visual word recognition and orthographic depth: A multilingual comparison. *Journal of Experimental Psychology: Human Perception and Performance* 13, 104–15.

Gentner, D., Imai, M. and Boroditsky, L. (2002) As time goes by: Evidence for two systems in processing space → time metaphors. *Language and Cognitive Processes* 17 (5), 537–65.

Gesi Blanchard, A.T. (1998) Transfer effects of first language proficiency on second language reading. In A.F. Healy and L.E. Bourne (eds) *Foreign Language Learning: Psycholinguistic Studies on Training and Retention*. Mahwah, NJ: Lawrence-Erlbaum Associates.

Geva, E. (1999) Issues in the development of second language reading: Implications for instruction and assessment. In T. Nunes (ed.) *Learning to Read: An Integrated View from Research and Practice* (pp. 343–67). Dordrecht, The Netherlands: Kluwer.

Geva, E. and Siegel, L.S. (2000) Orthographic and cognitive factors in the concurrent development of basic reading skills in two languages. *Reading and Writing* 12 (1–2), 1–30.

Gill, E. (1931) *An Essay on Typography*. London: Lund Humphries.

Gombert, J.È., Bryant, P. and Warrick, N. (1997) Children's use of analogy in learning to read and to spell. In C.A. Perfetti, L. Rieben and M. Fayol (eds) *Learning to Read: An Integrated View from Research and Practice* (pp. 221–35). Mahwah, NJ: Lawrence-Erlbaum Associates.

Goswami, U. (1999) The relationship between phonological awareness and orthographic representation in different orthographies. In M. Harris and G. Hatano (eds) *Learning to Read and Write: A Cross-Linguistic Perspective* (pp. 134–56). Cambridge: Cambridge University Press.

Goswami, U. and Bryant, P. (1990) *Phonological Skills and Learning to Read*. Hillsdale, NJ: Erlbaum.

Goswami, U., Porpodas, C. and Wheelwright, S. (1997) Children's orthographic representations in English and Greek. *European Journal of Psychology of Education* 12 (3), 273–92.

Goswami, U., Gombert, J.È. and de Barrera, L.F. (1998) Children's orthographic representations and linguistic transparency: Nonsense word reading in English, French, and Spanish. *Applied Psycholinguistics* 19 (1), 19–52.

Goswami, U., Ziegler, J.C., Dalton, L. and Schneider, W. (2003) Nonword reading across orthographies: How flexible is the choice of reading units? *Applied Psycholinguistics* 24 (2), 235–47.

Green, D.W. and Meara, P. (1987) The effects of script on visual search. *Second Language Research* 3 (2), 102–17.

Haggan, M. (1991) Spelling errors in native Arabic-speaking English majors: A comparison between remedial students and fourth year students. *System* 19 (1/2), 45–61.

Hanley, J.R., Tzeng, O.J.L. and Huang, H.-S. (1999) Learning to read Chinese. In M. Harris and G. Hatano (eds) *Learning to Read and Write: A Cross-Linguistic Perspective* (pp. 173–95). Cambridge: Cambridge University Press.

Hanson, V., Goodell, E. and Perfetti, C.A. (1991) Tongue-twister effects in the silent reading of hearing and deaf college students. *Journal of Memory and Language* 30, 319–30.

Harris, M. and Giannuoli, V. (1999) Learning to read and spell in Greek: The importance of letter knowledge and morphological awareness. In M. Harris and G. Hatano (eds) *Learning to Read and Write: A Cross-Linguistic Perspective* (pp. 51–70). Cambridge: Cambridge University Press.

Hatano, G., Kuhara, K. and Akiyama, M. (1981) Kanji help readers of Japanese infer the meaning of unfamiliar words. *Quarterly Newsletter of the Laboratory of Comparative Human Cognition* 3, 30–3.

Hayes, E.D. (1988) Encoding strategies used by native and non-native readers of Chinese Mandarin. *The Modern Language Journal* 72 (2), 188–95.

Haynes, M. and Carr, T.H. (1990) Writing system background and second language reading: A component skills analysis of English reading by native speaker-readers of Chinese. In T.H. Carr and B.A. Levy (eds) *Reading and its Development: Component Skills Approaches* (pp. 375–421). San Diego, California: Academic Press.

Holm, A. and Dodd, B. (1996) The effect of first written language on the acquisition of English literacy. *Cognition* 59, 119–47.

Huang, H.S. and Hanley, J.R. (1995) Phonological awareness and visual skills in learning to read Chinese and English. *Cognition* 54 (1), 73–98.

Huang, H.S. and Hanley, J.R. (1997) A longitudinal study of phonological awareness, visual skills, and Chinese reading acquisition among first-graders in Taiwan. *International Journal of Behavioral Development* 20 (2), 249–68.

Ibrahim, M. (1978) Patterns in spelling errors. *English Language Teaching* 32, 207–12.

Jackson, N.E., Lu, W. and Ju, D. (1994) Reading Chinese and reading English: Similarities, differences, and second-language reading. In V.W. Berninger (ed.) *The Varieties of Orthographic Knowledge I: Theoretical and Developmental Issues* (pp. 73–110). Dordrecht: Kluwer Academic Publishers.

Jackson, N.E., Chen, H., Goldsberry, L., Kim, A. and Vanderwerff, C. (1999) Effects of variations in orthographic information on Asian and American readers' English text reading. *Reading and Writing* 11 (4), 345–79.

James, C., Scholfield, P., Garrett, P. and Griffiths, Y. (1993) Welsh bilinguals' spelling: An error analysis. *Journal of Multilingual and Multicultural Development* 14 (4), 287–306.

Jared, D. and Kroll, J.F. (2001) Do bilinguals activate phonological representations in one or both of their languages when naming words? *Journal of Memory and Language* 44, 2–31.

Kajii, N., Nazir, T.A. and Osaka, N. (2001) Eye movement control in reading unspaced text: The case of the Japanese script. *Vision Research* 41 (19), 2503–2510.

Kato, K. (2004) Second language (L2) segmental speech learning: Perception and production of L2 English by Japanese native speakers. Ph.D thesis, University of Essex.

Ke, C. (1992) Dichotic listening with Chinese and English tasks. *Journal of Psycholinguistic Research* 21, 463–71.

Kess, J.F. and Miyamoto, T. (1999) *The Japanese Mental Lexicon: Psycholinguistic Studies of Kana and Kanji Processing*. Philadelphia/Amsterdam: John Benjamins.

Ko, H. and Lee, J.R. (1997) Chu xue shi zi cheng ren yu yin jue shi yu yue du neng li de guan xi [Phonological awareness and learning to read in illiterate adults]. *Journal of the National Chung-Cheng University* 7, 29–47.

Koda, K. (1987) Cognitive strategy transfer in second language reading. In J. Devine, P.L. Carrell and D.E. Eskey (eds) *Research in Reading in English as a Second Language*. (pp. 127–44). Washington, DC: TESOL.

Koda, K. (1988) Cognitive process in second language reading: Transfer of L1 reading skills and strategies. *Second Language Research* 4, 135–56.

Koda, K. (1989) Effects of L1 orthographic representation on L2 phonological coding strategies. *Journal of Psycholinguistic Research* 18, 201–22.

Koda, K. (1994) Second language reading research: Problems and possibilities. *Applied Psycholinguistics* 15, 1–28.

Koda, K. (1995) Cognitive consequences of L1 and L2 orthographies. In I. Taylor and D.R. Olson (eds) *Scripts and Literacy: Reading and Learning to Read Alphabets, Syllabaries and Characters* (pp. 311–26). Dordrecht: Kluwer Academic Press.

Koda, K. (1996) L2 word recognition research: A critical review. *Modern Language Journal* 80 (4), 450–60.

Kugelmass, S. and Lieblich, A. (1979) The impact of learning to read on directionality in perception: A further cross-cultural analysis. *Human Development* 22, 406–15.

Lado, R. (1957) *Linguistics across Cultures*. Ann Harbor, Michigan: University of Michigan Press.

Leong, C.K. (1997) Paradigmatic analysis of Chinese word reading: Research findings and classroom practices. In C.K. Leong and J. Malatesha (eds) *Applied Research in Reading and Spelling in Different Languages*. (pp. 379–417). Dordrecht, The Netherlands: Kluwer.

Leong, C.K. and Hsia, S. (1996) Cross-linguistic constraints on Chinese students learning English. In M.H. Bond (ed.) *The Handbook of Chinese Psychology*. Hong Kong: Oxford University Press.

Lesina, R. (1986) *Il manuale di stile*. Bologna: Zanichelli.

Levin, I., Patel, S., Margalit, T. and Barad, N. (2002) Letter names: Effect on letter saying, spelling, and word recognition in Hebrew. *Applied Psycholinguistics* 23, 269–300.

Li, W., Anderson, R.C., Nagy, W. and Zhang, H. (2002) Facets of metalinguistic awareness that contribute to Chinese literacy. In W. Li, J.S. Gaffney and J.L. Packard (eds) *Chinese Children's Reading Acquisition: Theoretical and Pedagogical Issues* (pp. 87–106). Dordrecht: Kluwer Academic Publishers.

Loizou, M. and Stuart, M. (2003) Phonological awareness in monolingual and bilingual English and Greek five-year-olds. *Journal of Research in Reading* 26 (1), 3–18.

Luelsdorff, P.A. (1986) *Constraints on Error Variables in Grammar: Bilingual Misspelling Orthographies*. Amsterdam/Philadelphia: John Benjamins.

Luelsdorff, P.A. (1990) Processing strategies in bilingual spellers. In J. Fisiak (ed.) *Further Insights into Contrastive Analysis* (pp. 187–205). Amsterdam/Philadelphia: John Benjamins.

Mann, V.A. (1986a) Phonological awareness: The role of reading experience. *Cognition* 24, 65–92.

Mann, V.A. (1986b) Temporary memory for linguistic and nonlinguistic material in relation to the acquisition of Japanese kanji and kana. In H.S.R. Kao and R. Hoosain (eds) *Linguistics, Psychology, and the Chinese Language* (pp. 155–67). Hong Kong: University of Hong Kong Press.

Miller, K., Chen, S.-Y. and Zhang, H. (in preparation) Where the words are: Judgments of words, syllables, and phrases by speakers of English and Chinese.

Morais, J., Bertelson, P., Cary, L. and Alegria, J. (1986) Literacy training and speech segmentation. *Cognition* 24, 45–64.

Mori, Y. (1998) Effects of first language and phonological accessibility on kanji recognition. *Modern Language Journal* 82 (1), 69–82.

Morikawa, K. and McBeath, M. (1992) Lateral motion bias associated with reading direction. *Vision Research* 32 (6), 1137–41.

Moser, D. (1991) Slips of the tongue and pen in Chinese. *Sino-Platonic Papers* 22.

Muljani, M., Koda, K. and Moates, D. (1998) The development of word recognition in a second language. *Applied Psycholinguistics* 19, 99–113.

Muter, V. and Snowling, M. (1997) Grammar and phonology predict spelling in middle childhood. *Reading and Writing* 407–25.

Nagy, W.E. and Anderson, R.C. (1999) Metalinguistic awareness and literacy acquisition in different languages. In D.A. Wagner, R.L. Venezky and B.V. Street (eds) *Literacy: An International Handbook* (pp. 155–60). New York: Westview Press.

Nassaji, H. and Geva, E. (1999) The contribution of phonological and orthographic processing skills to adult ESL reading: Evidence from native speakers of Farsi. *Applied Psycholinguistics* 20 (2), 241–67.

Nation, K. and Hulme, C. (1997) Phonemic segmentation, not onset-rime segmentation, predicts early reading and spelling skills. *Reading Research Quarterly* 32, 154–67.

Nunberg, G. (1990) *The Linguistics of Punctuation*. Stanford, California: CSLI Publications.

Odlin, T. (1989) *Language Transfer: Cross-Linguistic Influence in Language Learning*. Cambridge: Cambridge University Press.

Ohala, J.J. (1992) The costs and benefits of phonological analysis. In P. Downing, S.D. Lima and M. Noonan (eds) *The Linguistics of Literacy* (pp. 211–38). Amsterdam: John Benjamins.

Okada, T. (2002) Remarks on Japanese poor spellers of English. *Yamagata English Studies* 7, 21–41.

Oller, J.W. and Ziahosseiny, S.M. (1970) The contrastive analysis hypothesis and spelling errors. *Language Learning* 20, 183–9.

Osaka, N. and Oda, K. (1991) Effective visual field size necessary for vertical reading during Japanese text processing. *Bulletin of the Psychonomic Society* 29, 345–7.

Paap, K.R., Noel, R.W. and Johansen, L.S. (1992) Dual-route models of print to sound: Red herrings and real horses. In R. Frost and L. Katz (eds) *Orthography, Phonology, Morphology, and Meaning* (pp. 293–318). Amsterdam: North Holland.

Patterson, K.E. and Morton, J. (1985) From orthography to phonology: An attempt at an old interpretation. In K.E. Patterson, J.C. Marshall and M. Coltheart (eds) *Surface Dyslexia: Neuropsychological and Cognitive Studies of Phonological Reading* (pp. 335–59). Hillside, NJ: Erlbaum.

Perfetti, C.A. and Zhang, S. (1991) Phonological processes in reading Chinese characters. *Journal of Experimental Psychology: Learning, Memory and Cognition* 17 (4), 633–43.

Perfetti, C.A., Zhang, S. and Berent, I. (1992) Reading in English and Chinese: Evidence for a 'universal' phonological principle. In R. Frost and L. Katz (eds) *Orthography, Phonology, Morphology, and Meaning* (pp. 227–48). Amsterdam: North Holland.

Pinker, S. (1995) *The Language Instinct.* New York: Morrow and Co.

Pitman, I.J. (1961) Learning to read. *Journal of the Royal Society of Arts* 109, 149–180.

Prakash, P. (2000) Is phonemic awareness an artefact of alphabetic literacy?! Poster presentation, Association for Research in Memory, Attention, Decision Making, Intelligence, Language, Leaning and Organizational Perception - 11, Texas (October 13–14, 2000).

Prakash, P., Rekha, D., Nigam, R. and Karanth, P. (1993) Phonological awareness, orthography, and literacy. In R.J. Scholes (ed.) *Literacy and Language Analysis* (pp. 55–70). Hillsdale, NJ: Lawrence Erlbaum.

Pumfrey, P. (1985) *Reading Tests and Assessment Techniques.* London: Hodder and Stoughton.

Randall, M. and Meara, P. (1988) How Arabs read Roman letters. *Reading in a Foreign Language* 4 (2), 133–45.

Read, C.A., Zhang, Y., Nie, H. and Ding, B. (1987) The ability to manipulate speech sounds depends on knowing alphabetic reading. *Cognition* 24, 31–44.

Rickard Liow, S.J. (1999) Reading skill development in bilingual Singaporean children. In M. Harris and G. Hatano (eds) *Learning to Read and Write: A Cross-Linguistic Perspective* (pp. 196–213). Cambridge: Cambridge University Press.

Ryan, A. and Meara, P. (1991) The case of the invisible vowels: Arabic speakers reading English words. *Reading in a Foreign Language* 7 (2), 531–40.

Sampson, G. (1985) *Writing Systems.* Stanford: Stanford University Press.

Sassoon, R. (1995) *The Acquisition of a Second Writing System.* Oxford: Intellect.

Seidenberg, M.S. (1992) Beyond orthographic depth in reading: Equitable division of labor. In R. Frost and L. Katz (eds) *Orthography, Phonology, Morphology, and Meaning* (pp. 85–118). Amsterdam: North Holland.

Seidenberg, M.S. and McClelland, J.L. (1989) Eye movements while reading and searching spatially transformed text: A developmental examination. *Psychological Review* 96, 523–68.

Sergent, W.K. (1990) A study of the oral reading strategies of advanced and highly advanced second language readers of Chinese. PhD thesis, Ohio State University.

Share, D. and Levin, I. (1999) Learning to read and write in Hebrew. In M. Harris and G. Hatano (eds) *Learning to Read and Write: A Cross-Linguistic Perspective* (pp. 89–111). Cambridge: Cambridge University Press.

Shi, D. and Wan, Y. (1998) Guan yu dui wai Han zi jiao xue de diao cha bao gao [Report of a survey on Chinese character teaching to foreigner learners]. *Yuyan jiaoxue yu yanjiu* (1), 36–48.

Sokolik, M.E. and Smith, M.E. (1992) Assignment of gender to French nouns in primary and secondary language: A connectionist model. *Second Language Research* 8 (1), 39–58.

Sproat, R. (2000) *A Computational Theory of Writing Systems*. Cambridge: Cambridge University Press.

Staczek, J.J. and Aid, F.M. (1981) Hortografía himortal: Spelling problems among bilingual students. In G. Valdés, A.G. Lozano and R. García-Moya (eds) *Teaching Spanish to the Hispanic Bilingual: Issues, Aims, and Methods* (pp. 146–56). New York: Teachers College Press.

Sun, Y. (1994) Word printed frequency/familiarity and structure complexity effects on L1 and L2 word recognition processes in Chinese. In N. Bird, P. Falvey, A. Tsui, D. Allison, A. McNeill and R. Webb (eds) *Language and Learning*. Hong Kong: Hong Kong Education Department.

Tamaoka, K. and Menzel, B. (1994) Nihongo kyoiku ni okeru romaji shiyou shihan no ronriteki konkyo ni kansuru gengo shinrigakuteki kosatsu [To use or not to use Romaji: A psycholinguistic evaluation of the arguments against the use of romaji for teaching Japanese with learners of alphabetic mother tongues]. *Dokusho Kagaku* 38, 104–16.

Tannacito, D.J. (1995) *A Guide to Writing in English as a Second or Foreign Language: An Annotated Bibliography of Research and Pedagogy*. Alexandria, Virginia: TESOL.

Terrebone, N.G. (1973) English spelling problems of native Spanish speakers. In R. Nash (ed.) *Readings in Spanish-English Contrastive Linguistics*. Hato Rey, Puerto Rico: Inter American University Press.

Tolchinsky, L. and Teberosky, A. (1997) Explicit word segmentation and writing in Hebrew and Spanish. In C. Pontecorvo (ed.) *Writing Development: An Interdisciplinary View* (pp. 77–97). Amsterdam: Benjamins.

Totereau, C., Thevenin, M.G. and Fayol, M. (1997) The development of the understanding of number morphology in written French. In C.A. Perfetti, L. Rieben and M. Fayol (eds) *Learning to Read: An Integrated View from Research and Practice* (pp. 97–114). Mahwah, NJ: Lawrence-Erlbaum Associates.

Treiman, R.A. (1993) *Beginning to Spell: A Study of First-grade Children*. Oxford: Oxford University Press.

Tschichold, J. (1928) *The New Typography*. Berkeley: University of California Press.

Tversky, B., Kugelmass, S. and Winter, A. (1991) Cross-cultural and developmental trends in graphic productions. *Cognitive Psychology* 23 (4), 515–57.

Verhoeven, L. (1994) Transfer in bilingual development: The linguistic interdependence hypothesis revisited. *Language Learning* 44, 381–415.

Wade-Woolley, L. (1999) First language influences on second language word reading: All roads lead to Rome. *Language Learning* 49 (3), 447–71.

Wade-Woolley, L. and Geva, E. (1998) Processing inflected morphology in second language word recognition: Russian-speakers and English-speakers read Hebrew. *Reading and Writing* 11, 321–43.

Wang, M. and Geva, E. (2003) Spelling performance of Chinese children using English as a second language: Lexical and visual-orthographic processes. *Applied Psycholinguistics* 24, 1–25.

Wang, M., Koda, K. and Perfetti, C.A. (2003) Alphabetic and nonalphabetic L1 effects in English word identification: Lexical and visual-orthographic processes. *Cognition* 87 (2), 129–49.

Wimmer, H. and Landerl, K. (1997) How learning to spell German differs from learning to spell English. In C.A. Perfetti, L. Rieben and M. Fayol (eds) *Learning to Read: An Integrated View from Research and Practice* (pp. 81–96). Mahwah, NJ: Lawrence-Erlbaum Associates.

Wong, T.H. and Kao, H.S.R. (1991) The development of drawing principles in Chinese. In J. Wann, A.M. Wing and N. Sovik (eds) *Development of Graphic Skills: Research Prespectives and Educational Implications* (pp. 93–112). London: Academic Press.

Wyatt, V. (1973) An analysis of errors in composition writing. *English Language Teaching* 27 (2), 177–86.

Wydell, T.N. and Butterworth, B.L. (1999) A case study of an English-Japanese bilingual with monolingual dyslexia. *Cognition* 70, 273–305.

Yamada, J., Matsuura, M. and Yanase, Y. (1988) Does knowledge of Romaji facilitate English reading? *Journal of General Psychology* 115 (3), 229–39.

Yang, H.-M. and McConkie, G.W. (1999) Reading Chinese: Some basic eye-movement characteristics. In J. Wang, A.W. Inhoff and H.-C. Chen (eds) *Reading Chinese Script: A Cognitive Analysis* (pp. 207–22). Mahwah, NJ: Lawrence Erlbaum.

Yang, J. (2000) Orthographic effect on word recognition by learners of Chinese as a Foreign Language. *Journal of the Chinese Language Teachers Association* 35 (2), 1–18.

Part 1

Writing a Second Language Writing System

Chapter 2

L2 Japanese Kanji Memory and Retrieval: An Experiment on the Tip-of-the-pen (TOP) Phenomenon

NOBUKO CHIKAMATSU

Introduction

Kanji is a logographic script in the Japanese writing system. Every kanji character represents a meaning and functions as a morpheme in a word, or as a word by itself. Unlike many sound-based alphabetic or syllabic scripts, kanji has no systematic one-to-one grapheme–sound correspondence (GSC) rules. This may make its cognitive processing different from sound-based languages (Leong & Tamaoka, 1998). Yet native (L1) readers of Japanese acquire their own writing system and written language and function in them as efficiently and sufficiently as other L1 speakers do in their own languages. However, it is often a challenging task for second language (L2) learners of Japanese to acquire kanji. To develop an effective way to teach kanji, it is essential to understand the challenge encountered by non-native readers by examining their kanji retrieval patterns as compared to those of L1 speakers. The present study explores the issue of L2 kanji retrieval through the 'tip-of-the-pen' (TOP) phenomenon.

What is the TOP? In psycholinguistics the expression, the 'tip-of-the-tongue' phenomenon or 'TOT', indicates an intermediate stage of lexical recall. When speakers try to remember a word, they sometimes feel sure they know it, but the word is stuck on the tip of the tongue and they cannot say it. Brown and McNeill (1966) were the first to conduct an experimental study to explore this phenomenon with English words. When L1 English subjects were given a definition of a target English word and asked to write down the word, some subjects fell into the TOT state. The findings showed that the subjects in the TOT state often produced a response which was phonologically and/or semantically relevant to the target word, and had partial features, such as the initial and final phoneme, the number of syllables, the main stress of the target word. For instance, subjects were given a definition of the word 'sextant' and produced words such as 'sexton', 'secant' or 'sextet', or were given a definition of the word 'sampan' and produced 'sarong', 'saipan', 'sympoon', 'cheyenne', etc. Thus, Brown and McNeill proposed a model in which the mental lexicon is organized in a multiply indexed format, with first and last letters and the number of syllables and main stress of the word being the most accessible.

After many years, the TOT phenomenon is still a focus in psycholinguistic studies since it provides important insights into relationships between language production and memory (Schwartz, 2002). Recently, a variety of subject groups have been studied, such as bilinguals (Gollan & Silverberg, 2001), dyslexics (Faust & Sharfstein-Friedman, 2003) or older adults (White & Abrams, 2002), in order to explore their lexical retrieval and language production mechanism.

In the present study, this intermediate recall process of Japanese kanji was examined in both L1 and L2 readers to explore their memory and retrieval systems through a writing task. This process is named the 'tip-of-the-pen' (TOP), as if a kanji character in the word is stuck on the tip of the pen and cannot be written accurately, although the person thinks he/she knows it. Based on the observation of the TOP state and its error patterns among L1 and L2 readers, the organisation of the mental kanji lexicon, such as association among symbol, sound and meaning in kanji, is explored and discussed below.

Kanji

Kanji as logograph

The unique feature of the Japanese writing system is the coexistence of three different scripts: hiragana, katakana and kanji. Hiragana and katakana are sound-based, syllabic scripts in which each letter represents a syllable, such as hiragana お *o* or と *to*, or katakana オ *o* or ト *to*. The two kana scripts share the same syllabic sound representation. A newly encountered kana word can be pronounced correctly with grapheme–sound correspondence (GSC) rules as each letter systematically represents a sound unit. Hiragana is used primarily for grammatical or function words but is also used for some content words. Katakana is used for loan words, mainly from Western languages.

Kanji, on the other hand, is a meaning-based, logographic script in which each character represents a meaning or morpheme, such as 男 'man' pronounced as *o*, *dan* or *otoko*, or 都 'capital' as *to*, *tsu* or *miyako*. Each kanji character also has multiple readings, which vary according to context, for instance, the character 頭 which means 'head', can be pronounced: *toh*, *doh*, *zu*, *ju*, *saki*, *atama*, *kashira*, *kohbe*, *kaburi* and *tsumuri*. Each kanji has a great number of homophones, that is, kanji sharing the same pronunciation but representing different meanings; for instance, the following kanji, 木 'tree', 気 'feeling', 機 'chance', 輝 'to glow', 期 'period' and many others are all pronounced *ki*, i.e. are homophones. Thus, kanji does not have a systematic sound representation or a one-to-one relationship between sound and symbol; the visual form of the logographic script is, therefore, crucial to the identity of a character. Kanji is basically used for content words, such as nouns, verbs, and adjectives.

By convention, the script chosen to represent a word depends on word type and/or function, and all three scripts are combined in a single sentence, as seen in the following example in which the syllable *to* is transcribed in three different scripts.

男と トムは 京都に行った。
otoko to tomu wa kyohto ni itta.
'A man and Tom went to Kyoto.'

The hiragana and katakana scripts each consist of 46 different letters, plus diacritic marks for voicing, but there are large numbers of kanji. While kanji dictionaries used by Japanese natives contain anywhere between 12,000 and 55,000 entries (Atsuji, 2001), 1945 kanji characters, the so-called Jooyoo kanji, 'common use kanji', are selected as the standard for kanji usage in print, and taught from first through ninth grades in Japanese compulsory education. A recent corpus linguistic study (Chikamatsu *et al.*, 2000) found that, out of the 4476 entries in a corpus of one year's editions of a major newspaper, the 2000 most frequent kanji characters accounted for over 99% of the total kanji use. Thus, it is conventionally thought that Japanese adults need to know 2000 kanji to read Japanese newspapers or published materials in Japan.

In L2 Japanese instruction, because of the limited number of contact hours, only a small number of kanji are taught in class. Usually 300 to 500 characters are introduced in the beginning/intermediate textbooks commonly used for the first two years in US colleges (for instance, Makino *et al.*, 1998; Tohsaku, 1999). In advanced technical readings, such as economics, approximately 600 characters are required to comprehend the gist of academic articles or books (Shigaki, 1992). However, for L2 Japanese learners, memorizing even that relatively small number of kanji is often challenging.

Morphology of a kanji character

Each kanji is classified into six categories in terms of its intra-character structure and morphological features.[1] (The term 'morphology' is used here in its sense of 'shape, form, external structure or arrangement, especially as an object of study or classification' (OED, 1994), not in its linguistic sense of a 'branch of grammar'). Although widely known as 'iconic' or 'pictographic', the majority of kanji (60 to 80%) are classified as semantic–phonetic composites, consisting of semantic and phonetic constituents or 'radicals' (Tamaoka *et al.*, 2002; Tamamura, 1993). For instance, the character 銅 *doh* 'copper' consists of a semantic radical 金 on the left side, which denotes the categorical meaning 'metal', and a phonetic radical 同 on the right side, which indicates the pronunciation *doh*. The characters with the same semantic radical 金, such as 鉄 'iron', 銀 'silver' and 鋼 'steel', all belong to the same 'metal' category. Characters with the same phonetic radical 同, such as 同 'the same' 胴 'body' and 洞 'cave', share the same pronunciation *doh*. However, these functions of semantic and phonetic radicals are not always as transparent as the examples above. The meaning of a semantic radical may be less closely related to the whole meaning of the character. The pronunciation of a phonetic radical may also be different from the pronunciation of the whole character. In fact, such characters with phonetic cues may constitute less than half of the semantic–phonetic composites (see the summary in Koda, 2001).

The radicals are usually assembled with positional rules, as indicated below in Figure 2.1. Although there are exceptions, the positional constraints control the visual positional feature of a character by not allowing a right-side radical to be placed on the left, and vice versa.

Thus, the character's internal morphology is constrained by functional and positional intra-character rules to represent phonological, semantic, and visual information in its radicals. In contrast to the enormous number of characters, there are a relatively limited number of radicals. Two hundred and fourteen radicals were counted for the 1,945 Jooyoo kanji with the top 24 high frequency radicals comprising over 50% (Tamaoka *et al.*, 2002).

Kanji retrieval and memory

Decomposability and lexical units

Because of the high frequency of radical usage and morphological features, a radical may serve as a fundamental element in L1 Japanese kanji

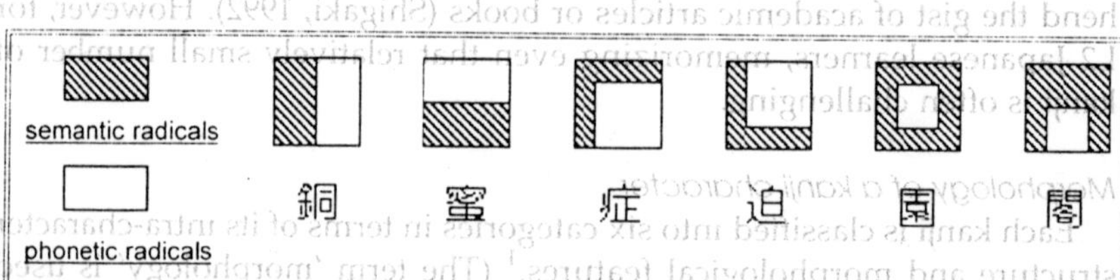

Figure 2.1 Positions of semantic and phonetic radical within the character

or Chinese lexicon. While a larger unit, i.e. a character or a whole word (compound), is claimed to be more salient in lexical storage and retrieval in previous L1 logographic studies (Hoosain, 1991; Yu *et al.*, 1984; Zhang & Peng, 1992; Zhang & Simon, 1985; Zhou & Marslen-Wilson, 1994), there is strong evidence for radicals themselves serving as lexical units in word recognition and memory (Flores d'Arcais *et al.*, 1994; Leong & Tamaoka, 1995; Saito *et al.*, 1994; Taft & Zhu, 1995).

The role of semantic radicals is more evident, due to their salient features in a character. For instance, Flores d'Arcais (1992) found interference from semantic radicals in a categorisation task. Subjects were presented with a pair of characters and asked to decide whether they belonged to the same meaning category (e.g. a body part) or not. When one character included a semantic radical closely related to the meaning of the other character, but the meanings of the two whole characters were completely unrelated, it took longer to respond than to the pairs without relevant radicals. Thus, the findings supported the lexical decomposition hypothesis, i.e. that a radical was recognised as a unit during character recognition. Other studies also supported the claim that semantic radicals were used to identify the meaning of unfamiliar words or pseudo-words (Flores d'Arcais & Saito, 1993; Flores d'Arcais *et al.*, 1995).

The role of phonetic radicals in lexical retrieval is somewhat weaker than the role of semantic radicals. Because of the lesser contribution of phonological radicals to the character's pronunciation, as mentioned above, the phonological information of the character seems usually to be accessed lexically through whole-character, rather than radical, activation (Hoosain, 1991). However, some studies show that phonological radicals are activated in lexical retrieval (Saito *et al.*, 1998), especially used for grapheme–sound correspondences in unfamiliar character recognition (Hue, 1992; Leong & Tamaoka, 1995; Seidenberg, 1985).

Thus, L1 speakers seem capable of decomposing a character into its components – as a result, radicals are stored and activated as a unit for character or word retrieval.

Intra-character structural and morphological awareness

The issue of decomposability leads to another question; intra-character structural and morphological awareness. In order to decompose a character into its components, the role of each component must be understood. Chan and Nunes (1998) examined awareness of functional and positional constraints of radicals among L1 Chinese children. Orthographic acceptability of positional constraints was investigated by switching radical positions legally in pseudocharacters (i.e. non-existing one-character words with the radicals in the correct positions) and illegally in non-characters (non-existing one-character words which violate compositional rules). The results showed that six-year-olds were able to use positional rules to judge non-characters unacceptable and pseudo-characters acceptable. To examine awareness of the functions of radicals, the subjects were asked to create and pronounce a character to refer to a newly introduced object (e.g. a person or plant from outer space). The results showed that six-year-old children could use semantic radicals appropriately for meaning, but could not use phonological radicals for pronunciation. On the other hand, nine-year-old subjects used both types of radicals appropriately and showed full understanding of the functions of radicals. Chan and Nunes (1998) concluded that morphological awareness (i.e. functional awareness of semantic radicals) is developed early in L1 Chinese acquisition although phonological radicals may take more time to acquire.

Thus, L1 readers have solid intra-character morphological awareness and decomposability; therefore, radicals serve as a crucial element in lexical retrieval. However, the role that radicals play in the L2 lexicon is still questionable. Koda (2001) reported her previous study in which semantic radical sensitivity for Japanese kanji was compared between L1 children and L2 learners. The subjects were asked to decide whether or not a visually presented character belonged to a certain semantic category. It was found that, while L2 subjects attended to semantic radicals for meaning judgement, they were less sensitive and efficient than L1 subjects, especially when the meaning of the semantic radical was not consistent with the meaning of the whole character. Koda also suggested that skilled L2 learners are sensitive to the morphological properties of radicals and are able to use radicals to extract information from a newly encountered character when morphological features contain reliable information.

Morphological analysis can also be applied to the reading of component characters in two-kanji compound words, but there is danger of over-reliance on morphological analysis in L2 reading strategies. Mori and Nagy (1999) pointed out the semantic 'semi-transparency' common in kanji words (e.g. a 'semi-transparent' word 月食 'lunar eclipse' with 月 'moon' and 食 'to eat' versus a 'transparent' word 月光 'moonlight' with 月 'moon' and 光 'light'), and examined learner strategy when guessing the meaning of new kanji compounds. The findings showed that the integration of morphological analysis and usage of contextual clues was the most efficient strategy. However, intra-word morphological analysis, i.e. analysing the meaning of each component character to discover the meaning of the whole compound, was not a successful strategy on its own, and was viewed as a low proficiency learner's strategy rather than high proficiency. Although the study focused on the character as a component unit of words rather than on the radical as a component unit of characters, this result suggests that novice L2 Japanese learners rely overly on radicals, which results in unsuccessful comprehension.

Multiple information activation

In addition to the issue of what unit information is stored in a logographic lexicon, discussed above, how information is stored is another important issue. Previous L1 logographic research proposed multiple information interactive activation, in which a single character or word is stored in a multiply-indexed mental dictionary with phonetic, semantic and visual representations, and those pieces of information are simultaneously activated for lexical retrieval (Saito & Shikata, 1988; Tan & Perfetti, 1998). In such a model, while phonological activation seems inevitable in any language regardless of orthographic features, including Chinese and Japanese kanji (Chua, 1999; Perfetti & Zhang, 1995; Perfetti *et al.*, 1992; Xu *et al.*, 1999), a stronger connection between visual symbol and meaning is often observed in logographic than alphabetic lexicons (Biederman & Tsao, 1979; Ju & Jackson, 1995; Morikawa, 1985; Paradis *et al.*, 1985; Weekes *et al.*, 1998).

Based on these observations, it is thought that kanji errors are often of semantic or orthographical, rather than phonological, origin. To examine this issue, Hatta *et al.* (1998) compared L1 adult and L2 novice writers' errors in two-kanji compound words. L1 errors were collected from academic writing samples and L2 errors from weekly kanji quizzes given in class. The results showed that a majority of L1 errors were phonological (e.g. 回 *kai* instead of 会 *kai* in 社会 *shakai* 'society'), semantic (e.g. 存 'exist' instead of 伏 'bend down' in 潜伏 *senpuku* 'concealment') or orthographic (e.g. 委 instead of 季 in 季節 *kisetsu* 'season'). Among these L1 errors phonological errors (60%) were much more common than semantic (43%) or orthographic (30%) despite the common belief. On the other hand, the dominant L2 error was non-kanji errors unrelated to any features of the target characters. Of the errors by L2 subjects 32% were 'one or two stroke addition and omission' (in which a radical was not accurately formed) while L1 subjects made such errors only 7% of the time. Instead, the majority (70%) of L1 non-kanji errors were classified 'mismatching of radicals' with the replacement of incorrect radicals, but such errors constituted 40% of L2 non-kanji errors. These observations indicate that a kanji character may be stored as radical assemblage in L1 lexicon, but rather as stroke assemblage in L2 lexicon. Therefore, it was concluded that the L1 kanji lexicon was organized at multiple information levels and radicals serve as a crucial lexical unit, but this was not the case in the L2 lexicon.

To sum up, in L1 logographic studies, the issues that have been widely discussed are: (1) decomposability; (2) intra-character structural and morphological awareness; (3) lexical unit; and (4) multiple information interaction for retrieval. Only a few L2 studies have examined these issues, and the internal mechanism of the L2 Japanese kanji lexicon is relatively unknown. Differences in proficiency, orthographic backgrounds, and cognitive processing strategies may cause different phenomena in kanji production in L1 and L2 subjects. Thus, the present study compared kanji production performance, TOP and errors in L1 and L2 subjects in order to understand the organisation and mechanism of the L2 kanji lexicon.

Present Study: The Kanji Tip-of-the-pen (TOP) Phenomenon Experiment

Subjects

Twenty-one native Japanese speakers and 18 non-native speakers participated in the present study at a large Midwestern university in the US. All the L2 subjects were college students enrolled in the second semester course of the second year of a degree in Japanese and had English as their first language. The L1 subjects were Japanese native college students or non-students who had resided in the US for nine months to four years at the time of the experiment. All had completed high school and at least a few years of university-level education in Japan.

Materials

A different set of 45 two-kanji character words with a target kanji on the right or left side were used for the L1 and L2 groups (see Appendix 1). To lead the subjects to fall into the TOP, it was not reasonable to use the same set of kanji words for the two subject groups. For L1 stimuli, 45 kanji were selected from among the 1945 Jooyoo kanji permitted for use in official publications by the Ministry of Education. All characters were semantic–phonetic composites; however, not all phonetic radicals represented exactly the same pronunciation as the whole kanji, even though they were, to some extent, similar to the pronunciation of the whole kanji. For L2 stimuli, 45 kanji characters were selected from approximately 350 characters that had been introduced in class. All 45 kanji characters were part of two-kanji compound words and had an *on*-reading (a kanji character often has multiple readings, an *on*-reading whose pronunciation derived from the Chinese language, and a *kun*-reading whose pronunciation originates in Japanese, such as 都 'capital' with on-reading *to* and kun-reading *miyako*; a two-character compound is commonly pronounced with the *on*-readings of its component characters, as in 都市 *toshi* 'urban city'). Inadvertently, one Japanese-derived compound with a kun-reading was selected. Since this stimulus could be confusing for L2 learners, it was dropped from the analysis, leaving 44 stimuli for the analysis.

Procedure

Kanji writing tests were conducted separately for the L1 and the L2 subjects, each lasting approximately two hours. At the beginning the main purpose of the experiment and the concept of the TOP were explained. L1 subjects were first presented orally with the pronunciation of a two-kanji word, then the dictionary definition in Japanese, followed again by the pronunciation. The sequence for L2 subjects was identical, except that an English definition was substituted for the Japanese definition. The subjects were then instructed to write the word containing the target kanji in a box provided at A on the answer sheet (see Appendix 2). The target kanji of interest was indicated in the bold boxes. Thus, subjects who were able to write both characters, or only the target character, immediately after the definition was given, were instructed to wait for the next question without proceeding to the following stage. Those unable to remember the target kanji at all were also instructed to wait for the next question. Those subjects who could not write the target kanji but felt they were in the TOP were instructed to answer questions B, C, D and E in order. Question B was about the general shape of the kanji, i.e. how each element of a character is assembled to construct a whole character. Six types of shape, as discussed above, were introduced with an example during the test directions. Question C referred to the number of strokes the character had. Since it seemed difficult for subjects to 'know' the number of strokes without knowing the intended kanji, during the instructions they were presented with five examples of kanji with 5, 8, 12, 15 and 18 strokes, and were asked to count them along with the experimenter. In Question D, space was provided on the right-hand side to jot down whatever form came to mind. Subjects were notified that this part of the test would not be scored. Lastly, Question E asked subjects to write their best guess at the target kanji. Subjects had 60 seconds altogether to answer each set of questions. Six sample items were given as a trial before the test.

Data analysis

Since different sets of test stimuli were used for L1 and L2 groups without any control over difficulty, frequency or transparency of each character, comparisons were made only at the descriptive level. The basis of control used in this analysis was whether the subjects self-claimed that they were in the TOP. Thus, the following analyses were conducted, based on the data that fell into the TOP conditions.

Categorisations of TOP

The first analysis was conducted with the TOP responses provided in Questions B through E. The TOP responses were classified into the following three categories based on the response in Question E:

(1) *Correct TOP:* a correct target character (e.g. 肪 'fat' *boh* in 脂肪 'body fat' *shiboh*),

(2) *Incorrect TOP with correct radicals:* an incorrect character or non-character which contained at least one of the constituent radicals of the target character (e.g. for the target 肪 'fat': 方, 防 or 妨 which all contain 方, or 朋 which contains 月),

(3) *Incorrect TOP with incorrect radicals:* an incorrect character or non-character with radicals totally unrelated to the target (e.g. 油, 法 or 亡 for the target 肪).

Kanji visual features

Since kanji is often viewed as a 'visual' script – a feature that may be emphasized in the process of learning – two 'visual' features, shape and complexity, were examined in the present study. The accuracy of the shape was calculated in percentages for each item by dividing the number of correct responses in Question B by the number of all TOP responses. Complexity, i.e. the number of strokes guessed in Question C, was also examined and submitted to a correlation coefficient with the 'correct' number of strokes for each target item.

Results and discussion

General characteristics of TOP

L1 transfer and the gap between recognition and production: Figures 2.2 and 2.3 show the number of TOP occurrences for the L1 and L2 groups respectively. Among L1 TOP responses, 30.5% resulted in a correct character, but 69.5% were incorrect. On the other hand, among L2 TOP responses, only 11.4% resulted in a correct character, and 88.6% were incorrect. A *t*-test was conducted to compare the occurrence of correct TOP responses between the two groups and it revealed a significant difference between the two groups ($t(37) = 2.981$, $p < 0.01$). In short, L1 subjects who fell in the TOP state could recall and write a target character at the end more accurately than L2 subjects. Thus, in many cases L2 subjects were apparently not looking for the target, but for something else, even though they declared that they were in the TOP. In other words,

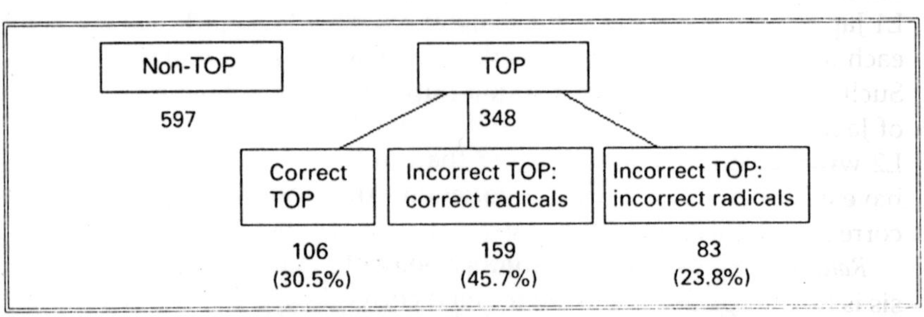

Figure 2.2 L1 natives' responses (out of 945 responses total)

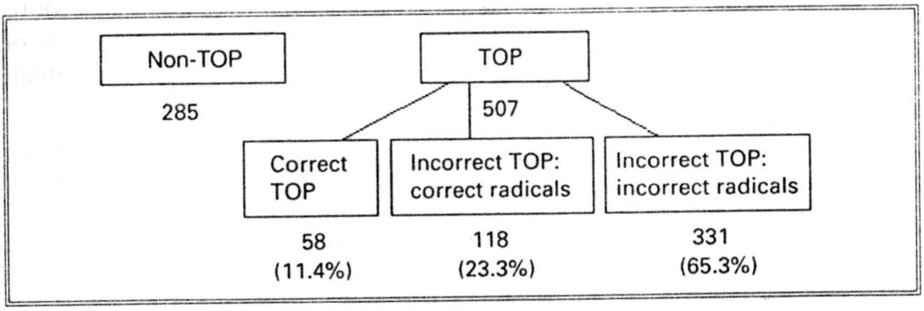

Figure 2.3 L2 non-natives' responses (out of 792 responses total)

TOP seems to be a more temporary phenomenon among L1 subjects than L2.

There are a couple of possible interpretations for the L2 learners' low frequency of correct TOP. First, it might be because of cognitive interference from their native language, i.e. sound-based alphabetic English. In the experiment, subjects were provided with the pronunciation of the word, which contained a target kanji. For the speakers of alphabetic languages, the connection between symbol and sound in their L1 is more systematic and direct due to the grapheme–sound correspondences (GSC). If they know the pronunciation of a word, it is often possible to spell the word properly in such sound-based languages. However, kanji does not have such systematic GSC. Therefore, the L2 subjects easily misjudged or overestimated their production ability for kanji-spelling when they heard the sound of the character. As a result, they felt overly confident about knowing the target kanji and self-declared TOP even though they did not know exactly how to write it. Thus, the L1 cognitive process of English might have led them into false TOP as the result of L1 transfer.

Another interpretation is that there is a considerable gap between recognition and production skills in kanji among L2 subjects. Recognition is easier than production in any language and kanji is no exception, even for L1 Japanese natives. It requires one to remember graphic details, such as each stroke and its assemblage, in order to write a character correctly. Such a production task could be even more challenging for L2 learners of Japanese. As a result, the gap between recognition and production in L2 writing could be much bigger than in the L1, and L2 learners could have easily misjudged their production skill, resulting in the low rate of correct TOP responses.

Radicals as a memory unit: Another point of interest in the present analysis is how often radicals were recalled correctly in TOP. While the L1 subjects responded to 69.5% of all TOP responses incorrectly at the end, approximately two-thirds of the incorrect answers contained a correct radical (see Table 2.1). In short, 76.2% of all the TOP responses contained at least a correct radical, and only 23.8% were totally irrelevant to a target character without any radicals in common. On the other hand, while the L2 subjects responded to 88.6% of all TOP responses incorrectly, approximately one-third of the incorrect answers contained a correct radical. In short, 34.7% of all the TOP responses contained at least a correct radical, but 65.3% did not have even one correct radical. A *t*-test was conducted to compare the occurrence of TOP responses with correct radicals (i.e. sum of Correct TOP and Incorrect TOP with correct radicals) between the two groups, and it revealed a significant difference, $t(37) = 7.253$, $p < 0.0001$. Thus, L1 subjects wrote radicals much more accurately than L2 subjects in the TOP state, even when they could not write down the correct character. This suggests that radicals are stored and retrieved as a solid lexical unit in the L1 lexicon, but not in the L2 lexicon. This result matches Hatta *et al.* (1998) where 80% of L1 errors were relevant to the target, and 70% of them contained a correct radical although they were placed in the wrong position. On the other hand, only 15% of L2 errors were relevant errors, and less than half (40%) contained a correct radical.

Kanji visual features

Kanji as a visual unit: Mean accuracy rates of shapes were 58.6% and 26.3% for L1 and L2 responses, respectively. A *t*-test revealed a significant difference between the two groups, $t(87) = 8.152$, $p < 0.0001$, that is, L1 subjects chose correct shapes more accurately than L2 subjects in the TOP state. Thus, for L1 subjects the figural feature of assemblage was retrieved well even at the intermediate retrieval stage before the actual target was fully accessed. On the other hand, L2 subjects did not seem to remember the shape if they did not remember a character thoroughly. This may be because the six patterns of assemblage were not familiar yet to L2 subjects. Or, it could be because the current L2 subjects had not acquired positional rules in a character and were not attentive to the assemblage patterns because of their limited kanji knowledge (of 350 characters). However, Chan and Nunes (1998) found that L1 Chinese first graders already understood positional constraints even with a similar amount of kanji knowledge (with approximately 500 characters). Therefore, the interpretation is just a speculation based on the present analysis.

The number of strokes was also examined. The mean number of strokes the subjects guessed in each kanji was used to calculate a correlation coefficient between 'guess' and the actual correct number of strokes of the target kanji. The result revealed significant correlation both for the L1 group ($r = 0.492$, $p < 0.001$) and for the L2 group ($r = 0.723$,

$p < 0.0001$). L2 subjects showed a high positive correlation while L1 subjects showed a moderate positive correlation. This outcome implies that it may be difficult for natives to figure out the stroke numbers because kanji is viewed as the assemblage of radicals rather than the assemblage of single strokes. On the other hand, a character may be visualised as a holistic image with fairly accurate complexity (or simplicity) by L2 subjects.

On the other hand, this may have been simply a result of instructional effects. At the early stage of kanji instruction, the teacher writes each character and counts each stroke aloud, and sometimes asks students to write a new character in the air with their hand by counting the number of strokes. As a result, the L2 subjects may have been more aware of the number of strokes. It was also possible that this was caused by the present test stimuli. The average for the target characters was 10.7 strokes, ranging from 4 to 18 strokes, in L2 stimuli, and 14.3 strokes, ranging from 8 to 19 strokes, in L1 stimuli. In short, the L2 subjects were presented with less complex characters, which had them guess the number of strokes more easily and accurately.

Error analysis

In addition to TOP analysis, error analysis was conducted. All the errors subject to this analysis were incorrect responses, yet real characters were found among incorrect TOP responses to Question E, as well as errors in Question A (which were not TOP responses). They were categorised into five error patterns on the basis of Saito & Shikata's study (1988). The five error types are: (1) phonetic errors; (2) graphic errors; (3) semantic errors; (4) compositional errors; and (5) contextual errors, as shown in Table 2.1. Errors were counted more than once as overlap errors when belonging to more than one category.

There were a total of 135 and 217 real character errors for L1 and L2 subjects, respectively (see Table 2.2). The percentages of error patterns were calculated using the total error numbers. Because of the overlapping error analysis, the sum is over 100%.

A single factor ANOVA with five levels (phonetic, graphic, semantic, compositional and contextual) was conducted for each subject group, and resulted in significant difference for L1 subjects, $F(4, 220) = 14.130$, $p < 0.0001$, as well as for L2 subjects, $F(4, 215) = 3.000$, $p < 0.05$. Planned multiple comparison tests were conducted to locate differences among the five error types for each subject group. For L1 errors, all paired comparisons were significant except for between phonetic and graphic, and between compositional and contextual (see Figure 2.4). Among L2 errors, contextual errors occurred significantly less frequently than any other errors, but no significant difference was found among the

Table 2.1 Error types and samples

Error types	*Descriptions*	*Examples*
Phonetic	The incorrect kanji has a similar pronunciation to the target.	L1: 演* *en* for 宴 *en* in 宴会 *enkai* (*also semantic)
		L2: 字, 寺, 時, 事 *ji* for 治 *ji* in 政治 *seiji*
Graphic	The incorrect kanji has a similar shape to the target.	L1: 督 for 暫 in 暫定
		L2: 米 for 来 in 来年
Semantic	The incorrect kanji has a similar meaning to the target.	L1: 歴* 'passage of time' for 暦 'calendar' in 旧暦 'old (lunar) calendar' (*also graphic/phonetic)
		L2: 金* 'money, gold' for 銀 'silver' in 銀行 'bank' (*also graphic)
Compositional	The incorrect character is the non-target character in the two-character compound instead of the target.	L1: 難 for 遭 in 遭難 *sohnan* 'missing'
		L2: 研 for 究 in 研究 *kenkyuu* 'research'
Contextual	The incorrect character is used or introduced frequently with the target in a different word context.	L1: 弔 (often used in 弔問 *chohmon* 'condolence') for 慰 in 慰問 *imon* 'consolation'
		L2: 練 (often used in 練習 *renshuu* 'practice') for 復 in 復習 *fukushuu* 'review'

*An overlap error is indicated with an asterisk, with the other classification in brackets.

other four factors, phonetic, graphic, semantic and compositional (see Figure 2.5).

Visual–phonetic association: Interestingly, L1 subjects made phonetic errors more often than semantic errors despite the common belief that semantic or graphic errors should be more common due to the orthographic features of the Japanese writing system. This may be explained as a task-oriented effect of writing in the present 'production' study where the sound representation was given first followed by the

Table 2.2 Error rates and frequencies

Errors	*L1 native*	*L2 non-native*
Phonetic	69.6% (94)	30.0% (65)
Graphic	54.8% (74)	27.7% (60)
Semantic	23.7% (32)	18.9% (41)
Compositional	3.0% (4)	15.2% (33)
Contextual	6.7% (9)	3.7% (8)
Total real kanji errors	(135)	(217)
Overlap errors	50.4% (68)	14.3% (31)
Unrelated errors	5.9% (8)	24.9% (54)

Brackets indicate the raw numbers of error frequency.

meaning to write a symbol. When a subject searched for a target kanji, several candidates associated with the phonological representation of the target were activated in the lexicon and one was wrongly chosen at the end. This interpretation is supported by Hatta *et al.* (1998) in which dominant phonetic errors were also observed in L1 free writing. Thus, unlike logographic 'recognition' where a visual representation is

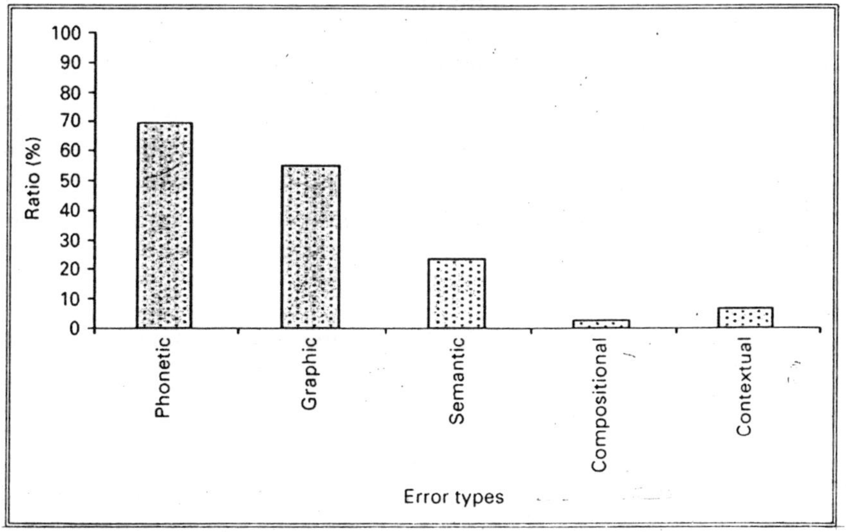

Figure 2.4 L1 natives' errors

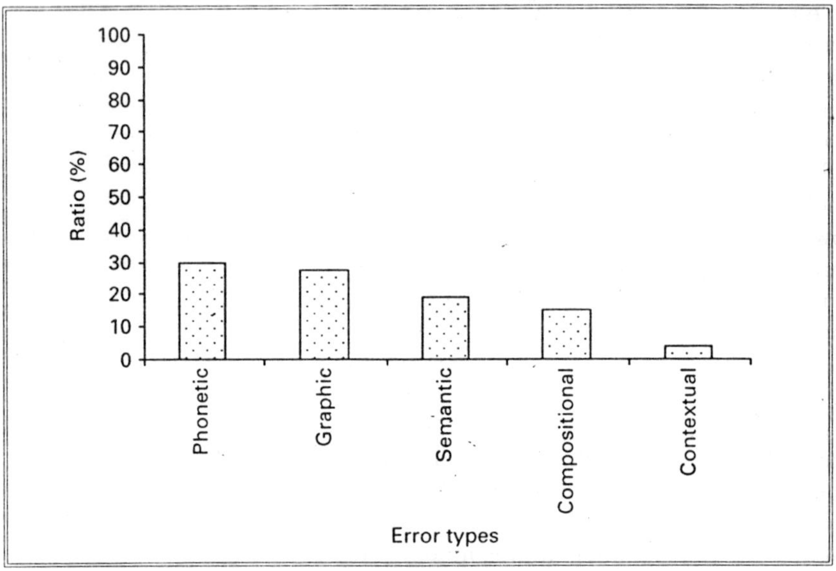

Figure 2.5 L2 non-natives' errors

converted into a semantic representation, often without sound mediation, in a writing task a concept (i.e. semantic representation) is converted into a symbol with automatic phonetic mediation despite its logographic feature. However, this automatic interactive phonetic activation may not be the case in the L2 lexicon, where multiple pieces of information are not strongly associated yet.

Character decomposability and radical functions: Of particular interest is the lack of difference between the occurrence of phonetic and graphic errors among the L1 errors. This may be explained by the large number of L1 phonetic–graphic overlap errors; that is to say, 59.6% (56 out of 94 cases) of L1 phonetic errors shared a graphically identical phonetic radical with the target, resulting in more cases of graphic errors. Interestingly, only 35.4% (23 out of 65 cases) of L2 phonetic errors had common radicals. The majority of L2 phonetic errors were characters with the same pronunciation as the target without any common phonetic radicals. Thus, while the L1 subjects made phonetic errors with common phonetic radicals, the L2 subjects often wrote an incorrect character as if a whole kanji character represented a sound unit. This could be the result of L1 cognitive transfer caused by the orthographic feature of sound-based English. In other words, even though a kanji is a logograph with the primary association between symbol and meaning, for L2 subjects it may not be easy to dissociate symbol and sound in kanji characters because of their L1 alphabetic features.

As for semantic errors, 68.8% (22 out of 32 cases) of the L1 semantic errors contained identical semantic radicals to the target, compared to 46.3% (19 out of 41 cases) of L2 errors. Radicals were frequently written correctly by L1 subjects even when whole characters were not recalled. It is probable that native speakers have a stronger sense of morphological rules, able to decompose a character into radicals. As a result, radicals could be stored and retrieved as information units. However, due to the low rate of recall of both phonetic and semantic radicals, it is thought that L2 subjects lacked morphological awareness or decomposability. As a result, radicals did not serve as a functional unit in L2 retrieval or memory to the same degree as in L1.

Multiple information activation: Another notable difference between L1 and L2 errors is the frequency of overlap errors. Over half of the L1 errors (50.4%) overlapped phonetic, semantic or graphic types, as compared to only 14.3% of L2 errors. While it was probably the case that L2 subjects simply did not know enough characters to produce such errors, this could also be explained by the multiple information activation model, mentioned above. In this model, a lexicon is organised with multiple levels of information, e.g. meaning, sound and shape, and those pieces of information are strongly connected and activated one after another in retrieval. The link between these levels in the network in the L1 lexicon is strong – as a result, L1 subjects produced many overlap errors. In the L2 lexicon, however, the lack of an established network means that this type of error is not observed very often. This interpretation is also supported by the relatively high rate of unrelated errors observed in L2 responses (24.9%), compared to L1 (5.9%).

Word decomposability: Another noteworthy finding is that substantial compositional errors were made by L2 subjects, i.e. statistically no fewer than phonetic, graphic, and semantic errors, but they were very rare in L1 errors. That is to say, L2 subjects often wrote the non-target character of the two-character words in the position of the target character. Only 3.0% of errors were of this type in L1 errors, compared to 15.7% of L2 errors. This indicates that in the L2 lexicon a character is often stored as part of a word, i.e. in the context in which the character is introduced or is used frequently. It suggests that native speakers can more effectively decompose larger units into smaller units (i.e. proceeding from a word to a character or from a character to a radical), while non-native speakers lack this ability.

Furthermore, more frequent compositional errors may have been the result of a weak connection between symbol and sound in the L2 lexicon. In the present writing test, the pronunciation and meaning of two-character compounds were given as cues for writing. In such a task, a compound could be easily decomposed into two constituent characters phonetically, but not semantically, as seen in 研究 *ken-kyuu* 'research'. If the phonetic representation is strongly associated to the visual symbol in each character, compositional errors should not occur often. Thus, L2 compositional errors may have been caused because the sound-symbol linkage was not well established yet for each character in the compound.

Conclusions

In the present study, TOP and error data collected from L1 and L2 writing samples were examined to discuss L2 Japanese learners' kanji knowledge and lexicon. To sum up, it suggests that:

(1) L2 learners of Japanese evidence a large gap between recognition and production skills;
(2) L1 orthographic transfer affects a learner's strategy and mechanism in L2 memory and retrieval;
(3) L2 learners lack intra-character structural and morphological awareness and the ability to decompose a character into radicals, or even a word into characters;
(4) radicals (both semantic and phonetic) do not serve as a solid memory unit in the L2 lexicon; and
(5) multiple information about a character (phonological, orthographic and semantic representations) is not strongly assembled or associated in the L2 lexicon.

Limitations

The present study has a number of limitations. First, different test materials were used for the two groups, and the two sets were not equally controlled in terms of morphological features, semantic or phonological transparency, familiarity, frequency, complexity, assemblage or position of the target character in a word. For instance, the target characters in L1 stimuli tended to have more obvious features as semantic–phonetic composites, which may have resulted in more visible intra-character functional awareness among L1 subjects. Practically, it was difficult to control these features because of the limited kanji knowledge among the L2 subjects. For instance, a substantial number of characters introduced at the early stage of kanji learning are pictographs (e.g. 火 'fire') or ideographs (e.g. 下 'under'). Many are composites with semantic and/or phonetic radicals, but a character often does not have a transparent phonological and/or semantic radical. Thus, L2 learners are not sufficiently exposed to kanji with apparent structural and morphological features. In addition, the usefulness of morphological rules is in question in kanji acquisition due to the semi-transparency of kanji, i.e. a constituent often has little or no relationship to the meaning or pronunciation of the whole character (Mori & Nagy, 1999). Due to this imbalance between the two sets of test stimuli, the present study remains at a descriptive and observational level.

Furthermore, the categorization criteria for error analysis or TOP are not well established yet since only a few kanji production studies have been conducted in either L1 or L2 research. The present study adopted Saito and Shikata's (1988) categorisation for error analysis, but the classification of phonetic, semantic, and orthographic errors was not straightforward due to the overlapping features of kanji, which may make interpretations more difficult to read in the analysis.

Pedagogical Implications

From the findings in the present study, some suggestions can be made for L2 kanji instruction, listed below.

Teaching intra-character rules: The evident lack of decomposability and intra-character functional awareness observed among L2 subjects raises the issue of whether or not intra-character rules should be taught explicitly in L2 kanji instruction. Rote learning is still widely used in L1 and L2 kanji instruction (Chan & Nunes, 1998; Tamaoka & Yamada, 2000), but limited exposure to written texts makes functional or morphological awareness more difficult in L2 kanji learning. One suggestion to facilitate understanding of intra-character features is to control the selection and order of character introduction based on the salient compositional features in L2 instruction. For instance, Yamashita and Maru (2000) conducted a survey study to rate the learning difficulty of new characters with different features. L2 novice subjects rated pictographs (e.g. 木 for 'tree') as the easiest, followed by katakana composites (e.g. 加, 外 which contain elements already learnt as katakana letters) and semantic composites (e.g. 好 'love' containing 女 'woman' and 子 'child') as somewhat easier, and semantic–phonetic composites (e.g. 油 'oil' *yu* containing semantic 氵 'water' and phonetic 由 *yu*) as the most difficult. The researchers suggested that the order of character introduction should be from pictograph, to katakana composites, semantic composites, and finally, semantic–phonetic composites, since learning takes place more efficiently when it is meaningful and related to existing knowledge.

Also, a relatively small number of radicals are in common use. Tamaoka *et al.* (2002) found that the top 10 and top 24 radicals accounted for 34% and 54% of Jooyoo kanji, respectively. It may be motivational and effective to teach intra-character features with these commonly used radicals. Of course, these suggestions have to be carefully incorporated into the early stage of L2 Japanese instruction, which may be difficult to carry out when the curriculum is often based on selected textbooks with specific grammatical features, vocabulary, and functions.

Meanwhile, over-reliance on morphological analysis for comprehension should be warned against, and the validity of morphological analysis should be attended to (Koda, 2001; Mori, 2002; Mori & Nagy, 1999).

Kanji in context: Due to semi-transparency or multiple readings of kanji, context may play a more crucial role in kanji comprehension than for other orthographies. Phonetic and semantic representation is realised only when a character is embedded in a word, or a word in a sentence. Therefore, decontextualisation of kanji may even be ineffective and harmful in kanji instruction. On the other hand, the present study found frequent compositional errors among L2 subjects, which suggests that L2 subjects are more likely to recall a kanji compound as a whole unit rather than as a unit assembling individual constituents, which could function as an independent unit for comprehension and production. To enhance these metacognitive and linguistic aspects of learning, for instance when a new word is introduced with the target character, other compounds with the target character could be reviewed or introduced simultaneously. It is important to have a learner compose a compound word and/or a sentence with the target character, or read a short paragraph with the target character embedded in context. This type of practice may help a learner strengthen the three linkages between symbol, meaning and sound of a character in the mental lexicon.

Recognition versus production: One implication of the present study was a large gap between L2 kanji recognition and production skills based on the low ratio of correct TOP occurrence (11.4%) among L2 subjects. One possible approach to enhance kanji production skills is to select high frequency radicals as functional lexical units, and to teach characters as an assemblage of those radicals rather than of several single strokes. Even if the radical is semantically or phonetically opaque in a given character, the knowledge of radicals may help a learner memorise and write characters more efficiently and precisely.

However, such a gap is noticeable even among L1 subjects, as only 30.5% of L1 TOP responses were correct TOP. Therefore, an important pedagogical issue here is to develop adequate recognition and production skills rather than filling the gap between them. One possible approach is to distinguish groups of kanji characters, some for reading and others for writing. In this way, learners can possibly focus on a smaller number of characters for writing with more attention, and be exposed to a greater number for recognition.

Nowadays computer word processing is becoming a common tool for Japanese writing and recognition skills are becoming crucial even for writing. Writing kanji on computers requires converting hiragana letters to the kanji equivalent by selecting from among several kanji homophone options. For instance, to type the kanji word 木, *ki* 'tree', one must first type the word phonetically in the Latin alphabet: KI. The computer application will display the hiragana representation, き. The user must then select the appropriate kanji for this word from among several homophones, all pronounced *ki*, such as 木, 気, 機, 輝, 期, etc. This process is completely different from writing kanji by hand, where every stroke of the character must be memorised and put together precisely, to form the proper character. In other words, writing kanji on a computer involves 'recognition' skills, rather than 'production' skills. The approach outlined above may therefore work from the early stage of kanji instruction (Chikamatsu, 2003).

The present discussion represents just the initial stage of the investigation of L2 kanji production and the study was limited in design. However, by looking at the response and error patterns in both native and non-native readers of Japanese, we have started to understand learners' difficulties and the organisation of the mental kanji dictionary. It is hoped that this information will help us find more effective ways for L2 kanji instruction in the future.

Acknowledgements

The original study was conducted with Jennifer Spenader. The author gratefully acknowledges De Paul University Research Council Leave Program for funding and the helpful suggestions of Drs Molly Mack and Jerome Packard.

Note

1. The six categories, so called 六書分類 *rikusho bunrui*, are:
   (1) *pictograph* (象形) which represents a shape of the object;
   (2) *ideograph* (指示) which expresses a concept such as quantity or quality;
   (3) *semantic composite* (会意) which consists of semantic components;
   (4) *semantic–phonetic composite* (形声) which consists of semantic and phonetic components;
   (5) *loan kanji* (仮借) which adopts the sound but not the meaning of the original character; and
   (6) *analogous kanji* (転注) which denotes a new meaning related to the original character.

References

Atsuji, T. (2001) *Kanji Dohraku* (The joy of kanji). Tokyo: Kodansha.

Biederman, I. and Tsao, I.C. (1979) On processing Chinese ideographs and English words: Some implications from Stroop-test results. *Cognitive Psychology* 2, 125–32.

Brown, R. and McNeill, D. (1966) The 'tip of the tongue' phenomenon. *Journal of Verbal Learning and Verbal Behavior* 5, 325–37

Chan, L. and Nunes, T. (1998) Children's understanding of the formal and functional characteristics of written Chinese. *Applied Psycholinguistics* 19, 115–31.

Chikamatsu, N. (2003) The effects of computer usage on L2 Japanese writing. *Foreign Language Annals* 36, 114–27.

Chikamatsu, N., Yokoyama, S., Nozaki, H., Long, E. and Fukuda, S. (2000) A Japanese logographic character frequency list for cognitive science research. *Journal of Behavior Research Methods, Instruments and Computers* 32, 482–500.

Chua, F.K. (1999) Phonological recoding in Chinese logograph recognition. *Journal of Experimental Psychology: Learning, Memory and Cognition* 25, 876–91.

Faust, M. and Sharfstein-Friedman, S. (2003) Naming difficulties in adolescents with dyslexia: Application of the tip-of-the-tongue paradigm. *Brain and Cognition* 53, 211–17.

Flores d'Arcais, G.B. (1992) Graphemic, phonological and semantic activation processes during the recognition of Chinese characters. In H.C. Chen and O.J.L. Tzeng (eds) *Language Processing in Chinese* (pp. 37–66). Amsterdam: North-Holland.

Flores d'Arcais, G.B. and Saito, H. (1993) Lexical decomposition of complex kanji characters in Japanese readers. *Psychological Research* 55, 52–63.

Flores d'Arcais, G.B., Saito, H., Kawakami, M. and Masuda, H. (1994) Figural and phonological effects in radical migration with kanji characters. *Advances in the Study of Chinese Language Processing* 1, 241–54.

Flores d'Arcais, G.B., Saito, H. and Kawakami, M. (1995) Phonological and semantic activation in reading kanji characters. *Journal of Experimental Psychology: Learning, Memory and Cognition* 21, 3–42.

Gollan, T.H. and Silverberg, N.B. (2001) Tip-of-the-tongue states in Hebrew-English bilinguals. *Bilingualism* 4, 63–83.

Hatta, T., Kawakami, A. and Tamaoka, K. (1998) Writing errors in Japanese kanji: A study with Japanese students and foreign learners of Japanese. *Reading and Writing: An Interdisciplinary Journal* 10, 457–70.

Hoosain R. (1991) *Psycholinguistic Implications for Linguistic Relativity: A Case Study of Chinese.* Hillsdale, NJ: Erlbaum.

Hue, C.W. (1992) Recognition processes in Chinese naming. In H.C. Chen and O.J.L. Tzeng (eds) *Language Processing in Chinese* (pp. 93–107). Amsterdam: North-Holland.

Ju, D. and Jackson, N.E. (1995) Graphic and phonological processing in Chinese character identification. *Journal of Reading Behavior* 27, 299–313.

Koda, K. (2001) Development of kanji knowledge among adult L2 learners of Japanese. In H. Nara (ed.) *Advances in Japanese Language Pedagogy* (pp. 1–29). Columbus, OH: National East Asian Language Resource Center, the Ohio State University.

Leong, C.K. and Tamaoka, K. (1995) Use of phonological information in processing kanji and katakana by skilled and less skilled Japanese readers. *Reading and Writing: An Interdisciplinary Journal* 7, 377–93.

Leong, C.K. and Tamaoka, K. (1998) *Cognitive Processing of the Chinese and the Japanese Languages*. London: Kluwer Academic Publishers.

Makino, S., Hatasa, Y. and Hatasa, K. (1998) *Nakama 1: Japanese Communication, Culture, Context*. New York: Houghton Mifflin.

Mori, Y. (2002) Individual differences in the integration of information from context and word parts in interpreting unknown kanji words. *Applied Psycholinguistics* 23, 375–97.

Mori, Y. and Nagy, W. (1999) Integration of information from context and word elements in interpreting novel kanji compounds. *Reading Research Quarterly* 34, 80–101.

Morikawa, Y. (1985) Stroop phenomena in the Japanese language (ii): Effects of character-usage frequency and number of strokes. In H.S.R. Kao and R. Hoosain (eds) *Linguistics, Psychology, and the Chinese Language* (pp. 73–80). Hong Kong: University of Hong Kong Centre of Asian Studies.

Oxford English Dictionary (OED) (1994) (CD-Rom edition). Oxford: Oxford University Press.

Paradis, M., Hagiwara, H. and Hildebrandt, N. (1985) *Neurolinguistic Aspects of the Japanese Writing System*. New York: Academic Press.

Perfetti, C.A. and Zhang, S. (1995) Very early phonological activation in Chinese reading. *Journal of Experimental Psychology: Learning, Memory, and Cognition* 21, 24–33.

Perfetti, C.A., Zhang, S. and Berent, I. (1992) Reading in English and Chinese: Evidence for a 'universal' phonological principle. In R. Frost and L. Katz (eds) *Orthography, Phonology, Morphology, and Meaning* (pp. 227–48). Amsterdam: Elsevier.

Saito, H., Kawakami, M. and Masuda, H. (1994) Kanji and kana recognition with migration paradigm. *Technical report of the Institute of Electronics, Information and Communication Engineers, NCL 94-9*, 15–22.

Saito, H., Masuda, H. and Kawakami, M. (1998) Form and sound similarity effects in kanji recognition. *Reading and Writing: An Interdisciplinary Journal* 10, 323–57.

Saito, H. and Shikata, Y. (1988) A minimal core model for associative memory: Hierarchy of strategy for kanji information retrieval. Nihon Ninchi Kagaku Kai (The Japanese Cognitive Science Society) (eds) *Ninchi kagaku no hatten* (Advances in Japanese Cognitive Science), Volume 1 (pp. 72–111). Tokyo: Kodansha Scientific.

Schwartz, B.L. (2002) *Tip-of-the-tongue States: Phenomenology, Mechanism, and Lexical Retrieval*. Mahwah, NJ: Erlbaum.

Seidenberg, M.S. (1985) The time course of phonological code activation in two writing systems. *Cognition* 19, 1–30.

Shigaki, M. (1992) Which kanji should the students of economics without a kanji-background learn? *Journal of Japanese Language Teaching* 76, 67–87.

Taft, M. and Zhu, X. P. (1995) The representation of bound morphemes in the lexicon: A Chinese study. In L.B. Fledman (ed.) *Morphological Aspects of Language Processing* (pp. 293–316). Hillsdale, NJ: Lawrence Erlbaum Associates.

Tamamura, F. (1993) Nihongo ni okeru kanji; Kanji in the Japanese language. *Journal of Japanese Language Teaching* 80, 1–14.

Tamaoka, K. and Yamada, H. (2000) The effects of stroke orders and radicals on the knowledge of Japanese kanji orthography, phonology and semantics. *Psychologia* 43, 199–210.

Tamaoka, K., Kirsner, K., Yanase, Y., Miyaoka, Y. and Kawakami, M. (2002) A Web-accessible database of characteristics of the 1,945 basic Japanese kanji. *Behavior Research Methods, Instruments and Computers* 34, 260–75.

Tan, L.H. and Perfetti, C.A. (1998) Phonological codes as early sources of constraint in Chinese word identification: A review of current discoveries and theoretical accounts. *Reading and Writing: An Interdisciplinary Journal* 10, 165–200.

Tohsaku, Y. (1999) *Yookoso: An Invitation to Contemporary Japanese* (2nd edn). New York: McGraw Hill.

Weekes, B.S., Chen, M.J. and Lin, Y.B. (1998) Differential effects of phonological priming on Chinese character recognition. *Reading and Writing: An Interdisciplinary Journal* 10, 201–22.

White, K.K. and Abrams, L. (2002) Does priming specific syllables during tip-of-the-tongue states facilitate word retrieval in older adults? *Psychology and Aging* 17, 226–35.

Xu, Y., Pollatsek, A. and Potter, M.C. (1999) The activation of phonology during silent Chinese word reading. *Journal of Experimental Psychology: Learning, Memory, and Cognition* 25, 838–57.

Yamashita, H. and Maru, Y. (2000) Compositional features of kanji for effective instruction. *Journal of the Association of Teachers of Japanese* 34, 159–78.

Yu, B., Jing, Q. and Sima, H. (1984) STM capacity for Chinese words and phrases under simultaneous presentation. In H.W. Stevenson and Q. Jing (eds) *Language Development and Neurological Theory* (pp. 290–311). New York: Academic.

Zhang, G. and Peng, D. (1992) Decomposed storage in the Chinese lexicon. In H.C. Chen and O.J.L. Tzeng (eds) *Language Processing in Chinese* (pp. 131–49). Amsterdam: North-Holland.

Zhang, G. and Simon, H.A. (1985) STM capacity for Chinese words and idioms: Chunking and acoustical loop hypotheses. *Memory and Cognition* 13, 193–201.

Zhou, X. and Marslen-Wilson, W. (1994) Words, morphemes and syllables in the Chinese mental lexicon. *Language and Cognitive Processes* 9, 393–422.

Appendix 1

Kanji stimuli

	L1 Native stimuli				*L2 Non-native stimuli*		
1	脂肪	26	老婆	1	調査	26	政治
2	哀愁	27	騎手	2	結婚	27	全然
3	鍛練	28	蜜蜂	3	会社	28	電車
4	手錠	29	墜落	4	新聞	29	問題
5	学閥	30	眺望	5	復習	30	石油
6	遺憾	31	基盤	(6	手紙)	31	質問
7	睡眠	32	絞殺	7	毎日	32	料理
8	迫力	33	捕鯨	8	家族	33	全部
9	開墾	34	悪癖	9	美術	34	漢字
10	旧暦	35	宴会	10	銀行	35	空港
11	暫定	36	慰問	11	仕事	36	説明
12	摩擦	37	腐食	12	練習	37	家内
13	捕虜	38	鳩舎	13	文法	38	専門
14	窮地	39	待遇	14	意味	39	試験
15	餓死	40	圏内	15	病院	40	今晩
16	漏電	41	搾取	16	音楽	41	切符
17	濃霧	42	撤回	17	映画	42	最初
18	装飾	43	応酬	18	立派	43	季節
19	感銘	44	噴火	19	宿題	44	歴史
20	蝶々	45	摘出	20	来年	45	番号
21	腹心			21	勉強		
22	右翼			22	数字		
23	店舗			23	住所		
24	遭難			24	研究		
25	威嚇			25	英語		

Appendix 2

Answer sheets

(Nonnative)

A.

If you cannot write the kanji, please proceed.

B. Circle the shape that you think is the most similar to it.

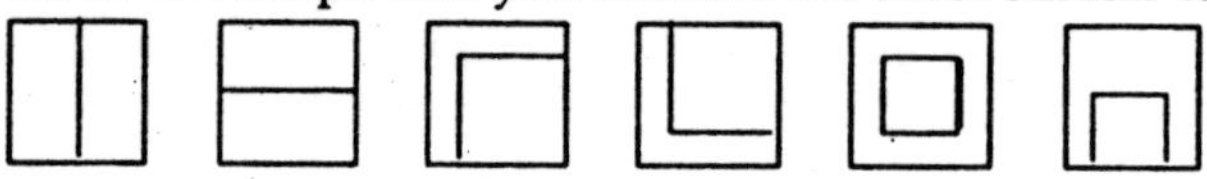

C. How many strokes do you think it has?

__________.

D. Use the space provided on the right side to try to write it.

E. Write the one that you think it is your best guess.

(Native)

A.

漢字が書けない時は、Bに進んで下さい。

B. 一番近いと思う型を、まるで囲んで下さい。

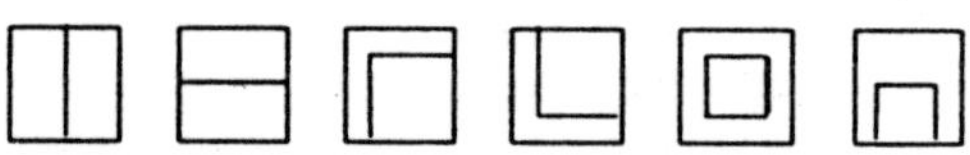

C. 画数は、いくつですか。

____

D. 右のスペースを使って、練習して下さい。

E. 一番近いと思う漢字を書いて下さい。

Chapter 3

The Role of the Phonological Strategy in Learning to Spell in English as a Second Language

ANS VAN BERKEL

Introduction

This chapter examines the acquisition of the English spelling system by Dutch learners during the first years of secondary education. Apparently, spelling is simply accepted as part and parcel of learning English, as English language teaching in the Netherlands devotes no systematic attention to this subject. From the very beginning, learners encounter all kinds of written forms, without any explanation of phoneme–grapheme correspondences (PGCs) or rules, and without any information about regular and exceptional spellings. Neither is instruction given about adequate spelling strategies or useful methods of learning the written form of English words by memory. Native speakers of English, who receive many years of instruction and training in orthography, may wonder whether L2 learners could ever master English spelling. Interestingly, most Dutch L2 learners do succeed in spelling English words correctly within a fairly short period of time. The question is how they manage to learn this complicated system.

When they start to learn English, Dutch L2 learners have a great deal of experience dealing with written language in their mother tongue. During primary education, they are taught the spelling system and instructed in the use of spelling strategies. By the end of primary school, Dutch children can be considered adult L1 spellers. Probably, in dealing with the written form of English words, Dutch learners will tend to apply the spelling skills they use in their mother tongue. To provide an understanding of what these spelling skills involve, Dutch L1 spelling acquisition will be discussed briefly, see Learning to Spell in Dutch L1, below. Since this process cannot be properly understood without at least some knowledge of the spelling system concerned, the main characteristics of the Dutch orthographic system will be introduced first. Having considered the Dutch system, the chapter will focus on the English spelling system. The two systems will then be compared in order to provide an impression of the kind of spelling problems that might be expected. Finally the results of research concerning L2 spelling acquisition by Dutch learners will be discussed.

This chapter concentrates solely on the acquisition of spellings corresponding to phonemes; the acquisition of morphological spellings is not examined.

The Dutch Spelling System

In view of a possible comparison of the Dutch and English orthographies, I would like to propose the following description. Dutch has an alphabetical spelling system, using the letters of the Roman alphabet. This does not mean, however, that the system is exclusively characterised by correspondence to phonemes. Morphology is also involved. As this paper focuses primarily on the acquisition of phoneme–grapheme correspondences, morphological spellings will be discussed only briefly. With morphologically complex words, Dutch spellers need to be aware of the required spelling of the morphemes, which often means that they have to ignore the phonological form. Examples can be taken from the domains of morphology: inflection, compounding and derivation. The inflected form <hij wordt> (he becomes) is composed of the root morpheme 'word' and the inflectional morpheme 't'. Although only /t/ is realised in the spoken form /wɔrt/, both <d> and <t> must be spelled in <hij wordt>. The compound 'postzegel' (stamp) is pronounced as /pɔse:χəl/, which could cause learners to spell the word as <*possegel>. However, 'postzegel' is made up of the words <post> and <zegel>, and both morphemes must be written. The affixes <lijk> and <ig> in the derived forms <gevaarlijk> (dangerous) and <gelukkig> (lucky) are unstressed and pronounced as /lək/ and /əχ/. Although the schwa usually appears as <e> in written language, the forms <*gevaarlek> and <*gelukkeg> are unacceptable. Our final example concerns the fact that voiced consonants in Dutch become devoiced when they appear in final position, e.g. /hɔnt/ occurs next to /hɔndə/. The forms that occur in the spoken language are not realised in the written language: <hond>, which is considered the basic form, is used to spell /hɔnt/, and occurs next to <honden>.

For a clear understanding of the system of phoneme–grapheme correspondences, it is important to note that the Dutch lexicon can be roughly subdivided into words that are originally Dutch and words of foreign origin, i.e. words adopted from Greek, Latin, French and English. Borrowed words, especially those of French and English origin, have largely retained their original pronunciation and spelling. Consequently, a considerable number of spellings (albeit in a relatively small portion of the language) deviate from the spelling system that applies to words of Dutch origin. This phenomenon, which concerns morphemes as well as phonemes, results in spellings that can be considered word specific. Examples include the <a> in 'tram' (pronounced as /trɛm/), the <a> in 'baby' (pronounced /beːbi/), and the <b> in 'club' (pronounced as /klʏp/).

In much of the non-foreign segment of the lexicon, Dutch PGCs are transparent. As shown in Table 3.1, short vowels correspond to only one possible spelling, as do most other vowels (except /a:/, /e:/, /o:/ and /y:/) and the consonants /h/, /v/, /w/, /z/, /ʃ/ and /ɳ/. These are prime examples of the alphabetical basis of the Dutch spelling system.

The remaining phonemes correspond to two spellings, the choice of which is determined by contextual rules. The two main spelling rules are related to the fact that Dutch has more vowel phonemes than the five vowel letters of the Roman alphabet. The single letters <a>, <e>, <i>, <o> and <u> function primarily as the spellings corresponding to the five short vowels. The spellings of the other vowels are rendered either by a combination of two different vowel letters (<oe>, <ui>, <ie> and <eu>), or by doubling the vowel letters (<aa>, <oo>, <ee> and <uu>). In pre-consonantal position, the phonemes /a:/, /e:/, /o:/ and /y:/ correspond to double vowel letters: 'haat', 'heet', 'boot' and 'fuut.' In open syllable position, however, '*haaten', '*heeten', '*booten' and '*fuuten' are not acceptable. Dutch spelling rules call for 'haten', 'heten', 'boten' and 'futen' in open syllable position, and for 'la', 'zo' and 'nu' in word final position. (Final /e:/ is written as <ee>, for example, in 'zee' (sea), to prevent confusion with the schwa in words like 'ze' (she).) Consequently, the letters <a>, <e>, <o> and <u> function not only as the spellings corresponding to short vowels, such as in 'lat', 'pet', 'zot' and 'hut', but also as spelling variants corresponding to long vowels. The second main spelling rule serves to prevent possible confusion. In syllable final (but not in word final) position, the consonant is doubled after short vowels, resulting not only in 'latten', 'petten', 'zotten' and 'hutten', but also in 'zitten'.

The remaining spelling rules are less important. The rule concerning /ŋ/ applies only to that phoneme: it is written <ng> 'bang', except before /k/, where the spelling is <n> 'bank'). The phoneme /j/ in post-vocalic position is written <i>, occurring in <aai> 'fraai', <ooi> 'mooi' and <oei> 'foei'. Post-vocalic <w> is preceded by <u> in <uw> 'duw' and in the groups <eeuw> 'sneeuw' and <ieuw> 'nieuw'.

The Dutch phoneme–grapheme correspondences can be subdivided into three categories:

(1) *Basic:* The basic category contains transparent correspondences, such as <a> in 'lat' or <aa> in 'haat' that function as the default spelling of the phonemes concerned.

Table 3.1 Dutch phoneme–grapheme correspondences (PGCs), subdivided into spelling categories

Phoneme	*Basic spelling*	*Contextual spelling*	*Word-specific spelling*
Short vowels			
/ɑ/	<a> lat		
/ɛ/	<e> pet		<ai> affaire; <è> carrière; <ê> enquête; <a> tram
/ɪ/	<i> pit		<y> gym
/ɔ/	<o> zot		
/ʏ/	<u> hut		
/ə/	<e> de		<u> museum
Long vowels			
/a:/	<aa> haat	<a> haten, la	
/e:/	<ee> heet, zee	<e> heten	<er> diner; <é> café; <ai> rails; <a> baby; <a-e> cake
/i:/	<ie> riet, rieten, drie		<i> vitrine; <y> type; <ea> team; <ee> keeper
/o:/	<oo> boot	<o> boten, zo	<au> auto; <eau> bureau; <oa> goal; <ow> show
/y:/	<uu> fuut	<u> futen, nu	
/u:/	<oe> voet, voeten, koe		<ou> route; <u> computer; <ew> interview
/ø:/	<eu> peut, peuter, sneu		
Diphthongs			
/œy/	<ui> buit, buiten, bui		<eu> fauteuil
/ɑu/			<au> heraut; <ou> bout, kou; <auw> lauw; <ouw> trouw
/ɛi/			<ei> feit; <ij> spijt; <y> nylon

(*continued*)

Table 3.1 *Continued*

Phoneme	*Basic spelling*	*Contextual spelling*	*Word-specific spelling*
Consonants			
/b/	<b> bel	<bb> rubber	
/d/	<d> daar	<dd> redden	
/f/	<f> fuif	<ff> koffer	
/χ/	<g> graag	<gg> vlaggen	<ch> lach
/h/	<h> hout		
/j/	<j> jaar	<i> mooi	<ill> taille; <y> yoghurt; <i> interview
/k/	<k> klok	<kk>klokken	<c> conflict; <qu> enquête
/l/	<l> lol	<ll> willen	
/m/	<m> mam	<mm> remmen	
/n/	<n> noen	<nn> zonnen	
/ŋ/	<ng> bang	<n> bank	
/p/	<p> pop	<pp> lappen	<b> club
/r/	<r> raar	<rr> karren	
/s/	<s> sis	<ss> sissen	<c> centrum; <zz> jazz
/t/	<t> tent	<tt> motten	<th> thee
/v/	<v> vet		
/w/	<w> wet	<uw> leeuw	
/z/	<z> zand		<s> visite
/ʃ/	<sj> sjaal		<ch> China; <sh> show
/ɳ/	<nj> oranje		<gn> champagne

(2) *Contextual:* Spellings determined by rules, such as <a> in 'haten' or <kk> in 'klokken', belong to the contextual category.

(3) *Word-specific:* This category consists of spellings of foreign origin and some historical spellings.

The basic status of spellings, such as <a>, <e>, <i>, corresponding to short vowels, or of <ie> and <eu> is clear: they are the only non-foreign spellings of the phonemes concerned. In the case of the long vowels, <aa>, <ee>, <oo> and <uu> are considered default spellings, mainly because they are the first spellings corresponding to these phonemes when they are introduced to children. These four spellings belong, therefore, to the basic category, whereas <a>, <e>, <o> and <u> are considered contextual spellings.

Aside from spellings of foreign origin, the word-specific category contains a few historical spellings of Dutch origin, namely those of the diphthongs /ɛi/ and /ɑu/ and the spelling <ch> for /χ/. Both diphthongs are represented by more than one spelling. None of the spelling alternatives, however, can be considered the default, either on the basis of frequency or for didactic reasons. Moreover, the alternatives are not determined by contextual rules. For that reason, all the spelling variants of these two phonemes are considered word-specific. The <ch> spelling is historical and is used in a limited number of words.

Table 3.1 presents the Dutch PGCs, subdivided into the categories discussed above.

Learning to Spell in Dutch L1

Judging by the teaching methods, the stages of spelling instruction in Dutch can be described roughly as follows. First, the basic spellings are presented, and children are trained in using phoneme–grapheme conversion rules. Since nearly all Dutch phonemes can be spelled using such rules, the *phonological strategy* appears to be highly suitable. In the next stage, when words consisting of more than one syllable are introduced, contextual spelling rules are learned. As discussed earlier, these involve consonant doubling after a short vowel ('petten', 'rokken', 'jassen', etc.) and the spelling of long vowels in open syllables ('weten', 'koken', 'laden', etc.). Children shift from the exclusive reliance on sound–letter relations to the use of spelling patterns as well: they use an *orthographic strategy*. Errors occur when spellers continue to use the phonological strategy, e.g. writing '*peten' instead of 'petten', or '*weeten' instead of 'weten'. Overgeneralisation of rules is another source of errors: '*boekken' instead of 'boeken', or '*laatten' instead of 'laten'.

Subsequently, the speller becomes acquainted with the morphological spellings, mainly involving the spelling of devoiced consonants in final position (/hɔnt/ spelled as <hond>) and the spelling of inflected forms (<hij wordt>). In the last years of primary school, morphology becomes increasingly important.

Although some frequent words with word-specific spellings are taught early in primary education, most word-specific spellings are introduced in the final years of primary school. As these are spellings of relatively low frequency, not determined by rules, children have to learn specific words with such spellings by memory. As long as pupils do not know the spelling of such words, their errors often testify to the use of a phonological strategy. The loan-word 'baby', for example, may be spelled as '*beebie', or 'keeper' as '*kieper'.

In Ellis' discussion of various stage models of English L1 spelling development (Ellis, 1994), it becomes clear that most models agree that two stages have to be distinguished: the alphabetic stage, characterised by exclusive phoneme–grapheme conversion, and the orthographic stage, characterised by the use of higher-order condition rules and by morphological insight. Besides, word-specific knowledge is necessary from the very beginning to spell words with low-frequency spelling (Ehri, 1986; Ellis, 1994; Frith, 1985). These stages do not occur only in the L1 acquisition of English orthography, but also seem to apply to L1 Dutch orthography.

As we can conclude from the discussion above, when children leave Dutch primary schools at age twelve, they have attained what can be considered an adult L1 spelling level. They are aware of the different kinds of correspondence between the spoken and written forms of words and have mastered various strategies for producing correct spellings. With known words, they will tend to retrieve the spelling from their mental lexicon, using a *lexical* spelling method. With unknown words, they are likely to use an *assembling* method, by converting phonemes into graphemes, applying spelling rules or making use of analogy (Barry, 1994).

Since spelling instruction is lacking in L2 education, Dutch spellers depend largely on their L1 spelling competence in learning the English spelling system. This brings us to several questions.

- Firstly, are the L1 spelling strategies, which appear to be related to the sub-categories of Dutch spelling, adequate in identifying the characteristics of the English orthographic system? This implies that the same sub-categorisation can also be found in English. To clarify this point, I will propose a description of the English spelling system, parallel to that used above for the Dutch spelling system.
- Secondly, which strategies do Dutch spellers prefer for their task? Dutch pupils are used to memorising words with foreign spellings. Do they apply that strategy in learning to spell in English? Do they try to discover rules, thus using an orthographic strategy? Or do they tend to apply the phonological strategy to English, a strategy that, as explained, is fairly well suited to learning Dutch spelling? It is important here to consider the issue of possible interference from L1 spelling knowledge. These questions will be discussed later.

The English Spelling System

Sub-categorising English phoneme-grapheme correspondences

Like Dutch orthography, the English system consists of spellings corresponding to phonemes on the one hand and morphological spellings on the other. Before discussing the PGCs, the morphological spellings will be dealt with briefly. The main characteristic of morphological spellings is that the written forms remain constant, whereas the spoken forms may vary (see Carney 1994, Chapter 2). The past tense morpheme <ed> relates to three spoken forms in 'worked', 'lived' and 'landed'. The word 'sanity' contains the written form of the root morpheme, 'sane', which explains why the consonant is not doubled after the short vowel. In the spoken form of 'cupboard', the two compounding words are hardly recognisable, in contrast to the written form.

One question that arises in examining PGCs is whether the sub-categories of basic, contextual and word-specific spellings that occur in Dutch can also be identified in English?. If so, which spellings fall into these respective categories?

As shown in Table 3.2, transparent PGCs seldom occur in English. Only the phonemes /æ/ and /θ/ correspond to a single spelling: <a> in 'cat' and <th> in 'thin', respectively. We could add some more cases, namely: /e/ corresponding to <e>; stressed /ɪ/ corresponding to <i>; /h/ corresponding

Table 3.2 English phoneme–grapheme correspondences, sub-divided into spelling categories

Phoneme	*Basic spelling*	*Contextual spelling*	*Word-specific spelling*
Short vowels			
/æ/	<a> cat		
/e/	<e> ten		<ea> bread; <ie> friend
/ɪ/	<i> pit		<ui> build; <y> gym
/ɒ/	<o> pot	<a> wash	<ou> cough
/ʌ/	<u> cut		<ou> young; <oo> blood; <o> monk
/ʊ/			<u> push; <oo> book; <o> wolf
/ə/	<e> the		

(*continued*)

Table 3.2 *Continued*

Phoneme	*Basic spelling*	*Contextual spelling*	*Word-specific spelling*
Long vowels			
/ɑ:/	<ar> card	<a> fast	<ear> heart; <er> clerk; <al> calm; <au> draught
/i:/			<ee> seem; <ea> team; <e> he; <e-e> theme; <ie> field; and others
/ɔ:/			<or> fork; <ore> more; <aw> law; <oa> broad; <ough> ought; and others
/ɜ:/			<er> her; <ir> girl; <ur> turn; <or> word; <ear> learn
/ju:/ [5]	<u> tulip	<u-e> tune; <ew> few	
/u:/			<oo> food; <u> ruler; <u-e> rule; <ue> blue; <ou> group; and others
Diphthongs			
/eɪ/	<a> lady	<a-e> name; <ay> day	<ai> rain; <ea> break; <eigh> eight; <aigh> straight; <ey> they; and others
/aɪ/	<i> tidy	<i-e> time; <y> fly; <ie> tie	<igh> night; <y-e> type; <eigh> height; <eye> eye
/ɔɪ/	<oi> coin	<oy> boy	
/əʊ/	<o> cosy	<o-e> home; <ow> show	<oa> coat; <ough> though; <ou> soul; <ol> folk
/ɑʊ/	<ou> house	<ow> cow, down	<ough> plough
/ɪə/			<ear> ear; <ere> here; <eer> cheer
/ɛə/			<are> care; <air> pair; <ear> wear; <ere> where; <eir> their

(*continued*)

Table 3.2 *Continued*

Phoneme	*Basic spelling*	*Contextual spelling*	*Word-specific spelling*
/ʊə/			<ure> pure; <oor> poor; <our> tour
Consonants			
/p/	<p> pop	<pp> apple	
/b/	<b> Bob	<bb> hobby	
/t/	<t> tent	<tt> bottle	
/d/	<d> dad	<dd> sudden	
/k/		<c> cat; <k> king; <ck> back	<ch> school
/g/	<g> grog	<gg> struggle	<gu> guide; <gue> league; <gh> ghost
/m/	<m> mum	<mm> summer	
/n/	<n> noon	<nn> funny	<kn> know; <gn> gnome
/ŋ/	<ng> sing	<n> think	
/f/	<f> fine	<ff> coffee, stuff	<ph> phone; <gh> laugh
/v/	<v> vote	<ve> have	
/θ/	<th> thin, bath		
/ð/	<th> this	<the> breathe	
/s/	<s> sing	<ss> missing, glass; <se> house	<c> cent; <ce> force; <sc> scene
/z/		<z> zoo; <s> easy; <zz> jazz; <se> please	<ze> freeze

(*continued*)

Table 3.2 *Continued*

Phoneme	*Basic spelling*	*Contextual spelling*	*Word-specific spelling*
/ʃ/	<sh> shellfish		<ch> chef
/tʃ/	<ch> church	<tch> kitchen, watch	
/dʒ/		<j> jam, jeep; <g> regent; <ge> change; <dg> budget; <dge> bridge	<g> gin, gel
/r/	<r> rain	<rr> narrow	<wr> wrong
/l/	<l> like	<ll> silly, will	
/j/	<y> yes		
/w/	<w> water	(/kw/) <qu> quarter	<wh> where; <u> suite
/h/	<h> hat		<wh> whole

to <h>; and /ʃ/ corresponding to <sh>, in leaving aside the low-frequency, word-specific spelling variants such as <ie> in 'friend', <ui> in 'build', <wh> in 'whole' and <ch> in 'chef'. Apparently, unlike Dutch, English has hardly any PGCs that can be classified into the basic category solely on the basis of their uniqueness. That is why the criteria for English were adapted on the basis of frequency. The frequency counts are taken from Carney (1994).[1] This study, which is based on a body of some 26,000 lemmata, presents both the lexical and the textual frequencies. Lexical frequency concerns only the frequency of the occurrence of a certain phoneme's spelling. Textual frequency refers to the frequency of the words in which the spelling occurs. Textual frequency will be examined here since discussion in this chapter is geared towards L2 teaching, and since, in their early stages of learning, the knowledge of L2 spellers is likely to consist of high-frequency words.

In adapting the criteria for English, it is useful to take note of the following, systematically occurring, relationship. Most spelling variants corresponding to a given phoneme are not only complementary, but together their coverage amounts to 80% or more. It follows that many spelling variants are predictable on this basis. The following examples are cases in point. The spellings <a> 'later', <a-e>[2] 'name' and <ay>

'day', corresponding to /eɪ/, are distinguished on the basis of their position in the word. Together, they cover 83% of the spellings of /eɪ/. The choice between <i> 'hiking', <i-e> 'time', <y> 'fly' and <ie> 'tie', corresponding to /aɪ/, is determined – once again – by contextual rules, and together they cover 80%. The spellings <ou> 'house' and <ow> 'owl', 'down', 'how', corresponding to /ɑʊ/, are equally distinguishable by context, and their total coverage is 99%. These examples should serve to illustrate that, in English, phoneme–grapheme conversions depend largely on contextual conditions.

Providing that the spelling variants covered at least 80% and complemented each other, they were subdivided into the basic and contextual categories. The most frequent variant was considered the default, basic spelling. Thus, <o> 'pot' and <oi> 'coin', for instance, are categorised as basic spellings of the respective vowels, and <a> (wash) and <oy> 'boy' as the contextual[3] ones. The same distinction was made in the case of consonants. Spellings, such as <b> 'but', <p> 'pot', <ch> 'teach', are considered the basic spellings of the consonants concerned, whereas <bb> 'hobby', <pp> 'happy' and <tch> 'watch', 'kitchen' are contextual.

In some cases, the categorisation of spelling variants requires more clarification. Each of the vowels /eɪ/, /aɪ/, /əʊ/ and /ju:/ corresponds to three spelling variants that follow the same pattern. In open syllable position a single vowel letter is used: 'lady', 'tidy', 'cosy' and 'tulip'. In words like 'name', 'time', 'home' and 'tune', <e> is added in word-final position. And in word-final position, <ay> 'day', <y> 'fly',[4] <ow> 'show' and <ew> 'few' occur. One might conclude that each spelling variant occurs in a specific context and should, therefore, be considered a contextual spelling. However, as the alphabetical names of the single vowel letters happen to be the same as the vowels in question, these are considered the default spellings and are categorised as basic.

A different approach to categorisation was taken as regarding the spellings of three consonants, namely /k/, /dʒ/ and /z/. For various reasons, it is not possible to consider any single spelling as the basic one with these consonants. The phoneme /k/ corresponds to <c> before the letters <a, o, u> and consonant letters (coverage 59%). It corresponds to <k> before the letters <e> and <i> and after consonant letters (coverage 21%). After short vowels, it is represented by <ck> (coverage 6%). If <c> were to be considered the basic spelling on the basis of frequency, the graphotactic context of the spelling <k> would be ignored. This is why all three spellings have been placed in the contextual category.

The phoneme /dʒ/ is usually written as <g> 'regent', 'gel', <ge> 'age' or <dge> 'budget', 'bridge'; total coverage 56%. The spelling <j> covers 29% and only occurs in word initial position 'jam', 'jeep', 'Jim', 'job', 'just', where it is the preferred spelling. If <g> were to be considered the basic spelling on the basis of frequency, <j> would not be the preferred choice in word-initial position. All three spellings were classified in the contextual category.

The phoneme /z/ is generally written as <s> (coverage of 93%). In word initial position, however, only <z> occurs. In keeping with the approach to categorisation described above, not only <se> and <zz>, but also <z> and <s> were considered contextual spellings.

As shown in Table 3.2, several phonemes lack basic *and* contextual spellings. These phonemes correspond only to word-specific spellings. This sub-categorisation is based on the fact that the spelling variants concerned do not meet the conditions outlined above: the different spellings do not complement each other on the basis of contextual rules. The frequency criterion does not apply either (none of the spellings reaches the frequency of 80% which is the minimum for being considered basic or contextual). It follows, therefore, that all spelling variants must be considered word-specific. Let us now turn to an example that illustrates this point. The main spellings corresponding to /i:/ are <e> 'Peter', <e-e> 'theme' and final <ee> 'see', with a total coverage of 38%. Non-final <ee> 'seem' adds another 26%, and <ea> 'sea', 'seam' covers 25%. Although <e>, <e-e> and final <ee> can be identified on the basis of context, the total coverage of these spellings is too low to predict spellings of /i:/.

The spellings discussed in the paragraph above are not the only ones in the word-specific category. As shown in Table 3.2, most phonemes with spellings in the basic and contextual categories correspond equally to one or more low-frequency spellings. For that reason, they were considered word-specific spellings.

Table 3.2 lists all the English PGCs. Since the textbooks used in the Netherlands focus primarily on teaching British English RP (Received Pronunciation), this pronunciation is followed here. Because of the high number of word-specific spellings in some cases, the number of examples is limited to five.

The Dutch and English systems: A comparative look

In comparing the Dutch and English systems, the differences stand out. Although both systems can be subdivided into the same kinds of spelling categories, the English orthography is likely to be more difficult to master than the Dutch spelling system for the following reasons:

(1) English has 44 phonemes and Dutch has 36, which explains the larger discrepancy between the number of phonemes and the available number of letters of the alphabet. Spellers of English need to learn more combinations of letters to cover all the phonemes.

Table 3.3 Basic L1 (English) = L2 (Dutch) spellings

<i> pit	<p> pop	<m> mum	<f> fine	<h> hat
<e> pet	<b> but	<n> noon	<v> vote	<l> like
<o> pot	<t> tent	<ng> sing	<s> sing	<w> water
	<d> day			

(2) English phonemes correspond to different spellings more often than in Dutch. Moreover, in a great many cases, they belong to the word-specific category. In English, spelling by ear will often lead to spelling errors. Spellers not only have to learn more contextual rules, but they also face the task of memorising more spellings.

Despite these differences, there are several PGCs in both languages that resemble each other closely. Table 3.3 presents the spellings concerned. Because all spellings are considered as basic spellings in both English and Dutch, these spellings will be called basic L1 = L2 spellings, and will be treated separately in the section on the importance of phonological strategy.

Use of the Phonological Strategy: What Kinds of Error Occur?

Introduction

If L2 spellers have not stored the written forms of words in their mental lexicon, they have to produce a possible spelling when asked to write. They may have identified spelling rules on their own, or may try to remember analogous forms, thus using an orthographic strategy. It seems plausible, however, that Dutch beginner L2 spellers will often rely on a phonological strategy. Evidence that points to the use of this strategy is usually based on error analysis. Spelling errors, such as '*exectly' (exactly), '*privite' (private), '*scolarship' (scholarship) (Cook, 1997), confirm the relevance of the phonological approach to L2 spelling. Learners also tend to draw on knowledge of their L1 spelling system in making errors such as these.

The examples in this and the next section stem mostly from the same data. These data were collected on two occasions in consecutive years: the first and second years of secondary school. In total, 173 pupils participated each year. They wrote 40 familiar words in a spot dictation, 29 of which were selected for further analysis: 'about', 'answer', 'bathroom', 'chairs', 'cleaning', 'clothes', 'colour', 'cupboard', 'desks', 'door', 'first', 'friends', 'girls', 'hungry', 'newspapers', 'only', 'page', 'right', 'rulers', 'sandwich', 'teacher', 'their', 'three', 'watch', 'white', 'windows', 'write', 'wrong', 'yellow'.

Three types of error

Three types of error may be distinguished:

(1) L1 errors: based on transfer of L1 phonological knowledge
(2) L2 errors: based on inadequate L2 spelling knowledge
(3) L1 = L2 errors.

L1 errors: Transfer of L1 phonological knowledge

When beginners base their phonological strategy on L1 knowledge, they tend to model their L2 spellings on L1 spellings. This can result in two outcomes.

(1) In cases where English phonemes also occur in Dutch, but with different spellings, the spelling is adapted. The main examples are /ʃ/ spelled as <sj> '*sjoe'/'shoe' and /j/ spelled <j> '*jello'/'yellow'. A special case is presented by the fact that consonant doubling in Dutch only occurs at the syllable juncture position, not at the end of words. Thus, words such as 'miss' and 'stuff' are written as '*mis' and '*stuf'.
(2) With new English phonemes that have a near-equivalent in Dutch, the spelling of the equivalent phoneme is produced.

There are many possible adaptations of English sounds to Dutch pronunciations (Gussenhoven & Broeders, 1976). In cases where the spelling of the Dutch near-equivalent is different from the English phoneme, spelling errors do occur (see Table 3.4).

Table 3.4 Spelling errors resulting from phonological adaptations

English phoneme	*Adapted to Dutch phoneme*	*Resulting spelling*
/ʌ/ cupboard	/ɑ/ lat	*capboard
/æ/ sandwich	/ɛ/ pet	*senwich
/ʊ/ book	/u:/ voet	*boek
/ɔ:/ daughter	/ɔ/ zot	*doter
/eɪ/ page	/e:/ heet	*peech
/əʊ/ clothes	/o:/ boot	*cloos
/aɪ/ white	/aj/ waai	*waait
/ɪə/ here	/i:r/ hier	*hier
/ɛə/ chair, there	/ɛr/ ver	*cher, *ther
/ʊə/ tour	/u:r/ toer	*toer
/g/ game	/k/ Kees	*keem

A special problem is presented by voiced consonants in final position, which do not occur in Dutch. A well-known pronunciation error that Dutch people make is the devoicing of consonants in words like 'bad', 'club' and 'dog'; this, in turn, results in spelling errors, such as '*bet', '*clup' and '*dok'.

Spellings as those listed in Table 3.4 only occur in the L1 as possible spellings of a given phoneme or its near Dutch equivalent, and will be called L1 errors in the research reported below.

L2 errors: Inadequate L2 spelling knowledge

Given that English language teaching in the Netherlands lacks any systematic instruction regarding the English spelling system, it seems unlikely that Dutch beginners would have any idea about the conditions underlying various spelling alternatives, or about the word-specific nature of many spellings. Thus, if the phonological strategy is based on inadequate L2 knowledge, it will often result in L2 variants that do not fit in the specific context, e.g. '*teatcher' ('teacher'; compare to 'kitchen') or '*roler' ('ruler'; compare to 'moving'). Spellings that only occur in L2 as possible spellings of a given phoneme will be called L2 errors below.

L1 = L2 errors

If the speller considers the relation between sound and spelling as a one-to-one correspondence and higher-level conditions are ignored, it follows that a vast number of L1 and L2 phonemes have identical spellings. For the researcher, it is difficult in these cases to determine which language the chosen spelling was based on. The form '*kliening' offers two examples of this phenomenon. Although <k> and <ie> are both basic L1 spellings, the L2 source of the error cannot be excluded, since in English both <k> and <ie> do occur as possible spellings of the phonemes concerned. Other examples include '*wotch' ('watch'; compare to English 'pot' and Dutch 'zot'), '*roelers' ('rulers'; compare to English 'shoe' and Dutch 'schoen') and '*frends' ('friends'; compare to English 'ten' and Dutch 'pet'). Spellings that occur in both English and Dutch and represent a given phoneme or its near equivalent in Dutch will be called L1 = L2 errors below.

Other errors

The three kinds of error discussed above (L1 errors, L2 errors and L1 = L2 errors) can clearly be interpreted as representing the target sound based on comparisons with existing spellings in the first or second language. They can be considered as instances of a phonological strategy. Not all errors fit into this pattern. There are at least two other sources of errors made by L2 beginners.

(1) One of the problems in learning spelling in one's mother tongue is that of mastering the letter forms. As English and Dutch use the

Table 3.5 New letter combinations with spelling errors

New combination	*Word*	*Error*
<ai>	chair	*chiar
<ea>	cleaning	*claening, *claning
<oa>	coat	*caot
<ow>	windows	*windous, *windouws
<ew>	newspaper	*neuwspaper
<th>	bathroom; clothes	*bahtroom; *clohtes
<gh>	eight; right	*eicht; *richth, *rihgt, *rigt, *richt
<tch>	kitchen	*kithen, *kitcen, *cithcen
<wh>	white	*with, *whiht, *wihte, *withe

same script (the Roman alphabet), this aspect of L2 spelling acquisition presents no problems. New combinations of letters, however, can give rise to difficulties. Table 3.5 lists most of the new letter combinations, accompanied by examples of spelling errors.

Such errors cannot be interpreted as caused by phonological adaptation or confusion of possible spellings. They cannot be categorised as errors due to the use of a phonological strategy. An analysis in terms of substitution, omission, reversal and insertion would probably be more suitable to handle them. Incidentally, such errors are not limited to new letter combinations. We also find for example '*freinds' (friends), '*hose' (house), '*rhoulers' (rulers), '*whitdose' (windows) and '*whong' (wrong).

(2) With phonemes that have no near equivalent in Dutch, learners are likely to represent the sounds roughly by inventing a spelling. Table 3.6 presents some examples.

Table 3.6 Invented spellings

English phoneme	*Phonological adaptation*	*Resulting spelling*
/θ/ bathroom	/s/	*badsroom
/ð/ clothes	/d/, /s/	*clodes, *cloos
/tʃ/ chairs	/tj/, /sj/	*tjers, *sjers
/dʒ/ page	/ts/	*peats

The above examples could be accepted as unsuccessful attempts at producing a correct spelling by the use of a phonological strategy. Other examples, however, are not that clear. Consider for example '*baddroom' (bathroom); '*clotts', '*clowts' (clothes); *trers (chairs) or '*peeth' (page). In the data to be discussed below, there appeared to be many such errors that cannot be clearly interpreted as based on a phonological strategy.

How Important is the Phonological Strategy?

The remaining discussion in this chapter will present two kinds of evidence that support the use of a phonological strategy: (1) error analysis (see below); and (2) the orthographic model presented earlier. This last approach will make clear that at first Dutch learners prefer a phonological strategy, but after a while they make equal use of an orthographic strategy (see below).

The results of error analysis

How important is the phonological strategy and what role does the mother tongue play in the first stage of spelling acquisition? To answer these questions, the data, already presented above, were collected. In the first and second years of secondary school, 173 pupils wrote familiar words in a spot dictation, 29 of which were selected for further analysis. Each error that occurred was counted separately. The form '*rhoulers' ('rulers') for example contains two errors: <*rh> and <*ou>.

In the first year, the mean error rate was 10.94 (standard deviation 7.6). In the second year, the mean decreased to 7.05 (sd 5.3). In order to study the importance of a phonological strategy, the errors were at first divided into two main categories.

(1) The first category consists of L1 errors, L2 errors and L1 = L2 errors taken together. They are referred to as PGC errors in Table 3.7.
(2) The second category comprises all the other errors, including those discussed in section Other errors. The common factor to these errors is that they cannot be clearly interpreted as based on a phonological strategy. They are referred to as 'other errors' in Table 3.7.

Table 3.7 PGC and other errors

	PGC errors	*Other errors*
Year 1 ($n = 173$)	5.83 (4.19)	5.11 (4.08)
Year 2 ($n = 173$)	4.62 (3.25)	2.43 (2.56)

Table 3.7 presents the mean number of PGC errors and other errors (out of 29 words; standard deviations in brackets).

In the first year the difference between the number of PGC errors and other errors, although small, was significant ($t = 3.13$; df = 172; $p < 0.01$), and it was significant in the second year as well ($t = 11.78$; df = 172; $p < 0.01$). Thus, the results show that in cases of doubt, L2 learners are usually able to choose a spelling that could possibly correspond to the phoneme in question. It would seem then that L2 learners do indeed use a phonological strategy. In order to evaluate the role of the first language in spelling properly, the PGC errors were divided into three sub-categories: L2 errors, L1 errors and L1 = L2 errors. (In the remainder of this discussion, the 'other errors' will be left out of consideration.) Table 3.8 presents the mean results for these three sub-categories (standard deviation in brackets).

Since it is impossible to draw any conclusions from L1 = L2 errors concerning the specific use of L1 or L2 knowledge, those errors were not included in the analysis of the results. In both the first and second years, the difference between the number of L2 errors and L1 errors appeared to be significant (first year: $t = -11.49$; df = 172; $p < 0.01$, second year: $t = -16.14$; df = 172; $p < 0.01$). Thus, in conclusion, it can be said that Dutch L2 learners prefer English spelling variants to Dutch spellings.

The results outlined so far can be summarised as follows. In the first two years of secondary school, Dutch learners use a phonological strategy to overcome their lack of spelling knowledge. As they prefer the English PGCs to the Dutch ones, L1 transfer does not appear to play a very important role. Although these results seem to provide sufficient evidence of a phonological strategy in L2 spelling, I am not all that convinced of the relevance of this result. The main point to remember here is that the phonological strategy discussed so far has only been demonstrated on the basis of errors. By the same token, we could draw an entirely different conclusion, namely that a phonological strategy leads to spelling errors! The question is: does this strategy also contribute to the acquisition of the English spelling system? I will try to answer this question in the next section.

Table 3.8 Errors subdivided into L2, L1 and L1 = L2 errors

	L2 errors	*L1 errors*	*L1 = L2 errors*
Year 1 ($n = 173$)	2.91 (2.14)	1.04 (1.39)	1.87 (1.78)
Year 2 ($n = 173$)	2.64 (1.85)	0.44 (0.74)	1.55 (1.54)

The acquisition of spelling categories

In the research discussed so far, L2 written products were studied from the perspective of errors, which show us what learners *cannot* do. Another way of examining the learning process is to take account of what learners *can* do, that is, to consider the number of correct answers. The question concerning the importance of the phonological strategy could then be reformulated as follows: to what extent can L2 spelling be explained on the basis of a phonological strategy? And what does L1 knowledge contribute? In order to answer the latter question, the basic category was divided into two sub-categories. The basic L1 = L2 category contains spellings that are also basic spellings in Dutch (see Table 3.3). The basic L2 category contains the remaining basic spellings, which are L2 specific.

In a previous study (Van Berkel, 1999; Van Berkel, 2004), I was able to demonstrate that, by the end of the first year of study, L2 spelling competence clearly depends on spelling categories. Few errors were made in the basic L1 = L2 category, followed by the basic L2 category. Contextual spellings caused more errors, but most errors occurred in the word-specific category. These outcomes applied to pupils across levels, the only exception being the group of the most talented learners whose results showed no difference between basic L2 and contextual categories. Thus it appears that a higher level of proficiency results in higher scores for the contextual category. One could conclude that good L2 spellers benefit over time from orthographic structure and begin to apply an orthographic strategy. In the research discussed in this paper, it was hypothesised that this tendency also occurs among less talented learners, provided that they are tested later in their development. So, to test this hypothesis, the data were gathered among average learners, who were tested at the end of their first and second years of secondary school.

The following hypotheses were formulated based on the fact that frequency and orthographic conditions were the main criteria for categorisation of the English spelling system.

(1) Given the high frequency and resemblance to Dutch, the results for the basic L1 = L2 category were expected to be very good. These spellings are prime examples of how Dutch learners might spell by ear without encountering any spelling problems.

(2) Given the high frequency and the unambiguous correspondence of the basic L2 category, this category was expected to have the lowest error rate as compared to the other specific English categories.

(3) Since contextual spellings occur less frequently, this category was expected to show lower scores than the basic L2 category in the first year of spelling acquisition. In the second year, however, L2 learners were expected to have identified orthographic regularities and

to show no difference in results between the basic L1 ≐ L2 category and the contextual category. In both years, the contextual category would lead to better results than the word-specific category.

(4) Because of their low frequency, word-specific spellings were expected to show the lowest scores.

To obtain a detailed overview of the pupils' spelling competence, the PGCs in the dictated words were sub-divided into spelling categories (see Table 3.2 for the sub-categorisation). There were 46 spellings in the basic L1 ≐ L2 category; 24 in the basic L2 category; 18 in the contextual category; and 17 in the word-specific category. Leaving aside the morphological <s> in 'chairs' and <ing> in 'cleaning', Table 3.9 presents some examples.

The analysis of pupils' responses differs completely from the method of error analysis presented above. Whenever an error occurs, the PGC concerned is crossed out, without interpretation of the error in terms of L1, L2 or other source. As can be seen in Table 3.10, PGCs may provoke various kinds of error, but all errors are treated alike when they concern the same PGC.

To gain insight into the learners' spelling competence, the correct PGCs per spelling category were totalled. The number of correct spellings per category was calculated for each year. The mean scores (in absolute values and in percentages) are presented in Table 3.11 (standard deviation in brackets).

The results were entered into a two-factor analysis of variance after the values of the scores on the basic L2, contextual and word-specific categories had been transformed proportionally to match the scores on the basic L1 = L2 category (to a maximum of 46). Effects were found for both 'category' ($F(3,516) = 185.51$; $p < 0.01$) and 'year' ($F(1,172) = 121.05$; $p < 0.01$). The interaction was also significant ($F(3,516) = 40.91$; $p < 0.01$). *Post hoc* tests (Bonferroni method) showed that in both the first and second years, the four mean scores were significantly different. As Table 3.11 indicates, the scores for first-year pupils followed expectations. The best results were achieved in the

Table 3.9 Examples of the dictation words subdivided into spelling categories

	Basic, L1 = L2	*Basic, L2*	*Contextual*	*Word-specific*
chairs		ch		air
cleaning	l, n		c	ea
white	t		i-e	wh

Table 3.10 Various incorrect spellings of words, subdivided into correct PGCs and errors

		Basic, L1 = L2		*Basic, L2*		*Contextual*		*Word-specific*	
Word	*Error*	*PGC*	*Error*	*PGC*	*Error*	*PGC*	*Error*	*PGC*	*Error*
chairs	*cheres			ch				air	*ere
	*chiars			ch				air	*iar
	*tjers			ch	*tj			air	*er
	*trers			ch	*tr			air	*er
cleaning	*claening	l, n				c		ea	*ae
	*claning	l, n				c		ea	*a
	*cleding	l, n	*d			c		ea	*e
	*kliening	l, n				c	*k	ea	*ie

Table 3.11 Results per spelling category

	Basic, L1 = L2 (max = 46)	*Basic, L2 (max = 24)*	*Contextual (max = 18)*	*Word-specific (max = 17)*
Year 1 ($n = 173$)	43.93 (2.65) 0.96 (0.06)	21.31 (2.08) 0.89 (0.09)	15.32 (2.29) 0.85 (0.13)	13.53 (2.58) 0.80 (0.15)
Year 2 ($n = 173$)	44.98 (1.30) 0.98 (0.03)	21.95 (1.68) 0.91 (0.07)	17.09 (1.18) 0.95 (0.07)	15.01 (1.77) 0.88 (0.10)

basic L1 = L2 category, followed by the basic L2 category, and by the contextual category. The word-specific spellings resulted in the lowest performance. In the second year, the scores improved in each category. It is important to note, however, that the results present a different picture. Although the scores on the basic L1 = L2 spellings were still the highest and the scores on the word-specific spellings the lowest, performance in the contextual category was better than it was in the basic L2 category, that is, better than predicted. It can be concluded, therefore, that over time all L2 spellers begin to learn rule-governed patterns. Apparently, they gain competence in applying an orthographic strategy.

Conclusion

In order to gain insight into the importance of the phonological strategy in learning the English spelling, the same data were analysed in two different ways. Error analysis made clear that Dutch beginners *do* use a phonological strategy, mainly based on L2 knowledge. However, a large part of the data (the 'other errors') had to be left out of consideration because these errors could not be clearly ascribed to the phonological strategy. The second method is not based on the analysis of errors. It takes the correct answers into account, sub-divided into spelling categories. In this approach no data have to be left out of consideration. With this method it is possible to gain more interesting results than in the first approach. It appeared that at first Dutch learners prefer a phonological strategy, but that after a while they equally use an orthographic strategy.

As in the first year of study, the results for the basic L2 category were better than for the other L2 categories, it was suggested that these results were due to the phonological strategy, because this strategy is highly suitable for spelling the basic spellings. In the second year of study the results for the contextual category improved, which led to the idea that the orthographic strategy had become more and more important, because only this strategy seems appropriate to spell contextual spellings. If this interpretation of the results is accepted, it means that English L2 spelling acquisition by Dutch learners follows the same sequence as the L1 acquisition of both the Dutch and the English spelling systems: in each learning process the use of the phonological strategy precedes the use of the orthographic strategy. However, this is not the only possible interpretation of the results.

Given the fact that instruction plays an important role in L1 spelling acquisition, whereas it is lacking in the L2 situation, one might wonder why the basic L2 spellings are mastered first and the contextual spellings afterwards. Or, why the phonological strategy is preferred first and the orthographic strategy is used only later, although Dutch spellers are used to both strategies in their L1. Taking the hypotheses formulated in the section on acquisition of spelling categories into account, it becomes clear that the acquisition of the various categories may be governed by frequency. That means that the reason for the basic L2 spellings being mastered before the contextual ones is not that the phonological strategy is preferred in the first stage of acquisition, but that the basic L2 spellings are the more frequent ones.

Notes

1. Carney's frequency counts (1994) also include spellings which must be considered morphological, and which consequently fall beyond the scope of this study. The most important examples concern: the schwa and unstressed /ɪ/ in affixes (such as '-ion', '-tion'), <y>, <age>, <be>; consonant doubling as a result of affixing, such as <cc> in 'account', or <pp> in appointment; and the spelling of consonants in affixes, such as /ʃ/ in 'station', /tʃ/ in 'adventure' and /j/ in 'opinion'.
2. In comparing the words <cat> with <Kate>, just like <them> with <theme>, <Tim> with <time>, <hop> with <hope> and <cut> with <cute>, it becomes clear that in words such as 'Kate', 'theme', 'time', 'hope' and 'cute' final <e> is part of the spelling of the preceding vowel. These spellings will be noted as <a-e>, <e-e>, <i-e>, <o-e> and <u-e> respectively.
3. Due to a lack of space, the English spelling rules will not be listed in this paper. An extensive treatment of main and local rules can be found for example in Venezky (1970, 1999) and Carney (1994).
4. The spellings <y> and <ie> alternate in that position. Carney (1994) postulates a 'three letter rule', according to which words with less than three letters are avoided in English. Compare <ie> in 'tie', 'pie', 'lie' with <y> in 'fly', 'dry', 'spy' (function words are excluded).
5. Following Hanna *et al.* (1966) as well as Carney (1994), /ju:/ and /u:/ are treated as two different items. Taking /ju:/ as one item, the spelling becomes fairly predictable: <u>, <u-e> and <ew> together cover over 80%. The figures for single /u:/ are as follows: taken together, <u>, <u-e> and <ue> cover 27%, and <oo> covers 39%. Since these spellings do not complement each other, and the frequency criterion does not apply, all /u:/ spellings are considered word-specific.

References

Barry, C. (1994) Spelling routes (or roots or rutes). In G.D.A. Brown and N.C. Ellis (eds) *Handbook of Spelling* (pp. 27–49). Chichester: John Wiley.

Carney, E. (1994) *A Survey of English Spelling*. London: Routledge.

Cook, V. (1997) L2 users and English spelling. *Journal of Multilingual and Multicultural Development* 18 (6), 474–88.

Ehri, L.C. (1986) Sources of difficulty in learning to spell and read. *Advances in Developmental and Behavioural Pediatrics* 7, 121–95.

Ellis, N.C. (1994) Longitudinal studies of spelling development. In G.D.A. Brown and N.C. Ellis (eds) *Handbook of Spelling* (pp. 155–77). Chichester: John Wiley.

Frith, U. (1985) Beneath the surface of developmental dyslexia. In K. Patterson, M. Coltheart and J. Marshall (eds) *Surface Dyslexia* (pp. 301–30). London: LEA.

Gussenhoven, C. and Broeders, A. (1976) *The Pronunciation of English*. Groningen: Wolters Noordhoff.

Hanna, P.R., Hanna, J.S., Hodges, R.E. and Rudorf, E.H. (1966) *Phoneme–grapheme Correspondences as Cues to Spelling Improvement*. US Department of Health, Education and Welfare, Office of Education.

Van Berkel, A.J. (1999) *Niet van Horen Zeggen. Leren Spellen in het Engels als Vreemde Taal*. [*Learning to Spell in English as a Second Language*]. Bussum: Coutinho.

Van Berkel, A.J. (2004) Learning to spell in English as a second language. *International Review of Applied Linguistics in Language Teaching* 42 (3), 239–257.

Venezky, R.L. (1970) *The Structure of English Orthography*. Den Haag: Mouton.

Venezky, R.L. (1999) *The American Way of Spelling: The Structure and Origins of American English Orthography*. New York: The Guilford Press.

Chapter 4

Orthographic Knowledge and First Language Reading: Evidence from Single Word Dictation from Chinese and Malaysian Users of English as a Foreign Language

MICK RANDALL

In this chapter we will examine the contribution that an analysis of dictation errors to targeted English words can make to an understanding of the orthographic knowledge of students of English as a Foreign Language (EFL). We shall report on two studies with Chinese[1] and Bahasa Malayu (BM) first language students, which were conducted to find out whether there are differences in the orthographic knowledge of these two groups as exemplified by the spelling errors which they made to selected word targets embedded in sentence contexts. As we shall argue below, in terms of language (phonological and syntactic) structure, BM and Chinese are highly similar. Thus, if orthographic errors are due to language structure, then speakers of both languages might be expected to produce similar spelling errors. However, in terms of writing system, BM and Chinese are quite different, with the former being written in the Roman alphabet with highly regular grapheme-to-phoneme conversion rules and the latter in a logographic (character) system which arguably does not require any phonological mediation to access word meanings. If the habits induced by first language reading/word recognition in these two highly differentiated scriptal systems have an effect on the way that these subjects approach recognising and storing words in English, then it is hypothesised that these differences will be discernible in the orthographic knowledge of the students and the types of error that they make in single word dictation tasks.

Two studies are reported here. One is of Malaysian secondary school students of mixed race (i.e. they had all been educated through the medium of BM yet were of different ethnic and first language backgrounds). The other study is of two entirely separate groups; a group of mainland Chinese (People's Republic of China or PRC) scholars in Singapore and a group of Malay-only students from a prestigious secondary school in Malaysia.

Theoretical Background

The relationship between dictation errors, orthographic knowledge and word recognition

It may seem odd at first sight to use dictation errors to try to draw conclusions about reading in different scripts. Traditionally, within first language pedagogies, dictation is viewed as a means of testing spelling knowledge, a sub-skill of writing. Within communicative second language learning (CLL) pedagogies, dictation is currently viewed as a way of training listening and understanding; the focus of attention has moved away from the micro-productive writing sub-skill to the more macro-receptive language skills of listening and comprehending. Indeed, as a classroom practice, modern CLL pedagogy views individual word dictation in a very poor light as the processes involved in word dictation bear little resemblance to real world communication. Such views are understandable if dictation is viewed as an exercise designed to increase oral competence in the language – one of the central goals of CLL. However, in this chapter, we shall be using single word dictation as an indicator of word knowledge, not of listening or phonological processing accuracy.

Whilst the effects of first language phonology must be borne in mind when looking at the errors generated, dictation errors can be used to examine the word knowledge of different users of English as L2 (we shall adopt here the term 'user' rather than 'speaker', see Cook, 1997). Figure 4.1 represents a general model of the cognitive processes involved in writing down an individual word dictated in a sentence context (an adaptation of Seidenberg and McClelland's (1989) 'triangle model' as presented in Adams, 1990).

In order to convert the sounds (phonemes) into letters (graphemes) the listener will have information both from the incoming speech signal and the ongoing sentence context with which to determine the actual written form of the word. In this model, there is a general interaction between four different processors: the phonological processor, which works on the incoming speech signal; the orthographic processor, which works on the written form of the language; the context processor, which provides information about the context within which the word appears; and the meaning processor, into which all the other processors feed. The phonological and orthographic processors will have access to information about the knowledge of the language possessed by the

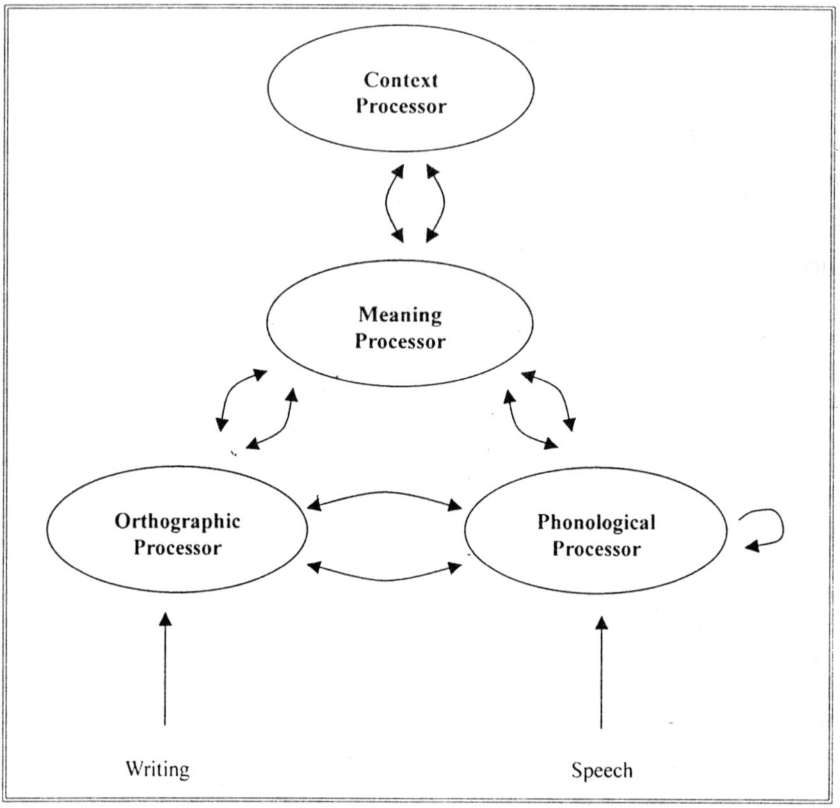

Figure 4.1 Model of cognitive processes involved in dictation

user. Under current parallel distributed processing (PDP) models of lexical recognition (for further discussion of PDP models and word recognition see van Heuven's chapter in this volume), each of these 'inputs' feeds information to, and receives positive and negative feedback from, the meaning processor, until a certain level of activation is reached and the word is selected. In addition, there is a similar two-way feedback exchange between the phonological and orthographic processors which may lead to direct word recognition without necessarily accessing the meaning system. To the degree to which such models also form the basis of processes involved in reading aloud, it is clear that both reading and writing need to employ some sort of orthographic processor for successful operation. Thus errors in output (spelling errors) will provide us with information about the orthographic knowledge of the student, knowledge which is equally used for word recognition and reading.

The technique of using targeted dictated words is one that has been used by Kibbel and Miles (1994) to investigate the orthographic knowledge of British dyslexic children. The studies in this chapter aim to use this general model of lexical access and the techniques employed by Kibbel and Miles to examine the orthographic knowledge of L1 Chinese and L1 Malay users of English as L2 through the analysis of errors to specified target words.

Dual route theories of lexical access

There is a large body of evidence from psychology and word recognition studies with both words and non-words, that English L1 users utilise both a non-lexical route and a lexical route to word recognition and production. These models, further refined in 'cascaded' dual route models (DRC) (Coltheart *et al.*, 2001; Patterson & Morton, 1985), identify the mechanisms by which L1 English users can convert the printed language into spoken output, i.e. reading aloud (see the introduction of this volume for a discussion of dual-route models). If such a mechanism is available for reading aloud, it should also be available for the reverse, for converting spoken into written language, i.e. dictation. A model of how such a dual route system might operate in a dictation task in given in Figure 4.2.

The non-lexical route describes the way that language users can 'mechanically' convert the sounds into graphemes and vice versa. The non-lexical route is here shown as consisting of two sub-systems. One is a grapheme–phoneme conversion mechanism (simply matching sounds onto letters) and the other is a 'body' sub-system (which utilises orthographical and phonological rhymes). Thus, this analytical route can either work serially through a word, converting phonemes into graphemes (when performing a dictation), or it can recognise whole 'chunks' made up of letters (rhymes) and assemble the syllable/word from the initial sound plus a chunk consisting of the peak and coda as a single element. This continuum from serial phonological assembly process, through onset/rhyme strategies and whole word phonology has been characterised as 'psycholinguistic grain size' by Goswami *et al.* (2001), who suggest that different languages use different psycholinguistic grain sizes.

In contrast, the lexical route consists of recognising words directly from their overall phonological shape, and then converting them into visual 'logogens'. A logogen is an 'evidence-collecting device with a threshold' (Coltheart *et al.*, 2001). Each word in a lexicon has a logogen which has a resting threshold depending on factors such as its frequency in the language. As information comes in from various sources (both the senses and other parts of the model such as the semantic system), the logogen becomes more activated until its threshold is activated. In the model as portrayed here, it is suggested that orthography can be accessed via a non-semantic route though the activation of visual

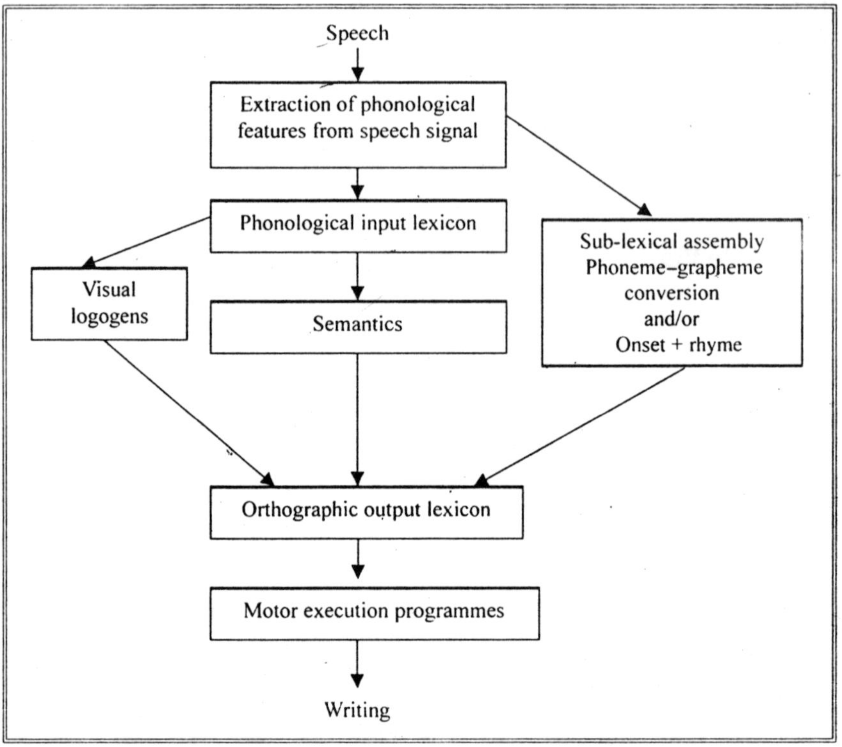

Figure 4.2 An adaptation of the DRC model of reading for dictation

logogens – stored whole-word images of lexical items. In fact, neither of these routes would operate in total isolation and information will be constantly interchanged between the non-lexical and lexical routes.

However, it is arguable that such a dual route approach to lexical access may be specific to L1 English users and be closely related to the complex orthographic system employed in English. In fact, the stable search patterns of visual arrays found with L1 English users have been found to be different with users of English with other first languages: Randall and Meara (1988) for example found that Arabic L2 users of English produced patterns quite different from those of L1 English users, as did BM users (Randall, 1991); so too, lexical access models may be quite different with users of English with other first languages. It is highly probable that the structure of the first language, in particular the orthographic structure, will play a central role in the cognitive processes used for word recognition and these processes will be reflected in the processes of written output which will be discernible in the errors produced by L2 users of English through dictation.

Linguistic and orthographic properties of Chinese and Bahasa Malayu

Koda (1996) argues that L2 reading processes are likely to be heavily influenced by, among other things:

- the similarity or dissimilarity between the language structure of the first and second language;
- the 'orthographic distance' between the two (the degree to which the two writing systems use similar scripts and/or levels of orthographic transparency);
- the transfer of processing experience from the first to the second language (Koda, 1996: 453).

In all these respects, Chinese and Bahasa Malayu are interesting languages as compared with English.

In terms of phonology, the two languages share a number of features which are quite different from English. Both languages have a relatively simple syllable structure as compared to English. BM has basically a CV or CVC syllable structure, with lexical items consisting of two syllables, and few consonant clusters, apart from a few loan words, none occurring in syllable/word final positions. Chinese is similar. In both Cantonese (the dialect largely used by the students in Study 1) and Mandarin (the dialect used by all the subjects in Study 2) all words are monosyllabic and most syllables are open, with only a restricted range of sounds (nasals) which can appear in the coda in Mandarin plus some stop consonants in Cantonese. Apart from the approximants that can follow the initial consonant in Mandarin, neither dialect has initial or final consonant clusters (Deterding & Poesjosoedarmo, 1998). In terms of vowels, both of the Chinese dialects and BM have a very different vowel system from English. Perhaps the most important difference is that neither of them uses vowel length as a distinctive phonemic feature and both have single vowels in areas where English makes more than one contrast (e.g. the front vowels /æ/ and /e/ in English are represented by a single-vowel phoneme /e/ in BM and the two Chinese dialects). Thus, if the errors made by students were being fed by the phonological features of the respective first languages, we could expect both sets of students to produce similar errors. We would expect:

- problems with clusters;
- problems with short and long vowel distinctions;
- problems with substitution of certain vowels.

Allied to the problem of clusters, final clusters in English play an important syntactical role, with the last consonant often being an inflectional morpheme, indicating past tense, plurality or person (in the present simple). Neither Chinese nor BM has any inflectional suffixes and neither do they mark plurality or tense by lexical affixation. Thus, arguing from a hypothesis which attributes errors to differences in syntactic structure, we would expect L1 users of both languages to produce similar error patterns to inflectionally modified English words.

In the second area for comparison between the languages, that of orthographic distance, we would expect to find a great deal of difference between L1 Chinese/L2 English users and L1 BM-L2 English users. Chinese has a logographic writing system where each character represents a separate semantic/lexical unit. Whilst there are studies which purport to show that phonology does play a part in character recognition in Chinese (Tan & Perfetti, 1998), the role that a serial phonological assembly route plays in character recognition, as against direct visual recognition, is much lower in Chinese than in an alphabetic language. In fact, it has been suggested that the Seidenberg and McClelland (1989) 'triangle model' of word recognition represented in Figure 4.1 may well become a 'hub and spoke' model in Chinese, with the meaning processor being the 'hub' and the orthographic, phonological and context processors acting as 'spokes', with access to the phonological form from the orthography and vice versa being solely through the meaning processor. Thus, Chinese and English would appear to be as distant in their orthographies as it is possible to get.

BM, on the other hand, in using an alphabetic script, would appear to be much closer to English. However, this apparent similarity (the use of an alphabetic system) is perhaps more apparent than real. A reader in BM, with its highly consistent grapheme–phoneme relationships (an orthographically highly regular language), will have no need to use a whole-word route to gain lexical access; a phonological assembly route will always produce successful lexical access. However, use of the phonological route alone will not always produce successful word recognition in English. Thus the necessity for the dual route model of lexical access, and the reading problems which derive from the loss or partial loss of the whole-word access route in aphasics (surface dyslexia).

If we consider the major distance between the scripts to be measured in terms of the use of logographic as against alphabetic principles, BM would appear to be closer to English than Chinese. If this is the case, we might then expect the Chinese L1 readers to make more errors than their BM L1 counterparts (the argument presented by Muljani *et al.*, 1998).

However, if we consider the third area for consideration, transfer of experience from L1 to L2 reading, the position is less clear cut. From the above discussion of word recognition procedures in Chinese, it would seem that the most likely process is that of holistic character recognition. It would thus seem sensible to assume that Chinese L1 readers would bring similar procedures to bear on word recognition in English.

Therefore, they would be expected to favour whole-word, lexical approaches to word recognition in English. Readers familiar with BM, in contrast, are more likely to transfer a non-lexical, phonological assembly process. One of the hypotheses that instigated this research is that the use of a whole-word lexical access approach would enhance the recognition of less phonologically 'transparent' words, i.e. words that do not use simple grapheme-to-phoneme correspondences but rely on more complex rhyme-based orthographic patterns. Thus, L1 Chinese readers might be expected to make less errors with these words than L1 BM readers.

In addition to the transfer of experience from reading in the first language to reading in the second, we also need to take into account the effect of the transfer of literacy *training* from L1 reading to L2 reading. Whilst initial literacy instruction in the L1 contains activities to enhance basic word recognition strategies, such training almost never happens in L2 reading. We have already discussed the difference in phonological syllable structure between BM and English and the difficulty that this might place on the recognition of clusters and of syllable-final clusters in particular. Although BM has an alphabetic writing system, it is quite possible that it uses a syllabic process based on its very regular CVCV structure. Thus words in BM would be processed as successive CV + CV syllables. There is good evidence from discussions with teachers that initial approaches to literacy in BM capitalise on this regularity, and that initial word building involves recognition of the consonant plus the vowel as a unit (e.g. recognising <bi>, <be>, <ba>, <bu>, <bo> as units) and not the individual phoneme blending approach used in much initial literacy teaching in L1 English contexts (/b/ + /æ/ + /t/). Therefore, we might expect a transfer of training effect in BM speakers which militates against the recognition and retention of final clusters, thus leading to a greater number of mistakes in this area amongst L1 BM users of English.

Study 1

The dictation procedure

As indicated above, both studies in this chapter followed a procedure similar to that used by Kibbel and Miles (1994). In that study, single words were dictated to students, followed by a sentence frame including the target word, followed by a repetition of the target word which the students were then asked to write down. The sentence frame in the Kibble and Miles study was largely to disambiguate homophones such as <brake>/<break> as the L1 English children would be expected to have an oral knowledge of all the words used. In the two studies in this paper, the role of the sentence frames was to try to eliminate, as far as possible, the effects of single word 'listening discrimination', i.e. the sentence frame was included to illustrate the meaning of the word, to allow the students to access a word from its meaning as well as its phonological form. We were primarily interested in the students' knowledge of known words rather than their ability to operate non-lexical phoneme-to-grapheme conversion principles.

In the first study with Secondary 1 students, the test was administered by trainee English language teachers studying in the UK, but back in Malaysia for teaching practice. They were not L1 English users but L1 BM users with a variety of English which has been characterised as mesolectal English of Malaysia and Singapore (Brown, 1986). Of particular interest to this study, their variety of English possessed certain crucial L1 transfer features such as simplification of final clusters, which we have noted above as differences between BM and English phonology.

The target words

In the Kibbel and Miles study, as the children were all native English speakers, oral word knowledge of real words could be assumed, and, in addition to probing the children's orthographic knowledge for real words, the study also involved their emerging orthographic knowledge with pseudo-word targets. However, in studies involving L2 users, use of pseudo-words is highly problematic, and indeed the selection of target words in terms of familiarity is also problematic. It can be argued that a real word which is unknown to a student is, in fact, equivalent to a pseudo-word or non-word to a L1 English user. As we are primarily interested in their knowledge of 'real words' in this study, the students were asked to also indicate after each word whether or not it was a word they knew, thus providing a check that we were gathering information about the way that known words were stored in their lexicon, rather than their knowledge of phonological assembly with non-word stimuli.

Similarly, research with L2 English users also has difficulty with the issue of word familiarity when selecting stimuli. With L1 English users it can be assumed that most relatively frequent words will be known orally by the children and that the task is therefore one of knowing if they know the written form. In the Muljani *et al.* (1998) study, where the focus was on gross effects of frequency and response latency, it was possible to select high frequency and low frequency words for study. However, the degree to which word frequency as measured by large corpus-based studies relates to ESL learner familiarity is not necessarily straightforward. As, in our studies, we were interested in words having different orthographic and morphological properties, it was not possible to control for word frequency. However, an attempt was made to allow for the effects of word familiarity. In the first study, the words were all taken from the list of words included in the Malaysian primary school syllabus.

In the first study, the words were grouped according to orthographical transparency. Thus words with less regular orthography such as <sharp> or <make> ('Rhyme' words) were contrasted with words with more transparent orthography such as <bag> or <crash> (Phonological, or 'Phon' words). The other factor examined in this first study was the effect of syllable structure, and, in particular, the presence of consonant clusters in the onset and coda of syllables. These targets were further sub-divided into those clusters in the coda which were part of the root word (e.g. <mist>, <land>) and those which consisted of a root word plus a morpheme (e.g. <missed>, <planned>). Thus, the words were grouped according to increasingly complex syllable structure (varying the number of consonants in initial and final syllable positions) and the degree of orthographic transparency (phon versus rhyme). In the final three categories, similar final clusters were differentiated according to whether the cluster contained an inflectional morpheme (± infl). The categories of words used and examples of the target words and their sentence contexts are given in Table 4.1.

The subjects

Two Secondary 1 classes (12–13-year-old students) from provincial secondary schools in different parts of Malaysia were used. They were native speakers of BM, Chinese (largely Cantonese) or Tamil, but they had all been educated through the medium of BM and had all learnt BM as their first writing system. No data were collected on the degree

Table 4.1 Examples of targets and sentence contexts for Study 1

	Type	*Target*	*Sentence context*
1	CVC (phon)	top	They were sitting on top of the hill.
2	CVC (rhyme)	pork	Pork comes from pigs.
3	CCVC (phon)	swim	We went to swim in the sea.
4	CCVC (rhyme)	brake	I stopped the car and put on the brake.
5	CVCC (phon)	belt	I'll wear my new leather belt tonight.
6	CVCC (rhyme)	month	Next month I shall finish school.
7	CCVCC (− infl)	grand	The palace looked very grand.
8	CVCC (+ infl)	missed	I missed my family when I went abroad.
9	CCVCC (+ infl)	planned	We planned a big party for his birthday.

A complete list of words and sentence contexts is given in Randall, 1997.

Table 4.2 First language backgrounds of students

	Bahasa Malaysia	*Chinese*	*Tamil*
Class 1	20	16	7
Class 2	32	5	1

of literacy that these children had obtained in their respective first languages. They were all studying English as a second language and their language backgrounds are shown in Table 4.2.

A comparison of the pattern of errors produced by the two classes in the different categories showed a large and highly significant correlation between the two classes, despite the difference in ethnic composition (Spearman's rho $= 0.95$, $n = 9$, $p < 0.01$). This would suggest that the pattern of errors in Class 1, which was then subjected to more detailed analysis, is not that different from another similar class in a different location. It also suggests that there may be little difference between the different L1 users in their pattern of errors in English, a suggestion which was then confirmed by the more detailed analysis of Class 1.

Results from Study 1

Rather than the difference we had hypothesised between the children of Malay and Chinese ethnic backgrounds, there emerged a high degree of similarity between the groups. There was a large and highly significant correlation between the rank order of the number of errors produced per student per category by the Chinese and Malay ethnic groups (Spearman's rho $= 0.97$, $n = 9$, $p < 0.01$). This would suggest that with this class there was no discernible effect of the first language on the error types produced within the categories; each group found certain word categories more difficult than others. There appeared to be a tendency for BM first language speakers to produce more errors than their Chinese counterparts (although this was not statistically significant), but in terms of difficulty across the stimulus types, they were very similar indeed.

In addition to this homogeneity of errors across the two groups, an analysis of the word types according to orthographical transparency showed no indication that the students were treating orthographically regular words any differently from orthographically more complex words. The error rates, shown in Figure 4.3, show no overall pattern, and on closer inspection the error rates probably owe more to familiarity than to orthographic complexity (error rates for certain words such as <broad>, <swarm>, <stalk> and <fold>, for which large numbers of students indicated unfamiliarity, tended to skew the overall error rates).

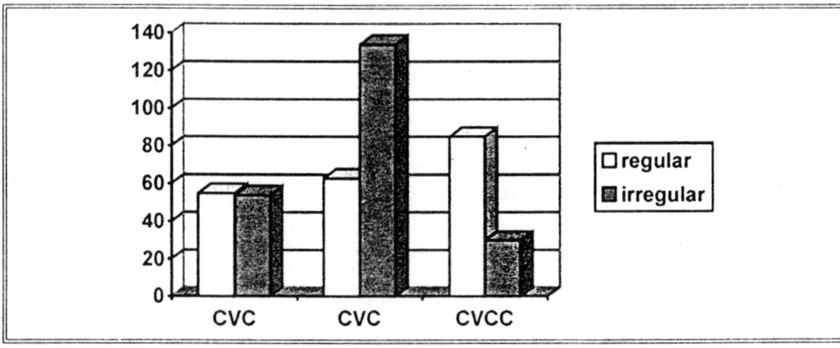

Figure 4.3 Number of errors produced in each word category

There were, as expected, a large number of errors due to problems with cluster processing, but what did emerge very strongly was the difference in error rates when the final cluster included an inflectional morpheme as against the situation where the final cluster was part of the root word. Table 4.3 indicates the dramatic difference in overall errors between words with or without inflectional morphemes.

It thus appears that students from all ethnic groups in this class have problems processing the final cluster when it contains an inflectional morpheme. This is further reinforced when we examine the type of errors that final CC clusters produce when an inflectional morpheme is or is not included in the root word (see Tables 4.4).

It is clear that initial and final consonant clusters do cause problems for the students, but that there are more problems in final positions and that these problems are of a final consonant deletion type. In the uninflected condition, a range of interesting errors are produced, some involving final consonant deletion, but often involving substitution to produce 'meaningful' words (c.f. <grand> – <friend>). However, in the inflected condition, the vast majority of the errors are of the same type: final morpheme omission.

Table 4.3 Number of errors produced in inflected and non-inflected words

Word category	*Error scores (tokens)*
CCVCC (uninflected)	66
CVCC (inflected)	248
CCVCC (inflected)	253

Table 4.4 CCVCC word errors for non-inflected words and inflected words

Target	*Total*	%	*Errors (token count)*
Non-inflected			
grand	11	26	brand [3]; rent [2]; friend [1]; grain [1]; rane [1]; grant [1]; run [2]
print	4	9	prin [1]; prind [1,]; prince [2]
stalk	28	65	stork [2]; storck [1]; store [6]; stor [6]; stall [3]; stock [7]; stoke [1]; stole [1]; stom [1]
Inflected			
dressed	33	77	dress [29]; drest [1]; drass [1]; rest [2]
planned	38	88	plan [35]; plan(t) [1]; plant [2]
smelled	36	84	smell [26]; smel [1]; smiel [1]; smile [1]; smelt [7]

Discussion of results from Study 1

The different language groups (including the Tamil students, although we need to be cautious given the small numbers involved) show a remarkably consistent overall pattern of error rates taken over the different categories. This argues for a strong effect from the homogeneity of the curriculum experienced by the different language groups, and effects of word familiarity fall into this category. In addition, the influence of BM, both in terms of initial literacy teaching and language form, is likely to be a highly dominant factor. All three language groups speak BM as a common language, have been taught throughout their school lives through the medium of BM, and attained initial literacy in BM. There do not appear to be any effects of the Chinese students' first language on error rates, thus suggesting that the language of initial literacy may be more important than the first language for orthographic knowledge in the second language.

The analysis of the processing of CC clusters in general, and the final CC clusters in particular, points to the problems that first language phonological structure can cause on output orthography. This aural processing problem with clusters will be reinforced by the grammatical and morphological difference between the languages and English; it is further exacerbated by the fact that in both these classes the teacher delivering the stimuli did not produce the final consonant in the cluster. Thus, if we are examining a simple phoneme–grapheme conversion process, the errors in both word types (i.e. the inflected and non-inflected) should be the same. In descriptive linguistic terms this could be characterised as a variety of English which consistently simplifies final CC clusters in the oral language (in the same way that certain consonants are elided in other varieties, including Standard English), but the elided consonants will still exist in the base representation of the words in the lexicon and are represented in the written form of the language. This would be parallel to the generative phonological mechanism which produces the surface representation 'significant' from 'sign', arguing that the silent <g> is part of the base representation of the lexeme <sign>. It would appear from these data that this explanation works when a word contains a final CC cluster in its root form: this knowledge is retained by the students and recognised in their spelling of the word, even if they are not sure what it is (i.e. a <t> might be substituted with a <d>). On the other hand, when this final consonant is a morpheme (e.g. a /t/ or /d/ past tense marker), its existence is not recognised by the student's underlying entry into the lexicon and consequently is not part of the written output. This would suggest that the errors are not simply generated by lack of input from the spoken variety (in this case both inflected and non-inflected clusters would be simplified in the same manner), but from some form of cognitive word-assembly process which involves the addition of affixes to the root form of the word.

These data indicate a substantial influence of BM on orthographical knowledge in English. However, it is not clear whether such influence derives from general language factors, from specific phonological factors of the use of the local variety of English in the delivery of the stimuli, or from general literacy practices in Malaysian schools and BM in particular. Specifically, it does not indicate any differences between L1 BM users and L1 Chinese users and their orthographic knowledge of English words. The second study, in being more rigorous about isolating language background, using an L1 English user to deliver the dictation, and controlling for language level, allowed us to see if any such difference can be determined.

Study 2

The dictation procedure

The procedure was the same as that for Study 1 except that the test was delivered by a native English speaker and the final cluster endings with inflectional morphemes were placed in sentence frames where there was no chance of elision of the final morpheme. To further reduce the 'listening comprehension' variable, in this second study subjects were given the sentence frame in a written form in addition to it being read out by the test administrator.

The target words

The word targets in the first study were all monosyllabic. In this second study, similar monosyllabic phonological/rhyme contrasts were included, but multi-syllabic targets with both derivational and inflectional morphemes were included. In order to control for word familiarity, in the second study, teachers familiar with students from the People's Republic of China and secondary schools in China were asked to rate the words and sentence contexts according to their perception of how familiar the words were to the students. Examples of the target words and their contexts are given in Table 4.5.

Table 4.5 Sample word targets and sentence contexts for Study 2

	Type	*Target*	*Context*
1	Monosyllabic: C coda	block	I live in an apartment block in the city.
2	Monosyllabic: CC coda [−infl]	grand	The president's palace looked very grand.
3	Monosyllabic: CC coda [+infl]	planned	I planned a trip to England with my friends.
4	Polysyllabic bases: phon reg	regular	My heart seems to be OK. My heartbeat is very regular.
5	Rhyme bases	heal	Some wounds heal very slowly, especially those on your knees.
6	Polysyllabic bases: CC coda [−infl]	intend	This is my last book. I intend it to be my best.
7	Polysyllabic bases: CC coda [+infl]	electrics	The electrics in the building were very unsafe.
8	Derivational morphology no change	complexity	The complexity of the problem made me give up trying to solve it.
9	Derivational morphology phon change	health	The health of so many older people depends on leading an active life.
10	Derivational morphology phon/orth change	intention	I'm sorry. It wasn't my intention to upset you.

The subjects

The second study used 73 (54 male and 19 female) PRC students studying English at the National Institute of Education in Singapore on an access year before entering university and 90 (53 female, 37 male) Malaysian Year 4 students from Maktab Rendah Sains Mara (Mara Science Junior Colleges) in Langawi in Malaysia. The average age of the PRC students was 19 (from 16 to 20) and the Malaysians were either 15 or 16 years old.

Data were collected from both groups concerning their literacy backgrounds, which were completely different. The PRC had a highly homogeneous educational background, having learnt to read in Mandarin and having been educated through the medium of Mandarin, prior to learning English as a Foreign Language in secondary school. The Malaysian students indicated that BM was their dominant language, although some reported profiles indicating balanced bilingualism. Most reported BM to be their language of initial literacy, although some reported learning to read in English simultaneously with BM.

Data was also collected about the reading level of both groups. The IELTS Test of General Academic Reading was given to the PRC students before they commenced their study and the same test was given to the Malaysian students after completing the dictation. The results for the tests show that both groups were closely matched in terms of English language reading proficiency; see Table 4.6.

Results from Study 2

In the first study there seemed to be a difference between the students from Chinese and Malay ethnic backgrounds in terms of the degree of accuracy, with the Chinese appearing to make fewer errors than the Malay students. As no information had been collected about language level, it was suggested that this might be a factor of language ability. As can be seen by the mean scores for the two groups in the second study, their language levels as measured by reading comprehension scores were very similar. Thus, language ability does not seem to be a significant variable in this study. However, there was a clear difference in error rates between the two groups. The Chinese students were much more accurate

Table 4.6 Mean reading comprehension scores for Chinese and Malaysian students

	Mean	*SD*	n
PRC	24.03	5.47	73
Malaysians	24.08	5.92	90

overall than the BM group. The mean error rate per student for the BM group was 31 and for the Chinese group it was 20.

This second study also indicated that both groups displayed problems with consonant clusters and with certain problematic vowel contrasts, again as predicted by the contrastive analysis of the two languages and English, but, as with the first study, the attempt to see any differences in the error rates between orthographically transparent and more complex words was unsuccessful. Both groups made few mistakes with the two types of word, almost certainly because the words chosen were too familiar to produce significant numbers of mistakes. In fact, the errors within the block which contained phonologically regular versus irregular monosyllabic words were dominated by one homophone error – <break> for <brake> – an error made highly consistently by both groups which would appear to be based on word frequency.

The most dramatic finding of the first study was the difference between the errors when the CC cluster was part of the root word and when it included an inflectional morpheme and this was quite consistent across the students of both Chinese and Malay ethnic backgrounds. However, the second study produced quite different findings in this respect.

Word Category 3 consisted of monosyllabic root words with an added morpheme. Table 4.7 shows the numbers of errors which can be attributed to the deletion of the final morpheme, separated according to the two groups.

This shows a clear difference between the two groups. It indicates both that the L1 BM users are highly likely to misspell words with final CC clusters by deleting the final consonant (e.g. 86% of the BM group deleted the final from <crossed> as against 1% of the Chinese group), and that this error is the most likely error type to be made by L1 BM users. This error type comprises over 90% of all the errors for five of the words in this category for the BM group, whereas for the Chinese users this type of error was a large factor in only two of the words, and then only accounting for 65% and 58% of the errors.

The difference between the two groups can be further demonstrated by examining the full responses from the two groups to four of the words in this category; see Table 4.8.

This clearly shows that the Chinese students have a greater range of error types than their BM counterparts. The Chinese errors are generated to a greater extent than the BM errors by other orthographic rules such as those in Table 4.9.

It is not that these error types are absent from the BM data, but clearly morpheme deletion far outweighs all other error types in the BM responses. It would seem that, although errors in the final CC clusters do appear in other types of word, when this CC cluster contains a final inflectional morpheme, then it is highly likely to be deleted. The same

Table 4.7 Malay and Chinese morpheme deletion

		Malaysians			*Chinese*		
Target word	*Response*	*Number of responses*	*% errors*	*% students*	*Number of responses*	*% errors*	*% students*
planned	plan	69	96	77	22	58	30
stocks	stock	11	39	12	2	8	3
boiled	boil	45	79	50	11	65	15
missed	miss	35	92	39	0	0	0
hopes	hope	18	86	20	0	0	0
joined	join	57	90	59	0	0	0
smiled	smile	56	97	62	0	0	0
crossed	cross	75	100	86	1	0	1
flats	flat	24	71	27	2	0	3
laughed	laugh	57	75	64	0	0	0

Table 4.8 Malay and Chinese errors for monosyllabic words with inflectional morphemes

Target		*Response*	*Number*	*% errors*
Malay	planned	plan	69	96
		planed	2	2
		fly	1	1
Chinese		plan	22	58
		planed	14	37
		plant	2	5
Malay	boiled	boil	45	79
		bowl	4	7
		boild	1	2
		boilt	1	2
		boils/boiling	3	6
Chinese		boil	11	65
		boild	1	6
		bohled	1	6
		borrowed	2	12
		brought	2	12
Malay	stocks	stock	11	39
		stops	3	11
		stop	1	4
Chinese		stock	2	8
		flock	2	8
		stops	8	32
		shops	4	16
		stores	4	16
Malay	joined	join	57	90
		joining	2	3
		joint	2	3
		joy	1	4
Chinese		join	0	0
		joinned	2	50
		joining	1	25

NB. No responses data removed, but included in % response.

Table 4.9 Chinese error types

Error type	*Examples*
Consonant doubling	*<planed> [−doubling], *<joined> [+ doubling]
Morpheme representation	*<plant> [<d/t> substitution, *<boilt> [<d/t>substitution]
Root word spelling	*<bohled> [vowel orthography], *<flock>, *<stops>, *<shops> [consonant substitution in CC clusters]
Root word substitution	*<borrowed>, *<brought>, *<stores>

does not hold when it is (or is perceived to be) part of the root word. This can be further illustrated by taking the BM students' responses to the inflected multi-syllabic words of Category 7; see Table 4.10.

It is abundantly clear from this that the pattern of errors for the BM group for <refined> is quite different from the other words in this

Table 4.10 Malay error responses to inflected multi-syllabic words

Target	*Morpheme deletion errors*	*Total number of errors*	*Responses*	*Number*
electrics	31	35	electricks	2
refined	12	71	refind	49
			refund	4
			refunded	2
dismissed	52	54	dismist	2
impressed	61	66		
confessed	32	55	confest	18
			confesed	2
reduced	57	68	rechoose	5
			refuse	1
			rejuice	1
			choose	1
telephones	44	50		
pretends	37	45	protects	2

category. It seems that, if the final CC cluster is perceived to be part of the root word, then the final consonant does not get deleted as it does with all the other target words. It is not that this type of error is absent from the Chinese data – <refind> was a common error in this data as well; but, within the Chinese responses to the multi-syllabic inflected words, there is again a far greater range of responses for the other inflected words, many of which reflect misspellings of the inflectional suffix, suggesting that the source of the error for <refined> can, at least partly, be attributed to a misspelling of the morpheme rather than to some integration of the final consonant into the root word (although undoubtedly this could be a cause for the prevalence of this error type in the Chinese data as well). What sets the BM data apart is the extremely high morpheme deletion type error across all these multi-syllabic words, except for <refined>, suggesting a difference in the orthographic representation for this word alone.

Conclusion

The errors generated by both studies have indicated that phonological differences between the first languages and English do play a part in the errors generated and thus confirmed that 'language distance' does contribute to L2 English users' orthographical knowledge of English. In both studies errors occurred in clusters, and certain vowel distinctions caused problems. However, 'orthographic distance' as a factor, as indicated by a simple alphabetic/logographic divide, was not borne out in this study. In the Muljani *et al.* (1998) study of response times to words of different frequencies, the alphabetic group showed a consistent advantage over the logographic L1 users in their reaction times. In this study, in terms of error rate, the logographic group showed an advantage over the alphabetic L1 users, with the Mandarin users being much more accurate than their BM counterparts despite very similar levels of language proficiency.

The other finding to emerge from these studies is the difference between the L1 BM users and L1 Chinese users in their errors in response to inflected words. From a contrastive analysis of the three languages involved (BM, Chinese and English), it is difficult to see how this difference can be explained in terms of language distance. As argued earlier, in terms of morpho-syntactical structure, both languages are equally different from English, and thus would be expected to face similar problems with English inflectional morphemes. In the first study, no difference was seen between the Malay and Chinese students when both were following a BM medium education system. This would suggest that BM as the initial language of literacy has a stronger effect on orthographic knowledge than does the first spoken language. The importance of the initial language of literacy was reinforced by the second study. When the two groups were from different educational and literacy backgrounds, there was a clear and substantial difference in the rate of morpheme deletion according to L1 background.

We must not discard the possibility that the above results could be due to the general educational backgrounds of the two groups and in particular the English language learning approaches used in the two education systems. It could be argued that the PRC students come from a very formal grammar-based method of studying English, which would make them more aware of grammatical features such as past tense morphemes, whereas the Malaysian students come from a more communicatively-based syllabus leading them to be less aware of the need for past tense morphemes. Although there may be some truth in this analysis, the study of English in Malaysian classrooms is still relatively formal, with quite a lot of emphasis on grammatical features. Furthermore, whilst this may provide a partial explanation for the difference between the groups in terms of morpheme deletion, it does not provide an explanation for the different error rates between the two groups. In fact, the similarity between the two groups in terms of language proficiency would tend to argue against an explanation based on English language knowledge.

However, a critical element of educational experience must be the influence of first language reading processes and their effect on literacy processes in the second language. Both studies have failed to find any evidence of a difference between the logographic and alphabetic writing system users in terms of their knowledge of regularly and less regularly spelt words. This, it is argued, could possibly be due to their familiarity with the word targets used in the studies, which therefore fail to generate significant numbers of errors.

However, it is possible to argue that a whole-word, logographic processing strategy might provide an explanation for the greater accuracy of the logographic group and their lower tendency to delete final morphemes. As we have argued, L1 BM users are likely to use non-lexical, serial processing processes based on the CVCV structure of BM. As this language does not include final clusters, serial processing will end when sufficient information is received to identify a word. If we use the logogen analogy for word recognition, with non-inflected words (e.g. <land>) word activation will take place once /læn/ has been received, with the mental lexicon providing the missing letter from the underlying representation. Similarly, the processing of inflected words (e.g. <planned>) will end when the base structure of the word has been accessed (i.e. /plæn/). However, in this case, without the use of context, there is no reason for the underlying representation of the word in the lexicon to provide the final consonant (morpheme). There may be only minimal use of the semantic processor, except to check that the root word exists. The L1 Chinese user, however, using a route which places much more emphasis on holistic visual representation, is more likely to access a visual 'picture' of the word to which the morpheme is connected. If character access in Chinese relies heavily on the use of semantic and contextual features, it is also possible that semantics and context will be used more by L1 Chinese users when accessing words in English. This will again help Chinese students to supply the past tense morpheme. The possible processing routes as used by the two groups are depicted in Figures 4.4 and 4.5.

It is clear that lexical representation is a complex matter, that there are a number of factors involved here and that more research is needed in this area. However, what these studies have demonstrated is that it is possible to see quite clear differences between language users by examining error rates in targeted dictation tasks, and that by analysing the types of error we can begin to understand the way orthographic knowledge of L2 English users is stored and, from that, begin to explore the way we can approach L2 reading instruction in English.

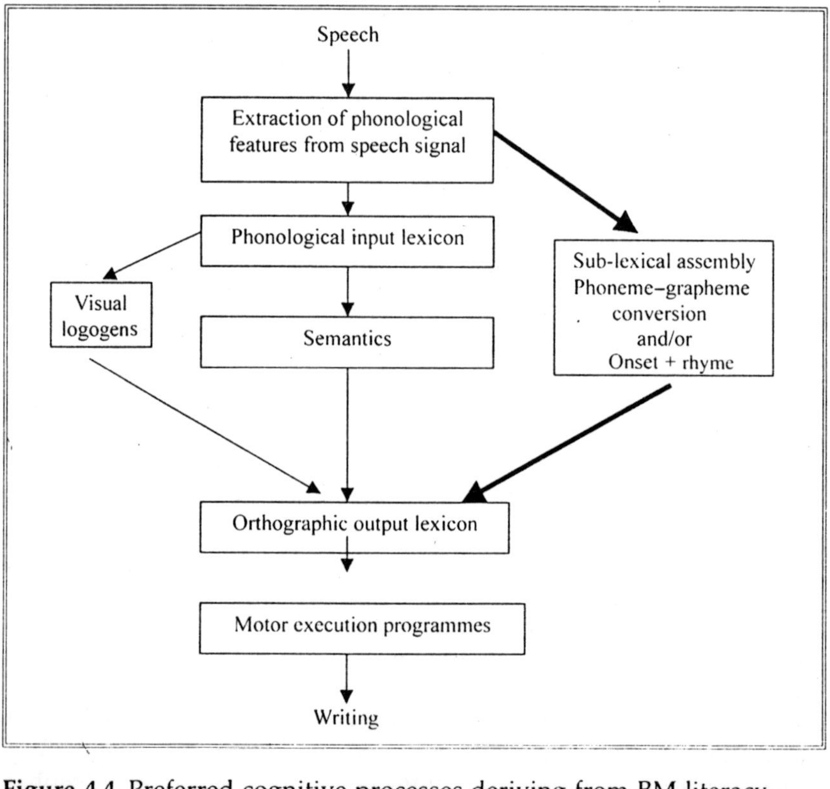

Figure 4.4 Preferred cognitive processes deriving from BM literacy

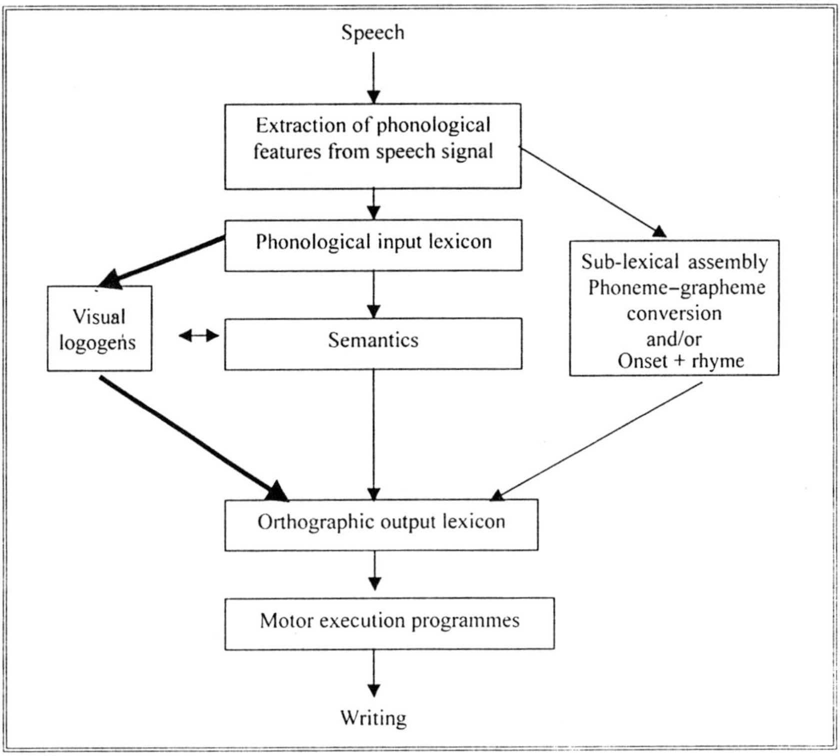

Figure 4.5 Preferred cognitive processes deriving from Chinese literacy

Note

1. The term 'Chinese' is used to refer generically to students of Chinese ethnic backgrounds and also to the spoken dialects of Chinese in general. The term is also used when referring to the written system of standard Chinese. The term 'dialect' is used when referring to the different spoken forms of Chinese. Thus, 'Mandarin' is used when referring to the standard spoken dialect of Chinese.

References

Adams, M.J. (1990) *Beginning to Read*. Cambridge, MA: MIT Press.

Brown, A. (1986) Pedagogical importance of consonantal features of the English of Malaysia and Singapore. *RELC Journal* 17 (2), 1–25.

Coltheart, M., Rastle, K., Perry, C., Langdon, R. and Ziegler, J. (2001) DRC: A Dual Route Cascaded model of visual word recognition and reading aloud. *Psychological Review* 108, 204–56.

Cook, V.J. (1997) L2 users and English spelling. *Journal of Multilingual and Multicultural Development* 18 (6), 474–88.

Deterding, D.H. and Poesjosoedarmo, G.R. (1998) *The Sounds of English.* Singapore: Prentice Hall.

Goswami, U., Ziegler, J., Dalton, L. and Schneider, W. (2001) Pseudohomophone effects and phonological recoding procedures in reading development in English and German. *Journal of Memory and Language* 45, 648–64.

Kibbel, M. and Miles, T.R. (1994) Phonological errors in the spelling of taught dyslexic children. In C. Hulme and M. Snowling (eds) *Reading Development and Dyslexia* (pp. 105–27). London: Whurr Publications.

Koda, K. (1996) L2 word recognition research: A critical review. *Modern Language Journal* 80 (4), 450–60.

Muljani, D., Koda, K. and Moates, D.R. (1998) The development of word recognition in a second language. *Applied Psycholinguistics* 19, 99–113.

Patterson, K.E. and Morton, J. (1985) From orthography to phonology: An attempt at an old interpretation. In K.E. Patterson, J.C. Marshall and M. Coltheart (eds) *Surface Dyslexia: Neuropsychological and Cognitive Studies of Phonological Reading* (pp. 335–59). Hove, UK: Lawrence Erlbaum Associates.

Randall, M. (1991) Scanning in different scripts: Does Jawi interfere with Bahasa Malaysia and English? *RELC Journal* 22 (4), 99–112.

Randall, M. (1997) Orthographical knowledge, phonological awareness and the teaching of English: An analysis of word dictation errors in English of Malaysian secondary school pupils. *RELC Journal,* 28 (2), 1–21.

Randall, M. and Meara, P. (1988) How Arabs read Roman letters. *Reading in a Foreign Language* 4 (2), 133–45.

Seidenberg, M.S. and McClelland, J.L. (1989) A distributed developmental model of word recognition. *Psychological Review* 96, 523–68.

Tan, Li-Hai and Perfetti, C.A. (1998) Phonological codes as an early constraint in Chinese word identification: A review of current discoveries and theoretical accounts. *Reading and Writing: An Interdisciplinary Journal* 10, 165–200.

Chapter 5

Learner Corpora and Handwriting

HAROLD SOMERS

Introduction

This chapter treats the question of handwriting in second-language acquisition (SLA) from the point of view of corpus linguistics, and in particular 'learner corpora'. We begin by introducing general issues in corpus linguistics, especially relating to annotation or 'mark-up' of manuscripts, and then consider the relevance of guidelines to the special case of a learner corpus of hand-written English. We illustrate our discussion with examples taken from a small corpus of English essays hand-written by Arabic-speakers.

Corpus Linguistics

According to McEnery and Wilson (1996), corpus linguistics is not a branch of linguistics, concentrating on one aspect or perspective of language use, but a *methodological* approach to linguistics in general. A 'corpus' is a collection of linguistic data, whether in its original form or transcribed from speech or, in our case, handwriting. Almost inevitably nowadays use of computers to store and manipulate the corpus is understood to be part of corpus linguistics. Furthermore, a corpus is usually understood to be a *motivated* collection of material, with explicit design criteria relating to its purpose, representativeness, balance, size, dynamism, and so on, and with a considerable degree of 'value added' in the form of annotation.

This annotation (or 'mark-up') can include general auxiliary information about texts in the collection such as the sex or age of author or intended reader, the source and date of the material, incidental information about the context of the material and so on. In addition, the text itself is usually annotated at any of a variety of linguistic levels. For example, transcriptions of speech may be marked up for phonetic and prosodic features. At the lexical level, texts may be annotated to indicate lemmatisation (identifying underlying forms of inflected words), word-sense (in the case of ambiguous forms), and so on. Grammatical annotation can include part-of-speech 'tagging' (where mark-up indicates grammatical category, for example, `covering:NN` for the noun sense versus `covering:VNG` for the present participle sense) or syntactic 'chunking' (where annotation indicates syntactic constituents like noun phrases). Semantic and pragmatic annotations can be proposed. The amount and level of mark-up is entirely dependent on the use to which the corpus is to be put. The general purpose is to add different types of information to the plain transcript. In computer terms 'mark-up' is material added to the actual data through a convention such as a 'mark-up language' (see below).

One thing to note is that mark-up is usually 'interpretive', that is, the result of someone's analysis of the data. So not all mark-up is uncontroversial, and users of already annotated corpora must understand that they may not agree with some of the annotations. Indeed, it may be that the mark-up has been done automatically, for example by a tagger (a program which automatically assigns part-of-speech annotations, or 'tags'), and only partially checked by a human.

Because of this, there are a number of conventions that most corpus linguists adhere to. Mark-up should be 'non-destructive': in other words, the raw corpus should be recoverable, so that you can dispense with any mark-up you don't need. The mark-up should be unambiguous and consistent, and should be fully documented. With this in mind, corpus linguists have converged on a consensual use of a Single Standardized General Mark-up Language (SGML) following the guidelines suggested by the Text Encoding Initiative (TEI).

SGML was developed in the 1980s to facilitate the portability of electronic manuscripts, that is independence from any particular computer software or hardware, so that resources could be more easily shared. SGML's conventions will be familiar to anyone who has looked at the source 'code' of web pages, which use HTML (HyperText Mark-up Language), a form of SGML.

Annotations in SGML are identified by tags enclosed in angle brackets <>. They usually come in pairs `<tag>...</tag>` to indicate the start and end of some textual feature, but they can stand alone, e.g. `<br>` in HTML indicating a line-break. Furthermore tags can have 'attributes', e.g. `<font size = 12>...</font>`. Beyond these basic rules, SGML is quite flexible, and the tags can be used for almost anything, at the user's discretion. For example, they could be used to indicate textual form or function, cf. `<it>italic</it>` versus `<emph>emphasis</emph>`. In the latter case the tag might be linked to a 'document type definition' which determines that text marked `<emph>...</emph>` should appear in italics.

Figure 5.1 shows a short example of text marked up in HTML for web pages, together with the text as it would appear in a web browser.

```
<font face='Arial'>This is an example
of marked-up text with some
<i>italics</i>, <b>bold-face</b>
and</font><font face='Times'> change of
type face.</font>
```

This is an example of marked-up text with some *italics*, **bold-face** and change of type face.

Figure 5.1 An example of marked-up text

The figure shows simple tag pairs like `<i>...</i>` and `<b>...</b>` for italics and bold face respectively, while the `<font>` tag includes an attribute naming the typeface.

While SGML is, as its name suggests, explicitly general, the TEI has sought to establish guidelines to encourage corpus linguists to annotate corpora in comparable ways, so as to facilitate the sharing of resources. Launched in 1987, the TEI (Sperberg-McQueen & Burnard, 1994; see also www.tei-c.org.uk/) is a joint venture of the Association for Computational Linguistics, the Association for Computing in the Humanities, and the Association for Literary and Linguistic Computing. Its guidelines are widely accepted as suggestions of best practice rather than prescriptions, and are very wide-ranging, covering text, speech, linguistic mark-up and, crucially for our purposes, manuscripts.

Guidelines on hand-written text mostly relate to ancient manuscripts and epigraphy (inscriptions on durable material), and we shall look at them in more detail below. As we shall see, they tend to focus on 'correction' and 'normalisation', where the editor 'believes the original to be erroneous', even sanctioning 'changes introduced for the sake of consistency or modernisation of a text'. We will discuss below how applicable these guidelines are to our particular interest.

Learner Corpora

Within the field of corpus linguistics, one application that is fast gaining recognition and interest is learner corpora, that is, corpora of language produced by second or foreign language (L2) learners. There have already been conferences and books dedicated to this topic (e.g. Granger, 1998b; Granger & Hung, 1998; Granger *et al.*, 2002), showing how such corpora can be used to track linguistic features of L2 use, whether lexical, grammatical or stylistic. These may include over- or under-use of specific features, incidence of errors, influence of the native or first language (L1), use of 'avoidance strategies', where learners achieve 'native-like' competence, what problem areas need most attention, and how learners with different L1s differ. Studies may be purely descriptive, may focus on data as evidence of psycholinguistic aspects of SLA, or may be aimed more at influencing teaching strategies. Examples of English learner corpora include *ICLE* (International Corpus of Learner English) (Granger, 1993; see also www.fltr.ucl.ac.be/fltr/germ/etan/cecl/Cecl-Projects/Icle/icle.htm), the *Longman Learners' Corpus* (www.longman-elt.com/dictionaries/corpus/lclearn.html) and the *Cambridge Learner Corpus* (uk.cambridge.org/elt/corpus/clc.htm), to name just three (for further listings see leo.meikai.ac.jp/~tono/lcresource.html).

Learner corpora are used in SLA research for example to illustrate over- and under-use of constructions, to study the development of interlanguage, to compare universal versus L1-specific learners' errors, and to compare native-like and non-native-like performance. Some researchers advocate using learner corpora in the classroom as illustrations of learners' errors, or as sources of material for error-correction exercises (see Granger, 1998a; Granger *et al.*, 2002).

Computer-based tools that can be used with learner corpora include concordances (lists showing the contexts in which certain words or phrases are used), and tools such as *WordSmith* (Scott, 2001), which can provide counts of words and word sequences, sorted in various ways, as well as information on word combinations. Part-of-speech tagging and grammatical analysis may also be useful.

One interesting aspect so far ignored in the literature on learner corpora is *handwriting* as an aspect of SLA. In particular, where the learner's first language uses a different writing system (WS1), acquisition and use of a second writing system (WS2) may be an important area for research, again from various points of view: SLA, teaching strategies and contrastive analysis in general.

This chapter looks in particular at the question of mark-up of handwriting in a learner corpus and tries to draw attention to some issues related to this question. Amongst the most important of these is the extent to which mark-up recommendations of bodies such as the TEI can be applied to such corpora, and whether it is possible to annotate such a corpus independent of any analysis of it. As a case study, we will look at examples from a small collection of English essays written by Arabic-speaking learners, collected in connection with a (more conventional) study of grammatical and lexical errors. The main goal of SLA research is, as Granger (1998b: 4) says, 'to uncover the principles that govern the process of learning a foreign/second language', and the main tools of this research are data from language use, metalinguistic judgments and student introspection. Learner corpora directly meet this first need, by providing a body of, usually genuinely produced, examples of L2 usage by students. There are of course drawbacks to the use of learner corpora, and, equally, issues regarding the design and collection of material, as there are with any corpus material. It is perhaps unnecessary to rehearse these here (see, again, Granger, 1998b).

The corpus which forms the basis of our case study below is by all standards a tiny one. It is a collection of 20 hand-written essays, each about 150 words in length, produced by adult learners of English, all with (Cairene) Arabic as their L1 and WS1. The essays, on the topic of the computer as an educational tool, were written as a follow-up to a listening comprehension exercise, and therefore tend to repeat many of the phrases and ideas expressed in the original. The corpus was collected as data for a study of lexical and grammatical interference, not explicitly for the study of handwriting. It was the task of converting the corpus to machine-readable form which alerted the current author to the specific problem of marking-up handwriting anomalies. Figure 5.2 shows a typical example and is a source of the examples below.

Granger (1998b) notes that keyboarding is currently the most common method of data capture, and indeed the only method for hand-written texts. But this process presents special difficulties for proof-readers: 'The proof-reader has to make sure he [sic] edits out the errors introduced during keyboarding ... but leaves the *errors* that were present in the learner text, a tricky and time-consuming task' (p. 11, emphasis added). Granger's use of the word 'errors' here raises an interesting point to which we will return. Borin (2002: 2) mentions the difficulty of 'resolving unclear handwriting and punctuation' when converting a learner corpus of hand-written Swedish to computer-readable form.

Regarding mark-up, which can be used to record textual features of the original data, Granger worries that it is also very time-consuming, and suggests that '[i]n the case of learner corpora, which tend to contain few special textual features, this stage can be kept to a minimum, although it should not be bypassed' (Granger 1998b: 12). We feel that this minimalistic approach is quite inappropriate for learner corpora, since one of the most striking features of L2 writing is that it contains anomalous language use that, if not annotated, might lessen the usefulness of the corpus. One obvious example is misspelling: consider that, if a misspelled word is left unmarked in a corpus, its presence may interfere with subsequent attempts to analyse the corpus, whether by parsing or by tagging, or more straightforward analyses such as concordances. Meunier's (1998) overview of tools available for corpus analysis makes no mention at all of the impact of anomalous usage on parsing, tagging and so on. It could certainly be argued that anomalies and errors in corpora can be very revealing. As the reviewers of this paper pointed out, the British National Corpus contains no instances of the misspelled word *<recieve>, whereas a Google search of the internet suggests that the word is misspelled about 4% of the time. As we mentioned above, conventionally mark-up should be non-destructive, which will enable us to search for misspellings of <receive> explicitly if we want to, but equally have those instances handled *as if* they were correctly spelled, if that is more appropriate.

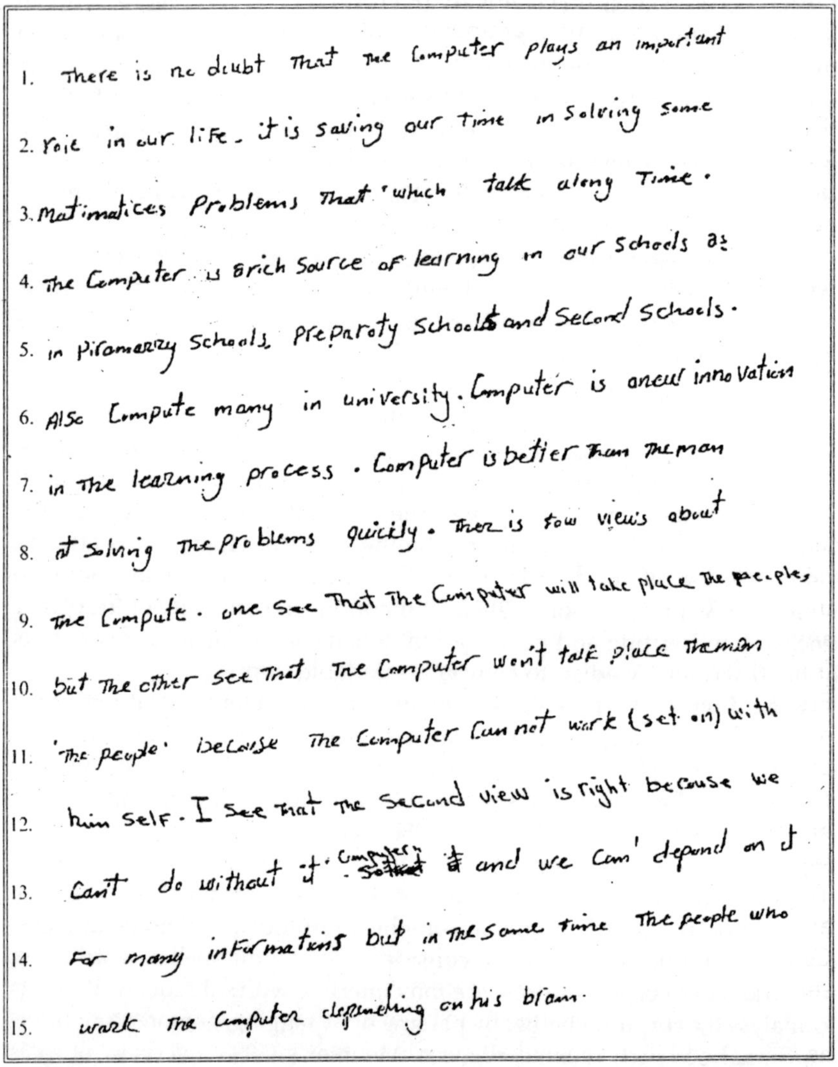
There is no doubt That The Computer plays an important
Roie in our life. it is saving our time in Solving some
Matimatices Problems That 'which talk along Time.
The Computer is Brich Source of learning in our Schools as
in Piramarry Schools, Preparoty Schools and Second Schools.
Also Compute many in university. Computer is anew innovation
in The learning process. Computer is better Than The man
at Solving The problems quickly. Ther is tow views about
The Compute. one See That The Computer will take place The peoples
but The other See That The Computer won't take place The man
'The people' because The Computer Can not work (set on) with
him self. I See That The Second view is right because we
Can't do without it. Computer it and we Can' depend on it
For many informations but in The Same time The people who
work The Computer depending on his brain.

Figure 5.2 An example of the raw corpus data (line numbers added)

In contrast, Dagneaux *et al.* (1998) describe the use of learner corpora in connection with computerised error analysis in which errors in the student's text are tagged with an appropriate 'error tag', which indicates the nature of the error as well as the (or rather, one of the) correct form(s).

The issue of learners' 'errors' is one that should not be ignored, and is especially relevant for marking up handwriting. While some of the things that learners write are unquestionably errors, e.g. <matimatices> for

<mathematics> (Figure 5.2, line 3), often things are not so clear-cut. One finds a whole range of grammatical infelicities, ranging from lack of number agreement, inappropriate prepositional complements and use (or omission) of articles, all of which might safely be tagged as errors, through to awkward use of tenses, choice of near synonyms and other lexical matters, which may be more an issue of judgement. In marking up a learner corpus, it would be preferable if tags could differentiate between those errors and anomalies that are objective, and those that more or less presuppose some analysis. For example, a tag of 'wrong tense' would presumably reflect some analysis of what the student was trying to say, rather than any ungrammaticality as such. As we will see when we come to consider handwriting, some of these issues are far from clear-cut.

Acquisition of a Second Writing System

Despite the large amount of literature in the field of SLA and in particular in the field of teaching English as a Second (or Foreign) Language, little has been written about 'the equally important subject of how to acquire the Latin alphabet as a second writing system, or how to change from any particular writing system to another' (Sassoon, 1995: 5). The work from which this quote is taken seems to be an almost unique exception. For example, Swan and Smith's highly recommended collection (1987) of language-by-language essays on L1 interference contains some examples of learners' handwriting, but generally says little about what to expect. Smith (1987), discussing Arabic speakers, has a few paragraphs on 'Orthography and punctuation' which include reading, writing and spelling problems, as do Wilson and Wilson (1987) discussing Farsi. Thompson (1987: 215) states merely that 'Japanese learners do not generally have great difficulty with English spelling or handwriting', while Chang (1987: 227) states that '[a]lphabetic handwriting . . . presents no serious problems for Chinese learners'.

Sassoon's (1995) focus seems to be mainly on children learning English as an L2 and her somewhat anecdotal approach is aimed at helping teachers develop strategies for overcoming problems which could be symptomatic of, or conversely the trigger for, deeper problems of linguistic and cultural assimilation. Nevertheless, her book is a good source of typical problems, with illustrations from learners with a wide variety of first writing systems.

Sassoon's book starts usefully by comparing the 'rules' of writing systems, including elements such as general direction of the writing, entry point and direction for individual letters ('ductus'), heights of letters and their composite parts (ascenders and descenders), alternate letter forms (upper and lower case, word-initial, medial and final), and spacing and joining of letters and words. In each of these aspects there is the possibility of interference from the WS1, if it differs. For some writing systems there is the additional problem of 'false friends', in this case letters which look similar but have a different value (e.g. Greek <P> with the phonetic value /r/ – but compare also Cyrillic lower-case <T> which in handwriting resembles an <m>). In other cases the interference is more generic, as exemplified by the problems Tamil writers have with joined-up writing, since their WS1 prescribes a clockwise ductus, whereas letter forms in English often require the opposite.

Sassoon then goes on to look at a number of interesting case studies, which are informative, but her treatment of them is not systematic. Subsequent chapters focus on writing materials and posture, assessment, teaching techniques, psychological and sociological aspects of handwriting, and, finally, typography. Although of interest, little of this is especially helpful to us in our quest for guidelines for marking up a hand-written corpus.

Mark-up Recommendations and Manuscripts

There is a considerable amount of literature on the electronic mark-up of manuscripts, mostly on the World Wide Web. Much of this work is related to more or less ancient documents, though original manuscripts of modern literary works are also subject to this kind of attention. In most cases, researchers look to the TEI guidelines for some basic suggestions, and agree that SGML-type mark-up is appropriate. Often, transcribers take it upon themselves to regularise features of the original text, to make them more readable to modern scholars (e.g. Hines, 1995). Most researchers find that they have to extend the TEI recommendations to meet their specific needs. The following extract regarding the work of the Electronic Text Center, University of Virginia, is typical:

> A primary goal of documentary editing is to preserve as many features of the original document as possible. To this end, we carefully transcribe each page, noting and preserving such features as line breaks, underlining, post-scripts scrawled in margins, changes in hand, and so forth. TEI includes a number of tags that enable an editor to describe these textual and non-textual features. For instance, we record information about the content and location of additions and deletions with the <add> and <del> tags, and we mark errors in the text and editorial emendations with <sic>, <corr>, and <orig reg>. [. . .] Even as we strive to replicate the original document as accurately as we can, we also want the text to be accessible to as many users as possible, for as many uses as imaginable. Of course, simply putting the text and its accompanying images up on the web makes a rare, unique document available to millions of users. These texts are fully searchable, so that

scholars can discover connections among documents that were previously unknown. (Spiro & Fay, 2001)

An interesting example of some relevance to us is the Lancaster Corpus of Children's Project Writing (Ormerod & Ivanic, 1999; Smith *et al.*, 1998), which is a corpus of transcribed texts written by 8–12-year-old children, freely available on the Web. The corpus includes images of the original material, which allow us to see more examples of handwriting anomalies. Unfortunately, for our purposes, the corpus is *not* marked up for 'letter (glyph) formation', and spellings have been regularised. As one of the project web pages states, 'the corpus will be of limited value in studying these phenomena' (www.ling.lancs.ac.uk/lever/docs/markup.htm).

In this section, we aim to summarise the TEI recommendations on manuscript mark-up, as described in Burnard and Sperberg-McQueen (1995), and to consider how these guidelines relate to our present problem.

In a section headed 'Editorial Interventions', the TEI guidelines distinguish between 'correction', where the editor 'believes the original to be erroneous', and 'normalization', or 'changes introduced for the sake of consistency or modernization of a text'. In the former case, one can either mark something as corrected, with the original indicated as an attribute of the `<corr>` tag, or, conversely, a self-explanatory `<sic>` tag is proposed, with the attribute `corr`. In either case, additional attributes can identify the editor responsible for the annotation, and the degree of certainty of the correction. Similarly for normalisation, one can indicate the original, with the correction as an attribute (`<orig>` with attribute `reg`) or the converse. We can illustrate these tags in relation to Figure 5.2, the first three lines of which might be tagged as in (1) below (we show here only the tags discussed so far, with the addition of `<lb/>` to indicate 'line break'). For the sake of illustration only, we use `<sic>` for clear-cut errors and `<corr>` for cases where we judge the text to be anomalous, though in doing so we are not necessarily advocating this distinction.

(1) `There is no doubt that the computer plays an important<lb/> role in our life. <sic corr = "It">it</sic> is saving our time in solving some<lb/> <sic corr = "mathematics">matimatices </sic> problems that "which" <corr orig = "talk">take</corr> <corr orig = "along">a long</corr> time.<lb/>`

The TEI guidelines also suggest that additions, omissions, and deletions can be indicated, using the tags `<add>`, `<gap>` and `<del>`. The first of these is for text inserted, and includes attributes indicating the

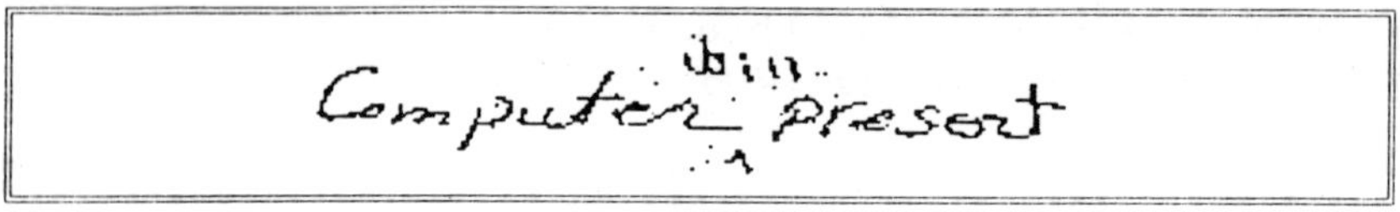

Figure 5.3 An example of an insertion

manner of the insertion. Figure 5.3 shows an obvious case where this tag could be used. In this case, the text might be marked up as in (2).

(2) `<add addtype = "superlinear">will</add>`

The <del> tag is of certain interest to us. It is used to indicate ‘a letter, word or passage deleted, marked as deleted, or otherwise indicated as superfluous or spurious [...]’. Attributes useful to us include the type or manner of deletion. Looking again at Figure 5.2, we see in line 5 that a correction has been made by overwriting (<schoold> changed to <schools>), while three lines from the bottom the words <so that it> have been crossed out and the word < computer'> in quote marks added (see below for discussion of punctuation marks). It is certainly a matter of consideration whether deletions should be rigorously recorded, but there is no doubt that certain kinds of self-correction can nevertheless be very revealing, as in Figure 5.4, which shows two examples of corrections which could indicate to a teacher or researcher a pattern of potential error.

The top example in Figure 5.4 shows a possible confusion regarding English morphology (present participle *-ing* versus agentive suffix *-er*), while the bottom example reflects a typical Arabic-speaker's phonological error (inserting a vowel before a word-initial consonant cluster *sp-*, which Arabic does not have) reflected as a spelling error. No matter that the learner in each case spotted and corrected the mistake. The appropriate tag in this case is presumably <del>, again perhaps with an attribute to indicate the manner of the deletion, as in (3) and (4), illustrating alternative possibilities. The attribute `rend` is recommended by the TEI to indicate how a particular annotation is rendered.

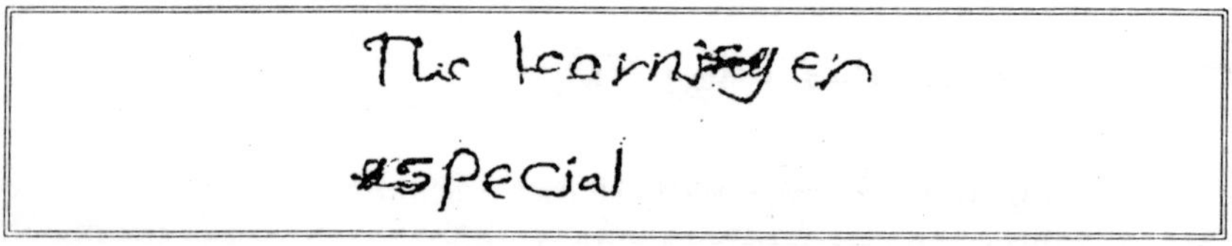

Figure 5.4 Two examples of revealing corrections

(3) `learn<del type = "linethrough">ing</del>er`
(4) `<del rend = "/">e</del>special`

Although, as we can see, the TEI guidelines give us some initial ideas, a number of interesting issues in the mark-up of learners' handwriting remain to be addressed.

Marking up learner handwriting

Perhaps a good place to start is to consider what elements of learner handwriting might be of pedagogic interest. In other words, what kinds of things might we want to mark up? Once again we note the tension between the notion of 'error' and, for want of a better word, 'anomaly', which can apply at all levels.

At the most abstract level, and of comparatively little interest to us here, are aspects of the text that go beyond the question of orthography and calligraphy. Style, syntax and lexical choice, for example, are of course of interest to the researcher, but do not generally relate to the question of handwriting. As we have seen, deletion and insertion may be revealing, but are well treated in existing TEI guidelines.

Our starting point might be **spelling**. Although at first sight this might seem straightforward, there are some interesting interactions between orthography and handwriting. Look again at Figure 5.3, this time concentrating on the words <computer> and what we assume to be <present>. On close inspection, the <n> of <present> closely resembles the <r> of <computer>; so how do we know that it is not a misspelling? Our judgment is guided by the plausibility of that error for this student, and also perhaps by our knowledge of the student's WS1. Figure 5.5 shows, in the space of just three lines, some of the difficulties facing us. On the first line, is that <invented> or <intented>? Is the second <m> in <humman> crossed out? Is that <depend> or <depond> or even <dopond>? And what exactly is the fourth word of the last line?

These are of course the kinds of decisions that teachers have to make when assessing students, but our purposes are somewhat different.

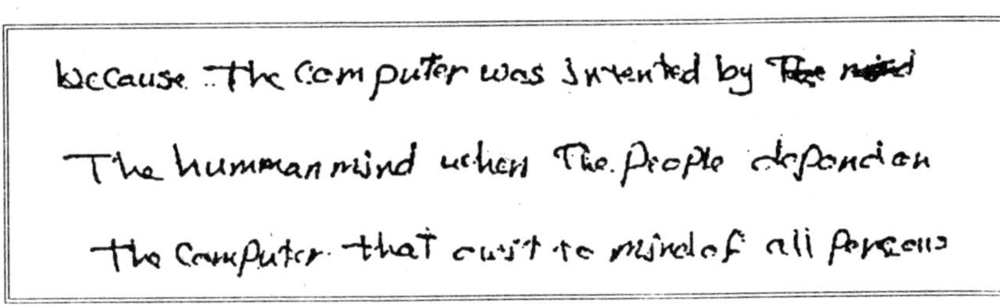

Figure 5.5 Some difficult decisions

Nevertheless, we probably use the same strategies, looking elsewhere in the text to see whether the student has made similar mistakes.

Spacing and **punctuation** are another major issue in our particular corpus. In Figure 5.2 we can see that the student consistently leaves a space before a full stop, which tends to be somewhat elevated. Should this be marked up or not? In the same example we see (line 4) <arich>, and (line 6) <anew> written with comparatively little space: is this significant? In this case we might be influenced by the fact that we find a similar phenomenon in other students' writing. Another feature that we find in Figure 5.2 in several places is unorthodox (in terms of the target orthography) punctuation: quote marks (lines 3, 11 and 13) are used as parenthetical markers here and also in other students' work. But this student also uses conventional brackets (line 11), though with unclear significance. One is reminded of the practice, taught in British primary schools, of indicating deletions with brackets and an <X>, <(thus)x>, since crossing out is for some reason discouraged.

We consider next what is perhaps the most basic aspect of writing, namely letter shape and choice among alternate forms, or 'allographs' (Sampson, 1985). In the Latin writing system, of course, there is a significant distinction between upper and lower case, but also, especially in handwriting, a number of insignificant distinctions between alternate forms. Figure 5.3 for example shows two forms of the letter <r>. To complicate matters further, for just under half the letters (give or take one or two borderline cases), the difference between upper and lower case is simply a matter of scale: compare <C> and <c>, <O> and <o>, <V> and <v>, etc. For the other letters the difference is both size and shape. In this respect our small corpus turns out to be full of difficult cases for mark-up, not surprisingly since the WS1 differs from the WS2 particularly in this respect: Arabic has different letter forms for initial, medial and final, but no upper–lower case distinction. Both Wilson and Wilson (1987) and Smith (1987) mention this as a problem.

Figure 5.6 shows an example of a student who consistently uses a large letter form for word-initial <c>s, but does use a smaller letter elsewhere (though compare <sourCe> in line 5, and <proCess> in line 8). Some of the <p>s are rather large too. Should we mark this up, and if so, how?

Figure 5.7 shows a similar case which extends to <c>s and <w>s. In this example, there is a more consistent pattern of using large letter shapes word-initially and smaller shapes elsewhere. Apart from that, the student's handwriting is comparatively neat, and the standard of English quite good. All of these factors could influence us to resist marking the letter forms as capitals.

A more intriguing case is illustrated in Figure 5.8. Here we can see three or four distinct <t> shapes. The <t> of the first word, <teacher> is

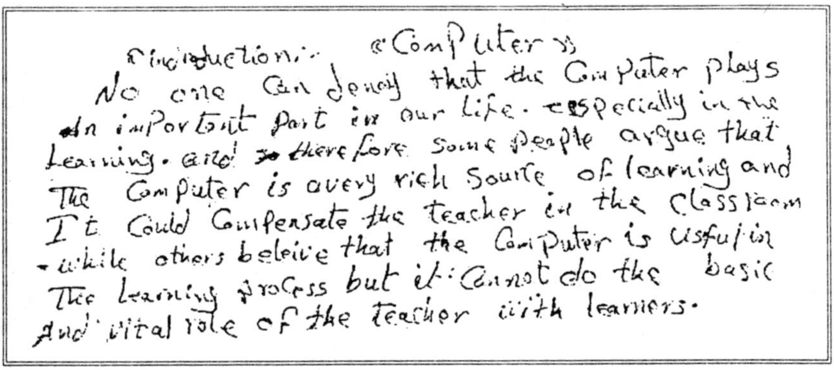

Introduction: «Computer»
No one Can deny that the Computer plays
An important part in our life. especially in the
Learning. and therefore some people argue that
The Computer is avery rich Source of learning and
It Could Compensate the teacher in the Classroom
- while others beleive that the Computer is usful in
The learning process but it Cannot do the basic
And vital role of the teacher with learners.

Figure 5.6 Failure to distinguish upper- and lower-case <c>

most like a conventional capital <t>. In <cannot>, <vital>, <it's> and the second <t> of <that>, we have a clear-cut lower-case letter. But the remaining cases are somewhat hybrid, with the crossbar on top of rather than cutting the vertical stroke, characteristic of the upper case variant, and the short exit stroke which suggests the lower case. And the <t> in <computer> is more like a capital <t>, but slanted backwards more like the other lower-case variants. In fact this student shows a systematic variation (also in the remainder of his essay, not shown here) where what we have called the hybrid form is used word-initially but not sentence-initially. The <t> in <computer> was probably meant to be lower case.

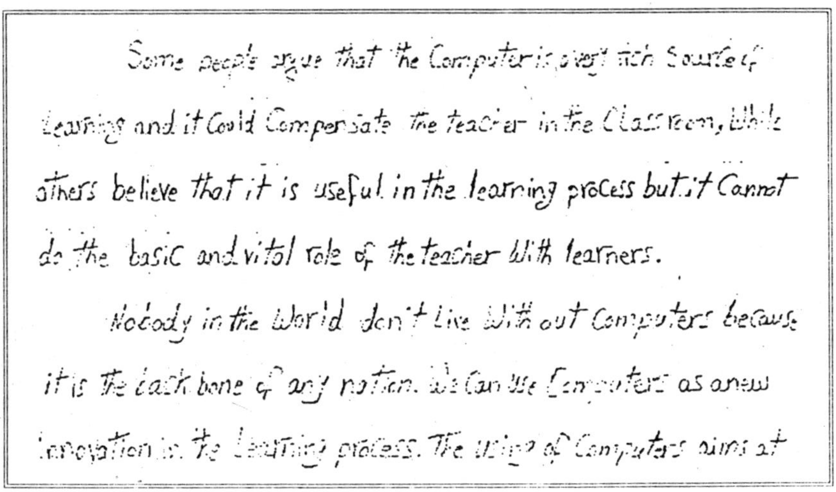

Some people argue that the Computer is avery rich Source of
Learning and it Could Compensate the teacher in the Classroom, While
others believe that it is useful in the learning process but it Cannot
do the basic and vitol role of the teacher With learners.
Nobody in the World don't Live With out Computers because
it is the back bone of any nation. We Can use Computers as anew
innovation in the Learning process. The using of Computers aims at

Figure 5.7 Consistent use of large letter shapes word-initially

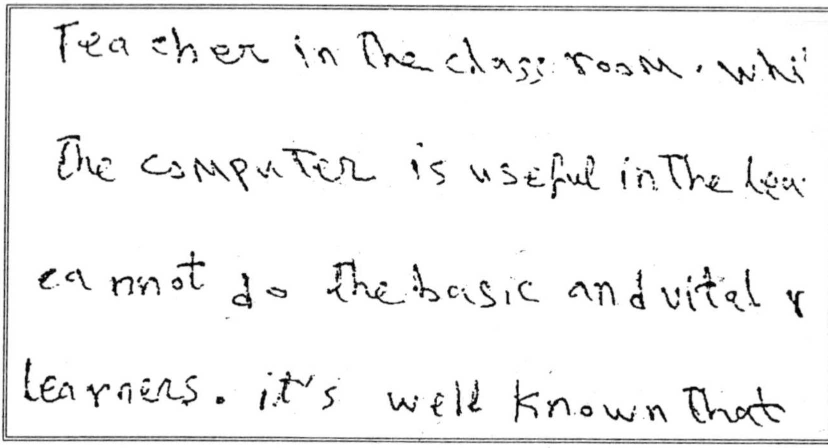

Figure 5.8 Three different <t> shapes

Notice that in all three cases we have been able to spot a more or less consistent pattern rather easily. Should this analysis of the data be reflected in our mark-up? And if so, would it not make more sense to capture the facts in the document header rather than marking up each individual case? One way to do this would be to define separate **entity references** as in (5). An entity reference allows you to define a <name> for a new character, associate with it a piece of mark-up, and then use it in the text as a kind of shorthand. Entity references are indicated in SGML by an ampersand & and a semi-colon ; . In this way one could also distinguish inappropriate use of apparent capitals, as in (6), which gives an entity definition for `&c1;` as 'an upper-case C which should be lower case', illustrated in (7), showing the end of Figure 5.7, line 3 in transcription.

(5) `<!entity t1 '[medial-T]'>`
(6) `<!entity c1 '<sic corr="c">C</sic>'>`
(7) *in the learning proCess but it Cannot . . .*
`in the learning pro&c1;ess but it &c1;annot...`

One final example is a clear case where a global comment in the document header would be most appropriate. Figure 5.9 shows an example which is unremarkable except for the somewhat idiosyncratic <r> shapes, which consistently extend over the following letter. This is clearly not ambiguous, or malformed in any sense, but may be something that one might want to reflect in the mark-up.

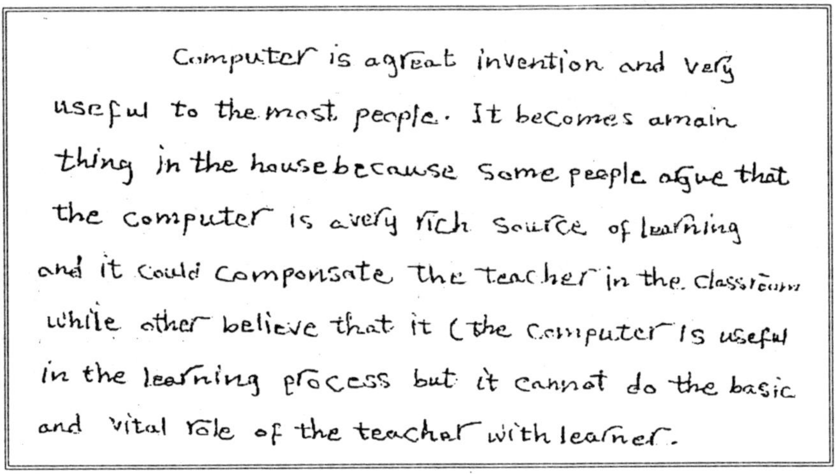
Computer is agreat invention and very useful to the most people. It becomes amain thing in the house because some people ague that the computer is avery rich source of learning and it could componsate the teacher in the classroom while other believe that it (the computer is useful in the learning process but it cannot do the basic and vital role of the teachar with learner.

Figure 5.9 Idiosyncratic but consistent <r> shapes

Conclusions

Our aim in this chapter has been to raise some issues, rather than to provide answers. It is apparent that we can mark up whatever we like, but how should we be guided? At one extreme, we could try to mark everything imaginable, so that the text could be more or less reconstituted on the basis of the mark-up, a bit like ball-by-ball scoring in cricket or baseball. More practically, we might be guided by the use to which the mark-up is going to be put, in which case we could not separate the notion of mark-up from the analysis of the corpus. Is that a bad thing?

Whatever one decides, notice that there are other areas where these issues might arise, with different decisions, for example corpus-based research on WS1 handwriting with young children, aphasics, etc.

Acknowledgements

I am grateful to Hossam Moharam for making his data available to me, to Lou Bernard for a number of discussions on this topic, and to Sylviane Granger for extensive comments on an earlier draft. Any errors and infelicities are mine and mine alone.

References

Borin, L. (2002) Bilaga 4: CrossCheck project status report. NADA, KTH Stockholm. www.nada.kth.se/theory/projects/xcheck/lagesrapport-021015.pdf. Accessed 20.8.03.

Burnard, L. and Sperberg-McQueen, C.M. (1995) TEI Lite: An introduction to text encoding for interchange. *Document No: TEI U 5.* www.hcu.ox.ac.uk/TEI/Lite/teiu5_en.htm. Dated June 1995; accessed 16.8.01; verified 20.8.03.

Chang, J. (1987) Chinese speakers. In M. Swan and B. Smith (eds) *Learner English: A Teacher's Guide to Interference and other Problems* (pp. 224–37). Cambridge: Cambridge University Press.

Dagneaux, E., Denness, S. and Granger, S. (1998) Computer-aided error analysis. *System: International Journal of Educational Technology and Applied Linguistics* 26, 163–74.

Granger S. (1993) The International Corpus of Learner English. In J. Aarts, P. De Haan and N. Oostdijk (eds) *English Language Corpora: Design, Analysis and Exploitation* (pp. 57–69). Amsterdam: Rodopi.

Granger, S. (ed.) (1998a) *Learner English on Computer.* London: Longman.

Granger, S. (1998b) The computer learner corpus: A versatile new source of data for SLA research. In S. Granger (ed.) *Learner English on Computer* (pp. 3–18). London: Longman.

Granger, S. and Hung, J. (eds) (1998) Proceedings of the First International Symposium on Computer Learner Corpora, Second Language Acquisition and Foreign Language Teaching (14–16 December 1998). Hong Kong: The Chinese University of Hong Kong.

Granger, S., Hung, J. and Petch-Tyson, S. (eds) (2002) *Computer Learner Corpora, Second Language Acquisition and Foreign Language Teaching.* Amsterdam: John Benjamins.

Hines, P. (1995) The Newdigate letters. *International Computer Archive of Modern and Medieval English Journal* 19, 158–61.

McEnery, T. and Wilson, A. (1996) *Corpus Linguistics.* Edinburgh: Edinburgh University Press.

Meunier, F. (1998) Computer tools for the analysis of learner corpora. In S. Granger (ed.) *Learner English on Computer* (pp. 19–37). London: Longman.

Ormerod F. and Ivanic, R. (1999) Texts in practices: Interpreting the physical characteristics of texts. In D. Barton, M. Hamilton and R. Ivanic (eds) *Situated Literacies: Reading and Writing in Context* (pp. 91–107). London: Routledge.

Sampson, G. (1985) *Writing Systems.* Stanford, California: Stanford University Press.

Sassoon, R. (1995) *The Acquisition of a Second Writing System.* Oxford: Intellect.

Scott, M. (2001) *WordSmith Tools* Version 3.0. Oxford: Oxford University Press.

Smith, B. (1987) Arabic speakers. In M. Swan and B. Smith (eds) *Learner English: A Teacher's Guide to Interference and other Problems* (pp. 142–57). Cambridge: Cambridge University Press.

Smith, N., McEnery, A. and Ivanic, R. (1998) Issues in transcribing a corpus of children's hand-written projects. *Literary and Linguistic Computing* 13, 217–25.

Sperberg-McQueen, C.M. and Burnard, L. (1994) *Guidelines for Electronic Text Encoding and Interchange*. Chicago and Oxford: Text Encoding Initiative.

Spiro, L. and Fay, C. (2001) Procedures for transcribing and tagging manuscripts, http://etext.lib.virginia.edu/tei/DocEdit.html. Accessed 13.8.01; verified 20.8.03.

Swan, M. and Smith, B. (eds) (1987) *Learner English: A Teacher's Guide to Interference and other Problems*. Cambridge: Cambridge University Press.

Thompson, I. (1987) Japanese speakers. In M. Swan and B. Smith (eds) *Learner English: A Teacher's Guide to Interference and other Problems* (pp. 212–23). Cambridge: Cambridge University Press.

Wilson, L. and Wilson, M. (1987) Farsi speakers. In M. Swan and B. Smith (eds) *Learner English: A Teacher's Guide to Interference and other Problems* (pp. 142–57). Cambridge: Cambridge University Press.

Chapter 6

A Corpus-based Study of Spelling Errors of Japanese EFL Writers with Reference to Errors Occurring in Word-initial and Word-final Positions

TAKESHI OKADA

Introduction

The two main concerns of this comparative corpus-based study are on the one hand to reveal whether Japanese writers of English as a foreign language (hereafter abbreviated as JWEFL) actually make peculiar spelling errors that are different from those generated by native speaker-writers of English (hereafter NSWE), and on the other hand, if that is the case, to explore the reasons why the JWEFL do so. Although the proportion of major errors made by the two groups of writers is similar, there are some idiosyncratic patterns among JWEFL-made errors. Their tendency to substitute particular sets of consonant letters and insert extra vowel letters is explicitly observed in the corpus. By paying attention to substitution errors that occur at the word-initial position and to insertion (or, more precisely, addition) errors that occur at the word-final position, this chapter claims that there is a serious interference from *romaji* (the Japanese romanisation system) on JWEFL, whereas NSWE are considerably influenced by a 'silent' word-final vowel letter <e>.

A rough sketch of two comparative spelling error corpora is given as well as some technical problems in constructing spelling error corpora in general. A discussion of lexical items follows, including semantic, syntactic, pragmatic, morphological and phonological properties of the word. In other words, in the JWEFL's mental lexicon, phonological information is seldom stored while morphological information (spelling) is retained fairly successfully via a vocabulary acquisition process that relies heavily on the visual image.

Comparative Error Corpora: Quantitative Difference

A few comments are necessary concerning the technical problems in collecting spelling errors that are compiled into a corpus. There are, in principle, two ways to collect hand-written spelling errors, i.e. misspellings. One is to collect them from running texts generated in, for example, free compositions or essay writing examinations; the other is from spelling tests. (In the present research, I exclude typos, i.e. errors generated in the process of key entry.)

Compositions or essays allow one to collect 'naturally occurring' errors. However, the actual number of times writers will produce the same word in running text is small, so that we cannot expect to obtain a large number of different misspellings. Moreover, in this circumstance, a writer is free to avoid spelling 'doubtful' words and can employ other words, whose spellings he/she is confident of, in their place. On the other hand, a greater number of attempts – and therefore many different instances of misspellings against a given target word – would be easily obtained from spelling tests. Suppose a spelling test containing a target word, say <spaghetti>, is given to 500 pupils, we are certain to encounter at least 30 variant misspellings.

Spelling tests given to English-speaking schoolchildren would provide a suitable error source to investigate to what extent native speakers rely on the phonological route in spelling, especially in the case when they do not know the correct form of a target word and try to reach it via phonological clues. But, although the JWEFL-made error corpus in this paper is composed of misspellings obtained from spelling tests in Japan, these misspellings have a different property, since, unfortunately, the standard spelling tests given in English speaking classrooms cannot be given in the Japanese setting, for various reasons. Japanese subjects usually do not rely on phonological clues to spell the target word; they try to retrieve the spelling from their lexical (visual) memory. If they are required to spell an unknown word when there is no visual entry in their memory, the Japanese writing system, romaji, has a bad effect on JWEFL, as we discuss later.

There are various types of romaji, two of which, Hepburn and *Kun-rei*, are shown in Table 6.1. Whereas *Kun-rei* (Cabinet order) style is institutionally taught in elementary schools, the Hepburn style is preferred in many cases where borrowed words have to be transcribed (Saeki & Yamada, 1977). The Hepburn style has the advantage over its competing systems of providing an easy way to transcribe certain alien pronunciations of borrowed words, mainly of English origin. It follows that the Hepburn style is also a help for English-speaking people to guess the original sound. In *Kun-rei* style, which all Japanese elementary school students have to learn, the Japanese word ローマ字 /roːmadʒi/ should be

Table 6.1 The English Roman alphabet and romaji letters

English	a	b	c	d	e	f	g	h	i	j	k	l	m
Hepburn style	a	b		d	e	f	g	h	i	j	k		m
Kun-rei style	a	b		d	e		g	h	i		k		m
English	n	o	p	q	r	s	t	u	v	w	x	y	z
Hepburn style	n	o	p		r	s	t	u		w		y	z
Kun-rei style	n	o	p		r	s	t	u		w		y	z

spelled <romazi>, not <romaji> since there is no <j> entry in the *Kun-rei* style. What makes things worse when Japanese people try to spell English words is the fact that romaji is taught before children start to learn English. Japanese children start learning romaji at the age of 10 at the beginning of their fourth year in elementary schools, but English is taught three years later, at the age of 13 in junior high schools. It is likely that many junior high school children at the basic learning level incorrectly assume that Japanese sounds transcribed in romaji have identical phonetic values to their corresponding English sounds. And the less aware Japanese writers are of the difference between the Japanese and the English sound systems, the greater the possibility of them trying to memorise (or encode) and even recall (or access) the English words in quite the wrong way.

Some quantitative differences between the two corpora are shown in Table 6.2. The NSWE corpus is nearly 4.5 times larger than the JWEFL-made error corpus in the number of target words and nearly 6.4 times larger in the number of types of misspellings. The rightmost column of the table shows how many 'error spots' occurred in the misspellings. A single misspelling can contain more than one 'error spot', as in <arubatoross> for <albatross>, which is identified as having one substitution error (employing <r> for <l>) and two insertion errors (adding extra <u> and <o>). The corpus consists of 4,777 different misspellings for 1,144 target words representing nearly 12,000 error spots. Note that the misspellings

Table 6.2 Quantitative differences between the two corpora

	Target words	*Misspelling types*	*Error spots*
JWEFL	1,144	4,777	11,915
NSWE	5,111	30,431	84,765
Total	6,255	35,208	96,680

in the corpus are types, not tokens; <hight>, for example, was written 181 times for <height>, but it has only one entry. (For a detailed description of the corpus, see the Appendix.)

Note that, although there is a quantitative difference between the two error corpora, there is a great similarity in the proportion of major spelling errors, as illustrated in Figure 6.1. The figure shows the properties of the following error types:

(1) Deletion (shortened as Del): one letter omitted, as in <albtross> for <albatross>.
(2) Insertion (shortened as Ins): one letter inserted, as in <alubatross>.
(3) Substitution (shortened as Sub): one letter wrong, as in <albatloss>.
(4) Transposition (shortened as Trp): an adjacent pair of letters transposed, as in <ablatross>.

This similarity in the proportion of spelling errors suggests that, in spite of the quantitative differences, the two comparative corpora adequately reflect the general tendency of spelling errors made by JWEFL and NSWE.

The next step is to investigate the qualitative differences. We will concentrate particularly on substitution errors occurring at the word-initial position and insertion errors occurring at the word-final position

Substitution Errors at the Word-initial Position

As often pointed out in the spell-checking literature, for instance Mitton (1996) or Yannakoudakis and Fawthrop (1983), the proportion of word-initial errors, and especially word-initial substitutions, out of all spelling errors is relatively low. This is indeed the case for both our groups as illustrated in Figure 6.2, which shows the proportion of

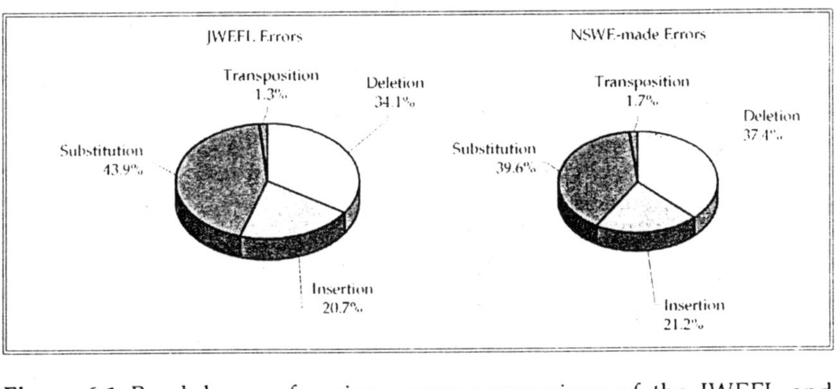

Figure 6.1 Breakdown of major errors: comparison of the JWEFL and NSWE corpora

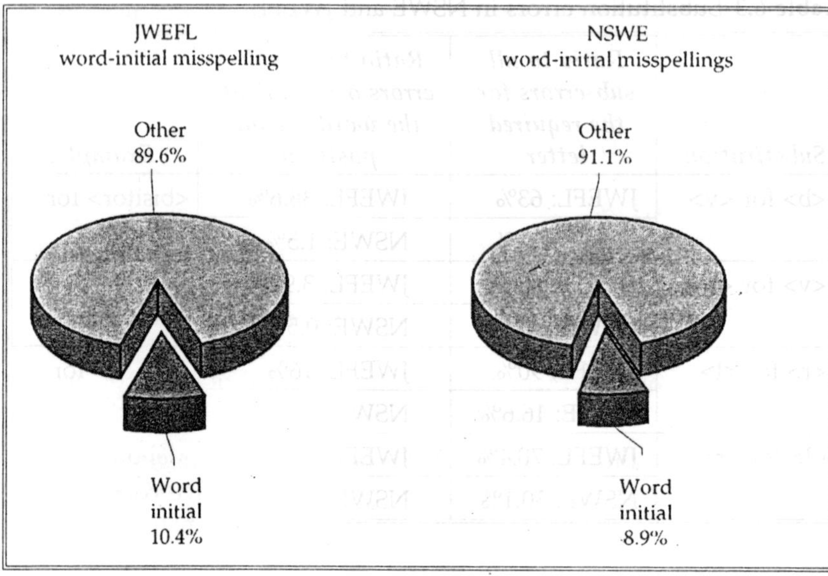

Figure 6.2 Proportion of word-initial errors

misspellings with word-initial errors set against other misspellings that begin with a correct letter.

The majority of spellcheckers are designed to detect and correct misspellings on the presupposition that the word-initial letter is correct. (However, Roger Mitton's spelling correction system is designed in order to cope with even word-initial errors, Mitton, 1996). What is more important for us is the fact that, although both corpora show a similar percentage of words with word-initial errors, their breakdowns show sharp contrast between the NSWE and JWEFL errors.

In Table 6.3 some peculiar tendencies can be observed among the errors made by the JWEFL. First, notice that in the second column JWEFL tend to use incorrectly those letters that are employed in the romaji chart (see Table 6.1), i.e. <b> and <r> are used more frequently than their counterparts, <v> and <l>. On the contrary, NSWE substitute <l> for <r> initially more than they substitute <r> for <l>.

Second, the JWEFL's tendency is more apparent in the third column. Out of 57 JWEFL-made misspellings that should start with initial <v>, only 32 (56.1%) actually start with it, while 22 (38.6%) misspellings start with <b> such as <bideo> for <video>, or <bisiter> and <bisitor> for <visitor>. In misspellings made by the NSWE, there are 678 instances that require word-initial <v>. The great majority of those misspellings, i.e. 612 (90.3%), correctly start with <v>, while only 10 (1.5%) incorrectly

Table 6.3 Substitution errors in NSWE and JWEFL

Substitution	*Ratio to all sub-errors for the required letter*	*Ratio to all sub-errors occurring at the word-initial position*	*Examples*
<b> for <v>	JWEFL: 63%	JWEFL: 38.6%	<bisitor> for <visitor>
	NSWE: 8.2%	NSWE: 1.5%	
<v> for <b>	JWEFL: 53.6%	JWEFL: 3.9%	<visiness> for <business>
	NSWE: 6.2%	NSWE: 0.5%	
<r> for <l>	JWEFL: 90%	JWEFL: 16%	<runch> for <lunch>
	NSWE: 16.6%	NSWE: 0%	
<l> for <r>	JWEFL: 70.4%	JWEFL: 9.3%	<labbit> for <rabbit>
	NSWE: 30.1%	NSWE: 0%	

start with <b> such as <boucher> for <voucher> or <bulgar> for <vulgar>. Note here that, although JWEFL never do so, NSWE incorrectly employ <f> for <v> 35 times (5.2%) as in <fagabond> for <vagabond>, <feiwed> for <viewed>, <firtues> for <virtues>, <fisited> for <visited>, <foucher> for <voucher>, or <falgar> for <vulgar>. This can be explained by presuming that for NSWE the contrastive pair of letters or sounds, i.e. the voiced and unvoiced contrast such as <v> and <f>, is sometimes confusing even if they are followed by a stressed vowel. The confusion among NSWE about the voiced and unvoiced contrast is also clearly observed in the reverse direction, i.e. substituting <v> for <f> such as in <vacilities> and <vasilities> for <facilities>, <vasinating> for <fascinating>, or <vundamental> for <fundamental>.

NSWE rarely start with <v> target words that require initial <b>, whereas JWEFL make 13 misspellings (3.9%) for 333 target words requiring word initial <b> as in <vassball> for <baseball>, <visiness> for <business> or <visy> for <busy>.

A similar tendency is also apparent in substitution errors where <r> is used for <l> and vice versa. While NSWE never use <r> incorrectly at the word-initial position in the 581 words where <l> is required, JWEFL employ <r> 23 times (16%) against 144 <l>s, for example <roughter> and <raughter> for <laughter>, <rettar> for <letter>, <rinking> for <linking>, <roop> for <loop> and <runch> for <lunch>. While NSWE never incorrectly use <l> for 1,786 word-initial <r>s, JWEFL use 15 (9.3%) incorrect <l>s for 161 <r>s required, as seen in <labit> and <labbit> for <rabbit>, <ladish> for <radish> and <lestrant> for <restaurant>.

It is well known that Japanese phonology does not distinguish /b/ from /v/ and /l/ from /r/. In addition to this, Japanese has the orthographical property of lacking either <v> nor <l>, as seen in the romaji inventory in Table 6.1. I assume that, when these factors are combined, they interfere strongly when JWEFL select the appropriate letter from a dubious pair. Though this general tendency is evident in the overall ratio of substitution errors, the word-initial position is where it emerges most explicitly.

As we have observed in Table 6.3, NSWE never make substitution errors involving the use of <l> for <r> or vice versa at the word-initial position. This is because they 'know' at least the word-initial sound, i.e. /l/ or /r/, while JWEFL do not 'know' the sound because the phonology of their mother tongue makes no distinction between the two sounds. (More precisely Japanese has neither /l/ nor /r/ sounds in a strict sense; the five Japanese syllables /ɽa/, /ɽi/, /ɽu/, /ɽe/, /ɽo/ – represented by the kana ら,り,る,れ,ろ – do not correspond exactly either to /la/, /li/, /lu/, /le/, /lo/ or to /ra/, /ri/, /ru/, /re/, /ro/.) Therefore, NSWE make few substitution errors at the word-initial position, while JWEFL, who do not know the exact word-initial sound, tend to get confused in choosing one of the appropriate letters.

However, in those cases when the word-initial sound does not directly correspond to the spelling, NSWE make more frequent errors than JWEFL do. Misspellings for target words with a 'silent' word-initial letter such as <p> in <psychology> or a digraph such as <ph> in <philosophy> are good instances. NSWE incorrectly use <s> or <f> (such as <sicology> or <sychology> and <filosify> or <filousify>) which seem to represent the word-initial sounds directly (Mitton, 1987). On the contrary, the fact that JWEFL do better than their English counterparts can be explained if we assume that they 'know' the forms of the target words instead of their sounds. From these observations we can claim that JWEFL rely on the lexical route in spelling, which is negatively affected by the Japanese phonological system and the romaji spelling system, whereas NSWE rely on the phonological route. If NSWE are not careful enough to spell out correctly 'hard spots' such as silent letters or double letters (Mitton, 1996), the result reflects the direct transcription of the sound of the target word.

Insertion Errors

Figure 6.3 illustrates the overall difference of errors made by the two groups of writers inserting either additional consonant letters or vowel letters.

This contrast makes it possible to claim that JWEFL make more incorrect insertions of vowels, which are indispensable for the Japanese syllabary with the open-vowel CV system. On the other hand, though deletions

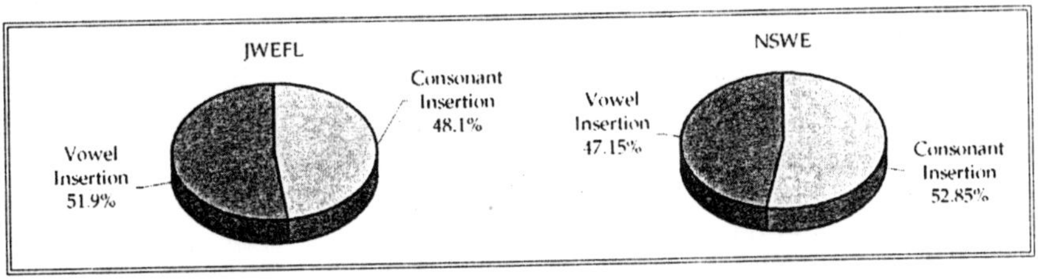

Figure 6.3 Insertion of consonant letters and vowel letters

are not dealt with here, it is observed that JWEFL delete fewer vowel letters than NSWE. This also suggests that JWEFL tend to retain as many vowel letters as possible in their misspellings. As Cook (1997) points out, JWEFL tend to use epenthetic vowels to pad out consonant clusters (CC) into consonant plus vowel plus consonant (CVC) structures.

Figure 6.4 shows that JWEFL tend to insert extra vowel letters in between consonant letters yielding CVC structures more frequently than NSWE do.

From the comparison above, word-final insertion (addition) of vowel letters which end up in a CV pattern are excluded, as we will give them a closer look later.

It is not easy to determine the actual sound of each vowel letter, which can represent a genuine vowel, a diphthong or a schwa sound, or may not even be pronounced at all, i.e. a silent letter. The vowel letter <e> is often used as a silent letter regardless of its position in the word. Figure 6.5

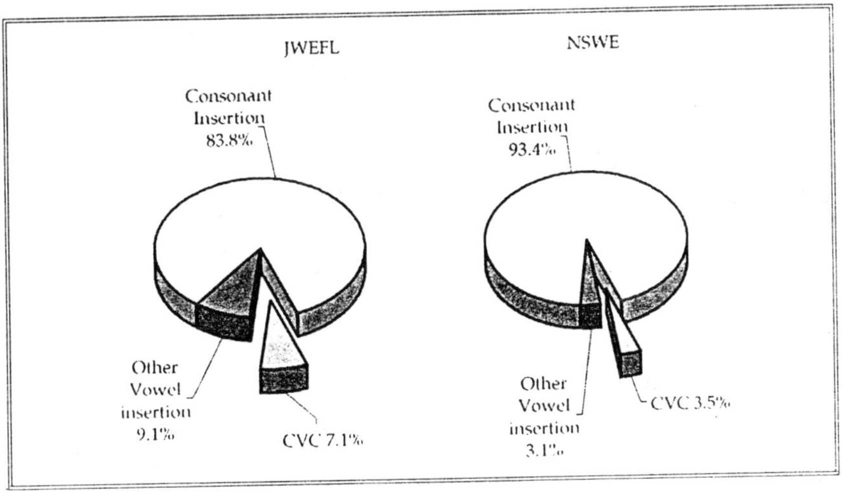

Figure 6.4 Vowel letter insertion errors yielding CVC

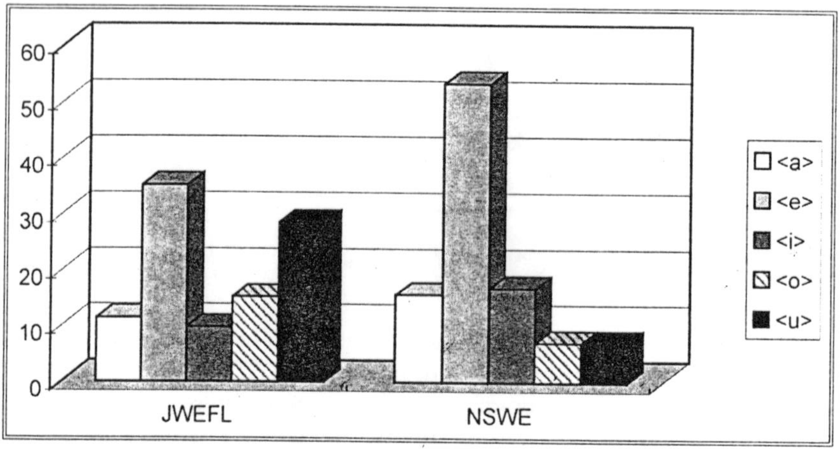

Figure 6.5 Vowel letters inserted between consonant letters

shows that NSWE insert the letter <e> quite often, whereas JWEFL frequently insert vowels such as <o> and <u> as well as <e> to avoid consonant clusters that are unfamiliar to their ears. This differs from the NSWE, for whom the four vowel letters other than <e> tend to retain their face value, i.e. their own individual corresponding sounds, since they seldom function as silent letters. A similar tendency can be observed in insertion errors, yielding extra syllables as shown in Figure 6.6. (For the syllable counting algorithm see Mitton, 1996.)

Cook (1997) claims that <a>, <e> and <i> cause the greatest problems among vowel substitutions. Cook gives a plausible explanation for

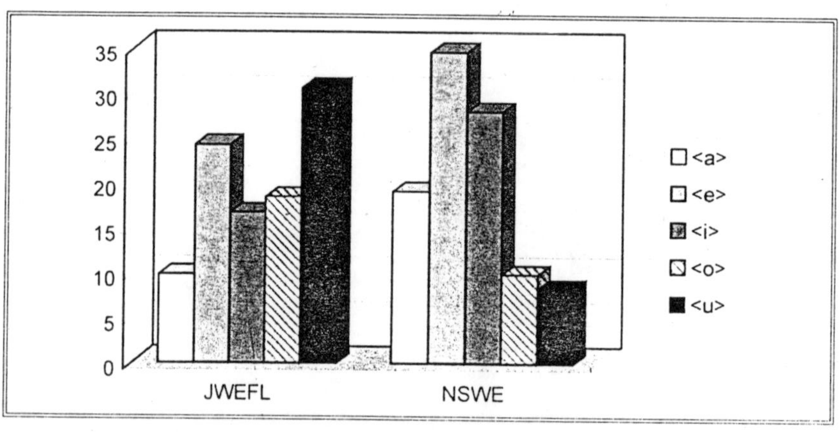

Figure 6.6 Syllable-creating inserted vowel letters

this: all three of the vowel letters can correspond to a single unstressed vowel, i.e. the schwa sound /ə/. For native speakers of English the unstressed sound /ə/ can be spelled in at least three ways, as in <about> /əbaʊt/, <the> /ðə/ and <method> /meθəd/. This is clearly supported by the <a>, <e> and <i> bars in Figure 6.6. On the other hand, JWEFL incorrectly insert <o> and <u> as frequently as the other three vowel letters. A convincing explanation is that for Japanese people, whose native language has only five vowel sounds, each vowel is definitely distinctive. In Japanese kana and even in romaji, each vowel letter has a one-to-one correspondence with the sound.

Let us now turn to the word-final position, where additional (extra) vowel letters yield CV structure. As we have noticed in investigating word-initial substitution errors, the opposite end of a word, i.e. the word-final position, is also a peculiar spot where a clear interference of the native language can be observed.

Figure 6.7 shows that the vowel letter <e> is overwhelmingly frequent at the word-final position, more prominently so in NSWE-made misspellings. Before exploring why <e> is so frequently added to the tail of a target word, notice that a JWEFL-specific inclination of adding another vowel letter, i.e. <u>, is explicitly observed at the word-final position (see Figure 6.8).

Let us examine the pronunciation of the word-final <e> more closely. There are 66,439 entries, excluding proper nouns, in the electronic

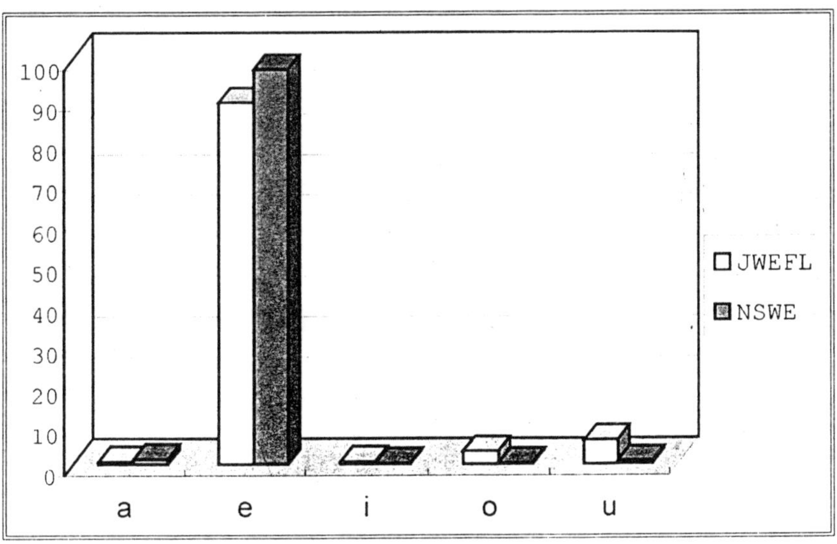

Figure 6.7 Word-final vowel letter insertion (addition)

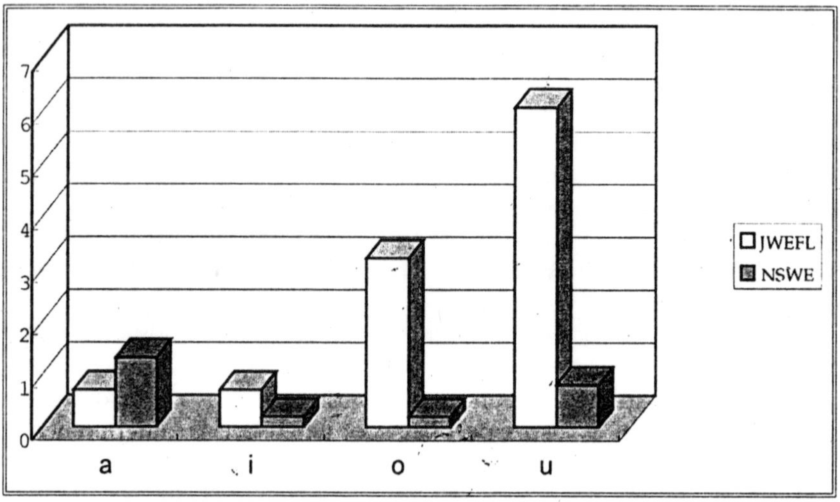

Figure 6.8 Vowel letter additions at the word-final position

version of the *Oxford Advanced Learner's Dictionary of Current English: 3rd Edition* (Mitton, 1986b). Among them, 7894 words (11.88%) have word-final vowel letters, including some foreign words; their breakdown is shown in Figure 6.9.

There are 544 words with final <a>, such as <area>, <data>, <media>, <sea> or <umbrella>; 107 words with final <i>, such as <alumni>, <nuclei>, <ski> or <taxi>; 355 words with final <o>, such as <auto>,

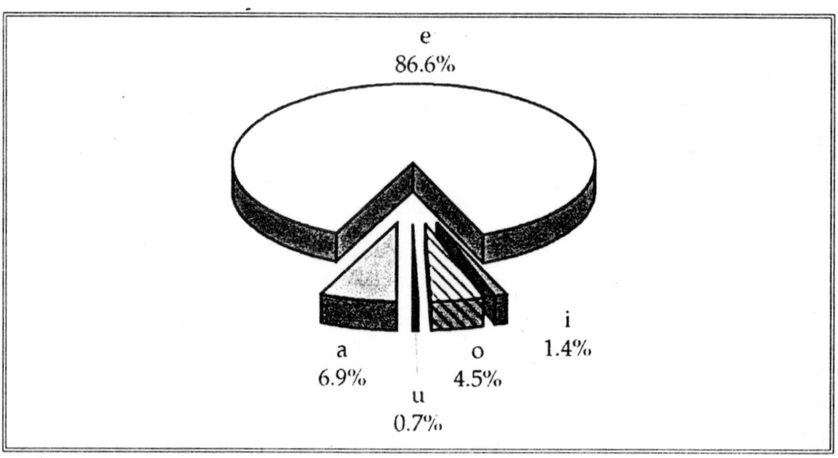

Figure 6.9 Breakdown of word-final vowel letters in the OALD

<ditto>, <embryo>, <into> or <zoo>. Only 53 words have final <u>, such as <bureau>, <menu>, <flu>, <plateau>, <thou> or <you>. Among the 6835 word-final <e>s, only 220 (3.22%) have actual phonetic manifestations. In other words, the great majority (96.78%) of word-final letter <e>s are not pronounced, i.e. a silent letter. In addition, among 220 word-final <e> letters that are not silent, 161 (73.18%) are pronounced as /i/. The other 59 word-final <e> letters are preceded by <u> and do not have a phonetic realisation, as in <avenue>, <continue>, <virtue>, etc. – in other words they are silent <e>s. This suggests that the word-final <e> letter is only pronounced as either /i/ or /iː/ in English. Moreover, the total of word-final <e>s on their own with an /i/ sound preceded by a consonant letter is only seven (4.35% against 161), such as <be>, <he>, <maybe>, <me>, <she>, <we> and <ye>. Another 154 non-silent <e>s are preceded by a second vowel letter such as <free>, <lingerie>, etc. (126 of them (81.82%) end with double letter <ee>.)

Of the 6615 silent <e>s, 133 (2.01%) have a special phonetic function, viz 'fairy' <e>s, the name coming from the immortal advice to primary school children 'Fairy <e> waves its magic wand and makes the vowel before it say its name'. I call them fairy <e>s in a narrow sense when they change the sound of their preceding vowel letters and, at the same time, there exist corresponding words that *lack* the word-final <e>. For example, the word final <e>s in <ate>, <cope>, <cute>, <kite>, <made> and so on are fairy <e>s, since each word has its counterpart without the final <e>, namely <at>, <bad>, <cop>, <cut>, <kit> and <mad> respectively. If we broaden the sense of fairy <e> to cover any word-final <e>s that simply alter vowels preceding them, such as in <admire>, <bone>, <fortitude>, <precede> or <smile>, their number would increase drastically.

Errors adding extra <e> at the word-final position are commonly observed in our comparative corpora, as illustrated in Figure 6.7. However, what is peculiar to JWEFL errors is the fact that, although English words with final <u> are rare, as we have seen in the electronic dictionary, and although NSWE make few addition errors with this vowel letter, JWEFL make this error frequently.

It is important to note that every Japanese word ends in a vowel (with the possible exception of nasals that may be treated as nasal vowels) while English words can end either in consonant or in a vowel. However, as we have seen above, the word-final <e> in English is almost always 'silent' and the great majority of English words end with consonants. It is reasonable to assume that errors in adding the final <e> are due to the fact that <e> is the most common vowel letter at the end of English words. Even JWEFL frequently make this addition error although Japanese has neither 'silent' nor 'fairy' <e>, since they are at least doing their best to spell English words. What is more interesting is that JWEFL add an extra <u> quite frequently, as in <Engrishu> for <English>, <albatrosu> for <albatross>, <animaru> for <animal>, <bigenesu> for <business>, <doresu> for <dress>, <grafu> for <graph>, <hankatifu> for <handkerchief>, <radishu> for <radish> or <cizazu> for <scissors>.

The overwhelming frequency of insertion (or addition) of <u> among misspellings made by the JWEFL might be explained from the viewpoint of the Japanese syllable system. Japanese has 111 syllables composed of a consonant and a vowel. There are five basic vowels, /a/, /e/, /i/, /o/, /u/; 12 basic consonants; one semi-vowel /w/; and a subset of consonants consisting of 16 phonemes. Among the basic Japanese vowels, /u/ and /o/ can combine with 25 consonants, thus generating 50 distinct syllables, while /e/ can combine only with 12 consonants and with one semi-vowel (generating a further 13 syllables). Furthermore, the fact that the inflectional endings of Japanese verbs usually end with a /u/ sound and that <u> is therefore the most familiar vowel letter may also explain the JWEFL's tendency to add <u> at the word-final position.

There seem to be three additional reasons for the interference of the Japanese orthographic system shown in the JWEFL-made spelling errors: the high tolerance of the Japanese language towards borrowed words of foreign origin, the writing system used to transcribe the borrowed words, i.e. katakana, and the popularity of word processors in Japanese daily life. It should be borne in mind that many borrowed words, mainly of English origin, have become so assimilated into modern Japanese that, even when JWEFL know that a given target is not an original Japanese word, they are so accustomed to writing it (and even pronouncing it) using katakana that they subsequently attempt to spell the word in romaji style, which they sometimes falsely believe represents English sounds. There is a close link between kana letters and romaji. Although the keys in Japanese keyboards are inscribed with the kana letters along with the Roman alphabet letters, very few Japanese people are accustomed to the kana entry system but instead use the alphabet to compose Japanese words and sentences, as exemplified in Figure 6.10. After a user keys in Japanese words and sentences in romaji, a piece of software called a front-end processor (FEP) converts them to hiragana and some portion of kana sequences are subsequently converted into katakana and kanji (Chinese characters). (It is interesting to note that once again in the *Kun-rei* style, kanji should be spelled kanzi.)

As Figure 6.10 shows, a borrowed word such as <England> is transcribed into Japanese katakana イングランド by typing the romaji form <ingurando>, which reflects the Japanese equivalent sounds for <England>. As a result, a Japanese person who tries to spell <England> may sometimes be affected by romaji spelling.

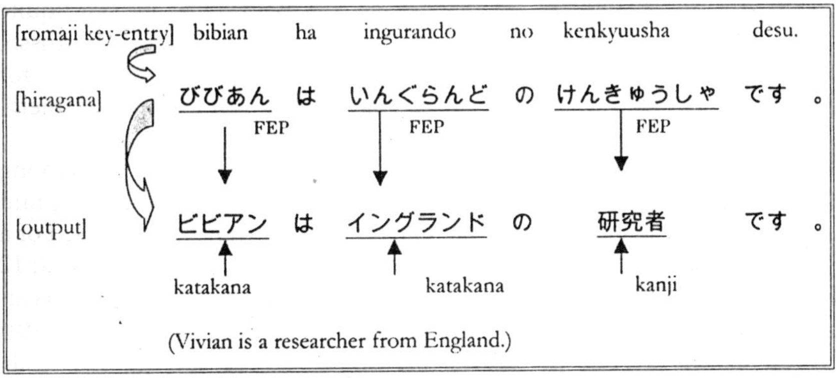

Figure 6.10 Japanese word processing

Conclusion

As we have seen, there are two major reasons for the peculiar errors of the JWEFL: one is the fundamental phonological difference between their native language and English; the other is a unique writing system, i.e. romaji, that directly transcribes Japanese sounds through letters of the roman alphabet.

In addition, we should assume that the vocabulary learning process of Japanese EFL learners can be vastly different from that of English native speakers. In other words, the idiosyncratic among JWEFL-made errors can be explained by postulating that the foreign language mental lexicon of the JWEFL is structurally different from that of the NSWE. Spelling requires knowledge of English phonology and the correspondence rules between the sound and the letter. When a person tries to spell a word, he/she makes use of all the possible knowledge stored in the mental lexicon (Ravid, 1996). In JWEFL's mental lexicon, the information about the pronunciation of a given target word is sometimes insufficient, or even deficient. As a result, weak JWEFL tend to suffer obvious interference from romaji, especially when they cannot rely on phonological clues (Okada, 2002). Let us quickly glance at an example of the vocabulary acquisition process of the average JWEFL.

In a common language laboratory situation, many Japanese EFL students have difficulty in comprehending slowly read material and fail to fill a suitable word in a gap such as:

> One international sports [ ] estimates that a quarter of a billion people around the world now participate in basketball at some level. (T. Okada (ed.) *Meeting America*, 1999: 27)

The gap should be filled with <authority>, which is one of the basic words in the Japanese high school EFL curriculum. But some of the students do not know (or perhaps have forgotten) the target word. After the listening comprehension practice, those who failed to grasp <authority>, usually try to 'memorise' the word in the traditional Japanese way of vocabulary building by memorising the English word <authority> together with its Japanese equivalent, 権威 /keɴi/ or something similar. Strikingly, many Japanese EFL learners have the wrong idea that a Japanese equivalent is a 'meaning' of the target English word. But a serious problem is the fact that a Japanese equivalent is not exactly the meaning of the target English word itself. Every lexical item has its own (1) concept, (2) collocation, (3) grammatical function (usage), (4) morphology (derivation, inflection), (5) spelling, (6) phonology, etc. (1) includes the word's connotation, associations or even subtle nuances, as well as its 'literal meaning'. The point here is that the Japanese learners' mental lexicon is structurally different from that of native speakers, where each item is stored together with all sorts of 'lexical' information. In the Japanese EFL learners' mental lexicon, each item is basically stored in one-to-one correspondence, i.e. one English word with one Japanese equivalent word. No other information usually accompanies each item: no actual concept, no information about its collocation, usage, spelling or sound. In other words, in the Japanese EFL learners' mental lexicon each English word is stored in isolation; it has no relation with other items.

A Japanese EFL learner who puts <authority> together only with 権威 /keɴi/ would stop there and he/she might get a wrong idea that he/she has learned/acquired a new word. As de Groot (2000) points out, this one-to-one style bilingual word list seems to be an attractive shortcut for foreign vocabulary learning, but it is not effective in long-term retention.

When the Japanese learner tries, or is forced, to spell <authority>, something complex can happen. If the learner still 'remembers' the correct visual form of the word, the output (i.e. the spelling) would be correct: we should say that the learner reached the appropriate goal via the lexical route, since there is not enough phonological information about English words in a Japanese EFL writer's mental lexicon. However, if he/she cannot retrieve the correct form from his/her FL mental lexicon, there would be a risk of romaji interference. If the target word <authority> has a single Japanese equivalent, the degree of inter ference would be low; however, the English word <authority> can also, unfortunately, be transcribed in 'Japanglish' オーソリティー in katakana. There is no schwa sound, /θ/ sound, or /r/ and /l/ contrast in オーソリティー /o:soɾiti:/. Things get more complicated when one tries to generate the katakana word オーソリティー using a word processor; he/she has to key in <o-sorithi> with romaji. Notice that <thi> in this romaji sequence does not stand for the /θi/ sound at all, but for the katakana sequence ティ /ti/. Therefore, the learner trying to spell English <authority> most likely gets lost in choosing the proper letters and is affected by romaji, since it is designed to transcribe Japanese syllables exclusively; as a result, he/she would generate spelling errors such as <ousority> or <ohsoliti>.

Japanese EFL learners 'learn' English from a textbook; they memorise English words visually, not aurally. In many cases a Japanese EFL learner probably knows the 'meaning' (Japanese equivalent), grammatical usage, and spelling, without knowing its phonetic form. We are not going to get into a serious discussion of the content of the mental lexicon itself here; a better idea is to compare the difference of information types. We can postulate that NSWE would make spelling errors when a given target word lacks its orthographic information, retaining phonological information in their mental lexicon. On the contrary, in the mental lexicon of Japanese EFL learners, quite a few items are not accompanied by their phonological information, while orthographic information is stored as visual images (Shuren *et al.*, 1996).

It is not always the case that the JWEFL experience interference from romaji; they are aware enough of the fact that English spelling differs from romaji to some extent. The deleterious effects of romaji appear only when the JWEFL get confused, and get lost in selecting the appropriate letter in spelling. The JWEFL do not primarily rely on the sound of the target words. This is because English is not used on a daily basis in Japan, and the English sound is less familiar to Japanese people than the form (i.e. the spelling) of English words. Japanese learners tend to acquire this foreign (not second) language on a 'letter' (i.e. visual) basis, so they rely more heavily on the lexical route in spelling. Consequently, they do not use the phonological route but they make frequent errors in selecting letters that are listed or not listed in the romaji chart, leading to the confusion we have explored especially at the word-initial and the word-final position.

The peculiarities of the Japanese ESL writers described in this chapter can be well demonstrated by means of an error corpus. Such corpora can also have practical applications, such as the creation of localised spell-checkers targeted at Japanese ESL learners and users, such as the one I have developed with Roger Mitton (Mitton & Okada, in preparation). Our joint experiment has shown that a spellchecker designed originally for native speakers of English can be easily adapted to cope with JWEFL-specific features and that these adaptations make a modest but worthwhile improvement to the spellchecker's performance when dealing with JWEFL-made errors.

References

Cook, V. (1997) L2 users and English spelling. *Journal of Multilingual and Multicultural Development* 18 (6), 474–88.

de Groot, P.J. (2000) Computer assisted second language vocabulary acquisition. *Language Learning and Technology* 4 (1), 60–81.

Furugouri, T. and Hiranuma, K. (1987) Statistical characteristics of English sentences written by the Japanese and detecting and correcting spelling-errors. *Mathematical Linguistics* 16, 16–26.

Mitton, R. (1986a) Birkbeck spelling error corpus: A collection of computer-readable corpora of English spelling errors (Version 2). The Oxford Text Archive (Text 0643) http://ota.ahds.ac.uk/

Mitton, R. (1986b) Electronic version of *the Oxford Advanced Learner's Dictionary of Current English: Expanded* (A.S. Hornby, A.P. Cowie and J.W. Lewis, eds). The Oxford Text Archive (Text 0710) http://ota.ahds.ac.uk/

Mitton, R. (1987) Spelling checkers, spelling correctors and the misspellings of poor spellers. *Information Processing and Management* 23 (5), 495–505.

Mitton, R. (1996) *English Spelling and the Computer.* Harlow: Longman.

Mitton, R. and Okada, T. (in preparation) The adaptation of a spellchecker for English spelling errors made by Japanese writers.

Okada, T. (1999) *Meeting America: Audio-visual English with 12 News Topics.* Tokyo: Tsurumi Shoten.

Okada, T. (2002) Remarks on Japanese poor spellers of English. *Yamagata English Studies* 7, 21–41. http://www.intcul.tohoku.ac.jp/okada/pdfs/poorspellers.pdf

Ravid, D. (1996) Accessing the mental lexicon: Evidence from incompatibility between representation of spoken and written morphology. *Linguistics* 34, 1219–46.

Saeki, K. and Yamada, H. (1977) *The Romanization of Japanese Writing: Hepburn vs. Kunrei System Controversies.* Tokyo: Nippon no Romazi Sya.

Shuren, J.E., Maher, L.M. and Heilman, K.M. (1996) The role of visual imagery in spelling. *Brain and Language* 52, 365–72.

Yannakoudakis, E.J. and Fawthrop, D. (1983) The rules of spelling errors. *Information Processing and Management* 19 (2), 87–99.

Appendix

The JWEFL-made error corpus is an amalgamation of the following seven sub-corpora summarised in Table 6.4, below.

(1) AEMH-error.txt

Misspellings extracted from English essays handwritten in class by 244 Japanese university students, 201 of them majoring in English. There were 20,299 running words in total; 393 of these

Table 6.4 JWEFL-made error corpus sources

File name	*Source*	*Target words*	*Attempts*	*Misspellings*
AEMH	244 university students	234	–	296
EXAMS	49 writers	151	213	162
HELC-JR	Junior high school students	431	3366	1921
HELC-SR	Senior high school students	187	673	346
SAMANTHA	Junior high + university students (333 in total)	53	7418	2071
SUZUKI	Senior high school students	43	–	46
FRGRI	88 university freshmen	324	–	366

were misspelled, which, after removal of duplicates, gives us 296 misspellings of 234 target words. For further details of the raw material, refer to the URLs of the original source files:

http://www.eng.ritsumei.ac.jp/lcorpus/data/asao01/
http://www.eng.ritsumei.ac.jp/lcorpus/data/asao02/
http://www.eng.ritsumei.ac.jp/lcorpus/data/shitara01/

(2) EXAMS-error.txt
One hundred and sixty-two misspellings of 151 target words, taken from the Japanese part of EXAMS.DAT included in the Birkbeck Spelling Error Corpus. This contains 213 attempts generated by 49 Japanese writers. The misspellings are taken from compositions written in examinations for the Cambridge First Certificate in English.

(3) HELC-JR-error.txt
Junior high-school students were given sentences to translate from Japanese into English in class. There were 286 target sentences and

the students produced 85,120 running words in total. The number of subjects per target sentence varied from 20 to 120. The sub-corpus contains 1921 misspellings of 431 target words (3366 attempts). The original source is maintained as *Hiroshima English Learners' Corpus No.1* by Shogo Miura at Hiroshima University, Japan.

(4) HELC-SR-error.txt
Similar to the previous corpus except with senior high-school students. There were 68 target sentences and 40,638 running words. The number of subjects per target sentence varied from 40 to 120. This sub-corpus contains 346 misspellings of 187 target words (673 attempts). The original source is maintained as *Hiroshima English Learners' Corpus No.2*. This and the previous sub-corpus are described at:

http://home.hiroshima-u.ac.jp/d052121/eigo1.html

(5) SAMANTHA-error.txt
Japanese university students were given a test of 53 English words. For each word, they were given a written definition in Japanese and an approximation in *katakana* to the English pronunciation. Three hundred and thirty-three people sat the test; 7418 of their attempts were incorrect, giving 2071 misspellings of 53 target words. The original error corpus, named SAMANTHA Error Corpus, is maintained by Takeshi Okada at Tohoku University, Japan.

http://www.e.intcul.tohoku.ac.jp/okada/corpora/Samantha/Samantha-top.html

(6) SUZUKI-error.txt
Personal collection of misspellings made by an unspecified number of Japanese high-school students in their classroom activities or in short tests. Collected by Michiaki Suzuki at Nan'yo High School, Yamagata, Japan. There are 46 misspellings of 43 target words.

(7) FRGRI-error.txt
Three hundred and sixty-six misspellings of 324 target words obtained from compositions written by 88 Japanese university freshmen not majoring in English. The students also submitted translations of their compositions. The list is given in an article written in Japanese: Furugouri and Hiranuma (1987).

For comparison, a corpus of errors made by English native speakers was created by combining several files from the Birkbeck Spelling Error

Table 6.5 NSWE-made error corpus sources

File name	*Source*	*Target words*	*Attempts*	*Misspellings*
CHES	202 10-year-old children	30	2,474	1,364
FAWTH1	Printed American sources	739	809	809
FAWTH2	3 adult poor spellers	484	1,084	557
GATES	Pupils in New York schools	3,390	144,179	4,401
MASTERS	American school + university	264	43,755	13,020
NFER1	83 Adult literacy students	40	838	495
PERIN1	42 Secondary school + adult literacy students	61	807	640
PERIN2	6 adult literacy students	538	658	625
PERIN2	176 14- and 15-years olds	40	1,678	901
PETERS1	156 children aged 9, 10 and 11	290	18,304	10,556
PETERS2	925 15-year-olds	1,618	4,147	2,576
UPWARD	163 15-year-olds	576	1,073	753
WING	40 university entrance candidates	185	237	191

Corpus, obtainable from the Oxford Text Archive. The result was a corpus of 34,658 misspellings of 5624 target words, representing over 220,000 attempts. Table 6.5 summarises the constituent files. FAWTH1, GATES and MASTERS were American, the rest were British. For further details of each original error file, refer to the description file that accompanies the corpus.

Chapter 7

Spelling and Pronunciation in Migrant Children: The Case of Italian-Swiss German Bilinguals

STEPHAN SCHMID

Introduction

This paper is concerned with the interaction between different types of linguistic knowledge in the mind of a bilingual. On the one hand it addresses the well-known issue of interference from one language to another, while on the other hand it explores the relationship between speech and writing. The general claim is that phonetics and phonology may contribute to a better understanding of the cognitive processes underlying the acquisition of a second language writing system.

The empirical research presented here deals with the language production of Italian children who live in German-speaking Switzerland. In particular, the analysis focuses on how these subjects realise, both in spelling and in pronunciation, two relevant features of Italian:

(1) the contrast between voiced and unvoiced obstruents; and
(2) the opposition between singleton and geminate consonants.

It will be demonstrated that the major difficulties encountered with these phenomena are due to the different phonological functions which the phonetic properties of voicedness and segmental duration display in the varieties of the bilinguals' repertoire.

The remainder of this chapter is organised as follows. The introduction raises some general questions about the notions of 'second language' and 'bilingualism' in connection with the acquisition of writing systems. Then follows a brief characterisation of the linguistic biography and repertoire of Italian-Swiss German bilinguals, in order to allow a better understanding of the linguistic processes which can intervene in their spelling of Italian. The next section provides a contrastive phonological analysis of four language varieties (i.e. Standard and Regional Italian on the one hand, and Standard and Swiss German on the other), focusing on the already mentioned features [±voice] and [±tense] as well as on the singleton/geminate contrast. Then follows a report on the results of classroom research, in which Italian-Swiss German bilinguals were tested in dictation and reading tasks. The final part answers the basic research question of this study, interpreting the findings in the light of a more general model of bilingual phonology.[1]

In the linguistics literature, there is a certain overlap between the notions of 'second language acquisition' (henceforth SLA) and 'bilingualism'. In a common-sense view, SLA can be regarded as the process through which monolingual adults acquire a new language, whereas bilinguals grow up, from their early childhood, using at least two different languages. Yet, as is well-known, there are many definitions of 'bilingualism', according to such differing criteria as the level of competence or the amount of language use (Romaine, 1995: 11–19); in fact, from a broader perspective, some scholars conceive of SLA as just a particular form of bilingualism.

The intersection of SLA and bilingualism becomes even clearer if one takes into account two additional criteria, namely the relative acquisitional chronology in the bilingual's biography and the specific medium of verbal communication (i.e. the distinction between spoken and written language). As far as speech is concerned, some people acquire language A as their mother tongue and then learn language B as a second language at school, but the spoken second language may turn out to be the first language through which literacy is achieved. This happens in quite a few diglossic situations, typically in linguistic minorities and in migrant communities. For instance, the children of the 6–8 million or so Moroccans who speak a Berber language normally learn to write Arabic as a first language at school, and the same situation holds for the 12 million or so Kurds who are predominantly literate in the Turkish language. As regards migrants, we must often rely on estimates, but it is reasonable to assume that the majority of the 40 million Hispanics in the USA have acquired literacy in English, not in Spanish; at least, this is supposed to apply to those born in North America. Now, if language A cannot build on an orthographic norm and a literacy tradition, language B often remains the sole code available for the purpose of written communication. In other circumstances, bilinguals may learn to write language A only after language B, so that – from a chronological point of view – the spoken first language A becomes a second language in writing.

We may suppose that neither of these scenarios, i.e. the complete lack of literacy or the acquisition of limited writing skills in the mother tongue, is unusual in the European context, given the existence of large immigrant communities in several countries. Up to now, researchers have mainly dealt with topics such as bilingual speech or spoken language attrition (Extra & Verhoeven, 1993, 1999); little attention has yet been paid to the bilinguals' knowledge of their writing systems.

When considering the different types of writing system used by bilinguals, one finds a broad variety of contact situations. Taking a European perspective, we may imagine the paths indicated in Table 7.1 towards the acquisition of a second language writing system.

The examples of languages and/or writing systems in the second and fourth columns are purely hypothetical and not linked to any real sociolinguistic context. Logically speaking, more contact patterns are possible, if one also takes into account the chronology or 'direction' of learning (for example, if the learner passes from a logographic script to a phonographic one, or vice versa). It is reasonable to assume that the 'distance', or the number of differences between the two writing systems, determines the degree of difficulty and the possibilities of interference in the acquisition process. The difficulties are probably greatest when one writing system is phonologically based and the other is not: consider the case of Chinese children living in the UK who start to memorise characters while already being familiar with the Roman alphabet. The second case, i.e. the mastering of a non-alphabetic but still phonographic writing system (e.g. a syllabary like *katakana*) is supposed to require less cognitive effort for a person literate in a western European language; still, this scenario is not supposed to be very frequent.

Instead, the third contact pattern – when two different alphabets are used by bilinguals – does occur among migrants. Such a situation has been investigated in Berkemeier's (1996) research on the children of German mothers living in Thessaloniki; these subjects were already familiar with Greek orthography and Cyrillic characters when they learnt to

Table 7.1 Types of contact between writing systems

First writing system	*Example*	*Second writing system*	*Example*
Phonographic	Roman (German)	Logographic	Chinese
Phonographic: alphabetical	Cyrillic (Russian)	Phonographic: syllabic	Hang'ul (Korean)
Alphabet 1: Greek	Greek	Alphabet 2: Roman	French
Alphabet 1: Roman	Spanish	Alphabet 2: Roman	Swedish

write German using the Roman alphabet. The same language pair appears in Hampel's (2000) study of the attrition of German orthography among Greek children who first went to school in Munich and then re-migrated to their home country. Both researchers reported several types of interference from the Cyrillic alphabet on the children's spelling of German.

The present study addresses the fourth pattern of contact, where both languages are written in the Roman alphabet. More precisely, it will deal with the spelling of the mother tongue by Italian children who live in German-speaking Switzerland. Little research seems to have been done on scenarios of this sort, perhaps the most common in western Europe. Nevertheless, one can quote Luelsdorff's extensive work (1986, 1991) on the spelling of English by German adolescents who are regarded as 'bilingual spellers', even if English clearly constitutes a foreign language for them. Not surprisingly, this research revealed a strong influence of German orthography on the L2 writing of English.

Italian Migrant Children in Switzerland

Despite a popular belief, most of the 7.3 million inhabitants of Switzerland are not 'naturally' multilingual. Instead, the country is divided into three monolingual regions (German, French, Italian, including both standard and regional varieties); only the Rhaeto-Romance citizens are reasonably bilingual with German. From a quantitative point of view, speakers are distributed as follows: German (63.6%), French (19.2%), Italian (7.6%), Rhaeto-Romance (0.6%), other languages (9%).

In fact Italian is an immigrant language as well, since it is spoken by more than 200,000 people in the German-speaking part of the country, where more than half of them are born. These second-generation immigrants typically claim to have acquired Italian as their first language in early childhood. In some families, an Italian dialect is also spoken at home, but most frequently the children have only a passive competence in it, since their parents have brought them up with a (non-standard) regional variety of Italian. It is important to note that these varieties of Italian do not coincide with the Italo-Romance dialects (which are autonomous linguistic systems), even if they are heavily influenced by them, in particular as far as pronunciation is concerned (Lepschy & Lepschy, 1977); in this respect, the parental dialects do have an indirect influence on the regional accent of the children's Italian. On the local side of the linguistic repertoire, the first variety to be acquired is Swiss German, which is used for a wide range of communicative needs; therefore, the dialect of the host society is spoken rather early in interaction among peers, for example at kindergarten. Standard German is taught later as a formal language at primary school; however, it is the first language in which literacy is achieved. Not all Italian children are given the opportunity to receive a formal education in their mother tongue: lessons in Italian – from two to four hours per week – are not obligatory; they start one year later and often take place in the pupils' spare time. As a consequence, their literacy is much more developed in German than in Italian.

To summarise, the children of Italian immigrants in German-speaking Switzerland are faced with a double diglossia, namely that of their ethnic group (which opposes the Italian language to an Italian dialect) and that of the country they are living in, which embraces both Swiss German and Standard German. The structure of this sociolinguistic repertoire can be characterised according to six parameters, shown in Figure 7.1, namely the order of acquisition and the level of competence for both spoken and written languages, as well as the dimensions of emotive preference and social prestige (De Rosa & Schmid, 2002a).

The 4-point-scales follow from the answers provided in a sociolinguistic questionnaire by the subjects of this study: a value of 1 corresponds to the variety which has been acquired first and is spoken most often, whereas a value of 4 indicates the latest acquired and less spoken variety (points 0 and 5 are simply artefacts of the diagram, since they do not form part of the questionnaire). For instance, on the basis of the first two parameters – order of acquisition and level of competence in spoken language – Italian and Swiss German can be regarded as the two central varieties of the repertoire (which are also most frequently employed in everyday life); in fact, code-switching between these two varieties is a widespread phenomenon in peer-group communication

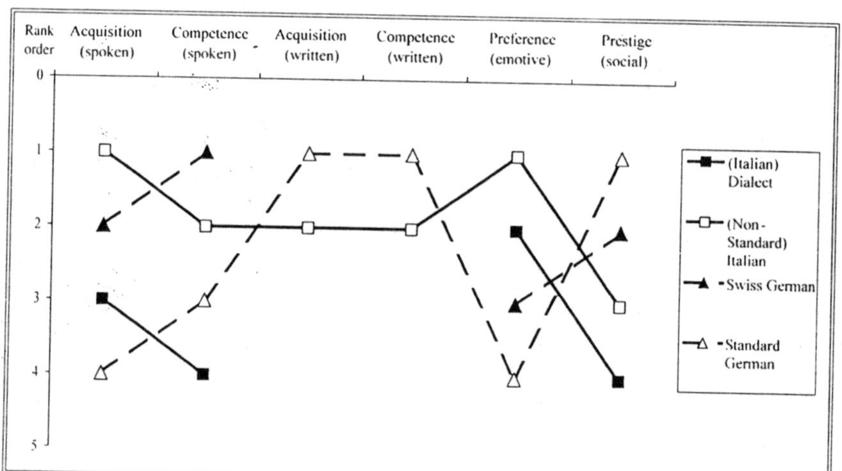

Figure 7.1 The sociolinguistic repertoire of the Italian/Swiss German bilinguals

(Schmid, 1992, 1993). As regards speaking, we note a shift from the ethnic varieties acquired first – Italian and Italian dialect – towards the varieties of the host society (Swiss German and German), in which a better level of competence is achieved. In writing, however, Standard German prevails over Italian both in acquisition order and in level of competence. A certain contrast between the ethnic and the local varieties follows again from the last two parameters, in that the Italian part of the repertoire is given a clear emotive preference over the German varieties, which, by contrast, are judged to have a greater social prestige.

Let us now illustrate some of the spelling problems faced by these subjects by commenting on typical errors found in their dictations (see below). Following a traditional error analysis approach (see, for example Lado, 1957: 93–109, chapter on 'How to compare two writing systems'), we discover three types of misspellings. First, there are problems due to certain structural properties of Italian orthography itself. Compared to French or English, the Italian language is commonly believed to be quite 'easy' to spell (and also to pronounce since its orthography adheres rather closely to the alphabetical ideal of a one-to-one-relationship between sounds and letters; etymological and morphological factors play only a marginal role (Lepschy & Lepschy, 1977)).

Nevertheless, the Italian spelling system contains a certain amount of allography, i.e. alternative correspondences for the same phoneme. For instance, the phoneme /k/ corresponds to three allographs <c>, <ch> and <q>, depending on the phonotactic context. The letter <c> is required before the front vowel /a/ and the back vowels /o/ and /u/, whereas <ch> is used before the front vowels /e/ and /i/ (compare the words <casa> 'house', <cosa> 'thing', <culla> 'cradle' with <che> 'what' and <chi> 'who', all pronounced with initial [k]). The allograph <q> occurs only before the approximant /w/ (for example in <questo> 'this'), which in turn is expressed by the same grapheme <u> as the vowel /u/.

In our data we find misspellings such as «cuelo» and «squdiero»[2] instead of <quello> and <scudiero> (Figure 7.2, lines 3 and 5), which testify to the difficulty of choosing between the allographs <c> and <q> before the letter <u>, as the child has not yet grasped the graphemic corollary of the phonological distinction between vowel and approximant. Misspellings of this kind are supposed to occur also in the writing of monolingual Italian children, in that they reflect an inherent problem of the orthographic norm, i.e. the lack of bi-uniqueness in grapheme–phoneme correspondences.

Bilingual children have to face a second difficulty as a result of their acquaintance with the writing systems of two languages. Any person who writes a second language with the Roman alphabet knows that spelling systems differ considerably in the way letters correspond to sounds. Not only may the other language present new phonemes, but the two

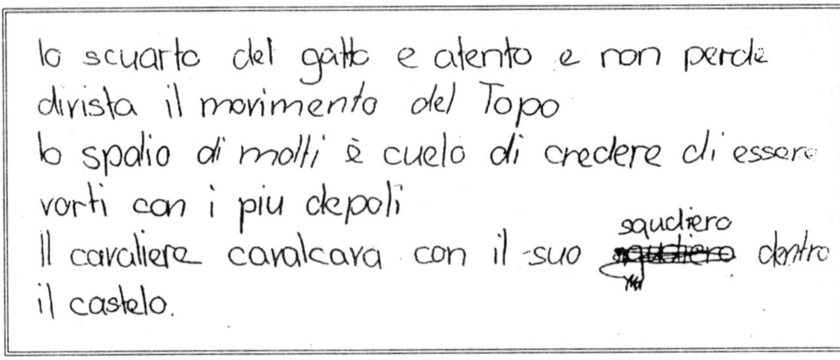
lo scuarto del gatto e atento e non perde
divista il movimento del Topo
lo spalio di molti è cuelo di credere di essere
vorti con i piu depoli
Il cavaliere cavalcava con il suo squdiero dentro
il castelo.

Figure 7.2 Italian dictation by a bilingual child living in German-speaking Switzerland

orthographies may use different graphemes for almost identical speech sounds; moreover, they often present different types of allography. For instance, Italian uses only one grapheme <f> for the sound /f/, against the two German allographs <f> and <v> (the voiced labiodental fricative /v/ is expressed by <w>: compare <Vater> 'father' with <Wasser> 'water'). In the bilingual child's dictation, the German <f v> allography underlies the misspelling «vorti» of the Italian word <forti> (Figure 7.2, line 4). Conversely, the phoneme /ʃ/ is expressed in German orthography with a trigraph <sch>, whereas Italian presents two allographs <sc> and <sci> according to the place of articulation of the following vowel (front versus back): again, in the bilinguals' dictations, we find the 'German' spelling of Italian words as in «restituische» instead of <restituisce>. Finally, a rare but clear type of interference appears with the use of upper-case letters for nouns, a German orthographic rule not shared by Italian (see the word «Topo» 'mouse' in line 2 of Figure 7.2).

However, in the bilinguals' dictations, we find a considerable number of misspellings that are of yet another kind. Note, for instance, the spellings of «squarto», «spalio» and «depoli» (lines 1, 3 and 4 of Figure 7.2) instead of <sguardo>, <sbaglio> and <deboli>; the fairly frequent substitution of the graphemes «p c» for <b g> points to a phonological problem related to the voicing contrast. Another error type involves the simplification of double consonants, as in «atento», «cuelo» and «castelo» instead of <attento>, <quello> and <castello> (lines 1, 3 and 6 of Figure 7.2). As we will see, however, the opposite kind of error also occurs, i.e. the replacement of <c> with «g» or the doubling of singleton consonants.

The present study focuses on this type of misspelling, trying to single out the various mechanisms which underlie the children's written language production. The basic research question concerns the relationship between orthographic and phonological competence: to what extent are misspellings determined by phonological factors? The second research question is more general and addresses the overall structure of the bilinguals' linguistic knowledge. Our methodological concern is twofold: on the one hand, we want to point out the advantage of a phonological analysis that looks both at abstract features and at their phonetic implementation; on the other hand, it is fruitful to consider the whole sociolinguistic repertoire of the bilinguals, taking into account both standard and substandard varieties.

A Sketch of Contrastive Phonological Analysis

In order to fully understand the many ways in which consonants like /p/ and /b/ are realised in the bilinguals' repertoire, we need to compare four language varieties: Standard Italian, Standard German, Swiss German and regional Italian. Such a comparison must take into account not only phonemic contrasts, but also allophonic rules. Moreover, the abstract feature analysis has to be complemented by a closer examination of the phonetic realisation of these speech sounds. Together with the feature [±voice], it becomes necessary, here, also to consider the feature [±tense].

The phoneme inventory of Standard Italian heavily exploits the contrast between voiceless and voiced obstruents, as one can see from the following minimal pairs (see Schmid, 1999: 135–8); the examples in (1) oppose the six plosives /p/ ~ /b/, /t/ ~ /d/ and /k/ ~ /g/, whereas those in (2) illustrate the distinctiveness of voicing in the labiodental fricatives /f/ ~ /v/ and the palato-alveolar affricates /tʃ/ ~ /dʒ/ (we do not consider here the contrasts between the alveolar fricatives and affricates /s/ ~ /z/ and /ts/ ~ /dz/, given their minor functional load).

(1)	/ˈpasta/ 'pasta'	~	/ˈbasta/ 'it is enough'
	/ˈmɔto/ 'movement'	~	/ˈmɔdo/ 'manner'
	/ˈkallo/ 'corn, horny skin'	~	/ˈgallo/ 'cock'
(2)	/ˈfɔʎʎo/ 'leaf'	~	/ˈvɔʎʎo/ 'I want'
	/ˈtʃiʎʎo/ 'lid'	~	/ˈdʒiʎʎo/ 'lily'

The opposition between the five pairs of phonemes – all identical with regard to place and manner of articulation – relies on the distinctive feature [±voice]. Moreover, this phonological contrast is implemented phonetically in a straightforward manner, by means of the absence versus presence of vocal-fold vibration during the closure/stricture phase of the obstruent; a periodic signal shows up in acoustic representations of these consonants, clearly visible as a 'voice bar' in the lower frequency range of a spectrogram (Albano Leoni & Maturi, 1995).

The situation in Standard German is somewhat more complex, in particular so far as the correspondence between the abstract phonological feature [±voice] and its phonetic realisation is concerned. According to current phonological analyses (e.g. Wiese, 1996: 10, 23), Standard German also opposes a series of voiceless obstruents to a series of voiced obstruents, as appears from the minimal pairs in (3) and (4):

(3) /paɪn/ 'pain' ~ /baɪn/ 'leg'
/tɔʀf/ 'peat' ~ /dɔʀf/ 'village'
/kʊs/ 'kiss' ~ /gʊs/ 'melting (of a metal) – founding'
(4) /'faːʀən/ 'drive, ride' ~ /'vaːʀən/ 'goods'

Nevertheless, the feature [±voice] gives rise to different surface forms, according to a variety of factors, depending both on the speaker (regional provenance, idiosyncratic behaviour) and on structural properties, such as the phonotactic position and the manner of articulation of the consonant (see Jessen (1998) for an extensive research review). It appears that the plosives /b d g/ are often pronounced without any participation of the vocal folds at all (thus as [b̥ d̥ g̊]), in particular at the beginning of an utterance, whereas the fricatives /z v/ are more likely to be voiced, especially in inter-vocalic and word-internal position. Word-initially, the contrast between /b/ and /p/ is guaranteed by means of an audible aspiration phase after the release of the unvoiced stop (as in English); thus, the word /paɪn/ is pronounced as [phaɪn]. In syllable-final position, underlying voiced obstruents are devoiced by a phonological rule of neutralisation, the so-called *Auslautverhärtung* (Wiese, 1996). Thus, all in all, the frequency of fully voiced obstruents in Standard German is rather low.

As a consequence of this rather complex picture, some German phoneticians differentiate between the two series of obstruents in German on the basis of the feature [±tense] and its basic phonetic correlate, aspiration (see, e.g. Jessen, 2001; Kohler, 1984). Here, we will reserve this feature for the slightly different pattern of Swiss German. What counts for the purpose of our contrastive analysis is the fact that obstruents of Standard German can be pronounced with vocal-fold vibration during the closure or stricture phase, something which will never occur in Swiss German dialects.

At this point, a brief excursion into the history of phonological theory is in order. It is worth noticing that [±tense] already figures in the list of distinctive features established by Jakobson *et al.* (1952: 36), who claim that 'in consonants, tenseness is manifested primarily by the length of their sounding period, and in stops, in addition, by the greater strength of the explosion'. Twelve years later, the first two of the founding fathers of distinctive feature theory dedicate an essay on tenseness to Daniel Jones; in it, they state that 'a typical example of tense and lax stops and fricatives, all of them produced without any participation of voice, is provided by the Swiss German consonantal pattern' (Jakobson & Halle, 1964: 100); in this view, 'tense' and 'lax' are synonymous with the terms *fortis* and *lenis* introduced by the Swiss dialectologist Josef Winteler (1876: 25).

Indeed, Swiss German lacks voiced obstruents altogether, instead establishing a phonemic opposition between tense and lax obstruents, which is exploited in numerous minimal pairs (in this case, from the dialect of Zürich):

(5)	/ˈhuːpə/ 'horn'	~	/ˈhuːb̥ə/ 'bonnet'
	/ˈl̩ɒtə/ 'lath'	~	/ˈlɒd̥ə/ 'shop'
	/kɛː/ 'given'	~	/g̊ɛː/ '(to) give'
(6)	/ˈhɒsə/ (to) hate'	~	/ˈhɒz̥ə/ 'hare'
	/ˈofə/ 'open'	~	/ˈov̥ə/ 'oven'

As has been proved by acoustic measurements and perception experiments, this contrast is realised phonetically mainly through a contrast of duration between the two types of consonants; in disyllabic words, for example, the average duration of a post-vocalic tense consonant is 2.7 times as long as that of a lax consonant in the same position (Willi, 1996). Moreover, on the spectrograms of the lax plosives, no voice bar can be found (Willi, 1996).

Now, quite astonishingly, the same phonetic type of consonant also occurs in regional varieties of Italian, but with a different phonological status. In fact, some varieties of southern Italian differ from the standard language, in that they have two additional allophonic rules converting tense voiceless sounds into lax ones (Lepschy & Lepschy, 1977: 71–2; Schmid, 1999: 151–2; De Rosa & Schmid, 2000: 59–63).

$$(7)\quad \begin{bmatrix} -\text{sonorant} \\ -\text{voice} \\ +\text{tense} \end{bmatrix} \longrightarrow [-\text{tense}]/\text{V}$$

$$(8)\quad \begin{bmatrix} -\text{sonorant} \\ -\text{voice} \\ +\text{tense} \end{bmatrix} \longrightarrow [-\text{tense}]\Big/\begin{bmatrix} -\text{consonantal} \\ +\text{nasal} \end{bmatrix}$$

Rule (7) applies to a wide range of central and southern varieties of Italian. It states that an unvoiced obstruent is realised as lax (i.e. [−tense]) when it occurs after a vowel: for instance, Standard Italian <poco dopo> 'a moment later' is pronounced as [ˈpɔːg̊o ˈdɔːb̥o]. According to rule (8) – which applies only to the south of Italy, not to the centre – an unvoiced obstruent is realised as lax when it occurs after a nasal: for instance, Standard Italian <tanto tempo> 'much time' may be realised as [ˈtand̥ə ˈd̥ɛmb̥ə]. This rule is variable to some extent, in the sense that sometimes the lax allophone may also be at least partially voiced. Neither process applies only word-initially, but they also apply across word boundaries; rule (7) is blocked only by another well-known *sandhi* process of Italian, the so-called *raddoppiamento fonosintattico* (phonosyntactic doubling) (Lepschy & Lepschy, 1977: 65–7).

The last type of misspelling we saw in Figure 7.2 has to do with double consonants. Also with regard to geminates, we find three different structural solutions in the repertoire of our bilinguals.

As is well-known, Italian has fully phonological geminates, which show up in numerous quasi-minimal pairs (Lepschy & Lepschy, 1977: 63; Schmid, 1999: 168–9).

(9)	/ˈnɔte/ 'notes'	~	/ˈnɔtte/ 'night'
	/ˈkasa/ 'house'	~	/ˈkassa/ 'cashbox'
(10)	/ˈkade/ 'he/she falls'	~	/ˈkadde/ 'he/she fell'
	/ˈbeve/ 'he/she drinks'	~	/ˈbevve/ 'he/she drank'

This holds true for 15 out of 21 consonants in Standard Italian, the exceptions being /z/, which exists only as a singleton consonant, and /ʃ ɲ ʎ ts tz/, which occur inter-vocalically only as geminates. Note, in particular, that geminates are not restricted to unvoiced obstruents, but frequently occur with voiced obstruents, as shown by the minimal pairs in (10). The regional varieties of central and southern Italy basically maintain the same pattern, with some minor differences; for instance, two additional consonants are 'intrinsically' long, namely /b/ and /dʒ/ (Lepschy & Lepschy, 1977: 70; Schmid, 1999: 169). Phonetically, the gemination contrast relies almost entirely on the time domain of the closure/stricture phase, the durations of geminates being close to twice those of singletons (Esposito & Di Benedetto, 1999; Giovanardi & Di Benedetto, 1998).

In Standard German, by contrast, the graphemic double consonants only serve as a means of signalling phonologically short vowels, as we see from the minimal pairs in (10):

(11)	<Ratte> /ˈʀatə/ 'rat'	~	<rate> /ˈʀaːtə/ '(I) advise'
	<schaffe> /ˈʃafə/ '(I) create'	~	<Schafe> /ˈʃaːfə/ 'sheep (pl.)'
	<Kamm> /kam/ 'comb'	~	<kam> /kaːm/ '(he/she) came'

Note that the double consonants of Standard German are always pronounced as short (DUDEN, 2000: 69–106).

As to the Swiss German dialects, the existence of geminates or the phonological status of consonantal length is a matter of theoretical debate, since there are at least four ways to analyse the traditional fortis/lenis contrast. One possibility is to maintain that the long obstruents of Swiss German are real geminates, which are one of the possible manifestations of the feature specification [+tense] (Jessen, 2001; Kohler, 1984). A second view dispenses with the feature [±tense], instead interpreting the durational differences between the two types of obstruents as a binary contrast between geminates and singletons, as claimed in Kraehenmann's (2001) study on the Turgovian dialect. A third proposal is based on a three-way opposition between lax, tense and geminate tense consonants; according to Ham (2001: 52), this pattern characterises the Bernese dialect. It lies beyond the scope of this study to evaluate these different proposals, also given that there are indeed considerable differences among Swiss German dialects as far as consonant length is concerned (Dieth & Brunner, 1943). Instead, a fourth alternative is adopted, in line with a more traditional understanding of the dialect spoken by our subjects; this solution dispenses with geminates, simply assuming a binary contrast between tense and lax obstruents (Willi, 1996: 19).

The interpretation of durational differences between speech sounds of the same category not only constitutes an analytical difficulty for the linguist but it also probably raises a serious problem for a bilingual who has to cope with such considerable structural diversity in four phonological systems. As we have seen, the duration of closure/stricture not only provides the relevant acoustic cue for the distinction between geminates and singletons in Italian, but it also constitutes – in our view – the main phonetic correlate of the feature [±tense]. There is, however, more to it than that: to a minor extent, a difference in duration even characterises the contrast between unvoiced and voiced obstruents. According to a phonetic universal based on physiological constraints, we can predict that, other things being equal, a voiced stop is shorter than a voiceless one (Maddieson, 1997: 624–7). In a sense, tenseness normally goes with voicelessnes, whereas laxness accompanies voicing. In Standard Italian and, by and large, also in Standard German, a negative correlation exists between the distinctive feature [±voice] and the redundant feature [±tense]. Swiss German, on the other hand, has abandoned the [±voice] contrast by converting [±tense] into a distinctive feature.

Therefore it is possible that, in the bilinguals' language production, gemination interferes with the realisation of the features [±voice] and [±tense]. But even if we leave aside the geminate versus singleton contrast, the varieties of the repertoire still vary enough to create misperceptions or reinterpretations. Table 7.2 gives an overview of the contrastive

Table 7.2 The features [±voice] and [±tense] in the bilinguals' repertoire

	Standard Italian	*Regional Italian*	*Standard German*	*Swiss German*
−voice, +tense	/p/ [p]	/p/ [p]	/p/ [p p^h]	/p/ [p]
−voice, −tense		[b̥]	[b̥]	/b̥/[b̥]
+voice, −tense	/b/ [b]	/b/ [b]	/b/ [b]	

analysis, demonstrating how the combinations of two features [±voice] and [±tense] result in three types of speech sound, which in turn are exploited differently in the four phonological systems. In particular, the intermediate category [−voice, −tense] serves as an allophone for opposite poles, belonging to the upper part in the Italian diasystem and to the lower part in the German diasystem.

In order to verify how the structural discrepancies between these phonological/graphematic systems are handled by bilinguals, classroom research was carried out, to be presented below.

Testing the Bilinguals' Spelling and Pronunciation: Two Classroom Experiments

Data were collected from 24 Italian children, living in a village on the lake of Zürich and aged from 12 to 15 years. This means that they have had extensive instruction in written German for 6–8 years, whereas the exposure to written Italian has been limited to a shorter span of time with regard both to the number of years and the amount of lessons per week (see above). As regards the regional origin of the families, it is important to note that the overwhelming majority of the parents come from southern Italy, in particular from Calabria (De Rosa & Schmid, 2002a: 216).

In order to analyse the children's realisations of Italian obstruents, we ran two experiments to elicit both written and oral data during the Italian language course. Twenty sentences were first read in a dictation exercise by the teacher (a native speaker from northern Italy) and written down by the pupils; subsequently, the children were recorded in a separate room while reading the same 20 sentences aloud. This material, which is reported in De Rosa and Schmid (2002a: 239–40), contains different kinds of obstruents occurring in 190 contexts, so that the subjects produced voiced and unvoiced obstruents, both as single consonants and as geminates. The obstruents occur in eight different phonotactic contexts, namely word-initially before vowels (#CV), word-initially after sibilants (#SC), between vowels both as single consonants (VCV) and as geminates (VCCV), before and after liquids (CL, LC), and finally after nasals (NC). All in all, this procedure yielded a corpus of 9120 tokens, i.e. 4560 written words and 4560 spoken words (the quantitative distribution of the contexts is illustrated in De Rosa and Schmid, 2000: 53–64). The evaluation procedure of the data consisted of an error analysis of the dictations and an auditory analysis of the pupils' tape recordings.

In the following discussion, the findings will be presented first from a qualitative and then from a quantitative point of view.

A first type of restructuring in the bilingual phonological and graphematic system of Italian shows up when the lax allophones – [b̥ d̥ g̊] etc. – of the regional varieties are related to the voiced obstruents of Standard

Table 7.3 Postvocalic lenition (or 'voicing') in Italian dictation and reading

Phoneme	*Orthographic word*	*Bilinguals' spelling*	*Phonemic representation*	*Bilinguals' pronunciation*	*English translation*
/p/	<rapinatore>	«rabinatore»	/rapina'tore/	[rab̥ina'toːre]	'robber'
/t/	<protegge>	«prodege»	/pro'tɛdʒdʒe/	[pro'd̥etʃe]	's/he protects'
/k/	<le pecore>	«le pegore»	/le 'pɛkore/	[le 'pɛg̊ore]	'the sheep'
/tʃ/	<giacimenti>	«giagimenti»	/dʒatʃi'menti/		'deposits'

Table 7.4 Hypercorrect postvocalic devoicing in Italian dictation and reading

Phoneme	*Orthographic word*	*Bilinguals' spelling*	*Phonemic representation*	*Bilinguals' pronunciation*	*English translation*
/b/	<la bicicletta>	«la picicletta»	/la bitʃi'kletta/	[la pitʃi'klɛtːa]	'the bicycle'
/d/	<giudicarlo>	«giuticarlo»	/dʒudi'karlo/	[dʒud̥i'karlo] [tʃuti'karlo]	'(to) judge it'
/g/	<Gabriele>	«Cabriele»	* /ga'brjɛle/	*[g̊a'brjeːle]	(first name)
/dʒ/	<giacimenti>	«ciacimenti» «cacimenti»	/dʒatʃi'menti/	[tʃatʃi'menti]	'deposits'

Italian /b d g/. Both in spelling and in reading, we do indeed find cases where a process of lenition applies to voiceless obstruents occurring after vowels.

In the dictations, the pupils represent /p t k tʃ/ with the graphemes «b d g gi», which correspond to the homorganic voiced phonemes. This is in accordance with their similar behaviour in the reading task, where the allophonic rule described in (7) leads to the lax, but voiceless, realisations [b̥ d̥ g̊].

As a reaction against this natural tendency, [b d g] may be considered as mere variants of their unvoiced counterparts /p t k/; this leads to an inverse application of the allophonic rule (7).

The phonosyntactic context of <giudicarlo> is intervocalic (<non puoi giudicarlo> 'you can't judge it'), whereas the first name <Gabriele> occurs at the beginning of the sentence. The two different pronunciations of <giudicarlo> indicate that we must distinguish two different outputs of the devoicing process, depending on whether the resulting consonant is fully devoiced and tense (a clear case of hypercorrection) or devoiced and lax (like a Swiss German lenis sound).

As is to be expected on the basis of rule (8), the bilinguals also show instances of lenition/voicing in the postnasal context (Table 7.5) (in the corpus, /p/ and /k/ do not occur in this position, so that the allophonic process could not apply).

In this context, too, we find the same contradictory behaviour as after vowels, since a hypercorrect reflex produces the devoicing of voiced consonants (Table 7.6).

The grapheme «c» in «incusto» represents the phoneme /tʃ/; similar misspellings are rather frequent, owing to the lack of bi-uniqueness between the phonemes /tʃ/ and /dʒ/ and the corresponding graphemes <c>, <ci> and <g>, <gi> (see Introduction).

As regards plosives after word-initial sibilants, we only observe devoicing (Table 7.7).

This result points to interference from Swiss German phonotactics, where lax sibilants are not allowed to occur in such a context; therefore, the feature [−tense] of the alveolar sibilant spreads towards the following consonant.

Similarly, a Swiss German pattern may intervene in the substitution of the voiced double consonants of Italian with tense singleton consonants, given that both Italian geminates and the Swiss German [±tense] contrast rely on a durational difference (Table 7.8).

For instance, the realisations of <giubbotto> indeed show a double degemination of /b/ and /t/, both in spelling and in pronunciation. Additionally, in <pioggia> and <protegge> the voiced geminate /dʒ/ undergoes not only degemination, but also 'devoicing'.

Conversely, we also find the opposite process, i.e. the hypercorrect gemination of singleton consonants (Table 7.9).

Table 7.5 Postnasal voicing in Italian dictation and reading

Phoneme	*Orthographic word*	*Bilinguals' spelling*	*Phonemic representation*	*Bilinguals' pronunciation*	*English translation*
/t/	<attento>	«attendo»	/at'tɛnto/	[a't:ɛndo]	'attentive'
/tʃ/	<cancellino>	«cangelino» «cangellino» «cangielino»	/kantʃel'lino/	[kandʒe'l:i:no]	'blackboard eraser'

Table 7.6 Hypercorrect postnasal devoicing in Italian dictation and reading

Phoneme	*Orthographic word*	*Bilinguals' spelling*	*Phonemic representation*	*Bilinguals' pronunciation*	*English translation*
/d/	<prende>	«prente»	/'prɛnde/	['prɛnte]	'he/she takes'
/dʒ/	<ingiusto>	«incusto»	/in'dʒusto/	[in'tʃusto]	'unfair'

Table 7.7 Postsibilant devoicing in Italian dictation and reading

Phoneme	*Orthographic word*	*Bilinguals' spelling*	*Phonemic representation*	*Bilinguals' pronunciation*	*English translation*
/b/	<sbaglio>	«spaglio» «spalio»	/'zbaʎʎo/	['sb̥aʎ:o]	'mistake'
	<sbatte>	«spate» «spatte»	/'zbatte/	['spa:te]	'he/she strikes'
/g/	<sguardo>	«scuardo» «scuarto»	/'zgwardo/	['skwardo]	'look' (n.)

Table 7.8 Degemination (and devoicing) in Italian dictation and reading

Phoneme	*Orthographic word*	*Bilinguals' spelling*	*Phonemic representation*	*Bilinguals' pronunciation*	*English translation*
/b/	<giubbotto>	«guboto» «cupotto»	/dʒub'bɔtto/	[dʒu'bɔːto] [tʃu'bɔːto]	'jacket'
/t/	<giubbotto>	«guboto»	/dʒub'bɔtto/	[dʒu'bɔːto] [tʃu'boːto]	'jacket'
	<sbatte>	«spate»	/'zbatte/	['spaːte]	'he/she strikes'
/k/	<soccorso>	«socorso»	/sok'korso/	[sɔ'kɔrso]	'help'
	<sacco>	«sacho»	/'sakko/	['sako]	'bag'
/dz/	<razzo>	«razo»	/'radzdzo/	['radzo]	'missile'
/tʃ/	<ghiaccio>	«giacio» «giaco»	/'gjatʃtʃo/		'ice'
/dʒ/	<pioggia>	«piocia»	/'pjɔdʒdʒa/	['pjɔdʒa] ['pjɔtʃa]	'rain'

Table 7.9 Gemination of single consonants in Italian dictation and reading

Phoneme	*Orthographic word*	*Bilinguals' spelling*	*Phonemic representation*	*Bilinguals' pronunciation*	*English translation*
/p/	<rapina>	«rappina»	/ra'pina/		'robbery'
/b/	<deboli>	«debboli»	/'deboli/	['dɛbːoli]	'weak' (m. pl.)
/t/	<protegge>	«prottece»	/pro'tɛdʒdʒe/	[pro'tːɛdːʒe]	's/he protects'
/k/	<le pecore>	«le peccore»	/le'pɛkore/		'the sheep' (pl.)
/ts/	<spazio>	«spazzio»	/'spatstsjo/	['spatːsjo]	'space'
/tʃ/	<piace>	«piacce» «biacce»	/'pjatʃe/	['pjatːʃe]	's/he likes'

It is reasonable to assume that most of these examples are due to hypercorrection, with some exceptions. As regards <deboli>, we can attribute both the phonetic and the graphetic realisation of /b/ to the regional norms of southern Italy, where intervocalic /b/ is always long; in the case of <spazio>, too, the actual spelling is motivated by the real pronunciation of intervocalic /ts/ not only in southern varieties, but also in Standard Italian (see above).

Moving on to a quantitative evaluation of the data, we first have to emphasise the very low percentage of deviations, which modifies the rather dramatic impression given of the dictation in Figure 7.2: with regard to the entire corpus, there are only 5.13% of spelling errors in the dictation exercise, and 7.89% of deviant pronunciations in the reading task. If we now compare the different phonological processes in the dictation and in the reading task, the picture in Figure 7.3 arises.

Note that the two weakening processes of voicing and lenition are distinguished only in speech, where indeed we can observe three different types of sound, namely tense unvoiced, lax unvoiced and lax voiced (e.g. [t], [d̥] and [d]); conversely, the graphic code forces subjects to make a binary choice between <t> and <d>, no grapheme being available for the intermediate category. This is why Figure 7.3 contains no score for lenition.

Now the results of our analysis show that voicing and lenition together represent the most frequent processes in reading (171 tokens), but affect spelling to a lesser degree (only 38 tokens). The opposite process of

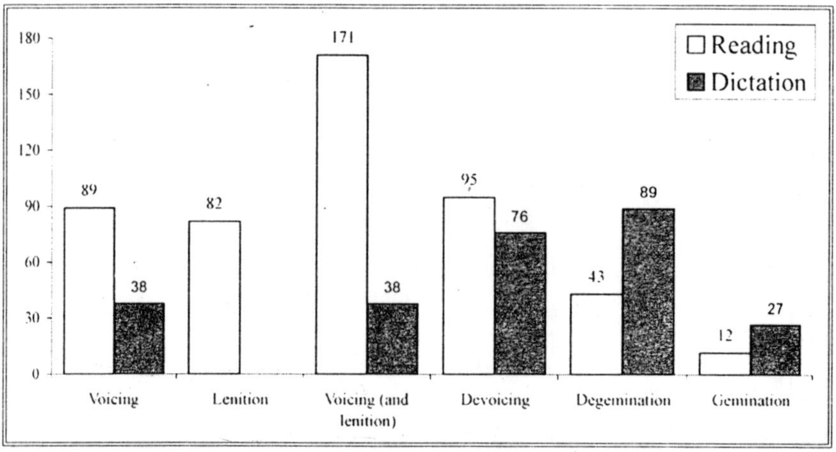

Figure 7.3 Total number of deviations revealing phonological processes in Italian dictation and reading

devoicing is present to more-or-less the same extent in dictations and in reading (76 and 95 tokens, respectively). Subjects appear to apply the allophonic rules (7) and (8) of southern Italian varieties in oral production, whereas they tend to avoid them in writing. The devoicing process results from two factors: namely, hypercorrection in the case of a fully tense devoiced consonant, or interference from Swiss German if the obstruent is realised as devoiced, but with a lax articulation.

The insecurity apparent with the voicing versus devoicing problem mainly affects pronunciation, whereas the contradictory behaviour related to gemination and degemination is more evident in the dictation task. However, the clear preference for degemination (89 tokens) might reflect a merely graphetic tendency to simplify double consonants and is not necessarily based on an underlying phonological representation. Similarly, the few cases of gemination (27 tokens) can be interpreted as a symptom of hypercorrection and orthographic insecurity; however, some graphetic double consonants do reflect underlying geminates, in particular as far as post-vocalic /b/ and intervocalic /ts/ are concerned.

Let us now consider the different phonotactic positions in which the consonants under analysis may occur. Figure 7.4 shows the percentages of deviations in relation to eight different contexts:

(1) word-initially before a vowel (#CV) like <p> in <le pecore>;
(2) after a word-initial sibilant (#SC) like <b> in <sbaglio>;
(3) between two vowels (VCV) like <d> in <giudicarlo>;
(4) as an intervocalic geminate (VCCV) like <tt> in <sbatte>;

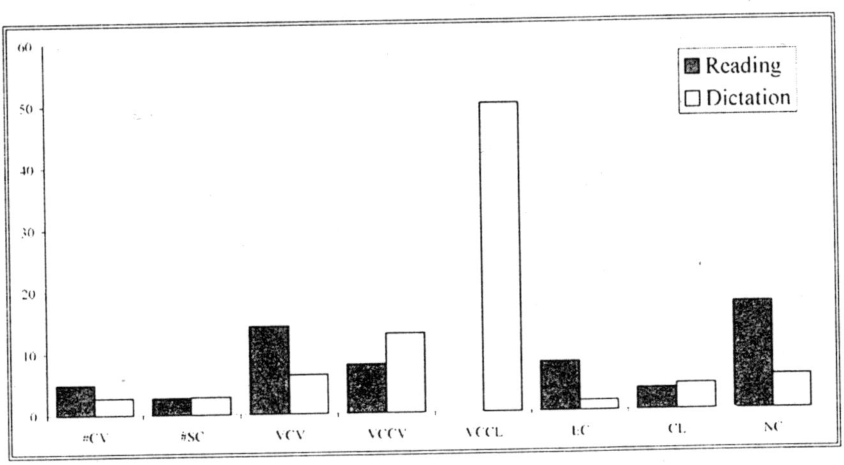

Figure 7.4 Deviations in Italian dictation and reading according to context (%)

(5) as a geminate between vowel and liquid (VCCL) like <bb> in <pubblicità>;
(6) after a liquid (LC) like <z> in <alza>;
(7) before a liquid (CL) like <p> in <prende>;
(8) after a nasal (NC) like <d> in <prende>.

Thus, a quantitative error analysis according to the phonotactic contexts largely confirms the foregoing analysis. In reading, deviations mainly occur with singletons after vowels and nasal consonants, whereas in the dictation task, geminates clearly constitute the critical point. As an example, consider the VCCL context, where half of our sample has simplified the double <bb> in the word <pubblicità> 'advertising'.

At this point, one might ask whether there is a quantitative relationship between deviations in reading and spelling errors in the individual subjects: do the ones with many errors in the dictation show the same kind of phenomena in their pronunciation?

The answer that emerges from Figure 7.5 is clearly negative. This figure shows a scattergram of subjects' scores for reading (on the x-axis) plotted against scores for dictation (on the y-axis); a clear correlation between the two would be indicated by a 'steep' regression line and a high coefficient

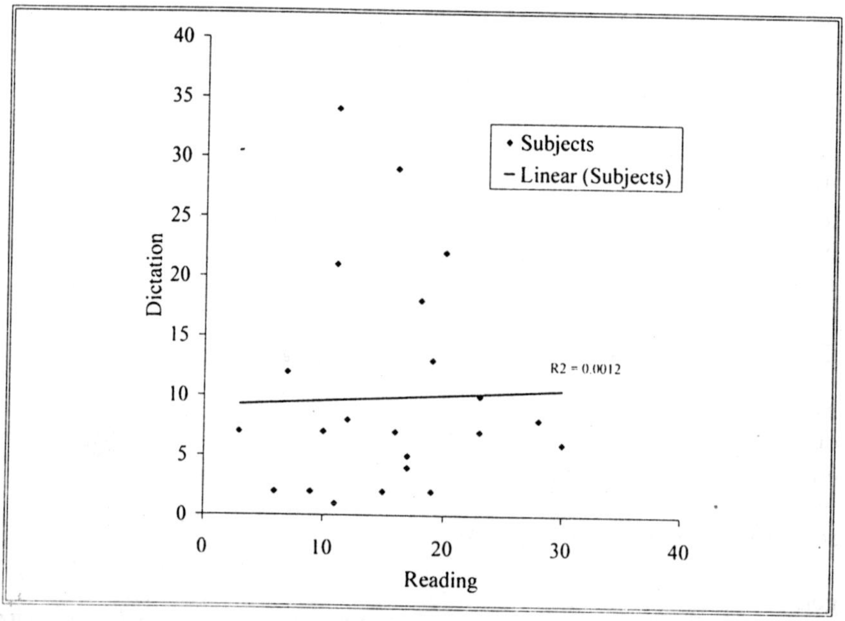

Figure 7.5 Subjects' deviations in Italian dictation and reading

of determination (R^2 close to 1). Instead, the graph clearly reveals the absence of any quantitative correlation between orthographic and phonetic competence, indicated by the very 'flat' linear regression and the very low coefficient of determination ($R^2 = 0.0012$). In fact, there are subjects with a rather standard-like pronunciation who make many spelling mistakes – for instance, with 11 deviations in the reading task and 34 in the dictation. But there are also subjects with high orthographic competence but clearly non-standard pronunciation, with six deviations in the dictation and 30 in the reading task (see De Rosa & Schmid (2002a: 222–38) for the profiles of the individual pupils).

Discussion

Do the spelling errors of Italian-Swiss German bilinguals have a phonological basis? Considering the results of the two classroom experiments, we can give a positive answer to the basic research question of this study. Obviously, the relationship between orthographic and phonological knowledge in bilinguals is not simple and deterministic, but there is evidence that at least some spelling errors are phonologically motivated. In particular, the voicing or devoicing of obstruents can be attributed to a difference in phonological structure between the four varieties of the bilinguals' repertoire, which mainly derives from the different distribution and status of the features [±voice] and [±tense]. Nevertheless, there is no direct quantitative correlation, whether we consider the corpus as a whole or we look at the spelling and reading of the individual subjects.

Moreover, the well-known phenomenon of hypercorrection has to be taken into account. In fact, there are two main strategies in dealing with the speech–spelling mismatch: either spellers keep as close as possible to the phonetic surface, or they try to inhibit the influence of the spoken (native) language on their writing. The same contradictory behaviour emerges in the way German spellers of English cope with their native rule of final obstruent devoicing: on the one hand, we find examples of 'phonetic realism', as appears from the devoiced final stop in «fint» instead of «find», but there are also attempts to realise graphetically a hypothetical underlying form, which lead to forms like «mead» instead of <meat> (Luelsdorff, 1991: 52). This second strategy testifies to the existence of a 'phonological awareness' in the acquisition of a second language writing system; from a developmental perspective, it reveals that some sort of learning is taking place at this stage.

It is true that some spelling errors, such as the simplification of geminates, could be motivated mainly by graphetic factors: writing one consonant instead of two obeys a sort of graphetic 'law of least effort'. However, if degemination is accompanied by devoicing (e.g. /dʒdʒ/ > /tʃ/

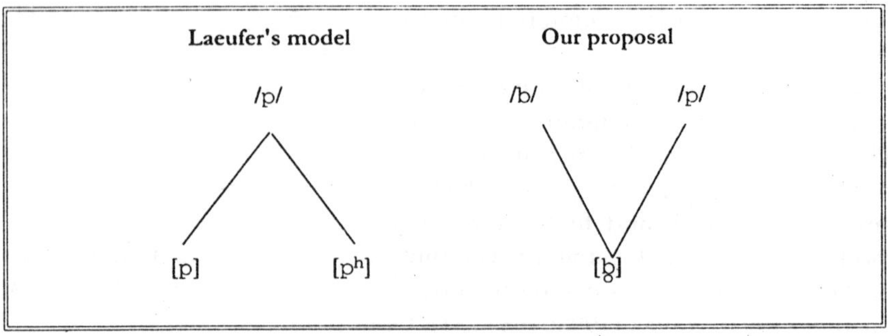

Figure 7.6 Two types of merging

in both the graphetic and the phonetic performance of Italian, it is likely to derive from contact with the phonological system of Swiss German, which dispenses with both voiced obstruents and geminates, instead using a longer closure duration as a cue for tenseness.

Taking as proven the strong phonetic and phonological bias in the spelling of our subjects, we may now turn to the second, more general research question: what are the driving forces in shaping the bilinguals' phonological representations of Italian? An initial finding to be stressed lies in the rather high standard of their spelling. Moreover, it appears that the main interference with the norms of Standard Italian does not come from the German part of the repertoire, but rather from the regional varieties of southern Italy. Above all, it is the latter model which leads to non-standard pronunciation and instances of hypercorrection.

Additional evidence for the strong influence of regional pronunciation norms comes from other allophonic processes appearing quite often in the speech of these children, like the intervocalic spirantisation of /tʃ/ or the affrication of /s/ after sonorants (De Rosa & Schmid, 2003: 175–6). In addition, many of the spelling errors found in our corpus have been detected in the writing of 'semi-literate' persons from central and southern Italy. Substitutions of, say, <t> with «d» (and vice versa) or of <tt> with «t» (and vice versa) are widely documented in letters of Italian prisoners of World War I and in autobiographies of foreign workers in Switzerland (see De Rosa & Schmid, 2000: 67–8 and references quoted therein).

To a lesser degree, however, interference from Swiss German does also occur. One typical pattern is the above-mentioned reinterpretation of voiced geminates as unvoiced singletons. A second example involves devoicing after word-initial sibilants, due to the transfer of a phonotactic constraint of Swiss German. A third case concerns the relatively frequent devoicing of the type /dʒ/ → /tʃ/, given that the Swiss German phoneme inventory has no lax counterpart of the tense palato-alveolar affricate (Keller, 1961: 45, 51).

To conclude, it might be interesting to interpret our findings in the light of a more general consideration of the linguistic competence of bilinguals. The last decade has seen a growing interest in aspects of 'bilingual' phonology and phonetics, which has led both to a substantial body of empirical research and to the formulation of a number of theoretical models. In this field, the overlapping of bilingualism and SLA is particularly striking, as can be seen from the reviews of the literature in Laeufer (1997), Yavas (1998: 193–231), Obler and Gjerlow (1999: 123–8) and Guion (2003: 98–102); nevertheless, the useful bibliographies provided by Joaquim Llisterri try to separate the two phenomena (http://liceu.uab.es/%7Ejoaquim/).

It lies beyond the scope of this contribution to compare our findings with such a large variety of studies; instead, we will concentrate on one specific model proposed by Christiane Laeufer (1997). Drawing on Weinreich's (1953) ground-breaking ideas, this author proposes a typology of bilingual phonological systems, basically distinguishing between 'coexistent systems', 'super-subordinate systems', and 'merged systems'; a similar typology, called the 'integration continuum', has been proposed in Cook (2002).

According to Laeufer's model, the simultaneous acquisition of two languages in different social contexts leads to the development of 'coexistent systems', which function in rather independent ways. This would apply in the case of an 'ideal' bilingual who has learnt the two languages in separate environments since his or her early childhood and has achieved a native-like competence in both of them. By contrast, foreign language learning in a formal setting typically yields 'super-subordinate systems', where the perception and storage of an L2-phonology is strongly based on the representations of the first language, leading to the well-known phenomenon of 'foreign accent'. Finally, individuals who learn two first languages at the same time are supposed to develop a 'merged system', where one and the same phonological system is associated with different phonetic implementations for the two languages. This type of bilingual system may arise when two languages are acquired simultaneously in the same context. The research review done by Laeufer (1997: 331–40) proves that all three types of bilingual phonological system are substantiated by experimental studies on the VOTs (voice onset times) produced by bilinguals with different language pairs.

Comparing the results of the present study with Laeufer's typology, we can conclude that, on the whole, native-like production testifies to two coexistent phonological systems in Italian-Swiss German bilinguals; it is precisely the strong influence of the regional varieties of Italian that underpins the similarity of their language production to that of monolingual speakers of Italian. Yet, as we have seen, there are some instances of interference from Swiss German phonological patterns, such as the replacement of voiced by voiceless lax obstruents, in particular after sibilants and in the case of palato-alveolar affricates. Finally, we also find forms which exhibit the partial merging of two phonological systems.

As an example of merging, consider the pronunciation [tʃuḍi'g̊arlo] of the expression /dʒudi'karlo/ 'to judge it', which contains two voiceless lax stops, [ḍ] and [g̊]. Now, the first lax plosive [ḍ] results from the devoicing of the voiced phoneme /d/ and is probably due to interference from Swiss German. The same holds for the devoicing of the word-initial affricate /dʒ/ → /tʃ/, due to the above-mentioned structural gap in the Swiss German phoneme inventory. Conversely, the second lax plosive [g̊] is derived from the allophonic lenition of unvoiced /k/, as prescribed by rule (7) of the southern Italian varieties. Thus, one and the same type of obstruent is generated by two different structural forces, one 'interlingual' and the other 'intralingual'. Note that this sort of merging is different from that in Laeufer's model, which predicts two phonetic implementations of a unified underlying representation. In our case, we have quite the opposite, namely the derivation of one and the same type of surface realisation from two different phonological forms (see Figure 7.6).

It therefore seems reasonable to modify Laeufer's model slightly by stating that a typology of bilinguals' phonological systems must be conceived of as a continuum rather than a series of discrete categories with clear-cut boundaries. In the case of Italian-Swiss German bilinguals, we are mostly dealing with coexistent and separate systems. However, a certain amount of interference between the different systems must be allowed for. Merging does occur, but only marginally, in that the phonological representations of two different systems may produce the same kind of phonetic output.

Notes

1. This study would not have been possible without the fundamental contribution made by Raffaele De Rosa, who drew my attention to the phenomena discussed here and collected all the data. Subsequently, we together carried out the basic steps of the present analysis. In a sense, this paper represents a revised and extended version of De Rosa and Schmid (2002b); needless to say, I alone am responsible for any possible errors.
2. In representing the linguistic data, the following conventions are adopted: square brackets [] are used for phonetic realisations, i.e. the actual pronunciation of a sound or a word; double angled brackets « » enclose the graphetic realisations produced by the informants, i.e. their real spelling.

References

Albano Leoni, F. and Maturi, P. (1995) *Manuale di fonetica* (new edition 2002). Roma: Carocci.

Berkemeier, A. (1996) *Kognitive Prozesse beim Zweitschrifterwerb. Zweitalphabetisierung griechisch-deutsch-bilingualer Kinder im Deutschen.* Frankfurt: Peter Lang.

Cook, V.J. (2002) Background to the L2 user. In V.J. Cook (ed.) *Portraits of the L2 User* (pp. 1–28). Clevedon: Multilingual Matters.

De Rosa, R. and Schmid, S. (2000) Aspetti della competenza ortografica e fonologica nell'italiano di emigrati di seconda generazione nella Svizzera tedesca. *Rivista italiana di dialettologia* 24, 53–96.

De Rosa, R. and Schmid, S. (2002a) Convergenze e divergenze tra grafia e pronuncia in scolari italiani nella Svizzera tedesca. In M.T. Vigolo and A. Zamboni (eds) *Saggi dialettologici in area italo-romanza. Sesta raccolta* (pp. 213–40). Padua: CNR.

De Rosa, R. and Schmid, S. (2002b) On the relationship between spelling and pronunciation in Italian Swiss-German bilinguals. In A. James and J. Leather (eds) *New Sounds 2000* (pp. 97–106). University of Klagenfurt.

De Rosa, R. and Schmid, S. (2003) Phonetic and orthographic performance of Italian-Swiss German bilinguals: The case of obstruents and the features [±voice] and [±tense]. In L. Costamagna and S. Giannini (eds) *La fonologia dell'interlingua. Principi e metodi di analisi* (pp. 163–78). Milan, Franco Angeli.

Dieth, E. and Brunner, R. (1943) Die Konsonanten und Geminaten des Schweizerdeutschen experimentell untersucht. In A. Steiger (ed.) *Sache, Ort und Word. Festschrift Jakob Jud* (pp. 737–62). Genève: Droz.

DUDEN (2000) *Ausspracheworterbuch.* Mannheim: Dudenverlag.

Esposito, A. and Di Benedetto, M.-G. (1999) Acoustical and perceptual study of gemination in Italian stops. *Journal of the Acoustical Society of America* 106, 2051–62.

Extra, G. and Verhoeven, L. (eds) (1993) *Immigrant Languages in Europe.* Clevedon: Multilingual Matters.

Extra, G. and Verhoeven, L. (eds) (1999) *Bilingualism and Migration.* Berlin: Mouton de Gruyter.

Giovanardi, M. and Di Benedetto, M.-G. (1998) Acoustic analysis of singleton and geminate fricatives in Italian. *WEB-SLS. The European Student Journal of Language and Speech.* http://www.essex.ac.uk/web-sls/papers/98-01/98-01.html.

Guion, S. (2003) The vowel systems of Quichua-Spanish bilinguals. *Phonetica* 60, 98–128.

Ham, W. (2001) *Phonetic and Phonological Aspects of Geminate Timing.* New York/London: Routledge.

Hampel, D. (2000) *Regressive Interimsprache.* Frankfurt: Peter Lang.
Jakobson, R., Fant, G. and Halle, M. (1952) *Preliminaries to Speech Analysis.* Cambridge, MA: MIT Press.
Jakobson, R. and Halle, M. (1964) Tenseness and laxness. In D. Abercrombie *et al.* (eds) *In Honour of Daniel Jones* (pp. 96–101). London: Longmans.
Jessen, M. (1998) *Phonetics and Phonology of Tense and Lax Obstruents in German.* Amsterdam: Benjamins.
Jessen, M. (2001) Phonetic implementation of the distinctive auditory features [voice] and [tense] in stop consonants. In T. Hall (ed.) *Distinctive Feature Theory* (pp. 237–94). Berlin: Mouton de Gruyter.
Keller, R.E. (1961) *German Dialects. Phonology and Morphology.* Manchester University Press.
Kohler, K. (1984) Phonetic explanation in phonology: The feature fortis/lenis. *Phonetica* 41, 150–74.
Kraehenmann, A. (2001) Swiss German stops: Geminates all over the word. *Phonology* 18, 109–45.
Lado, R. (1957) *Linguistics Across Cultures.* Ann Arbor: The University of Michigan Press.
Laeufer, C. (1997) Towards a typology of bilingual phonological systems. In A. James and J. Leather (eds) *Second-Language Speech* (pp. 325–340). Berlin: Mouton de Gruyter.
Lepschy, G. and Lepschy, A.L. (1977) *The Italian Language Today.* London: Hutchinson.
Luelsdorff, Ph. A. (1986) *Constraints on Error Variables in Grammar: Bilingual Misspelling Orthographies.* Amsterdam: Benjamins.
Luelsdorff, Ph. A. (1991) *Developmental Orthography.* Amsterdam: Benjamins.
Maddieson, I. (1997) Phonetic universals. In W. Hardcastle and J. Laver (eds) *The Handbook of Phonetics Sciences* (pp. 617–39). Oxford: Blackwell.
Obler, L. and Gjerlow, K. (1999) *Language and the Brain.* Cambridge University Press.
Romaine, S. (1995) *Bilingualism* (2nd edn). Oxford: Blackwell.
Schmid, S. (1992) Code-switching among Italian bilinguals in German-speaking Switzerland. In A. Giacalone Ramat (ed.) *Code-Switching Summer School* (pp. 293–4). Strasbourg: European Science Foundation.
Schmid, S. (1993) Lingua madre e commutazione di codice in immigrati italiani di seconda generazione nella Svizzera tedesca. *Multilingua* 12, 265–89.
Schmid, S. (1999) *Fonetica e fonologia dell'italiano.* Torino: Paravia Scriptorium.
Weinreich, U. (1953) *Languages in Contact.* The Hague: Mouton.
Wiese, R. (1996) *The Phonology of German.* Oxford: Clarendon.

Willi, U. (1996) *Die segmentale Dauer als phonetischer Parameter von 'fortis' und 'lenis' bei Plosiven im Zürichdeutschen.* Stuttgart: Steiner.

Winteler, J. (1876) *Die Kerenzer Mundart des Kantons Glarus in ihren Grundzügen dargestellt.* Leipzig.

Yavas, M. (1998) *Phonology. Development and Disorders.* San Diego: Singular.

Part 2

Reading a Second Language Writing System

Chapter 8

Are the L1 and L2 Word Reading Processes Affected More by Writing System or Instruction?

PHIL SCHOLFIELD and GLORIA SHU-MEI CHWO

Introduction

Does the writing system of a language affect how we read it? Does how we were taught to read words have any actual effect on how we do it? These are fundamental questions to which we offer a modest contribution by studying the way in which sixth grade schoolchildren read words for their meaning in L1 Chinese and L2 English in two contexts where word reading is taught in widely differing ways: Hong Kong and Taiwan.

This chapter concerns word reading, also known as word recognition or decoding. But what is its role in the reading process as a whole? When we read in what is arguably the default real-life way, i.e. reading text silently and with prime attention paid to the message, clearly part of what we are doing involves decoding the written forms of individual words in the text – words predominantly already known to us and stored in our mental lexicons. This may seem obvious, but in fact the role attributed to written word recognition and comprehension in the overall reading process has been evaluated very differently in theories of reading in the past. In the heyday of the bottom-up view of reading (LaBerge & Samuels, 1974) it was seen as central: reading was essentially a succession of acts of word recognition cumulatively built up to yield a representation of the meaning of a text. In the days of the extreme top-down approach (Goodman, 1967) it was seen as somewhat marginal: reading was basically prediction relying far more on prior knowledge of content than on decoding of words to yield an interpretation of text. Today mostly some form of interactive view is adopted (as proposed for instance by Rumelhart, 1977) which gives a more even role to bottom-up word decoding and top-down prediction: both activities go on simultaneously and inform each other. Hence it is not surprising that studies show that readers with better scores on tests of word reading ability are generally better also on tests of text comprehension (e.g. Chabat *et al.*, 1984, for L1 English; Koda, 1992, for L2 Japanese).

Within this wider context of research on reading, then, it remains important to broaden our understanding of the way in which written word recognition actually takes place, in both the first and second language, and the factors affecting it – the realm where reading connects with writing systems. Research studies in this area, such as ours, usually focus on the processing of words in isolation, not in text, so that the effects of any reader prediction from prior text or background knowledge are eliminated and the processes of pure word decoding can be determined. Furthermore the research methods required are typically of the computer-based laboratory experimental type. This is because, in order to study online processing of the automatic and subconscious type which goes on when someone identifies a written word and accesses its meaning in his/her mental lexicon, we largely need to rely on timed experiments where we can see how fast, and how accurately, readers recognise different types of word presented in various ways which allow us to make deductions about how they may have been processing them. These mental processes are not really open to study by asking readers to think aloud and self report them, though that is a technique used effectively to explore the more conscious levels of the reading process, such as how readers try to determine the meaning of an unknown word or perform 'higher' level processes such as predicting.

Factors in Word Reading

The two routes

Even within the narrow field of word recognition in reading there is an extensive and complicated literature, from which we will now consider a small portion that is relevant to our own study. A natural starting point is the two general kinds of model or 'routes' that are often proposed to account for how written words are decoded individually (e.g. Seidenberg, 1985). These have already been described in the Introduction to this volume, using the labels 'lexical' and 'phonological' to distinguish them, so we will not recapitulate their description here. Clearly they apply potentially to word reading as much as to word writing/spelling. However, a point of importance for our study concerns the involvement of phonology even in the so-called lexical route. This route involves word recognition which, unlike the phonological route, was at one time thought to bypass sound altogether, linking a word's written shape directly to its meaning (Coltheart, 1978), though sound could of course be accessed 'postlexically': hence it is also sometimes called the direct route. However, there is increasing evidence that 'phonological recoding' also often occurs in the lexical route prelexically: i.e. sound is accessed from the written shape on the way to the meaning, albeit not as a series of segments but as a holistic word sound shape or 'addressed phonology'. Contrast the phonological route, where sounds are always imagined to be accessed prelexically, as 'assembled phonology', i.e. via individual phonemes or phoneme sequences linked to units of the writing system.

Treiman *et al.* (1981) and Tzeng *et al.* (1977) for example show that even in Chinese, where the writing system is widely supposed to favour the lexical route (see below), words are read via sound. Many studies in this area however suffer from the fact that the experimental task is partly oral (e.g. the words have to be spoken aloud or 'named') so could prompt phonological recoding for that reason, and may measure retention and recall rather than recognition in silent reading alone. Perfetti and Zhang (1995), however, in a study similar to ours, showed that even where similarity of meaning, not of sound, has to be judged between pairs of Chinese characters, judgments are slowed not only on semantically similar pairs but also on phonologically similar ones, suggesting that sound as well as meaning gets accessed when reading a character. They further importantly varied stimuli exposure times to show no evidence for 'a precedence of semantic activation over phonological information' (p. 31) and propose a 'Universal Phonological Principle' that writing is *always* read with some access to phonology, regardless of route, as there is a 'preference for phonological representations in working memory' (p. 31). However, there remain others convinced of the 'Universal Direct Access Hypothesis' (Baluch & Besner, 1991) which holds that word reading occurs always by a visual route, with phonology used only when required by reader, task or word characteristics. Nevertheless, overall nowadays the difference between the two routes is seen, not so much that one (phonological) involves sound and the other (lexical) does not, but as a matter of relative dominance in each of phonological or visual (ortho)graphic code activation, the features of processing that our study will measure, and that one involves breaking up the written and phonological form of a word while the other handles these more as wholes.

Not only is the precise nature of the routes debated, but also how exclusive and distinct they are. A modern view is that they are in reality not so much alternatives as options which a reader can exploit 'interactively' to a greater or lesser extent. This view is inherent in connectionist models of word recognition which do not distinguish discrete routes at all, but allow for a continuum of possibilities between them (Seidenberg & McClelland, 1989). The balance of preference for one extreme or the other has been found to depend on a number of factors (Seidenberg, 1985).

Four of these are:

- word frequency, where high frequency words have been shown to favour the lexical route (Seidenberg, 1985);
- word familiarity, where unknown (in studies, often unreal) words require the phonological route (Treiman *et al.*, 1981);
- task, where tasks like 'word naming' or judging similarity of sound require sound to be accessed so favour the phonological route (Perfetti & Zhang, 1995);
- age, where younger children (e.g. first grade) have been argued to find the lexical route conceptually easier (Hsia, 1995).

In our study these four factors were controlled as the words to be read were chosen for their relatively high frequency and familiarity in both places where the research was conducted, the children were all of similar age (sixth grade), and the task required access to meaning not sound. We now turn to the two focal factors in our study which might affect the degree or involvement of graphic shape or sound in the word recognition process.

Our study concerns readers whose first language is Chinese, a language written in a writing system very different from that used for their L2 English; indeed the type of writing system is often claimed as a major factor affecting the processing route that readers use, depending on its 'depth': see coverage of the Orthographic Depth Hypothesis (ODH) in the Introduction. The English writing system is relatively shallow, in that there are numerous, if complicated, systematic ways in which its small number of written symbols (letters or short letter sequences) correspond to sounds: other alphabetic systems such as the alphabet used for Iberian Spanish are shallower still. This will not be further detailed here. Chinese, however, uses a deep writing system consisting of thousands of logographic symbols (characters). Though most are constructed from two or more component characters which recur elsewhere, it is hard to find many systematic correspondences between any component of the written form of a word and its sounds (though there may be better links between some components of characters and aspects of the meaning). There are varied claims, such as that 40% of compound characters (which in turn comprise around 80% of all characters) have a phonetically useful component character (Huang & Hanley, 1995). An example would be the character 工 /kuŋ/ gōng 'work' which appears also as a component in the characters 功 (/kuŋ/ gōng 'merit'), 杠 (/kaŋ/ gàng 'thick pole'), 扛 (/kʰaŋ/ káng 'carry on the shoulder'), 紅 (/xuŋ/ hóng 'red') and 江 (/tɕiaŋ/ jiāng 'river'), but not in 供 (/kuŋ/ gōng 'supply') or in dozens of other characters with similar pronunciations. Clearly the usefulness of such a component as an indication of the sounds to aid word reading is limited, but such evidence *is* used by

Chinese readers when they meet unknown characters (Seidenberg, 1985). The Orthographic Depth Hypothesis claims that the deeper the system, the more the lexical route will be used simply because the writing system does not provide enough systematic information to support the phonological route (Frost *et al.*, 1987). Furthermore, the logographic symbols of deep systems typically provide more visual cues than do shallower systems to aid use of the lexical route, as they differ from each other in more ways than can arise where only 26 letters of an alphabet are available to write words with (Lee *et al.*, 1986). Some studies have supported the ODH: for example Chen and Juola (1982) found that alphabetic and logographic writing systems activated different encoding of words in memory by native speakers (and so, by implication, different processing when reading): Chinese characters favoured visual/graphic recognition and English words a more even mix of graphic and phonological strategies.

The key point for our study is that, if the ODH truly identifies a dominant factor, then we would expect differences between how English and Chinese words are processed when reading, but no differences between people in Hong Kong and Taiwan in this respect. In both places the English words are written in the same L2 writing system, and any transfer of processing habits from reading L1 words should be the same (as reported, for example, in Hsia (1995), who found evidence for transfer of instruction-induced phonological awareness of L1 Chinese to L2 English phonological awareness). In both places the Chinese words are also written in the same L1 writing system, the traditional unsimplified characters (in contrast with the People's Republic of China apart from Hong Kong, where simplified versions of some characters are standard), and there is no reason to expect the difference between the dominant spoken languages, Cantonese and Mandarin respectively, to have any effect. However, in fact we feel that another, somewhat neglected, factor in determining the word reading process may outweigh the ODH, and create differences between Hong Kong and Taiwan.

Reading instruction

This second major factor that we are concerned with is early instruction in word reading, where broadly we find two kinds of approach used for writing systems such as the English one, closely matching the two routes described earlier (Chall, 1983). In the first, often called 'phonics', the teacher focuses on making readers aware of the individual graphic components of written words and of what sounds they correspond to. Typically words are practised spoken letter-by-letter or assembled from cards for individual letters or letter sequences (e.g. <b-oo-k>), or treated in rhyming sets that demonstrate grapho-phonological correspondence patterns, e.g. English <pain, stain, rain> or <pot, pet, pit>, and explicit rules may be given about the letters of the alphabet, e.g. 'In words like <late, complete, like, poke, use>, the final <e> makes the preceding vowel sound its name'. In the extreme form, some kind of phonemic transcription may be used before or alongside the usual writing system, such as the Initial Teaching Alphabet used for a time in the UK in the 1960s (see Pitman & St. John, 1969). In the second approach, often called the 'look and say' or 'whole-word' method, the teacher focuses on rapid visual recognition or copying of the graphic shape of a word as a whole, often using word-picture flash-cards to involve meaning, and the sound shape is handled holistically, or in chunks not smaller than syllables, and is not a focus of attention. Often this goes along with focusing less on practising reading words aloud and in isolation (common in phonics), more on reading them silently in wider contexts (e.g. compound words or sentences or texts), which allows some top-down skills of meaning prediction to be developed alongside (called the 'whole language' approach). Though these methods are usually described for the teaching of L1 English word reading, they also occur in L2 English contexts. From a survey we conducted, we found that in Taiwan phonics is used (without transcription) while Hong Kong predominantly uses the whole-word (and whole-language) method. Hence, if instruction has an effect, we might expect it to show up as differences in measures of word recognition in these two places.

For logographic writing systems, the whole-word approach can be used much as described above and, again, is found so used in Hong Kong for L1 Chinese, with a very occasional use of romanised transcription to elucidate pronunciation. However, the equivalent of phonics used for L1 Chinese in Taiwan is slightly different in that there is little in the way of grapho-phonological correspondence rules to teach. The teacher may focus on making readers aware of the individual components of compound characters that represent sound but, as already indicated, these components rarely give a systematic clue to sound and more attention is often paid to those components (often called radicals) which give a somewhat better clue to the meaning of the whole character (and which may be taught also in the whole-word approach). However, words are often read aloud in isolation in phonologically (and/or graphically and semantically) related pairs or sets and there is emphasis on segmenting the sound shape of a word, typically with the use of transcription, even though the usual written form (character) cannot be broken up to match. In China (excluding Hong Kong) the romanisation Pinyin is systematically learnt alongside the characters and serves this purpose (and is given after characters in this chapter for those familiar with it); in Japan kana (a shallow syllabary) is often used alongside what is normally written in kanji (i.e. Chinese characters) at early stages. In Taiwan a Chinese-script transcription is used, which is called *Zhuyin Fuhao* and represents a Chinese syllable (corresponding to one character) with between one and three symbols which each correspond one-to-one with one or two phonemes, often plus another symbol for the tone. Examples: 木 /mu/ 'mù' (tree) (and 目 /mu/ 'mù' (eye) and every other /mu/ homophone) is transcribed ㄇㄨˋ with a symbol for each phoneme and one for the tone, as is 我 /wo/ 'wŏ' (I, me) ㄨㄛˇ, while 媽 /ma/ 'mā' (mother) is represented with just two symbols ㄇㄚ, as the level tone is left untranscribed; we see a symbol for a diphthong in 賣 /mai/ 'mài' (sell) ㄇㄞˋ and for vowel + nasal in 黃 /xuaŋ/ 'huáng' (yellow) ㄏㄨㄤˊ. Children are taught to read this system in school before characters are introduced and it is then used alongside the characters up to 6th grade; even when the semantically relevant component of a character is isolated for attention, its own Zhuyin Fuhao pronunciation may be presented as well as that for the whole character (our own survey, and Lee *et al.*, 1986).

From the above it seems likely overall that, for English, phonics would straightforwardly lead to greater use of the phonological route by readers, with a dominant part played by sound in the process, and whole-word would lead to greater reliance on the lexical route, with some phonological recoding but greater attention to overall graphic shape. For Chinese, the lexical route is inevitably dominant but phonics would lead to greater phonological recoding within that route than would the whole-word method. Overall, therefore, in our study we expect that, if instruction shows an effect, it will be in the form of a stronger phonological element in the word reading of Taiwanese children, and a greater graphic/visual element in the word recognition of Hong Kong children, though both aspects will be present in some degree for all subjects.

Summary

Many studies of the effects of writing system type or instruction have tended to provide at best indirect evidence of effects on the word reading process as they have instead targeted effects on some or all of the other three following reader variables:

(1) Phonological awareness is typically measured with purely oral tests of a person's ability to identify rhyming words, say a word with the first sound omitted, and the like, in a specific language; hence a subject with high scores might be expected to favour access to the sound of a word when reading it, though that is not directly measured.

(2) Visual discrimination ability is measured independently of language by ability to spot matching shapes among a set of slightly different

shapes, and the like; hence a subject with high scores might be expected to favour reliance purely on the graphic shape of a word when reading it, though that is not directly measured.

(3) Word reading ability is often measured by how accurately subjects can read aloud isolated words in a language (untimed), some of which may not be known to them, which means that, unlike in much 'real' reading, they have to access or try to figure out the sound but may not access the meaning; hence a subject with high scores might be one who favours access to the sound in the word recognition process, though that is not directly measured.

The prevailing evidence (e.g. Huang & Hanley, 1995) is that for English readers both instruction and writing system type affect phonological awareness, in that phonics and a relatively shallow L1 alphabetic system enhance it; however, high phonological awareness goes with better reading ability much more strongly than does visual discrimination ability only for L1 English readers, not Hong Kong readers of L2 English for whom the reverse holds (Taiwan readers of English were not in that study). For L1 Chinese readers, writing system favours visual discrimination ability, but phonic instruction also enhances phonological awareness (in Taiwan versus Hong Kong, also found by Read *et al.* (1986) for Chinese adults who had learnt pinyin versus those who had not); however, visual discrimination ability correlates with reading ability better than phonological awareness does in both places (though phonological awareness does so a little better in Taiwan than Hong Kong). Insofar as one can deduce any implication about the actual process of word reading, this would all seem to imply that in Hong Kong one might expect less phonological than graphic involvement in word recognition in both languages. In Taiwan there should be greater phonological involvement. This is what we wish to establish. However, rather than using any of the three above measures, we shall attempt to tap into the word recognition process more directly with the instrument described below.

The Hypotheses in the Study

(1) If instruction affects the word reading process, then due to their more graphic-oriented instructional background, we expect Hong Kong subjects to judge the semantic similarity of Chinese word pairs with faster response time and lower error rate where there is sound similarity than where there is graphic similarity between the two words in a pair (where their training will lead them to be more distracted). Due to their more phonic-oriented instruction, the reverse should be true of Taiwan subjects: i.e. they will be more distracted by pairs with sound similarity, and respond more slowly and with greater error than on graphically similar pairs.

(2) The two groups should also show the same differences when reading L2 English due both to L1 to L2 processing transfer, and to the instructional methods used in the second language for the same reasons as above.

(3) If, on the other hand, the effects of writing system dominate instruction, there should for all subjects, regardless of place, be the same interactive effect of language and pair type on scores, since Chinese logographic writing is supposed to generally favour graphic word recognition, and English alphabetic writing supposedly favours the use of grapho-phonological correspondences. That is they should be slower and less accurate on graphically similar word pairs than on phonologically similar ones in Chinese, and the reverse on English pairs.

Furthermore:

(4) There is no reason to expect differences in overall L1 Chinese reading between the two places (when types of word pair are not considered separately).

(5) There is reason to expect Hong Kong subjects to be better overall than Taiwanese in reading L2 English due to the different currency of English in the community, and the greater number of hours of English classes in school, despite our efforts to control such factors (see below).

(6) We expect no differences between groups in the way the distracter word pairs are decoded (identical pairs and ones different in sound, graphic form and meaning).

(7) Responses should be fastest on identical word pairs, i.e. there should be some distraction effect of both phonological and graphic similarity for subjects in both places.

Method

Design

The design has two groups, from the key places Taiwan and Hong Kong, with two within-subjects factors – two languages (Chinese L1 and English L2) and two critical types of word pair experimentally manipulated: phonologically similar but different in graphic shape and meaning; graphically similar but different in phonological shape and meaning. Two other types of word pair were used as distracters: identical, and totally different (in sound, written form and meaning). The dependent variables are latency/response time and accuracy/error rate. The word pairs are described under Materials below: the essential assumption behind their use is that the more a subject accesses a word's sound while reading it, the more they will be distracted by phonologically similar word pairs, and so respond slower and less accurately; conversely, the greater reliance the reader places on the graphic form of a word when trying to recognise it and access its meaning, the more they should be distracted by words that are graphically similar, and so respond slower and less accurately.

Schools and subjects

In both Hong Kong and Taiwan children usually start school in kindergarten aged four or five years and enter primary school aged six or seven, but while in Hong Kong English is a feature of the education alongside Cantonese from the start, in Taiwan instruction has long been only in Mandarin at this level. However, there is an ongoing development in Taiwan to introduce English from first grade in select schools and the Education Department is introducing this as a general feature of the primary curriculum (from Sept 2001 it has been launched generally from fifth grade onwards). Anticipating this, English has been introduced in a large number of private kindergartens. Against this background it was important to target subjects with comparable L1 and L2 exposure from an early age, so the Taiwan school was one which in fact had English well established in the curriculum from kindergarten onwards.

Besides this, Hong Kong is a community where English has a significant role in daily communication in business, administration, etc. and as a medium of instruction in subjects other than English at secondary level (13+). In short, it has the role of a 'second language' as distinct from its purely 'foreign language' status in Taiwan where none of the above are true. The best we could do to control for this factor was to select primary school students, of an age and L2 competence not yet likely to be heavily influenced by out-of-school exposure or the lack of it, and of course not yet embarked on secondary education with its differences in medium of instruction.

At the same time we needed subjects who were familiar with a reasonable number of Chinese characters and had an English vocabulary, familiar in both written and spoken form, sufficient for the tests. They needed to have been exposed to the different instructional methods long enough for these to have had an effect, if any were to be found. They also needed to be cognitively mature enough to concentrate and handle the test task. All these considerations led us to target primary students of sixth grade (aged around 12).

Following a postal survey, a primary school was identified in each place which was willing to participate, and suitably matched in the above respects as well as being of similar size, with a similar number of classes, and attracting children with a similar mix of middle class and working class backgrounds: Tunghai Primary School and Taichung County in Taiwan; and Fuk Wing Street Government Primary School (morning shift) in Hong Kong. Tunghai Primary (est. 1956, 770 students) is one of the limited number of schools with a full English component in the curriculum and is seen as a possible model for primary schools in the future in Taiwan. Fuk Wing Street (est. 1958, 740 students) is a typical local school following the usual Hong Kong National Curriculum. The schools devoted similar numbers of hours per week to Chinese classes (around five hours), but there was an unavoidable difference in time spent on English: the Hong Kong school spent more time than the Taiwan school (approximately three and a quarter hours versus two).

In each school, after gaining the appropriate permissions, approximately half of the sixth grade children participated in the experiment, chosen as every second child seated in class and evenly divided between sexes: 60 from Taiwan and 70 from Hong Kong.

Materials

The reason for choosing a simultaneously presented word-pair judgment task (similar to Perfetti & Zhang (1995) who presented one word slightly ahead of the other) was largely because this format was judged the easiest to handle for children of the targeted age, who were not familiar with any type of computer-based psychometric tests. We focussed on judgment of meaning similarity, rather than phonological or graphic similarity, partly for the same reason and also because we wanted to tap processing in which the meaning of the word being read was definitely accessed, closer to 'real' reading, which is not guaranteed to happen in a task where only graphic or sound similarities have to be judged.

The aim was to test words that were known to the subjects, not words unknown to subjects either as a whole, or in their written form, which would necessarily be processed differently when seen for the first time. A preliminary list of word pairs for the experiment was compiled from standard frequency lists (e.g. Kučera & Francis, 1967; Liu *et al.*, 1975), but since children do not typically learn words following adult L1 frequency bands, familiarity was checked by submitting the prospective pairs to teachers of Chinese and English in both places to judge whether sixth grade students would have met the members of the pairs in their respective school language syllabuses or not, and be familiar with their sound, written form and meaning. Fifteen Chinese and 12 English teachers were polled in Taiwan, 13 Chinese and eight English teachers in Hong Kong. Further checks were made against the school syllabus and textbook wordlists. In the end it was not possible to create enough suitable word pairs using only words which were judged familiar by a large majority of teachers. However we were able at least to follow a principle that pairs were only chosen which had very similar familiarity judgments in the two places, so if a word in a pair was at all unfamiliar, it would be equally so for all subjects. Examples: 山 /ʂan/ 'shān' (Cantonese saan[1]) (mountain) - 刪 /ʂan/ 'shān' (Cantonese saan[1]) (erase) 93% in Taiwan and 92% in Hong Kong; <serial> /sɪərɪəl/ - <cereal> / sɪərɪəl/ 33% in Taiwan and 38% in Hong Kong.

Chinese word pairs

All words in Chinese were one character and one syllable long in this study. The various types were as follows, laid out in Table 8.1 below.

Phonologically similar word pairs (PWP) in Chinese were identical in pronunciation (including tone) both within Mandarin and within Cantonese (though often differing between those), but differed in meaning and in character constituents and/or number of strokes.

Graphically similar word pairs (GWP) shared a component character element, but had a different meaning-related component character, with a few strokes difference.

Same word pairs (SWP) simply repeated the identical character.

Different word pairs (DWP) were different in sound, graphic shape and meaning.

English word pairs

English words were one or two syllables long in English, see Table 8.2. PWP had the same pronunciation but different meaning, and spelling, differing typically both in one consonant and the representation of the vowel sound, with up to two letters difference in length. GWP differed in first consonant and vowel sound and meaning, but were spelt identically

Table 8.1 The four types of Chinese word pairs (with transcriptions)

		Mandarin transcriptions		*Cantonese transcriptions*	
Types of word pair	*Examples*	*IPA*	*Pinyin*	*Romanisation*	*Meanings*
PWP (Phonologically similar word pairs)	東	tuŋ	dōng	dung[1]	east
	冬	tuŋ	dōng	dung[1]	winter
GWP (Graphically similar word pairs)	紅	xuŋ	hóng	hung[4]	red
	江	tɕiaŋ	jiāng	gong[1]	river
SWP (Same word pairs)	些	ɕie	xiē	se[1]	few
	些	ɕie	xiē	se[1]	few
DWP (Different word pairs)	些	ɕie	xiē	se[1]	few
	長	$tʂ^haŋ$	cháng	zoeng[2]	long

Table 8.2 The four types of English word pairs (with transcriptions)

Types of word pair	*Examples*		*IPA transcriptions*	
PWP (Phonologically similar word pairs)	right	write	raɪt	raɪt
	him	hymn	hɪm	hɪm
GWP (Graphically similar word pairs)	mother	bother	mʌðə	bɒðə
	most	cost	məʊst	kɒst
SWP (Same word pairs)	flower	flower	flaʊə	flaʊə
DWP (Different word pairs)	wind	shop	wɪnd	ʃɒp

but for one letter. SWP simply repeated the same word, while DWP differed in sound, spelling and meaning.

Three forms of the test were prepared in each language, using different sets of word pairs, to be administered to different, randomly selected, subsets of subjects. Each form contained 7 PWP, 7 GWP, 14 SWP and 14 DWP, interspersed in systematically varied sequences.

Apparatus

PCs running the Experimental Run Time System (ERTS) program version 3.26 (Beringer, 1996) were used to present the word pair stimuli and capture the responses with accurate millisecond timing.

Procedure

With the cooperation of local teachers, subjects were taken from class in small groups to a separate room where computers had been set up. Instructions were given orally (in Cantonese or Mandarin) and in English on screen telling them to press the appropriate key as fast as possible to indicate if they thought 'Yes, the words in this word pair have similar meaning' or the opposite. Subjects were encouraged not to worry about earlier answers if they felt they had made a mistake, or pressed the wrong key, as it was more like a game than a test, and no school grades would be affected by their performance.

The L1 test was given before the L2 one, to lessen anxiety. Using the experience of the pilot study, in each test 10 practice items were given, during which time the table and chair height could be adjusted to the child and a check made that they knew which keys to press (the right and left Alt keys marked 'similar' and 'different' in the first language) and had their fingers positioned correctly. Subjects then pressed the space bar to start. Pairs were presented 1.5 cm apart in the centre of the screen, with words in one cm square spaces, black on a light yellow background, for a maximum of 5000 ms, with 500-ms pauses between exposures. Each test took about three minutes and subjects did not report any great difficulty, though several reported thinking they had at times pressed the wrong key.

After the test, subjects filled in a questionnaire in which they had to indicate their first language and brief biographical data and educational background, so we could check if any did not belong to the populations we wished to sample in this respect.

Data analysis

In the background questionnaire 17% of the Taiwan subjects reported Hakka or Taiwanese as their first language rather than Mandarin, though Mandarin is the official language learnt by all and exclusively used in school. Subsequent analyses yielded very similar results whether or not these subjects were included, so they have been included in results reported below, as have some subjects who claimed to be Chinese-English bilinguals. Due to computer glitches, the records of responses of some subjects were incomplete: subjects with usable data numbered 56 in Taiwan and 68 in Hong Kong.

The data was analysed in SPSS and item response times submitted to alpha reliability checking within each commonly defined subset of word pairs within each test form. A few items which were unduly lowering alpha were omitted so that in the end alphas for the subsets averaged to produce scores for pair types ranged from 0.54 to 0.94, mean 0.81. It was not felt surprising that with child subjects new to this type of test it was not possible to obtain alphas above 0.8 for all sets. Mean alphas were understandably higher for the sets of more straightforward SWP (0.858) and DWP (0.882) distracter pairs in both languages than for PWP (0.754) and GWP (0.750).

For the response time analyses below, only times for correct responses were used, which leads to further subjects being dropped, though analyses using all response times, and logs of response times, all produced similar results. The accuracy data were extremely non-normal, but since the arcsine transformed data were not appreciably more normal, and did not generate different significant results, we have retained the raw data (scored 0 wrong, 1 correct) in analyses below.

Results

We performed three-way ANOVAs with place, pair type and language as factors, adopting $p = 0.01$ as the threshold for significance.

Response time results

Table 8.3 gives the mean response times and standard errors for both L1 and L2 responses, in both Taiwan and Hong Kong, on the focal word pairs of interest, PWP and GWP, and on the distracter pairs.

Table 8.3 Descriptive statistics for all response times

		Taiwan				*Hong Kong*			
		Chinese		*English*		*Chinese*		*English*	
Word pair type		*M*	*SE*	*M*	*SE*	*M*	*SE*	*M*	*SE*
PWP	ms	1870	78	1801	72	1606	73	1305	68
GWP	ms	1691	72	1747	85	1744	67	1386	80
SWP	ms	1235	55	1182	37	1168	49	941	33
DWP	ms	1827	73	1741	74	1690	66	1328	67

With respect to the main hypotheses of interest (1 and 2), reflected in the pair type by place interaction (Tables 8.3 and 8.4 and Figure 8.1), we find clear evidence that responses are faster on PWP than GWP in Hong Kong, and the reverse in Taiwan, as predicted. This testifies to the effects of instruction, and is uniform across languages, as there is no significant language by pair type by place interaction. Furthermore, the fact that the language by pair type effect is not significant shows that there is no effect of writing system consistent with the Orthographic Depth Hypothesis (hypothesis 3). If such an effect had been dominant, subjects would have systematically recorded different response times in Chinese for GWP versus PWP than in English, regardless of place, with

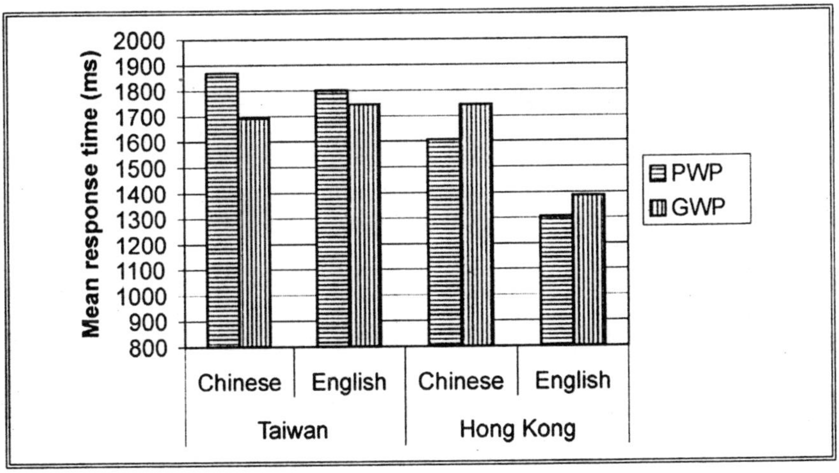

Figure 8.1 Response time results for phonologically similar (PWP) and graphically similar word pairs (GWP)

Table 8.4 ANOVA response time results for phonologically similar (PWP) and graphically similar (GWP) word pairs

Effect	*df*	F	p
Language (Chinese vs English)	1, 111	11.55	0.001
Pair type (PWP vs GWP)	1, 111	0.01	0.915
Place (Taiwan vs Hong Kong)	1, 111	10.10	0.002
Language by Place	1, 111	10.62	0.001
Pair type by Place	1, 111	11.91	0.001
Language by Pair type	1, 111	0.48	0.490
Language by Pair type by Place	1, 111	3.40	0.068

responses to GWP slower on Chinese and responses to PWP slower on English.

The results for the distracters (same and different word pairs, SWP and DWP) were also analysed (Tables 8.3 and 8.5 and Figure 8.2), primarily as a form of construct validation. As we had assumed, all subjects found it vastly easier to judge identical words than different ones (whose response times were similar to the mean response times for PWP and GWP

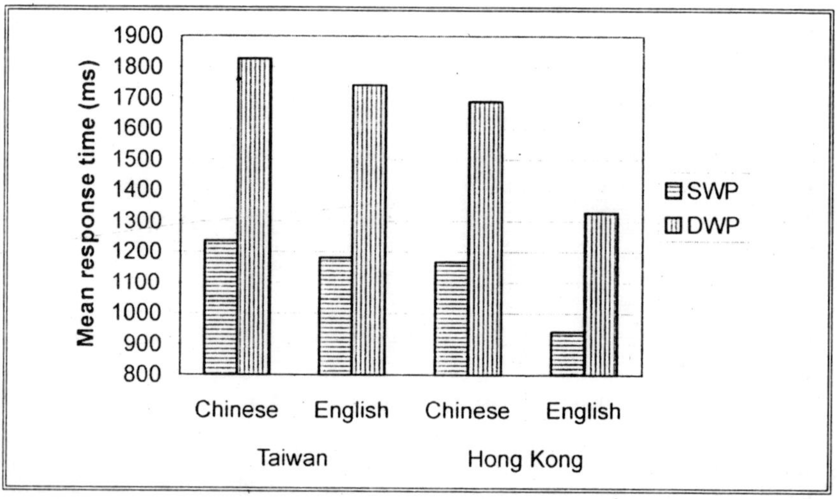

Figure 8.2 Response time results for same (SWP) and different (DWP) word pairs

Table 8.5 ANOVA response time results for same and different word pairs

Effect	*df*	F	p
Language (Chinese vs English)	1, 118	29.34	<0.001
Pair type (SWP vs DWP)	1, 118	294.33	<0.001
Place (Taiwan vs Hong Kong)	1, 118	10.41	0.002
Language by Place	1, 118	11.19	0.001
Pair type by Place	1, 118	4.06	0.046
Language by Pair type	1, 118	4.01	0.047
Language by Pair type by Place	1, 118	1.50	0.223

together), thus supporting the general accuracy of the instruments and procedures (hypotheses 6, 7).

However, both the analyses above show some further effects that we had not entirely anticipated, in the significant language, place and language by place effects (hypotheses 4, 5). In follow-up paired comparisons, and as seen in Figures 8.1 and 8.2, Hong Kong subjects proved significantly faster than Taiwanese on all English pairs, and they were also much faster than themselves on Chinese. Descriptively, Hong Kong subjects were also slightly faster than Taiwanese ones on Chinese, and Taiwanese subjects were also slightly faster on English than Chinese, but these differences are highly non-significant. The response time means for all pairs combined were: Hong Kong–Chinese 1574.6, English 1261.8; Taiwan–Chinese 1659.0; English 1636.4. These effects are independent of pair type and constitute a separate issue from the one we were targeting primarily.

We had expected Hong Kong subjects to be faster than Taiwanese on English, due to differences in the role of English in the educational and social environments mentioned earlier (hypothesis 5), but we had not expected them to be faster than their own performance in L1 Chinese. This may suggest that the effects of the ESL rather than EFL environment in Hong Kong, and greater number of hours on English in school, compared with Taiwan, had a powerful effect, to the extent that subjects were able to respond more rapidly to L2 than L1 stimuli. Also this result may reflect the fact that in assessing word familiarity and attempting to match it between the two places we relied necessarily on separate sets of teachers. Possibly what Hong Kong teachers rated as familiar English words were, due to the ESL context and extra hours of teaching English, in fact considerably *more* familiar to their students than those the Taiwanese teachers regarded as familiar to *their* students. Obviously

Table 8.6 Descriptive statistics for all accuracy scores

Word pair type	*Taiwan*				*Hong Kong*			
	Chinese		*English*		*Chinese*		*English*	
	M	*SE*	*M*	*SE*	*M*	*SE*	*M*	*SE*
PWP	0.72	0.03	0.69	0.03	0.68	0.03	0.83	0.03
GWP	0.75	0.04	0.78	0.04	0.74	0.03	0.78	0.04
SWP	0.90	0.02	0.93	0.02	0.94	0.02	0.96	0.02
DWP	0.81	0.03	0.78	0.03	0.86	0.02	0.89	0.02

it is not impossible to obtain faster response times in the second language (English) than in the first if the L2 words are very easy and the L1 ones more difficult relative to subjects' competence. Furthermore, different teachers judged each language, so it was not possible to be certain of the calibration of the familiarity judgments for the English words with those for the Chinese ones.

Accuracy results

Table 8.6 gives the mean accuracy scores for both L1 and L2 responses, in both Taiwan and Hong Kong, on the focal word pairs of interest, PWP and GWP, and on the distracter pairs.

With respect to our main hypotheses (1–3), the results are as expected in three out of four ways (Table 8.7 and Figure 8.3). Higher accuracy goes with lower response time for both graphically and phonologically similar pair types in both languages in Taiwan, and in English only in Hong Kong. The anomaly, which produces the significant three-way interaction

Table 8.7 ANOVA accuracy results for phonologically similar (PWP) and graphically similar (GWP) word pairs

Effect	*df*	F	p
Language (Chinese vs English)	1, 119	6.76	0.001
Pair type (PWP vs GWP)	1, 119	4.93	0.028
Place (Taiwan vs Hong Kong)	1, 119	0.44	0.509
Language by Place	1, 119	6.06	0.015
Pair type by Place	1, 119	3.23	0.075
Language by Pair type	1, 119	0.86	0.357
Language by Pair type by Place	1, 119	9.24	0.003

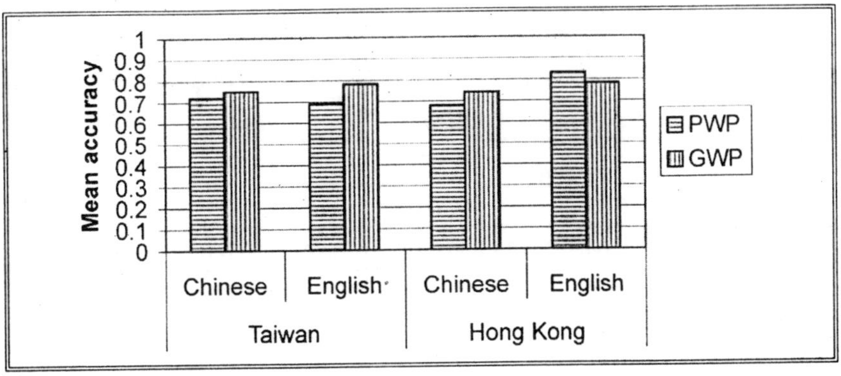

Figure 8.3 Accuracy results for phonologically similar (PWP) and graphically similar (GWP) word pairs

effect, is that the reverse holds for L1 Chinese in Hong Kong. Here the shorter response times go with greater error on PWP, where greater error on GWP was expected, hence the place by pair type interaction is not quite significant. One way of interpreting this would be to say that on L2 English the dominant effect of instruction on accuracy is confirmed (hypothesis 2), just as it was for response time, while on L1 Chinese the writing system effect determines lower accuracy but not longer response time (hypotheses 1 and 3). But is this possible? Why should the response time and accuracy results conflict? While in online word recognition studies it is often conventionally assumed that response time and accuracy results should be related (faster speed – greater accuracy), we do not feel that this should necessarily be so. Response time reflects what

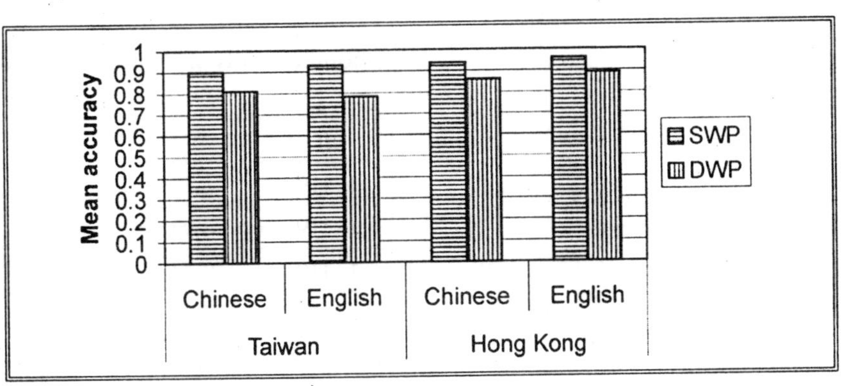

Figure 8.4 Accuracy results for same (SWP) and different (DWP) word pairs

Table 8.8 ANOVA accuracy results for same (SWP) and different (DWP) word pairs

Effect	*df*	F	p
Language (Chinese vs English)	1, 119	0.77	0.383
Pair type (SWP vs DWP)	1, 119	57.65	<0.001
Place (Taiwan vs Hong Kong)	1, 119	5.82	0.017
Language by Place	1, 119	1.06	0.305
Pair type by Place	1, 119	3.21	0.076
Language by Pair type	1, 119	1.61	0.207
Language by Pair type by Place	1, 119	5.51	0.021

subjects may or may not be paying attention to during the process by which a response to a task is computed, while accuracy reflects the product of that computation, which may also be affected by other things, such as the quality of stored knowledge or competence that is accessed during processing. Hence a longer response time may sometimes yield greater accuracy rather than less. It could be that although Hong Kong subjects are more distracted and slowed by graphic similarities than by sound similarities, regardless of language (and consistent with hypotheses 1 and 2), this serves to focus their attention on the fine details of graphic shape more than do PWP; then since for Chinese, due to the nature of the writing system, they (and maybe Taiwanese also) have stored high quality visual shapes for characters, they are able to use the extra time to end up with a more accurate judgment for GWP in L1.

The SWP and DWP accuracy results (Tables 8.6 and 8.8 and Figure 8.4) straightforwardly match the response time results in that subjects are universally better on SWP than on any other word pairs, with accuracy 90% or better (hypotheses 6 and 7). Furthermore, if accuracy results for all pairs are pooled, there is support for the finding from the response time analysis that Hong Kong subjects are notably better on English than Chinese, and indeed better than the Taiwanese subjects on both languages (hypotheses 4 and 5). The accuracy means for all pairs combined were: Hong Kong–Chinese 0.805, English 0.865; Taiwan–Chinese 0.793; English 0.793.

Conclusion

Clearly our work provides further support for the Universal Phonological Principle mentioned earlier, in that, regardless of what route may be used, phonology emerges as playing a role in reading both English and Chinese words in both Hong Kong and Taiwan. Even in Hong Kong, sound similarity slows judgments considerably compared with the 'same word' distracters. There are two things we cannot be categorical about, however, given our design.

First, we cannot be certain *when* access to phonology occurs in the time course of computing the judgment decisions. We cannot totally rule out that some of the effects observed are postlexical, taking place during the part of the task after the words' meanings have been accessed and while the similarity of meaning is being judged. However, we feel this is unlikely, given that the judgment itself did not require any access to sound, and findings such as those of Perfetti and Zhang (1995), which suggest phonology is an essential constituent of 'at-lexical' identification, where it always co-occurs with a word's graphic and meaning constituents to constitute a three-constituent word identity. They claim the evidence from time course studies so far suggests it is semantics, rather than phonology, that is delayed at the character level. The stronger bonding of graphic and phonological form, compared with that of graphic form and meaning (Van Orden & Goldinger, 1994), may operate even in Chinese to explain this.

Second, our study was not designed to distinguish between the processing of either graphic or phonological information in a holistic way versus a segmented way. Hence we cannot say for example if Taiwanese readers were accessing addressed (lexical route) phonology or assembled (phonological route) phonology in either language. Further work would be needed to establish that.

However, the main strength of our study lies in its demonstration, in a more direct way than arises from the many phonological awareness studies, that phonic versus whole word instruction does have an effect on the level of phonological versus graphic activation in the word reading process and that this works in parallel for the same subjects reading in two quite different writing systems, one deep and one less so, and hence supposedly differentially favouring access to phonology. Hence, though the Orthographic Depth Hypothesis may yet have a place in explaining the size and nature of the sound units used in the reading process, it was not in our study supported by any difference in the amount of access to phonology, while the often neglected instruction-based hypothesis clearly was strongly supported. The greater instruction-induced activation of phonology in Taiwan is consistent with the greater phonological awareness identified in other Taiwanese studies, though we did not measure phonological awareness directly ourselves and it is of course a purely phonological variable not necessarily associated with the degree of involvement of phonology in word reading, though often imagined to be. The result is all the more striking as our study focussed on *real, familiar* words read *silently* for *meaning*, all factors which are thought to disfavour phonological activation.

Our design does not of course allow us to determine whether the similarities found between L1 and L2 word recognition are predominantly due to transfer of L1 processing habits induced by L1 instruction, or directly due to L2 instruction. Very likely both are operative. Also of course we cannot say if any of the effects we found would persist in later life, when subjects become distanced from classroom influences on how reading is done.

Finally, the big question for pedagogical applications of such research is, if teaching does affect *how* people read, can we show that any one method is superior to any other, and teach accordingly? Despite some findings in the phonological awareness literature, clearly our study gives no evidence that reading with more or less activation of phonology is superior since neither response time nor accuracy differed overall between Chinese children taught with the two methods, and the differences for English have other more plausible explanations in the differences in the wider role of English in the school and social environment. On this vexed question, the jury remains out.

References

Baluch, B. and Besner, D. (1991) Visual word recognition: Evidence for strategic control of lexical and nonlexical routines in oral reading. *Journal of Experimental Psychology: Learning, Memory, and Cognition* 17, 644–52.

Beringer, J. (1996) *Experimental RunTime System*. Frankfurt: BeriSoft Corporation.

Chabat, R., Zehr, H., Prinzo, O. and Petros, T. (1984) The speed of word recognition subprocesses and reading achievement in college students. *Reading Research Quarterly* 19, 147–61.

Chall, J. (1983) *Learning to Read: The Great Debate*. New York: McGraw-Hill Book Company.

Chen, C. and Juola, J. (1982) Dimensions of lexical coding in Chinese and English. *Memory and Cognition* 10, 216–24.

Coltheart, M. (1978) Lexical access in simple reading tasks. In G. Underwood (ed.) *Strategies of Information Processing* (pp. 151–216). New York: Academic Press.

Frost, R., Katz, L. and Bentin, S. (1987) Strategies for visual word recognition and orthographical depth: A multilingual comparison. *Journal of Experimental Psychology: Human Perception and Performance* 13, 104–15.

Goodman, K. (1967) Reading: A psycholinguistic guessing game. *Journal of the Reading Specialist* 6, 126–35.

Hsia, S. (1995) How beginning reading theories account for second language reading: Implications for teaching word recognition and reading and for pedagogical research in second language reading. *Singapore Book World: Asian Reading Congress 1995. National Book Development Council of Singapore in Association with Society for Reading and Literacy* 25, 117–32.

Huang, H. and Hanley, J. (1995) Phonological awareness and visual skills in learning to read Chinese. *Cognition* 54, 73–98.

Koda, K. (1992) The effects of lower-level processing skills on FL reading performance: Implications for instruction. *The Modern Language Journal* 76, 502–12.

Kučera, H. and Francis, W. (1967) *Computational Analysis of Present Day American English*. Providence, RI: Brown University Press.

LaBerge, D. and Samuels, S.J. (1974) Toward a theory of automatic information processing in reading. *Cognitive Psychology* 6, 293–323.

Lee, S., Stigler, J. and Stevenson, H. (1986) Beginning reading in Chinese. In B. Foorman and A. Siegel (eds) *Acquisition of Reading Skills* (pp. 123–50). Hillsdale, NJ: Lawrence Erlbaum.

Liu, I.-M., Chuang, C.-J. and Wang S.-C. (1975) *Frequency Count of 40,000 Chinese Words* (in Chinese). Taipei, Taiwan: Lucky Books Company.

Perfetti, C. and Zhang, S. (1995) Very early phonological activation in Chinese reading. *Journal of Experimental Psychology: Learning, Memory and Cognition* 21, 24–33.

Pitman, J. and St. John, J. (1969) *Alphabets and Reading: The Initial Teaching Alphabet*. London: Pitman.

Read, C., Zhang, Y., Nie, H. and Ding, B. (1986) The ability to manipulate speech sounds depends on knowing alphabetic writing. *Cognition* 24, 31–45.

Rumelhart, D. (1977) Toward an interactive model of reading. In S. Dornic (ed.) *Attention and Performance VI* (pp. 573–603). Hillsdale, NJ: Lawrence Erlbaum.

Seidenberg, M. (1985) The time course of phonological activation in two writing systems. *Cognition* 19, 1–30.

Seidenberg, M. and McClelland, J. (1989) A distributed development model of word recognition and naming. *Psychological Review* 96, 523–68.

Treiman, R., Baron, J. and Luk, K. (1981) Speech recoding in silent reading: A comparison of Chinese and English. *Journal of Chinese Linguistics* 9, 116–25.

Tzeng, O., Hung, D. and Wang, D. (1977) Speech recoding in reading Chinese characters. *Journal of Experimental Psychology: Human Learning and Memory* 3, 621–30.

Van Orden, G. and Goldinger, S. (1994) The interdependence of form and function in cognitive systems explains perception of printed words. *Journal of Experimental Psychology: Human Perception and Performance* 20, 1269–91.

Chapter 9

Effects of Second Language Reading Proficiency and First Language Orthography on Second Language Word Recognition

NOBUHIKO AKAMATSU

Cross-linguistic effects have been one of the central issues in second language (L2) reading research, in that features of the L2 learners' first language (L1) influence their L2 word recognition. Critical orthographic properties of the first language are considered to play a crucial role in the development of L2 word recognition (Koda, 1996). It has been reported that L1 orthographic features determine:

(1) the type of information on which L2 readers dominantly depend during word-recognition processing (e.g. Chikamatsu, 1996; Koda, 1990, 1998; Mori, 1998);
(2) sensitivity towards intra-word information (e.g. Koda, 1999, 2000; Muljani *et al.*, 1998);
(3) efficiency in processing the components of a word (e.g. Akamatsu, 1999, 2003; Brown & Haynes, 1985).

These findings give the impression that L2 reading researchers are converging on the idea that L2 word-recognition processes are shaped by L1 orthographic features. There are, however, several studies reporting contradictory results (e.g. Akamatsu, 2002; Jackson *et al.*, 1994, 1999). Furthermore, recent studies questioning a simplistic view of L1 effects on L2 reading suggest that L2 reading researchers scrutinize cross-linguistic effects in L2 reading (e.g. Gholamain & Geva, 1999; Koda, 2002).

The present study explores the relationships between L2 reading proficiency and cross-linguistic effects on word recognition. Specifically, the purpose of this study is to investigate whether L2 reading proficiency influences the effects of a non-alphabetic L1 orthography on L2 word-recognition processes.

The relationships between writing systems and reading have attracted attention in L1 reading research. Researchers working with the Orthographic Depth Hypothesis (ODH), for example, found evidence that the extent to which a written form (symbol) represents its corresponding phonological form (sound) determines one's word-recognition processes (e.g. Frost, 1994). Other reading researchers instead highlight similarities, rather than differences, in word-recognition processes among different writing systems. Seidenberg, for example, suggests that what determines word-recognition processes is not orthographic properties such as orthographic depth, but one's accumulative knowledge of spelling (Seidenberg, 1985, 1992). He claims that, regardless of differences in writing systems, all skilled readers process written words via both visual and phonological mediation; the familiarity of printed words determines whether visual or phonological mediation is utilised. Specifically, the words which one is often exposed to and familiar with are recognised on a visual basis, whereas less familiar, low-frequency words are processed via phonological mediation.

These contradictory views of the relationships between writing systems and reading seem to reflect the debates on the transfer of L1 word-recognition processes to L2 reading. Koda (1988, 1990), for example, applying the Orthographic Depth Hypothesis to L2 reading research, suggests that L1 orthography affects L2 word-recognition processes. She found that the Japanese, who have a deep L1 orthography, dominantly utilised orthographic information in recognising English words, whereas the Arabic and Spanish, whose L1 orthography is shallow, relied on phonological information rather than orthographic information in processing English words. Chikamatsu (1996) also found similar results. Examining the performance of Chinese and American learners of Japanese in a lexical decision task, she found that L2 learners with a relatively deeper L1 orthography (i.e. Chinese) were more dependent on orthographic information in L2 word-recognition processes.

Holm and Dodd (1996) also suggest that word-recognition skills developed in a first language may be transferred to a second. They examined the basic word-recognition skills of (ESL) learners with varying L1 backgrounds (i.e. People's Republic of China, Hong Kong, and Vietnam), using different types of task which tap such phonological processing skills as phoneme segmentation, phoneme manipulation and rhyme judgment. The results underscored the poor performance of the Chinese-L1 learners of ESL from Hong Kong; although those from the People's Republic of China shared the same L1 orthography (i.e. Chinese), they showed better phonological processing skills than the Hong Kong group. Holm and Dodd (1996) paid attention to the use of *pinyin* as a possible reason for the difference between the Chinese and Hong Kong groups.

Pinyin, an alphabetic system employing Roman letters, was developed in the People's Republic of China to represent the phonology of the Chinese characters. It has been used to facilitate initial learning of reading Chinese. In Hong Kong, on the other hand, *pinyin* was not introduced. Children in Hong Kong learn to read Chinese in a traditional 'look and say' manner, without the use of an alphabetic system to facilitate the mapping of a character to its corresponding phonological representation. Because the noticeable difference between the Chinese and Hong Kong groups was the use of *pinyin* before their exposure to English, Holm and Dodd concluded that early exposure to the alphabetic scripts enhanced the L2 learner's phonological awareness. Similar results were also reported by Huang and Hanley (1994), who looked into the differences in phonological processing skills in English between Hong Kong children and Taiwanese children.

Akamatsu (1999, 2003) claims that orthographic differences between a L1 and a L2 result in a deficit in L2 word-recognition efficiency. Comparing ESL readers with an alphabetic L1 background (Persian[1]) and those with a non-alphabetic L1 background (Chinese, Japanese), he investigated whether L1 orthographic differences affect L2 word-recognition processes. Asking the ESL learners to read English words printed in normal case and in alternating case, he examined the extent to which case alternation affects ESL readers' word-recognition processing.

Akamatsu (1999, 2003) found that the Chinese and Japanese learners of ESL were more adversely affected by the visual distortion of a written word than were the Persian-L1 learners of ESL. This finding was observed in the context of single word naming as well as text reading. He suggested that, because only Persian has the same orthographic features as English, the Persian-L1 learners of ESL benefited from L1 processing experience, resulting in more efficient word-recognition processes than L2 learners with a non-alphabetic L1 background (i.e. Chinese and Japanese). Brown and Haynes (1985) also reported that the Japanese learners of ESL had more difficulty translating alphabetic symbols into spoken units than ESL learners with a phonologically-based L1 writing system (i.e. Spanish and Arabic).

Viewed collectively, cross-linguistic studies applying the Orthographic Depth Hypothesis or focusing on orthographic differences often find L1 orthographic effects on L2 word-recognition processes. These findings suggest that L1 orthographic features play such a fundamental role in shaping one's word-recognition mechanisms that one may not be able to restore the mechanisms suitable for L2 word recognition. Nonetheless, this does not imply that L1 orthographic features affect L2 word-recognition processes in every aspect; there are some studies reporting similarities in word-recognition processes among L2 readers with varying L1 backgrounds.

Jackson and her colleagues, for example, highlight universal properties of the human mind, rather than specific properties of L1 orthography, in determining L2 word-recognition processes (Jackson *et al.*, 1999). They provided five types of passage, including one printed in alternating case, to learners of EFL from Taiwan, Korea, and Hong Kong, and asked them to read the passages for comprehension. Jackson and her colleagues found no differences in case-alternation effects on reading speed between the EFL learners with a phonologically-based L1 orthography (i.e. the Koreans) and those with a non-phonological L1 orthography (i.e. the Taiwanese). Furthermore, the EFL learners from Hong Kong, who had relatively earlier exposure to English, showed fewer effects of case alternation on reading speed than did the other two EFL groups, suggesting that the timing of L2 readers' exposure to the target language and writing system is more important.

Akamatsu (2002) also emphasises commonalities in L2 word-recognition processes, regardless of differences in the nature of L1 orthography. Applying a converging view among L1 reading researchers that words are processed similarly in all languages (e.g. Baluch & Besner, 1991; Massaro & Cohen, 1994; Seidenberg, 1992), he focused on the relationships between word-frequency and word-regularity effects, and L1 orthographic effects on L2 word-recognition processes.

Word-frequency effects are shown by the way in which high-frequency words are processed more quickly and accurately than low-frequency words; likewise, word-regularity effects are indicated by the quicker and more accurate processing of regular words that follow spelling-to-pronunciation correspondence rules. What makes these effects significant in L1 reading research is the relationship between the two effects; regularity effects are usually modulated by word frequency in word recognition. That is, regularity effects appear only with low-frequency words; high-frequency irregular words are processed as quickly as regular high-frequency words (e.g. Seidenberg, 1985; Seidenberg *et al.*, 1984).

Seidenberg (1985) proposes that the lack of regularity effects in the processing of high-frequency words results from word recognition via visual mediation. When one is often exposed to high-frequency words, the lexical access of these words can be carried out with the orthographic information. The orthographic representations of low-frequency words, on the contrary, are not strong enough to trigger the corresponding semantic information. Accordingly, low-frequency words are processed on a phonological basis, which is influenced by spelling-to-pronunciation correspondence rules. This word-recognition procedure is considered convincing evidence of universality in word-recognition processes because similar findings have been observed in different languages (e.g. Seidenberg, 1985).

Replicating Seidenberg's (1985) study, Akamatsu (2002) examined whether L1 orthographic differences affect the relationship between word-frequency and word-regularity effects in L2 word recognition. Providing monosyllabic English words of varying frequency and regularity to fluent ESL readers with a phonologically-based L1 orthography (Persian) and a non-phonological L1 system (Chinese, Japanese), he asked them to name each word as quickly and as accurately as possible. Results showed that regardless of L1 orthographic differences, the L2 readers named low-frequency regular words more quickly than low-frequency irregular words; no such regularity effects, however, were found in the naming of high-frequency words. These findings led Akamatsu to conclude that, regardless of L1 differences, fluent L2 readers recognise words in the same manner by using such lexical properties as word frequency and regularity. He also underscored similarities in word-recognition processes between a first language and a second language because the results were almost identical to those of Seidenberg's (1985) study with English-L1 adult readers.

Koda (2002) shows her reservations about a simplistic view of cross-linguistic effects on L2 reading and points out the necessity of more studies scrutinising L1 effects on L2 reading. In a series of studies comparing Chinese (with a non-phonological first language orthography) and Korean (with a phonological L1 orthography) learners of ESL, Koda examined L1 effects on critical basic skills and knowledge underlying L2 word recognition. She found that although the Chinese and the Korean ESL learners did not differ in phonemic awareness skills in English, the extent to which phonemic awareness skills contributed to L2 decoding varied due to the influence of L1 processing experience on L2 reading (Koda, 1998). Furthermore, while the Koreans showed high correlations between decoding, reading comprehension and phonemic awareness, the Chinese did not show such a pattern. She also found that in spite of no differences in decoding abilities, the Koreans were more sensitive towards intra-word information in English words (Koda, 1999) and that the Chinese, who were slower than the Koreans in analysing intra-word structures, were more efficient in using morphological and contextual information in sentence processing (Koda, 2000).

These collective results suggest that, although L1 effects on L2 word recognition may not appear at an observable level, the nature of L1 orthography may still have a sustained impact on L2 word-recognition processes at a deeper level. In other words, 'disparate L1 processing experience apparently produces little quantitative difference in L2 decoding skills, but [...] L1-based variations may account for qualitative (i.e. procedural) differences in processing behaviors among L2 learners' (Koda, 1999: 60). Namely, some aspects of L2 word-recognition skills, which develop primarily through accumulated L2 reading experience, are mostly free from cross-linguistic effects. In other respects, however, L1 processing experience largely influences the development of L2 word-recognition processes, resulting in particular characteristics in L2 word-recognition processes that reflect the nature of the L2 learner's L1 writing system.

In summary, cross-linguistic studies of L1 effects on L2 reading often suggest that L1 orthographic features affect L2 word-recognition processes and thus L2 word-recognition processes vary according to the nature of L2 learners' L1 orthography (e.g. Koda, 1999, 2000). In certain aspects of L2 reading, however, L2 readers demonstrate similar word-recognition processes regardless of their L1 differences (e.g. Akamatsu, 2002; Jackson *et al.*, 1999). Reflecting these contradictory findings, recent studies subject the cross-linguistic effects to closer analysis to grasp such a complex mechanism of L1 effects on L2 reading.

There are several critical issues to discuss before the debates on L1 orthographic effects on L2 word recognition reach the final stage; L2 research needs to address at least the two issues:

(1) which aspect of L1 orthographic features affect L2 word recognition, and;
(2) to what extent L1 orthographic features affect L2 word-recognition processes.

The first issue has been explored in several studies (e.g. Koda, 1998, 1999, 2000), but the second question appears not to have been fully examined. One way of addressing the second issue is to examine the relationship between L2 reading proficiency and the impact of L1 effects on L2 word recognition.

Suppose that a certain L1 orthographic property affects L2 word-recognition processes. If the impact of this L1 orthographic effect remains constant regardless of differences in L2 reading proficiency, one can assume that the respective L1 orthographic property profoundly influences the development of L2 word recognition. In contrast, if L2 reading proficiency can reduce the degree of the L1 effect, resulting in similar word-recognition processes among skilled L2 readers with varying L1 backgrounds, then the influence of the particular L1 orthographic property on L2 word recognition may not be so robust.

The present study examined whether the degree of L1 orthographic effects on L2 word recognition varies according to L2 reading proficiency. Focusing on the efficiency of processing the constituent letters, the study investigated the degree to which L1 orthographic features affect Japanese learners of English with differing L2 reading proficiency. The efficiency of processing the constituent letters was chosen as the target aspect of L2 word-recognition skills because previous studies (e.g. Brown & Haynes, 1985) often report that L2 readers with a non-phonological L1 orthography (e.g. Japanese, Chinese) demonstrate a large impact of L1 effects in this particular aspect of word-recognition processes. The main research question of the study was whether an increase in L2 reading proficiency can reduce the degree of L1 orthographic effects on the efficiency of processing the constituent letters in an English word.

Case alternation (i.e. cAsE aLtErNaTiOn) was applied in this study for in-depth analyses of L2 word-recognition mechanisms. Due to the nature of case mixing, case manipulation has been popular in L1 reading research. For example, different types of case manipulation have been used to investigate:

(1) the word shape effect on reading (e.g. Fisher, 1975; Smith, 1969);
(2) the size and nature of perceptual units in word recognition (e.g. Taylor *et al.*, 1977);
(3) the locus of the superiority effects of words over non-words in word recognition (e.g. Bruder, 1978; Coltheart & Freeman, 1974), and;
(4) basic processes in word recognition (e.g. Ehri & Wilce, 1982; Kinoshita, 1987).

The purpose of case manipulation varied according to the nature of research investigations. Nonetheless, this deformation measure was applied because of its significant advantage: although words printed in mixed case have lost word-shape cues, they still preserve spelling patterns, which are important cue values for words. This particular feature allows researchers to look into basic word-recognition processes, which may not appear in data based on the processing of words printed in normal case. In other words, case manipulation could generate data which could provide a plausible basis for inferences about word-recognition mechanisms.

For the purpose of this study, case alternation (mixing lowercase and uppercase letters in an alternating way) was considered to be suitable because the unfamiliar appearance of case-alternating words forces one to pay attention to sequences of individual constituent letters (Paap *et al.*, 1984). It has been reported that skilled readers' recognition of familiar words is not dependent upon word-shape information; skilled readers are not affected by such visual distortion of words as case manipulation (e.g. Adams, 1979). Likewise, there are some studies reporting that the readers who are less efficient in using intra-word information (e.g. grapheme-to-phoneme correspondence rules) tend to be more adversely affected by case alternation (e.g. Baron & Strawson, 1976; Besner & Johnston, 1989). These results, therefore, suggest that if a reader is sensitive to intra-word information and efficient in processing the constituent letters, he or she may not be adversely affected by case alternation, which still preserves spelling patterns. Thus, the impact of case alternation on word recognition could be used as an index of how efficiently one amalgamates the constituent letters in an English word.

There are two hypotheses in this study. The first hypothesis states that a high level of L2 reading proficiency could conceal or reduce L1 orthographic effects on the efficiency of processing the constituent letters in an English word. Thus, more proficient L2 readers should demonstrate a smaller impact of case alternation on word-recognition performance than less proficient L2 readers. An alternative hypothesis is suggested by the findings of previous studies favouring the effects of non-phonological L1 orthographic features on L2 word-recognition processes. Taking the accumulated empirical evidence into consideration, one could speculate that the nature of L1 orthography influences L2 word-recognition processes so deeply that L2 reading proficiency could not affect the degree to which L1 orthographic features affect L2 word-recognition processes. Thus, regardless of differences in L2 reading proficiency, case alternation should affect the processing efficiency of L2 readers with a non-phonological L1 orthography in an equal or a similar manner.

Method

Participants

Two groups were compared. Twenty-three Japanese-L1 learners of EFL who were undergraduate students in a department of English in a Japanese university participated in this study. For an ESL group, the data set of the Japanese participants in Akamatsu's (1999) study was used; they were 16 Japanese-L1 learners of ESL who were graduate students at a Canadian university.

The EFL participants took the same English proficiency test used in Akamatsu (1999); the vocabulary and reading-comprehension section of the Test of English as a Foreign Language (TOEFL) (Educational Testing Service, 1991). The scores of the ESL group (M = 63.8, SD = 2.5) were significantly higher than those of the EFL group (M = 52.1, SD = 2.8) [$t(37) = 13.39$, $p < 0.0001$]; the ESL and EFL groups were labeled as a more proficient and a less proficient group, respectively.

Materials

Replicating Akamatsu (1999), this study used a naming task with the same stimuli, consisting of 40 high-frequency and 40 low-frequency monosyllabic English words. For each frequency-type, there were 20 regular and 20 exception words. Table 9.1 indicates the proportion of stimuli of varying word length, frequency, and regularity. Each stimulus item was used twice in two different case-types (lowercase and alternating case); the total number of stimuli provided to each participant as test trials was therefore 160.

Three word frequency lists were used to calculate the frequency of stimulus words: *American Heritage Word Frequency Book* (Carroll *et al.*, 1971), *Computational Analysis of Present-Day American English* (Kucera &

Table 9.1 Distribution of the stimulus words according to the number of constituent letters

	3-letter-words	*4-letter-words*	*5-letter-words*	*Examples*
High-frequency and regular	2	13	5	both, bOtH
High-frequency and exception	2	13	5	have, hAvE
Low-frequency and regular	2	13	5	tray, tRaY
Low-frequency and exception	1	13	6	tomb, tOmB

Francis, 1967), and *Cambridge English Lexicon* (Hindmarsh, 1980). Each of the three lists used a different pool of words. *American Heritage Word Frequency Book* was created using the words that students from Grades 3–12 in the United States would encounter in major textbooks. Kucera and Francis' word-frequency list, focusing on adults' print exposure, was based on a pool of words that adults would encounter in daily life. The target population of the *Cambridge English Lexicon* was ESL students in Britain and it was based on words in textbooks used for ESL students in Britain. With respect to word regularity, Berndt and his colleagues' list of probabilities for grapheme-to-phoneme correspondences in English was used as a reference (Berndt *et al.*, 1987).

Design

The analysis used a 2 × 2 × 2 × 2 factorial design, with reading proficiency in English (more proficient and less proficient), stimulus case-type (lower and alternating case), stimulus frequency-type (high- and low-frequency) and stimulus regularity-type (regular and exception words) as factors. The data were analysed both by participant and by item. In the participant analysis, the reading proficiency in English was used as a between-subjects factor; in the item analysis, it was used as a within-subjects factor.

Procedure

The experiment consisted of two sessions; in each session the experimental task was administered individually. The interval between sessions was approximately one week.

Each session consisted of two blocks, each of which provided a written instruction, eight practice trials and 40 test trials. The 40 test trials consisted of 10 stimulus items randomly selected from each of the four categories (i.e. high-frequency regular and exception, and low-frequency regular and exception), and the order of presentation of stimulus case-type, frequency-type and regularity-type was counterbalanced across participants.

Each test trial began with an asterisk appearing on the screen for 500 msec to mark the fixation point. Another 500 msec after the disappearance of the fixation mark, the stimulus item was presented and it was displayed until the onset of the participant's vocal response. A masking stimulus (i.e. ######) appeared after the disappearance of the stimulus item for 50 msec. There was a 1-second interval between trials.

Each stimulus word was presented individually in the centre of the screen of a personal computer connected to a real-time clock. The participant was asked to name each stimulus word as quickly and as accurately as possible. The participant read the word aloud into a microphone connected to a voice key of the computer. Reaction time (i.e. latency from the onset of the stimulus to the onset of the participant's response) was automatically recorded via the experimental laboratory software SuperLab. Inappropriate responses (e.g. mispronunciation errors, noise and low voice) were recorded by the experimenter.

Results

The data were analysed using MANOVA across participants and across stimulus items. Tables 9.2 and 9.3 list the means and standard

Table 9.2 The mean reaction times and standard deviations for more and less proficient groups under all conditions

	Reaction time (ms)	
Stimulus	*More proficient readers*	*Less proficient readers*
Lower case		
High-frequency and regular	634.7 (57.2)	740.2 (73.4)
High-frequency and exception	649.3 (63.7)	770.6 (81.8)
Low-frequency and regular	672.9 (70.0)	842.8 (109.9)
Low-frequency and exception	735.7 (103.0)	921.4 (185.5)
Alternating case		
High-frequency and regular	830.6 (165.5)	934.1 (152.1)
High-frequency and exception	872.9 (167.2)	966.4 (154.3)
Low-frequency and regular	1026.4 (238.4)	1169.8 (210.5)
Low-frequency and exception	1022.6 (225.4)	1232.5 (203.5)

Values enclosed in parentheses represent standard deviations.

Table 9.3 The mean error percentages and standard deviations for more and less proficient groups under all conditions

Stimulus	Errors (%)	
	More proficient readers	*Less proficient readers*
Lower case		
High-frequency and regular	0.0 (0.0)	1.5 (2.4)
High-frequency and exception	1.3 (2.2)	4.6 (4.5)
Low-frequency and regular	1.6 (3.0)	6.3 (7.1)
Low-frequency and exception	7.5 (7.3)	12.4 (6.9)
Alternating case		
High-frequency and regular	3.8 (4.3)	3.7 (4.8)
High-frequency and exception	3.8 (5.3)	8.7 (7.4)
Low-frequency and regular	4.4 (5.4)	13.7 (11.2)
Low-frequency and exception	7.8 (8.4)	13.5 (6.3)

deviations for reaction-time and response-accuracy scores (error percentages) for each group under all conditions.

Reaction time

The item analyses revealed that the less proficient group's response accuracy for nine low-frequency exception words ('couch', 'grind', 'pear', 'pearl', 'pint', 'sweat', 'sword', 'tomb', 'worm') was lower than 40%; they were omitted from the analysis. Furthermore, reaction-time scores greater than 2SD from the mean for each participant, across all conditions, were replaced with a value of 2SD from the mean.

The analysis of reaction time (RT) was based on correct responses only. All the main effects were statistically significant.

The more proficient group (M = 805.6, SD = 210.4) recognised stimulus words more quickly than did the less proficient group (M = 947.2, SD = 224.2); by participant: $F(1, 37) = 12.05$, $p < 0.01$; by item $F(1, 134) = 606.86$, $p < 0.0001$.

Lowercase words (M = 759.1, SD = 138.6) were named significantly more quickly than alternating-case words (M = 1019.3, SD = 228.3); by participant: $F(1, 37) = 153.30$; by item $F(1, 134) = 213.51$, $p < 0.0001$ for both.

High-frequency words (M = 809.4, SD = 116.1) were recognised faster than were low-frequency words (M = 968.9, SD = 254.9); by participant: $F(1, 37) = 163.93$; by item $F(1, 134) = 70.70$, $p < 0.0001$ for both.

Regular words (M = 868.1, SD = 223.5) were named significantly more quickly than exception words (M = 910.1, SD = 233.6); by participant: $F(1, 37) = 27.98$, $p < 0.0001$; by item $F(1, 134) = 4.49$, $p < 0.05$.

There was a significant two-way interaction between case type and word frequency (by participant: $F(1, 37) = 57.70$, $p < 0.0001$; by item $F(1, 134) = 9.39$, $p < 0.01$), reflecting the fact that the frequency effect was larger for alternating-case words than for lowercase words. The interaction between reading proficiency and frequency was also significant (by participant: $F(1, 37) = 8.87$, $p < 0.01$; by item $F(1, 134) = 45.10$, $p < 0.0001$), indicating that the less proficient group were more affected in word-recognition time by word frequency than were the more proficient group. The three-way interaction among case type, word frequency, and word regularity was found to be statistically significant only by participant ($F(1, 37) = 4.61$, $p < 0.05$). In naming lowercase words, high-frequency exception words were recognised as quickly as high-frequency regular words, while low-frequency regular words were recognised more quickly than low-frequency exception words ($p < 0.01$). In naming alternating-case words, on the other hand, the participants demonstrated no regularity effects in naming either high- or low-frequency words.

No statistical significance emerged in the interaction between reading proficiency and case type. This reflects the fact that the more proficient group were affected by case alternation as adversely as the less proficient group, suggesting that reading proficiency in English did not influence the degree to which the Japanese-L1 readers of English slowed down in naming English words printed in alternating case (see Figure 9.1).

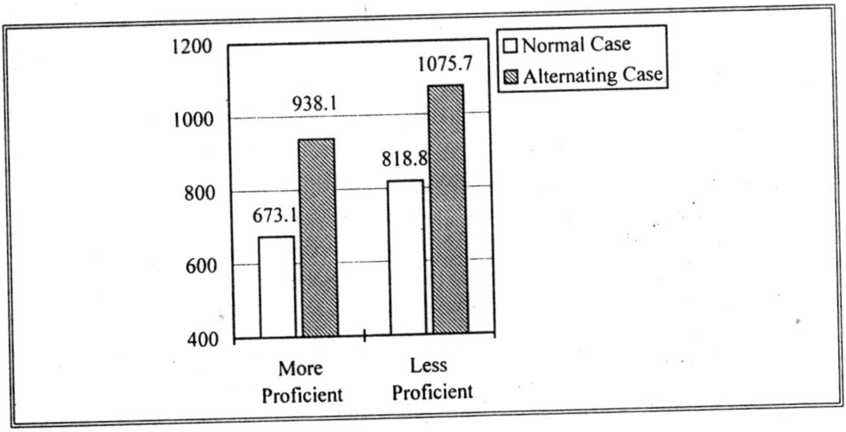

Figure 9.1 Mean reaction-time scores (ms) for each group on lowercase and alternating-case items

Response accuracy

There were three types of response error: consistent incorrect pronunciation, low voice or noise, and mispronunciation. Consistent incorrect pronunciation was coded for the response to the stimulus word whose phonological representation (pronunciation) was incorrectly established by a participant, but whose semantic representation (meaning) was correct. Mispronunciation was coded when a participant responded incorrectly to a stimulus word in spite of knowing its correct pronunciation and meaning. In the response-accuracy analysis, response-error percentage was calculated only on the basis of mispronunciation-type response errors.

As observed in the reaction time analysis, all the main effects were statistically significant.

The more proficient group (M = 5.3, SD = 9.3) recognised stimulus words more accurately than did the less proficient group (M = 10.7, SD = 11.6); by participant: $F(1, 37) = 15.19$, $p < 0.001$; by item $F(1, 152) = 79.68$, $p < 0.0001$.

Lowercase words (M = 6.8, SD = 10.4) were named significantly more accurately than alternating-case words (M = 10.1, SD = 11.4); by participant: $F(1, 37) = 11.97$; by item $F(1, 152) = 7.99$, $p < 0.01$ for both.

The response-error percentage for high-frequency words (M = 3.6, SD = 5.1) was lower than that for low-frequency words (M = 13.3, SD = 13.0); by participant: $F(1, 37) = 51.47$; by item $F(1, 152) = 22.92$, $p < 0.0001$ for both.

Regular words (M = 4.7, SD = 7.2) were named significantly more accurately than exception words (M = 12.3, SD = 12.8); by participant: $F(1, 37) = 26.30$, $p < 0.0001$; by item $F(1, 152) = 7.99$, $p < 0.01$.

The two-way interaction of reading proficiency by frequency was significant (by participant: $F(1, 37) = 7.17$, $p < 0.05$; by item: $F(1, 152) = 14.73$, $p < 0.001$), indicating that only the less proficient group showed statistically significant differences in error percentage between high-frequency words (4.6%) and low-frequency words (11.5%) ($p < 0.0001$). Although the more proficient group also demonstrated frequency effects (2.2% for high-frequency words; 5.3% for low-frequency words), statistical significance did not emerge.

The case-type by word-regularity interaction was significant by participant only ($F(1, 37) = 4.68$, $p < 0.05$). This appears to reflect the fact that the regularity effects in lowercase words were larger than in alternating-case words. The three-way interaction among case type, word frequency, and word regularity was also significant by participant only ($F(1, 37) = 6.9$, $p < 0.05$). In naming lowercase words, high-frequency regular words (0.8%) were recognised as accurately as low-frequency regular words (2.9%), while low-frequency regular words (3.9%) were

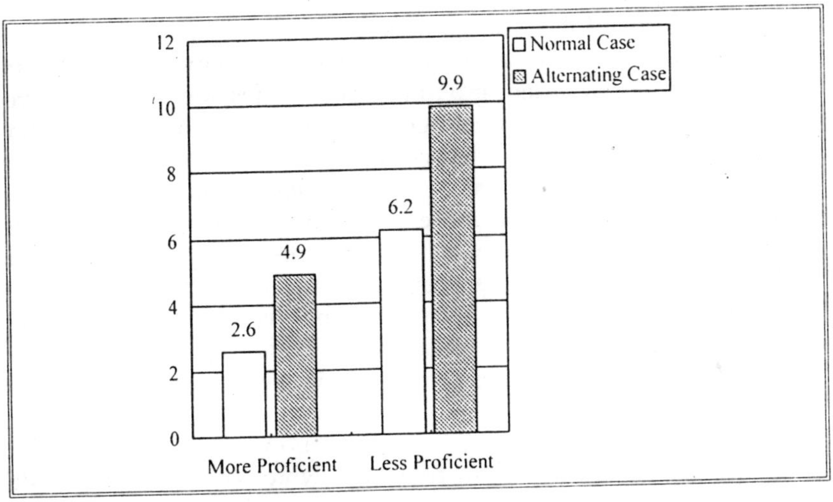

Figure 9.2 Mean error percentages for each group on lowercase and alternating-case items

recognised more accurately than were low-frequency exception words (9.9%). In naming alternating-case words, however, such differences between high- and low-frequency words were not found; there were no regularity effects in either high-frequency words or low-frequency words.

As observed in the RT analysis, the interaction between reading proficiency and case type was found to be statistically not significant in the response-accuracy analysis. This result suggests that, although the less proficient group were slightly more adversely affected by case alternation than the more proficient group, the difference was not large enough to result in statistical significance. Thus, it seems that an increase in reading proficiency in English did not influence the degree to which case alternation affected the word-recognition accuracy of Japanese-L1 readers of English (see Figure 9.2).

Discussion

Results underscored the robustness of the main effects for four variables: word frequency, word regularity, case type and L2 reading proficiency. As expected, high-frequency words were recognised more quickly and more accurately than low-frequency words; regular words were processed more quickly and more accurately than exception words. Furthermore, lowercase words were named more quickly and more accurately than alternating-case words; more proficient L2 readers recognised English words more quickly and more accurately than less proficient L2 readers.

The superiority of the more proficient group was also highlighted in the significant interaction between reading proficiency and word frequency. The more proficient group showed smaller differences in both word-recognition time and accuracy between high- and low-frequency words than did the less proficient group. In other words, the impact of low-frequency words was relatively smaller for the more proficient L2 readers, suggesting that the more proficient group were more often exposed to low-frequency words than were the less proficient group. This relation between reading proficiency and word-frequency effects has been pointed out in the comparison between L1 and L2 readers (e.g. Akamatsu, 1999; Muljani *et al.*, 1998). Word-frequency effects are usually modulated by reading proficiency in word recognition; highly proficient readers process low-frequency words as quickly and as accurately as high-frequency words, resulting in no word-frequency effects. Thus, the smaller impact of low-frequency words on word-recognition processes for the more proficient L2 readers in this study appears to imply that L2 reading experience (i.e. exposure to L2 words) contributes to L2 word-recognition speed and accuracy.

Results also showed that case alternation interacted with word frequency and word regularity in different manners. Regardless of differences in L2 reading proficiency, the differences in word-recognition time between high- and low-frequency words were much larger for words in alternating case than for those in lower case. This may be simply due to scaling effects: because the participants had to slow down when processing alternating-case words, the impact of word frequency on word-recognition time increased. However, such differences were not observed.

However, with respect to the interaction between case type and word regularity, statistical significance emerged in word-recognition accuracy rather than in word-recognition time; the differences in word-recognition accuracy between regular and exception words in lower case were larger than those in alternating case. It seems that the effects of word regularity on word-recognition accuracy disappeared with the loss of word-shape information due to case alternation. The same impact of case alternation was observed in the significant three-way interaction among case type, word frequency, and word regularity in both word-recognition time and accuracy. Regardless of differences in L2 reading proficiency, high-frequency regular words in lower case were recognised as quickly and as accurately as low-frequency exception words in lower case. Low-frequency regular words in lower case, on the contrary, were recognised more quickly and more accurately than were low-frequency exception words in lower case. In naming alternating-case words, however, L2 readers demonstrated no such regularity effects either in word-recognition time or accuracy.

An important finding of this study was the lack of a statistically significant interaction between reading proficiency and case type in either word-recognition time or accuracy. This finding supported the second hypothesis of this study that the nature of L1 orthography affects L2 word-recognition processes so deeply that L2 reading proficiency could not influence L1 orthographic effects on the efficiency of processing the constituent letters in an English word. This hypothesis was proposed on the basis of the accumulated empirical evidence of previous studies of the effects of non-phonological L1 orthographic features on L2 word-recognition processes.

Previous studies suggest that the nature of L1 orthographic features plays a fundamental role in the development of various aspects of L2 word-recognition, such as sensitivity towards L2 intra-word information (e.g. Koda, 1999; Muljani *et al.*, 1998), L2 phonological awareness (e.g. Holm & Dodd, 1996; Huang & Hanley, 1994), L2 morphological awareness (e.g. Koda, 2000), and efficiency in L2 word-recognition processing (e.g. Akamatsu, 1999, 2003; Brown & Haynes, 1985). In Akamatsu's (1999, 2003) studies, for example, L2 readers with a non-phonological L1 orthography (Chinese and Japanese) demonstrated less efficiency in word-recognition processing in English than those with a phonological L1 background (Persian). He explains that the inefficiency may result from differences in the course of word-recognition development between a phonological and non-phonological orthography.

In learning to read in English, children go through different phases before they can recognise words by sight; among the developmental phases of sight word reading, the amalgamated alphabetic phase is vital in order to acquire full knowledge of letter-sound correspondence rules (Ehri, 1992, 1995). Only after one goes through the amalgamated alphabetic phase and understands how the constituent letters are connected to the corresponding sounds, can one read sight words via grapheme-to-phoneme correspondence rules. In other words, 'complete and repeated attention to sequences of individual letters' enables one to read sight words in a skilful manner (Adams, 1990: 130).

In learning to read a non-alphabetic language, however, it seems that one does not need to experience a phase like the amalgamated alphabetic phase. *Kanji* is known as a deep orthography in which the relation between sound and print is complex and thereby the orthographic information of a word is unreliable for its phonological retrieval (Taylor & Taylor, 1995). The majority of *kanji* characters have two types of phonological representation: the *on*-reading (*on-yomi*, or 'Chinese pronunciation') and the *kun*-reading (*kun-yomi*, or 'Japanese pronunciation'). The *on*-reading reflects the historical and dialectal, phonological features of original Chinese characters. Because some *kanji* characters were introduced more than once from different regions in China or in several historical periods, those kanji have multiple on-readings, i.e. more than one Chinese-derived pronunciation. According to the database developed by Tamaoka *et al.* (2002), 262 kanji characters have multiple on-readings among the 1,945 basic kanji characters (which cover approximately 99% of all kanji characters used in Japanese newspapers). The *kun*-reading, on the other hand, is based on the Japanese translation of the original Chinese character, and thus, phonologically, it bears no relation to the *on*-reading (Taylor & Taylor, 1995).

With respect to the *on*-reading, one simply must retrieve it from memory. Normally there are few, if any, phonological clues in the components of a *kanji* character. In contrast, to retrieve the *kun*-reading, one could use a basic component called the phonetic radical, although the predictability of appropriate pronunciation from the phonetic radicals is relatively low (Kess & Miyamoto, 1999). The phonological retrieval from the phonetic radical does not involve the computational processing of the components of a word but simply retrieving the phonological forms from the radicals as a whole.

Akamatsu (2003) proposes that not encountering the amalgamated alphabetic phase in a first language may cause L2 readers with a non-alphabetic L1 background to become inefficient in processing the constituent letters in an alphabetic word. He argues that critical phases of development in learning to read words by sight differ according to the nature of orthography and that such differences may result in particular cross-linguistic effects on L2 word-recognition processes. Furthermore, considering the present study's findings, one could speculate that L1 orthographic features may deeply affect L2 word-recognition development.

As mentioned above, this study found no statistically significant interaction between reading proficiency and case type in either word-recognition time or accuracy. This lack of interaction indicates that regardless of differences in reading proficiency in English, Japanese-L1 readers of English were adversely affected by case alternation in word-recognition speed and accuracy. In other words, an increase in L2 reading proficiency could not diminish the degree of non-phonological L1 orthographic effects on the efficiency of processing the constituent letters in an English word. This appears to imply that even a high level of L2 reading ability could not eliminate, or even reduce, transfer effects that are specific to L1 word-recognition processing. This finding also suggests that L2 readers with the same L1 processing experience may develop their L2 word-recognition processes in a similar manner.

In a first language orthography, through cumulative exposure, one improves word-recognition ability, and develops word-recognition skills and strategies. Although there may be some individual differences, L1 processing experience (e.g. the amount of print exposure) is considered as a major factor in determining one's word-recognition processes (e.g. Frost, 1994; see Seidenberg, 1992 for an alternative view). In a second language, in contrast, both L1 and L2 processing experiences intertwine in contributing to L2 word-recognition development (Koda, 2000). Thus, L2 readers, who are equally exposed to L2 print, may develop different L2 word-recognition processes deriving from their particular L1 processing experiences. Likewise, L2 readers with the same L1 processing experience could show different L2 word-recognition ability, if the amount of their L2 print exposure differs.

In Koda's (1999) study, for example, the Koreans (L2 readers with an alphabetic L1 background) and the Chinese (L2 readers with a non-alphabetic L1 background) were equally proficient in L2 reading and word-recognition processing, and yet, the Koreans were more sensitive towards intra-word information in English words. Moreover, the contribution of phonological awareness to L2 decoding was greater for the Koreans than for the Chinese, even though there were no differences in phonemic awareness skills between the Koreans and the Chinese[2] (Koda, 1998). Interpreting these differences between the Koreans and the Chinese learners of ESL as cross-linguistic effects on L2 word-recognition processes, Koda (1998, 1999, 2000) proposed the notion of quantitative and qualitative differences in L2 word recognition. She argued that L1 processing experience tends to result in little difference in observable L2 word-recognition performance (i.e. quantitative difference), whereas L1 effects may reflect the foundational skills or processes underlying L2 word-recognition (i.e. qualitative difference).

In contrast with Koda's (1998, 1999) studies, the present study focused on L2 readers with the same L1 orthographic background who differed in L2 reading proficiency and found that L2 processing experience produced little difference in the efficiency of processing the constituent letters in English words for the Japanese learners of ESL. In other words, L2 readers with a non-phonological L1 background did not differ in the ability to amalgamate the component letters of an alphabetic word, even though they varied in L2 reading proficiency and word-recognition performance. Thus, following Koda's notion of quantitative and qualitative differences in L2 word-recognition processes, this finding suggest that L2 readers with the same L1 orthographic background can be different at an observable level (i.e. quantitatively different) and yet be the same in such a critical underlying ability for alphabetic readers as processing constituent letters (i.e. qualitatively the same). This underscores the profound impact of L1 orthographic effects on qualitative differences in L2 word-recognition processes.

In summary, this study investigated whether L2 reading proficiency influences the degree to which L1 orthographic features affect L2 word-recognition processes. Results showed that, regardless of differences in

L2 reading proficiency, case alternation adversely affected the L2 word-recognition performance (word-recognition speed and accuracy) of Japanese-L1 readers of ESL to the same degree. This suggest that L2 processing experience produces little difference in the efficiency of processing the constituent letters in an English word for L2 readers with a non-phonological L1 orthography, thereby underlining the impact of L1 orthographic effects on L2 word-recognition processes.

Acknowledgements

I am very grateful to Vivian Cook and Benedetta Bassetti for their insightful comments on the early version of this chapter. I also acknowledge their patience. Preparation for this chapter was supported with the aid of Doshisha University's Research Promotion Fund (2001).

Notes

1. The Persian alphabet, which was slightly modified from Arabic, consists of 32 letters. All the letters are primarily used as consonants; three of them are also used as vowels. These three letters represent half of the six spoken vowels in Persian. The other half of the vowels are represented by diacritics, usually omitted in text. Diacritic spelling is used only for children or beginning readers (Thackston, 1978).
2. This may appear to contradict the results of the study, namely, that L1 orthographic features affect L2 word-recognition processes; the focus of Koda's study, however, differed from that of this study. Koda explored L1 effects on L2 phonological awareness skills, while this study investigated L1 effects on the efficiency of processing the constituent letters in a L2. Thus, these seemingly different findings suggest that L1 orthographic features do not necessarily affect every aspect of L2 word-recognition processing.

References

Adams, M. (1979) Models of word recognition. *Cognitive Psychology* 11, 133–76.

Adams, M. (1990) *Beginning To Read: Thinking and Learning about Print*. Cambridge, MA: The MIT Press.

Akamatsu, N. (1999) The effects of first language orthographic features on word recognition processing in English as a second language. *Reading and Writing: An Interdisciplinary Journal* 11 (4), 381–403.

Akamatsu, N. (2002) A similarity in word-recognition procedure among L2 readers with different L1 backgrounds. *Applied Psycholinguistics* 23 (1), 117–33.

Akamatsu, N. (2003) The effects of first language orthographic features on second language reading in text. *Language Learning* 53 (2), 207–31.

Baluch, B. and Besner, D. (1991) Visual word recognition: Evidence for strategic control of lexical and nonlexical routines in oral reading.

Journal of Experimental Psychology: Learning, Memory and Cognition 17 (4), 644–52.

Baron, J. and Strawson, C. (1976) Use of orthographic and word-specific knowledge in reading words aloud. *Journal of Experimental Psychology: Human Perception and Performance* 2 (3), 386–93.

Berndt, R., Reggia, J. and Mitchum, C. (1987) Empirically derived probabilities for grapheme-to-phoneme correspondences in English. *Behavior Research Methods, Instruments, and Computers* 19 (1), 1–9.

Besner, D. and Johnston, J. (1989) Reading and the mental lexicon: On the uptake of visual information. In W. Marslen-Wilson (ed.) *Lexical Representation and Process* (pp. 291–316). Cambridge, MA: MIT Press.

Brown, T. and Haynes, M. (1985) Literacy background and reading development in a second language. In H. Carr (ed.) *The Development of Reading Skills* (pp. 19–34). San Francisco: Jossey-Bass.

Bruder, G. (1978) Role of visual familiarity in the word-superiority effects obtained with the simultaneous-matching task. *Journal of Experimental Psychology: Human Perception and Performance* 4, 88–100.

Carroll, J., Davies, P. and Richman, B. (1971) *The American Heritage: Word Frequency Book*. New York: American Heritage Publishing.

Chikamatsu, N. (1996) The effects of L1 orthography on L2 word recognition: A study of American and Chinese learners of Japanese. *Studies in Second Language Acquisition* 18, 403–32.

Coltheart, M. and Freeman, R. (1974) Case alternation impairs word identification. *Bulletin of the Psychonomic Society* 3, 102–4.

Educational Testing Service (1991) *Reading for TOEFL* (2nd edn). Princeton, NJ: Official TOEFL Publication.

Ehri, L. (1992) Reconceptualising the development of sight word reading and its relationship to recoding. In P. Gough, L. Ehri and R. Treiman (eds) *Reading Acquisition* (pp. 107–43). Hillsdale, NJ: Lawrence Erlbaum Associates.

Ehri, L. (1995) Phases of development in learning to read words by sight. *Journal of Research in Reading* 18, 116–25.

Ehri, L. and Wilce, L. (1982) Recognition of spellings printed in lower and mixed case: Evidence for orthographic images. *Journal of Reading Behaviour* 14 (3), 219–30.

Fisher, D. (1975) Reading and visual search. *Memory and Cognition* 3, 188–96.

Frost, R. (1994) Prelexical and postlexical strategies in reading: Evidence from a deep and a shallow orthography. *Journal of Experimental Psychology: Learning, Memory, and Cognition* 20 (1), 116–29.

Gholamain, M. and Geva, E. (1999) Orthographic and cognitive factors in the concurrent development of basic reading skills in English and Persian. *Language Learning* 49 (2), 183–217.

Hindmarsh, R. (1980) *Cambridge English Lexicon*. Cambridge: Cambridge University Press.

Holm, A. and Dodd, B. (1996) The effect of first written language on the acquisition of English literacy. *Cognition* 59, 119–47.

Huang, H. and Hanley, J. (1994) Phonological awareness and visual skills in learning to read Chinese and English. *Cognition* 54, 73–98.

Hung, D. and Tzeng, O. (1981) Orthographic variations and visual information processing. *Psychological Bulletin*, 90, 377–414.

Jackson, N., Lu, W.-H. and Ju, D. (1994) Reading Chinese and reading English: Similarities, differences, and second-language reading. In V. Berninger (ed.) *The Varieties Of Orthographic Knowledge I: Theoretical and Developmental Issues* (pp. 73–110). Dordrecht, The Netherlands: Kluwer Academic Publishers.

Jackson, N., Chen, H., Goldsberry, L., Kim, A. and Vanderwerff, C. (1999) Effects of variations in orthographic information on Asian and American readers' English text reading. *Reading and Writing: An Interdisciplinary Journal* 11 (4), 345–79.

Kess, J. and Miyamoto, T. (1999) *The Japanese Mental Lexicon: Psycholinguistic Studies of Kana and Kanji Processing*. Amsterdam: John Benjamins.

Kinoshita, S. (1987) Case alternation effect: Two types of word recognition? *The Quarterly Journal of Experimental Psychology* 39A, 701–20.

Koda, K. (1988) Cognitive process in second language reading: Transfer of L1 reading skills and strategies. *Second Language Research* 4, 135–56.

Koda, K. (1990) The use of L1 reading strategies in L2 reading: Effects of L1 orthographic structures on L2 phonological recoding strategies. *Studies in Second Language Acquisition* 12, 393–410.

Koda, K. (1996) L2 word recognition research: A critical review. *The Modern Language Journal* 80 (4), 450–60.

Koda, K. (1998) The role of phonemic awareness in second language reading. *Second Language Research* 14, 194–215.

Koda, K. (1999) Development of L2 intraword orthographic sensitivity and decoding skills. *Modern Language Journal* 83 (1), 51–64.

Koda, K. (2000) Cross-linguistic variations in L2 morphological awareness. *Applied Psycholinguistics* 21 (3), 297–320.

Koda, K. (2002) Writing systems and learning to read in a second language. In W. Li, J. Gaffney and J. Packard (eds) *Chinese Children Reading Acquisition: Theoretical And Pedagogical Issues* (pp. 225–48). Boston, MA: Kluwer Academic Publishers.

Kucera, H. and Francis, W. (1967) *Computational Analysis of Present-Day American English*. Providence, RI: Brown University Press.

Massaro, D.W. and Cohen, M.M. (1994) Visual, orthographic, phonological, and lexical influences in reading. *Journal of Experimental Psychology: Human Perception and Performance* 20, 1107–28.

Mori, Y. (1998) Effects of first language and phonological accessibility on Kanji recognition. *The Modern Language Journal* 82 (1), 69–82.

Muljani, D., Koda, K. and Moates, D. R. (1998) The development of word recognition in a second language. *Applied Psycholinguistics* 19 (1), 99–113.

Paap, K., Newsome, S. and Noel, R. (1984) Word shape's in poor shape for the race to the lexicon. *Journal of Experimental Psychology: Human Perception and Performance* 10, 413–28.

Seidenberg, M. (1985) The time course of phonological code activation in two writing systems. *Cognition* 19, 1–30.

Seidenberg, M. (1992) Beyond orthographic depth in reading: Equitable division of labor. In R. Frost and L. Katz (eds) *Orthography, Phonology, Morphology, and Meaning* (pp. 85–118). Amsterdam: Elsevier Science.

Seidenberg, M., Waters, G., Barnes, M. and Tanenhaus, M. (1984) When does irregular spelling or pronunciation influence word recognition? *Journal of Verbal Learning and Verbal Behavior* 23, 383–404.

Smith, F. (1969) Familiarity of configuration vs. discriminability of features in the visual identification of words. *Psychonomic Science* 14, 261–63.

Tamaoka, K., Kirsner, K., Yanase, Y., Miyaoka, Y. and Kawakami, M. (2002) A Web-accessible database of characteristics of the 1,945 basic Japanese kanji. *Behavior Research Methods, Instruments and Computers* 34, 260–75.

Taylor, G., Miller, T. and Juola, J. (1977) Isolating visual units in the perception of words and nonwords. *Perception and Psychophysics* 21, 377–86.

Taylor, I. and Taylor, M. (1995) *Writing and Literacy in Chinese, Korean, and Japanese*. Amsterdam: John Benjamins.

Thackston, W. (1978) *An Introduction to Persian*. Tehran, Iran: Soroush Press.

Chapter 10

Bilingual Interactive Activation Models of Word Recognition in a Second Language

WALTER J. B. VAN HEUVEN

Introduction

Reading is a most intriguing human cognitive skill. Humans are able to read texts at an average rate of 300 words per minute (Rayner & Pollatsek, 1989). During this process readers must not only identify line segments as letters and letter strings as words, but they must also derive the meaning and sound of the sequence of words in each sentence. A central component of reading is visual word recognition, a process that has been studied extensively by cognitive psychologists over the last 30 years. While this research has mainly focused on the recognition process in monolinguals, in the last decade research on bilingual visual word recognition has increased considerably. This is important because more than 50% of the world's population is bilingual (Grosjean, 1982).

Research on bilingual visual word recognition stimulates our understanding of the underlying representations and mechanisms of the language system of the bilingual but also that of the monolingual. In this chapter, I begin with a short overview of some empirical findings concerning the characteristics of the visual word recognition system of a bilingual reader. These characteristics have been used to develop computational models of this process. Next, I will outline why computational modelling is a very useful tool to understand and analyse the visual word recognition system. This will be further illustrated when I describe bilingual interactive activation models that are able to simulate a number of empirical findings of visual word recognition in a second language.

Issues and Findings in Bilingual Visual Word Recognition

Research on bilingual visual word recognition has mainly been concerned with the question of whether word reading in one language is affected by the knowledge of words from the other language. If a bilingual were just two monolinguals in one person, the two language systems would be completely separated. However, a more likely possibility would be that bilinguals have one combined language system for both their languages. In the literature, these positions have been investigated in relation to the issue of storage (memory) and access to words (processing) of both languages. The focus in the literature has been on contrasting (1) language selective access in independent lexicons with (2) language non-selective access into an integrated lexicon (Van Heuven *et al.*, 1998). Both viewpoints are depicted in Figure 10.1. According to the first viewpoint (Figure 10.1, left), the word recognition process of bilinguals is not affected by their knowledge of the other language, while according to the second viewpoint (Figure 10.1, right) the influence of the knowledge of the other language on word recognition in one language can be noticed. These theoretical viewpoints on bilingual visual word recognition have been investigated in different experimental tasks in the first (L1) or second (L2) language of the bilingual, using various sorts of stimulus material. In the next sections, I will describe word types that have been used by researchers in experiments and their findings.

Before I do so, I need to comment on the type of bilinguals used by researchers. Many bilinguals are not perfect balanced bilinguals who learned both languages simultaneously from birth. Most are non-balanced bilinguals who learned the second language after the age of about 10 and who became proficient in it as students. They use their second language for study and leisure, but not necessarily every day or

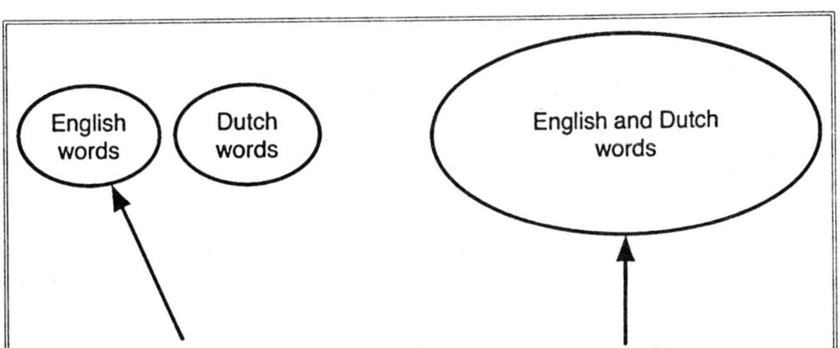

Figure 10.1 Two viewpoints on lexical organisation and processing. Left: (1) selective access in independent lexicons (e.g. to English words only). Right (2) non-selective access to an integrated lexicon of Dutch and English words

regularly. The participants in the experiments reported below are, unless noted otherwise, such non-balanced bilinguals.

I should also point out that the research overview presented here is not complete as it focuses on studies that investigated effects of cross-linguistic identity and similarity (for overviews see Dijkstra, in press; Grainger, 1993; Keatley, 1992). Furthermore, these studies are important for the current chapter because their findings have been used to develop and evaluate interactive activation models of bilingual word recognition.

Cross-linguistic identity: Homographs and cognates

One of the interesting aspects of bilingual readers is that the two languages that they have learned can be closely related (e.g. Dutch and English). As a consequence, words from both languages are often spelled identically. For example, the English word 'room' is also a Dutch word, but its meaning in Dutch is completely different from that in English, namely 'cream'. Identically spelled words between two languages but with a different meaning are called *interlingual* (or *interlexical*) *homographs* or false friends. In contrast, words that are written the same and have (largely) the same meaning in both languages are called *cognates* (e.g. <storm>). In Dutch and English, words with the same written form (which I will refer to in this chapter as 'orthography') are quite common. In fact, there are more than 1080 written words between 3 and 6 letters in length that are words in Dutch as well as in English (Timmermans, 1996). About one-fifth are interlingual homographs (with a different meaning) while the others are cognates (having more or less the same meaning).

Cognates and interlingual homographs have two interesting aspects that can be used to investigate bilingual word recognition. First, because interlingual homographs (henceforth also referred to as 'homographs') exist in two languages, the number of times they are encountered by a bilingual in each language can be different (e.g. the English reading of <room> is more frequent than the Dutch reading of <room>). Thus, there can be a difference in relative frequency between the two readings. Second, while the orthographic form in the two languages is identical for cognates and homographs, homographs have a completely different meaning in each language. Furthermore, pronunciation of homographs and cognates in each language can be similar – the Dutch-English cognate 'film' is pronounced as /fɪlm/ in both languages – or different – pronunciation of the Dutch-English homograph 'room' in English is /ruːm/ while the pronunciation in Dutch is /roːm/. These issues of frequency and similarity in terms of orthography and phonology can be used to investigate bilingual visual word recognition, because a selective access model would not predict any effect of the relative frequency differences and orthographic/phonological overlap of homographs and cognates because the storage of words and access to them are language specific, while a non-selective access model would predict effects of these characteristics because words of both language become active in an integrated lexicon. Related questions are, for example, how do bilinguals distinguish the two meanings of a homograph? And does the context in which these words occur have an effect on how they are processed? Consider, for example, words from the second language presented in a pure list of L2 words versus those presented in a mixed list of L1 and L2 words.

Dijkstra *et al.* (1998b) conducted a series of experiments to investigate the effects of the relative frequency differences of the two readings of homographs and cognates. They also investigated the role of stimulus list composition. In their first experiment, Dutch-English bilinguals performed an English lexical decision task. Participants in this task have to decide as quickly as possible whether a letter string presented on the screen is a correct English word (e.g. <list>) or not (e.g. <blan>) and press the corresponding response button. In this experiment, homographs and cognates were intermixed with English control words and pseudowords. For homographs, the word frequency (low or high) of homographs was varied orthogonally in Dutch and English. The results revealed that response times to homographs were not significantly different from those to English control words. This finding might be seen as support for a selective access model of bilingual word recognition, because participants were not affected by the Dutch reading of the homographs. However, reaction times to cognates presented in the same experiment were significantly faster than to English control words, supporting the view of non-selective access to an integrated lexicon.

The next two experiments of Dijkstra *et al.* (1998b) also supported the latter view because the result pattern indicated that bilinguals were not able to read homographs without being affected by Dutch words presented in the same list. While in the first experiment participants conducted an English lexical decision task in a purely English list context (no purely Dutch words were presented), the word list in the second experiment contained also purely Dutch words. Participants were instructed to press the 'No' button in case of such Dutch words, because they are not English words.

Reaction times to interlingual homographs were now much slower than to English control words. In the third experiment, subjects conducted a generalised lexical decision task in which they had to press the 'Yes' button when a string of letters was a Dutch or an English word and the 'No' button when the string was not a word. This third experiment led to much faster reaction times for interlingual homographs. Only a model assuming non-selective access to an integrated lexicon can account for this pattern of results.

The same conclusion was drawn by De Groot *et al.* (2000) who also conducted three experiments with interlingual homographs. In their first experiment they used a translation recognition task in which Dutch–English bilinguals had to decide whether or not two words presented simultaneously on the screen were translation equivalents. The other two experiments used the lexical decision task. The overall pattern of results revealed slower reaction times to homographs than to control words, supporting the viewpoint of non-selective access to an integrated lexicon. Note that the size of the inhibition effects in both De Groot *et al.* (2000) and Dijkstra *et al.* (1998b) varied with the relative frequency of the Dutch and English reading of the interlingual homograph. For example, in the second experiment of Dijkstra *et al.* (1998b), when the frequency of the Dutch reading was higher relative to the English frequency, stronger inhibition effects were found.

As indicated above, apart from their relative frequency in the two languages, homographs and cognates differ in the similarity of their pronunciation. Dijkstra *et al.* (1999) pointed out that this overlap in phonology has been neglected in many studies. In the case of the Dutch-English cognate <film>, the pronunciation in Dutch and English is very similar (/fɪlm/), while in the case of the cognate <type> the pronunciation is very different (e.g. Dutch /ti:pə/ and English /taɪp/). Dijkstra *et al.* (1999) investigated the role of such cross-linguistic similarity of orthography (O), phonology (P) and semantics (S) in two experiments. Dutch-English cognates (with similar meaning) were selected with either a similar pronunciation in Dutch and English (SOP items, e.g. <film>) or a different pronunciation (SO items, e.g. <type>). In addition, homographs (with different meaning) were selected with either a similar pronunciation in Dutch and English (OP items, e.g. <brief> pronounced as /bri:f/ in both Dutch and English) or a different phonology (O items, e.g. <room>). Furthermore, items were selected with a similar meaning and phonology but a different orthography in Dutch and English (SP items), such as the English word <cliff> and the Dutch word <klif>, which have the same meaning and phonology (/klɪf/). Finally, English words were selected with a similar pronunciation to Dutch words but with a different orthography and meaning (P items), such as the English word <leaf> and Dutch <lief> ('sweet'), both pronounced as /li:f/.

Using these items, Dijkstra *et al.* (1999) conducted experiments in L2 English with Dutch–English bilinguals involving English lexical decision and progressive demasking. In a progressive demasking experiment, the presentation of a target word is alternated with the presentation of a mask (e.g. a row of hash marks <####>). The sequence starts with a long presentation of a mask (e.g. 300 ms) followed by a short presentation (e.g. 15 ms) of the target string. In the subsequent sequences, the presentation time of the mask decreases while the presentation time of the target increases. The participants have to press a button as soon as they have identified the target word. This progressive demasking technique is less sensitive to strategies than lexical decision and therefore is a better reflection of the visual word recognition process (Snodgrass & Mintzer, 1993). The lexical decision and progressive demasking results revealed that, relative to English control words, overlap in semantics and orthography produced a facilitation effect, while overlap in phonology produced an inhibition effect. Again, this pattern of results can only be explained by a bilingual model of word recognition that assumes non-selective access to an integrated lexicon.

Cross-linguistic similarity: Orthographic neighbours

Another stimulus type that has been used to study the bilingual word recognition system is words that are orthographically similar but not identical across languages. For example, the English word <cord> and the Dutch word <bord> ('plate'), differ in only one letter. Such orthographically similar words are called *orthographic neighbours*. Coltheart *et al.* (1977) defined a neighbour as a word that can be created by changing a single letter of a target word. Research on monolingual readers has shown that the number (*neighbourhood density*) and frequency (*neighbourhood frequency*) of orthographic neighbours affect target word processing. For example, the English word <evil> differs from the word <burn> in terms of their neighbourhood density: <evil> has no orthographic neighbours in English while <burn> has several orthographic neighbours in English (e.g. <turn>, <born>, <barn> and <bury>). An example of neighbourhood frequency differences between words are the English words <burn> and <bowl>. Both words have seven orthographic neighbours and about the same word frequency but they differ in the number of neighbours that have a higher word frequency than themselves: <bowl> has no neighbours that have higher frequency, while <burn> has two neighbours that have a higher frequency (<born> and <turn>). For overviews of effects of neighbourhood density and frequency in monolingual visual word recognition and naming aloud see Andrews (1997), Mathey (2001) and Perea and Rosa (2000).

In the case of bilingual participants, neighbours of a target word (e.g. L2 English word <cord>) can originate not only from the target language (e.g. L2 English neighbour <cold>) but also from the non-target language (e.g. L1 Dutch neighbour <bord>, 'plate'). Neighbours provide a unique way to investigate the two fundamental questions in bilingual research of access method and memory organisation, because participants are not aware of such neighbours. Note that in the case of homographs and cognates participants might become aware of the existence of a homograph or cognate in the other language. However, Dijkstra *et al.* (2000) have shown that participants can 'overlook' Dutch–English homographs in a Dutch go/no-go task (press a button when the word is a Dutch word) when the frequency of the English reading is much higher than the Dutch reading. Neighbourhood effects are assumed to arise during word identification, not during a late decision process. This is important because the effects of within- and between-language neighbours allow for a test of the independent versus integrated lexicon hypotheses. The independent lexicon hypothesis predicts that only within-language neighbours will affect target word processing, while the integrated lexicon hypothesis predicts that both within- and between-language neighbours will affect target word processing when word access is language non-selective.

Van Heuven *et al.* (1998) investigated the effects of within- and between-language neighbours in a series of experiments with Dutch–English bilinguals and English monolinguals. They selected English words that had either a few or many neighbours in English (within-language neighbours) and Dutch (between-language neighbours), and Dutch words with a few or many neighbours in Dutch (within) and English (between). For Dutch target words, increasing the number of Dutch neighbours led to slower responses from bilinguals. For English target words, increasing the number of English neighbours facilitated the response of bilinguals and monolinguals. More importantly, for both Dutch and English target words, neighbours of the other non-target language inhibited target word processing in bilinguals. Inhibitory effects of non-target neighbours on target word presentation have also been found in a lexical decision task with French–Spanish bilinguals (Font, 2001). In both French (L1) and Spanish (L2) longer reaction times were observed to words with larger number of neighbours in the non-target language. Only a model that assumes non-selective access to an integrated lexicon can account for these results.

Neighbours have also been found to affect target word processing in a masked priming paradigm (Forster, 1987; Segui & Grainger, 1990). In this paradigm a prime and a target letter string are presented in sequence. The presentation sequence starts with a mask (e.g. a row of hash marks <####>), followed by a very brief presentation of the prime in lower case (e.g. <both>), which is immediately followed by the target letter string in upper case (e.g. <BATH>). Participants are instructed to make a lexical decision on the target string presented in upper case. The prime is presented for a very short time (e.g. 30–60 ms) so that participants do not become aware of it. Bijeljac-Babic *et al.* (1997) used the masked priming technique to investigate the effects of orthographically related L1 and L2 word primes (neighbours) on target word processing. In two experiments, French-English bilinguals performed a lexical decision task on targets from L2 (English) in one experiment and on targets from L1 (French) in the second. In both experiments, neighbour primes from L1 and L2 significantly slowed down target word processing. Recently, Schulpen (2003) replicated the results of this second experiment with Dutch–English bilinguals in a Dutch lexical decision task. Orthographically related L2 (English) word primes inhibited L1 (Dutch) target word processing – English prime word <large> and Dutch target word <LARVE> – relative to unrelated word primes – English prime word <group>. Again, only a non-selective access model with an integrated lexicon is able to account for these results.

Cross-linguistic similarity: Homophony

The masked priming technique has also been used to study the effect of phonological overlap between primes and targets. In the monolingual domain, word and non-word primes that are homophonic (same pronunciation) with the target word facilitate target word recognition relative to non-homophonic primes. For example, the French non-word prime <lont> facilitates the French target word <LONG>, because both prime and target are pronounced similarly as /lɑ̃/ (Ferrand & Grainger, 1993). In the bilingual domain, Brysbaert *et al.* (1999) found that L2 target word processing in Dutch–French bilinguals was affected by homophonic word primes (homophones) and homophonic non-word primes (pseudohomophones), not only from the second language but also from the first. For example, the Dutch non-word prime <soer>, which sounds like the French word <sourd> /su:r/ according to the Dutch spelling-to-sound correspondences, affected the identification of the French target word <SOURD>. This finding showed that phonological representations of both languages are activated simultaneously by spelling–sound connections from both L2 and L1. Van Wijnendaele and Brysbaert (2002) demonstrated that phonological priming is also possible from L2 to L1. Again, only a model that assumes non-selective access can account for these cross-linguistic phonological priming results.

The role of phonology in L2 word recognition tasks has also been investigated using single word presentation. In the second experiment of Nas (1983), English words, pseudowords and pseudohomophones were presented to Dutch-English bilinguals in an English lexical decision task. The pseudohomophones in this experiment were constructed by changing the spelling of Dutch words according to English spelling-to-sound rules. For example, the Dutch word <triest> was changed into the pseudohomophone <treast>. Rejection latencies to those pseudohomophones were much slower than to control (non-homophonic) pseudowords (e.g. <prusk>). Thus, when bilinguals perform a task in the second language, the spelling–sound correspondences of the L2 can activate L1 phonological representations that affect visual word processing in the L2. These results also support the viewpoint of non-selective access.

The studies reported in this overview used cross-linguistically identical or similar words of both languages. Their results showed that L2 word processing is affected by L1, and so they are by a large majority in favour of a bilingual model of visual word recognition with an integrated lexicon in which access is language non-selective (parallel access to words of both languages).

The BIA Model

In the early 1980s, a group of algorithmic models were developed called *connectionist models*. These contain interconnected processing units (*nodes*). Activation flows through these units and units influence each other's activation via excitatory and inhibitory connections. One of the first models of this kind was the Interactive Activation (IA) model (McClelland & Rumelhart, 1981). This computational model was developed to account for context effects in letter perception. The IA model has so-called 'localist representations', referring to the presence of one computational unit for each concept or entity. Thus a visual feature, a letter, or a word is represented by one node in the network. A network with localist representations mirrors the structure of the knowledge it contains (Hinton *et al.*, 1986). The designer of a localist network preprograms the connections and weights between the nodes. A related yet different type of network model, generally called *parallel distributed processing (PDP) models*, uses *distributed* representations rather than *localist*. In these models concepts are represented as a pattern of activation over several nodes.

Both types of network model have advantages and disadvantages. In the bilingual domain, models of both approaches have been developed (see Thomas and Van Heuven, in press). In this section and those following, I will provide some in-depth analysis of bilingual interactive activation models, which use localist connectionist representations, beginning with a description and analysis of the bilingual interactive activation (BIA) model (Dijkstra & Van Heuven, 1998; Dijkstra *et al.*, 1998a; Van Heuven *et al.*, 1998). The BIA model is an extension of the IA model (McClelland & Rumelhart, 1981) to the bilingual domain and it implements non-selective access to an integrated lexicon.

Structure and processing

The BIA model consists of four layers of nodes: an input layer with visual letter features, a letter layer with letters for each letter position, a word layer with words from two languages (e.g. English and Dutch words), and a language node layer with a language node for each language. These are represented in Figure 10.2. The BIA model contains only words of a fixed length, just like the IA model, for example, only 4-letter Dutch and English words.

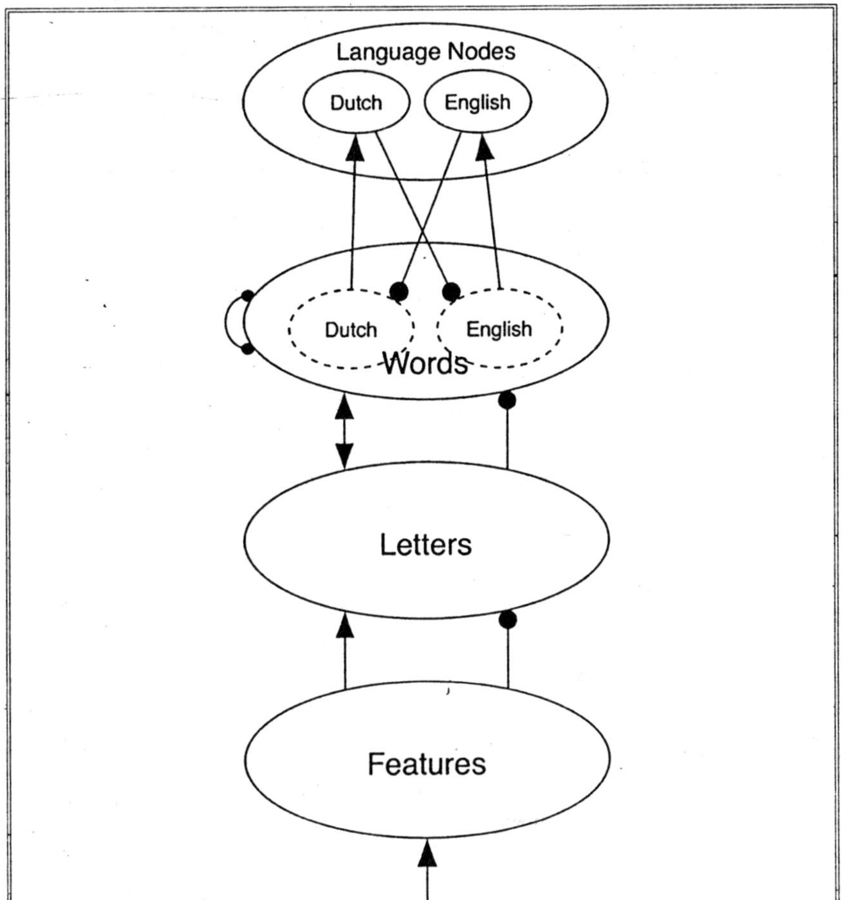

Figure 10.2 The architecture of the Bilingual Interactive Activation (BIA) model. Excitatory connections are indicated by arrows (with arrow heads pointing in the direction of activation spreading), inhibitory connections by ball-headed lines

To explain how this model works, I will describe four important characteristics of the BIA model. Note that the first three are shared with the original IA model, which is embedded in the BIA model.

(1) Word frequency differences are implemented in the model by varying the *resting-level activation* of word nodes. A node of a word with the highest frequency receives a resting-level activation of 0. The resting-level activations of all other word nodes are assigned

values between −0.92 and −0.01, proportional to the log of the frequency of the word (McClelland & Rumelhart, 1988). A consequence of these differences in resting-level activations is that word nodes with higher resting-level activations will become activated more quickly than word nodes with lower resting-level activations. For example, a common word such as <bath> is activated faster in the model because it has a higher resting-level activation than a rare word such as <balm>. Therefore the model recognises common words faster than rare words.

(2) Word nodes compete with each other at the word level. This mechanism is called *lateral inhibition.* The higher the word node is activated, the more strongly it will inhibit other activated word nodes. This mechanism is also important, because it magnifies the small initial resting-level activation differences (that is why it is called the 'rich-get-richer' effect, McClelland & Rumelhart, 1981). Thus, when the letter string <bath> is presented to the model, not only is the English word node of <bath> activated in the model but also word nodes of similar written words (e.g. neighbours <both>, <path>) and all these word nodes compete with each other.

(3) Words that are activated at the word level activate the letters that they contain through *top-down feedback.* For example, the word <took> excites the letter <t> at the first position, the letter <o> at the second and third positions and the letter <k> at the fourth letter position. An interesting aspect of this top-down feedback is that activated words with the same letters at the same positions (e.g. <book>, <cook>) will reinforce their shared letters (e.g. <o>, <o>, and <k>). The more words that share these letters, the more their activation level increases; this is called the 'gang' effect (McClelland & Rumelhart, 1981).

(4) Words in the BIA model send activation to the language node to which they belong. These language nodes are then able to inhibit the activated words of the other language. This *top-down inhibition* enables the model to suppress the influence of the other language. It is important for the behaviour of the model that this top-down inhibition can be asymmetric, and therefore different for each language. Thus, an English word <cook> activates the English language node which in turn can inhibit activated Dutch words (e.g. <rook>, <dook>, <kook>).

These four mechanisms are important for the behaviour of the model. So what happens when an input string is presented to the model? First, the string is converted to a set of visual features at each letter position. Then, at the beginning of each processing cycle, these letter features excite those letters that contain these features and inhibit letters that do *not* have these features. Activated letters at each letter position then excite words that contain these letters at the same position and inhibit words that do not have the letter at that position. For example, if the letter <b> is activated at the first position, it will excite words like <book> and <back>, because these words have this letter at the first position. However, it will inhibit words that do not have the letter <b> at the first position, such as <task> and <able>.

At the word level, activated words inhibit each other (lateral inhibition). Furthermore, words excite the letters that they contain (top-down feedback). In addition, words activate the language node to which they belong. For example, the word <book> will activate the English language node, and the word <berm> will activate the Dutch language node. Furthermore, language nodes can inhibit activated words of the other language. The amount of excitation and inhibition that each node receives and the new activation value of the node is calculated at the end of each processing cycle. After this updating, the whole cycle starts again. Over time, some nodes become more active while others become less active. Figure 10.3 shows what happens over time at the word level when the Dutch word <vers> is presented to the model,

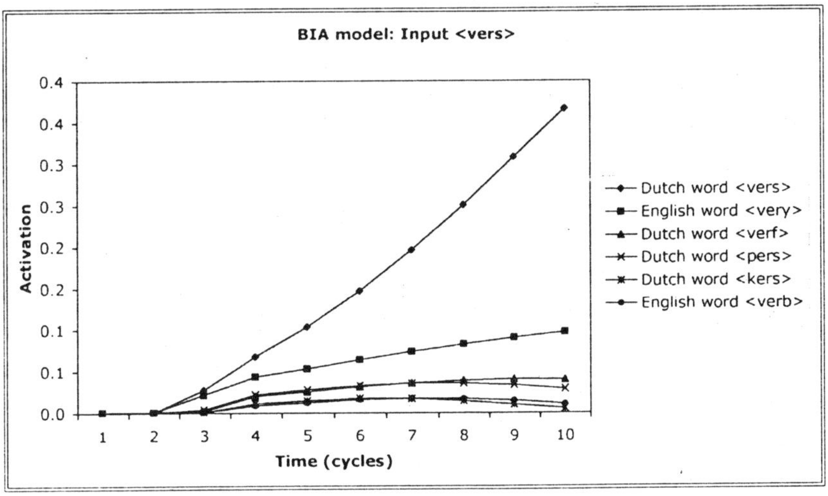

Figure 10.3 Activation curves of word nodes activated at the word layer when the Dutch word <vers> is presented to the BIA model (only the first 10 time cycles are shown). In this simulation there was no language node to word inhibition (parameters were set to zero). All other parameters were identical to the Interactive Activation (IA) model (McClelland & Rumelhart, 1981). The BIA model contained all 4-letter Dutch and English words

presented as successive time-cycles during which <vers> becomes more and more active compared to its Dutch neighbours <verf>, <pers> and <kers> and its English neighbours <very> and <verb>. The whole simulation process ends when a word node reaches a certain activation level, i.e. when <vers> has an activation value of at least 0.7. This activation level is called the *identification threshold* and is generally set a little below the maximum activation that a node can reach.

The BIA model has a number of parameters (e.g. letter-to-word excitation and letter-to-word inhibition) that are used to set the weights between the nodes. These weights determine how much excitation and inhibition flows between and within the layers. All parameter settings of the BIA model are identical to the IA model. However, a few parameters are unique for the BIA model: the word-to-language excitation parameter and the top-down inhibition parameters that control how much inhibition is sent from each language node to all words of the other language. These latter parameters are assumed to vary under particular task demands (Dijkstra & Van Heuven, 1998). For example, bilinguals might be able to reduce the influence of non-target language words on target word processing by suppressing non-target language word candidates during word identification when the task is limited to one language.

The BIA model implements non-selective access to an integrated lexicon. Thus, as can be seen in Figure 10.3, it is not only Dutch words that are activated when the Dutch word <vers> is presented to the model but also orthographically similar English words such as <very> and <verb>. Furthermore, both Dutch and English words compete with each other at the word level in the same way as words within a language. Thus, at the word level the model does not distinguish between Dutch and English words.

The BIA model is not only able to simulate a perfect, balanced bilingual who has mastered both languages perfectly, but also a less perfect (non-balanced) bilingual. For a perfect bilingual, word frequencies of words from both languages are assumed to be comparable. For a less proficient bilingual who has encountered the L2 words less frequently, the frequencies of L2 words have to be adjusted. In Van Heuven *et al.* (1998) the resting-level activation range of the L2 words was reduced. As a consequence, the highest frequency words were especially reduced in their frequency and so they are activated more slowly. With this mechanism, the model is able to simulate the slower reaction times to L2 words in non-balanced bilinguals.

The processing mechanisms of the BIA model seem very simple. However, because of interactions between the nodes in the network, its behavior can be quite complex and difficult to predict. It is therefore necessary to conduct actual simulations with the model. Furthermore, the model might exhibit unpredicted behavior that can lead to new predictions that can be tested in experiments. For example, unexpected interactions between primes and targets, so called shared neighbourhood effects, were observed in simulations with the IA model. This led to predictions concerning the effect of the size of the shared neighbourhood on target word processing, which were subsequently confirmed in a masked priming experiment (Van Heuven *et al.*, 2001).

Simulations with the BIA model

A number of simulations have been conducted with the BIA model. For example, it was able to account for effects of within- and between-language neighbours (Van Heuven *et al.*, 1998). Not only could the model account for the inhibition effect of between-language neighbours in L2 and L1, but also for the different effects of within-language neighbours in L2 (facilitatory) and L1 (inhibitory). Two aspects of the BIA model turned out to be important to obtain a good fit for the overall pattern of results. First, the word frequencies of L2 words were reduced by lowering their resting-level activations because the participants in the study were non-balanced bilinguals. With this frequency adjustment, the model already provided a very good fit. Secondly, the fit increased further when some top-down inhibition from only the Dutch language node to all English word nodes was introduced (Dijkstra & Van Heuven, 1998; Dijkstra *et al.*, 1998a; Van Heuven *et al.*, 1998).

In addition, the BIA model was able to account for the within- and between-language masked priming effects of Bijeljac-Babic *et al.* (1997). Simulations of these experiments were conducted with a French and English lexicon incorporated in the BIA model. To simulate masked priming, primes were presented on the first cycle and replaced by the target word on the third cycle. The model was able to simulate the inhibitory effect of orthographic word primes from L1 and L2 relative to unrelated word primes in both languages. Furthermore, effects for the L2 proficiency groups in the second experiment of Bijeljac-Babic *et al.* (1997) were correctly simulated by the BIA model (Dijkstra *et al.*, 1998a).

Simulation of interlingual homograph effects turned out to be more difficult. The BIA model assumes that interlingual homographs are characterised by two representations, one for each language. Because both homographs are identical in their written form, their activity at the word level becomes about equal (any activation differences are due to frequency differences). The two representations compete because of lateral inhibition while they reinforce each other through feedback from the word level to the letter level. The net effect of these mechanisms is that both word nodes are activated strongly but none of them reaches the activation threshold. This model behaviour is not correct, because in real life bilingual humans are able to recognise homographs. However, a homograph can reach the threshold when a language node sends inhibition to one of the representations. With this top-down inhibition mechanism, Dijkstra and Van Heuven (1998) were able to simulate the pattern of correct responses in the Dutch go/no-go experiment of Dijkstra *et al.* (2000).

Limitations and problems of the BIA model

Although the BIA model is successful in simulating a number of empirical findings, it has a number of problems and limitations. I will focus now on a few of these limitations and problems (for an extensive discussion see Dijkstra & Van Heuven, 2002). First of all, the BIA model does not contain any phonological and semantic representations. Consequently, the model is unable to account for effects of phonology and semantics in visual word recognition. For example, the BIA model cannot account for the effects of the phonological and/or semantic overlap in the recognition of homographs and cognates. Secondly, the model is limited to the recognition of words of a fixed length, e.g. four letters. Thirdly, language nodes have both functional and representational characteristics. For example, the language nodes can inhibit words of the other language, whereby the effects of the other language are reduced. However, Dutch-English bilinguals were not able to inhibit Dutch words in an English lexical decision experiment in which Dutch words (requiring a 'No' response) were included (the second experiment in Dijkstra *et al.*, 1998b) when this would reduce Dutch interference. In other words, this top-down inhibition does not seem to exist. To be able to overcome these limitations and problems, Dijkstra and Van Heuven (2002) proposed a revised and extended BIA model, which they called the BIA+ model.

Introduction to the BIA+ Model

The BIA+ model is a theoretical framework for bilingual word processing proposed by Dijkstra and Van Heuven (2002). I will start with a description of the basic architecture of this theoretical model.

Architecture of the BIA+ model

The BIA+ model consists of two systems: an identification system and a task/decision system, shown in Figure 10.4. The identification system is a partly independent module that subserves the identification of words. This system incorporates orthographic, phonological and semantic layers. These layers are fully interconnected so that orthography activates phonology and vice versa at both the sublexical and lexical levels. In addition, orthographic and phonological word forms activate semantic representations. Furthermore, language nodes are activated but, unlike

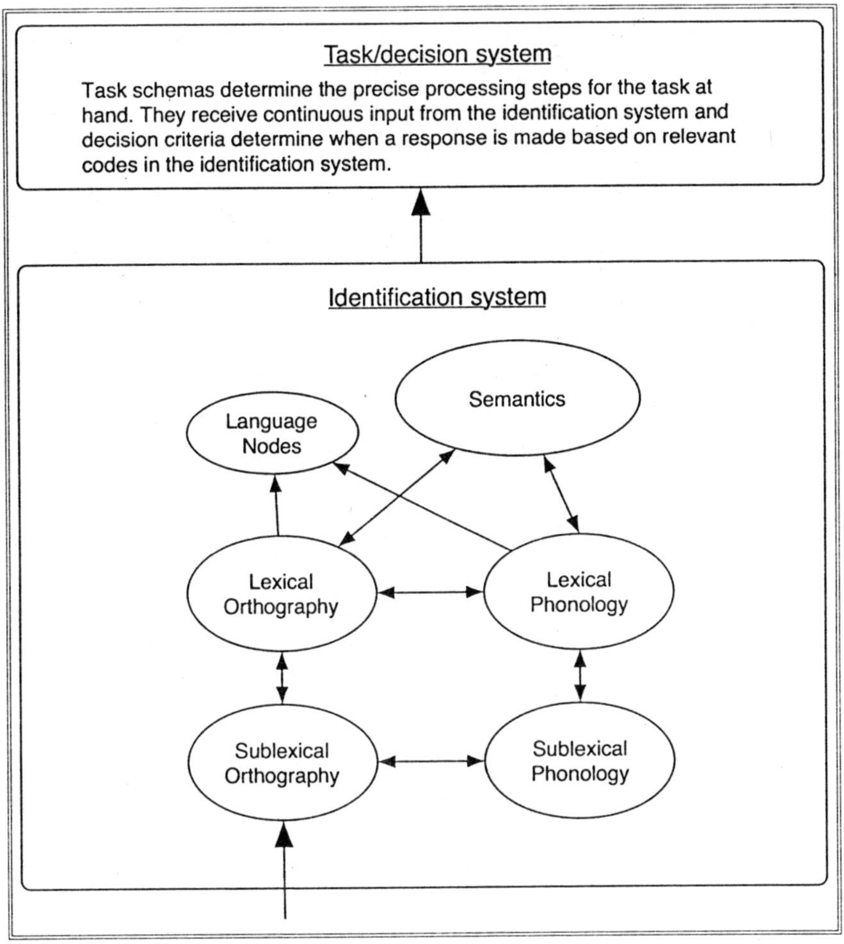

Figure 10.4 The BIA+ model, a theoretical framework of bilingual word recognition. Excitatory connections are indicated with arrows while inhibitory connections within each layer are omitted

in the BIA model, they cannot affect the activation of words from the other language. The language nodes are only used as language-tags so that the model 'knows' to which language each word belongs.

The identification system of the BIA+ model

The identification system of the BIA+ model has both lexical and sublexical connections between orthography and phonology. In this way the model implements the theory of multiple routes for reading words aloud (Coltheart *et al.*, 1993). According to this theory, a word can be pronounced using two or three information processing routes. One route is called the *direct route*. In this route the phonology of a word is looked up in memory. This direct route is implemented through the connection between orthographic and phonological word forms. The second route is called the *sublexical route*. It transforms letters and letter clusters into phonemes. The sublexical connection between orthography and phonology in the BIA+ model reflects this second route. Finally, the third possible route, in which phonology is looked up through semantics, is implemented in the BIA+ model in terms of connections between orthographic and phonological word nodes on the one hand and semantic nodes on the other.

The identification system of the BIA+ assumes (just like the BIA model) non-selective access to an integrated lexicon. Thus, at the orthographic and phonological word level, words of both languages are fully interconnected. Input at the sublexical orthographic level activates orthographic word representations in a language independent way. The same holds for the connection between sublexical and lexical phonology because connections are language independent. In the BIA+ model homographs have two representations at the orthographic and phonological word level. This allows the model to capture the frequency dependent inhibition effects for homographs observed in Dijkstra *et al*. (1998b).

Task/decision system of the BIA+ model

The task/decision system of the BIA+ model receives continuous input from the identification system. This system uses so-called *task schemas* (Green, 1998) that determine which task-specific response procedures have to be applied to the task at hand. These procedures can be implemented using simple activation thresholds in one or more layers of the identification system. However, more complex thresholds that reflect different strategies might be used as well. For example, a lexical decision could be based not only on the correct identification of a word but also on a quick guess based on the overall activity in the lexicon. Thus, when there are many word nodes activated in the lexicon (due to the activation of many neighbours), the likelihood that the input string is a word increases, so participants might adopt the strategy to press the 'Yes' button in such cases before the word is identified. Such a guessing strategy was implemented in the IA model by Grainger and Jacobs (1996), who introduced a total word activity threshold (sigma) that uses the summed activity at the word level to make a fast guess about the presented item.

An important characteristic of the BIA+ model is that the identification system functions independently from the task/decision system. The task/decision system cannot affect the activity of nodes within the identification system. An important question is what kind of information outside the BIA+ model is able to affect the two systems of the model. Dijkstra and Van Heuven (2002) made a distinction between linguistic and non-linguistic context effects. In the BIA+ model only linguistic context can affect the activation of nodes in the identification system. In contrast, non-linguistic context can affect the task/decision system of the BIA+ model (see Dijkstra & Van Heuven, 2002, for an extensive discussion of these issues). Linguistic context refers to, for example, sentence context, while non-linguistic context effects refer to the participants' expectations based on instruction or task demands.

Implementation of BIA+: The SOPHIA model

The BIA+ model proposed by Dijkstra and Van Heuven (2002) is a verbal-theoretical model. Recently, Van Heuven and Dijkstra (2003, in preparation) have started to implement the identification system of the BIA+ model in an interactive activation network, called the Semantic, Orthographic and PHonological Interactive Activation model (SOPHIA). As acknowledged by Dijkstra and Van Heuven (2002: 182), 'implementing phonological and semantic representations in an interactive activation model poses serious problems for the modeller'. In particular, the mapping between letters and phonemes is complex, especially for irregular languages such as English. For example, in English, the letter <i> in the word <pint> /paɪnt/ is pronounced differently from the letter <i> in the words <hint> /hɪnt/ and <mint> /mɪnt/. Another example is the letter cluster <ough> which is pronounced differently in the words <tough> /tʌf/, <cough> /kɒf/, <though> /ðəʊ/ and <through> /θruː/. In the monolingual domain, various solutions have been proposed for this sublexical mapping between letters and phonemes (Dijkstra, 2001). For example, in the dual-route cascaded (DRC) model of reading aloud (Coltheart *et al.*, 2001), sublexical mapping is implemented using context-dependent grapheme-to-phoneme rules.

At the moment the SOPHIA model incorporates only monosyllabic words. The model makes a distinction (for each syllable) between onset (O), nucleus (N) and coda (C) representations (letter and phoneme clusters) at the orthographic and phonological sublexical level, because mappings between single letters and phonemes are difficult as explained above. Note that the onset contains only consonants, and the nucleus only vowels (thus identical to CV distinction). These Onset-Nucleus-Coda (ONC) representations at the orthographic level are used as input representations. A similar input scheme has also been used in the monolingual model of Plaut *et al.* (1996). In the SOPHIA model, connections between orthographic and phonological ONC representation perform the conversion between letters and phonemes.

The links between orthographic and phonological ONC representations and the weights of these connections are determined by the specific words and their frequencies that are read into the model. When words are read into the model, orthographic and phonological wordforms are divided into three letter and phoneme clusters for onset, nucleus, and coda respectively. Taking the example of the English word <book>, the onset <b>, nucleus <oo> and the coda <k> representations are entered into the model. Next, the phonological wordform of <book>, i.e. /bʊk/, is divided into the onset /b/, nucleus /ʊ/ and coda /k/. Next, the onset letter cluster <b> is connected to the phonological onset cluster /b/, the nucleus letter cluster <oo> connected to the phonological nucleus /ʊ/ and the coda letter <k> to the coda phoneme /k/. The weights of these representations are then assigned values based on their frequency of occurrence in the language.

What happens when a letter string is presented to the SOPHIA model? When the word <link> is presented to the model, the onset <l>, the nucleus <i> and the coda <nk> are activated. These letter clusters subsequently activate both the whole word orthographic representation of <link> and the corresponding phonological ONC clusters at the phoneme cluster layer. Next, the orthographic word activates its associated phonological representation, and at the same time the activated phonemes activate the whole phonological representation of /lɪŋk/. The same processing mechanisms described for the BIA model (under Structure and processing above) also apply to the SOPHIA model. Thus, there is lateral inhibition at each layer in the model and top-down feedback flows from higher levels to lower levels. The architecture of SOPHIA is shown in Figure 10.5. So far, only the orthographic and phonological parts of the SOPHIA model are implemented.

Simulations with SOPHIA

The current implementation of SOPHIA is able to simulate various orthographic and phonological effects observed with monolinguals (Van Heuven & Dijkstra, in preparation). In the simulation presented below I describe two exploratory sets of simulations with the SOPHIA model focusing on bilingual data sets. The same set of parameters was used in all the simulations reported here. The monosyllabic English and Dutch wordform lexicons used in the simulations were extracted from the CELEX database (Baayen *et al.*, 1993), which is a large lexical database of Dutch, English, and German words.

Interlingual homographs

In the first simulation study that I will consider, the SOPHIA model was used to simulate the frequency-dependent inhibition effects observed

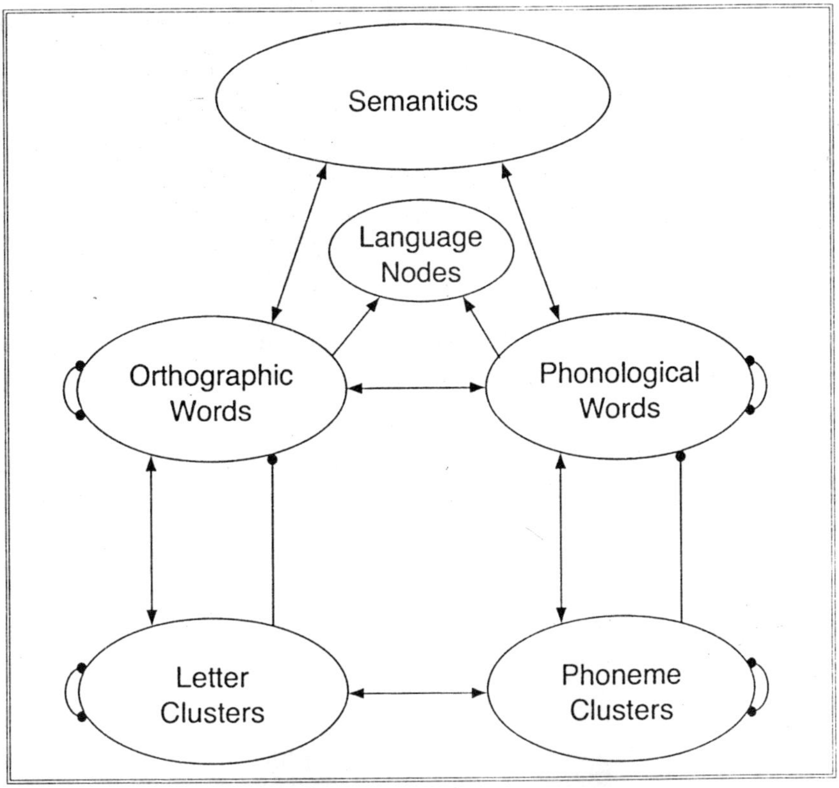

Figure 10.5 The architecture of the Semantic, Orthographic, Phonological, and Semantic interactive activation (SOPHIA) model. Excitatory connections are indicated by arrows, and inhibitory connections by ball-headed lines

with homographs in the second experiment of Dijkstra *et al.* (1998b), described above. In Figure 10.6a the mean response times for the Dutch-English homographs with a low and high frequency in Dutch are presented together with the mean response times of the English control words. All response times to homographs are slower than to control words; homographs with a high frequency reading in Dutch are slower than those with low frequency reading in Dutch.

To simulate word identification in the lexical decision task, an identification threshold of 0.7 was set at the orthographic word layer. The first simulation was conducted with the SOPHIA model incorporating Dutch and English words to simulate the performance of a Dutch-English bilingual reader.

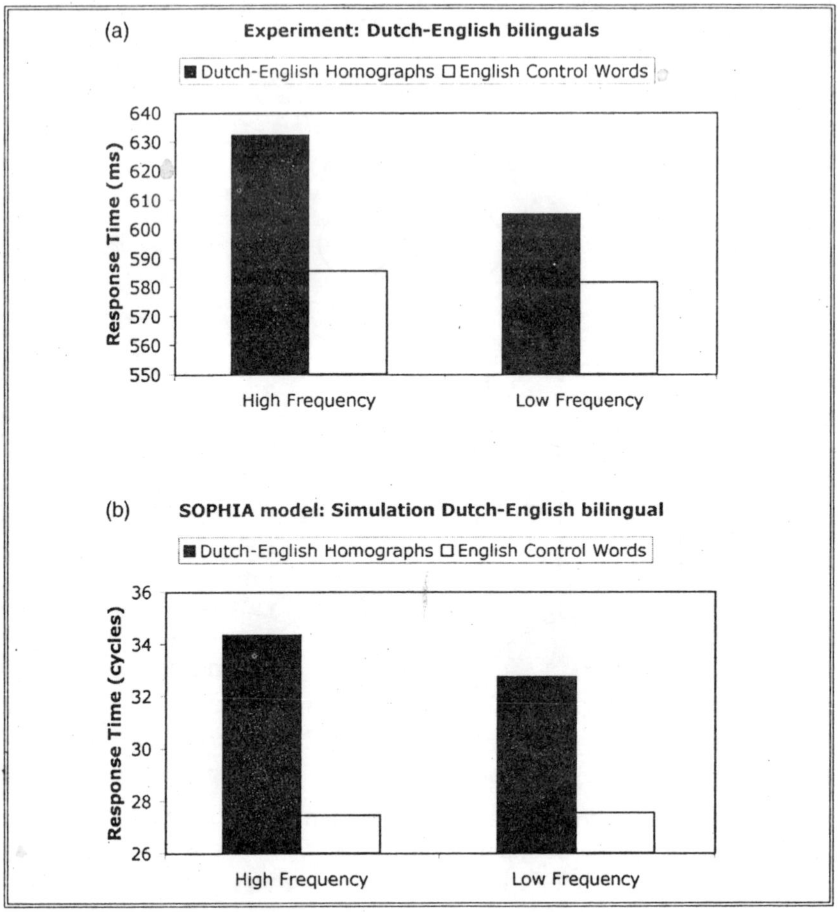

Figure 10.6 (a) Reaction times of the second experiment of Dijkstra *et al.* (1998b) for Dutch–English homographs with high or low frequencies in Dutch, and English control words. (b) Simulation results of Dijkstra *et al.* (1998b) with the SOPHIA model simulating a Dutch-English bilingual reader

The simulation revealed, just as the experiment, overall slower responses to homographs than to English control words. In addition, the response times were higher when the frequency of the Dutch reading of the homographs was high than when it was low (Figure 10.6b). The results of the experiment and the simulation are similar, as can be seen by comparing Figure 10.6a with 10.6b. In fact, the Pearson correlation between the means of the experiment and the simulation was 0.95 ($p < 0.06$). Note, however, that the model made many errors for homographs because the Dutch orthographic representation of the homograph reached the identification threshold instead of the English representation. More simulation work has to be conducted to investigate how to reduce the number of errors for homographs. Furthermore, simulation of the two other experiments of Dijkstra *et al.* (1998a) will have to wait until the task/decision system is implemented.

A very interesting aspect of conducting computer simulations is that one can use the model to check whether words from different conditions in an experiment are indeed well-matched. For example, the homographs and control words of Dijkstra *et al.* (1998b) were matched in English frequency and word length. Thus, for an English monolingual who does not know any Dutch, response times to homographs and controls should be similar. Dijkstra *et al.* (1998b) did not conduct such a control experiment. However, with the SOPHIA model such a control experiment (simulation) can be easily conducted. The result of such simulation with the SOPHIA model is shown in Figure 10.7. As expected the response times are very similar for homograph and control conditions. Thus, we can conclude that according to the SOPHIA model the word materials of Dijkstra *et al.* (1998b) are well matched.

Pseudohomophones

To investigate the ability of the SOPHIA model to account for cross-linguistic phonological effects, SOPHIA's response to pseudohomophones was examined using the materials from the second experiment of Nas (1983). The pseudohomophones of this study sound like Dutch words only when they are pronounced using English spelling-to-sound

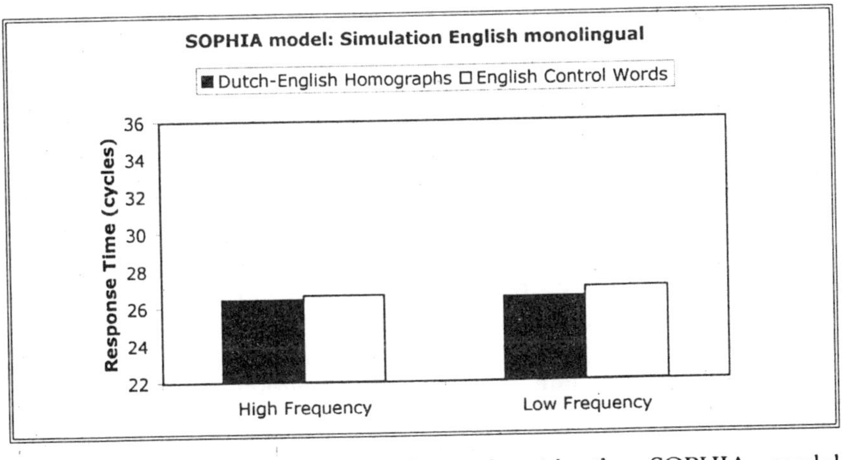

Figure 10.7 Simulation results obtained with the SOPHIA model simulating an English monolingual reader with the stimulus materials of Dijkstra *et al.* (1998b)

conversion rules. For example, applying the English conversion rules, the pseudohomophone <treast> is pronounced as the Dutch word <triest>, namely as /tri:st/. The results of Nas (1983) revealed much slower rejection latencies to these words than to non-homophonic pseudowords (e.g. <prusk>). The SOPHIA model cannot simulate rejection latencies because a task/decision system is not yet implemented. However, in the future such a mechanism might be implemented using a rejection threshold such as that implemented by Grainger and Jacobs (1996). The rejection threshold in Grainger and Jacobs' model is affected by the total activation at the word level. Strong activation at the word level makes the model run longer before it will reject, while little activation makes the model reject quicker. Before this kind of mechanism is implemented in the SOPHIA model, the overall activity in the model can be used as an indication of rejection times when a pseudoword is presented to the model. First, the ability of the SOPHIA model to activate the correct phonology of an English pseudohomophone was tested in a simulation with the model that incorporated only English words. An example of an English pseudohomophone is the letter string <bloo>, which is pronounced by English monolingual readers as the word <blue>, namely /blu:/. As can be seen in Figure 10.8, the phonological representation /blu:/ is correctly activated by the model when the input string <bloo> is presented to it.

Next, the pseudohomophone <treast>, taken from the stimulus materials of Nas (1983), was presented to the SOPHIA model that contained both Dutch and English words, simulating a balanced Dutch-English bilingual reader. Figure 10.9a shows that the phonological representation /tri:st/ of the Dutch word <triest> is strongly activated. Therefore, the SOPHIA model seems to correctly predict that a 'No' response would take much longer compared to such response to a non-homophonic pseudoword (e.g. <prusk>).

The SOPHIA model can be further used to conduct an interesting simulation for which there is no experimental counterpart. Nas (1983) constructed pseudohomophones such as <treast>, that activates the phonology of <triest> only when English spelling-to-sound correspondences are used. Thus, Dutch monolinguals should not activate the phonological representation of <triest> because they have not acquired English spelling-to-sound correspondences. This prediction was tested with the SOPHIA model simulating a Dutch monolingual reader.

Remarkably, the simulation of the pseudohomophone <treast> revealed that the SOPHIA model including only *Dutch* words was able to activate the phonology of <triest> (Figure 10.9b) as well. Simulations with other pseudohomophones from Nas (1983) showed that the Dutch word forms from which they were derived were activated, even though

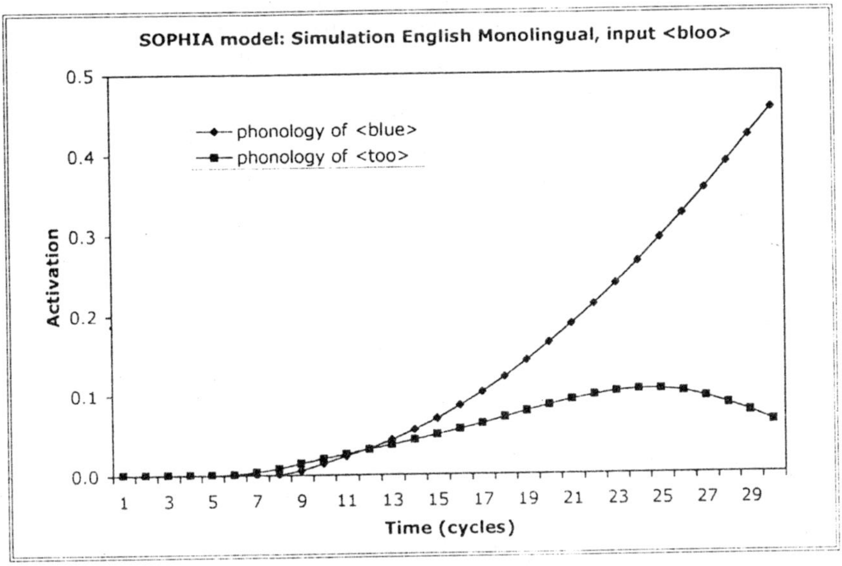

Figure 10.8 Activation curves of activated nodes at the phonological wordform level when the English pseudohomophone <bloo> was presented to the SOPHIA model with only an English lexicon (simulating an English monolingual reader)

the model did not have any English spelling-to-sound correspondences. How is this possible? In the case of the pseudohomophone <treast>, simulations revealed that Dutch spelling-to-sound mappings played a role. The SOPHIA model, which was used to simulate a Dutch monolingual, lacks English words that map the letter cluster <ea> to the phoneme /i:/ to activate the correct phonology of <treast> like the English words <least> and <feast>. However, it turns out that there are also Dutch words that map <ea> to the phoneme /i:/, for example the Dutch-English cognate <team>, which is pronounced the same in Dutch and English /ti:m/. Other pseudohomophones from Nas (1983) activated the English phonology for other reasons: for the letter string <deef>, activation of the correct phonology /di:f/ by the monolingual model can be explained by the activation of the Dutch orthographic neighbour <dief>, which in turn activates its corresponding phonological representation /di:f/.

Thus, these simulations with the SOPHIA model reveal that there are problems with the stimulus materials in Nas (1983). However, these problems do not affect his conclusion of a common lexical store, although the simulation shows that the observed effect might not only be due to bilinguals applying English spelling-to-sound rules.

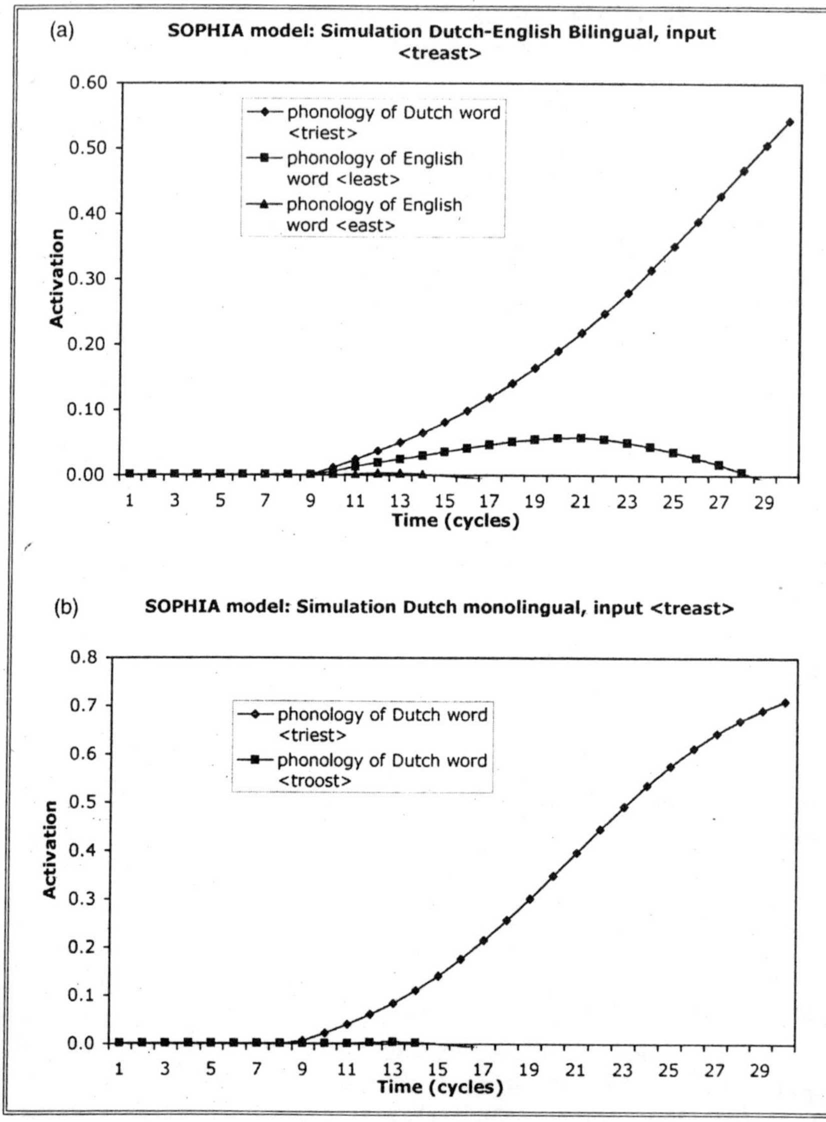

Figure 10.9 Activation curves of activated nodes at the phonological wordform level when the pseudohomophone <treast> was presented to the SOPHIA model: (a) with English and Dutch words (simulating a Dutch-English bilingual reader); and (b) with only a Dutch lexicon (simulating a Dutch monolingual reader)

Summary and Conclusions

In this chapter, I described bilingual interactive activation models of bilingual word recognition. The first of such models to be implemented in the literature, the BIA model, was able to simulate various empirical findings. Although generally rather successful, it had some problems and limitations, which led to the theoretical BIA+ model. Next, I described the SOPHIA model that implements the identification system of the BIA+ model. Simulations with the SOPHIA model showed that this new model is able to account for some additional findings. Of course, more modelling work has to be done to fully evaluate SOPHIA's performance, but the preliminary simulation results obtained with the SOPHIA model clearly look promising.

Models such as those described in this chapter can be used to simulate the performance not only of bilingual but also of monolingual readers, or even any type of reader with varying knowledge of L2. This flexibility of computational modelling allows for additional tests of the theory and the experimental materials and makes it possible to derive new predictions. Furthermore, the connections in a computational model can be easily modified, or even be removed, to simulate, for example, various reading impairments. Also, interactive activation networks pick up effects of the statistical characteristics of languages that might be difficult to notice otherwise. Thus, interactive activation models with localist representations not only provide a good and adequate framework for the computational modelling of visual word recognition in bilingual readers, but turn out to be a useful tool for researchers trying to understand and develop such models as well.

Acknowledgements

I would like to thank Ton Dijkstra for his comments on earlier versions of this chapter.

References

Andrews, S. (1997) The effects of orthographic similarity on lexical retrieval: Resolving neighborhood conflicts. *Psychological Bulletin and Review* 4, 439–61.

Baayen, H., Piepenbrock, R. and Van Rijn, H. (1993) *The CELEX lexical database (CD-ROM)*. Philadelphia, PA: University of Pennsylvania, Linguistic Data Consortium.

Bijeljac-Babic, R., Biardeau, A. and Grainger, J. (1997) Masked orthographic priming in bilingual word recognition. *Memory and Cognition* 25, 447–57.

Brysbaert, M., Van Dyck, G. and Van de Poel, M. (1999) Visual word recognition in bilinguals: Evidence from masked phonological priming. *Journal of Experimental Psychology: Human Perception and Performance* 25, 137–48.

Coltheart, M., Davelaar, E., Jonasson, J.T. and Besner, D. (1977) Access to the internal lexicon. In S. Dornic (ed.) *Attention and Performance VI* (pp. 535–55). New York: Academic Press.

Coltheart, M., Curtis, B., Atkins, P. and Haller, M. (1993) Models of reading aloud: Dual-route and parallel-distributed processing approaches. *Psychological Review* 100, 589–608.

Coltheart, M., Rastle, K., Perry, C., Langdon, R. and Ziegler, J. (2001) DRC: A dual route cascaded model of visual word recognition and reading aloud. *Psychological Review* 108, 204–56.

De Groot, A.M.B., Delmaar, P. and Lupker, S.J. (2000) The processing of interlexical homographs in translation recognition and lexical decision: Support for non-selective access to bilingual memory. *Quarterly Journal of Experimental Psychology* 53A, 397–428.

Dijkstra, A. (2001) Word recognition and lexical access II: Connectionist approaches. In D.A. Cruse, F. Hundsnurscher, M. Job and P. R. Lutzeier (eds) *Lexikologie – Lexicology* (Article 265). Berlin: Walter de Gruyter.

Dijkstra, A. (in press) Bilingual visual word recognition and lexical access. In J.F. Kroll and A.M.B. de Groot (eds) *Handbook of Bilingualism: Psycholinguistic Approaches*. Oxford: Oxford University Press.

Dijkstra, A. and Van Heuven, W.J.B. (1998) The BIA model and bilingual word recognition. In J. Grainger and A.M. Jacobs (eds) *Localist Connectionist Approaches to Human Cognition* (pp. 189–225). Mahwah, NJ, USA: Lawrence Erlbaum Associates.

Dijkstra, A. and Van Heuven, W.J.B. (2002) The architecture of the bilingual word recognition system: From identification to decision. *Bilingualism: Language and Cognition* 5, 175–97.

Dijkstra, A., Grainger, J. and Van Heuven, W.J.B. (1999) Recognition of cognates and interlingual homographs: The neglected role of phonology. *Journal of Memory and Languages* 41, 496–518.

Dijkstra, A., Timmermans, M. and Schriefers, H. (2000) Cross-language effects on bilingual homograph recognition. *Journal of Memory and Language* 42, 445–64.

Dijkstra, A., Van Heuven, W.J.B. and Grainger, J. (1998a) Simulating competitor effects with the Bilingual Interactive Activation Model. *Psychologica Belgica* 38, 177–96.

Dijkstra, A., Van Jaarsveld, H. and Ten Brinke, S. (1998b) Interlingual homograph recognition: Effects of task demands and language intermixing. *Bilingualism* 1, 51–66.

Ferrand, L. and Grainger, J. (1993) The time-course of orthographic and phonological code activation in the early phases of visual word recognition. *Bulletin of the Psychonomic Society* 31, 119–22.

Font, N. (2001) Rôle de la langue dans l'accès au lexique chez bilingues: Influence de la proximité orthographique et sémantique interlangue sur la reconnaissance visuelle de mots. PhD thesis, Université Paul Valery, Montpellier.

Forster, K.I. (1987) Form-priming with masked primes: The best match hypothesis. In M. Coltheart (ed.) *Attention and Performance XII* (pp. 127–46). London: Erlbaum.

Grainger, J. (1993) Visual word recognition in bilinguals. In R. Schreuder and B. Weltens (eds) *The Bilingual Lexicon* (pp. 11–25). Amsterdam/ Philadelphia: John Benjamins.

Grainger, J. and Jacobs, A.M. (1996) Orthographic processing in visual word recognition: A multiple read-out model. *Psychological Review* 103, 518–65.

Green, D.W. (1998) Mental control of the bilingual lexico-semantic system. *Bilingualism* 1, 67–81.

Grosjean, F. (1982) *Life with Two Languages: An Introduction to Bilingualism.* Cambridge, MA: Harvard University Press.

Hinton, G.E., McClelland, J.L. and Rumelhart, D.E. (1986) Distributed representations. In D.E. Rumelhart, J.L. McClelland and the PDP Research Group (eds) *Parallel Distributed Processing: Explorations in the Microstructure of Cognition, Volume 1. Foundations* (pp. 77–109). Cambridge, MA: Bradford Books.

Keatley, C.W. (1992) History of bilingualism research in cognitive psychology. In R.J. Harris (ed.) *Cognitive Processing in Bilinguals* (pp. 15–49). Amsterdam: Elsevier.

Mathey, S. (2001) L'influence du voisinage orthographique lors de la reconnaissance des mots écrits. *Canadian Journal of Experimental Psychology* 55, 1–23.

McClelland, J.L. and Rumelhart, D.E. (1981) An interactive activation model of context effects in letter perception, Part 1: An account of basic findings. *Psychological Review* 88, 375–405.

McClelland, J.L. and Rumelhart, D.E. (1988) *Parallel Distributed Processing: Explorations in the Microstructure of Cognition: A Handbook of Models, Programs, and Exercises.* Cambridge, MA: Bradford Books.

Nas, G. (1983) Visual word recognition in bilinguals: Evidence for a cooperation between visual and sound based codes during access to a common lexical store. *Journal of Verbal Learning and Verbal Behavior* 22, 526–34.

Perea, M. and Rosa, E. (2000) The effects of orthographic neighborhood in reading and laboratory word identification tasks: A review. *Psicológica* 21, 327–40.

Plaut, D.C., McClelland, J.L., Seidenberg, M.S. and Patterson, K. (1996) Understanding normal and impaired word reading: Computational principles in quasi-regular domains. *Psychological Review* 103, 56–115.

Rayner, K. and Pollatsek, A. (1989) *The Psychology of Reading*. Hillsdale, NJ: Lawrence Erlbaum Associates.

Schulpen, B. (2003) Explorations in bilingual word recognition: Cross-model, cross-sectional, and cross-language effects. PhD thesis, University of Nijmegen.

Segui, J. and Grainger, J. (1990) Priming word recognition with orthographic neighbors: Effects of relative prime-target frequency. *Journal of Experimental Psychology: Human Perception and Performance* 16, 65–76.

Snodgrass, J.G. and Mintzer, M. (1993) Neighborhood effects in visual word recognition: Facilitatory or inhibitory? *Memory and Cognition* 21, 247–66.

Thomas, M.S.C. and Van Heuven, W.J.B. (in press) Computational models of bilingual comprehension. In J.F. Kroll and A.M.B. de Groot (eds) *Handbook of Bilingualism: Psycholinguistic Approaches*. Oxford University Press.

Timmermans, M. (1996) Blocking the mother tongue: Inhibitory effects of a second language on accessing interlingual homographs. Master thesis, Nijmegen University.

Van Heuven, W.J.B. and Dijkstra, A. (2003) Modeling bilingual visual word recognition: The SOPHIA model. Presented at the XIII Conference of the European Society for Cognitive Psychology. Granada, Spain.

Van Heuven, W.J.B. and Dijkstra, A. (in preparation) SOPHIA: A computational model of monolingual and bilingual visual word recognition.

Van Heuven, W.J.B., Dijkstra, A. and Grainger, J. (1998) Orthographic neighborhood effects in bilingual word recognition. *Journal of Memory and Language* 39, 458–83.

Van Heuven, W.J.B., Dijkstra, A., Grainger, J. and Schriefers, H. (2001) Shared neighborhood effects in masked orthographic priming. *Psychonomic Bulletin and Review* 8, 96–101.

Van Wijnendaele, I. and Brysbaert, M. (2002) Visual word recognition in bilinguals: Phonological priming from the second to the first language. *Journal of Experimental Psychology: Human Perception and Performance* 28, 616–27.

Chapter 11

The Effect of L1 Reading Processes on L2: A Crosslinguistic Comparison of Italian and Japanese Users of English

MIHO SASAKI

Introduction

L2 reading research reveals that differences in readers' L1 writing systems (L1WS) affect their L2 reading (Chikamatsu, 1996; Holm & Dodd, 1996; Muljani *et al.*, 1998; Wade-Woolley, 1999): learners who use alphabetic writing systems in their first language show facilitation in reading an alphabetic second language writing system (L2WS), compared to those who use non-alphabetic writing systems in their L1WS. For example, Muljani *et al.* (1998) found that Indonesian learners of English performed English word recognition better than Chinese learners of English. This suggested that such differences arose from different experiences of reading: both the L1WS and L2WS for the Indonesian learners were alphabetic while the L1WS of Chinese learners of English was non-alphabetic.

The current study investigates the effects of the different reading processes involved in alphabetic and non-alphabetic L1WSs on reading performance in English as a L2WS. Reading processes refer to cognitive processes in reading, i.e. the way in which a written form is processed to arrive at the meaning, activating various types of information. The study contrasts two groups of L2 users of English with alphabetic versus non-alphabetic L1WS backgrounds, i.e. Italian versus Japanese, in order to examine their word recognition performance in English. Two questions are raised about the effects of writing system background. Firstly, would users of different writing systems develop different reading processes? In other words, can variation in writing systems be one of the factors involved in generating cross-linguistic differences in reading performance? Secondly, would L2 users read a second language differently because of their experience of a L1WS?

The chapter first describes cross-linguistic variation in writing systems, and variation in acquisition of L1WSs, followed by a review of previous L2 word recognition studies in terms of the influence of L1WSs. The second part of the chapter reports the results of an L2 English word recognition experiment and examines the relationship between writing systems and L1 and L2 reading processes.

Cross-linguistic Variations in Writing Systems

The writing system is a central system that represents the rules of symbol-to-sound correspondences connecting the spoken form and the written form in a language. Writing systems vary in terms not only of the script type such as the Roman alphabet or Japanese kana, but also of the unit of orthographic representation. This paper divides writing systems into two types in terms of orthographic unit, alphabetic and non-alphabetic. The English and the Italian writing systems are alphabetic since they are based on correspondence between written symbols and phonemes; the kanji and kana of the Japanese writing system are non-alphabetic in that they correspond to morphemes and syllables respectively. The written unit of correspondence then varies between a phoneme and larger units such as a syllable or a morpheme.

Reading in alphabetic writing systems

Alphabetic writing systems differ with regard to their spelling-to-sound correspondences, i.e. orthographic regularity, according to the *Orthographic Depth Hypothesis* (ODH) (Frost *et al.*, 1987; Katz & Frost, 1992). For example, the Italian writing system has consistent 'shallow' correspondences between spellings and phonemes, i.e. one-to-one correspondences, whereas the English writing system has inconsistent 'deep' correspondences, i.e. many-to-many correspondences. In English, there are several ways to spell a phoneme, e.g. the phoneme /e/ is spelled <e> in <bed> but <ea> in <bread> and the phoneme /u:/ is spelled <oo> in <fool> but <ui> in <bruise>. Conversely, there are several ways to pronounce a spelling, e.g. <ea> is pronounced /i:/ in <heal> but /e/ in <health>, <gh> is pronounced /g/ in <ghost>, /f/ in <enough>, but silent in <though>, while <th> is pronounced /ð/ in <there> but /θ/ in <theatre>. It is often difficult even for skilled English readers to retrieve a correct sound from an unknown spelling. This inconsistency of English spelling–sound correspondences allows the orthography to signal lexical features visually and morphologically. Thus, the English writing system is deemed to function in some ways as a morphophonemic writing system instead of a phonologically based system (Carney, 1994; Chomsky & Halle, 1968; Venezky, 1970). Another characteristic of a deep writing system is the large number of homophones, where the same sounds are spelled differently, e.g. /eə/ <pair/pear>, /ʌ/ <sun/son>, and /n/ <night/knight>.

The Orthographic Depth Hypothesis claims that the difference in orthographic depth across writing systems leads to processing differences for cognitive tasks such as naming and lexical decision (Katz & Frost, 1992). It predicts that reading in a shallow orthography utilises phonological coding more than reading in a deep orthography because of its consistency between phonology and orthography. In contrast, reading in a deep orthography is assumed to utilise more visual and morphological elements. However, the ODH does not imply exclusive phonological coding in reading a shallow orthography; rather both phonological coding and visual-orthographic coding are assumed in *any* writing system. Therefore, orthographic depth is one of the factors that indicates a preference for the use of phonological coding.

Recently, several studies have proposed another view of orthographic variation and processes, i.e. the 'grain size' of units (Goswami *et al.*, 1998, 2003; Ziegler *et al.*, 2001). This concerns the size of a processing unit in word reading. The grain size varies from 'small', such as the link between graphemes and phonemes, to 'large', such as the link between *word bodies* and phonological rhymes or that between spelling and sound at whole-word level. The *word body* or *body* has been considered an important unit in English reading acquisition. For example, Treiman *et al.* (1995) reported that in monosyllabic English words (consonant-vowel-consonant: C_1VC_2) such as 'leap', vowel-consonant units (i.e. -VC_2, or word-body units) such as <-eap> provide more consistent pronunciations than either vowel units (V) or consonant-vowel units (C_1V-). They argue that the consonant that follows the vowel help to reduce the ambiguity associated with the vowel, thus -VC_2 units help to regulate the links between spelling and sound in the English writing system. Their further investigation using a naming task with simple C_1VC_2 words revealed that adult readers utilised -VC_2 units in addition to single graphemes. Therefore, phonological coding in English requires processing at a variety of grain sizes including grapheme, word body and even whole-word. In contrast, orthographically consistent languages such as Italian rely on a small grain size, i.e. a grapheme–phoneme level, of processing. Thus, orthographic regularity in alphabetic writing systems influences phonological coding during reading as well as the grain size of units. In sum, the different units of written language which are mapped into the spoken forms predict different cognitive processes of written language across different types of writing system.

Reading in non-alphabetic writing systems

Reading processes in alphabetic writing systems are greatly affected by orthographic regularity. However, are non-alphabetic systems read in the same way as alphabetic ones? Several previous studies on the Japanese writing system have proved that kanji and kana involve different reading processes (Feldman & Turvey, 1980; Saito, 1981; Sasanuma, 1975). Kanji characters do not need to be phonologically activated since the phonological representation is word specific and a character represents a meaning directly. However, recent studies have provided evidence that phonology plays an important role in reading kanji (Morita & Matsuda, 2000; Saito *et al.*, 1998; Sakuma *et al.*, 1998; Wydell *et al.*, 1993). Wydell *et al.* (1993) found homophone interference for processing two-character kanji words in a semantic category judgement task as previously found in English (Van Orden, 1987): for example 'rows' was affected by the word 'rose' implied by the category name 'flower'. In addition, Wydell *et al.* (1993) found significant orthographic interference: when homophone words were orthographically similar to implied words, they produced longer response times and more errors. However, the homophone interference was larger than the effect of orthographic similarity. Interference was strongest when both phonological and orthographic similarity interacted. Reading kanji invokes both orthographic (visual symbol pattern) and phonological (symbol–sound correspondence) information. Similarly, experimental studies support the view that orthographic information is as crucial to Japanese and Chinese word recognition as phonological information (Leck *et al.*, 1995; Sakuma *et al.*, 1998; Weekes *et al.*, 1998).

The activation of phonological information has been also studied in terms of lexical involvement. Studies in English word reading and recognition have shown that phonological coding uses automatic and rapid access and may occur prior to semantic activation (e.g. Lesch & Pollatsek, 1993). Perfetti and Tan (1998) also demonstrated in a same-different judgment task with stimulus onset asynchrony (SOA) that phonological activation occurred earlier than semantic activation in the reading of single Chinese characters. They suggested that phonological information would be available earlier than some semantic information when the orthographic forms and phonological forms are highly determinate. However, it is possible that in reading Chinese for meaning phonological activation can be at the lexical level rather than at the pre-lexical level if form–meaning relationships are as determinate as form–form relationships (Tan & Perfetti, 1998). Since the mapping of writing onto spoken language is at a character–morphosyllabic level in Chinese (DeFrancis, 1989), orthographic form–meaning relationships and orthographic form–phonological form relationships can be equally close.

Compared to Chinese, Morita and Matsuda (2000) revealed that, in Japanese kanji reading, both semantic and phonological activation would occur automatically and simultaneously, although it was easier to ignore phonological information than to ignore semantic information when examining recognition of two-character kanji words involving homophones and synonyms with the SOA. Kanji seems to connect to meaning more strongly than to phonology because of its multiple pronunciations. Since the mapping of writing onto spoken language is at a character-morpheme or even a (two-kanji) word-meaning level in Japanese, orthography–meaning relationships are presumed to be more closely linked than orthography–phonology relationships.

In summary, cross-linguistic variations of writing systems include variation of representation units across writing systems and variation of orthographic regularity and orthographic grain size among alphabetic writing systems. Previous studies suggest that although phonological information is activated automatically in any writing system, supporting the *Universal Phonological Principle* (Perfetti *et al.*, 1992), the difference in mapping the phonology onto the written form leads to a considerable difference in the use of phonological information among different writing systems. Thus, a writing system can influence reading processes. This perspective is also maintained by empirical studies in L2 reading processes to be discussed later.

Acquisition of reading in a first language

Just as writing systems vary, so does the acquisition of L1 reading and writing across writing systems. These differences are related to the difficulty of the writing system for children. The three writing systems investigated in this paper, English, Italian and Japanese, show a clear contrast in this respect. Children take a longer time to master the English writing system compared with children acquiring other alphabetic writing systems. They are not expected to learn to read and spell within the early years of schooling, and so they do not become fluent users of the system until the age of 10 or 11. On the other hand, Italian children learn to read and spell within only six months from the start of formal literacy instruction at age six or seven (Cossu, 1999). By contrast, most Japanese children learn kana by the end of the first year in primary school (age six or seven) and then continue to learn around 2000 official kanji by the age of 15. However, since many more than this are in common use, even adults often come across a new kanji. There are also many kanji which they read and understand, but cannot write.

From a different perspective, the incidence of reading disorders such as developmental dyslexia seems also to be affected by various characteristics of the writing system. Dyslexia is widely known to be related to phonological processing deficits, where children have difficulty establishing links between letters and sounds (Bruck & Treiman, 1990; Snowling, 2000). It has been reported that, when a writing system has a consistent relationship between letters and sounds, i.e. is shallow, the incidence of dyslexia is lower than in writing systems with a complex system. For example, dyslexics are half as numerous in Italy as in Britain (Paulesu *et al.*, 2001). In Japan and China, where Chinese characters are mainly used, an awareness of dyslexia itself is still not widespread. In such meaning-based writing systems, although phonological processing is important, reading and spelling may rely more on visual-orthographic information than on phonological coding. Without any compositional sound cues, kanji learning is essentially by rote and whole characters are remembered as words. Wydell and Butterworth (1999) provided evidence of an English-Japanese bilingual who was dyslexic only in English. They postulated that any language where the orthographic unit representing sounds is at the level of a whole symbol (letter, syllable, Chinese characters, etc.), as in Italian, kana, or kanji, should not produce a high incidence of developmental phonological dyslexia. These cross-linguistic variations in L1 reading acquisition therefore also support the view that the development of reading processes in different languages varies according to the writing system, thus confirming that writing systems and reading processes are strongly related.

Acquisition of reading in a second language

While Italian children start to learn English during the third year of primary school (age eight or nine), the formal teaching of English in Japan starts in secondary school (age 12 or 13). Japanese children learn the Roman alphabet at the age of nine or 10 as a supplementary orthography in the Japanese writing system called Romaji; however, it is taught through Japanese phonology, i.e. syllables, which have very regular correspondences between symbols and sounds. Thus, some confusion with the Romaji system is likely when children start to learn the English writing system.

The acquisition of reading and spelling in the second language differs from that in the first language because L2 readers already have reading experiences with their first language, i.e. they have established reading processes through another writing system. Does acquisition of another writing system encourage developing 'new' reading processes for L2 users? Koda (1996: 453) clearly describes factors involved in L2 reading acquisition:

(1) variation of L2 reading experience itself;
(2) structural similarity or non-similarity between L1 and L2 writing systems; and
(3) transfer of L1 processing experience.

These factors are each interpreted into the L2 proficiency effect, the L1–L2 writing system distance effect and the L1 reading process effect on L2. The effects of L1–L2 writing system distance and L1 reading processes indicate that acquisition of L2 reading processes can be affected by the first language in terms of its structure and processing experience.

Previous L2 reading studies have provided evidence that L1–L2 orthographic distance affects L2 reading acquisition (Haynes & Carr, 1990; Holm & Dodd, 1996; Koda, 1999). Moreover, various studies comparing L2 users from different L1 alphabetic and non-alphabetic writing system backgrounds found that users of the Chinese and the Japanese writing systems rely more strongly on orthographic information than users of alphabetic writing systems in reading their second language (Akamatsu, 2003; Chikamatsu, 1996; Koda, 1989; Muljani *et al.*, 1998; Wade-Woolley, 1999; Wang & Geva, 2003; Wang *et al.*, 2003). Wade-Woolley (1999) found that lower-intermediate Japanese learners of English were faster and more accurate than their Russian counterparts on tasks requiring an awareness of legitimate orthographic patterns and Russians were significantly more accurate at deleting specified phonemes than Japanese, i.e. their different strategic strengths in reading English depended on their L1 writing systems. Chikamatsu (1996) examined Chinese and English learners of Japanese in terms of strategies for reading kana. The Chinese learners relied more on visual information whereas the English learners relied more on phonological information. Furthermore, Wang *et al.* (2003) compared Chinese and Korean learners of English in a semantic category judgment task to examine the influence of phonological and orthographic similarity and found that Korean learners were affected by phonological similarity while Chinese learners were affected by orthographic similarity. They concluded that Chinese learners rely less on phonological information and more on orthographic information in English word reading than Korean learners.

Thus, previous studies comparing L2 readers with contrastive L1WS backgrounds have agreed on the different consequences of L2 reading performance, namely that L1 reading processes are transferred to L2 reading. Along with L1 reading studies, the view that the L1WS affects the reading processes is supported in L2 reading studies.

The Present Study

Based on the previous L2 reading studies, the current study investigates the following two aspects of L2WS reading:

(1) the effect of different L1 orthographic backgrounds (alphabetic versus non-alphabetic); and
(2) the effect of L1 orthographic regularity (shallow versus deep).

An experiment was designed to examine the use of phonological information in word recognition in terms of these two aspects. Japanese and Italian L2 users of English were compared as different L1WS groups. The Japanese writing system is non-alphabetic and uses different scripts from English, while the Italian writing system is alphabetic and employs the same Roman alphabet as English. According to the studies discussed above (e.g. Muljani *et al.*, 1998), Japanese readers will show negative effects of the L1WS compared to Italian readers because of the dissimilarity in the L1 and L2 writing systems. It is hypothesised that Italian readers will be more efficient (i.e. more accurate and faster) than Japanese counterparts at recognising English words because of their familiarity with the alphabetic correspondence and the script.

In addition, an effect of an L1 shallow orthography on reading an L2 deep orthography was investigated in Italian performance of English. If L1 reading processes also influence L2 reading, Italian users of English would read English differently from English users because the Italian writing system has regular correspondences between symbols and sounds, unlike the English writing system. Italian readers would have facilitation over English homophones because of their L1 reading processes in a shallow orthography. Table 11.1 summarises the contrastive features of the three writing systems, English, Italian and Japanese.

In summary, the hypothesis tested in this study is that L2 reading will be affected by L1–L2 writing system distance in terms of the representation unit as well as orthographic regularity. It follows that:

- Japanese users of English will be less efficient at recognising English words compared to Italian users because of their experience with the non-alphabetic L1WS.
- Italian users of English will be more efficient at recognising English homophone words, even compared to English L1 users, because of their experience with regular symbol–sound correspondences in their L1WS.

Experiment

Participants

Italian and Japanese intermediate-level L2 users of English studying at a university in the UK were recruited. Their proficiency and use of

Table 11.1 Representation units and orthographic depth

<table>
<tr><th colspan="2" rowspan="2">Unit of representation</th><th colspan="2">Orthographic depth</th></tr>
<tr><th>Shallow ←</th><th>→ Deep</th></tr>
<tr><td colspan="2">Alphabetic
Phoneme</td><td>Italian</td><td>English</td></tr>
<tr><td rowspan="2">Non-alphabetic</td><td>Syllabic
Syllable</td><td>Kana</td><td></td></tr>
<tr><td>Chinese character
Morpheme</td><td></td><td>Kanji</td></tr>
</table>

English were measured by their scores on Nation's (1990) vocabulary test, length of stay in English-speaking countries (5 months to 2.5 years), and self-assessment of daily use of both English and their first language. The average length of stay for the Japanese users in England (16.4 months, SD = 0.69) was calculated to be longer than that of the Italian users (8.8 months, SD = 0.35), after eliminating those scoring below 'university level' on the Nation vocabulary test. The daily use of the two languages was established by asking 'What is the percentage of use of English compared to your first language on an average day?' to show sufficient use of and exposure to English. In total, 14 Italian and 14 Japanese students participated in the experiment. Fifteen native English L1 users also participated as a control group.

Materials

The words for the experiment were chosen from the most frequent 3000 words (i.e. those with three to five black diamonds) listed in the *COBUILD Learner's Dictionary of English* (1996). Target words were all one or two syllable words, controlled for abstractness and concreteness. In order to equalise the appearance of loan-words and cognates for both L2 groups (naturally irrespective of the script and spelling differences), the percentages of such words in the experimental words were calculated: 39.9% of the English words exist as loan-words in Japanese whereas only 10.1% of them exist in Italian; however none of the English words had cognates in Japanese, while 27.7% of the English words had cognates in Italian, e.g. 'total-totale' and 'force-forza'. Adding cognate and loan-word appearance rates, in total 37.8% of the experimental English words were related to Italian words. Thus, it is assumed that cognate/loan-word effects between the two writing systems on this experiment would not be manifest.

Task

The experiment was carried out using PsyScope (Cohen *et al.*, 1993) on a Macintosh G3 laptop computer. Accuracy and response times (RTs) were recorded. As shown in Table 11.2, the experiment consisted of two phases. Phase 1 was an odd-one-out test to choose a semantically different word from a set of four words shown on a screen simultaneously, for example, to choose 'tail' from 'tail, cat, lion, tiger'. Participants were told that the correct answers were obvious. Phase 2 was a recognition test where target words were presented one by one on screen. Participants were asked to push the 'yes' button if they saw a specific word in Phase 1, and to push 'no' if they had seen the word not seen in Phase 1, as accurately and as quickly as possible. The words presented in Phase 2 were categorised into three different types in terms of their relationship with

Table 11.2 Examples of the experimental word types

Word type	*Presentation in Phase 1*				*Word in Phase 2*	*Correct answer*
Homophone	tail	cat	lion	tiger	tale	No
	trip	fare	travel	journey	fair	No
Repeated	horse	cow	donkey	fuel	fuel	Yes
	profit	benefit	loss	gain	loss	Yes
New	–	–	–	–	phone	No
	–	–	–	–	trend	No

the words presented in Phase 1:

(1) homophone words of the four words presented in Phase 1 (homophone words), e.g. 'tail' (in Phase 1) – 'tale' (in Phase 2);
(2) same words as the words in Phase 1 (repeated words), e.g. 'fuel' (in Phase 1) – 'fuel' (in Phase 2);
(3) words not seen in Phase 1 (new words).

Therefore, the correct answers were 'no' for homophone words and new words, but 'yes' for repeated words. Phase 2 included 24 homophone words, 40 repeated words and 16 new words, making 40 'yes' trials and 40 'no' trials in total. The error rates therefore include two types of error: (1) 'no' response errors (repeated words) and (2) 'yes' response errors (homophone and new words). The comparison between homophones and repeated words is based on the different types of error, whereas the comparison between homophones and new words is based on the same type of error.

Four sets of Phase 1 and 2 were created; thus each recognition test consisted of 20 target words. Words in each set were automatically randomised for each participant. In order to avoid any direct activation of phonological or graphic features of words from short-term memory, participants were asked to count to 50 aloud between Phase 1 and Phase 2. A practice set was given before starting the first set and a break was given between the second and third sets if required.

Phase 1 presented orthographic, phonological and semantic priming; Phase 2 tested how these three types of priming affect subsequent word recognition. Homophone words were used to investigate subjects' strategy with phonological information; if they use word phonology to retrieve visually presented words, they are likely to make mistakes with homophone words. According to previous L1 word recognition studies, these homophone effects are seen in both English and Japanese (Van Orden, 1987; Wydell *et al.*, 1993). Only the results from Phase 2 were analysed.

Results

Mean error rates and correct RTs in the recognition test (Phase 2) for Japanese, Italian, and English groups were submitted to a 3 × 3 mixed ANOVA. The subject analysis (*F*1) is a combination of a 'between-subjects' factor (first language) and a 'within-subjects' factor (word type). Conversely, in the item analysis (*F*2), language was a within-items factor and word type was a between-items factor. Overall mean performance and standard deviations are given in Table 11.3.

The main effect of word type was significant for both the error rate ($F1(2, 80) = 18.81$, $p < 0.001$; $F2(2, 77) = 8.41$, $p < 0.001$) and the RT ($F1(2, 80) = 49.15$, $p < 0.001$; $F2(2, 77) = 46.08$, $p < 0.001$), i.e. the overall responses demonstrated the contrast between word types: homophone words, repeated words and new words. The main effect of language group was found significant in the error rate only by item ($F1(2, 40) = 2.02$, $p = 0.15$; $F2(2, 154) = 6.15$, $p < 0.01$) and both by subject and item in the RT ($F1(2, 40) = 6.88$, $p < 0.01$; $F2(2, 76) = 110.15$, $p < 0.001$ by a multivariate test (Pillai's Trace)). Irrespective of word type, language group provided a contrasting effect in RTs but not in error rates. Significant interactions between word type and language group were found in the error rate ($F1(4, 80) = 5.10$, $p < 0.01$; $F2(4, 154) = 7.57$, $p < 0.001$) and in the RT only by item ($F1(4, 80) = 1.91$, $p = 0.12$; $F2(4, 154) = 5.40$, $p < 0.001$). (Note: supported by significant differences by item, the main effect of language group in error rate and the interaction between word type and language group in RT can be marginally significant according to a one-tailed hypothesis.)

The effect of word type within each language group by subject was analysed by a one-way within-subjects ANOVA (*F*1). The analysis-by-item was conducted by a one-way between-subjects ANOVA (*F*2).

Table 11.3 Mean error rates and RTs for each condition by language group (standard deviations are shown in brackets)

	Homophone		*Repeated*		*New*	
	Error rate (%)	*RT (ms)*	*Error rate (%)*	*RT (ms)*	*Error rate (%)*	*RT (ms)*
Japanese	27.38 (14.31)	1411 (306)	9.64 (5.79)	1113 (219)	8.04 (8.98)	1263 (257)
English	13.33 (8.36)	1363 (256)	6.17 (4.90)	1048 (176)	10.42 (11.49)	1165 (288)
Italian	14.58 (9.77)	1111 (172)	11.43 (8.97)	916 (88)	8.04 (11.35)	964 (133)

The error rate data indicated that Japanese and English were significantly affected by word type but not Italian (Japanese: $F1(2, 26) = 24.41$, $p < 0.001$; $F2(2, 77) = 13.78$, $p < 0.001$) (English: $F1(2, 28) = 3.44$, $p < 0.05$; $F2(2, 77) = 5.31$, $p < 0.01$). The RT data showed all language groups were affected by word type (Japanese: $F1(2, 26) = 16.62$, $p < 0.001$; $F2(2, 77) = 34.81$, $p < 0.001$) (English: $F1(2, 28) = 17.79$, $p < 0.001$; $F2(2, 77) = 23.15$, $p < 0.001$) (Italian: $F1(2, 26) = 18.42$, $p < 0.001$; $F2(2, 77) = 17.90$, $p < 0.001$). The effects of homophone words (homophone versus repeated and homophone versus new) were observed within each language group by pairwise comparisons with Bonferroni adjustment (significance level set at $p < 0.05$) by subject. Homophone words showed higher error rates and longer RTs than repeated words for both the Japanese and English groups (Japanese: $p < 0.001$ both in error rate and in RT) (English: $p < 0.05$ in error rate and $p < 0.001$ in RT). However, the Italian group showed significant differences between homophone and repeated words only in RT ($p < 0.001$). According to comparisons between homophone words and new words, Japanese also showed a significant difference both in error rate ($p < 0.001$) and RT ($p < 0.05$) while English and Italian groups showed a difference only in RT ($p < 0.05$ for English; $p < 0.01$ for Italian). Japanese users were strongly affected by homophones both in error rate and RT, while Italian users were affected in RT only. Figure 11.1 shows comparisons of the mean error rates and the mean RTs of the three language groups for each word type.

The effect of language group on each word type by subject was analysed by a one-way between-subjects ANOVA. The analysis-by-item was conducted through a one-way within-subjects ANOVA. In terms of

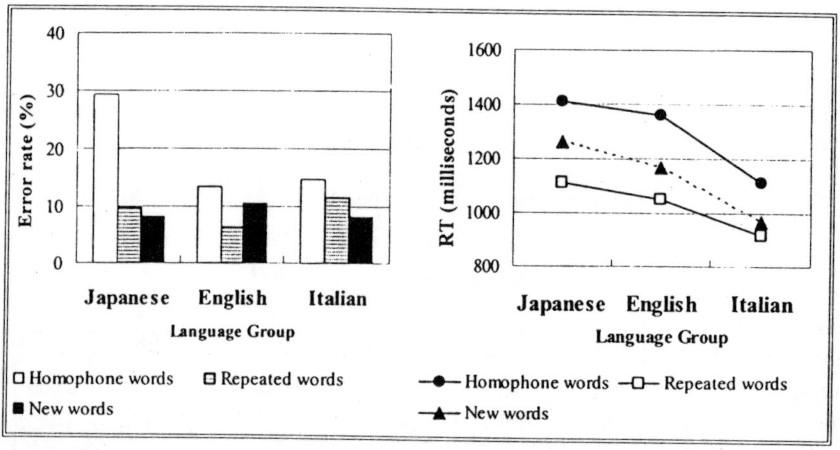

Figure 11.1 A comparison of error rate and the reaction time by language group

error rate, the effect of language group was significant only in the homophone word condition ($F1(2, 40) = 7.04$, $p < 0.01$; $F2(2, 46) = 11.25$, $p < 0.001$). In the RT data, the effect of language group was significant in all three word type conditions (homophone: $F1(2, 40) = 5.18$, $p < 0.01$; $F2(2, 46) = 35.66$, $p < 0.001$; repeated: $F1(2, 40) = 4.90$, $p < 0.05$; $F2(2, 78) = 21.47$, $p < 0.001$; new: $F1(2, 40) = 5.80$, $p < 0.01$; $F2(2, 46) = 20.32$, $p < 0.001$). In line with the hypotheses, Japanese responses were compared with Italian responses. The post-hoc comparison (Tukey HSD) by subject indicated significant differences between the Japanese and Italian groups. Japanese homophone word responses showed significantly higher error rates and longer RTs than Italian responses ($p < 0.05$ in error rate; $p < 0.01$ in RT). In terms of the other two word type conditions, although the error rates of repeated and new words did not show any difference between these two groups, Japanese took significantly longer than Italian in both word types ($p < 0.05$ for repeated words; $p < 0.01$ for new words). Thus, the data provided evidence that the Japanese group was less efficient at English word recognition compared with the Italian group.

Furthermore, Italian homophone responses were compared to English responses in order to observe the effect of orthographic depth. While the error rate data did not show a significant difference, the RT data indicated that Italian users were significantly quicker than English to respond correctly ($p < 0.05$). Thus, Italian users were more efficient at responding to homophone words than English users. Moreover, although the RT differences between Italian and English did not reach the significant level in the two other word types by post-hoc comparisons ($p = 0.10$ for repeated words; $p = 0.07$ for new words, two-tailed), Italian readers were relatively faster than English readers on these conditions, too.

Additionally, the effect of spelling similarity between homophone word pairs was also analysed. Orthographic similarity of a homophone word in Phase 1 (e.g. 'tail') and the pair which appeared in Phase 2 (e.g. 'tale') was calculated in Van Orden's procedure based on Weber's measure of graphic similarity (see the formulas in Van Orden, 1987). The 24 homophone word pairs were categorised into two spelling similarity groups: less similarly spelled pairs and similarly spelled pairs (e.g. the pair such as 'suite-sweet' was categorised into the former, while the pair 'heel-heal' was the latter). Figure 11.2 shows a comparison between these two types of homophone words for error rates and RTs. The responses for similarly spelled homophone words were submitted to a one-way ANOVA in order to compare language group effects by subject. There was a significant difference both in error rate ($F(2, 48) = 4.97$ $p < 0.05$) and in RT ($F(2, 48) = 17.05$, $p < 0.001$). The post-hoc comparison indicated that Japanese users showed significantly higher error rate than both English users ($p < 0.05$) and Italian users ($p < 0.05$). The RT data

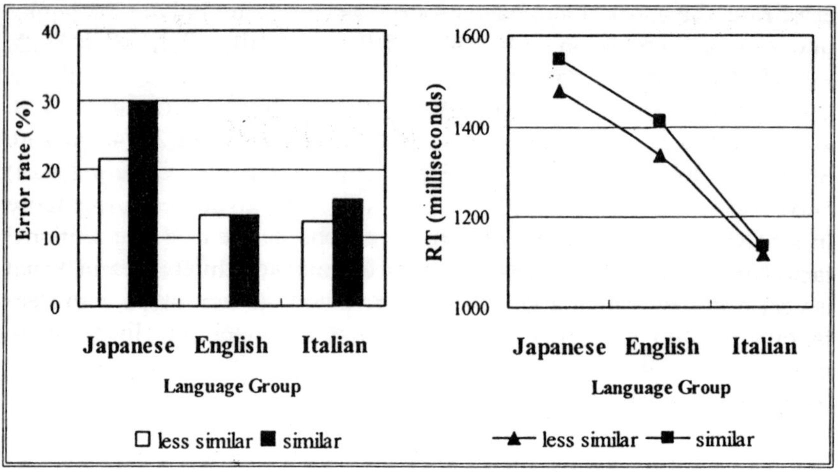

Figure 11.2 A comparison of the spelling similarity effects on homophone responses

revealed that the difference was due to the Italian group's faster responses than both the Japanese ($p < 0.001$) and the English groups ($p < 0.01$). The difference between the English and the Japanese groups did not reach significance ($p = 0.15$). The less similarly spelled homophones showed significant differences by language group only for RT ($F(2, 18) = 4.13$ $p < 0.05$) due to the faster responses of the Italian group.

In summary, the stronger homophone interference in Japanese responses compared to that of English and Italian was mainly attributed to similarly spelled homophones.

Discussion

The responses (i.e. the error rates and the RTs) between three language groups, Italian, Japanese and English, in English word recognition were compared in relation to their orthographic backgrounds. The results support the hypothesis that a difference between alphabetic and non-alphabetic L1 orthographic backgrounds affects L2 English reading processes. The Japanese group showed the highest error rate and the longest response time in recognition of the homophone words out of the three groups, indicating their inefficiency in recognising words in an unfamiliar alphabetic writing system. Moreover, the current results support the second hypothesis that L1 orthographic regularity affects L2 English reading processes. The Italian group was faster than the English group at recognising homophone words, although there was no difference in accuracy between the two groups.

These data corroborate the two dimensions of cross-linguistic variation in writing systems described earlier: the varying unit of orthographic representation and orthographic regularity. In other words, the effects of similarity and non-similarity in L1–L2 writing systems are attributed to at least two different features: effects of the similarity and non-similarity of what a symbol represents (i.e. a phoneme, a syllable or a morpheme) and effects of the similarity and non-similarity of the degree of regularity in symbol–sound correspondence. The script type forms an additional factor of variation. Thus, the Japanese writing system (kanji and kana) is very different from that of English in terms of the script type, representation unit and regularity in correspondence. Therefore, the Japanese users of English were affected by several types of non-similarity between the L1 and L2 writing systems.

The Japanese users of English in this experiment showed significant homophone interference in reading English, which suggests they use phonology in reading, i.e. provides evidence for the universal phonological principle. This is also consistent with the previous studies dealing with homophone responses in English L1 users (Van Orden, 1987) and in Japanese kanji reading (Wydell *et al.*, 1993). However, their homophone interference in error rate was much larger than the English group and the Italian group. This can be explained by the effect of non-similarity in L1–L2 scripts: for example, distinguishing two similarly spelled words in an alphabet script would be more difficult for Japanese than for Italians who were familiar with the same script. Secondly, it can be explained by the difference between L1–L2 representation units because the Japanese L1WS does not represent the phoneme level of sounds. The previous studies discussed above indicated that kanji readers rely more on visual-orthographic information than phonological information. In the current data, the comparison of less similarly spelled homophone responses across the language groups did not show any advantage for Japanese users. Instead, the Japanese users made significantly more errors than both the English and Italian groups for the similarly spelled homophone responses. Similar results were found in Wang *et al.* (2003) where Chinese and Korean learners of English were compared. Japanese users were not as sensitive to the phoneme level of phonological representation as Italian users even when it was orthographically different. This may be because they were unfamiliar with the script as well as the phoneme level of the orthographic representation. Rather, they seemed to have a tendency to use whole-word phonology, possibly as in reading two-kanji compound words, which generated strong homophone interference.

On the other hand, Italian users were not affected by homophones. Moreover, their responses were faster than Japanese and even than English users. This implies they use reading processes from their shallow L1 writing system in English. The Italian writing system provides reliable correspondences of graphemes to phonemes to yield correct pronunciation of the word. Thus, it is plausible that readers of Italian are used to recognising words in constantly smaller units (i.e. single letters or letter-strings) than in English word bodies or words. In such reading processes, English homophone words would not be seen as homophones at first. In this way, Italian users were not affected by homophones as much as English users so their correct responses for homophones were faster than those of English. However, it is not sufficient to speculate that the use of whole-word phonology was non-existent for Italian readers in this task, since the error rate of the homophone words was similar to their English counterparts, even though there was no significant difference in the Italian's error rates among word type. Recent cross-linguistic studies suggest that reading speed by readers of a shallow orthography is faster than that by deep orthographic readers; Paulesu *et al.* (2000) for instance provided evidence that Italian students read words and non-words faster than English students.

Thus, the current data indicate that Japanese users of English relied more on whole-word phonology when recognising visually presented English words while Italian users of English relied more on the phoneme level of correspondence than any other size of units. Therefore, the use of phonological information differed between Japanese and Italian. Furthermore, neither of the L2 groups seemed to show the same processes as English L1 readers. In other words, because L2 readers have specific reading processes in each L1WS, the reading processes in L2WS should be different from those of the native readers. As the grain size of reading units hypothesised (e.g. Goswami *et al.*, 1998), English phonological coding requires processing at a variety of grain sizes such as graphemes, word bodies and whole-words. The fact that the two L2 groups (i.e. alphabetic L1WS and non-alphabetic L1WS groups) were different at reading English and the group with alphabetic L1WS background performed more efficiently than the other group was consistent with the previous studies discussed above (Mujani *et al.*, 1998; Wang *et al.*, 2003; etc.). The current study also provides new evidence that L2 users with a shallow alphabetic L1WS perform more efficiently than L1WS users in a particular L2 word recognition task, suggesting positive transfer of L1 reading processes.

The participants in the experiment were no longer taking English courses and they were using English in their academic life. Therefore, their level of English is supposed to be sufficient to conduct an English word recognition task. With relation to the effect of L2 proficiency on word recognition, a further study by Sasaki (2004) employed advanced Japanese users of L2WS English in the same word recognition task but found no difference from the English counterpart. Thus, the negative effect of non-similarity in L1–L2 writing systems does not appear to be sustained in advanced-level L2 reading. Negative transfer from the first language can be overcome by developing different reading processes from those used in the L1WS after sufficient L2 reading experience.

In conclusion, the study supports the view that the reading processes in an L1WS writing system would affect L2 reading performance, thus leading to differences in L2 reading performance between users with different orthographic backgrounds. Japanese intermediate-level users of L2WS when reading English words use the phoneme level of phonological coding less but whole-word phonology more, while their Italian counterparts use more phoneme level of phonological coding but less whole-word phonology. The data provide evidence for an L1WS effect on the L2WS in terms of two dimensions of variation in writing systems, namely the unit of orthographic representation and orthographic regularity.

References

Akamatsu, N. (2003) The effects of first language orthographic features on second language reading in text. *Language Learning* 53 (2), 207–31.

Bruck, M. and Treiman, R. (1990) Phonological awareness and spelling in normal children and dyslexics: The case of initial consonant clusters. *Journal of Experimental Child Psychology* 50, 156–78.

Carney, E. (1994) *A Survey of English Spelling*. London: Routledge.

Chikamatsu, N. (1996) The effects of L1 orthography on L2 word recognition. *Studies in Second Language Acquisition* 18, 403–32.

Chomsky, N. and Halle, M. (1968) *The Sound Pattern of English*. New York: Harper & Row.

COBUILD Learner's Dictionary of English (1996) London: HarperCollins.

Cohen J.D., MacWhinney B., Flatt M. and Provost J. (1993) PsyScope: A new graphic interactive environment for designing psychology experiments. *Behavioral Research Methods, Instruments, and Computers* 25 (2), 257–71.

Cossu, G. (1999) The acquisition of Italian orthography. In M. Harris and G. Hatano (eds) *Learning to Read and Write: A Cross-linguistic Perspective* (pp. 10–33). Cambridge: Cambridge University Press.

DeFrancis, J. (1989) *Visible Speech: The Diverse Oneness of Writing Systems*. Honolulu: University of Hawaii.

Feldman, L.B. and Turvey, M.T. (1980) Words written in kana are named faster than the same words written in kanji. *Language and Speech* 23, 141–7.

Frost, R., Katz, L. and Bentin, S. (1987) Strategies for visual word recognition and orthographic depth: A multilingual comparison. *Journal of*

Experimental Psychology: Human Perception and Performance 13 (1), 104–15.

Goswami, U., Gombert, J.E. and de Barrera, L.F. (1998) Children's orthographic representations and linguistic transparency: Nonsense word reading in English, French, and Spanish. *Applied Psycholinguistics* 19 (1), 19–52.

Goswami, U., Ziegler, J.C., Dalton, L. and Schneider W. (2003) Nonword reading across orthographies: How flexible is the choice of reading units? *Applied Psycholinguistics* 24 (2), 235–47.

Haynes, M. and Carr, T.H. (1990) Writing system background and second language reading: A component skills analysis of English reading by native speaker-readers of Chinese. In T. Carr and B. Levy (eds) *Reading and Its Development: Component Skills Approaches* (pp. 375–421). New York: Academic Press.

Holm, A. and Dodd, B. (1996) The effect of first written language on the acquisition of English literacy. *Cognition* 59, 119–47.

Katz, L. and Frost, R. (1992) Reading in different orthographies: The orthographic depth hypothesis. In R. Frost and L. Katz (eds) *Orthography, Phonology, Morphology, and Meaning* (pp. 67–84). Amsterdam: Elsevier.

Koda, K. (1989) Effects of L1 orthographic representation on L2 phonological coding strategies. *Journal of Psycholinguistic Research* 18 (2), 201–22.

Koda, K. (1996) L2 word recognition research: A critical review. *The Modern Language Journal* 80 (4), 450–60.

Koda, K. (1999) Development of L2 intraword orthographic sensitivity and decoding skills. *The Modern Language Journal* 83 (1), 51–64.

Leck, K.J., Weekes, B.S. and Chen, M.J. (1995) Visual and phonological pathways to the lexicon: Evidence from Chinese readers. *Memory and Cognition* 23, 468–76.

Lesch, M.F. and Pollatsek, A. (1993) Automatic access of semantic information by phonological codes in visual word recognition. *Journal of Experimental Psychology: Learning, Memory and Cognition* 19, 285–94.

Morita, A. and Matsuda, F. (2000) Phonological and semantic activation in reading two-kanji compound words. *Applied Psycholinguistics* 21, 487–503.

Muljani, D., Koda, K. and Moates, D.R. (1998) The development of word recognition in a second language. *Applied Psycholinguistics* 19, 99–113.

Nation, I.S.P. (1990) *Teaching and Learning Vocabulary.* Boston: Heinle & Heinle.

Paulesu, E., McCrory, E., Fazio, F., Menoncello, L., Brunswick, N., Cappa, S.F., Cotelli, M., Cossu, G., Corte, F., Lorusso, M., Pesenti, S., Gallagher, A., Perani, D., Price, C., Frith, C.D. and Frith, U. (2000) A cultural effect on brain function. *Nature Neuroscience* 3 (1), 91–6.

Paulesu, E., Demonet, J.F., Fazio, F., McCrory, E., Chanoine, V., Brunswick, N., Cappa, S.F., Cossu, G., Habib, M., Frith, C.D. and Frith, U. (2001) Dyslexia: Cultural diversity and biological unity. *Science* 291, 2165–7.

Perfetti, C.A. and Tan, L.H. (1998) The time course of graphic, phonological, and semantic activation in Chinese character identification. *Journal of Experimental Psychology: Learning, Memory and Cognition* 24 (1), 101–18.

Perfetti, C.A., Zhang, S. and Berent, I. (1992) Reading in English and Chinese: Evidence for a "universal" phonological principle. In R. Frost and L. Katz (eds) *Orthography, Phonology, Morphology, and Meaning* (pp. 227–48). Amsterdam: Elsevier.

Saito, H. (1981) Use of graphemic and phonemic encoding in reading Kanji and Kana. *The Japanese Journal of Psychology* 52 (5), 266–73 (in Japanese).

Saito, H., Masuda, H. and Kawakami, M. (1998) Form and sound similarity effects in kanji recognition. *Reading and Writing* 10, 323–57.

Sakuma, N., Sasanuma, S., Tatsumi, F. and Masaki, S. (1998) Orthography and phonology in reading Japanese kanji words: Evidence from the semantic decision task with homophones. *Memory and Cognition* 26 (1), 75–87.

Sasaki, M. (2004) Acquisition of reading processes in the first and the second writing systems. PhD thesis, University of Essex.

Sasanuma, S. (1975) Kana and Kanji processing in Japanese aphasics. *Brain and Language* 2, 369–83.

Snowling, M. (2000) *Dyslexia*. Oxford: Blackwell.

Tan, L.H. and Perfetti, C.A. (1998) Phonological codes as early sources of constraint in Chinese word identification: A review of current discoveries and theoretical accounts. *Reading and Writing* 10 (3–5), 165–200.

Treiman, R., Mullennix, J., Bijeljac-Babic, R. and Richmond-Welty, E.D. (1995) The special role of rimes in the description, use, and acquisition of English orthography. *Journal of Experimental Psychology: General* 124 (2), 107–36.

Van Orden, G.C. (1987) A rows is a rose: Spelling, sound and reading. *Memory and Cognition* 15, 181–98.

Venezky, R.L. (1970) *The Structure of English Orthography.* The Hague: Mouton.

Wade-Woolley, L. (1999) First language influences on second language word reading: All roads lead to Rome. *Language Learning* 49 (3), 447–71.

Wang, M. and Geva, E. (2003) Spelling performance of Chinese children using English as a second language: Lexical and visual-orthographic processes. *Applied Psycholinguistics* 24, 1–25.

Wang, M., Koda, K. and Perfetti, C.A. (2003) Alphabetic and non-alphabetic L1 effects in English word identification: A comparison of Korean and Chinese English L2 learners. *Cognition* 87 (2), 129–49.

Weekes, B.S., Chen, M.J. and Lin, Y.-B. (1998) Differential effects of phonological priming on Chinese character recognition. *Reading and Writing* 10 (3–5), 201–21.

Wydell, T.N. and Butterworth, B. (1999) A case of an English-Japanese bilingual with monolingual dyslexia. *Cognition* 70, 273–305.

Wydell, T.N., Patterson, K.E. and Humphreys, G.W. (1993) Phonologically mediated access to meaning for Kanji: Is a rows still a rose in Japanese Kanji? *Journal of Experimental Psychology: Learning, Memory and Cognition* 19 (3), 491–514.

Ziegler, J.C., Perry, C., Jacobs, A.M. and Braun, M. (2001) Identical words are read differently in different languages. *Psychological Science* 12 (5), 379–84.

Part 3

Awareness of Language and Second Language Writing Systems

Chapter 12

Learning to Read Across Writing Systems: Transfer, Metalinguistic Awareness, and Second-language Reading Development

KEIKO KODA

Introduction

Children develop sensitivity to the particular regularities of spoken language well before formal literacy training commences. Such sensitivity is generally assumed to regulate both perception and interpretation of linguistic input – thereby guiding and facilitating subsequent language learning and processing (Ellis, 2002; MacWhinney, 1987; Slobin, 1985). Although the sensitivity evolves through learning and using a given language, it is distinct from linguistic knowledge in that it denotes a basic understanding of the language's general structural properties, independent of specific linguistic instantiations (Bialystok, 2001). Among English-speaking children, for example, syntactic *awareness* reflects the realisation that the order in which words are presented determines sentence meaning. However, an abstract notion of this sort differs from syntactic *knowledge* – an understanding of the canonical word order (subject-verb-object) in English sentences.

Insofar as reading is embedded in two interrelated systems – language and orthography – linking the two is a requisite for reading acquisition in all languages (Perfetti, 2003). It generally is accepted, consequently, that structural sensitivity, emanating from oral language experience, substantially expedites the pivotal learning-to-read task – deducing how spoken language elements are mapped in the writing system. The current consensus, in fact, holds that learning to read is fundamentally *metalinguistic*, entailing the recognition of spoken language elements, units of graphic symbols, and their relationships (e.g. Fowler & Liberman, 1995; Goswami & Bryant, 1992; Nagy & Anderson, 1999). In this context, *metalinguistic awareness* is defined as the ability to identify, analyse and manipulate language forms.

Although the early phases of literacy acquisition depend on children's rudimentary understanding of linguistic regularities, this initial sensitivity is refined progressively through experience with processing print, gradually becoming more explicit (e.g. Bowey & Francis, 1991; Perfetti *et al.*, 1987; Tolchinsky, 2003). In this sense, literacy and metalinguistic awareness are developmentally interdependent. This reciprocity gives rise to two major implications: metalinguistic awareness is shaped to accommodate specific properties of the language elements and the writing system; and therefore the precise nature of metalinguistic awareness varies systematically from language to language.

Second-language reading, obviously, is unique in that virtually all operational aspects are cross-linguistic, involving two or more languages. The dual-language involvement, seemingly, results from the inevitable transfer occurring during second-language processing, irrespective of the learner's intent (e.g. Akamatsu, 1999; Djikstra & van Heuven, 1998; Koda, 2000; Muljani *et al.*, 1998; Wang *et al.*, 2003a). Inasmuch as transferred competencies continue to mature through print processing experience in the target language (e.g. Koda, 1999, 2000; Koda *et al.*, 1998), second-language skill development can be regarded as procedural amalgamation, evolving from cross-linguistic interactions between transferred first-language competencies and second-language visual input. Given that linking language elements with the writing system is universally required for reading acquisition, we can logically assume that first-language metalinguistic awareness, once transferred, facilitates learning to read in a new language. Despite the potential significance, however, metalinguistic competencies – particularly, their relation to first- and second-language writing systems – remain largely unexplored in second-language research. In an attempt to reduce this gap, the goal of this chapter is to explore the distinct ways in which first- and second-language writing systems shape the evolution of second-language metalinguistic awareness, as well as subsequent reading skill development. It should be noted, at the outset, that the word 'competence' is used inclusively in the subsequent sections to refer to linguistic knowledge, processing skills and cognitive abilities.

Theoretical Underpinnings

Reading is a complex, multi-dimensional, pursuit, entailing a large number of sub-component processes. In second-language reading, the complexity increases exponentially, because, as noted above, virtually all operations involve two, or more, languages. To understand how second-language reading skills develop, it is necessary to consider what 'dual language involvement' means; how it affects learning to read in an unfamiliar language; and how the aggregate consequences can be empirically examined. Although it is commonly observed that reading skills, once developed in one language, readily transfer to another language (e.g. Akamatsu, 1999; August *et al.*, 2001; Durgunoglu *et al.*, 1993; Koda, 1998, 1999, 2000; Wang *et al.*, 2003a), little is known about which specific skills actually transfer, how and to what extent transferred skills contribute to second-language reading development, and whether the transfer occurs in the same manner – and to the same degree – across learners with diverse first-language orthographic backgrounds.

To address these vital, largely untapped, questions, brief summaries of the relevant theories are helpful. Language transfer is central to the current conceptualisation because it clarifies the very concept of dual-language involvement, explaining procedural variations attributable to diverse first-language learning-to-read experiences. Metalinguistic awareness is also fundamental in comparing the requisite competencies for reading acquisition across languages. Careful analyses of writing-system properties in a particular language should permit the identification of metalinguistic capabilities directly related to learning to read in that language. Therefore, systematic comparisons of these capabilities in diverse languages should also permit the categorisation of shared learning-to-read requirements across languages. Such categorisation is essential in second-language research because it helps achieve accurate predictions of the extent to which transferred first-language competencies facilitate second-language reading development.

Cross-language transfer of reading competencies

Although reading-skill transfer has been studied over the past three decades, a clear consensus has yet to emerge as to what actually transfers, in part because of the somewhat polarised views of reading. One faction sees reading as an indivisible whole, while another views it as a constellation of separate components. Based on the conviction that language is acquired as a whole through communication, and communicative use of language is intrinsic in reading, proponents of the holistic view posit that reading is learned holistically as a meaning-making process (Goodman, 1967, 1969). Since meaning construction does not vary from one language to another, there should be little difference in the learning-to-read process across languages. The early transfer research, taking this view, focused on two primary issues: the interrelationship between first- and second-language reading abilities (e.g. Cummins, 1979, 1991; Cummins *et al.*, 1981; Legaretta, 1979; Skutnabb-Kangas & Toukomaa, 1976; Troike, 1978); and the conditions that either inhibit or facilitate reading-skill transfer from the first to the second language (e.g. Clarke, 1980; Devine, 1987, 1988). By defining reading as a single, unitary construct, these early studies generally disregarded the component skills underlying efficient processing of print information. As a result, little attention is given to what precisely is transferred from one language to another, and how transferred skills contribute to second-language reading development.

In more recent studies, however, reading is seen as a constellation of closely related mental operations. Inasmuch as this view incorporates multiple skills, it allows the tracing of possible relationships between corresponding skills in first- and second-languages. Thus, the componential view is well suited for studying reading skill transfer. More critically, the multiple-skills approach also makes it possible to examine the relative extent to which varying first-language skills contribute – directly and indirectly (through their corresponding second-language skills) – to second-language reading performance. Since second-language readers vary along a number of dimensions, such as first-language reading ability, second-language linguistic knowledge, and similarity in learning-to-read experiences in the two languages, we cannot assume that transfer occurs in the same manner either across all component skills, or among all second-language learners. Systematic competency dissections should enable us to determine the relative contributions of various first-language reading skills, and, in so doing, to distinguish transferable from non-transferable competencies.

Roles of metalinguistic awareness in reading acquisition

Because metalinguistic awareness is multi-dimensional in nature, its facets can be defined and measured in conjunction with various language features (e.g. Adams, 1990; Stahl & Murray, 1994; Yopp, 1988). In recent times, interest in metalinguistic awareness has risen sharply among reading researchers. The facilitating benefits of metalinguistic awareness can be illustrated in two ways. First, for reading acquisition to occur, the child must understand that graphic symbols correspond to speech units; what each symbol represents; and how they can be combined to form a word. Lacking these basic insights, written symbols are perceived as nonsense scribbles, and their learning is unduly painstaking, because it is apparently both useless and meaningless. Second, an understanding of the segmental nature of spoken language promotes analytical approaches to language processing, simply because the concept of segmentation bolsters the capacity for analysing the internal structure of words in order to identify known elements in an unfamiliar string of letters. Without the analytical competence, reading words becomes an all-or-nothing process, preventing the child from extracting partial information from a novel string of symbols. Under such circumstances, reading capacity is likely to be limited to words previously encountered and retained.

The roles of metalinguistic awareness in alphabetic literacy – English, in particular – have been extensively studied over the past two decades. While English orthography is alphabetic, bound by phonemic constraints, it tends to preserve morphological information in its graphic representation. Reflecting this duality, many of the investigations on record have concentrated on the phonological and morphological aspects of metalinguistic awareness. Evidence from phonological awareness research has led to the widely-endorsed conviction that to master an alphabetic script, children must not only recognise that words can be divided into sequences of phonemes, but also must acquire the capability to analyse a word's internal structure to identify its phonemic constituents. Reading studies, in fact, show that children's sensitivity to the segmental structure of spoken sounds is directly related to their ability to read and spell words (e.g. Stahl & Murray, 1994; Stanovich, 2000; Stanovich *et al.*, 1984; Yopp, 1988); phonological segmentation capability is a powerful predictor of reading success among early and middle-grade students (e.g. Bryant *et al.*, 1990; Juel *et al.*, 1986); and reading progress is significantly enhanced by phonological awareness training (e.g. Bradley & Bryant, 1991).

The contribution of morphological awareness to literacy acquisition has also been noted. For example, children's capability of analysing a word's morphological constituents systematically relates to reading ability (e.g. Carlisle, 1995; Carlisle & Nomanbhoy, 1993; Fowler & Liberman, 1995); considerably more errors of omitting inflectional and derivational morphemes occur in the writing and speaking of less skilled readers (e.g. Duques, 1989; Henderson & Shores, 1982; Rubin, 1991); and the ability to use morphological information during sentence comprehension distinguishes skilled from less-skilled high-school readers (Tyler & Nagy, 1989, 1990). Interestingly, different patterns of metalinguistic contributions have been reported in a recent study involving native Mandarin-speaking children. Reflecting the prominence of grapheme–morpheme connections in Chinese characters, morphological awareness was found to be a stronger predictor of literacy acquisition in Chinese than phonological awareness (Li *et al.*, 2002).

Viewed collectively, findings from both phonological and morphological awareness studies make it plain that metalinguistic capabilities facilitate literacy learning in several distinct ways and, more critically, that the specific facets of the awareness underlying reading development in a particular language are allied with properties of its writing system.

Metalinguistic awareness as a window for investigating reading skill transfer in second-language reading development

Tracing reading-skill transfer is a challenging enterprise. Since validation of 'cross-language transfer' entails an empirical demonstration of similar processing behaviours across languages, we must consider what competencies are expected to evolve from processing experience in both first and second languages. Without clear descriptions of the expected processing behaviours in the first language, it is virtually impossible to determine whether observed response patterns in the second language are an accurate manifestation of reading skill transfer.

Metalinguistic awareness offers two major advantages as a basis for examining cross-language transfer. First, since diverse facets of metalinguistic awareness are related to print information processing, first-language literacy experience can be translated into specific metalinguistic capabilities. This in turn provides a solid basis for predicting which specific capabilities are 'transfer ready' at a given point in time among a particular group of second-language learners. Second, since the aspects of metalinguistic capabilities directly contributing to decoding mastery are shaped through print information processing (e.g. Bowey & Francis, 1991; Perfetti *et al.*, 1987; Vellutino & Scanlon, 1987), such capabilities are believed to reflect the specific ways spoken-language elements are graphically represented in the writing system. This means that the metalinguistic competencies likely to transfer can be identified through analysis of properties of the first-language writing system. The metalinguistic capabilities underlying efficient decoding in the target language can also be categorised by analysing the second-language writing system. Hence, systematic comparisons of the two writing systems involved should enlarge our understanding of the specific ways first-language literacy experience influences learning to read a second language.

In sum, metalinguistic studies, to date, have yielded a number of significant implications directly relevant to cross-language transfer in second-language reading development. Listed below, they encapsulate the fundamental premises underlying a theoretical framework through which specific contributions, generated by transferred competencies, can be conceptualised and examined empirically.

- Children form sensitivity to the regularities of spoken language during oral language development.
- Writing systems are structured to capture these regularities, and therefore, learning to read necessitates the linking of spoken language elements and units of graphic symbols.
- Metalinguistic sensitivity precipitates a recognition of the specific ways spoken language elements are mapped in the writing system.
- Such sensitivity becomes increasingly explicit through cumulative print processing experience.
- The nature of metalinguistic awareness varies in languages in accordance with properties of their writing systems.

The Framework of the Transfer Facilitation Model

In keeping with the above postulations, the Transfer Facilitation Model represents an attempt to explain how transferred metalinguistic awareness promotes second-language reading development among second-language learners across age groups. The rationale underlying the formulation of such a model is simply that, despite the commonly-held belief that first- and second-language reading competencies are closely related, to date our understanding of the mechanisms conjoining literacy experiences in two languages is still very limited. Elucidating the mechanisms involved – leading to subsequent empirical examinations – will yield important clues for clarifying other critical issues in second-language reading development, such as: the optimal ages for providing second-language literacy instruction for learners already literate in their first languages; the functions of oral language proficiency in literacy acquisition; and possible variations in the developmental sequence in first- and second-language literacy. Given the strong probabilities that metalinguistic awareness transfers across languages and also that the transferred competencies enhance second-language reading acquisition, there is reason to explore the phenomena inherent in cross-language reading-skill transfer.

In a sense, the Transfer Facilitation Model is a particular instantiation of the Functionalist approach to language learning and processing. In Functional theories, language is viewed as a set of relationships between forms and functions (Van Valin, 1991). Since such relationships do not embody closely-matched, one-to-one correspondences, they are regarded as correlational, and are described in terms of probability rather than absolute rules. In the same vein, language learning is seen as the internalisation of form–function relationships, implicit in linguistic input, through cumulative processing experience (MacWhinney & Bates, 1989). Input frequency, therefore, is closely aligned with learning outcomes (Ellis, 2002). The more frequently particular patterns of form-to-function mappings are experienced, the more rapid and effortless the mappings become. In this approach, accordingly, processing automaticity is viewed as a non-deliberate, non-volitional activation of well-established mapping patterns initiated through input (Logan, 1988).

The conception of experience-based learning, outlined above, not only explains why first-language literacy experience is central to second language reading, but also provides an empirical basis for tracing and comparing the impacts of such experience across learners. As a case in point, within this line of reasoning, transfer can be defined as automatic activation of well-rehearsed first-language mapping procedures, triggered by second-language input, irrespective of the learner's intent. Non-volitional first-language activation, in fact, has been observed in laboratory experiments, examining second-language lexical processing among adult bilingual learners (e.g. Djikstra & van Heuven, 1998; Dijkstra *et al.*, 1998; Jiang, 2002). Critically, this view presumes that, for cross-language transfer to occur, elements to be transferred must be well-rehearsed and established in the first language; and also that transferred elements should continuously evolve through second-language print-processing experience in order to accommodate properties of the writing system of the new language.

Assuming such automatic first-language involvement, the critical question is how transferred elements facilitate second-language reading development. Although the model presumes that reading skill transfer occurs in virtually all processing operations, the current elucidation centres on metalinguistic awareness for the reasons noted in the previous sections. Inasmuch as the initial task of learning-to-read, in all languages, uniformly entails the linking of language elements with units of graphic symbols (Perfetti, 2003), the proposed model assumes that second-language visual input is filtered through transferred first-language metalinguistic capabilities. In light of the universality in basic learning-to-read requirements, it is also presumed that transferred metalinguistic awareness provides useful top-down assistance, guiding the task of linking language elements and graphic symbols in a new language. With such assistance, the task should be more deductive in second-language literacy learning, necessitating far less input for its completion. Moreover, since underdeveloped metalinguistic capabilities are not likely to transfer, differences in first-language literacy experience, and in the resulting metalinguistic sophistication, should be a strong predictor of initial reading achievement among second-language learners.

Beyond the initial phase, however, acquiring the skills to extract accurate phonological and semantic information from visual word displays necessitates metalinguistic acumen attuned to the specific way in which relevant lexical information is graphically represented. The proposed view of transfer, as noted above, presupposes that second-language metalinguistic awareness emerges from the continuous interplay between transferred first-language metalinguistic sensitivity and second-language visual input, gradually transforming itself into optimal utility in the new language. It is further assumed that such transformation is achieved more easily when the first- and second-language writing systems involved share similar properties, because less adjustment is necessary when the two systems are closely related. Presuming that the evolving second-language awareness serves as a foundation through which second-language print information extraction skills are shaped, the orthographic distance should also be a significant factor in explaining individual differences in the rate at which second-language reading skills develop. Based on these premises, the model has generated four hypotheses.

First, to the extent that metalinguistic competencies are common across languages, *transferred capabilities contribute to second-language reading acquisition*. The first hypothesis is, therefore, that a strong relationship exists between first-language metalinguistic capabilities and the initial stages of reading development both within and across languages. The relationship is particularly obvious among young second-language learners whose first-language metalinguistic awareness is still developing and varies widely.

But, unlike simultaneous literacy acquisition, successive learning involves second-language learners who are already literate in their first languages. Theoretically, their prior metalinguistic 'experience' should provide substantial facilitation in detecting regularities inherent in second-language visual input. Insofar as a high level of maturation is a precondition for transfer, it follows that first-language reading ability is a strong indicator of how well one can read a second language. The proposed transfer model predicates that first-language metalinguistic insights, when transferred, offer substantial assistance to literate second-language learners, in deducing how language elements correspond with graphic symbols in the new writing system. The second hypothesis is, therefore, that *first-language metalinguistic sophistication is a reliable predictor of the rate at which corresponding second-language metalinguistic awareness matures.*

Because the distance between the first- and second-language writing systems tends to vary considerably among disparate learners (e.g. Spanish learners of English versus Chinese learners of English), such variance must also be taken into consideration. When the method of representing specific linguistic information is similar between the two writing systems, information extraction procedures are also likely to be analogous – if not identical. Thus, transferred metalinguistic sensitivity should substantially facilitate second-language print information extraction. The direct implication is that, when the two writing systems share similar structural and representational properties, transferred competencies require minimal processing experience in the second language for fine-tuning. The model hence offers a plausible explication of why decoding competence is acquired more rapidly by learners with some first-language backgrounds than those with others. Consequently, a third hypothesis can be formulated: *the distance between the two writing systems accounts for the differential rates of second-language metalinguistic awareness, and subsequent decoding skill development among learners with diverse first-language orthographic backgrounds.*

Finally, within Functionalist paradigms, the model further presumes that second-language metalinguistic awareness evolves through continuous interactions between transferred first-language competencies and second-language visual input. Since such cross-linguistic interplay typically results in sustained assimilation of processing experiences in both languages (e.g. Muljani *et al.*, 1998; Wang *et al.*, 2003a), the resulting second-language competencies are expected to vary systematically across diverse first-language groups. Hence, the final hypothesis is that *variations in second-language processing efficiency are attributable, in part, to differential procedural requirements imposed by first-language writing systems, and in part to varying amounts of experience with the target language visual input.*

The model's central claims can be summarised as follows:

- *Facilitation from shared metalinguistic awareness competencies:* The aspects of metalinguistic awareness shared across languages, once developed in one language, facilitate the initial task of learning to read in another language, because the basic requirements for the task are also common across languages.
- *Contribution of first-language metalinguistic sophistication:* First-language metalinguistic insights regarding how language elements are graphically represented in the writing system, when transferred, establish a solid foundation for developing a functional understanding of the corresponding relationships in a second language, thereby facilitating the formation of second-language metalinguistic awareness and subsequent decoding skill development.
- *First- and second-language orthographic distance effects:* The aspects of transferred metalinguistic awareness, attuned to the properties specific to the first-language writing system, need to be adjusted to those in the second language through processing experience with the target-language visual input. Because degree of adjustment is determined essentially by how closely the two writing systems are related, the development of second-language metalinguistic awareness and decoding skills requires different amounts of print information processing experience among learners with similar, and dissimilar, first-language orthographic backgrounds.
- *Cross-linguistic variations in second-language metalinguistic awareness:* Second-language decoding skills develop through interaction between transferred first-language metalinguistic competencies and second-language visual input, and, as a result, newly acquired skills, reflecting both first- and second-language writing systems, vary systematically across learners with diverse first-language orthographic backgrounds.

The predictive validity of these claims is evaluated in the following section through a review of empirical studies.

Roles of Metalinguistic Awareness in Second-Language Reading Development

Facilitation from shared metalinguistic awareness competencies

In view of the irrefutable contributions of metalinguistic awareness to early reading development, the question is how the learning-to-read process among school-age second-language learners differs from that of their monolingual counterparts. Presumably, young second-language learners are handicapped by a double-bind. Generally, they lack adequate oral language command at the point when second-language literacy learning commences, and unlike adult learners, they have limited prior literacy experience in the first language. Inasmuch as the primary objective in the initial 'learning-to-read' phase is developing skills with which to map spoken-language elements onto graphic symbols, success in this phase largely depends on metalinguistic understanding of what is to be mapped. Young second-language learners, because of limited oral communication experience in the target-language, are likely to be less sensitive to the functional significance of linguistic features. Conceivably, they may undertake the 'learning-to-read' task without either adequate knowledge of the actual linguistic elements, or the metalinguistic facilitation guiding mapping skill development. Moreover, because of their limited prior literacy experience, we cannot assume that all children have a clear understanding that print represents speech. In the absence of such a basic concept, linguistic knowledge, however developed, cannot automatically be used to 'decipher' print information.

Are there, then, mechanisms to facilitate learning-to-read for these children with a dual handicap? One possibility, seemingly, is phonological awareness – the child's growing understanding of the segmental nature of spoken words. The conviction emanating from first-language reading research is that phonological awareness, a by-product of oral language experience, precedes and supports initial literacy acquisition. The awareness serves as a basis for decoding development in typologically diverse writing systems, including logographic Chinese (Ho & Bryant, 1999; Li *et al.*, 2002). The Transfer Facilitation Model posits that the segmental understanding, once developed in one language, can facilitate learning to read in another language, irrespective of their orthographic distance. It can be predicted, therefore, that the early stages of second-language reading development among young learners rely heavily on metalinguistic sensitivity, in general, and phonological awareness specifically, much like first-language literacy acquisition.

Earlier studies investigated the extent to which phonological awareness relates to word-reading ability among school-age second-language learners. Cisero and colleagues (1992), for example, contrasted English monolingual and Spanish-dominant bilingual first-grade children in phoneme detection performance, and concluded that in both groups, competent readers were superior in phonemic analysis to their less-competent counterparts. Similarly, in a study on Spanish-dominant bilingual first graders, Durgunoglu *et al.* (1993) determined that first-language phonological awareness is a powerful predictor of subsequent word recognition skills in both languages. These studies thus extended earlier first-language research conclusions to bilingual populations. The Durgunoglu *et al.* (1993) study, moreover, points to the strong possibility that phonological awareness, developed in one language, can enhance literacy acquisition in another.

Subsequent studies, employing a large battery of tasks in both first and second languages, focused on the inter-lingual connections among a wide range of component skills. Collectively, their findings suggest that significant relationships exist in a variety of corresponding skills; poor readers are uniformly weak in phonological skills in both languages; their deficiencies usually are 'domain-specific' and not primarily attributable to non-phonological factors (e.g. Abu-Rabia, 1995; August *et al.*, 2001; Carlisle & Beeman, 2000; Cormier & Kelson, 2000; da Fontoura & Siegel, 1995; Gholamain & Geva, 1999; Verhoeven, 2000; Wade-Woolley & Geva, 2000). Da Fontoura and Siegel (1995), for instance, examined literacy development among Portuguese-English bilingual children in each of their two languages. Measuring and comparing phonological skills, syntactic knowledge and working memory, the researchers found high correlations between corresponding skills in the two languages. They also determined that reading problems were associated with phonological skill deficits. In a study with second grade children who were simultaneously learning to read English and Hebrew, Wade-Wooley and Geva (2000) also acquired evidence of cross-linguistic relations between phonological skills and word-reading ability. Gholamain and Geva (1999), by comparing yet another set of component skills (decoding, letter naming speed and working memory) among children learning to read English and Persian, once again found significant relationships between corresponding skills both within and across languages.

Taken as a whole, these findings make it plain that phonological awareness plays a vital role in reading acquisition in both first and second languages. Even more significantly, phonological awarenesses in the children's two languages are developmentally interdependent. It is not yet clear, however, the extent to which such interdependence results from the commonalty of alphabetic scripts involved in most of the studies on record. On one hand, we can speculate that cross-linguistic connections are reduced when learners deal with two orthographically unrelated languages, while, on the other, it seems equally plausible that strong inter-lingual connections remain – regardless of orthographic typology – because the aspects of phonological awareness required for reading acquisition do not vary much from language to language. Empirical data is currently limited, in the main, to children learning to read two alphabetic orthographies. Further investigations are needed to enhance our understanding of inter-lingual relationships between phonological awareness and decoding skill acquisition in biliteracy development involving orthographically unrelated writing systems.

Contribution of first-language metalinguistic sophistication

Inasmuch as aspects of metalinguistic awareness are common across languages, once developed, they can provide substantial facilitation in the formation of structural sensitivity in another language. Consequently, metalinguistically 'trained' adult second-language learners should be adept at deducing how spoken-language elements relate to units of graphic symbols in a new language. Studies on adult learners of Japanese and Chinese offer some insights on the issue. With the growing interest in logographic literacy, an increasing number of studies have appeared that address the development of character-knowledge among second-language learners of logographic languages. Their findings generally suggest that character-specific awareness evolves relatively early among these learners, but, until then, they appear to learn and process characters holistically in all-or-nothing manners.

In an instructional study, Dwyer (1997) for example examined ways of facilitating kanji learning among beginning learners of Japanese. His data demonstrated that systematic presentations of phonetic radicals when introducing new characters facilitated the mastery of kanji pronunciations, and that simultaneously presenting a group of kanji, sharing no common graphic elements, was beneficial in remembering character meanings. His results thus suggest that even beginning learners utilise character components to learn and recall characters, supporting the conviction that sensitivity to a character's internal components among second-language learners evolves early in kanji-knowledge development. Similarly, Ke (1998) found that, after one year of Chinese study, his college-level participants were aware of the utility of radicals in building character-knowledge; and also that such awareness was a direct consequence of their character-recognition ability. Using a think-aloud protocol analysis, Everson and Ke (1997) determined that, while intermediate learners depended on rote-memorisation approaches to character identification, advanced learners were more analytical, invoking character segmentation and radical-information retrievals.

Wang *et al.* (2003b) explored how adult second-language learners of Chinese acquire sensitivity to the second-language orthographic structure. Using two experimental tasks (lexical decision and naming), the researchers showed that lexical processing among American learners of Chinese was considerably impaired by visual complexity, radical combination violations and radical misplacement. These results corroborate those from other Chinese-learning studies described above, suggesting that beginning learners of Chinese, despite their limited print exposure, become sensitised to the internal structural properties of Chinese characters. Even more critically, such sensitivity – an understanding of the visual-orthographic constraints – appears to guide character information processing among second-language learners of Chinese with alphabetic first-language backgrounds.

In a psycholinguistic experiment, Koda and Takahashi (submitted) compared radical awareness among native and non-native kanji users through semantic category judgement. In the experiment, participants were asked to decide whether a presented character (e.g. 'lake') belonged to a specific semantic category (e.g. 'body of water'). Their findings demonstrated that the groups benefited similarly from semantic radicals when extracting semantic information from single-character words. However, the groups' responses differed when the characters and radicals provided conflicting information, as in the case of the 'water' radical used in a character whose meaning had no relevance to 'water' (e.g. 'decide'). While judgment speed among native kanji users declined considerably in processing characters whose semantic radicals conveyed conflicting information, their accuracy rate remained the same, presumably because they took time to decide. Reaction times among non-native participants, in contrast, were minimally affected, but their error rates increased perceptibly, seemingly because they disregarded the incongruity. Apparently, native Japanese readers detected the mismatch, but novices did not. The findings thus indicate that second-language learners are sensitised to the basic function of semantic radicals and attentive to their information during kanji processing. However, they still need to become aware that not all radicals provide valid information, as well as to develop the skills of differentiating valid from invalid information and incorporating valid information selectively during kanji recognition.

To sum up, studies involving second-language learners of Chinese and Japanese repeatedly suggest that adult learners of logographic languages are progressively sensitised to the functional and structural properties of character components, and gradually rely on this sensitivity both in learning new characters and retrieving stored character information. Of greatest moment, however, such sensitivity readily develops with somewhat restricted character-learning experience (usually 250–400 characters) among metalinguistically adroit adult learners. This contrasts sharply with children learning to read Chinese as their first language, who require knowledge of roughly 2000 characters to develop similar metalinguistic insights (Shu & Anderson, 1999).

First- and second-language orthographic distance effects

Cross-language transfer occurs during second-language decoding development, irrespective of the distance between the two writing systems. However, the degrees of facilitation brought about by transferred first-language metalinguistic awareness are likely to vary because the distance imposes varying modifications on the transferred competencies. If so, orthographic distance should be responsible, in part, for the rate at which second-language metalinguistic awareness develops among learners with diverse first-language backgrounds, which, in turn, explains differences in their print information extraction efficiency. Although systematic probing of the relationship between orthographic distance and second-language metalinguistic awareness has yet to occur, initial inquiries into the orthographic distance effects on second-language decoding development are currently under way. Studies involving ESL learners demonstrate that more accurate and rapid performance transpires among those with alphabetic, than non-alphabetic, first-language backgrounds (e.g. Dhanesschayakupta, 2003; Green & Meara, 1987; Koda, 2000; Muljani *et al.*, 1998). The critical question in this research is how shared properties facilitate second-language print information extraction through cross-language transfer.

Muljani *et al.* (1998) shed significant light on the issue by testing the effects of orthographic distance on second-language intra-word structural sensitivity. Comparing lexical-decision performance (deciding whether or not a given string of letters is a real word) among proficiency-matched ESL learners with related (Indonesian, i.e. Roman-alphabetic) and unrelated (Chinese, i.e. logographic) first-language orthographic backgrounds, the study revealed that intra-word structural congruity (i.e. spelling-pattern consistency) between the two alphabetic languages (Indonesian and Chinese) benefited lexical judgement among Indonesian, but not Chinese, participants. Indonesian superiority, however, was far less pronounced on the items whose spelling patterns were unique to English (i.e. not present in Indonesian). These findings suggest that although related orthographic backgrounds induce general facilitation in lexical processing, accelerated efficiency occurs only at the operations dealing with properties shared between the two languages and thus posing identical processing requirements. Hence, it appears that orthographic distance not only explains overall performance differences among learners with related and unrelated first-language backgrounds, but it also underscores the ways in which first-language experience facilitates second-language lexical processing.

To sum up, research findings seem to suggest that orthographic distance is a strong predictor of second-language decoding development. To date, however, the hypothesised role of metalinguistic awareness, as a factor mediating the observed connection between orthographic distance and second-language decoding efficiency, has yet to be empirically tested. Given the explanatory potential of this factor, future research should directly examine the relationship between orthographic distance and second-language metalinguistic awareness, as well as that between second-language metalinguistic awareness and decoding efficiency among learners with diverse first-language orthographic backgrounds.

Cross-linguistic variations in second-language metalinguistic awareness

Traditionally, in second-language research, limited attention has been given to the cognitive interplay between the two languages during second-language lexical processing. Of late, however, systematic investigations of such cross-linguistic interactions have been initiated through comparisons of metalinguistic awareness among second-language readers.

In a series of studies, Koda and associates (Koda, 2000; Koda *et al.*, 1998) show that processing experiences in both first and second languages predict differences in morphological awareness development among ESL learners with typologically similar and dissimilar first-language backgrounds (typologically similar: Korean, i.e. alphabetic-syllabary orthography, linear-sequential morpheme organisation; typologically dissimilar: Chinese, i.e. logographic orthography, non-linear non-sequential morpheme organisation). Korean superiority, attributable to their typologically similar background, was found in some, but not all, aspects of second-language morphological awareness. Although Korean learners outperformed the Chinese in the awareness aspects directly related to the structural properties shared between English and Korean, the two ESL groups did not differ in other aspects pertaining to the features unique to the target language. Their findings, as noted in the previous section, would seem to suggest that information extraction efficiency in the operations involving the linguistic features specific to the target language is gained mainly through second-language print processing experience. The clear implication is that, since the development of information extraction efficiency necessitates second-language visual input, it is unaffected by differences in first-language processing experiences.

In related studies, Koda (1998, 1999) compared phonological awareness and orthographic sensitivity among proficiency-matched Korean (alphabetic) and Chinese (logographic) ESL learners. While intra-word segmentation is central to phonological processing in alphabetic systems, it is not mandatory in logographic orthographies. It was hypothesised, therefore, that intra-word analysis experience among Korean ESL learners would facilitate the acquisition of metalinguistic competence in manipulating segmental phonological information. It was further hypothesised that accelerated phonological awareness among Korean ESL learners would enhance their decoding development. Results complicated the already complex picture. Contrary to the predictions, the groups did not differ in either phonological awareness or decoding. However, a clear contrast existed in the extent to which the two variables were related to reading comprehension. In the Korean data, phonological awareness decoding and reading performance were closely interconnected, but no direct relationships were observed in the Chinese data. The contrast was interpreted as suggesting that the two ESL groups rely on different processing competencies during reading comprehension. The study did not reveal what those competencies were, but the fact that Korean Hang'ul is typologically similar (alphabetic), although orthographically unrelated, to the English writing system could imply that typological similarity alone may not be sufficient to achieve the anticipated magnitude of facilitation, stemming from transferred skills in second-language decoding development.

In a more recent study (Wang *et al.*, 2003a), first-language orthographic influence was examined using a category judgment task. In the study, participants were first presented with a category descriptor, such as 'flower,' and then with a target word. The task was to decide whether the word was a member of the given category. The task would have been simple if real category-member words, such as 'rose,' had appeared. Instead, target words were manipulated either phonologically or graphically. Phonologically manipulated targets were homophones of category-member words. Using the above example, instead of showing the word 'rose,' its homophone 'rows' was presented. Graphically manipulated targets words were visually similar, but non-homophonic, to category-member words (e.g. 'fees' for 'feet'). The primary hypothesis was that the two ESL groups would respond differently to the two types of manipulation: Korean participants would be more likely to accept homophonic targets as category members, while Chinese would make more false positive responses to graphically similar targets. The data demonstrated that phonological and graphic similarity both significantly interfered with category judgement performance of both ESL learner groups. But, as predicted, the magnitude of interference, stemming from each type of manipulation, varied noticeably between the groups: Korean learners made significantly more errors by accepting homophonic items, whereas Chinese participants' errors were attributable to their false positive responses to graphically similar targets. Here again, the results clearly indicate that the two groups rely upon different information during semantic information extraction, and more critically, that these differences are related to their first-language orthographic experiences.

Hence, empirical findings, to date, suggest that structural sensitivities evolving from first- and second-language orthographic experiences are *both* operative during second-language processing, jointly affecting second-language decoding skill development.

Summary and Future Research Agendas

This synthesis – based on insights from language-transfer and metalinguistic awareness research – provides a fitting introduction to the Transfer Facilitation Model. Formulated as a unified framework, the model clarifies the specific ways in which first- and second-language writing systems shape second-language metalinguistic awareness, which, in turn, facilitates second-language reading development. In essence, the model postulates, first, that metalinguistic sensitivity evolves gradually through print processing experience; and, second, that transferring across languages, such sensitivity provides second-language learners with top-down guidance in formulating reliable connections between spoken language elements and graphic symbols in the new writing system.

A considerable body of studies with both child and adult second-language learners demonstrate that first-language metalinguistic capabilities are readily usable in other languages, and transferred capabilities play an important role in second-language reading development. As a consequence, substantial variations in the structural and functional properties of first-language writing systems can give rise to major differences in the rate and manner in which second-language metalinguistic awareness and decoding skills are acquired. Of the greatest moment, however, it is very likely that literate second-language learners, because of their prior metalinguistic training, may acquire an understanding of how elements of a new language relate to its writing system much more rapidly, and with far greater ease, than beginning first-language readers. In short, first-language metalinguistic awareness can make critical contributions, in multiple ways, to second-language literacy acquisition.

In light of the impact that transferred metalinguistic awareness plays in second-language reading development, two avenues appear to hold strong promise for expanding current research. First, little information is available about the nature of metalinguistic competencies, as well as their development in languages other than English. Since different writing systems have distinct ways of representing speech, metalinguistic understanding of how the writing system works should vary across languages. Systematic probing of the print–speech relationships in diverse writing systems would shed substantial light on the precise metalinguistic foundation literate learners bring to reading acquisition in a second language. Such analyses will also help establish systematic ways of estimating first- and second-language orthographic distance, which, in turn, facilitates accurate predictions of the relative ease with which decoding skills develop among learners with diverse first-language orthographic backgrounds.

Second, because decoding efficiency is a critical prerequisite to successful comprehension (Gough & Tunmer, 1986; Hoover & Gough, 1990), the long-term effects of initial decoding variance associated with first- and second-language writing systems are worthy of systematic explorations. Inability to extract accurate, and/or sufficient, word-meaning information impedes comprehension, because it creates an extremely weak, perhaps non-existent, semantic basis for text-meaning construction. Because of the strong possibility that second-language learners acquire decoding competencies through interplay between transferred first-language metalinguistic competencies and second-language visual input, diverse first-language learning-to-read experiences could result in initial variations in decoding competence. Decoding variance, in turn, could have disparate effects on the ways comprehension skills develop among contrasting first-language groups.

Different reading skills are acquired at different developmental stages, entailing diverse sets of prerequisite elements. Metalinguistic contributions to the acquisition of distinct reading skills, therefore, can only be understood through detailed, multi-faceted analyses, clarifying what skills are needed to accomplish major operations in text information extraction and integration during meaning construction; which specific structural features (e.g. orthographic, morphological, syntactic) are relevant to each of those skills; and how abstract structural understanding facilitates their acquisition. Further elucidation of metalinguistic awareness effects on reading acquisition, both within and across languages, coupled with empirical validations, will undoubtedly foster innovative approaches to investigating second-language reading development.

References

Abu Rabia, S. (1995) Learning to read in Arabic: Reading, syntactic, orthographic and working memory skills in normally achieving and poor Arabic readers. *Reading Psychology* 16, 351–94.

Adams, M.J. (1990) *Beginning to Read*. Cambridge, MA: The MIT Press.

Akamatsu, N. (1999) The effects of first language orthographic features on word recognition processing in English as a second language. *Reading and Writing* 11 (4), 381–403.

Anderson, R.C. and Li, W. (in press) A cross-language perspective on learning to read. In A. McKeough and L. Phillips (eds) *International Perspectives on Literacy*. Hillsdale, NJ: Lawrence Erlbaum.

August, D., Calderon, M. and Carlo, M. (2001) Transfer of skills from Spanish to English: A study of young learners. *NABE News*. At http://www.cal.org/pubs/articles/skillstransfer-nabe.html. Accessed March 2004.

Bialystok, E. (2001) *Bilingualism in Development*. Cambridge: Cambridge University Press.

Bowey, J.A. and Francis, J. (1991) Phonological analysis as a function of age and exposure to reading instruction. *Applied Psycholinguistics* 12, 91–121.

Bradley, L. and Bryant, P. (1991) Phonological skills before and after learning to read. In S.A. Brady and D.P. Shankweiler (eds) *Phonological Processing in Literacy* (pp. 37–45). Hillsdale, NJ: Lawrence Erlbaum.

Bryant, P., MacLean, M. and Bradley, L. (1990) Rhyme, language, and children's reading. *Applied Psycholinguistics* 11, 237–52.

Carlisle, J. (1995) Morphological awareness and early reading achievement. In L. Feldman (ed.) *Morphological Aspects of Language Processing* (pp. 189–209). Hillsdale, NJ: Lawrence Erlbaum Associates.

Carlisle, J.F. and Beeman, M.M. (2000) The effects of language of instruction on the reading and writing achievement of first-grade Hispanic children. *Scientific Studies of Reading* 4, 331–53.

Carlisle, J.F. and Nomanbhoy, D. (1993) Phonological and morphological development. *Applied Psycholinguistics* 14, 177–95.

Cisero, C.A., Carlo, M.S. and Royer, J.M. (1992) Can a child raised as English speaking be phonemically aware in another language? Paper presented at the annual meeting of the American Educational Research Association, San Francisco, CA, April.

Clarke, M.A. (1980) The short circuit hypothesis of ESL reading – or when language competence interferes with reading performance. *Modern Language Journal*, 64, 203–209.

Cormier, P. and Kelson, S. (2000) The roles of phonological and syntactic awareness in the use of plural morphemes among children in French immersion. *Scientific Studies of Reading* 4, 267–94.

Cummins, J. (1979) Linguistic interdependence and educational development of bilingual children. *Review of Educational Research* 49, 222–51.

Cummins, J. (1991) Interdependence of first- and second-language proficiency in bilingual children. In E. Bialystok (ed.) *Language Processing in Bilingual Children* (pp. 70–89). New York: Cambridge University Press.

Cummins, J., Swain, M., Nakajima, K., Handscombe, J. and Green, D. (1981) *Linguistic Interdependence in Japanese and Vietnamese Students*. Report prepared for the Inter-America Research Associates, June. Toronto: Ontario Institute for Studies in Education.

da Fontoura, H.A. and Siegel, L.S. (1995) Reading, syntactic and memory skills of bilingual Portuguese-English Canadian children. *Reading and Writing: An International Journal* 7, 139–53.

Devine, J. (1987) General language competence and adult second language reading. In J. Devine, P.L. Carrell and D.E. Eskey (eds) *Research on Reading English as a Second Language* (pp. 73–86). Washington, DC: TESOL.

Devine, J. (1988). A case study of two readers: Models of reading and reading performance. In J. Devine, P.L. Carrell and D.E. Eskey (eds) *Interactive Approaches to Second Language Reading* (pp. 127–30). New York: Cambridge University Press.

Dhanesschayakupta, U. (2003) Transfer of cognitive skills among Chinese and Thai ESL readers. Unpublished doctoral dissertation, University of Pittsburgh.

Dijkstra, T. and Van Heuven, W.J.B. (1998) The BIA model and bilingual word recognition. In J. Grainger and A.M. Jacobs (eds) *Localist Connectionist Approaches to Human Cognition* (pp. 189–225). Mahwah, NJ: Erlbaum.

Dijkstra, T., Van Jaarsveld, H. and Ten Brinke, S. (1998) Interlingual homograph recognition: Effects of task demands and language intermixing. *Bilingualism: Language and Cognition* 1, 51–66.

Duques, S.L. (1989) Grammatical deficiencies in writing: An investigation of learning disabled college students. *Reading and Writing* 1, 309–25.

Durgunoglu, A.Y., Nagy, W.E. and Hancin, B.J. (1993) Cross-language transfer of phonemic awareness. *Journal of Educational Psychology* 85, 453–65.

Dwyer, E.S. (1997) Getting started the right way: An investigation into the introduction of Kanji study to neophyte Japanese learners. Ph.D. dissertation, The University of Texas at Austin.

Ellis, N. (2002) Frequency effects in language processing: A review with implications for theories of implicit and explicit language acquisition. *Studies in Second Language Acquisition* 24, 143–88.

Everson, M.E. and Ke, C. (1997) An inquiry into the reading strategies of intermediate and advanced learners of Chinese as a Foreign Language. *Journal of the Chinese Language Teachers Association* 32, 1–20.

Fowler, A.E. and Liberman, I.Y. (1995) The role of phonology and orthography in morphological awareness. In L.B. Feldman (ed.) *Morphological Aspects of Language Processing* (pp. 157–88). Hillsdale, NJ: Lawrence Erlbaum.

Gholamain, M. and Geva, E. (1999) The concurrent development of word recognition skills in English and Farsi. *Language Learning* 49 (2), 183–217.

Goodman, K.S. (1967) Reading: A psycholinguistic guessing game. *Journal of the Reading Specialist* 6, 126–35.

Goodman, K.S. (1969) Analysis of oral language miscues: Applied psycholinguistics. *Reading Research Quarterly* 5, 9–30.

Goswami, U. and Bryant, P. (1992) Rhyme, analogy, and children's reading. In P.B. Gough, L.C. Ehri and R. Treiman (eds) *Reading Acquisition.* Hillsdale, NJ: Erlbaum.

Gough, P. and Tunmer, W. (1986) Decoding, reading, and reading disability. *Remedial and Special Education* 7, 6–10.

Green, D.W. and Meara, P. (1987) The effects of script on visual search. *Second Language Research* 3, 102–17.

Henderson, A.J. and Shores, R.E. (1982) How learning disabled students' failure to attend to suffixes affects their oral reading performance. *Journal of Learning Disabilities* 15, 178–82.

Ho, C.S.-H. and Bryant, P. (1999) Different visual skills are important in learning to read English and Chinese. *Educational and Child Psychology* 16, 4–14.

Hoover, W.A. and Gough, P.B. (1990) The simple view of reading. *Reading and Writing: An Interdisciplinary Journal* 2, 127–60.

Jiang, N. (2002) Form-meaning mapping in vocabulary acquisition in a second language. *Studies in Second Language Acquisition* 24, 617–38.

Juel, C., Griffith, P.L. and Gough, P.B. (1986) Acquisition of literacy: A longitudinal study of children in first and second grade. *Journal of Educational Psychology* 78, 243–55.

Ke, C. (1998) Effects of language background on the learning of Chinese characters among foreign language students. *Foreign Language Annals* 31, 91–100.

Koda, K. (1998) The role of phonemic awareness in L2 reading. *Second Language Research*, 14, 194–215.

Koda, K. (1999) Development of L2 intraword structural sensitivity and decoding skills. *Modern Language Journal* 83, 51–64.

Koda, K. (2000) Cross-linguistic variations in L2 morphological awareness. *Applied Psycholinguistics* 21, 297–320.

Koda, K. and Takahashi, T. (submitted) Role of radical awareness in lexical inference in Kanji. Manuscript submitted for publication.

Koda, K., Takahashi, E. and Fender, M. (1998) Effects of L1 processing experience on L2 morphological awareness. *Ilha do Desterro* 35, 59–87.

Legaretta, D. (1979) The effects of program models on language acquisition of Spanish speaking children. *TESOL Quarterly* 13, 521–34.

Li, W., Anderson, R.C., Nagy, W. and Zhang, H. (2002) Facets of metalinguistic awareness that contribute to Chinese literacy. In W. Li, J.S. Gaffney and J.L. Packard (eds) *Chinese Children's Reading Acquisition: Theoretical and Pedagogical Issues* (pp. 87–106). Boston: Kluwer Academic.

Logan, G.D. (1988) Toward an instance theory of automization. *Psychological Review* 95, 492–527.

MacWhinney, B. (1987) Applying the Competition Model to bilingualism. *Applied Psycholinguistics* 8, 315–27.

MacWhinney, B. and Bates, E. (eds) (1989) *The Crosslinguistic Study of Sentence Processing*. Cambridge: Cambridge University Press.

Muljani, M., Koda, K. and Moates, D. (1998) Development of L2 word recognition: A Connectionist approach. *Applied Psycholinguistics* 19, 99–114.

Nagy, W.E. and Anderson, R.C. (1999) Metalinguistic awareness and literacy acquisition in different languages. In D. Wagner, R. Venezky and B. Street (eds) *Literacy: An International Handbook* (pp. 155–60). New York: Garland.

Perfetti, C.A. (2003) The universal grammar of reading. *Scientific Studies of Reading* 7, 3–24.

Perfetti, C.A., Beck, I., Bell, L.C. and Hughes, C. (1987) Phonemic knowledge and learning to read are reciprocal: A longitudinal study of first grade children. *Merrill-Palmer Quarterly* 33, 283–319.

Rubin, H. (1991) Morphological knowledge and writing ability. In R.M. Joshi (ed.) *Written Language Disorders* (pp. 43–69). New York: Kluwer Academic.

Shu, H. and Anderson, R.C. (1999) Learning to read Chinese: The development of metalinguistic awareness. In J. Wang, A. Inhoff, and H.-C. Chen (eds) *Reading Chinese Script: A Cognitive Analysis* (pp. 1–18). Mahwah, NJ: Lawrence Erlbaum.

Skutnabb-Kangas, T. and Toukomaa, P. (1976) *Teaching Migrant Children's Mother Tongue and Learning the Language of the Host Country in the Context of the Socio-cultural Situation of the Migrant Family.* Helsinki: The Finnish National Commission for UNESCO.

Slobin, D.I. (1985) (ed.) *The Crosslinguistic Study of Language Acquisition* (Vol. 2). Hillsdale, NJ: Erlbaum.

Stahl, S.A. and Murray, B.A. (1994) Defining phonological awareness and its relationship to early reading. *Journal of Educational Psychology* 86, 221–34.

Stanovich, K.E. (2000) *Progress in Understanding Reading: Scientific Foundations and New Frontiers*. New York: Guilford Press.

Stanovich, K.E., Cunningham, A.E. and Cramer, B.B. (1984) Assessing phonological awareness of kindergarten children: Issues of task comparability. *Journal of Experimental Psychology* 38, 175–90.

Tolchinsky, L. (2003) *The Cradle of Culture*. Mahwah, NJ: Erlbaum.

Troike, R.C. (1978) Research evidence for the effectiveness of bilingual education. *NABE Journal* 3, 13–24.

Tyler, A. and Nagy, W. (1989) The acquisition of English derivational morphology. *Journal of Memory and Language* 28, 649–67.

Tyler, A. and Nagy, W. (1990) Use of derivational morphology during reading. *Cognition* 36, 17–34.

Van Valin, R.D. (1991) Functionalist linguistic theory and language acquisition. *First Language* 11, 7–40.

Vellutino, F.R. and Scanlon, D.M. (1987) Phonological coding, phonological awareness, and reading ability: Evidence from a longitudinal and experimental study. *Merrill-Palmer Quarterly* 33, 321–63.

Verhoeven, L. (2000) Components in early second language reading and spelling. *Scientific Studies of Reading* 4, 313–30.

Wade-Woolley, L. and Geva, E. (2000) Processing novel phonemic contrasts in the acquisition of L2 word reading. *Scientific Studies of Reading* 4, 295–311.

Wang, M., Koda, K. and Perfetti, C.A. (2003a) Alphabetic and non-alphabetic L1 effects in English semantic processing: A comparison of Korean and Chinese English L2 learners. *Cognition* 87, 129–49.

Wang, M., Perfetti, C.A. and Liu, Y. (2003b) Alphabetic readers quickly acquire orthographic structure in learning to read Chinese. *Scientific Studies of Reading* 7, 183–208.

Yopp, H.K. (1988) The validity and reliability of phonemic awareness tests. *Reading Research Quarterly* 23, 159–77.

Chapter 13

Effects of Writing Systems on Second Language Awareness: Word Awareness in English Learners of Chinese as a Foreign Language

BENEDETTA BASSETTI

Introduction

Much research has shown that second language learners and users read and write their second language writing system differently from its native users, as a consequence of knowing another writing system. A relatively smaller amount of research shows that learners and users of a second language writing system (L2WS) also have a different knowledge of the linguistic units represented by their L2WS, compared with its native users. Native users of different writing systems are affected in their analysis of the spoken language by the linguistic units that their writing system represents as discrete units (by means of graphemes and orthographic conventions). When they learn a second language, they may encounter a L2 writing system that represents different linguistic units as discrete units. In that case, these multi-competent L2WS users may develop a different awareness of the linguistic units in their second language compared with native users of the target language because they know more than one writing system.

The present research shows that English learners of Chinese have different concepts of the Chinese word compared with Chinese natives, as a consequence of knowing both the English and Chinese writing systems. The word is the metalinguistic unit *par excellence* for English speakers, and their encounter with the Chinese writing system, that represents morphemes but not words as discrete units, may lead to a variety of reactions.[1] The conflict between a L1 writing system that represents words and a L2 writing system that represents morphemes can be solved by relying on the L1WS to determine word boundaries in the L2, but the impact of the L2WS can affect various aspects of L2 awareness and use. The conflict can be solved in different ways by different L2 learners, ranging from the integration of the two views of language to the complete rejection of the new view of language conveyed by the L2 writing system.

The first language writing system and second language awareness

Writing systems represent the flow of spoken language as a sequence of distinct linguistic units with clear boundaries. For instance, while phonemes overlap in speech (Lively *et al.*, 1994), they are represented as discrete units in alphabetic writing systems. But not all writing systems represent the same linguistic units: while the graphemes of alphabetic writing systems represent phonemes, the graphemes of other writing systems represent consonants, syllables or morphemes.

Cross-orthographic research shows that writing systems affect the ability to identify and manipulate linguistic units in their users. In general, literate speakers tend to be aware of those linguistic units that are represented in their writing system. For instance, users of alphabetic writing systems are aware of phonemes, while users of syllabic writing systems are aware of syllables. Awareness of linguistic units is not related to literacy *per se*. Language users who are literate are still not aware of linguistic units that are not represented in their writing system, though present in their speech; for instance, Japanese children cannot perform some tasks that require awareness of phonemes, even though they are literate (Leong, 1991), because their writing system represents morphemes and morae but not phonemes; English adults can perform tasks that require awareness of words, which are represented as individuated units separated by spacing in their writing system, but not tasks requiring awareness of syllables or phrases, whose boundaries are not marked in their writing system (Miller *et al.*, in preparation). Writing systems affect awareness of linguistic units independently of characteristics of the language: this is obvious when comparing native speakers of the same language who are users of different writing systems. For instance, literate Chinese natives, whose writing system represents monosyllabic morphemes, cannot perform some phonemic awareness tasks which can be performed by Chinese natives who learnt *pinyin*, a transcription system based on the Roman alphabet (Read *et al.*, 1987); Kannada-speaking children, whose writing system is a semi-syllabary, cannot perform some phonemic awareness tasks which can be performed by blind Kannada children, who are users of an alphabetic *braille* (Prakash, 2000). This suggests the existence of *orthographic relativity*, whereby language users analyse language differently according to which units are represented in their writing system: phonemes for English speakers, morae for Japanese speakers, morphemes for Chinese, words for English, etc. (see Bugarski's 'graphic relativity', Bugarski, 1993).

If users of different writing systems are aware of different units, what are second language users aware of? Bilingualism helps children develop some aspects of phonological awareness (Bruck & Genesee, 1995), but this does not extend to awareness of phonemes, which is only learnt through exposure to a phonemic writing system. Bilingual children are no better than monolinguals at phoneme substitution or phoneme counting tasks (Bialystok, 2001; Bialystok *et al.*, 2003). But, if they learn to read their L1 writing system and become aware of the linguistic units it represents, they can use this awareness to analyse their L2, and perform differently from, or even better than, literate monolinguals; for instance, Hebrew users of English as a Second Language segment English words into phonemes differently from English natives (Ben-Dror *et al.*, 1995); literate English-Greek bilingual children outperform literate English monolinguals in some English phonemic awareness tasks (Loizou & Stuart, 2003). Bilingualism *per se* does not make L2 users more aware of linguistic units than monolinguals, but once they acquire awareness of a linguistic unit by exposure to one writing system, L2 users can apply this awareness to other languages.

Word awareness in English and Chinese natives

The present study deals with *word awareness*, that is to say the conscious knowledge of the word as a linguistic unit. Word awareness is demonstrated by the ability to understand and use the term 'word', to identify words in a written or spoken text and to distinguish them from other linguistic units, so that morphemes or phrases are not considered 'words'. According to orthographic relativism, word awareness should only develop in users of those writing systems that represent words as discrete units, and it should not be present in illiterates or in those literates whose writing system does not mark word boundaries.

English is one of the writing systems that mark word boundaries; it represents *orthographic words*, i.e. strings of letters preceded and followed by spacing (*interword spacing*). In line with orthographic relativism, literate English adults understand what a 'word' is and can distinguish it from other linguistic units. Using the most widespread test of word awareness, the *word segmentation task*, Miller *et al.* (in preparation) presented a group of English natives with a series of sentences written without interword spacing (such as <icecreamisthemostpopulardessertinsummer>), and asked them to segment the sentences by drawing a line between words. Answers were almost unanimous, showing that English adults understand the meaning of 'word' and can identify words. On the other hand, research repeatedly showed that English preliterate children are *not* word aware: they do not understand what a 'word' is (Downing, 1970), they do not understand that the spacing between strings of letters in writing separates linguistic units (Meltzer & Herse, 1969), they cannot say whether phonemes, syllables or sentences are words or not (Downing & Oliver, 1974); and when asked to identify words in speech they identify phonemes, sentences or other linguistic units (Ferreiro, 1997). When they learn to read a word-spaced writing system, children then go through a stage where they can count written words but not spoken words (Ferreiro, 1999), and after about two years of literacy, they can consistently identify spoken words the same way as adults. Illiterate English adults also cannot identify words (for instance, they cannot identify the number of words in 'television', 'forever', 'four oxen' or 'the White House') and in general seem to think that dividing speech into words is 'meaningless' (Scholes, 1993).

Unlike the English writing system (but like Thai, Burmese, Tibetan, Japanese and other writing systems), Chinese does not mark word boundaries. Spacing is used to separate Chinese graphemes, the *hanzi* or *zi* (汉字, /xan tsɨ/). Again confirming orthographic relativism, Chinese natives (both children and adults) are not aware of words; indeed Chinese did not have a term for 'word' until the concept was imported from the West at the beginning of the 20th century (Packard, 1998). When performing a word segmentation task, Chinese natives segment the same text into words differently from each other, are inconsistent with their own previous segmentations, identify whole phrases as words and sometimes do not understand instructions asking them to identify 'words' (Hoosain, 1992; King, 1983; Miller, 2002; Sproat *et al.*, 1996). Interestingly, Chinese natives who learnt pinyin (the Chinese romanisation system, which uses interword spacing) segment Chinese texts differently from Chinese natives who only know hanzi (Tsai *et al.*, 1998). This shows that exposure to a word-spaced writing system affects word awareness even among native speakers of the same language. In an interesting cross-linguistic experiment, Miller and his colleagues (in preparation) compared Chinese and English natives' segmentations of the same sentences, presented in Chinese and English respectively. They found that while English natives reached an almost 100% agreement on their word segmentations, Chinese natives had a significantly lower agreement rate (Miller *et al.*, in preparation).

While it appears that users of non-word-spaced writing systems are generally not aware of words, literate Chinese natives might represent a special case because of characteristics of their writing system. Each Chinese grapheme (hanzi) represents one morpheme and its corresponding spoken syllable (with very few exceptions). For instance, 爱 represents the morpheme 'to love' and the corresponding syllable /ai/ (in the standard variety of Chinese). Chinese lexical items can be mono- or polymorphemic; in written Chinese they are correspondingly mono- or multi-hanzi. For instance: /ai/ (爱, 'to love'); /ai ʐən/ (爱人, 'spouse'), etc. In this way, the writing system assigns one specific written form to each morpheme: while the syllable /ji/ can be written with various hanzi (以, 已, 乙, 倚, 蚁, etc.), the writing system indicates that the /ji/ in /ji waŋ/ ('before') is written with the same hanzi as the /ji/ in /ji tɕiŋ/ ('already') but not as the /ji/ in /ji ʂaŋ/ ('above-mentioned'). This means that the spoken /ji waŋ/ can be analysed as the two morphemes 'already-past' and /ji tɕiŋ/ as 'already-pass through', but /ji ʂaŋ/ ('above-mentioned') is not 'already-above', but 'at-above'. The same hanzi also often represents more than one morpheme, so that it may represent some that are lexical items and some that are not; when reading, the context of the sentence determines whether a hanzi represents a lexical item or a component of a polymorphemic lexical item. So 生 represents a verb in 她生孩子了 ('she gave birth to a baby'), the second morpheme in 陌生人 ('foreigner'), the third morpheme in 研究生 ('researcher'), and so on. This gives the false impression that 生 represents a lexical item, when in fact it is the written representation of different homophonic morphemes. It is by now clear that the hanzi plays a central role in the Chinese writing system and that its importance and versatility conceal the role of the lexical item.

Going back to language awareness, since their graphemes represent monosyllabic morphemes, Chinese natives can segment language into syllables (Miller *et al.*, in preparation) and, for each syllable, identify the correct hanzi among the many homophonic hanzi that could represent it. For instance, they can say that /ai tɕʰiŋ/ ('love') contains two syllables, and that the first one is written as 爱 rather than 艾, 碍, 隘, 暧 or other homophonic hanzi. The ability to identify syllables with the corresponding morpheme/hanzi is an important aspect of language awareness for Chinese children acquiring literacy (Li *et al.*, 2002), which illiterates do not have (Chao, 1976). The hanzi is recurrent in Chinese linguistic activities: text length is calculated in hanzi, dictionaries are searched by hanzi, etc. (Chao, 1968). Given the importance of the hanzi in their writing system, not surprisingly most Chinese natives think of their language as made of hanzi (Hannas, 1997; T'ung & Pollard, 1982). The status of the hanzi as the metalinguistic unit for Chinese natives is just as salient as the status of the 'word' as the metalinguistic unit for English natives. Hanzi does not mean 'a group of strokes inscribed inside a square', just like the English 'word' does not mean 'a series of letters comprised within two spaces'; hanzi are the linguistic units that everybody is aware of, recognizes and uses to talk about language. And the central role of the hanzi obfuscates the role of the word for Chinese natives, in probably the same way as the central role of the word obfuscates the role of the morpheme for English natives. In this, English and Chinese natives do not differ: they are all aware of the linguistic units that are represented in their writing system.

Word awareness in L2 users

The evidence reviewed above supports the view that word awareness only develops with literacy in a word-spaced writing system. But does this also apply to L2 users? There is evidence that bilingualism facilitates the development of some aspects of language awareness (Cook, 1997). Are L2 users aware of words in the absence of literacy? The answer seems to be negative: bilingual prereaders are not better than monolinguals at counting words in a text (Ricciardelli, 1992) or at word segmentation and word judgement tasks (Nicoladis & Genesee, 1996); word counting in bilingual children is positively affected only by their literacy, not by their bilingualism (Edwards & Christophersen, 1988). For instance, although preliterate American children performed better than Chinese-English bilingual children in English word segmentation, a group of Chinese-English bilingual children learning to read English in the first year of primary school outperformed the American native speaker children who could not read (Hsia, 1992). Word awareness acquired through exposure to a writing system can be used to analyse another language: French-English bilingual children who are literate only in French can segment English texts in words as well as literate English children (and even perform better in the segmentation of bimorphemic compound words such as 'snowman') (Bialystok, 1986). It is clear that the ability to segment a text into words, or to decide whether something is a word, only develops with literacy in a word-spaced writing system; but once word awareness is acquired via one writing system, it can be used to analyse another language even in the absence of literacy in that language, and then bilinguals can even enjoy an advantage over literate monolinguals.

The Present Study

Word awareness develops in English natives as a consequence of learning to read English, and does not develop in literate Chinese natives. Since English represents orthographic words and Chinese does not, literate English speakers might use their word awareness to analyse L2 Chinese. Their concept of the Chinese word could therefore be different from that of native Chinese speakers. Given that, once word awareness is acquired, it can be used to analyse a second language, do English learners of Chinese as a Foreign Language (CFL) apply their word awareness to identifying words in Chinese? Do they have a different concept of the Chinese word compared with Chinese natives?

In order to investigate this question, a Chinese word segmentation task was given to a group of English CFL learners and a group of Chinese natives. On the basis of previous findings, two hypotheses were proposed: (1) English CFL learners will mark shorter words; and (2) English CFL learners will show higher levels of intragroup agreement on their word segmentations. The first hypothesis was proposed because previous research had shown that Chinese natives who learnt the pinyin romanization system (which represents orthographic words) marked more word boundaries (i.e. shorter words) than Chinese natives who did not learn it (Tsai *et al.*, 1998); it was reasoned that English CFL learners' prolonged exposure to the English writing system should have even stronger effects than a limited exposure to pinyin and should result in shorter words than those marked by pinyin-literate Chinese natives. The second hypothesis was proposed because previous research had shown that English natives segmenting English words reach almost 100% agreement, but Chinese natives segmenting Chinese have much lower levels of agreement (Miller *et al.*, in preparation); it was reasoned that if L1 word awareness can be used to analyse the second language, English CFL learners who reach such high levels of agreement in their first language should reach higher levels of intragroup agreement on Chinese segmentation than Chinese natives.

The two hypotheses were tested by means of two word segmentation tasks (a text and a sentence segmentation task respectively), whereby participants were asked to segment the materials into words. For both tasks, a one-factor between-subjects quasi-experimental design was used to test the effects of the first language writing system (English and Chinese) on average word length and on intragroup agreement rates.

Participants

Sixty English-speaking learners of Chinese as a Foreign Language (CFL) were recruited at various British universities. They were users of English as an L1 and as an L1 writing system, enrolled in third- or fourth-year Chinese language courses. Ninety per cent of respondents rated their own Chinese reading skills as good or proficient.

The 60 Chinese natives were native users of the standard variety of Chinese and of the Chinese writing system. They were matched to the English group in terms of educational background, had all learnt pinyin (the Chinese romanisation system) in school and most of them knew at least one additional Chinese language besides Standard Chinese, as is the norm in the People's Republic of China. Since knowledge of English could affect the results, they were given an English vocabulary test (Schmitt *et al.*, 2001) to check that their knowledge of English was non-existent or minimal.

Materials and procedure

Participants were given a set of printed materials containing two texts (for the text segmentation task) and nine sentences (for the sentence segmentation task). The written instructions invited them to draw a square around each word in the text, and a final questionnaire included demographic information. The Chinese texts were two short descriptive passages taken from a Chinese encyclopaedic dictionary (Cihai Bianju Weiyuanhui, 1989). In total they were 342-hanzi long and contained 300 valid word boundaries (hanzi not followed by a punctuation mark). The nine sentences were taken from a previous study (Hoosain, 1992) and consisted of seven hanzi (with six valid word boundaries) each. Materials were judged by a native Chinese language teacher as appropriate for the target L2 learners. The hanzi in the text were highly frequent: 99% belonged to the 'frequent' category in a hanzi frequency dictionary (Shanghai Jiaotong Daxue, 1988). In the final questionnaire, 95% of the English respondents reported that the Chinese materials were not difficult.

Results

Results from the text segmentation task revealed that the effect of L1 Writing System was significant. The average word length, i.e. the average number of hanzi per word, was significantly different between the two groups, with English learners of Chinese as a Foreign Language showing a significantly shorter average word length compared with the Chinese natives ($M = 1.79$, $SD = 0.14$ and $M = 2.78$, $SD = 0.81$ respectively, see Figure 13.1).

An independent group *t*-test revealed a significant difference between the two group means ($t_{1,118} = -9.397$, $p < 0.001$). In line with the first hypothesis, the English CFL learners segmented text into shorter words compared with Chinese natives.

Results from the sentence segmentations revealed a significant effect of L1 Writing System on intragroup agreement rates, with English learners of Chinese as a Foreign Language showing a significantly higher agreement rate than Chinese natives (Figure 13.2). The agreement rate on each sentence was calculated by means of an Index of Commonality, which expresses the frequency of agreements as a proportion of the total number of comparisons as a figure ranging from 0 to 1. The average agreement rate for the English CFL group was 0.65 ($SD = 0.18$); for the Chinese group it was 0.24 ($SD = 0.05$), showing that English CFL learners agreed on significantly more sentence segmentations than Chinese natives. (As the Index of Commonality was based on agreement on each segmentation of the whole sentence, the levels of agreement are relatively low.)

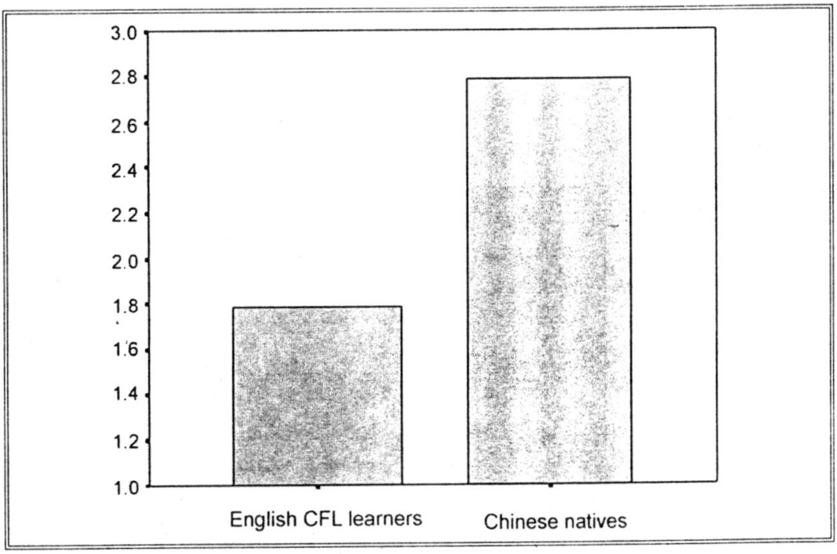

Figure 13.1 Average word length (in hanzi) by group

A repeated measures *t*-test by item revealed that the difference between the two groups was significant ($t_{1,8} = 6.83$, $p < 0.001$), showing that, in line with the second hypothesis, the English CFL learners had a higher intragroup agreement rate than the Chinese natives.

Analysis of results

Since both groups were segmenting the same materials in the same language and writing system, differences can only be attributed to differences in word awareness, and not to differences between the languages and/or writing systems being segmented, as could be the case with cross-linguistic comparisons. These results show that English learners of Chinese have a different approach to Chinese word segmentation to Chinese natives, and agree more with each other's approach to identifying words. But on the other hand they are also affected by the Chinese language and writing system. The English group was far from the almost 100% agreement that English natives show when segmenting English materials. This is due to characteristics of the Chinese writing system, notably the lack of interword spacing and the important role of the morpheme/hanzi.

In line with the hypotheses, exposure to a first language writing system that marks word boundaries resulted in shorter words and higher agreement rates in the segmentation of a second language, but it is not clear why this should be so. In order to understand why English CFL learners identify shorter Chinese words than Chinese natives,

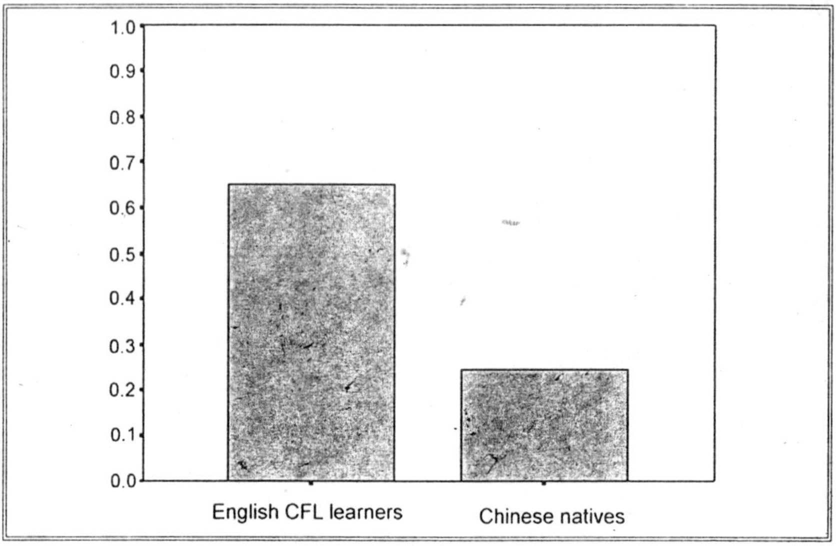

Figure 13.2 Intragroup agreement rates by group

further analyses were performed on the linguistic units marked as words by both groups.

Reasons for different word lengths

Two main differences between the Chinese and the English groups seem to have led to differences in word lengths. English CFL learners mostly treated function words as words, while Chinese natives considered them as both words and affixes (affixed to the preceding, or sometimes following, content word). English CFL learners also segmented nominal compounds in smaller units, while Chinese natives considered them as single words. For instance, let us consider the following seven-hanzi phrase:

Chinese text:	十	七	世	纪	的	欧	洲
Transcription:	/ʂɨ	tɕʰi	ʂɨ	tɕi	tɤ	ou	tʂou/
Hanzi meaning:	Ten	seven	age	epoch	*de*	Europe	continent
English translation:	The Europe of the Seventeenth century						

This is how it was segmented by most English CFL learners (dots represent where participants drew word boundaries):

十七•世纪•的•欧洲 ('Seventeenth century *de* Europe', four words).

Most Chinese natives segmented it as follows:

十七世纪的•欧洲 ('Seventeenth-century-*de* Europe', two words)

or

十七世纪•的•欧洲 ('Seventeenth-century *de* Europe', three words).

The results from the Chinese group are in line with previous findings that Chinese natives consider compounds and phrases as words and attach function words to content words (Hoosain, 1992; King, 1983). T-test comparisons were performed on the two groups' treatment of *de* (the most frequent function word in Chinese) as a word and on the treatment of four-hanzi nominal compounds as words, and both differences were statistically significant (Figures 13.3 and 13.4). Obviously when nominal compounds are considered one word and function words are affixed to content words, the average word will be longer than when nominal compounds are segmented and function words considered words.

Reasons for different agreement rates

Going back to the short phrase presented above, the distinction between the two groups' segmentations was not as clear-cut as it looked above. At closer view, the segmentation patterns of the Chinese group were much more complex. While 83% of Chinese participants considered 欧洲 ('Europe') as one word, another 12% considered 十七世纪的欧洲 all as one word ('17th-century-*de*-Europe'), and the remaining 5% considered 的欧洲 ('*de*-Europe') as one word. Regarding 十七世纪的 ('Seventeenth century *de*'), as many as five different segmentations were suggested:

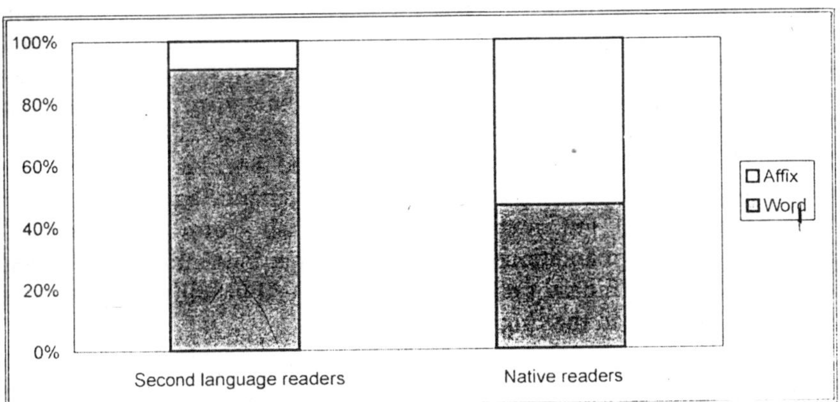

Figure 13.3 Segmentation of *de* by group

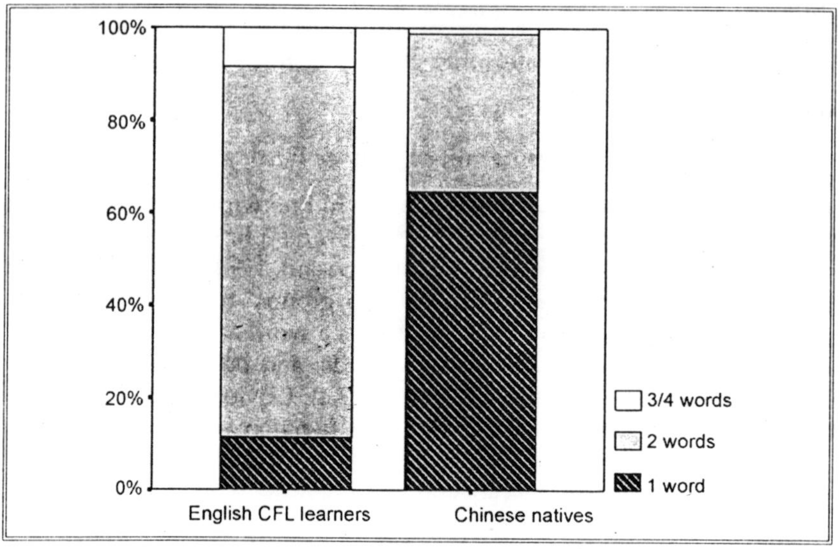

Figure 13.4 Segmentation of four-hanzi nominal compounds by group

十七世纪的
十七世纪•的
十七•世纪的
十七•世纪•的
十•七•世纪•的

Obviously such a variety of segmentations on such a short string explains the high levels of disagreement on word segmentation in the Chinese group. With regard to the English CFL learners group, although 85% of English participants segmented the phrase as 十七•世纪•的•欧洲 ('Seventeenth century *de* Europe'), it is worth noting that another 10% considered 十七世纪 ('Seventeenth-century') as one word, in line with the Chinese natives' segmentation, and the remaining 5% segmented 'seventeen' in two words, 十 and 七 ('ten' and 'seven'). Compared with the English group, the Chinese group presented a wider variety of segmentation, with a lower percentage of participants agreeing on one main segmentation, but interestingly the English group also presented some minority segmentations. This explains the low intragroup agreement rate of the Chinese group, and the higher but still relatively low level of agreement in the English group.

Besides differing on the levels of intragroup agreement, the two groups also differed in the levels of self-consistency (intrajudge agreement). When the text contained the same lexical item twice, the English CFL learners tended to treat the same hanzi or hanzi strings in the same way throughout, but Chinese natives treated the same hanzi or hanzi strings differently in the same text. This characteristic of the Chinese natives' performance had already been noted in the literature with reference to the segmentation of *de* and of the negation *bu* (King, 1983). In the present research, this lack of self-consistency appeared both in the segmentation of *de* (which occurred 12 times in the text) and in the segmentation of nominal compounds (two compounds occurred twice each). The English CFL learners showed significantly higher self-consistency in the segmentation of both *de* and the repeated compounds, but they too were not 100% self-consistent.

But why do Chinese participants show lower levels of intragroup agreement and self-consistency in word segmentation? This is because the two groups' approaches to word segmentation are different. The Chinese use a higher number of word segmentation strategies and a wider variety of them compared with the English CFL learners.

Word segmentation strategies

In the final questionnaire, participants were asked to describe their word segmentation criteria. An analysis of the answers revealed quantitative and qualitative differences between the two groups. English CFL learners applied fewer and less varied segmentation criteria, and while some criteria were common to both groups, others were only mentioned by one group or the other.

The following are typical descriptions of how an English CFL learner segments Chinese text into words:

> 'Whether in English it is a word or not'
> 'Counted English equivalent as one word + Chinese grammatical particles as one word.'

Translation into English was the most frequently reported strategy in the English CFL group, reported by 36% of respondents, 47% of whom indicated it as their only strategy. This could partly explain the higher levels of intragroup agreement and self-consistency[2].

The Chinese group reported more varied and complex word segmentation strategies, which included various criteria, sometimes organised in a sequence as in the following example:

> 'I use the following stages: (1) I first segment the sentence into subject and predicate; (2) I then segment each part into the smallest units according to the word's meaning and word class, but at the same time I consider completeness of meaning, I don't simply segment according to word class, for instance: 学生生活 ['student-life'] and 锻炼身体 ['body-building'] [make one word]; (3) Finally, I rely on intuition, and the rhythm when I read it.' [all translations by the author]

Although not all the Chinese participants gave such elaborate answers, some of their answers contained as many as five different word segmentation criteria, while the overwhelming majority of English participants (81%) reported only one criterion. Using more than one criterion naturally leads to more varied segmentations.

Besides reporting different numbers of criteria, the two groups also reported using different criteria. For instance, as mentioned above, the most frequently used criterion in the English group was translation into English; this hardly ever occurred in the Chinese group (who had no or minimal knowledge of English). The most striking difference is the overwhelming use of syntactic strategies by the Chinese group (dividing subject, verb and object; dividing nouns, verbs, adverbs and adjectives; etc.) reported by 45% of respondents. While a couple of English CFL learners reported using 'grammar', they did not explain how they used it.

Arguably the most interesting difference is that the Chinese group reported the use of prosodic strategies for word segmentation. For instance, one of the Chinese respondents wrote:

> 'I segment according to the spoken intonation. [...] When we speak, there are always some pauses, and I use these pauses to segment.'

A variety of prosody-based criteria were reported, including pauses in speaking or in reading, intonation and rhythm. While such criteria were reported by 18% of Chinese respondents, the English group did not report them at all (only one respondent reported using the 'tempo of the text'). This prosodic approach could explain why *de* was not considered a word (phonologically it behaves as a clitic). It could also explain its apparently inconsistent treatment by the Chinese group, which could be determined by prosodic context, as proposed by King (1983).

Sometimes the two groups reported using similar criteria, but from different viewpoints. If all criteria are classified by type of strategy (semantic strategies, syntactic strategies, intuition, etc.), it appears that both groups mostly used semantic strategies, which include considering the meaning of each hanzi, considering words as units of meaning, analysing the sentence meaning, etc. But while English CFL learners mostly looked at the meaning of single hanzi or words, the majority of Chinese respondents were preoccupied with the meaning of longer units and stressed the importance of keeping units of meaning together within the same word. For instance, one Chinese participant wrote:

> 'I do a complete segmentation depending on the meaning of the whole sentence, I don't just mechanically segment into the smallest words. That way, one loses coherence and completeness of meaning.'

This probably explains why the Chinese group did not segment nominal compounds into smaller words.

Segmentation strategies can explain the differences in word length and intragroup agreement between the two groups, as well as differences in the two groups' self-consistency. When only one strategy is used, and it mostly consists of English translation (as is the case with English CFL learners), the same hanzi or hanzi string will be segmented in the same way by different participants and by the same participant on different occasions. When different participants apply different criteria, and each participant employs more than one criterion (so that different criteria can take priority in different contexts), this leads to the more varied segmentations seen in the Chinese group.

Discussion

It appears that English learners of Chinese as a Foreign Language have a different concept of the Chinese word compared with Chinese natives. The two groups not only differ in how they identify words, they also differ in their view of what constitutes a Chinese word: for most Chinese natives it is a syntactic unit, while for most English CFL learners it is the equivalent of an English word; for both groups a word is a unit of meaning that cannot be further segmented, but for English CFL learners this means a mono- or disyllabic unit, while for Chinese natives this includes longer compounds and phrases; for Chinese natives it is also a prosodic unit that can be identified by means of pauses and intonation units, a possibility that never occurs to English CFL learners.

But the Chinese word awareness of English CFL learners is not simply a consequence of cross-orthographic influence. They can use their L1 English word awareness to analyse L2 Chinese; but, unlike French-English bilingual children, who use their awareness of French words to segment English (Bialystok, 1986), CFL learners cannot simply 'transfer' their L1 word awareness because they are affected by characteristics of the Chinese language and writing system. English CFL learners obtain lower intragroup agreement rates and self-consistency when segmenting Chinese than they would obtain in segmenting English texts. This is due to the Chinese writing system: it is partly due to its lack of interword spacing, and partly to the centrality of the morpheme/hanzi that imposes itself on CFL learners as well. Those English CFL learners who considered 十七世纪 ('Seventeenth-century') as one word have developed a concept of word (or at least of the Chinese word) which is different from the concept of word in monolingual English natives and in line with the Chinese concept of an unbreakable unit of meaning; those who divided 十七 'seventeen' into two words ('ten' and 'seven') were influenced by the important role of the morpheme/hanzi; in both cases, their segmentations are not the results of simply translating into English. The percentage of English participants who at least occasionally showed such 'Chinese-style' segmentations testifies to the impact of the Chinese language and writing system on their concept of the Chinese word. The effects of the Chinese writing system also surface in the descriptions of their word segmentation criteria: there is the difficulty of deciding what a word is in the absence of interword spacing ('Difficulty in deciding whether to split up names, esp. names of centres, e.g. 人口研究中心 [Population Research Centre] all one word? Or three separate ones?') and there is the centrality of the hanzi as a unit of meaning; one felt 'Each character is a word; however there are many two character phrases that are words'. And in fact a few CFL learners reported difficulty in deciding what constitutes a Chinese word: 'A difficult question to answer'; 'I don't really know!'. Even the authority of reference tools becomes questionable when tools in the two languages differ: while one learner showed a typical reliance on the authority of dictionaries: 'If I know I can find it in the dictionary it must be a word', another noted: 'It's difficult because 中华人民共和国 [People's Republic of China] will probably appear as ONE word in the dictionary'.

The multi-competent L2 user and language awareness

These results support the theory of multi-competence, that is the knowledge of two or more languages in one mind (Cook, 1991). Literate L2 users not only have two or more languages in their minds, they also have two or more writing systems (see discussion in the introduction to this book). Their use and their knowledge of their languages and writing systems are different from the use and knowledge of native users of the target language and writing system, and are influenced by the two (or more) languages and the two (ore more) writing systems in the multi-competent L2 user's mind. In this way, the multi-competent English learner/user of Chinese as a Foreign Language has a different knowledge of the Chinese language to Chinese natives.

English CFL learners have a different concept of the Chinese word, compared with natives. But what is actually happening in the minds of these L2WS users? Do they have a different concept of the Chinese word coexisting with their concept of the English word, or is their overall concept of word changing? In addition to the results from this research, informal conversations with other CFL users revealed interesting cases: an Italian CFL user reported discovering the existence of morphemes when she started studying Chinese and then applying the same concept to her first language; an English CFL user, asked to translate some Chinese sentences into English, wrote all the English compounds corresponding to two hanzi in the Chinese text (such as 桌布, <tablecloth>) as two separate English orthographic words (<table cloth>) and wrote: 'I'm not sure what constitutes a word really – for example table cloth – is that two words in English? Is it the same in Chinese?'. While this is of course anecdotal evidence, it is still interesting.

On the other hand, other CFL users think that words are self-evident and universal units of language analysis. They criticise the Chinese natives' view of language as made of hanzi and their habit of putting hanzi together to create new words that do not exist in dictionaries (e.g. Hannas, 1997). The negative view of the Chinese lack of word awareness also creeps into Chinese language textbooks, as in the following (co-authored by a CFL user): 'Most Chinese still think of their language as consisting of characters rather than words' (T'ung and Pollard, 1982: 2). Although the authors explain that this view facilitates Chinese reading, and proceed to teach both spoken words and hanzi, they do not explain why the Chinese think their language is made of hanzi, and the use of the word 'still' implies that this view is incorrect rather than different. And while some CFL users work to produce word-based Chinese reference tools (e.g. the ABC Dictionaries series: DeFrancis, 1996; or the word index to a hanzi dictionary, Mair, 2003), other CFL users comment that these word dictionaries might be more difficult to use than hanzi dictionaries (Light, 1998). And while some CFL users fight to get romanised library catalogues written in words rather than syllables, according to the 'rational aggregation of Sinitic syllables into words', others find syllable-based catalogues easier to search or to produce because they have 'absolutely no faith in [their own] ability to separate the words correctly' (see Chinese Kenyon archives, 2000).

It appears that there is much variability in how English-speaking CFL users react to the impact of a different writing system and related views of language. While reliance on L1 word awareness is their main approach to identifying L2 words, CFL learners show signs of developing a new concept of the Chinese word different from the concept of the English word, as a consequence of exposure to the Chinese writing system.

Orthographic relativism and Chinese word awareness

These research findings support orthographic relativism, the view that writing systems affect their users' views of language. Previous research showed that native speakers of the same language analyse their first language differently if they learnt to read it through the medium of different writing systems (Prakash, 2000; Read *et al.*, 1987); the present study shows that L1 and L2 users show different awareness of the same linguistic units in the same language if they were exposed to different first language writing systems.

But how many of these differences can be attributed to the participants' L1 writing system, rather than to bilingualism? Given the lack of orthographic conventions for word boundaries, both English and Chinese natives trying to segment Chinese find themselves in the same situation as preliterates or illiterates. But while the word segmentations of Chinese natives are reminiscent of the word segmentations of English preliterates, those of English CFL learners are not. This is evident in at least three aspects:

(1) English preliterates mostly do not consider function words as words, but either attach them to the following content word or ignore them altogether; Chinese literates also often considered function words to be affixes, and interestingly a small percentage of them ignored function words altogether, i.e. did not mark them as either words or parts of words.
(2) Both English preliterates and Chinese literates often do not segment compounds and phrases in smaller words.
(3) Both English preliterates and Chinese literates sometimes rely on prosody to identify words: stress units for English children; intonation groups, potential pauses, etc. for Chinese literates.

English CFL learners mostly do not show such features of preliterates' word segmentation: function words are mostly considered words, compounds and phrases are segmented and prosodic clues are not taken into account. Interestingly, this is in line with the spacing conventions of the English writing system, where function words are represented as orthographic words – 'in', 'on' and 'the' (unlike some function words in the Arabic and Hebrew writing systems, see Bauer, 1996); compounds are variable, going from 'table napkin' to 'table-knife' to 'timetable' (unlike in the Dutch writing system); and prosodic boundaries are not reflected in spacing conventions (unlike in the Thai or Khmer writing systems, see Coulmas, 1999; Diller, 1996). It therefore appears that previous experience of learning a word-spaced writing system is at least partly the cause of the differences between the Chinese and English participants' view of the Chinese word. Of course this parallel between Chinese adults and English preliterates cannot be taken as evidence that the differences between Chinese and English users of Chinese are due to their respective writing systems. To demonstrate this causal link it would be necessary to compare CFL learners with different L1 writing system backgrounds. The next step could be a comparison of English and Japanese CFL users, because the Japanese writing system does not mark word boundaries with spacing, some of its graphemes (*kanji*) represent morphemes, and the alternation of morphemic and syllabic graphemes (*kanji* and *kana*) segments the written text differently from English orthographic conventions.

In conclusion, native users of English and Chinese have different concepts of the Chinese word and different approaches to word segmentation. The presence of two writing systems in the minds of these multi-competent L2 and L2WS users may lead to a new awareness of the Chinese word, and possibly of the word.

Acknowledgements

The study reported here formed part of the author's doctoral thesis (Bassetti, 2004), which was supported by a Postgraduate Studentship by the Economic and Social Research Council.

Notes

1. Whether the word is a valid linguistic construct or not is irrelevant here; a construct does not need to be scientifically valid in order to affect people's thinking.
2. It is interesting to note that the L1WS orthographic conventions are sometimes also present in the word segmentations of professional linguists; when trying to identify word boundaries for previously unwritten languages, linguists sometimes rely on the orthographic conventions of English or French (see criticism in Van Dyken & Kutsch Lojenga, 1993).

References

Bassetti, B. (2004) Second language reading and second language awareness in English-speaking learners of Chinese as a foreign language. PhD thesis, University of Essex.

Bauer, T. (1996) Arabic writing. In P.T. Daniels and W. Bright (eds) *The World's Writing Systems* (pp. 559–64). Oxford: Oxford University Press.

Ben-Dror, I., Frost, R. and Bentin, S. (1995) Orthographic representation and phonemic segmentation in skilled readers: A cross-language comparison. *Psychological Science* 6 (3), 176–81.

Bialystok, E. (1986) Children's concept of word. *Journal of Psycholinguistic Research* 15, 13–32.

Bialystok, E. (2001) *Bilingualism in Development: Language, Literacy, and Cognition*. Cambridge: Cambridge University Press.

Bialystok, E., Majumder, S. and Martin, M.M. (2003) Developing phonological awareness: Is there a bilingual advantage? *Applied Psycholinguistics* 24, 27–44.

Bruck, M. and Genesee, F. (1995) Phonological awareness in young second language learners. *Journal of Child Language* 22, 307–24.

Bugarski, R. (1993) Graphic relativity and linguistic constructs. In R.J. Scholes (ed.) *Literacy and Language Analysis* (pp. 5–18). Hillsdale, NJ: Lawrence Erlbaum.

Chao, Y.-R. (1968) *A Grammar of Spoken Chinese*. Berkeley: University of California Press.

Chao, Y.-R. (1976) Rhythm and structure in Chinese word conceptions. In Y.-R. Chao (ed.) *Aspects of Chinese Sociolinguistics* (pp. 275–92). Stanford: Stanford University Press.

Chinese Kenyon archives (2000) Archives of the 'Chinese@kenyon.edu mailing list'. At http://lbis.kenyon.edu/services/archive/ ~ chinese/2576.html.

Cihai Bianju Weiyuanhui (1989) *Ci Hai*. Shanghai: Shanghai Cishu Chubanshe.

Cook, V.J. (1991) The poverty of the stimulus argument and multi-competence. *Second Language Research* 7 (2), 103–17.

Cook, V.J. (1997) The consequences of bilingualism for cognitive processing. In A.M.B. de Groot and J.F. Kroll (eds) *Tutorials in Bilingualism: Psycholinguistic Perspectives* (pp. 279–99). Mahwah, NJ: Lawrence Erlbaum Associates.

Coulmas, F. (1999) *The Blackwell Encyclopedia of Writing Systems*. Oxford: Blackwell Publishers.

DeFrancis, J. (1996) *ABC Chinese-English Dictionary*. Honolulu: University of Hawaii Press.

Diller, A. (1996) Thai and Lao writing. In P.T. Daniels and W. Bright (eds) *The World's Writing Systems* (pp. 457–66). Oxford: Oxford University Press.

Downing, J.A. (1970) Children's concepts of language in learning to read. *Educational Research* 12, 106–12.

Downing, J.A. and Oliver, P. (1974) The child's concept of a word. *Reading Research Quarterly* 9 (4), 568–82.

Edwards, D. and Christophersen, H. (1988) Bilingualism, literacy and meta-linguistic awareness in preschool children. *British Journal of Developmental Psychology* 6, 235–44.

Ferreiro, E. (1997) The word out of (conceptual) context. In C. Pontecorvo (ed.) *Writing Development: An Interdisciplinary View* (pp. 47–60). Amsterdam: Benjamins.

Ferreiro, E. (1999) Oral and written words. Are they the same units? In T. Nunes (ed.) *Learning to Read: An Integrated View from Research and Practice* (pp. 65–76). Dordrecht, The Netherlands: Kluwer.

Hannas, W.C. (1997) *Asia's Orthographic Dilemma*. Honolulu: University of Hawaii Press.

Hoosain, R. (1992) Psychological reality of the word in Chinese. In H.-C. Chen and O.J.L. Tzeng (eds) *Language Processing in Chinese* (pp. 111–30). Amsterdam: Elsevier Science Publishers.

Hsia, S. (1992) Developmental knowledge of inter- and intraword boundaries: Evidence from American and Mandarin Chinese speaking beginning readers. *Applied Psycholinguistics* 13 (3), 341–72.

King, P.L. (1983) Contextual factors in Chinese pinyin writing. PhD thesis, Cornell University.

Leong, C.K. (1991) From phonemic awareness to phonological processing to language access in children developing reading proficiency. In D.J. Sawyer and B.J. Fox (eds) *Phonological Awareness in Reading: The Evolution of Current Perspectives.* New York: Springer-Verlag.

Li, W., Anderson, R.C., Nagy, W. and Zhang, H. (2002) Facets of metalinguistic awareness that contribute to Chinese literacy. In W. Li, J.S. Gaffney and J.L. Packard (eds) *Chinese Children's Reading Acquisition: Theoretical and Pedagogical Issues* (pp. 87–106). Dordrecht: Kluwer Academic Publishers.

Light, T. (1998) Review of *ABC Chinese English-Dictionary* [sic] edited by John DeFrancis with Bai Yuqing, Victor H. Mair, Robert M. Sanders, E-tu Zen Sun, and Yin Binyong. *Journal of the Chinese Language Teachers Association* 33 (1), 115–6.

Lively, S.E., Pisoni, D.B. and Goldinger, S.D. (1994) Spoken word recognition: Research and theory. In M.A. Gernsbacher (ed.) *Handbook of Psycholinguistics.* San Diego: Academic Press.

Loizou, M. and Stuart, M. (2003) Phonological awareness in monolingual and bilingual English and Greek five-year-olds. *Journal of Research in Reading* 26 (1), 3–18.

Mair, V.H. (2001) *ABC Dictionary of Sino-Japanese Reading.* Honolulu: University of Hawaii Press.

Meltzer, H.S. and Herse, R. (1969) The boundaries of written words as seen by first graders. *Journal of Reading Behavior* 1, 3–14.

Miller, K. (2002) Children's early understanding of writing and language: The impact of characters and alphabetic orthographies. In W. Li, J.S. Gaffney and J.L. Packard (eds) *Chinese Children's Reading Acquisition: Theoretical and Pedagogical Issues* (pp. 17–29). Dordrecht: Kluwer Academic Publishers.

Miller, K., Chen, S.-Y. and Zhang, H. (in preparation) Where the words are: Judgments of words, syllables, and phrases by speakers of English and Chinese.

Nicoladis, E. and Genesee, F. (1996) Word awareness in second language learners and bilingual children. *Language Awareness* 5 (2), 80–90.

Packard, J.L. (1998) Introduction. In J.L. Packard (ed.) *New Approaches to Chinese Word Formation: Morphology, Phonology and the Lexicon in Modern and Ancient Chinese* (pp. 1–34). Berlin, New York: Mouton de Gruyter.

Prakash, P. (2000) Is phonemic awareness an artefact of alphabetic literacy?! Poster presentation, Association for Research in Memory, Attention, Decision Making, Intelligence, Learning and Organizational perception - 11, Texas (October 13–14, 2000).

Read, C.A., Zhang, Y., Nie, H. and Ding, B. (1987) The ability to manipulate speech sounds depends on knowing alphabetic reading. *Cognition* 24, 31–44.

Ricciardelli, L.A. (1992) Bilingualism and cognitive development in relation to threshold theory. *Journal of Psycholinguistic Research* 21 (4), 301–16.

Schmitt, N., Schmitt, D. and Clapham, C. (2001) Developing and exploring the behaviour of two new versions of the Vocabulary Levels Test. *Language Testing* 18, 55–81.

Scholes, R.J. (1993) On the orthographic basis of morphology. In R. Scholes (ed.) *Literacy and Language Analysis* (pp. 73–95). Hillsdale, NJ: Erlbaum.

SJDHBZ, Shanghai Jiaotong Daxue Hanzi Bianmazu (eds) (1988) *Han zi xin xi zi dian* [*Dictionary of Chinese Character Information*]. Beijing: Kexue Chubanshe.

Sproat, R., Shih, C., Gale, W. and Chang, N. (1996) A stochastic finite-state word-segmentation algorithm for Chinese. *Computational Linguistics* 22 (3), 377–404.

Tsai, C.-H., McConkie, G.W. and Zheng, X.J. (1998) *Lexical parsing by Chinese readers.* Paper presented at the Advanced Study Institute on Advances in Theoretical Issues and Cognitive Neuroscience Research of the Chinese Language, University of Hong Kong. At http://www.geocities.com/hao520/research/papers/cht_asi.htm.

T'ung, P.-C. and Pollard, D.E. (1982) *Colloquial Chinese.* New York: Routledge.

Van Dyken, J.R. and Kutsch Lojenga, C. (1993) Word boundaries: Key factors in orthography development. In R.L. Hartell (ed.) *Alphabets of Africa* (pp. 3–20). Dakar: UNESCO-Dakar Regional Office.

Chapter 14

Phonological Awareness and Spelling Skill Development in Bilingual Biscriptal Children

LILY H.-S. LAU and SUSAN J. RICKARD LIOW

The importance of phonological awareness for reading development (Ehri, 1998; Goswami & Bryant, 1990; Wagner & Torgesen, 1987) and remedial intervention (Foorman *et al.*, 1998; Hatcher *et al.*, 1994) has been widely reported for British and American unilingual children (see Rayner *et al.*, 2001, for a review). Similarly, when these children first learn to spell English words, their ability to segment and transcribe speech sounds appears critical (e.g. Caravolas *et al.*, 2001; Treiman *et al.*, 1994). Nevertheless, for English-knowing bilingual children living elsewhere, the use of phonological awareness for early reading and spelling development is likely to be more variable for at least three reasons. First, concurrent exposure to an orthography that is more transparent than English enhances phonological awareness (e.g. Durgunoglu *et al.*, 1993 on Spanish-English speaking children). Skill transfer between orthographies can also impede the development of phonological awareness, especially if bilingual children are taught visual strategies for one or both of their languages (Rickard Liow, 1999; Rickard Liow & Tng, 2003, on Mandarin-English speaking children). This suggests that specific combinations of orthographies can affect the nature of literacy acquisition in bilingual children. The second reason is that teachers vary in the emphasis they place on phonological awareness in bilingual classrooms, even when the main medium of instruction is English. For unilingual English-speaking children, the advantages and disadvantages of various approaches to literacy instruction are routinely debated (see Bruck *et al.*, 1998, for a comparison). Finding optimal methods for teaching particular sub-types of English-knowing bilingual children is likely to prove even more of a challenge. Third, exposure to oral forms of language at home can also influence reading and spelling in alphabetic (Caravolas & Bruck, 1993) and logographic scripts (Cheung *et al.*, 2001; McBride-Chang & Ho, 1999).

The disparity between unilingual and bilingual processing of English words, resulting from skill transfer between orthographies, teaching methods, and oral language exposure, persists well into adulthood (Holm & Dodd, 1996; Morais *et al.*, 1979; Read *et al.*, 1986). After school entry, the underlying factors become more difficult to separate, so we wondered how soon processing differences are observable between sub-types of bilingual children, given that any influence of home language probably starts very early. In this chapter, we address this question by looking at the early spelling skills of three different groups of 5–6-year-old bilingual children in Singapore who were using English as either their L1 or L2 writing system.

Language Backgrounds in Singapore

Singapore has four main ethnic groups (Chinese, 76.8%; Malay, 13.9%; Indian, 7.9%; and others, 1.4%, Department of Statistics, 2001), and there are four official languages: Mandarin, Bahasa Malaysia, Tamil and English. Tamil is the most widely taught Indian language in Singapore, but Tamil-English speaking children represent the smallest sub-type of bilinguals, and were outside the scope of this study; Mandarin brings together the Chinese population although many speak other languages at home (e.g. Hokkien, Cantonese, Teo Chew, Hakka); Bahasa Malaysia (or the similar Bahasa Indonesia) is spoken in neighbouring countries as well as by the ethnic Malay population in Singapore; English is now the language for commerce, and the main medium of instruction in schools and universities. In informal settings, colloquial forms of English and Bahasa Malaysia, known as Singlish and Pasar respectively, are widely used and understood.

Singapore has adopted China's system of simplified characters for writing in Chinese. From the early years of primary school (seven years and older) pupils are taught *pinyin*, the romanised script for standard Mandarin phonology, alongside the simplified characters, and kindergartens begin this process. Bahasa Malaysia is written in the Rumi script, except for documents relating to Islam which are usually in Jawi (Arabic). The letters used in the Rumi alphabet are the same as those for the English alphabet, except that <q> and <x> are only found in foreign loan words. There are some novel blends (e.g. <ny>, <ng> and <sy>) and <e> carries two phonemic forms; otherwise Rumi is very regular. This kind of orthographic transparency allows beginners to rely heavily on phonological awareness for reading and spelling (see Oney & Durgunoglu, 1997, on Turkish; Wimmer & Goswami, 1994, on German). For Bahasa Malaysia, Rickard Liow and Lee (2004) report that beginner spellers in primary school can often encode long, low-frequency words correctly. Relatively few vowel pairs and consonant clusters make this task much easier in Bahasa Malaysia than in English.

To ensure that Singapore citizens retain a sense of their ethnic culture and can communicate in their family language, all pupils in government schools must learn to read and write in their 'mother tongue' as a second language. This means that most Singaporean children are English-knowing bilinguals when they enter school (6–7 years old) and they will become biscriptal (Mandarin-English, Malay-English or Tamil-English) by the end of their secondary education. The Singapore Ministry of Education refers to English as the first language (L1) and mother tongue as the second language (L2), but pre-school children's actual first and second languages depend on family usage at home and on what kind of kindergarten they attend. We selected kindergarten pupils who used English, Bahasa Malaysia or Mandarin as their first oral and written language. Once in school, their first writing system quickly becomes English, but in the pre-school period most kindergartens teach some writing and spelling skills in either Malay Rumi or Chinese characters. Parents often choose kindergartens that encourage the family's home language because English is emphasised in the schools.

Cross-linguistic Transfer in Spelling

In previous work with Singaporean 9–10 year olds, Rickard Liow and Poon (1998) used homophone judgment and non-word spelling tasks to show that the transparency of the first language's orthography affects the development of phonological awareness in English, the second language. The 57 pupils in their study were all ethnic Chinese children from the same English-medium primary school, but their mother tongue was Chinese (Mandarin, Cantonese, Hokkien), Bahasa Indonesia or English, so the influence of exposure to a particular orthography could be seen in the absence of differences in teaching methods. Rickard Liow and Poon's results showed that Bahasa Indonesia L1 pupils had the highest level of phonological awareness, followed by the English-L1 pupils, and then the Chinese-L1 children.

More recent work elsewhere has proved consistent with these findings. Wang and Geva's (2003) comparison of younger Cantonese-speaking ESL children (mean age 7:3 years) from Hong Kong with native English-speaking children (mean age 7:4 years) in Canada, also suggested that having a non-alphabetic first language (i.e. Chinese characters learned without *pinyin*) is associated with low levels of phonological awareness. Both these studies showed that Chinese ESL children's exposure to a logographic script makes them less likely to rely on phonological processing for English than English-speaking unilingual children who are taught letter-sound correspondences. However, Caravolas and Bruck (1993) suggested that differences between bilingual groups could also be attributable to aural linguistic experience. They looked at the effect of oral language input on the phonological awareness of Czech- and English-speaking 4–6-year-old Canadian children. Exposure to Czech increased awareness of complex onsets and this led to more advanced spelling skills by the end of Grade 1. This seminal paper supports the view that early reading and writing skills are founded partially on aural experience of the home language, not just on script and pedagogical differences.

The purpose of our study was to extend the work on beginner spellers' differential use of phonological awareness by looking at 5–6-year-old bilingual children from the three largest language background (LB) groups in Singapore: the English-LB group had English as their first language (L1) and Mandarin as their second language (L2); the Chinese-LB group had Mandarin as L1 and English as L2; and the Malay-LB group had Malay as L1 and English as L2. All the children in our study spent about 75 minutes per day learning English in the same kindergarten, so teaching method was neither a factor, nor a potential confound.

We considered analysing samples of free writing because even 3–4 year olds invent spellings that include letter names, and result in phonologically plausible 'words' (see Treiman, 1993). However, most kindergarten children in Singapore are taught to write by a system of letter sequences learned by rote (i.e. reciting constituent letters '<c> <a> <t> spells *cat*') rather than by transcription of speech sounds. We also decided against the use of a standardised spelling test of whole words as the main means of assessing phonological awareness because we feared floor effects. Finally, we settled on an adapted version of Treiman *et al.*'s (1994) ingenious Flaps Spelling Test (described later) because it allows children to respond at the level of a single letter, and it taps phonological processing very directly.

Flaps and Children's Spelling

In some varieties of spoken English, notably American English, medial stop consonants in certain contexts undergo a process known as 'flapping'. This means they are pronounced with the tongue tapping rapidly against the alveolar ridge before it drops away (Ladefoged & Maddieson, 1996) rather than with full plosion. Speakers flap when bi-syllabic words contain a single medial /t/ or /d/ that is preceded by an unstressed vowel and followed by a vowel or a vowel plus /r/. For example, when flapped, the /d/ in 'riding' and the /t/ in 'later' are both voiced, so that the /t/ sounds like a /d/. Children who rely heavily on phonological information should choose the letter <d> to spell words with t-flaps as well as words with d-flaps, e.g. for <w a_e r>, they choose <d> instead of <t> even with a context sentence for 'water'; in other words mistakes are more likely in words with flapped /t/ 'water' than in words with flapped /d/ 'riding' since this allophone of /d/ will still correspond to the letter <d>. From here on we will use the terms 'd-flap' and 't-flap' to refer to words that contain flapped /d/ and /t/.

This over-use of phonological information when spelling flaps was first observed by Read (1975) in unilingual American English-speaking children. Soon after, Beers and Henderson (1977) systematically analysed pre-schoolers' early writing efforts, and found that words containing t-flaps were often spelled with a <d> for example 'water' as <woord>, and 'sweater' as <sweder>. Ehri and Wilce (1986) then used a cross-sectional design and looked at the spelling of words containing t- and d-flaps in first graders (up to 6.9 years), second graders (up to 7.7 years), and fourth graders (up to 9.6 years). They also found a <d> bias overall, but there were differences across the cohorts: <d> errors on words with t-flaps decreased with age. Ehri and Wilce suggested this is because once children become more experienced with print, they learn the conventional spellings of flapped words. This explanation is consistent with reports that the importance of phonological awareness declines with age (Comeau *et al.*, 1999; Wagner *et al.*, 1994).

More recently, the results of a four-year longitudinal study of French-speaking children (aged 6:6 to 10 years) by Sprenger-Charolles *et al.* (2003) suggest that effective phonological processing in reading facilitates the construction of the orthographic lexicon. This makes sense because children cannot rely extensively on visual recognition until they have developed a sizeable orthographic lexicon, so aural experience is specially salient. In other words, if phonological processing and orthographic processing are reciprocally related, early attempts at writing necessarily involve making links between speech and print.

Treiman's (1993) study of first graders' (up to seven years old) free writing is also relevant here. Their performance was better on words without flaps than on words with flaps, but unlike Ehri and Wilce's (1986) children, they made the same number of errors on words with /t/ and /d/ flaps. Treiman's explanation for this difference was that Grade 1 children had already observed that flaps are often spelled with <t>, i.e. they had already begun to develop a rudimentary orthographic lexicon which eliminated the bias towards <d> for words containing t-flaps.

The Flaps Spelling Test

Treiman *et al.* (1994) subsequently designed the Flaps Spelling Test and used it to make a cross-sectional comparison of kindergarten children (6.08 years old), first graders (seven years old) and second graders (eight years old). The test is a forced-choice task that simply requires children to write either a <d> or <t> in a blank space within the target word which is spoken in context. It comprises five words with t-flaps (e.g. 'city'), five words with d-flap words (e.g. 'lady'), and five control words with a medial /t/ or /d/ that is not flapped, e.g. 'sometimes'). Along with four practice items, the 15 experimental words were presented on audio-tape in random order, within a sentence context. With this new Flaps Spelling Test, Treiman's results were more consistent with those of Ehri and Wilce (1986): performance was poorer on flapped words than control words, better on d-flaps than t-flaps, and performance on t-flaps improved from kindergarten to second grade.

These changes in performance with age suggest that print exposure limits the <d> bias, but we wanted to address the related question of whether the <d> bias is influenced by early linguistic experience. More specifically, we wondered how the development of phonological awareness, gauged through flaps spelling, might be influenced by home language. According to Lim (in press), the flapping of /t/ and /d/ also occurs in the widely spoken colloquial form of English (Singlish), and almost all Singaporean children are also regularly exposed to American English through television and computers. For these reasons, we assumed kindergarten children would readily comprehend flapped high frequency words spoken in context even if their L1 was not English.

From Rickard Liow and Poon's (1998) earlier work on bilingual Singaporean children, we made some predictions about the spelling performance on Treiman *et al.*'s (1994) flaps test for the three different language background groups. First, the English L1/Mandarin L2 children's home language is English, so we could expect to replicate the results of Ehri and Wilce (1986) and Treiman *et al.* (1994) and find a <d> bias in words with t-flaps. However, the teaching methods for reading and spelling in English are based on visual memory and rote-learned letter sequences, rather than phonological decoding and encoding between print and speech. For this reason, our English-LB children were expected to rely on a rudimentary orthographic lexicon for reading and have poorer phonological awareness for spelling than unilingual children (see Bruck *et al.*, 1998). If so, the English-LB children's bias towards the letter <d> for words with t-flaps might be less pronounced than that of unilingual children, or more like performance in Treiman's (1993) earlier study. Second, the Chinese-LB children (Mandarin L1, English L2) may be less likely to rely on phonological processing for English because they speak more Chinese at home and have been exposed to a logographic script. Although alphabetic *pinyin* eventually encourages phonological awareness (Rickard Liow & Tng, 2003) the Chinese-LB children's exposure might be too limited in kindergarten to have much effect on early spellings of English words. Thus for the Chinese-LB children, performance should be close to chance for all three conditions (d-flaps, t-flaps and control words) even on a forced-choice task. Finally, we expected the Malay-LB (Bahasa Malaysia L1/English L2) children to have the most well-developed phonological awareness, and thus be more prone to <d> bias in words with t-flaps. This is because alongside Singlish, Malay-LB children are exposed to a home language that has a transparent orthography. Even though the emphasis in Bahasa Malaysia lessons is initially on CV syllables (see Rickard Liow & Lee, 2004), rather than single letter-sound correspondences, this phonic training may have begun to transfer to English spelling. Thus, unlike Caravolas and Bruck (1993), we predicted that the simple syllable structures of spoken Rumi would facilitate early spelling in beginners.

To summarise, we expected the Malay-LB children to have the best phonological awareness, and so for words with t-flaps, they should show the poorest performance (i.e. more <d> bias), followed by the English-LB children, and then the Chinese-LB children. On words with d-flaps and control words, the Malay-LB children might perform better than the English-LB children; both these groups should perform better than the Chinese-LB children.

If Treiman *et al.*'s (1994) flaps spelling test does reveal that English-knowing bilingual children's phonological awareness is variable, such that Malay-LB < English-LB < Chinese-LB for t-flaps, Malay-LB > English-LB > Chinese-LB for d-flaps and control words, then the free spelling ability and oral proficiency of the three groups would also be of interest. To assess these, we administered a standardised spelling task, and collected data on auditory vocabulary for each child's reported first and second language.

Experimental design and test administration

Treiman *et al.*'s (1994) 15-item flaps test comprises three types of word: those with t-flaps, those with d-flaps and control words. Two words from the flaps spelling test were changed because they were thought to be outside the vocabulary of kindergarteners in Singapore: 'quarter' and 'meadow' were changed to 'water' and 'tidy' (see Appendix 1 for a copy of the answer sheet) and all the experimental words were flapped when dictated. We also administered Schonell's (1961) spelling test (100 words arranged in order of difficulty, with norms for UK children from five to 14 years) and a multilingual version of the British Picture Vocabulary Scale (MPVS, see Rickard Liow *et al.*, 1992, for details). With the consent of the kindergarten principal and the children's parents, a total of 80 native Singaporean kindergarten pupils (aged 5–6 years) who were attending a government kindergarten in Singapore took part: 29 were Malay-LB, 21 were Chinese-LB, and 30 were English-LB. The language background of these children was first determined using responses to a questionnaire (see Rickard Liow & Poon, 1998, for details) and then verified with the MPVS vocabulary scores. The mean age of the 80 children was 5.62 years, $SD = 0.27$, (Malay-LB $M = 5.60$ years, $SD = 0.22$; Chinese-LB $M = 5.61$ years, $SD = 0.29$; English-LB $M = 5.64$ years, $SD = 0.31$). A one-way ANOVA showed that the three groups were not different in age ($F(2, 79) = 0.13$, $p = 0.877$).

All testing sessions were conducted during normal school hours in a quiet room by the first author. The language background questionnaire was administered individually to all second year pupils in the kindergarten to exclude those with languages outside the scope of the study (e.g. Tamil speakers), and to allocate all the remaining children to one of the three language background groups, i.e. Malay-LB, Chinese-LB and English-LB. The classes were then divided into small groups with 5–7 pupils in each. At the start of each session, the children were informed and assured that the testing would not contribute towards their official term grades. The first group session involved the Schonell spelling test, which was discontinued after 10 consecutive failures, and the 75 MPVS vocabulary items in the child's reported L1, whilst the second group session involved the flaps test ($n = 15$ words with five t-flaps, five d-flaps, five control words, as well as four practice trials) and a further 75 MPVS vocabulary items in the child's reported L2.

The procedure for the Schonell spelling test was unchanged (see Schonell, 1961) but, along with the flaps spelling test items, the target words were tape-recorded using the same female voice (RP). For each flaps test item, the number of the word on the answer sheet was spoken, followed by the word itself after two seconds, and then the word in a context sentence after five seconds, and then the word by itself again after 10 seconds. This provided ample time for children to put a circle around the <t> or <d> after listening to the target word three times.

Results and discussion

Before analysing the flaps spelling data, we re-confirmed group allocation using the MPVS vocabulary test scores for each child's L1 and L2, and tested for differences between the language background groups for English vocabulary and Schonell spelling ability. The results of a one-way ANOVA for English vocabulary scores showed that there was a significant difference between language groups ($F(2,79) = 5.69$, $p = 0.005$), and *post hoc* tests established that the English-LB children's scores were higher than those of both the Chinese-LB children ($t(49) = 2.63$, $p = 0.011$, $d = 0.71$) and Malay-LB children ($t(57) = 2.98$, $p = 0.004$, $d = 0.73$). For this reason, we included English vocabulary as a covariate in the subsequent flaps test analyses. Similarly, a one-way ANOVA on the raw scores for the Schonell spelling test showed a significant difference between language groups ($F(2, 79) = 3.62$, $p = 0.03$), and tests established that the English-LB children ($M = 4.53$; $SD = 7.29$)

performed better than the Malay-LB children ($M = 0.41$; $SD = 0.91$), ($t(57) = 3.02$, $p = 0.004$, $d = 0.74$) but there were no differences between the Malay and Chinese-LB children ($M = 2.67$; $SD = 7.41$), ($t(48) = 1.63$, $p = 0.110$), nor between the Chinese and English-LB children ($t(49) = 0.89$, $p = 0.376$). Note that the mean Schonell scores were low for all three groups confirming that we were looking at beginner spellers, but spelling ages (SAs) were almost equivalent to British unilingual norms for their mean chronological age (5 years 7 months: English-LB SA = 5 years 5 months; Malay-LB SA = 5 years 0 months; Chinese-LB SA = 5 years 3 months).

For the flaps spelling test, the main measure of phonological processing, all 15 items were attempted by all the children, and none gave the same response throughout the test (i.e. all <t> or all <d>). Responses were scored as either 1 (hit) for correct response or 0 (miss) for incorrect response (max = 15). As the children had only two spellings from which to choose (<t> or <d>), we needed to exclude guesses. To check whether responses differed from chance (0.50), we conducted two-tailed *t* tests for each flap-type.

Table 14.1 shows that the English and Malay-LB children were significantly different from chance for all three conditions, i.e. these two groups were not just guessing. The Chinese-LB children were above chance (0.62) only for words with d-flaps, so we will not discuss their performance on words with t-flaps or control words. To test whether performance on t-flaps was Malay-LB < English-LB < Chinese-LB, and on d-flaps and control words was Malay-LB > English-LB > Chinese-LB, a 3 × 3 ANCOVA was carried out with language group (Malay, English, Chinese) as the between-participants variable, flap-type (t-flap, d-flap and control) as the within-participants variable, and English vocabulary and Schonell scores as covariates. Results showed that both English vocabulary and Schonell scores had the same effect across groups, and neither

Table 14.1 Mean proportion correct for the three language groups for each condition of the forced-choice flaps test (standard deviation in brackets)

Language background	***Flap-type***		
	t-Flap	***d-Flap***	***Control***
English ($n = 30$)	0.74* (0.22)	0.80* (0.17)	0.73* (0.30)
Chinese ($n = 21$)	0.59 (0.23)	0.62* (0.24)	0.62 (0.29)
Malay ($n = 29$)	0.40* (0.22)	0.60* (0.22)	0.62* (0.23)

*Significantly different from 0.5 (chance) according to two-tailed *t*-tests

interacted with flap-type, so we were reasonably confident that potential confounds were minimal. The predicted interaction between language background group and flap-type was (borderline) significant ($F(3, 137) = 2.49$, $p = 0.052$, $eta^2 = 0.06$) and one-way ANOVAs revealed significant differences across the three groups for t-flaps ($F(2, 79) = 17.27$, $p = 0.001$) and d-flaps ($F(2, 79) = 7.99$, $p = 0.001$). Subsequent *t*-tests (with Bonferroni corrections) confirmed that for t-flaps the Malay-LB children's performance was significantly poorer than that of the English-LB children ($t(57) = 5.96$, $p = 0.001$, $d = 1.23$), see Figure 14.1.

For words with t-flaps, the Malay-LB children showed the expected <d> bias, suggesting their spelling is strongly influenced by the phonological properties of dictated words. Meta-phonological skills must either transfer soon after the Malay children start attending Bahasa Malaysia lessons (cf. Rickard Liow & Poon, 1998), and/or their home language does affect literacy acquisition, though probably not by the same mechanism that Caravolas and Bruck (1993) postulated for their (slightly older) Czech children. The influence of phonological awareness was less dominant for the English-LB children, who showed less <d> bias to words with t-flaps. For words with d-flaps, the performance of the Malay-LB and Chinese-LB children was significantly poorer than that of the English-LB children ($t(57) = 3.87$, $p = 0.001$, $d = 0.91$; $t(49) = 3.15$, $p = 0.003$, $d = 0.83$ respectively). For control words, the three LB groups showed no difference in performance ($F(2, 79) = 1.60$, $p = 0.209$). This is of interest because data from the Schonell spelling test had already established that the English-LB group's use of visual and phonological skills appears to

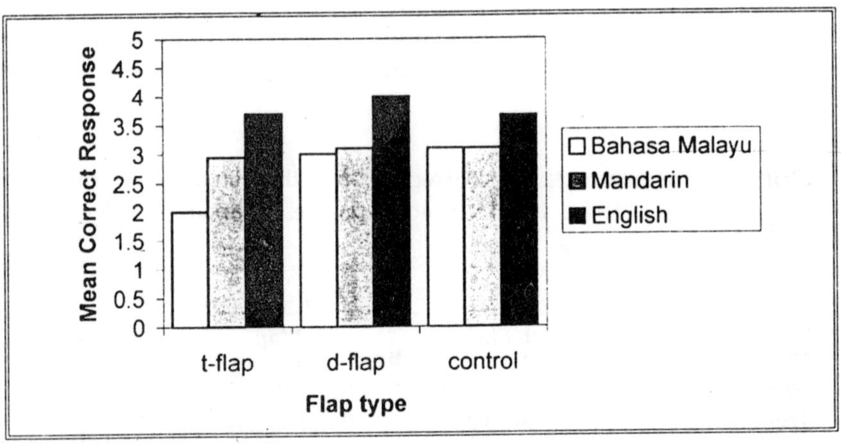

Figure 14.1 Performance on t-flaps, d-flaps, and control words for each language group

assist early whole-word spelling in English, yet differences were masked on the single letter forced-choice flaps test.

We also conducted within-group analyses of flap-type. For the Malay-LB children there were differences in performance on flaps ($F(2, 56) = 8.40$, $p = 0.001$, $eta^2 = 0.23$, see Figure 14.1 again) with d-flaps better than t-flaps ($t(28) = 3.81$, $p = 0.001$, $d = 0.71$) and control words also better than t-flaps ($t(28) = 3.30$, $p = 0.003$, $d = 0.61$), but there were no differences in their performance for d-flaps and control words. Again, this suggests phonological processing prevailed for the Malay-LB group. In contrast, the English-LB children, who were the best spellers overall, showed no difference in performance across t-flaps, d-flaps and control words. The lack of bias for the English-LB group appears consistent with the view that reciprocal development of orthographic and phonological processing skills, described by Sprenger-Charolles *et al.* (2003), is optimal.

To summarise the results, the Chinese-LB pupils were at chance for t-flaps and control words, but the main prediction that Malay-LB < English-LB for t-flaps was supported. Pairwise comparisons revealed better spelling performance overall by the English-LB children when compared to both the Malay-LB (English $M = 3.79$, $SE = 0.16$; Malay $M = 2.70$, $SE = 0.16$; $t(57) = 5.16$, $p = 0.001$, $d = 1.12$) and Chinese-LB children (English $M = 3.79$, $SE = 0.16$; Chinese $M = 3.05$, $SE = 0.19$; $t(49) = 2.72$, $p = 0.009$, $d = 0.73$). This pattern on the flaps test was consistent with the small, but reliable, differences in scores on the Schonell test which has a more representative sample of words. It seems, therefore, that a combination of phonological awareness and early development of an orthographic lexicon is optimal for bilingual children learning to spell English words. Exposure to English (or Singlish) at home is sufficient for the English-LB children to achieve this balance, although it may be less readily attainable by beginners with Bahasa Malaysia and Mandarin as a mother tongue.

Concluding Remarks

A modified version of Treiman *et al.*'s (1994) Flaps Spelling Test detected early differences in phonological processing amongst English-knowing bilinguals attending a kindergarten in Singapore. Perhaps the most striking finding is that *none* of the three bilingual subtypes showed exactly the same pattern of performance as the youngest cohorts of American unilingual children in Ehri and Wilce (1986) and Treiman *et al.*'s (1994) studies. The Malay-LB children's performance was closest to that of English-speaking unilingual children. They showed the typical <d>-bias on words with t-flaps, but they were not better on control words than words with d-flaps. This heterogeneity in the use of phonological awareness, both across the Singaporean bilinguals and between unilinguals and bilinguals, provides further evidence that differences in aural language experience (Caravolas & Bruck, 1993), as well as script exposure (Rickard Liow, 1999; Rickard Liow & Poon, 1998; Rickard Liow & Tng, 2003), can influence the early spelling attempts of first language (English-LB) bilingual children, as well as the second language (Malay-LB and Chinese-LB) children. The data we have presented suggest that a Malay-English bilingual child tends to over-rely on phonology when spelling English words, whilst the phonological awareness of an age-matched Chinese–English bilingual child, who is studying in the same kindergarten, is very limited.

English-knowing Chinese speakers already represent a very large group of all bilinguals, and the use of English as a medium for instruction is set to increase substantially in Malaysia and other parts of SE Asia. Finding ways to optimise second language spelling and reading skills in these complex multilingual settings presents quite a challenge for teachers and researchers alike (see Durgunoglu, 2002, for a review).

References

Beers, J.W. and Henderson, E.H. (1977) A study of developing orthographic concept among first-grade children. *Research in the Teaching of English* 11, 133–48.

Bruck, M., Treiman, R., Caravolas, M., Genesee, F. and Cassar, M. (1998) Spelling skills of children in whole language and phonics classrooms. *Applied Psycholinguistics* 19, 669–84.

Caravolas, M. and Bruck, M. (1993) The effect of oral and written language input on children's phonological awareness: A cross-linguistic study. *Journal of Experimental Child Psychology* 55, 1–30.

Caravolas, M., Hulme, C. and Snowling, M.J. (2001) The foundations of spelling ability: Evidence from a 3-year longitudinal study. *Journal of Memory and Language* 45, 751–74.

Cheung, H., Chen, H.-C., Lai, C.Y., Wong, O.C. and Hills, M. (2001) The development of phonological awareness: Effects of spoken language experience and orthography. *Cognition* 81, 227–41.

Comeau, L., Cormier, P., Grandmaison, E. and Lacroix, D. (1999) A longitudinal study of phonological processing skills in children learning to read in a second language. *Journal of Educational Psychology* 91, 29–43.

Department of Statistics (2001) *Census of Population 2000: Demographic Characteristics.* Singapore: Ministry of Trade and Industry.

Durgunoglu, A.Y. (2002) Cross-linguistic transfer in literacy development and implications for language learners. *Annals of Dyslexia* 52, 189–204.

Durgunoglu, A.Y., Nagy, W.E. and Hancin-Blatt, B.J. (1993) Cross-language transfer of phonological awareness. *Journal of Educational Psychology* 85, 453–65.

Ehri, L.C. (1998) Grapheme–phoneme knowledge is essential to learning to read words in English. In J.L. Metsala *et al.* (eds) *Word Recognition in Beginning Literacy.* (pp. 3–40). Mahwah, NJ, US: Erlbaum.

Ehri, L.C. and Wilce, L.S. (1986) The influence of spellings on speech: Are alveolar flaps /d/ or /t/? In D.B. Yaden and S. Templeton (eds) *Metalinguistic Awareness and Beginning Literacy* (pp. 101–14). Portsmouth, NH: Heinemann Educational Books Inc.

Foorman, B.R., Francis, D.J., Fletcher, D.J., Schatschneider, C. and Mehta, P. (1998) The role of instruction in learning to read: Preventing reading failure in at-risk children. *Journal of Educational Psychology* 90, 37–55.

Goswami, U. and Bryant, P.E. (1990) *Phonological Skills and Learning to Read.* London: Lawrence Erlbaum.

Hatcher, P.J., Hulme, C. and Ellis, A.W. (1994) Ameliorating early reading failure by integrating the teaching of reading and phonological skills: The phonological linkage hypothesis. *Child Development* 65, 41–57.

Holm, A. and Dodd, B. (1996) The effect of first written language on the acquisition of English literacy. *Cognition* 59, 119–47.

Ladefoged, P. and Maddieson, I. (1996) *The Sounds of the World's Languages.* Oxford, UK: Blackwell.

Lim, L. (in press) Sounding Singaporean. In L. Lim (ed.) *Singapore English: A Grammatical Description.* Amsterdam/Philadelphia: John Benjamins.

McBride-Chang, C. and Ho, C.S.-H. (1999) Developmental issues in Chinese children's character acquisition. *Journal of Educational Psychology* 92, 50–5.

Morais, J., Cary, L., Alegria, J. and Bertelson, P. (1979) Does awareness of speech as a sequence of phones arise spontaneously? *Cognition* 7, 323–31.

Oney, B. and Durgunoglu, A.Y. (1997) Beginning to read in Turkish: A phonologically transparent orthography. *Applied Psycholinguistics* 18, 1–15.

Rayner, K., Foorman, B.R., Perfetti, C.A., Pesetsky, D. and Seidenberg, M. (2001) How psychological science informs the teaching of reading. *Psychological Science in the Public Interest* 2, 31–74.

Read, C. (1975) *Children's Categorization of Speech Sounds in English (NCTE Research Report No. 17).* Urbana, IL: National Council of Teachers of English.

Read, C., Zhang, Y., Nie, H. and Ding, B. (1986) The ability to manipulate speech sounds depends on knowing alphabetic reading. *Cognition* 24, 31–44.

Rickard Liow, S.J. (1999) Reading skill development in bilingual Singaporean children. In M. Harris and G. Hatano (eds) *Learning to Read and Write: A Cross-linguistic Perspective* (pp. 196–213). Cambridge: Cambridge University Press.

Rickard Liow, S.J. and Lee, L.C. (2004) Metalinguistic awareness and semi-syllabic scripts: Children's spelling errors in Malay. *Reading and Writing: An Inter-disciplinary Journal* 17, 7–26.

Rickard Liow, S.J. and Poon, K.K.L. (1998) Phonological awareness in multilingual Chinese children. *Applied Psycholinguistics* 19, 339–62.

Rickard Liow, S.J. and Tng, S.K. (2003) Biscriptal literacy development of Chinese children in Singapore. In C. McBride-Chang and H.-C. Chen (eds) *Reading Development in Chinese Children* (pp. 215–28). Westport, CT: Praeger Publishers.

Rickard Liow, S.J., Hong, E.L. and Tng, S.K. (1992) *Singapore Primary School Norms for the Multilingual British Picture Vocabulary Scale: English, Mandarin and Malay.* Working paper no. 43, Department of Social Work and Psychology, National University of Singapore.

Schonell, F.J. (1961) *The Psychology and Teaching of Reading* (4th edn). New York: Philosophical Library.

Sprenger-Charolles, L., Siegel, L.S., Bechennec, D. and Serniclaes, W. (2003) Development of phonological and orthographic processing in reading aloud, in silent reading, and in spelling: A four-year longitudinal study. *Journal of Experimental Child Psychology* 84, 194–217.

Treiman, R. (1993) *Beginning to Spell: A Study of First-grade Children.* New York: Oxford University Press.

Treiman, R., Cassar, M. and Zukowski, A. (1994) What types of linguistic information do children use in spelling? The case of flaps. *Child Development* 65, 1318–37.

Wagner, R.K. and Torgesen, J.K. (1987) The nature of phonological processing and its causal role in the acquisition of reading skills. *Psychological Bulletin* 101, 192–212.

Wagner, R.K., Torgesen, J.K. and Rashotte, C.A. (1994) Development of reading-related phonological processing abilities: Evidence of bi-directional causality from a latent variable longitudinal study. *Developmental Psychology* 30, 73–87.

Wang, M. and Geva, E. (2003) Spelling performance of Chinese children using English as a second language: Lexical and visual-orthographic processes. *Applied Psycholinguistics* 24, 1–25.

Wimmer, H. and Goswami, U. (1994) The influence of orthographic consistency on reading development: Word recognition in English and German children. *Cognition* 51, 91–103.

Appendix 1

Flaps spelling test answer sheet (with condition shown)

Name: ______________ **Class:** ______________

Please write the correct letter (t or d) for each word.

Practice Words			
_ap	t or d	_oor	t or d
_une	t or d	_ig	t or d
Test Words			
ci_y (t)	t or d	wa_er (t)	t or d
bo_y (d)	t or d	no_ice (t)	t or d
birth_ay (c)	t or d	un_o (c)	t or d
some_imes (c)	t or d	ti_y (d)	t or d
mo_or (t)	t or d	swea_er (t)	t or d
un_ie (c)	t or d	gar_en (d)	t or d
la_y (d)	t or d	un_il (c)	t or d
mo_el (d)	t or d		t or d

Key: (t) = word with t-flap; (d) = word with d-flap; (c) = control
Adapted from Treiman *et al.* (1994) by changing 'quarter' to 'water' and 'meadow' to 'tidy'.

Part 4

Teaching a Second Language Writing System

Chapter 15

Different and Differing Views on Conceptualising Writing System Research and Education

THERESE DUFRESNE and DIANA MASNY

Introduction

This paper is one of a series on literacy, language, second language learning, focus-on-form, writing system research and systemic change paving the way to conduct inquiry and research from a post-structural position or way of thinking and demonstrating that commensurability is necessary between systems. Atkinson (2003a, b) and Leki (2003) have stated separately on different occasions and in their most recent publications that:

> second language (L2) writing has been somewhat undertheorised, not in terms of developing or debating specific aspects of L2 writing but in terms of connecting what researchers do to broader intellectual strands, domains, and dimensions of modern thought and contemporary lived experience. (Leki, 2003: 103)

In this chapter, we view writing system research as being situated within the broader domain of second language writing.

In choosing post-structuralism, we respond to a plea to try to do more to explore wider dimensions of conceptualisation and develop broader theoretical thinking on issues and claims made with reference to writing systems in general and to second language in particular. The chapter does this in three ways. The first is through the adoption of a post-structural conceptual position taken to collect, analyse and interpret data in second language teaching and learning. The second is through the use of an educational research lens to examine data that might prove to be essential when looking at the not-yet well established 'intersection between second language writing and second language acquisition' as Kubota (2003: 33) states. The third is to conceptually frame the paper within Dufresne's theory of knowledge (2002) as applied to learning and language learning and within Masny's Multiple Literacies Theory (2002).

The argument often brought up about the inability to broach the wide gap between second language acquisition research and second language writing research, including writing system research, is that they use different paradigmatic lenses to focus upon research (Dufresne, 2002). Since different and differing paradigms are involved in the two aforementioned research disciplines, 'questions in one framework make little if any sense in another framework', according to Lincoln and Guba (2000: 176). There is incommensurability between the two paradigms regarding knowledge. Second language acquisition mainly goes about researching knowledge as if it were part of the physical world and science, whereas second language writing research regularly centres on how to go about knowing about the social world. As Kubota (2003) reiterates in reference to the two disciplines, while second language writing primarily has a pragmatic concern for learner performance at a discourse level, much of second language acquisition research has a focus on competence on the morphosyntactic level. However, somewhere along the way, the two do meet. Sometimes this meeting of different research foci and different research conceptualisations causes a collision, which has recently been tagged as being a voice of dissent perhaps drowning in the larger sea of second language acquisition research. At times, second language acquisition research politely tolerates second language writing research by not silencing it in an attempt to smooth out the ripple created in that tranquil sea. At other times, they influence each other given that second language writing research and second language acquisition research can be considered as parallel issues. While both areas of research target some aspect of language, their concerns differ.

In sum, this paper is based upon several premises. The first premise is that one area of research can contribute to another and that they have something to learn from one another from time to time. Secondly, different ways of looking at language in a language learning situation, be it under strictly controlled laboratory conditions and/or in a classroom, can only shed more light upon written language, the object under investigation, thereby giving that quasi-object more substance as more is learned about second language learning. Research should thereby lead to a deeper understanding of what takes place when a student attempts to use a writing system that is *other* than what the student would consider to be hers/his. Moreover, it should enable all second language researchers to reflect upon what they actually do when the focus is on product alone instead of process and what kind of knowledge is being generated by the research conducted.

With regard to the lenses used in this paper, in addition to looking at data through Masny's Multiple Literacies Theory (MLT) (2002), second language acquisition and second language writing (i.e. teaching and learning of a second language) are examined through the effects of focus-on-form and Dufresne's theory of the Telling Maps (2002). Long and Robinson (1998) define focus-on-form as an occasional shift of attention to linguistic code features by the teacher and/or by students that can be triggered by perceived problems of comprehension and perception that occur in a classroom situation. In this way, focus-on-form can be classified as a form of consciousness-raising that makes one become aware of some aspect of the target language. It can also be considered as dealing in part, though not exclusively, with writing systems since focus-on-form could refer to 'a set of visible or tactile signs used to represent units of language in a systematic way', as in the definition of a writing system given by Coulmas (1996: 560). The caveat is that a student must first have a general understanding of what has been said and/or written.

Because oral and/or written comprehension are the bases upon which focus-on-form depend, an exemplar has been selected from data taken from a second language student learning French in an immersion classroom in Canada. Within the selected setting, all students understand the teacher and are able to read French quite independently. However, the rate of freedom from error for all students in the classroom is high, making their attainment of accepted established target language norms in the French language system low.

A second exemplar has been taken from a longitudinal study documenting ways of becoming through a lens of second orthography, language and literacy in Gujarati and English in England.

Paradigms

A paradigm can be defined as a deeply held shared system and set of beliefs among stakeholders regarding how to go about doing something like teaching, learning and research. In other words it is a set way of thinking that dominates actions and ways of learning about the world. According to Guba and Lincoln (1994, 1998), a paradigm is made up of three interrelated but separate parts. These are its paradigmatic ontology, epistemology and methodology. The nature of reality and truth are the focus of ontology. How we come to know the world and the relationship between the knower and what can be known are encompassed in epistemology. At issue in methodology are the specific ways in which we gain knowledge. In other words, a paradigm deals with conceptualisation, which creates a way of thinking and a belief-system that influence actions and decisions. For example, in second language research more often than not, ontology, epistemology and methodology are considered as being one and the same. The emphasis is on how to go about conducting research, the controls that must be imposed upon it and its research validity and that it is *value-free*. In a recent issue of *TESOL Quarterly* (2002, Volume 36, number 4) for example, 80% of the articles were quantitative in nature. The articles had an introduction, a review of the literature and then moved into methodology, with a focus on data analysis, results and their interpretation. The issue of ontology and epistemology was not brought to the fore. When language is researched as a science, the positioning of ontology (knowledge) and epistemology (what can be known) is intrinsically wrapped up in the way research is and must be conducted (methodology). It is from methodology that knowledge and what can be learned is captured and understood. Quantitative methods are favored instead of qualitative methods; the former are considered as being scientific. This paper has no intention of revisiting the paradigm wars that were launched, fought and won in other disciplines (see for instance Donmoyer *et al.*, 2000). In fact when there is nothing beyond methodology in research, both qualitative and quantitative methods actually form part of the same general belief system. At issue are the limitations and consequences that these conceptualisations and paradigmatic beliefs have on research on second language writing which includes language teaching and learning.

In short, a paradigm signals a worldview, a relationship between the knower (the individual), forms of knowledge and how they intersect in space and time. For many years, if not decades, the field of second language learning viewed the world through the lens of a binary mode (literacy/illiteracy; correct/incorrect, acceptable/unacceptable ...) within positivism and post-positivism. This worldview is often referred to as the received mainstream view – an account linked to logical empiricism. Schwandt (2000: 196) informs us that: 'Logical empiricism worked from a conception of knowledge of correct representation of an independent reality and was/is almost exclusively interested in the issue of establishing the validity of scientific knowledge claims'. In other words, these paradigms are mainly concerned with the rational reconstruction of scientific knowledge. As such, the received view has acquired tremendous legitimacy. These methodologically driven paradigms derive their traditions from the natural sciences with their desires for replication, laboratory-like controls and results that can be generalised and have universal appeal.

Post-structuralism

The subject of post-structuralism is to conceptualise, to reconceptualise and, in reference to the topic of this paper, to examine underlying educational and research tenets. These might be considered as philosophical issues but they form the bases and belief tenets upon which research is conducted. As such, they must be part of a look at the inner workings of any paradigm including research in general (Lather, 2000; St. Pierre, 2000a, b) for they influence language learning, language education and all aspects of language acquisition research. Within this framework, the definition of a concept is paradigm-specific. For example, the concept of literacy within post-positivism is taken up differently from how it would be taken up in post-structuralism. The concept of literacy would be taken up in post-positivism as a question related to literacy/illiteracy and related issues. In post-structuralism, literacy would be focused on processes of literacy and how reading the word and the world would influence the reading of self for example. In sum, post-structuralism brings about a critical reflection upon the dynamics of structure or structuralism (Payne, 1997).

What then is a concept? A concept is defined *in situ* and in relation to and with other concepts that intersect with it and with which it interferes. Findings in neuroscience regarding context and hemispheric specialisations support this in that, as Wolfe (2001: 46) explains, 'Our understanding of what we read or our comprehension of what we hear depends on the context in which it occurs and it is the right hemisphere working in concert with other areas of the brain that decodes the external information, allowing us to create an overall understanding of what is said or what is read'. This cannot be ignored when researching second language writing systems. New knowledge introduced upon an established *how the world works and how it should work* is like trying to fit into a new pair of shoes and thinking that they should be as comfortable as the old pair that must be discarded. It is uncomfortable and has a good chance of being rejected.

Following along the same lines, another characteristic of a concept is consistency. A concept organises heterogeneity and reorganises heterogeneity into the sameness and distinctness of its formerly heterogeneous elements. We do not like instability. When a student is presented with new knowledge through focus-on-form, for example, there could be an attempt to organise and reorganise that *other* knowledge *to fit*. Under these circumstances, this attempt causes the system to seek to regain and maintain the stability it had and has lost through the introduction of new knowledge.

In speaking of organisation in neuroscience, Wolfe (2001: 104) states that: 'One of the most effective ways to make information meaningful is to associate or compare a new concept with a known concept, to hook the unfamiliar with something familiar so the brain can organise that information'. This is not a traditional statement involving something like prior knowledge of a verb tense in French or restructuring. It implies that the experiences of the student as a whole can and must be tapped in order to support writing ability. It also implies that the one-to-one correspondence sought between teaching and learning in the transmission paradigm traditional in teaching is nothing more than information and that a distinction must be made between learning as knowledge and learning as information gathering.

For the last characteristic of the definition of concept, May's (1994) interpretation is retained. May (1994: 35) states that: 'A concept must be understood as a productive force that reverberates across a conceptual plane in that field or system'. As such, a concept is paradigm-specific. It is very powerful in framing what we know, what we can know and how we can go about imparting knowledge and assessing knowledge. It also determines the importance of knowledge and assigns a norm to that knowledge. Within this definition, a concept condones, sanctions, overlooks, forgives, silences, informs and misinforms.

In sum, concepts are used in different ways not only across disciplines but also within disciplines. There is a proliferation of meanings assigned to concepts taken up by many disciplines: applied linguistics, psycholinguistics, anthropology, sociology and cultural studies, just to name a few. The proliferation of meanings assigned to a concept calls for an examination of conceptual frameworks that situate a concept. Conceptual frameworks cannot be created without understanding paradigmatic contexts.

As a result, there is considerable debate and chaos with regard to multiple meanings assigned to a concept. Chaos and complexity are trademarks of post-modern science. These forms of science, asserts Dufresne (2002: 134): 'are not interested in traditional problem-solving. They focus on the unknown and the impossibility of defining initial conditions thereby defying any possibility of relying on rational explanation to explain an observation'. This paper situates itself within the boundaries of post-modern science and explores an alternative paradigm that might prove to be valuable to research. In other words, this paper reconceptualises problems related to second language learning, writing systems and literacy and it does so using a non-traditional paradigm.

Teaching–learning Paradigms and Second Language Acquisition

When Schmidt (1993) referred to applied linguistics and the possible role that consciousness (focus-on-form is part of this) might play or be allowed to play in research, he was dealing with conflicting paradigms and reminded us that: 'Deeply held philosophical beliefs often colour our positions so that there is the widely held belief among second language researchers that introspection is unreliable and that subjective data thus elicited is not the domain or realms of science' (Schmidt, 1993: 220). He pointed out that this point of view was inherited from behaviourism and that it had far-reaching implications even for non-behaviourists.

With this statement second language acquisition and teaching and learning a second language not only form parallels but intersect. The traditional teaching-learning paradigm is based upon closely intertwined ideas of social efficiency and scientific management. Social efficiency links to theories of hereditary differences whereas scientific management is related to associationist and behavioural learning theories which may or may not be commensurate to one other. Pressures exerted by these theories, according to Shepard (2001: 1068), have not spared second language teaching and learning.

There has been, though, a paradigm shift in education in certain areas of Canada and the United States (Dufresne, 2001). Traditional teaching-learning paradigms are being replaced, as exemplified by the Quality Paradigm Shift in Education from the Alaska Department of Education (Bonsting, 1995) and the new programme published by the Minister of Education of Québec (Ministère de l'Éducation du Québec, 2001).

Many of the new paradigms are considered as a form of constructivism, constructionism and/or socio-constructivism in that they espouse a theory of knowledge where learning and meaning-making are constructed by the learner who is the primary agent of the action of learning. As Schwandt (2000) reiterates, humans do not discover knowledge or find it, they construct or build knowledge. Moreover, this knowledge is added to and modified according to experience. Linked to French Immersion, a student becomes more proficient in the language through the experience of learning in the target language. Knowing is not merely the 'impression of sense data on the mind of the learner. Rather the mind of the learner is actively engaged in making use of impressions at the very least forming abstractions or concepts' (Schwandt, 2000: 197). In this framework, the learner tries to make sense of experience by continually testing and modifying constructions in light of new experience and what the learner knows of how the world works.

As a result, focus-on-form and its use as a language learning and teaching tool seldom occur in subject areas that are taught in French in an immersion setting. An example is a subject like mathematics which is taught in French. In classroom observations performed to date, the freedom from error sought is freedom from mathematical error in basic operations. It involves the application and development of mathematical thinking rather than freedom from language errors.

Focus-on-form, however, still continues to be used in French literacy classes within immersion programmes. To date, a paradigmatic shift has not affected its use as a language teaching-learning tool within the teaching of French as a subject in an immersion programme. Conceptually, focus-on-form and a definition of literacy as decoding/encoding belong to the traditional paradigm of teaching-learning. The paradigm is one that involves transmission of language information done very often by a teacher. There is a hope attached to it that somewhere along the way, a student will reach targeted norms, achieve accuracy and develop a relative freedom from error through correction in oral and/or written forms using a binary mode like that of a right answer and a wrong answer. Conceptually, what can be known is thought of in terms of correct/incorrect. In other words, there can only be one form of knowledge taken up by the student and this knowledge is thought of as teacher-controlled and controllable by the teacher. Process has little or no importance in this paradigm. In learning, the student is rewarded for being right and penalised for being wrong.

Moreover, when focusing-on-form, both second language acquisition research and research on second language writing within this traditional paradigm centre on the product, norms of correctness and, to a lesser degree, norms of acceptability when it comes to establishing the binaries upon which a judgment will be formed by a researcher. In this way, norms must serve as frames of reference in judging grammaticality as well as acceptability of their foci, be it on the level of discourse, the phonological and/or the morphosyntactic level, for example. More often than not, the primary source of this normalisation is the native speaker and the second language learner is judged according to how well s/he has reached this norm of freedom from error and/or conversely how far away s/he is in reference to the established norm. The language data may be collected in a strict laboratory setting and/or a classroom depending upon the foci.

The research on focus-on-form that took place in the 1990s was also greatly influenced by the same type of thought. Here we are referring to the work done in Canada on input enhancement and second language question formation (White *et al.*, 1991), adverb placement in second language acquisition (White, 1991) and timing in focus-on-form (Lightbown, 1998) for example. This shared conceptualisation drove the research on focus-on-form and other research on 'consciousness raising'.

In contrast, the deep-seated change in learning theory (constructivism) that is presently occurring worldwide involves a reformed view of language learning. As part of constructivism, learning to write is situated and it is considered and assessed as part of a process. At its bare minimum, learning cannot be understood apart from its social context and content. The paradigm can be looked at as a growing-continuant involving processes. Very little is known about the learning continuant processes and the resulting exchange of information that could lead to knowledge. We do know that these processes cross and traverse disciplines and fields (Masny & Dufresne, in press). Product is field-specific.

It is judged according to its correctness, i.e. the mechanics of writing. In contrast, the learning processes and knowledge-building are not field-specific. They involve the development of thought and would be evaluated according to this development, i.e. learning how to write/ content – the act of writing. The paradigm is based upon ontology (knowledge: truth and reality; reality is constructed) and epistemology (what can be known about how students learn in general, and that applies to second language learning as well). The result is that methodology (how to go about creating knowledge, researching) focused only on product is put into a position of secondary importance. In other words, the paradigm deals with a deep-seated change in learning theory. It involves a reformed view of learning and knowledge-creation that very often has longitudinal continuant processes as its foci. The emphasis is on authentic writing situations using longitudinal exemplars of student writing which will eventually create a process norm. A student's writing process is documented and assessed using descriptive rubrics arising from student exemplars which serve as raw data for example.

What happens on a regular basis throughout the longitudinal documenting of a student's language learning in a French immersion setting? Is the introduction of error correction through focus-on-form effective? If it is, just how effective is it and under what circumstances would allowing a writing system to reorganise itself toward correctness work? Are there factors that have been overlooked when the world of the teacher and the world of the student collide?

The murkiness: When worlds collide, do writing systems re-organise?

To reflect upon these questions, let us move into learning to read French through an English lens. The two languages have differing writing systems and they divide time and space quite differently. What can happen when different and differing worlds, those of a French teacher and those of an English student learning French, collide in a classroom concerning focus-on-form, freedom from error, the seeking of accuracy in a second language and the use of correction using the same script but different orthographies?

The vignette that follows will serve as a data sample to address this question. It is taken from observational data collected during a pilot study in preparation for a longitudinal study. The study was conducted in an early French Immersion program in Canada. The pilot study involved videotaping four Grade 4 participants during four French classes over a two-week period. Because of an impending work-to-rule by the teachers, only two of the participants were included in the pilot.

The videotapes were used as a trigger as well as a record of what had taken place in these classes. Students were asked to find a place on video where they were featured and to answer questions as to what was going on during the class and address the corrections that had been forwarded either by the teacher or by other students. The teacher used various techniques including focus-on-form in order to make her students conscious of correctness in French. Most of these were used during the French class rather than the classes that were held in French like maths and social science.

French Immersion students were reading, drawing and writing about bears (les ours) in class. The conversation between student and teacher took place in French.

> The teacher-directed conversation turned to whether a bear could shovel snow or not.
>
> In response to the teacher-asked question: Do you know what shoveling means?
>
> Andrew, one of the students, made shoveling motions with his arms.
>
> The teacher then asked what he was doing with the snow.
>
> The answer from the student was that you shovel (it).
>
> Pushing the issue further, the teacher asked Andrew what he did to the snow when he shoveled it.
>
> Andrew's response was that you threw it.

The teacher then repeated what Andrew had said and told him that you take the snow away, and that it was a very good answer. She told Andrew that he was right, that a bear did not need to shovel snow, thanked him and called on another student.

It was at this point that the two worlds, that of Andrew and that of the teacher, started to collide.

> Andrew pointed to the picture in the textbook, held up his writing workbook and interrupted her saying that sometimes a bear needed to shovel.
>
> The teacher retorted that they were talking about bears and repeated 'if you were a bear' to Andrew indicating that bears do not shovel snow, people do.
>
> Not to be dismissed, Andrew raised his voice and insisted that sometimes it was necessary for a bear to shovel.
>
> The teacher repeated 'sometimes'. It was a statement and not a question asked of the student.
>
> Andrew answered in the affirmative as if it had been asked as a question.

The teacher repeated the affirmation after Andrew and went on to state that she did not know that 'a bear had to shovel sometimes'. She asked Andrew to think about it and then to tell her how a bear would have a need to shovel and then she pointed to the bear in the book to make certain that they were actually talking about the same thing.

Andrew, ever persistent, insisted that a bear would need to shovel in order to go out and find food ('pour chercher et manger').

The teacher then came back to the subject and asked him whether this would be done with a shovel ('avec une pelle?').

Andrew had to admit that it would not ('non').

The teacher repeated his negation, told him they would discuss it another time and went back to the book informing students that they would find out what a bear does in winter for the rest of the allotted time and to complete the written exercise on bears.

In French, the use of the verb 'pelleter' is very specific unless used metaphorically. It is an action accomplished with a shovel. For Andrew, in English, shovelling is an action that can conceptually be undertaken without a specific tool like a shovel. He was thinking and using English and trying to convey the English notion of shovelling to his teacher. In English, a bear can use its paws to shovel or dig. A bear can remove snow from the entrance to its cave, for example. This was not evident in the exchange that took place and neither Andrew nor the teacher was able to grasp the nuances behind shovelling as it is usually used in the two languages.

Andrew had been focusing on form but he was not focusing on what the teacher was trying to convey. Moreover, there is evidence that while Andrew had initially given the right answer, his level of knowledge concerning shovelling in French does not mesh with his understanding of shovelling in English. Neuroscience states that experience(s) and prior knowledge form networks in the brain (Wolfe, 2001). Information that fits into an existing network has a better chance of being retained and accepted than information that does not. Andrew was trying to fit 'pelleter' into his knowledge while the teacher had her own world with which to contend.

The story does not end there. Having witnessed the incident and viewed the videotape several times, the researcher (T. Dufresne) was well aware of the events that had taken place. As part of a linguistic pilot study at the time, she wanted to discuss interpretations of the word 'shovel' and its differences in English and in French to see if there was any correlation with Andrew's interpretation. That was not to be, for in the interview that immediately followed the class, Andrew avoided the question of shovelling altogether. The interview was held in both French and English.

When asked to explain either in English or in French or in both languages what he had seen in the video concerning the story cited above,

Andrew told the researcher: 'they had been talking about bears and why they wanted to be a bear and she (referring to the teacher) wanted to know: c'est quoi pelleter? (What is shoveling?) and so I was trying to answer . . . answer the question'.

When asked what he had said, he responded: 'J'ai dit comme une pelle que tu lances (Like a shovel that you throw)'.

When the researcher asked Andrew what the teacher had said, he shrugged his shoulders and he called an end to that interview.

There is cause for reflection at this point. Were Andrew and the researcher communicating about the same thing? Andrew had provided a slightly different twist to the events and, moreover, he had shifted the power to his corner perhaps indicating that he had grasped the concept that in French, one has to use a shovel to throw snow ('comme une pelle que tu lances'). Since Andrew had called the interview to an end, the researcher was unable to verify any interpretation assigned to the events. In any case, one thing that was ascertained was that Andrew was not seeing the video in the same way as the researcher. The interpretations of that video were commensurate with what had taken place in the first interview.

Three days later, at Andrew's request, the researcher again met with Andrew. He indicated that he would not mind seeing that particular section of videotape once more. This time Andrew decided that the interview was going to take place in English. They viewed the same section of video and after talking a while about other things than what he had seen on the video, the researcher asked him once again to describe what he had just seen. Andrew replied that: 'what I had been doing was in my head cause I do a lot of shovelling and my Dad talks to me in French about shovelling so I knew what it was'.

When the researcher inquired as to whether the teacher understood what he was trying to say, he replied in the affirmative. The researcher then asked him to explain what he had told her and at that point he said that he wanted to re-view the video because he could not remember.

After viewing again, Andrew informed the researcher that: 'it was because they were talking about shovelling so what I did was to try to remember last year shovelling my neighbor's walkway . . . and I was trying to answer the question'.

The researcher then asked him what particular question he was answering.

His response was: 'Est-ce que le . . . Does the bear have to shovel?'

When asked whether he was able to say the same thing in French, Andrew's response was: 'Est-ce que *le ours *besoin de pelleter? (Does a bear need to shovel?)'.

The researcher then inquired: 'Et puis, est-ce que l'ours a besoin de pelleter? (And so does a bear need to shovel?)'.

His answer was a definite no.

The researcher asked Andrew to explain why not and he responded: 'Parce *que il *dormi tout le . . . tout l'hiver (because it sleeps all winter)'.

When asked: 'Est-ce que des fois l'ours, il pellette? (Does a bear sometimes shovel?)', Andrew again replied, 'Non, jamais. (No, never.)'

Have different worlds collided on several planes and on different levels in this vignette? There was a conflict in relation to Andrew and the teacher as far as the factual content of Andrew's utterance was concerned. Moreover, the teacher contested the grammaticality of Andrew's utterance while Andrew did not seem to have grasped this even later in the week. There had been explicit correction by the teacher on at least two levels and possibly even implicit correction on other levels as well.

In sum, the kind of learning that is going on and how it is happening cannot be ascertained, according to Dufresne and Masny (2001). It was obvious that Andrew had not grasped the fine points of the use of the verb 'to shovel' in French when first videotaped. After that we cannot be certain, although he uses the verb with no difficulty. He certainly had grasped some of the distinction but in the first interview he refused to admit that he had. He also refused to discuss the teacher's reaction and her correction of the point he was trying to make. It is only much later that same week that Andrew seems to have come to terms with the video and he introduces new elements that are not on the video but which he states were present in his head at the time it was filmed. In addition, he is very definite in French about the fact that a bear does not shovel nor does a bear ever need to shovel. He has told the researcher in no uncertain terms that he knows what shovelling is because he shovels snow with his father.

Andrew was faced with a sort of language paradox. Conceptually, he knew what shovelling was; what he did not know at the time of the videotaping in the French class was that the concept of shovelling has a semantic field that is much narrower in French than it is in English. He seemed to progress toward the notion at times during different interviews but at the end he resolved it by saying that a bear never needs to shovel and he left it at that.

The vignette presented seems to support the fact that there are many different and differing ways by which problem solving, problem solving situations and the tasks associated with problem solving can be perceived. This is conveyed, in part, through language. In the light of what we now know from research in neuroscience (according to Sylwester, 2002), having a student deliberately focus attention on anything could possibly enable that student to learn as long as that information somehow matches information that is already stored. In this way, the student can make sense of the information and meaning-making can occur.

Beyond the word, there is a world and that world is imparted through language, in part. Andrew was the recipient of that world through the word but there is also a possibility of interpreting this as Andrew's becoming part of that world and word as a result of the will to power through text, as Masny (2001, 2002) explains in Multiple Literacies Theory (MLT).

There are good indications in the vignette that while Andrew had not grasped the significance of the French shovelling in detail, he was well on his way to allowing the French conceptualisation of shovelling to enter his world. In this way he was touched by text, its imposition and by a conceptualisation involving a division of time and space that was not his own but that he seemed to have come to accept at least concerning bears.

Needless to say, situated within the educational framework in which this occurred, the approach taken in the teaching of French using focus-on-form within the immersion program was not only conceptually troubling, but the two frameworks were incommensurate. The teacher used a transmission model of correction and students were expected to take up the correction.

What happened in the class between the teacher and Andrew involved paradigmatic differences. It also dealt with effectuating a systemic change through reading, writing and an oral discussion that arose out of the two. As Truebu (2001) states, these distinctions should not be set aside as trivial for they make a world of difference. Through the lens used in this chapter, Andrew is focusing-on-form which is the occasional shift of attention to linguistic features either by the teacher and/or by students that can be triggered by perceived problems of comprehension and perception that occur in a classroom situation (Long & Robinson, 1998). The situation demonstrates that while there is a link between teaching and learning, there is an uncontrollability factor that is involved. There is a gap that exists between the two. Through correction, it was possible for experience through the word and world to intrude upon what Andrew knew of the world and how it worked. It interacted and connected with this knowledge and possibly troubled that knowledge base. This caused a systemic rupture and there was most probably mediation that took place with what

Andrew knew thereby changing his knowledge of how things work and should work.

How did the type of consciousness-raising used through focus-on-form enable Andrew to do that? There was resistance to the type of knowledge Andrew was trying to acquire. The resistance disrupted what Andrew thought he already knew about a bear shovelling. Focus-on-form has the ability to open the closed spaces or aporia (Derrida, 1996, 1998) by first creating doubt (Dufresne, 2002). However, there is resistance to change and *other* knowledge until there is a reaffirmation of how things work and correctness assigned as to how things are. Once Andrew was able to go through this, there was a possibility that a new link and new knowledge involving change could be made thereby enabling knowledge to become other than what it was. This type of knowledge, which is absolutely necessary in learning a language, is much more than information gathering and simple processing. Rather, learning engages selection processes involving an exchange of information which have the potential to intervene and reorganise systems and, in the case in question, it causes and enables language learning to occur.

Language learning goes beyond looking at lexical items, grammar, punctuation, mastering linguistic strings and syntax. It must also be able to reflect the conceptual framework involved in the target language behind problem solving within situations and contexts that respect the worldview of that target language. It must enable a student to link, explore, focus and work within this paradigmatic framework and to do so in a 'safe' atmosphere. The data that follow demonstrate what happens when a student is allowed to do just that.

When worlds collide: Learning to write in a second orthography and a different script (Gujarati-English)

These data, taken from Kenner (2000), explicate how a student explores orthographies and scripts within a theory of Multiple Literacies (Masny, 2002), which is situated within a post-structuralist paradigm. Within Multiple Literacies Theory (MLT), events (that is, 'creations . . . selected and assessed according to their power to act and intervene rather than to be interpreted', (Colebrook, 2002a: xliv)) take place through different orthographies and different forms of literacy. Literacy relates to text that goes beyond the written word. Text can also mean reading notations, signs and symbols involving oral, visual and tactile forms.

Text as notations, signs, symbols takes on meaning within a particular society or a subgroup of that society. That particular social group establishes its meanings or *readings*, thereby imposing a constant upon the writing system. Literacy as a social construct consists of words, gestures, attitudes, ways of speaking, writing and valuing. In other words, literacy refers to ways of becoming in the world. An integral part of MLT is the processes involved in reading the world, the word and self. An individual engages in differing and different literacies. Accordingly, as an individual talks, reads, writes and values, construction of meaning takes place within a particular context and *in situ*. This act of meaning construction that qualifies as literate is culturally driven. In addition, it is shaped by the sociopolitical and sociohistorical productions of a society and its institutions to name a few.

Within MLT, the individual is reading the world, the word and self in the context of the home, school and community (local, national and international). This entails on the part of the individual a personal as well as a critical reading. Personal literacy focuses on reading oneself as one reads the world and the word; it contributes to the shaping of one's worldview. It is a way of becoming, based on construction of meaning that is always in movement, always in transition. When personal literacy contributes to a way of becoming, it involves fluidity and ruptures within and across differing literacies.

Critical literacy acknowledges that transformation is taking place. What remains to be seen is how the transformations happen, how they get taken up. When reading the world and the word in a critical way, social, cultural, economic, historical and political values are attached to literacies. At issue is the question of which literacies link to which values and in what context. Moreover, critical literacy involves reading oneself in school, home and community.

Let us consider the school. There is the expectation that children in school will display school-based literacies often considered literacies of normalisation. The power of normalisation can seriously challenge an individual's reading of self in reading the world and the word in school. When tensions arise or, as Dufresne (2002) states, when worldviews collide in the individual, transformations take place. The individual will seek stability in the midst of chaos. The question remains: how will the learner seek stability when his/her worldview collides with school norms? Community norms? The individual has moved.

Community-based literacies refer to an individual's reading of literate practices of a community. Because community-based literacies appear not to have the same legitimacy as school-based literacies, they are often marginalised and called upon in contexts outside the classroom. In this manner an individual's reading of the world, the word and self in the context of home, school and community create opportunities to construct and reconstruct his or her way of becoming.

School-based literacy refers to the process of communication in reading the world, the word and self in the context of school. It also includes social adaptation to the school milieu, its rites and rituals. School-based literacy emphasises conceptual readings that are critical to school success. Such literacies are mathematics, science, social sciences, technologies and multimedia. While these literacies are important for school membership, they cannot be devoid of links or partnerships with home and community.

In sum, the literacy of a social group is rooted in oral, visual and tactile forms that are woven into religion, gender, race, culture, ideology and power. The concept of literacy is actualised according to a particular context in time and in space in which it operates (Masny, 2001). For this reason, we refer to a literacy affecting a specific field and literacies which traverse different disciplines and fields in the reading of the world, word and self. In short, literacies involve constant movement in the processes of becoming *other.*

A case in point is Kenner's study (2000). Over a period of three years, Kenner documented the literacy practices of Meera (ages four to seven) as she engaged in Gujarati and English literacies at home, the community and school in South London, England. Like English, the Gujarati writing system operates from left-to-right. Gujarati is a phonemic writing system with certain diacritic marks showing vowels.

In the following examples, Meera displayed her literacy creations. At age four at home, she sat next to her mother who is writing a letter in Gujarati. Meera produced 'her own wavy-line writing' and said 'I am writing a letter'. At the same time at the nursery, Meera developed her knowledge of the English writing system. One day, her mother guided her in copying her name in Gujarati.

Later that day, Meera produced her own set of symbols different from English and said: 'It's Gujarati. It's my sister's name' (Kenner, 2000: 18). She went on to produce her own symbols which she named Gujarati. According to Kenner, Meera's experiences in both literacies occur simultaneously and often within the same text. Her environment in the nursery incorporates the presence of home texts, materials which she has seen used in the family and community contexts, or which have been written by her mother on the classroom chalkboard. Her mother is a regular contributor to the nursery.

Kenner is able to document that Meera's Gujarati literacy at school interacts with her development of writing at home. A similar stance advocated by Masny (1995) focuses on ways children engage in multiple literacies at home and in daycare through the presence of and engagement of literacy artifacts from the home and community.

At age five, Meera said that she does not speak Gujarati. Yet, she still continues to write Gujarati at school. By age seven, she claimed she can write animal names in Gujarati, as seen in Figure 15.1. She produced four lines and wrote the names of three animals. Her first animal appears on the second line and she wrote ⟨fox⟩ in English. She then proceeded to write ⟨frog⟩ and ⟨elephant⟩ on the third and fourth line respectively and approximates Gujarati orthography. She used Gujarati

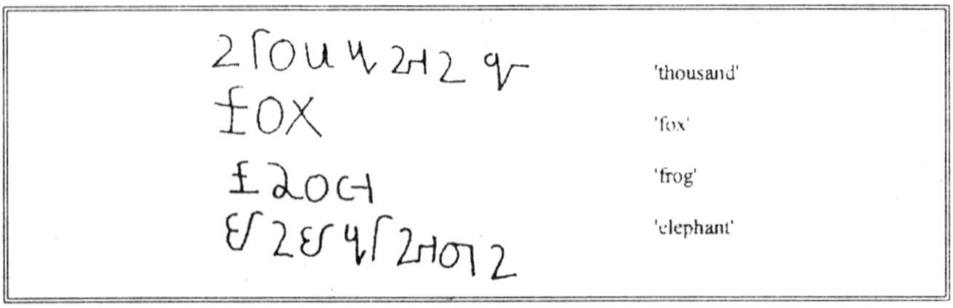

Figure 15.1 Meera's writing of animal names (from Kenner, 2000, with permission)

letters to produce English sounds. Within a traditional paradigm, Meera would be said to be transliterating.

Within a post-structural paradigm, Meera took up these creations and assessed them according to their power to act and intervene in her life. Meera used Gujarati notations to represent English words. She applied Gujarati script to look like English words. How can creating experiences with writing systems, that: (1) move beyond conventional and normalising scripts; and (2) create notations, transform Meera's ways of becoming a reader-writer? How are the processes of reading, writing, scripts and orthographies within the home, school and community affecting Meera? Have these different worlds collided? Meera produced texts and she is becoming a *text* influenced by different literacies. In short, Meera is an effect of continuous investment and reinvestment in family and school literacy practices. Dufresne (2002: 218) states that: 'Language, in this framework, is not a way to carry signs that carry meaning to some subject who in turn will interpret them in order to get the right or correct meaning/referent. Rather, language is an event that is productive that produces speakers/readers/writers and has the potential to do so. Readers are an effect of language use but they are neither uniquely an effect of language nor is language touted as being the sole representative of experience'.

Kenner's study of Meera's literacies serves as an entry point for the emerging complexity of research. There are additional studies that centre on what the learner is thinking about and reflecting as s/he is going about learning a second script, be it English, Hebrew (Mor-Sommerfeld, 2002) or Chinese (Bell, 1995), for example.

What more would Meera's talk about her language and literacies reveal? What do learners disclose regarding their encounters with an L2 orthography and a different script? How are these disclosures different from those made about the L1 orthography and the L1 script? Reading/writing with a lens of second orthography and a different script signals a transformation within the processes of becoming *other* through investment of reading the world, the word and self (Multiple Literacies Theory).

Reflections

In this chapter, we have attempted to demonstrate that commensurability is necessary between systems. When these systems are incommensurate, as they were in the case of Meera and of Andrew and his teacher, equilibrium is sought at all costs. This was part of Meera and Andrew's becoming *other* and learning a language that was *other.* A combination of things, including the insertion of doubt, caused an aporia, an opening or gap to form between certainty of how things worked and how they could work. After this occurred, both Meera and Andrew could draw the necessary links for *other* learning to occur and for knowledge to become other than what it was. As Kumashiro (2000: 35), who draws upon the work of Felman (1995), states: 'Unlearning one's worldview can be upsetting and paralyzing leading to the paradoxical position of learning and unlearning'.

Perhaps with Andrew, we have encountered what Britzman (1998) refers to as a resistance to knowledge, which is often a way to repress what our worldview cannot accommodate. In terms of neuroscience, Meera and Andrew found nothing to match and to help make sense of the writing system. In finding nothing, Andrew, for example, wanted to discard the information and his brain refused to attend to the information presented. Meera adapted what she knew of one system and tried to make it work in another. The question is: what would Meera have done had her adaptation of the Gujarati writing system to English been challenged? How would she have responded had her reality of how things worked in English been corrected? Would there have been much difference in her responses in comparison to Andrew?

Meera and Andrew involved a desire to ignore the incompatibility between languages. Both tellings can be mapped in what Dufresne (2002) refers to as Telling Maps. They indicate that there can be resistance to new knowledge that is deemed as *other* on the level of ontology. In other words, new knowledge can cause worlds to collide. It may cause an established language system to rupture and destabilise it at the level of epistemology. If destabilisation occurs, stability and equilibrium are sought at all costs. When this happens, there is a good probability that paradigmatic change will begin to occur. Moreover, the effectuated change may or may not be the one that was initially sought.

Is a paradigmatic change in conducting research also not necessary so that it can be reflective of what we now know about how learning occurs? Isn't a research change necessary so we learn more about the processes involved in language learning and writing systems within different theories of knowledge and literacy?

According to Lather (2000), to provoke thought is to trouble the boundaries. In both cases cited, through the lens of second language writing systems, the intention of this paper was to provoke thought about a multiplicity of literacies theory which conceptually involves reading the world, the word and self in post-modern times (Masny, 2002) and its link to Dufresne's theory of knowledge and learning (2001, 2002). The paper takes up the thought of: (1) script and orthography as notations, involving creative processes ever in a state of becoming *other*; (2) the learner who seeks constancy and strives for stability at all costs; and (3) the flow responding to experience(s) which intervenes, thereby allowing literacy to move beyond, extend, and transform a multiplicity of literacies so that 'we create and select not on the basis of who we are but how we might become', as Colebrook (2002b: 96) implores.

References

Atkinson, D. (2003a) L2 writing in the post-process era: Introduction. *Journal of Second Language Writing* 12, 3–15.

Atkinson, D. (2003b) Writing and culture in the post process era. *Journal of Second Language Writing* 12, 49–63.

Bell, J.S. (1995) The relationship between L1 and L2 literacy: Some complicating factors. *TESOL Quarterly* 29 (4), 687–704.

Bonsting, J.J. (1995) The Quality Paradigm Shift in Education. Alaska Department of Education. Online document: www.educ.state.ak.us.

Britzman, D. (1998) *Lost Subjects, Contested Objects: Toward a Psychoanalytic Inquiry of Learning*. Albany, NY: State University of New York Press.

Colebrook, C. (2002a) *Understanding Deleuze*. Crows Nest, AU: Allen & Unwin.

Colebrook, C. (2002b) *Deleuze*. New York: Routledge.

Coulmas, F. (1996) *The Blackwell Encyclopedia of Writing Systems*. Cambridge, MA and Oxford, UK: Blackwell Publishers.

Derrida, J. (1996) *Apories: Mourir-s'attendre aux 'limites de la vérité'* [Aporias: Dying-awaiting one another at the limits of truth]. Paris: Les éditions de Galilée.

Derrida, J. (1998) *Of Grammatology.* (G.C. Spivik, trans). Baltimore, MD: The John Hopkins University Press. (Corrected edition. Original work published in 1967.)

Donmoyer, R., Lather, P. and Dillard, C. (2000, April) Paradigm talk revisited: How else might we characterize the proliferation of research perspectives within our field? Presentation at the Annual Conference of the American Educational Research Association, New Orleans.

Dufresne, T. (2001) Le poststructuralisme: Un défi à la mondialisation des savoirs. [Poststructuralism: A challenge to globalisation of knowledge]. In L. Corriveau and W. Tulasiewicz (eds) *Mondialisation, politiques et pratiques de recherche* [Globalisation, politics and research] (pp. 53–68). Sherbrooke, QC: Éditions du CRP.

Dufresne, T. (2002) Through a lens of difference OR when worlds collide: A post-structural study on error correction and focus-on-form in language and second language learning. PhD thesis, University of Ottawa.

Dufresne, T. and Masny, D. (May, 2001) The Makings of Minority Education: the Québec educational curriculum reforms/Éléments de l'éducation aux minorités: Les réformes des programmes d'éducation au Québec. Presentation at Canadian Society for the Study of Education (CSSE) 29th annual conference as part of Canadian Association for Curriculum Studies – Association canadienne pour l'étude du curriculum (CACS): Québec, QC.

Felman, S. (1995) Education and crisis, or the vicissitudes of teaching. In C. Caruth (ed.) *Trauma: Explorations in Memory* (pp. 13–60). Baltimore, MD: The John Hopkins University Press.

Guba, E.G. and Lincoln, Y.S. (1994) Competing paradigms in qualitative research. In N.K. Denzin and Y.S. Lincoln (eds) *Handbook of Qualitative Research* (pp. 105–17). Thousand Oaks, CA: Sage Publications.

Guba, E.G. and Lincoln, Y.S. (1998) Competing paradigms in qualitative research. In N.K. Denzin and Y.S. Lincoln (eds) *The Landscape of Qualitative Research: Theories and Issues* (pp. 195–220). Thousand Oaks, CA: Sage Publications.

Kenner, C. (2000) Biliteracy in a monolingual school system? English and Gujarati in South London. *Language, Culture and Curriculum* 13 (1), 13–18.

Kubota, R. (2003) New approaches to gender, class, and race in second language writing. *Journal of Second Language Writing* 12, 31–47.

Kumashiro, K. (2000) Toward a theory of anti-oppressive education. *Review of Educational Research* 70 (1), 25–53.

Lather, P. (2000) Drawing the line at angels: Working the ruins of feminist ethnography. In E. St. Pierre and W. Pillow (eds) *Working the Ruins: Feminist Post-Structural Theory and Methods in Education* (pp. 284–312). New York, NY: Routledge Press.

Leki, I. (2003) Coda: Pushing L2 writing research. *Journal of Second Language Writing* 12, 103–5.

Lightbown, P. (1998) The importance of timing in focus-on-form. In C. Doughty and J. Williams (eds) *Focus-on-form in Second Language Acquisition* (pp. 76–90). Cambridge, UK: Cambridge University Press.

Lincoln, Y.S. and Guba E.G. (2000) Paradigmatic controveries, contradictions, and emerging confluences. In N.K. Denzin and Y.S. Lincoln (eds) *Handbook of Qualitative Research* (163–188). Thousand Oaks, CA: Sage.

Long, M.H. and Robinson, P. (1998) Focus-on-form: Theory, research and practice. In C. Doughty and J. Williams (eds) *Focus-on Form in Classroom Second Language Acquisition* (pp. 15–41). Cambridge: Cambridge University Press.

Masny, D. (1995) Literacy development in young children. *Interaction* 6 (1), 21–4. Available online at http://www.cfcefc.ca/docs/cccf/00000049.htm.

Masny, D. (2001) Pour une pédagogie axée sur les littératies [Toward a pedagogy based on literacies]. In D. Masny (ed.) *La culture de l'écrit: Les défis à l'école et au foyer* [The written culture: Challenging the school and the home] (pp. 15–26). Outremont, QC: Les Éditions Logiques.

Masny, D. (2002) Les littératies: Un tournant dans la pensée et une façon d'être [Literacies: A way of being or an alternative way of thinking]. In R. Allard (ed.) *Actes du colloque pancanadien sur la recherche en éducation en milieu francophone minoritaire: Bilan et perspectives* [Proceedings of the pan-Canadian Colloquium on Research in Minority French Education]. Québec: ACELF; Moncton, NB: Centre de recherche et de développement en éducation (CRDE). Available online at http://www.acelf.ca/publi/crde/articles/14-masny.html.

Masny, D. and Dufresne, T. (in press) La littératie critique: Les enjeux de la réussite d'une école exemplaire et les réformes en éducation [Critical literacy: What's at stake in the success of an exemplary school in the context of educational reforms]. In J.C. Boyer (ed.) *Entre le savoir intuitif et la littératie critique: enjeux épistémologiques et praxéologiques* [From Intuitive Knowledge to Critical Literacy: Studies on Epistemology and Praxis]. Montreal: les éditions Logiques.

May, T. (1994) Difference and unity in Gilles Deleuze. In C.V. Boundas and D. Olkowski (eds) *Gilles Deleuze and the Theater of Philosophy* (pp. 33–50). New York: Routledge.

Ministère de l'Éducation du Québec (2001) *Education in Quebec*. Online document: www.meq.gouv.qc.ca.

Mor-Sommerfeld, A. (2002) Language mosaic. Developing literacy in a second new language: a new perspective. *Reading: Literacy and Language* 36 (3), 99–105.

Payne, M. (1997) (ed.) *A Dictionary of Cultural and Critical Theory*. Malden, MA and Oxford, UK: Blackwell Publishers.

Schmidt, R. (1993) Awareness and second language acquisition. *Annual Review of Applied Linguistics* 13, 206–26.

Schwandt, T.A. (2000) Three epistemological stances for qualitative inquiry. In N.K. Denzin and Y.S. Lincoln (eds) *Handbook of Qualitative Research* (2nd edn) (pp. 189–213). Thousand Oaks, CA: Sage Publications.

Shepard, L. (2001) The role of classroom assessment in teaching and learning. In V. Richardson (ed.) *Handbook of Research on Teaching* (pp. 1066–101). Washington, DC: American Educational Association.

St. Pierre, E. (April, 2000a) *Refusing to Write it up*. Paper presented at the 2000 Annual Meeting of American Educational Research Association, New Orleans, LA.

St. Pierre, E. (2000b) Methodology in the fold and the irruption of transgressive data. *Qualitative Studies in Education* 10 (2), 175–89.

Sylwester, R. (2002, February) A praise-worthy brain in search of a brain-worthy school. Leadership Symposium, Laval, QC.

Truebu, H. (2001) Interpreting Menchu's account: Socio-cultural and linguistic contexts. Online document at http://ccwf.cc.utexas.edu.

White, L. (1991) Adverb placement in second language acquisition: Some effects of positive and negative evidence in the classroom. *Second Language Research* 7, 133–66.

White, L., Spada, N., Lightbown, P. and Ranta, L. (1991) Input enhancement and L2 question formation. *Applied Linguistics* 12, 416–32.

Wolfe, P. (2001) *Brain Matters: Translating Research into Classroom Practice*. Alexandra, VA: Association for Supervision and Curriculum Development.

Chapter 16

Second Language Writing Systems: Minority Languages and Reluctant Readers

TINA HICKEY

Introduction

Many language learners are presented with learning a second language writing system that appears not to diverge markedly from the writing system of their first language. Rather than having to deal with a logographic system or learn a new alphabet, these learners find that their first language literacy maps quite conveniently onto their second language literacy. However, as Bernhardt (2003) notes, even where the mapping is convenient, the mere existence of a first language makes the second language reading process considerably different, because of the nature of the information stored in memory. Even languages using the same alphabet can differ in the transparency of their orthography.

Second language reading cannot be viewed simply as the interaction between first language reading skills and second language proficiency. Leloup (1993) and Bernhardt and Kamil (1995), for example, show that other factors such as motivation to read in the language contribute significantly to attainment in second language reading. Teachers are well aware of the difficulties in encouraging second language learners to read, but this challenge becomes all the greater when that language is a minority language, with fewer resources available to the young reader. Here we will look at the issue of promoting the reading of such a minority language, Irish, among young English speakers in Ireland.

Irish belongs to the Celtic branch (comprising Irish, Scots Gaelic, Welsh and Breton) of the Indo-European family, and is thought to have been brought to Ireland around 300 BC by the invading Gaels. The term 'Irish' is used to refer to the Celtic language spoken in Ireland, to distinguish it from Scots Gaelic. Both Irish and English are official languages of the Republic of Ireland. While small Irish-speaking communities exist, mainly on the western seaboard, most of the rest of the Republic is English-speaking. Figures from Census 2002 show that approximately 1.57 million persons over three years of age (42% of the respondents to that question) were recorded as being 'able to speak Irish'. Of those, however, only 22% (339,541) were reported as speaking Irish on a daily basis and most of these (77%) were school-goers (aged 5–19 years). Irish is a compulsory school subject for most pupils from school entry at the age of four years, and most learn the language as a single subject. A minority of 25,000 children (about 6% of the total primary school population) attended Irish-medium primary schools outside Irish-speaking districts in the 2003–2004 school-year (Gaelscoileanna, 2004). Even in areas officially designated as Irish-speaking, only 33,789 (54%) of the respondents aged over three who reported themselves as 'able to speak Irish' in Census 2002 answered that they spoke Irish on a daily basis.

In this chapter the orthography of Irish will first be described briefly, and then some of the problems of L2 readers of Irish will be explored. Issues concerning the materials available for L2 readers of this language will then be discussed and finally there will be a brief description of a small intervention study aimed at improving children's L2 reading by increasing their exposure to Irish texts.

Irish and Irish Orthography

Irish is a Celtic language with an unmarked order of VSOX (Verb-Subject-Object-Other). The following description of Irish orthography is based on *Graiméar Gaeilge na mBráithre Críostaí* (Na Bráithre Críostaí, 1999), *Foclóir Póca* (An Gúm, 1986), Ó Baoill (1996), Ó Baoill and Ó Riagáin (1990), M. Ó Murchú (1977), S. Ó Murchú (1998), Ó Sé (1990, 2000) and Ó Siadhail (1989). The Irish alphabet (adapted from Latin before the end of the 6th century AD) comprises five vowels and 13 consonants:

< a b c d e f g h i l m n o p r s t u >

and represents approximately fifty basic sounds in the language. The letters <j, k, q, v, w, x, y, z> are also used in loan words. The five spoken vowels of Irish can be either short or long, giving ten sounds, and a length mark (*síneadh fada*) is placed above the vowel (<á>, <é>, <í>, <ó>, <ú>) to indicate its lengthening, e.g. <ba> /ba/ 'cows' versus <bá> /baː/ 'understanding'. Vowels on which no stress is placed are pronounced as schwa /ə/ but this is not represented orthographically.

A special script for written Irish was used from the end of the sixteenth century, in an attempt to represent Irish manuscript writing, since Roman letters were considered to be too closely associated with English and Elizabethan domination. However, during the revival movement and after the foundation of the State in the early 20th century, there was increasing pressure to adopt Roman type because of its easier availability and its more 'progressive' appearance (M. Ó Murchú, 1977: 284). Eventually the decision was made to use only Roman type in primary school textbooks by 1963.

While the script now used for written Irish is familiar to readers of English, the orthographical system differs significantly from English, and has been described by M. Ó Murchú (1977) as 'bewildering' to newcomers. This is in spite of the standardisation that occurred in the period following independence in 1922, when spellings that dated from classical Irish (1200–1650) in many cases were simplified to represent modern pronunciations (Ó Baoill & Ó Riagáin, 1990). In other cases, however, this standardisation introduced inconsistencies and a number of other difficulties (see, for example, M. Ó Murchú (1977) and Ó Sé (1990)).

One of the more 'exotic features' (M. Ó Murchú, 1977: 269) of Irish phonology that is expressed in its orthography is the contrast between slender (palatalised) and broad (non-palatalised or velarised) consonant forms. Orthographically the quality of the spoken consonant is indicated by preceding or succeeding it with a slender or broad vowel. The following examples show minimal pairs of broad and slender consonants, with the palatalised consonant marked with a following /'/ according to the norms of Irish phonetic transcription:

<bó>	/boː/	=	/b^{u}ʊː/	'cow'	<beo>	/b'oː/	=	/b^{i}oː/	'alive'
<buí>	/biː/	=	/b^{u}iː/	'yellow'	<bí>	/b'iː/	=	/b^{i}iː/	'be'

The non-palatalised consonants on the left can be described (Ó Siadhail 1989: 5) as having a weak *u*-quality, and the palatalised consonants on the right as having a weak *i*-quality, but henceforth the convention of indicating palatalisation by /'/ is followed here.

Irish orthography, like Welsh orthography (see Spencer & Hanley, 2003) is more transparent than English, but there is still considerable variability. Despite the official standardisation of Irish that aimed to shorten spellings, many words still look longer than their pronunciation would indicate, often because of the use of spellings from an earlier period of the language. M. Ó Murchú (1977) noted that Irish orthography has no parsimonious way of representing diphthongs and he criticised the decision taken during standardisation to retain traditional spellings for these words. For example, the diphthongs /au/ and /ai/ can be represented in Irish in a variety of ways:

/au/ spelling	Irish word containing /au/		Meaning
<a>	<am>	/aum/	'time'
<abha>	<abhainn>	/aun'/	'river'
	<leabhar>	/l'aur/	'book'
<ea>	<ceann>	/k'aun/	'head'
<amha>	<samhradh>	/saurə/	'summer'

/ai/ spelling	Irish word containing /ai/		Meaning
<ai>	<caint>	/kain't'/	'talk'
<adh>	<adhmad>	/aiməd/	'wood'
	<radharc>	/rairk/	'view'
<oigh>	<oigheann>	/ain/	'oven'

A feature of the Irish language is its initial mutations, whereby the start of words, including verbs, nouns and adjectives, are either lenited (made more lenis in articulation) or eclipsed (whereby a voiced segment becomes nasalised and a voiceless segment becomes voiced). For example, <póca> /po:k·/ 'pocket', when lenited (e.g. after the first person singular possessive) becomes <phóca> /fo:k·/ and when eclipsed (e.g. after the first person plural possessive) is <bpóca> /bo:k·/. Lenition is marked orthographically by the insertion of a <h> after the initial stop, fricative or /m/, and eclipsis is marked by the prefixing of certain consonants to stops and /f/, or of <n> to a vowel. Both lenition and eclipsis change the pronunciation of the original consonant and result in complex word-initial consonant clusters that can present difficulties for L1 readers of English. Thus, readers need to learn the following grapheme–phoneme correspondences for lenited consonants:

<ph> = /f/ <bh> = /w/ <th> = /h/ <dh> = /ɣ/ <ch> = /x/
<phr> = /fr/
<fh> = /Ø/ <mh> = /w/ <sh> = /h/ <gh> = /ɣ/ <chr> = /xr/

The following are possible word-initial combinations on eclipsed consonants:

<bp> = /b/ <mb> = /m/ <dt> = /d/ <nd> = /n/ <gc> = /g/
<ng> = /ŋ/ <bhf> = /w/ <ngr> = /ŋr/ <tsr> = /tr/ <mbr> = /mr/

Thus, Irish uses an alphabet that is familiar to English readers, and it shares some sounds and segments with English, but it also has a different set of rules to represent different sounds and morphosyntactic processes. While it is not as deep an orthography as English, it nevertheless presents the child embarking on Irish reading (the majority of whom have only just 'cracked the code' for English) with considerable challenges. A flavour of the complexity for English readers of Irish orthography is given by a humorous writer, Myles na Gopaleen (1987: 263), who presented the following passage of English following Irish orthographical rules (fairly loosely):

> 'Irish & Related Matters'
> Aigh nó a mean thú ios só léasaigh dat thí slíps in this clós, bhears a bíord, and dos nod smóc bícos obh de trobal obh straigein a meaits. It is só long sins thí did an anasth dea's bhorc dat thí tincs 'manuil leabear' is de neim obh a Portuguis arditeitear. [Lamhd láftar]
> I know a man who is so lazy that he sleeps in his clothes, wears a beard, and does not smoke because of the trouble of striking a match. It is so long since he did an honest day's work that he thinks 'manual labour' is the name of a Portuguese agitator. [Loud laughter]

Children Learning to Read Irish

In the Republic of Ireland, children fall into three main categories as readers of Irish:

(1) *L2 readers of Irish in English-medium schools.* Children start learning Irish as a single subject from school entry at age four. They begin reading in English, and the emphasis is on developing oral Irish skills in the first three years before the inclusion of Irish reading at age 7–8, in Grade 2.

(2) *L2 readers of Irish in all-Irish schools.* In these schools Irish is the medium of instruction from age four. Initial literacy is usually taught in Irish, the majority's L2, with pre-reading occurring in the first year, and a move to more formal Irish reading at the end of that year or the start of the second year of school (Senior Infant grade).

(3) *L1 readers in Gaeltachtaí (Irish-speaking communities).* In these schools Irish is the official medium of instruction, but children whose mother-tongue is Irish are usually mixed with L2 learners of Irish whose families are English-speakers or who have moved into their areas. The approach to Irish reading is similar to that in the all-Irish schools.

Thus, there are children who acquire their first literacy in English, their L1, and then move on quite soon to read in Irish as well, while others acquire their first literacy in Irish either as their L1 or as their L2, and later acquire literacy in English. The curriculum notes that it is expected that children will generalise the skills from reading one language to the other, but there tends to be little discussion with children of the differences between the languages in terms of orthography, and teachers complain of a dearth of materials with which to present the grapheme–phoneme rules of Irish to beginners. Thus, even though Irish has a more shallow orthography than English, the teaching of Irish reading tends to be oriented mainly towards reinforcing language items learned orally, with little systematic identification of regular grapheme–phoneme correspondences during Irish reading classes, and little use of phonics for L2 readers in particular.

The Problems of Young Readers of Irish

Research (see for example Oakhill, 1999) shows that successful readers interact with a text, and are constantly using their knowledge of the orthography and syntax of the language, integrating the meaning of words and sentences with their world knowledge in order to comprehend a text. L2 readers and poor L1 readers are more likely to get tripped up by the mechanics of reading, and have to spend more time on the lower levels of processing (Urquhart & Weir, 1998). Research on Irish reading (Hickey, 1991, 1992) showed some of the problems of young L2 readers of Irish, such as:

(1) limited reading skills;
(2) limited L2 proficiency;
(3) limited access to resources and low motivation to read in Irish;
(4) limited parental support for L2 reading.

Such problems are outlined briefly below.

Limited reading skills

- **Decoding to non-words or to the wrong word category:** The decoding of L2 readers is more likely to result in a non-word or the wrong type of word than is the case in their L1 reading. This is because they are more dependent on how an individual word looks than on what meaning they expect in that context. Some examples of decoding to non-words in the Irish reading of a group of children in Grade 3 are:

  [ar an] <tsráid>/traːd'/ '[on the] street' — read as <trasid> /trasid/ (non-word)
  <feirm> /fer'm/ 'farm' — read as <federum> /federum/ (non-word)

  Examples of decoding to the wrong word class are:

  <tharraing> 'pulled' /harəŋ'/ — read as [an] <t-arán> /taraːn/ '[the] bread'
  [ar] <Thiarnán> boy's name /hiərnaːn/ — read as <tháinig> /haːn'ig'/ 'came'

- **Decoding to similar words:** Less skilled L2 readers may decode an unknown word as one they do know if it looks similar to it. These errors again show dependence on how the word looks, rather than on predicting meaning. For example, the following errors occurred among children in Grade 3 (Hickey, 1992):

  <muintir> /mwiːtər'/ 'family' read as <múinteoir> /muːn't'oːr'/ 'teacher'

  [a] choileán /kwil'aːn/ [his] 'puppy' read as <ceol> /k'oːl/ 'music'

  L1 readers and more proficient L2 readers also make errors, but their substitutions tend to fit better with the meaning in the text, rather than depend on a word's appearance alone. For example, a more able reader in Grade 3 made the following substitutions:

  <seanathair> /s'anahər'/ 'grandfather' read as <seanfhear> /s'anar'/ 'old man'

  <in am> /in'aum/ 'in time' read as <in ann> /in'aun/ 'able to'

  ('it was time to milk the cows' read as 'he was able to milk the cows')

- **Encoding in English sounds:** It has long been recognised that less proficient L1 readers often encode phonologically and subvocalise as they read, and this is thought to be an effort to aid memory processing, since auditory short-term memory is better in terms of retention than visual short-term memory (Crowder, 1976; Muchisky, 1983). The more difficult the text, the more subvocalisation occurs. Phonological encoding also occurs in L2 reading (Hatch, 1974; Muchisky, 1983), but the problem is that it is frequently based on L1 sounds. For example, the following are some of the English substitutions that occurred in the Irish reading of children in Grade 3 (Hickey, 1992):

Irish word	**Correct Pronunciation**	**English substitution**	**Meaning**
<siad>	/s'iəd/	<said>	'they'
<ann>	/aun/	<Ann>	'there'
<féach>	/f'eːx/	<fetch>	'look'
<beag>	/b'eg/	<beg>	'little'

- **Slower processing hinders comprehension:** Droop and Verhoven (2003) note that limited exposure to the L2 writing system results in weaker word representations and thus to slower and less accurate reading. The decoding of non-proficient L2 readers is less automatic because of their restricted knowledge of the grapheme–phoneme correspondence rules and orthographic constraints of the L2. This means that the lower-level decoding takes up more of the processing time. Even learners with advanced L2 proficiency and good L1 reading skills read differently in their second language than in their first because their less automatic L2 word recognition skills impede their ability to focus on text meaning. Some researchers (Favreau & Segalowitz, 1982; Kellaghan & Macnamara, 1967; Segalowitz & Hébert, 1990) have found that even bilinguals with advanced L2 skills read about 30% more slowly in their second language than in their first. Hickey (1991) found that children in Grade 3 read aloud in English, their first language, at a rate of 115 words per minute, but in Irish at a rate of only 75 words per minute. Advanced balanced bilinguals have also been shown (Favreau *et al.*, 1980) to behave rather like poor L1 readers when reading in their second language, showing less of an ability to process words as wholes in their L2 than in their L1, thus accounting for their slower rate in reading their second language. This slower reading rate makes it more difficult to extract meaning from texts. Reading rate is improved by practice, but it is those readers with the slowest rate who find L2 reading most difficult. The 'Matthew Effect' (Stanovich, 1986) summarises the position of children in this situation, who do not develop sufficiently automatised decoding and word recognition skills to allow them to enjoy reading; as a result of the fact that they do not enjoy reading they avoid it, and thus they are less likely to develop the automatised reading skills they need to break out of this vicious circle.

Limited language proficiency

There is an extensive literature on the effects of limited second language proficiency on second language reading, which can only be briefly outlined here. Learners' limited L2 proficiency may 'short-circuit' the L2 reading process (Bernhardt & Kamil, 1995; Bossers, 1991; Clarke, 1980) and cause even skilled L1 readers to revert to less effective reading strategies in their second language. Verhoeven (2000) showed that the smaller second-language vocabularies of L2 learners seriously impedes their reading.

Limited access to resources and low motivation to read in Irish

The problem of L2 reading resources involves both supply and use: while there are fewer suitable texts available in Irish than in English, even those which are available tend not to be used, because of a strong reliance on textbooks for Irish reading. Nor can it be assumed that using only textbooks overcomes the problem of linguistic suitability: Ní Argáin (1990) noted that the majority of teachers in her study of the readability of Irish graded readers for Grade 5 believed these books to be too difficult linguistically. In addition, she found that 68% of the teachers surveyed believed that the material did not awaken children's interest and did not represent their experience.

In a survey of teachers' attitudes to Irish (INTO, 1985) only 22% indicated that their pupils read Irish books other than their textbooks, and only 29% reported that they read or told stories in Irish to their pupils. While these data are not recent, teachers report that these already low levels of Irish leisure reading have dropped even further in the meantime. Hickey and Ó Cainín (2003) found that over 80% of Grade 2 children surveyed in an English-medium school reported that they never did any leisure reading in Irish.

The low frequency of Irish leisure reading needs to be set against the background of low levels of leisure reading in English also. Martin and Morgan (1994: 90) noted in their study of reading in Ireland (part of the International Association for the Evaluation of Educational Achievement (IEA)), that:

> In terms of frequency of reading, it seems that Irish children [aged 9 years] read [in their first language] rather less than children in other countries. This is true of all kinds of reading material, except newspapers . . . The amount of time children spend reading may be linked to the level of resources for reading that are available in schools, which is also low in Ireland by international standards . . . Given the evidence on the strong association between access to reading resources and reading achievement, improvement in such resources may be a worthwhile and promising approach to encouraging independent reading and standards of reading achievement.

Thus, research would indicate that the low frequency of English L1 reading and of Irish L2 reading, in addition to limited suitable reading resources, is likely to impact negatively on achievement in reading Irish. Fuller (1987) and Martin and Morgan (1994), in reviewing large-scale evaluations of reading, recommended providing enhanced access to books in order to improve L1 reading achievement. It is reasonable to expect that greater access to suitable Irish materials would also have some positive effects on reading in Irish. Some of the issues concerning Irish reading resources are discussed below.

Limited parental support for L2 reading

Parents' support for L1 reading is considered central, and parents' support for their children's L2 reading would be equally valuable.

However, parents may be unable to assist with L2 reading because of their own limited proficiency in the language. Harris and Murtagh (1999) found that only 34% of the parents of Grade 6 pupils help with Irish reading homework (reading and spelling), but about half of those who do not help cited their own poor level of Irish competence. Most parents need help and material support before they feel confident to read aloud to their children in Irish, reflecting their own poor attainment in Irish reading in school.

Reading Resources in Irish

Leisure reading books in Irish may be:

- international publications translated into Irish;
- written in English locally (i.e. by Irish authors) and translated;
- composed in Irish.

Translations have historically made up a large proportion of Irish children's books, but in recent years there has been growth in the number of books which have been developed specifically for the Irish market, though in some cases these may start out as stories written originally in English (though not published) which publishing houses have then translated into Irish.

The central problem with translations is that most of the books whose rights are bought are aimed at native speakers of the original language, and thus there can be a gap between the interest level of a translated book and its language difficulty. A significant problem with translating texts is that the non-indigenous story concepts and constraints of fitting text around original graphics and layouts can result in the language difficulty of the translated text being greater than that of the original, due to unfamiliar vocabulary and compression of text. For example, the text to be translated may contain rhymes, or word play, or may have grammatical features that are considerably more difficult in the translation than in the original. Some of these issues are discussed in relation to the example of a translation below.

Oíche Mhaith, a Bhéirín

Can't You Sleep, Little Bear? is a very popular prize-winning picture book by Martin Waddell (1988), and it was translated into Irish as *Oíche Mhaith, a Bhéirín* (Waddell, 1989) (literally 'night good bear-little' (Good Night Little-Bear)). The main characters in the English text are Big Bear and Little Bear and the story begins as follows (the line breaks of the originals are preserved in these examples and the Irish text is given in bold):

<Once there were two bears,
Big Bear and Little Bear.>

However, the Irish translation of this passage is:

<Bhí dhá bhéar ann tráth,>
(Were two bear there once) 'Once there were two bears'
<Béar Mór agus Béirín.>
(Bear Big and Bear-diminutive) 'Big Bear and Little-Bear'

The adjectives 'mór' (big) and 'beag' (little) would be familiar to most young L2 learners of Irish, but the translation opts instead to use the diminutive 'Béirín', which also changes the spelling of the first part of the word (from <Béar> to <Béir[ín]>) resulting in less linkage between the names of the two characters in the Irish text than in the English original. On the other hand, this allows the translator to avoid the very complex marking that would be necessary in Irish on the adjective in the vocative case 'a Bhéir Bhig' (bear little, vocative). This is an example of a situation that an author who was composing a text in Irish might avoid by choosing character names that were less complex in the language.

The second sentence of the English text is meant as an amusing aside, referring to the picture, and allows the text to show the difference in capitalisation between names and common nouns.

<Big Bear is the big bear, and Little Bear is the little bear.>

The second sentence in the Irish text eschews a similar amusing statement of the obvious, and instead offers a much more complex sentence, using the copula in the past tense.

<Béar fásta ba ea Béar Mór, agus babaí béir ba ea Béirín.>
(Bear grown was Bear Big, agus a-baby of-bear was Bear-dim.)
'Big Bear was grown, and Little-Bear was a baby.'

Irish requires the use of the copula rather than the verb 'to be' for identification and states of being. The copula is a focus of errors among English-speaking learners of Irish, who tend to overextend the verb 'to be' to copula constructions. While learners have difficulty enough with the present tense of the copula, they are even less familiar with the past tense copula used in this sentence <ba ea>. This past tense was selected in the Irish translation even though the English original (above) was in the present and clearly referenced the accompanying picture.

The Irish translation of this sentence also introduces a new term 'fásta' (grown) which is a more difficult concept for children than 'mór' (big).

A more fundamental problem arises with the tense of the next three sentences, which are in the simple past in English:

<They played all day in the bright sunlight. When night came, and the sun went down, Big Bear took Little

Bear home to the Bear Cave.
[New Page] Big Bear put Little Bear to bed . . . >

Waddell here used the simple past, and the first two sentences are ambiguous, in that they could be referring to the events of one day (since it continues on the next page to a particular night's events) or to actions that took place every day for the two bears. The Irish translation opted to use the Habitual Past Tense for the first two sentences, a tense that occurs very rarely in normal conversation (and did not occur at all in the observation of young L1 speakers of Irish in Hickey, 1999):

<Chaithidís an lá ar fad ag súgradh faoi sholas na gréine>
(play-Hab-Past-3rd per. pl.) the day in all at playing under light of the sun
'They-used-to-spend all day playing under the light of the sun'
<San oíche nuair a théadh an ghrian faoi thugadh Béar Mór Béirín abhaile go dtí Pluais na mBéar>
(in-the night when go-HabPast the sun down take-HabPast Bear Big Bear-dim home to Cave of-the Bears)
'In the night when the sun used-to-go down, Big Bear used-to-take Little Bear home to the Bear Cave'
[New Page] **<Oíche amháin, chuir Béar Mór Béirín a luí. . . . >**
(night one, put-Past Bear Big Bear-dim to sleep. . .)
'One night, Big Bear put Little Bear to bed. . .'

Rather than adopt the Habitual Past Tense which is unusual in the speech of young children even in their mother-tongue, it would have been possible, without damaging the story significantly, to present the first two sentences also as referring to the events of one day, i.e. in the simple past. In addition it would have been possible to avoid the genitive 'gréine' on 'grian' 'sun' as follows:

<Lá amháin, chuaigh siad amach ag súgradh faoin ngrian.>
day one, went they out at playing under-the sun
'One day they went out playing in the sun.'
<Nuair a thit an oíche, chuaigh siad abhaile go Pluais na mBéar.>
when fell the night, went they home . . . . to . . . . . . Cave of-the Bears
'When night fell, they went home to the Bear Cave.'
<Chuir Béar Mór Béirín a luí . . . >
'Big Bear put Little Bear to bed. . .'

While this might not be as literary a translation, it would present fewer obstacles for the young reader. As it stands, even on the first page of this book, the young Irish reader has encountered significantly more complex language than in the English original. The author in English has chosen his words very carefully in order to be accessible to young children, but the translator has attempted to be true to the literary language, which can often mean presenting the young reader with more difficult language than in the original.

In this story Waddell delights in offering children a different world in which ordinary objects are transmuted to their equivalents in the bear world. Thus he uses 'Bear Cave', 'Bear Chair' and 'Bear Book'. However, Irish makes compounds of some such combinations, resulting in words that are considerably more challenging to the young reader than the original:

- *Bear Chair*; 'Béarchathaoir': <béar> and <cathaoir> Where the young reader of the English text is presented with two short capitalised nouns, the young reader of Irish finds a 13-letter compound <béarchathaoir>. In addition, the second part of this compound must be altered by an initial mutation on the noun <cathaoir> 'chair', making its identification in the compound even more difficult for the young reader.
- *Bear Book*; 'Béarleabhar': <béar> and <leabhar>. In this case there is no lenition on the second noun, because /l/ is not lenited. However, the young Irish reader is again confronted by an 11-letter compound, where the <ea> in the second noun encodes a different sound /au/ from the <éa> of the first noun which is pronounced /e:/.

M. Ó Murchú discussed the issue of compounding and comprehensibility of terminology in Irish and made the following recommendation (1993: 61): 'In contemporary Irish, a noun + qualifier should as a rule be preferred to a qualifier + noun: *clár ama* [table of time] is more natural now than *amchlár* [timetable].' The decision to use qualifier + noun compounds in the Irish translation could be justified as an attempt to highlight Waddell's wordplay in English, but it results in lexemes that are far more complex than their equivalents in the English original, and pose serious challenges for the young L2 reader. A possible compromise might have been at least to hyphenate these words, so that children were helped to segment the compounds. Standard Irish does not hyphenate in such contexts, but S. Ó Murchú (1977) recommends using hyphens for clarity in poetry and literature, and young readers especially would benefit from them.

The compounds draw attention to the fact that the translation presents the Irish reader with significantly more long words than the English reader. Analysis showed that while 7% of the word tokens in the English text consisted of words which were seven letters or longer, in the Irish translation twice that number (14%) of all the tokens consisted of seven or more letters (and 10% had eight or more letters, compared with less than 2% of the English word tokens). Conversely, the Irish reader of this story also has more one-letter words (6%) and two letter words (20%) than the English reader of this story (1% and 13%). Significant differences in the distributional patterns of languages are likely to impact most on the child who is at the early stages of L2 reading. The implications of word length distribution in Irish compared to English for L2 teaching are explored in Hickey (in preparation).

Table 16.1 presents a comparison between the English and Irish editions of *Can't you sleep little Bear?* A measure of Irish readability is currently in development by the author, but in this preliminary analysis Lix and the percentage of common words are calculated to give a preliminary comparison of the readability of the two texts. Lix is a simple measure (based on mean length of sentence and the proportion of words that are seven letters or longer) that has been used in cross-linguistic studies of readability (Bjornsson, 1983). The figures show that the Irish translation is several grades more difficult than the English original, even without taking into account the difference in language proficiency in the target readerships.

Table 16.1 Can't You Sleep Little Bear? and Oíche Mhaith, a Bhéirín

	Can't you sleep, little bear?	*Oíche Mhaith, a Bhéirín*
Word Types	184	226
Tokens	974	1043
Sentences	79	82
Sentence Length (words)	12.33	12.72
Proportion of seven-letter-words or longer	6.9%	13.6%
Lix	19	27
Approximate grade level	Grade 2[a]	Grade 5–6[b]
Reading age (approx.) (years)	8–9	11–12
Publisher's recommended age (years)	N/A	6–9
Proportion of Word Types found in 100 most common words in children's books[c]	36%	32%

[a]Based on Flesch-Kincaid and Lix (Bjornsson, 1983) score for English original.
[b]Based on Lix scores (Anderson, 1983) for Irish translation.
[c]The English corpus used for the common words comparison is the Children's Printed Word Database and the Irish corpus is the Institiúid Teangeolaíochta Éireann (ITÉ) *Corpus of Children's Books in Irish*, analysed by the author.

Overall, the Irish text appears significantly more difficult than the English one, and its language difficulty and reading level are such as to make it accessible only to L2 readers who would be likely to find it babyish and inappropriate to their interests. The orthography of the language results in young Irish readers being presented both with more very long words and also more very short words (see Hickey, in preparation) than in English, and this change in distributional pattern is likely to impact on reading fluency.

The inflectional and mutation systems of Irish result in less word stability, which means that children see fewer tokens of the same exact word, and more variant types. This lack of stability is likely to require higher frequencies of exposure to words and their variants before their decoding can become automatised. Increasing the exposure to L2 texts is, however, difficult, since there tends to be low motivation to read the target language if children feel the books are both too difficult *and* below their interest level. Tackling one aspect of this, the difficulties with decoding, can increase the possibility of children feeling a sense of achievement and satisfaction in reading a book in their second language, even if one aimed at a slightly younger age group. The following section looks at one way of increasing the frequency of L2 reading and tackling some of the decoding problems of young L2 readers.

Encouraging Extensive L2 Reading

Communicative approaches to language teaching view L2 reading as a valuable and integral part of the process of language learning. There is a body of research which points to the advantages for language learning of second language reading. As Day and Bamford (1998: 4) note:

> In an ideal world, are there any reading teachers who would NOT want their students to a) read a great deal and b) enjoy reading? It is unlikely. But such aims may seem remote, unattainable and even irrelevant to the job at hand ... The second language reading lesson can avoid being merely an empty ritual ... by addressing the two aims of students reading a great deal and students enjoying reading.

One approach that has achieved increases in L2 reading is the Book Flood, whereby children are given access to a wide range of generally suitable leisure reading materials in their second language, without strict controls for reading difficulty. Positive effects of Book Floods studied by Elley (1991) include:

- Increased motivation to read;
- increased enjoyment;
- Improved:

- word recognition;
- oral language;
- reading comprehension;
- listening comprehension;
- vocabulary;
- grammar.

In the Book Floods studied by Elley the range of books available varied between 48 and 250, and the children involved were as young as six years in some studies. Projects ran for periods as short as three months up to three years.

A related method of increasing exposure to L2 texts is Extensive Reading, which is defined by Day and Bamford (1998: xiii–xiv) as follows:

> Extensive reading is an approach to the teaching and learning of second language reading in which learners read large quantities of books and other materials that are well within their linguistic competence. [It] is appropriate at all stages of language learning.

Another approach found to be effective in promoting L2 reading is the provision of tape support for texts. Hickey (1991) showed that children read a taped Irish book significantly more often than an untaped one, and were able to read the taped books more accurately and fluently. This positive effect has also been found in other studies of taped books in supporting L1 reading (e.g. Gamby, 1983). It was decided to try to assess the suitability and feasibility of adapting the Book Flood/Extensive Reading approach and the Taped Book method to the teaching of Irish reading, through a case study of one group, aiming to examine the feasibility and effect of using a number of real Irish books and tapes with 33 children in a Grade 2 class (aged 7–8 years) in a Dublin English-medium school.

Taped Book Flood

Procedure

The trial began in January at the start of the second term with a graded reader (selected by the teacher) that had been taped by the researchers and teacher. This allowed the children to familiarise themselves with using taped books both in school and at home, using the kind of text which was familiar to them. A letter was sent to parents explaining the scheme and outlining how they could help. The Taped Book Flood intervention took place between February and the end of May, with gaps for the Easter holidays and teacher illness. The children's reading fluency was pre-tested in early January, and post-tested in early June. Survey data were collected from the children and parents in November and again in early June.

Fifty picture books were chosen, and divided into three levels of difficulty. The range of appropriate materials available for the least proficient readers was limited, and some extracts from early graded readers (stories and poems) were prepared as 'stand-alone' booklets in order to give them a sense of success on completing a 'book'. Non-commercial tapes were prepared by the researcher and the teacher, and the reading rate was kept slow, to allow the children to keep up with the tape. Both sides of the tape contained looped readings of just one story, and short tapes were used to minimise rewinding. Each child was provided with a Walkman suitable for young children (with a volume limiter in operation). Two 'listening stations' were also used, allowing groups of five children to hear a tape at the same time. The books were displayed in the library corner, in separate plastic zip-lock bags containing the book and a boxed tape. Children chose their own book, sometimes on the recommendation of the teacher or another child.

The class had 30-minute Irish reading sessions four mornings a week, when the children read while listening to their Walkmans or at the listening stations. The teacher and researcher circulated among them, helping children with questions or listening to them read extracts. Throughout, the children were urged to work at understanding the text, and the use of pictorial cues was discussed with them. Discussion with the children indicated that many believed it was 'wrong' to try to guess the meaning of a word in context, and that they believed instead that they ought to stop and ask the teacher. These discussions allowed some exploration of the value of making guesses in context, using all the available cues, and checking the guess as they went along.

After reading and listening to their story at least eight times, each child could change books if they felt ready to read part of the story aloud. Later a rota of groups was introduced to allow easier identification of children who needed more help, and every third day children in two groups (who had had their books for at least one session) read aloud briefly to the teacher or researcher, or discussed problems. In addition, children were regularly asked to listen to and read their taped Irish book as homework.

Children's response to the taped books

Seventy-one per cent of the children liked the taped books when they were first introduced, and 8% were neutral. More able readers were more likely to report liking them, while those who had difficulties with Irish reading were more likely to be wary of them. Personality factors influenced how long children wanted to keep books: some enjoyed being able to move on to a new book quickly and worked at meeting the requirements to do that, while others wanted to keep a book for longer, in some cases because they wanted to master it fully, and in other cases because they realised that keeping the same book required less effort than working on a new book. Teacher absence and school holidays sometimes meant children had to stay on the same book over periods of two weeks or more, and in the post-trial survey, two-thirds reported that they had wanted to change Irish books more often. This desire to read new books is, in itself, very positive and illustrates their raised motivation to read in the L2, and their sense of achievement on completing one book and progressing to another. The children believed that they were making progress in Irish reading: 61% of the children reported their Irish reading to be 'much improved' by the trial, and another 35% believed it to be a 'bit better'. A sense of pride was also engendered in the 72% who felt that their parents were impressed by their Irish reading skills as the trial continued.

How much did they read?

The children could be divided into roughly three groups: 31% read between three and eight books in the trial period, 28% read nine to 11 books, and 41% read more than 12 books. At the extremes, three children read five books or fewer, and five children read 12 books or more.

Results: Improved fluency

The children were stratified into three levels of Irish proficiency, based on their results in the test of Irish listening skills (ITÉ Béaltriail Gaeilge Rang 2). From these results, 20 children were chosen for individual tests of reading aloud in Irish before and after the Taped Book Flood. They were tested individually on reading passages from three texts, two from graded readers below their grade level (which they had not studied as class textbooks) and one from a leisure reader, none of which were in the sample of taped books. Their reading aloud was taped and analysed for reading speed and accuracy. The mean pre- and post-test scores for reading fluency among this sample are presented in Figure 16.1 (data are presented on the 16 children for whom full pre- and post-test data were collected, sorted by their initial reading fluency). A paired *t*-test showed the differences to be significant ($p < 0.0001$).

In the pre-test, seven children with lower levels of Irish competence in this group read in Irish at rates of less than 40 words per minute, a speed which imposes severe burdens on short term memory for comprehension. The post-test data show that all but one of the children were able to read the test passages more fluently, with increases of between 20% and 70% in reading speed. (The child who made no increase in reading fluency, C, had begun attending a learning support teacher for help with his reading difficulty.) Children who had higher scores in Irish competence

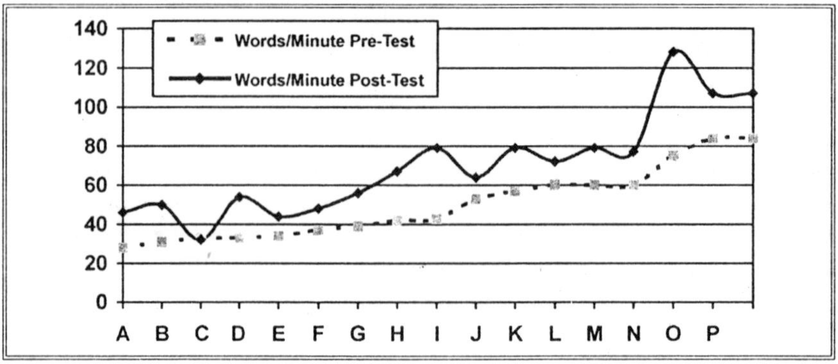

Figure 16.1 Reading fluency in pre- and post-tests (A–P = individual children, ordered by initial fluency)

read aloud at speeds of about 80 wpm, and in the post-test the most able reached a reading fluency of about 130 wpm.

Of course, this is in no way to presume that being able to read an L2 text aloud fluently is the same as reading it for meaning: teachers are well aware that students can at times competently decode texts they do not understand. However, if the decoding is itself extremely slow, or highly inaccurate (as the next section discusses), then the entire process of reading for meaning is short-circuited. Thus, it is not suggested that improving reading fluency is the solution to these children's problems with their L2 reading, but rather that improving their lower-level skills is an important step towards helping their higher-level reading skills. It is also worth noting that the children's improved fluency extended to intonational contours that helped them to group phrases together, and to read more expressively, which must be more conducive to reading for meaning than the halting reading of apparently disconnected words which had been the strategy adopted by the weaker readers in particular.

Reading accuracy

Accuracy in decoding is central to reading comprehension. Figure 16.2 shows that the children showed wide variability in the pre-test in the accuracy of their reading aloud, ranging from only 40% of the words in each passage being read accurately to 80% among the more proficient. In fact, seven children were able to read only about half of the words accurately in the pre-test, despite the fact that the test passages were judged to be below their grade-level. In the post-test, they all showed improved accuracy, but the weakest made the largest gains, and at the post-test all read the test passages with at least 80% accuracy levels. A paired *t*-test showed the differences to be significant ($p < 0.0001$).

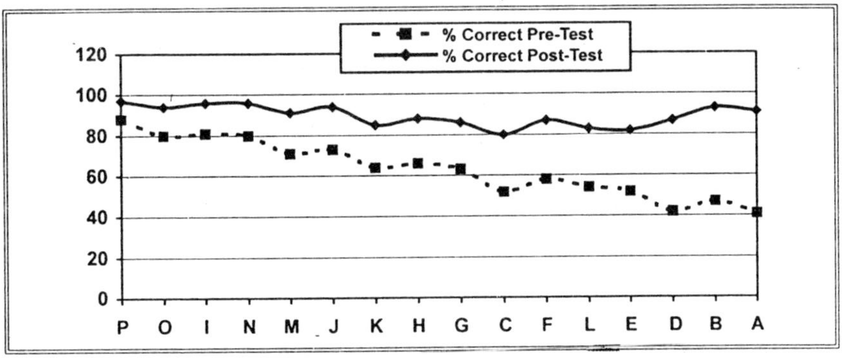

Figure 16.2 Accuracy in reading aloud (% words correct in pre- and post-test) (A–P = Children ordered by magnitude of difference from left to right)

One effect remarked on by the children's teacher and clearly evident from their post-test readings was their use of more natural intonation in reading, with more accurate decoding, phrasing and expression. While it is possible that 13 weeks of normal Irish instruction would have effected some improvement in the children's overall decoding accuracy, it is less likely that it would have achieved such a noticeable effect in orienting the children towards reading in Irish with natural intonation, or a similar increase in motivation to read (and complaints about not being able to read more books).

Children's attitude to Irish

Learners of Irish often view the language very negatively, and believe that it is of little worth to them. The intervention was found to have some effect on the children's attitudes to Irish. In the pre-trial survey, only 52% of the children agreed that Irish was an important school subject, compared to 72% in the post-test. Similarly, while 20% in the pre-test agreed with the statement that 'I don't really try very hard to learn Irish at school', only 10% agreed post-test. It would appear that the extra effort and resources devoted to Irish reading, and the children's sense of achievement, helped some children to feel at least a little more positive towards the subject.

Survey of parents' response

Parents were asked their opinions regarding their children's standard of Irish reading and 84% reported that their child's reading had improved since the introduction of taped Irish books. Almost three-quarters reported that their child's attitude to Irish and Irish reading had improved, and almost two-thirds said that they listened to the tape with their child at least once a week. Almost four-fifths believed using taped-Irish leisure readers was more effective than exclusive use of a class textbook. Some of the parents' comments on the trial are given below:

> My daughter really enjoyed the Irish Reading Project. She thinks her Irish has really improved and she enjoys reading the Irish books.
>
> I think that the tape accompanying the reader is an excellent idea and helps especially with pronunciation and fluency. I think it also helps to make the Irish language more 'real' for the children.
>
> A very positive project – making Irish fun and giving them control over their own learning.
>
> I felt the project gave my child a confidence that she did not previously have. I would be delighted to buy the books and tapes if available.

Among the small number of critical responses, one parent reported that the tapes were too fast for her child, while another remarked that they were too slow. Another parent did not accept that repeated listening is required to reap the benefits of the taped books and was reluctant to encourage this. Only one parent commented that her child found some of the translated *Spot* books used for the least proficient readers 'too babyish' because they were like her baby sister's. Interestingly, one parent objected to the tape presenting a 'prescriptive' (native-speaker-like?) pronunciation of Irish, stating that she thought the child's own pronunciation superior; it is difficult to imagine a parent making a similar argument with regard to the learning of a more widely valued language such as French, but it may reflect a Dublin parent's greater familiarity with the less dialectal Irish spoken by learners than with the Irish of native-speakers. This points to the value of discussing with parents and children what their aims and expectations are with regard to the learning of Irish.

Teacher's comments

The teacher was struck by the children's motivation to read the taped Irish books. As the term progressed, he reported that it became obvious who had been listening to the tapes at home, because the natural rhythms of Irish were present in their reading of the books. He commented that homework was helped by having the tapes in that the children had backup even if their parents could not help with Irish. Parents' spontaneous feedback to the teacher was also extremely positive.

The primary difficulty noted by the teacher lay in classroom management, and judging how much time he could allocate from the recommended hour per day for the Irish curriculum. Overall, the teacher found the Irish Taped Book Flood to be very effective, although he suggested some reorganisation. He recommended grouping the children by Irish reading ability and having the less proficient in two groups (with five in each) use listening stations more often. He argued that having these groups read a smaller number of texts (about six) chosen by the teacher would facilitate the teacher's monitoring of their progress, and give the children a sense of working together. However, it would be important to ensure that the more able readers, who relished the chance to read more extensively in the trial, would continue to have daily independent reading-while-listening sessions. It would also be necessary to monitor whether restricting the texts for the weaker readers would negatively affect those children's motivation.

Researcher's suggestions

It would be easier for the less able children to approach a book independently if the Taped Book Flood were linked with daily sessions of the teacher reading aloud. This would help to orient children to books they might choose to read later themselves. Regular sessions of the teacher reading aloud would also allow some exploration of reading strategies to deal with unknown words or phrases. Regular short sessions focusing on frequent words or clusters would also support the children's independent reading. Post-reading dramatisations of the stories were both effective and popular: for example a number of children who had read the Irish version of the *Three Little Pigs* staged a lively version complete with a director/prompter who was able to supply lines to each actor from memory. Establishing reading groups of children who are on the same book would allow them to prepare such presentations on a more regular basis. Building the reading-while-listening into homework in a more regular and central way would also be beneficial, as there was a tendency for it to be added to other Irish homework such as workbook use, rather than given the main focus.

Conclusions

There are a number of ways of tackling some of the problems of learning to read an L2 writing system, and the attendant problem of low motivation to read it. Briefly summarised they are:

- Target decoding problems directly (e.g. difficult consonant clusters) rather than leaving it to children to notice patterns. Poor lower-level skills are obstacles to automatisation and reading for meaning.
- Encourage teachers (and parents if possible) to read aloud in the L2 every day so that children are helped to understand and enjoy the experience of reading in their L2.
- Use the strategies that work for L1 reading, such as exposing children to as wide a range of texts as possible, rather than relying exclusively on limited exposure in whole-class work to graded

readers. Allow children to move at the appropriate pace for them, rather than approaching L2 reading only as a whole-class activity.

- Provide taped support for young L2 readers to help them with decoding and to increase their motivation to read L2 texts frequently even when their L2 reading proficiency is low.
- Actively elicit parental support by setting up and resourcing Shared L2 Reading programmes, informing parents of the importance of their participation and praise for their children's progress in motivating children.
- Develop school-wide programmes for L2 reading, where children have a clear appreciation of the value the school attaches to reading in both L1 and L2, and with children in older classes writing texts for younger classes and reading aloud to them.

This study showed that children responded with great enthusiasm to the opportunity to read a range of taped books in their L2, rather than working slowly and painstakingly with the class through a graded reader. They felt a sense of achievement on completing even a very simple book in their L2 with the help of the tape, and the results of the fluency and accuracy analyses showed that they were closer to reading the texts in a meaningful way, rather than approaching Irish reading only as an exercise in decoding individual words when reading their class textbook.

These results demonstrate the value of broadening children's experience of L2 reading to include real books, with supports, rather than relying exclusively on a graded reader. However, there are practical difficulties centring on the supply of suitable books and the issue of translation and overall levels of language difficulty and readability are currently being examined (Hickey, in preparation).

Overall, these results are positive enough to indicate that the Taped Book Flood approach could fruitfully be pursued even with young L2 readers with very limited proficiency, and they underline the value of providing such support materials commercially. The provision of tapes or CDs to accompany L2 texts is shown to be a valuable aid in motivating and supporting early L2 readers in particular. Finally, parents' positive responses to the tape-support for their child's Irish reading indicates that this constitutes a valuable way of helping parents to help their children with L2 reading homework, which should be explored more fully.

Acknowledgements

This study was funded by Institiúid Teangeolaíochta Éireann and the National Reading Initiative of the Department of Education and Science.

References

Anderson, J. (1983) Lix and Rix: Variations on a little-known readability index. *Journal of Reading* 26, 490–6.

An Gúm (1986) *Foclóir Póca*. Baile Átha Cliath: An Gúm.

Bernhardt, E. (2003) Challenges to reading research from a multilingual world. *Reading Research Quarterly* 38 (1), 112–17.

Bernhardt, E. and Kamil, M. (1995) Interpreting relationships between L1 and L2 reading: Consolidating the linguistic threshold and the linguistic interdependence hypotheses. *Applied Linguistics* 16 (1), 15–34.

Bossers, B. (1991) On thresholds, ceilings and short-circuits: The relation between L1 reading, L2 reading and L2 knowledge. *AILA Review* 8, 45–60.

Bjornsson, C. (1983) Readability of newspapers in eleven languages. *Reading Research Quarterly* 18 (4), 480–97.

Clarke, A. (1980) The short-circuit hypothesis of ESL reading – or when language competence interferes with reading performance. *Modern Language Journal* 64, 203–9.

Crowder, R. (1976) *Principles of Learning and Memory*. Hillsdale, NJ: Erlbaum.

Day, R. and Bamford, J. (1998) *Extensive Reading in the Second Language Classroom*. Cambridge: Cambridge University Press.

Droop, M. and Verhoeven, L. (2003) Language proficiency and reading ability in first- and second-language learners. *Reading Research Quarterly* 38 (1), 78–103.

Elley, W. (1991) Acquiring literacy in a second language: The effect of book-based programs. *Language Learning* 41 (3), 375–411.

Favreau, M. and Segalowitz, N. (1982) Second language reading in fluent bilinguals. *Applied Psycholinguistics* 3, 329–41.

Favreau, M., Komoda, M. and Segalowitz, N. (1980) Second language reading: Implications of the word superiority effect in skilled bilinguals. *Canadian Journal of Psychology* 34, 370–80.

Fuller, B. (1987) What school factors raise achievement in the third world? *Review of Educational Research* 57, 255–92.

Gaelscoileanna (2004) All-Irish Education Outside the Gaeltacht 2003–2004: Statistics. At www.iol.ie/gaelscoileanna.

Gamby, G. (1983) Talking books and taped books: Materials for instruction. *The Reading Teacher* 36, 366–9.

Harris, J. and Murtagh, L. (1999) *Teaching and Learning Irish in Primary School*. Dublin: Institiúid Teangeolaíochta Éireann.

Hatch, E. (1974) Research on reading in a second language. *Journal of Reading Behaviour* 6 (1), 53–61.

Hickey, T. (1991) Leisure reading in a second language: An experiment with audiotapes in Irish. *Language, Culture and Curriculum* 4 (2), 119–31.

Hickey, T. (1992) *Teaching Irish in Primary School: Practical Approaches/ Múineadh na Gaeilge sa Bhunscoil: Moltaí Praiticiúla*. Dublin: Bord na Gaeilge and Reading Association of Ireland (RAI).

Hickey, T. (1999) *Luathoideachas trí Ghaeilge sa Ghaeltacht*. Gaillimh: Údarás na Gaeltachta and Institiúid Teangeolaíochta Éireann.

Hickey, T. and Ó Cainín, P. (2003) Second-language reading: Taping over the cracks. In G. Shiel and U. Ní Dhálaigh (eds) *Other Ways of Seeing: Diversity in Language and Literacy* (pp. 147–57). Dublin: Reading Association of Ireland.

Hickey, T. (in preparation) Word length distribution and the young reader of Irish.

INTO (Irish National Teachers' Organization) (1985) *Survey of Teachers' Attitudes to the Irish Language*. Dublin: INTO.

Kellaghan, T. and Macnamara, J. (1967) Reading in a second language in Ireland. In M. Jenkinson (ed.) *Reading Instruction: An International Forum*. (pp. 231–40). Newark, Delaware: International Reading Association.

Leloup, J. (1993) The effect of interest level in selected text topics on second language reading comprehension. Unpublished PhD dissertation, Ohio State University.

Martin, M. and Morgan, M. (1994) Reading literacy in Irish schools: A comparative analysis. *The Irish Journal of Education* 28 (Special Monograph Edition), 3–101.

Muchisky, D. (1983) Relationships between speech and reading among second language learners. *Language Learning* 33, 77–102.

Myles na Gopaleen (1987) *The Best of Myles*. Dublin: Grafton Books.

Na Bráithre Críostaí (1999) *Graiméar Gaeilge na mBráithre Críostaí*. Baile Átha Cliath: An Gúm.

Ní Argáin, C. (1990) Sóléite nó doléite? Staidéar ar shoiléiteacht théacsleabhar Gaeilge sa bhunscoil. *Oideas* 35, 35–55.

Oakhill, J. (1999) Reading: Acquisition. In B. Spolsky (ed.) *Concise Encyclopedia of Educational Linguistics*. (pp. 431–40). Oxford: Elsevier Science Ltd.

Ó Baoill, D. (1996) *An Teanga Bheo: Gaeilge Uladh*. Baile Átha Cliath: Institiúid Teangeolaíochta Éireann.

Ó Baoill, D. and Ó Riagáin, P. (1990) Reform of the orthography, grammar and vocabulary of Irish. In I. Fodor and C. Hagége (eds) *Language Reform: History and Future* (pp. 173–95). Hamburg: Helmut Buske Verlag.

Ó Murchú, M. (1977) Successes and failures in the modernization of Irish spelling. In J. Fishman (ed.) *Advances in the Creation and Revision of Writing Systems* (pp. 267–89). The Hague: Mouton.

Ó Murchú, M. (1993) Some general observations: An Ghaeilge bheo 2000 AD. (The Irish Language Alive 2000 AD.) *Teangeolas* 32, 59–61.

Ó Murchú, S. (1977) Úsáid an fhleiscín i scríobh na Gaeilge (Use of the hyphen in written Irish). *Éigse* 17 (1), 115–22.

Ó Murchú, S. (1998) *An Teanga Bheo: Gaeilge Chonamara*. Baile Atha Cliath: Institiúid Teangeolaíochta Éireann.

Ó Sé, D. (1990) Súil ghéar ar litriú na Gaeilge (A sharp eye on the spelling of Irish). *Teangeolas* 28, 16–18.

Ó Sé, D. (2000) *Gaeilge Chorca Dhuibhne*. Baile Átha Cliath: Institiúid Teangeolaíochta Éireann.

Ó Siadhail, M. (1989) *Modern Irish: Grammatical Structure and Dialectal Variation*. Cambridge: Cambridge University Press.

Segalowitz, N. and Hébert, M. (1990) Phonological recoding in the first and second language reading of skilled bilinguals. *Language Learning* 40, 503–38.

Spencer, L. and Hanley, J. (2003) The effects of orthographic consistency on reading development and phonological awareness: Evidence from children learning to read in Wales. *British Journal of Psychology* 94, 1–28.

Stanovich, K. (1986) Matthew effects in reading: Some consequences of individual differences in the acquisition of literacy. *Reading Research Quarterly* 21 (4), 360–407.

Urquhart, A. and Weir, C. (1998) *Reading in a Second Language: Process, Product and Practice.* London: Longman.

Verhoeven, L. (2000) Components in early second language reading and spelling. *Scientific Studies of Reading* 4, 313–30.

Waddell, M. (1988) *Can't You Sleep, Little Bear?* London: Walker Books.

Waddell, M. (1989) *Oíche Mhaith, a Bhéirín*. Dublin: An Gúm.

Chapter 17

Written Language and Foreign Language Teaching

VIVIAN COOK

Since the decline of audiolingualism as a teaching method, there has been little public debate about the respective roles of spoken language and written language in language teaching or about how to teach the writing system itself. This chapter argues that it is time to start thinking again not only about the general relationship between spoken and written language in language teaching but also about how to teach the specifics of writing. It is then concerned with the acquisition of an L2 writing system in foreign language teaching classrooms. The term 'writing' is used here in the general superordinate sense which subsumes both writing and reading; the discussion thus extends beyond the writing system to the uses of the system. The question is how teaching should use writing at the beginners level rather than at more advanced levels of writing, which have received more attention. The chapter looks at teaching through the lens of specimen coursebooks. It draws on Cook (2004) for its general concept of writing systems and for some of the details of L2 writing systems and on the overall idea of multi-competence – one mind with two languages (Cook, 2002). More general discussion of teaching materials for beginners from an L2 user perspective can be found in Cook (2003).

The Relationship of Spoken and Written Language in Language Teaching

The priority of spoken over written language has been a constant theme in language teaching methodology (Banathy & Sawyer, 1969) and it formed article 1 of the International Phonetic Association in the 1880s: 'Foreign language study should begin with the spoken language of everyday life' (cited in Stern, 1983). The audiolingualism of the 1960s established the first principle of 'scientific language teaching' as 'Speech before writing' (Lado, 1964). The over-riding importance of the spoken language is implicit in almost all language teaching methods at the start of the twenty-first century. The major exception is the teaching of languages with character-based scripts (Chinese and Japanese) where the writing system has always played a crucial role in the early stages of teaching.

The reasons advocated for the primacy of speech are usually derived from the pronouncements of linguists, say Lyons (1968: 38) 'the spoken language is primary and ... writing is essentially a means of representing speech in another medium'. The linguistic arguments used to justify the primacy of speech are typically:

- children acquire their first language in spoken form before written: 'Because many people acquire languages by hearing them first, many teachers prefer to expose students to the spoken form first' (Harmer, 1998: 53);
- spoken language existed in many countries long before written;
- many languages today still essentially lack a writing system, like Swiss German or Ulster Scots;
- many individuals are illiterate, the world-wide illiteracy rate for the year 2000 being 20.6% (*UNESCO Statistical Yearbook*, 2000).

While these statements are unquestionably true, they say nothing direct or relevant about L2 acquisition itself or about the desirability of teaching spoken rather than written language to students who are already literate.

In addition teachers sometimes claim that:

- some students only need the second language in spoken form;
- some students demand to be taught the spoken form;
- early writing may cause interference in speaking from the written forms in sound-based scripts.

Again, true as these statements may be, they show only that a proportion of students need speaking or that there is some caution to be used in teaching writing, not that writing should be taught as a secondary form of language. It is probably equally true that some students need written language, demand written language and may have interference in writing from speech (for example the frequent use of full stressed forms of English auxiliaries 'will' and 'shall' rather than their usual reduced spoken form ''ll' /l/). The claims of both linguists and teachers seem to be based on an implicit view that all writing systems are sound-based, rather than conceived in terms of meaning-based systems.

In many ways the whole tradition of teaching European languages since the Reform Movement of the 1880s has been to pretend that the first language does not exist in the foreign language teaching classroom and to make the students start from scratch as if they did not already have another language. So far as the teaching of the written language is concerned, this fails to recognise that becoming literate in a first writing system has already changed the learner in ways that cannot be undone. To be specific:

- *literate people reason in a more abstract way* (Luria, 1976). People who have learnt to read have different perceptions of the world and store information differently from those who have not (Goody, 2000). The actual brains of literate people differ from those of non-literates (Petersen *et al.*, 2000).
- *literate people perceive language differently.* Literate English people believe there are more sounds in 'ridge' /rɪdʒ/ than in 'rage' /reidʒ/ (Derwing, 1992) because of the extra letter <d> in the written form. English children do not 'hear' the phoneme /n/ till after they have acquired the letter <n> (Treiman *et al.*, 1995). As Olson (1996: 100) puts it, 'Writing systems create the categories in terms of which we become conscious of speech'. Written English is pre-analysed into words by spaces, into types of nouns by capital letters and into grammatical constructions by commas, full stops and semi-colons. The very units of language we perceive vary according to our L1 writing system; the phonemes and words that exist for speakers of alphabet-based writing systems may be far from the minds of those using a syllable-based writing system, let alone one based on morphemes.

It is then time for language teaching methodology to reconsider its emphasis on the spoken language in the beginning stages. While there may still be valid grounds for the primacy of spoken language, there is no reason why it should be accepted on the grounds of the beliefs of the 1880s or the largely irrelevant arguments of linguists.

Learning to Use a Second Language Writing System

What in fact do people need to know to be able to read and write in a second language? Let us sum up the types of information covered in many chapters of this book, using English as the main example of a second language, i.e. a sound-based, far from transparent, alphabetic system. The areas are not in any particular order.

(1) *Students have to learn the appropriate direction of reading and writing,* whether left-to-right as in English, right-to-left as in Arabic, top-to-bottom in columns as in some traditional Japanese and Chinese (or occasional English street signs), or the complexities of Hindi where vowels are placed at the beginning of the word before the consonants.

Though changing direction undoubtedly creates problems in acquiring an L2 writing system, at least initially, particularly with the complex eye-movement involved in reading, little has been documented. It probably contributes to the well-known slowness of Chinese readers of English compared to other L2 readers (Haynes & Carr, 1990), at least for those Chinese readers still using the traditional column arrangement. Arabic students in England have reported that their children attempt to write English from right-to-left, though such mirror writing is not uncommon among native English children.

(2) *Students have to learn to make and recognise the actual letter or character shapes.* Variation between languages partly depends on the medium, whether keyboard, pen or brush, but also on movement – English makes circles predominantly in an anti-clockwise direction, Japanese in a clockwise direction – and on sequence of construction – English makes vertical lines before horizontal, Japanese the reverse (Sassoon, 1995). Letters may also have contextually determined forms, say the 97 or so necessary for linking the 28 letters of Arabic; interestingly the font devised by Gutenberg for the German Bible in 1455 originally had over 300 different letter forms to mimic the variation in handwriting. Of course for many users the basic skill nowadays is the ability to type text in at a keyboard, whether a PC or a mobile phone.

In terms of recognition, students also have to be able to see the different versions of a letter as the same, say the three alphabets <a A *a*> or the differences between serif and sans-serif fonts <A A>, let alone differences in handwriting say <I I J J> for capital <I> (see Sassoon (1999) for an extensive discussion). This extends to variations in font, for example the older fonts for German such as <ß> rather than <ss> as in <beiß> (bite) and the difference between so-called serif (lines of varying width) and sans-serif (lines of uniform thickness) scripts in Japanese, say せんしゅう versus せんしゅう.

Clearly L2 students' handwriting shows the transfer from the L1WS, both from sound-based L2WSs with different alphabets – Greek use of <α> for <a> in English <αrises> (arises) – and from characters to letters – the Japanese use of horizontal before vertical strokes in English <E> for capital <E>. This transfer of physical actions from the L1WS to the L2WS is perhaps only documented by Sassoon (1995).

The computer has added new dimensions to this. At one level the keyboard itself may differ from one writing system to another. It is impossible to key in a tilde < ~ > by itself on some Spanish keyboards as it is incorporated into separate letters, i.e. <ñ> or <ã>. Inputting characters in word processing Chinese and Japanese is complex; for example a typical word-processing programme requires the user to type the words in roman letters, say <hatarakisugi> (to work too much); the programme automatically converts this into *hiragana* syllabic symbols namely はたらきすぎ, then this is converted into *kanji* characters 働き過ぎ (sometimes involving a choice between alternative *kanji* for the same pronunciation).

Additionally there are transliteration systems that allow Greek speakers to use the Roman alphabet for e-mails (Tseliga, 2003). Crucially the access to many character dictionaries depends upon knowing the order in which the strokes of the character are made, now much less available to the user because the keyboard has cut down on the need to write characters stroke by stroke.

(3) *Students have to learn to use the phonological processing route* for relating letters and sounds in an alphabet-based writing system such as English, so that they can link written <bus> to spoken /bʌs/ and vice versa. In less transparent alphabetic writing systems, they need to use complex correspondence rules.

Mistakes with phoneme–grapheme correspondence rules are common in L2 students' work in English (Cook, 1997), for instance vowel alternations such as <a>/<e> in <catagories>, <e>/<i> in <defenetely>, <a>/<i> in <privite>, alternations of <s>, <c>, <z>, <t> in <immence> or <amasing>. The difficulties with the phonological route are:

- The L2 phonological system, which the L2 learner may not use in the same way as a native speaker – in this case similar to the problems of children who have not yet developed the adult system or who speak with a dialect accent that is not the one reflected in the standard correspondence rules.
- The projection of the learners' L1 phonological system on the L2WS, say the lack of final voicing in German revealed in English spelling 'recognice'. Japanese students have <l>/<r> problems with <blackets>, <grobal>, <sarary> (salary) etc, showing they do not use the /l~r/ contrast in the same way as native speakers. It may of course be difficult to distinguish such phonological transfer from deficiencies in knowledge of the L2WS.
- The correspondence rules that govern the relationships between letters and sounds in a particular language. The correspondence rules that English employs for showing say 'short' versus 'long' vowels are hardly appreciated by L2 learners, whether consonant doubling <accomodation>, <forgoten> or silent <e> in <mor> or <mane> (man). Nor are the three spelling systems of English (Albrow, 1972): *basic* as in final /k/ corresponding to <ck> 'mock', *romance* as in final /k/ corresponding to <que> 'baroque', and *exotic* as in final /k/ corresponding to <k> 'amok'.

(4) *Students have to learn to use the lexical, morpheme-based processing route.* In an orthographically deep alphabet-based writing system they

need this route to deal with individual words and meanings, so that they can, say, link <does> with /dʌz/ in one direction and /jɒt/ with <yacht> in the other; in character-based systems they need this route to deal with the character-to-meaning correspondences for example between 人 and the meaning 'person', or in reverse between 'person' and 人; 'benevolence' and 仁, 'Ren' (surname) and 任 (all pronounced /ʐən/). In English, according to Seidenberg (1992), perhaps the most frequent 200 words have to be processed as one-off items by this route. Students show many mistakes with words that have to be remembered as idiosyncratic items such as <rong> for <wrong> and <payed> for <paid>.

The lexical route is also used for direct access to the lexicon within the Chomskyan model of spelling as lexical representation: the fact that there is a single plural 's' morpheme is shown by spelling it as <s> despite the variation in pronunciation between /s/ in 'books', /z/ in 'rugs', and /ɪz/ in 'badges'; the links between different forms of the same word are maintained by preserving the spelling, the letter <o> is used in <photograph> and <photographer> despite corresponding to /əu/ and /ɒ/ respectively. However, while it clearly takes some time for children to perceive the common feature of 'ed' in 'played', 'liked' and 'watched' (Nunes *et al.*, 1997), adult L2 learners seem not to have the same difficulty (Cook, 2004).

(5) *Students have to learn orthographic regularities in less transparent writing systems*, in English for instance:
- the three letter rule that distinguishes content from function words ('in/inn', 'an/Ann' and 'I/eye/aye').
- the constraints on letters not occurring in final position, say <v>, <j> or <h> (apart from a handful of items such as <spiv>, <raj> and <blah>).

Again these orthographic regularities provide a frequent source of error for students, the use of final <ck> rather than <k> 'thik', of double <o> as in 'wood' but not of double <aa> (apart from say <baa>), of final but not initial <ll> ('dull' versus 'llud'), of silent <e> in reading as a clue to the preceding vowel, and so on. L2 learners develop these orthographic regularities along with the sound- and meaning-based routes (Cook, 2004).

(6) *Students have to learn to use punctuation marks and other typographic features* that show different structural relationships in the sentence, <John's book?>, or provide clues to reading aloud, say potential pauses shown by commas in lists such as <apples, oranges, pears and lemons>. The actual punctuation marks differ slightly in form across languages, for instance the goose-feet quotation marks used in French <le verbe«avoir»>, the initial upside-down Spanish question marks <¿> and exclamation marks <¡> and

the hollow punctuation mark < 。> and listing comma <,> of Chinese. Typography in the broad sense ('the structuring and arranging of visual language', Baines & Haslam, 2002: 1) also plays a crucial part in the interpretation of the page. Though little studied, these features form an important aspect of reading and writing in an L2 writing system.

(7) *Students have to cope with the creative use of spelling* and other typographical devices in shop-names such as 'Kidz Kutz Hair Design' (Kids Cuts). Novel spelling also occurs frequently in text messages 'C U 4 T' (see you for tea) and other computer-mediated communication, now perhaps the commonest form of written language for many users. L2 users too may need to master the features of e-mail, for example Arabic-speaking businessmen using English for communicating with each other.

(8) *Students have to learn to use the forms and functions of written language,* so that they can use the appropriate words and grammar for, say, writing an e-mail rather than making a phone-call, have greater lexical density in more formal genres (Biber, 1995) and so on. At the most general level, this has to some extent been catered for in language teaching, as we see below.

In general adding an L2WS to a L1WS can lead to issues resulting from:

- the influence of one writing system on another, i.e. an aspect of transfer;
- the creation of a new system;
- language-internal contradictions, interlocking phonological as well as orthographic systems; etc.

Some of these problems are also found in children learning an L1 writing system, some only in the acquisition of an L2 writing system because of the knowledge of the L1WS already present in the learner's mind. Some of these eight areas outlined above are common to all writing systems, some peculiar to one or two; some 'obvious' and giving little trouble, others leaving problems that persist throughout people's lives. But it would be very hard to function as a reader or writer in a second language without them.

Written Language in Modern Language Teaching Coursebooks

Let us now look at some of the ways in which written language is utilised in a sample of beginners courses, limiting ourselves to the acquisition of alphabetic L2 writing systems. The course-books have been chosen to provide useful illustrations, rather than to be statistically representative of good current coursebooks: namely six adult low-level courses: four for English – *Atlas* (Nunan, 1995); *Reward* (Greenall, 1994); *Changes* (Richards, 1998); *Headway Elementary* (Soars & Soars, 1993) – and two for other languages – *Ci siamo* (Guarnuccio & Guarnuccio, 1997) for Italian and *Libre Echange* (Courtillon & de Salins, 1995) for French. *Changes, Libre Echange* and *Atlas* claim to be suitable for beginners, *Reward* for 'intermediate', *Headway* for 'elementary'; *Ci siamo* does not specify level. Any criticisms of these courses implied below are not aimed at undermining these courses, which have many other virtues; my own beginners' EFL course *People and Places* (Cook, 1980) had very similar characteristics. All the courses apart from *Ci siamo* are monolingual and are stand-alone volumes.

The most crucial aspect to look at for language teaching is the overall functions of written language within the L2 user's world outside the classroom and the uses for it within the classroom. The written language found in the coursebooks falls into a limited set of categories:

(1) *Scripted dialogues*
A typical example comes where two characters are introducing each other.

> Permesso?
> Avanti.
> Buongiorno.
> Buongiorno. Io sono la signora Pasotto. Lei come si chiama?
> Mi chiamo Lucy, cioè Lucia ... Lucia Burns. (*Ci siamo*, 1)

All the coursebooks use scripted textbook dialogues, far more well-formed and cohesive than any natural spoken language (Cook, 1970). Occasionally, as in *Libre Echange*, they are taken from authentic film-scripts – again invented rather than authentic speech. The main use of these written texts is to present spoken language in written form. However, paradoxically, the spoken language portrayed is far from ordinary, more like the well-scripted dialogues of a play or film. The dialogues are neither fish nor fowl, far from speech written down but equally far from normal written language in vocabulary, syntax and lexical density.

(2) *Written elements in teaching tasks*
The written language is also used as an integral part of teaching:

- *language explanation*
  Elements such as grammar are explained to students in written language, as in:

  > J'ai loué ... Ici, le participe passé est employé avec le verbe « avoir » et il est invariable. (*Libre Echange*: 32)

Even the first lessons of these course-books use the authentic written language of grammar discussion, with a technical L2 vocabulary way outside the usual limits of beginners – 'participe', 'verbe' (*Libre Echange*: 32); 'adjectives', 'conjunction', 'wh question' (*Atlas*: 16), or 'Naming objects', 'Asking and saying where things are', 'Prepositions of place' (*Changes*: 17). It is debatable whether these explanations are addressed to the beginner students or are intended for the teacher or designed for later reference purposes. Sometimes these explanations are given in the first language (*Ci siamo*).

- *conveying L2 word meaning*
  A perpetual problem in language teaching is how to convey the meaning of words in the second language. From the Direct Method through the Audiovisual Method down to the present day, a common technique is ostensive definition through the presentation of pictures with labels. *Ci siamo* (p. 136) uses Michelangelo's David with 24 labelled parts including 'il dito' (finger) and 'la spalla' (shoulder) (but with a discreet added item 'la foglia' (leaf)). Similar is the use of picture captions 'À la terrasse d'un café chic' (on the terrace of a smart café) (*Libre Echange*: 91), though this is often turned into an exercise of finding a name for a picture. This technique then represents a straightforward everyday use of written language, found in notices, encyclopaedias etc.
- *giving instructions for teaching exercises*
  Students' books provide written directions for the activities they have to do, for example:

  > Look at the pictures and find these places. Label the pictures. (*Atlas*: 25)

  This represents a normal function of written language in the style of instructional texts such as cookbooks, for instance the dominance of imperatives, but is again way above the spoken language of the students in terms of grammar and vocabulary.
- *asking comprehension questions*
  Another unavoidable element in language teaching is checking whether the students have understood, in these courses often covered by written questions:

  > Who are they? Listen to their conversations. Spell their surnames. (*Changes*: 6)

  The overall point is checking on comprehension of elements of spoken or written text through written language, sometimes in disguised ways. Outside educational contexts, it is rather unusual to be, say, quizzed on today's headlines after we read the newspapers.

(3) *Providing exercise props*
The written language can also provide material for practising the spoken language:

- *lists of words*
  Many activities rely on lists of words:

  > Match the foods and drinks to the words in the chart ... apples, carrots, bread, butter, beef, coffee... (*Changes*: 37)

  Little outside the educational context provides a model or a purpose for these isolated bits of written language. The only parallel might be making a speech from notes, which is self-prepared and far more complex.
- *realia*
  Information necessary for the exercise can be conveyed through realia and graphics, such as catalogues:

  > i jeans 1 avorio L.50.00, 2 nero L.79.00, 3 prélavé L.73.000 ... (*Ci siamo*, 124–125)

  Maps are particularly popular whether San Francisco (*Atlas*), London (*Changes*), Dublin (*Reward*) or Urbania (*Ci siamo*). While these represent a normal use of written language for display and information, the students are learning the names for the clothes etc. rather than deciding what to buy, i.e. a codebreaking rather than a decoding activity. The written language is the 'block' language of noun phrases, proper names, prices etc. rather than being 'full' sentences or having textual coherence.
- *fill-in forms and charts*
  Students fill in copious amounts of information into charts and the like:

  > DAILY PLANNER Monday Morning ...... Afternoon ... Evening ...... (*Atlas*: 31)

  and forms:

  > CARTE INTERNATIONALE D'EMBARQUEMENT 1. M/Mme/ Mlle _____ Nom ___ ... (*Libre Echange*: 39)

  Mostly their response is a single written word or phrase rather than a complete sentence or paragraph, usually acting as the basis for a later oral exchange. While it is of course necessary to fill in such forms from time to time in everyday life, this is usually an unavoidable chore. The language is fragments and isolated words. Most of the charts and forms in the coursebooks have no outcome other than providing material for a teaching exercise.

- *sentence completion*
  Perhaps the most ancient teaching technique gets students to fill in blanks in sentences before saying them aloud:

  > Et ...... laitues, il y a ...... laitues? (*Libre Echange*: 84)

  or to construct sentences from jumbled words:

  > Rearrange the words to make questions and answers and then practice them: you/where/live/do ... (*Atlas*: 20)

  In a sense this exploits the permanency of written language so that the whole sentence can be present simultaneously for the student to play with, again using written language in a way unparalleled outside a classroom.
- *making up sentences*
  Students are given questions and answers in a jumbled order and have to pair them appropriately, for example *My perfect weekend* as seen by Stephen from Leeds and Paula from Nottingham (*Reward*: 90). Sentences are also constructed from jumbled words:

  > How many statements and questions can you make from these words?
  > I dessert she want any steak don't fries they coffee some he wants (*Atlas*: 83).

  This too is a purely pedagogical use of written language, inconceivable outside a classroom, relying finally on reading aloud.

(4) *Written texts*
Some coursebooks also present written language through continuous texts longer than a single sentence:

- *short information texts*
  Cultural information is often conveyed through short texts, typically about 50 words long:

  - biographies: Beryl aged 95 from Nottingham (*Changes*: 95);
  - first person accounts: Sun Hee Shi talks about her birthday (*Changes*: 88);
  - factual accounts: *Amazing Animals* ('Did you know the kangaroo can't walk at all?', *Changes*: 81).

  Only *Reward* features a real short story, by Roald Dahl, and extracts from books such as Paul Theroux's *The Kingdom by the*

Sea. These short texts resemble pieces of travel guides or children's textbooks rather than normal reading. Little of our everyday reading consists of passages of this type (particularly when they are pretexts for arranging information in columns or completing sentences).

- *letters*
  Specimens of letters occasionally form a basis for the students' own writing, for instance refusing an invitation (*Atlas*: 98) or telling a friend about Italian pastimes (*Ci siamo*: 47).

Let us then sum up the conclusions about beginners coursebooks reached in this section:

- Scripted dialogues are primarily a way of teaching spoken language by providing a permanent record, not of teaching aspects of the written language itself.
- Written language is often a device for explaining, giving instructions etc., i.e. a kind of meta-language of teaching rather than a way-in to writing itself.
- Written language within teaching activities is mostly a pretext for spoken exercises, involving uses of language seldom encountered outside textbooks.
- Texts are mostly restricted to short quasi-factual biographies etc., with some longer texts about 'interesting facts', seldom recognisable as text types that would occur outside a teaching context.

These features seem typical of the coursebooks. Though they may be taught differently by different teachers, there is no reason to think that the average beginner will encounter a totally different range of written language than that represented in these coursebooks.

None of the courses explicitly teach any of the areas 1–8 listed above in any depth. A few courses implicitly teach aspects of the phonological processing route (3) – the different sound correspondences of <c> and <g> are briefly mentioned in *Teach Yourself Italian* (Vellacio & Elston, 1998, p. 21) and *Ci siamo* (p. 27), those for <s> in *Changes* (p. 17); most of them mention the letter names, called 'pronunciation' by *Atlas* (p. 25), and encourage students to spell words out loud using them (*Changes*: 10). Nor is there any attention to punctuation. The elements in the French writing system that differ from other European languages, such as the accents, goose-feet and cedilla, are untreated in *Libre Echange*, unless concealed in pronunciation practice such as *Le «e» tombe parfois* (*Libre Echange*: 85). Not only do these coursebooks distort the nature of written language in using it as a prop for spoken language but they also fail to approach written language systematically.

Taking English as a target L2WS, we can summarise what a proper coursebook might include:

(1) *direction.* students with L1WSs with a right-to-left direction such as Arabic need to be guided into the left-to-right nature of English.
(2) *letter formation.* Students with different alphabets in the L1WS, such as Greek, or with characters, need to be helped in the basics of letter recognition and production.
(3) *phonological processing.* Students need to learn the correspondence rules for the English writing system; students from meaning-based L1WSs need to be told the extent to which the English writing system depends upon phoneme–grapheme correspondence.
(4) *lexical processing.* Students need to be encouraged to treat English as partially meaning-based one-off symbols, say for common words and for unique words.
(5) *orthographic regularities.* Students need to know the rules that govern the pure arrangements of letters other than those that depend on letter–sound correspondences.
(6) *punctuation and typography.* Students may need instruction on the marks and layout themselves or on their specific use in English.
(7) *creativity.* Students need to appreciate the systematic deviations from the standard spelling system used in English.
(8) *functions.* Students need to know the ways in which the resources of the writing system can be used in different genres and for different purposes.

The disappointment about the coursebooks is not so much that they are doing anything wrong in terms of teaching the writing system as that they simply do not bother to cover any of these points. Yet each page they present has potential difficulties for the student coming from another writing system. Take a specimen page, say page 17 from *Atlas,* in terms of typography. This is headed '2 This is my Sister' across a full colour photo of two heads; it consists of four exercises of different types illustrated with full-colour drawings, one being of five smiling people representing a family.

- headings are in sans-serif <Warm-Up> and text in serif <Look at the picture>, a common distinction say in British newspapers but not universal.
- turns in dialogues are prefaced by speakers labelled A and B and a colon:

A: What's your name?

but without quotation marks. However some sub-headings to 'Unit Goals' are given in italics as quotations with double quotation marks

"My name is Tony Shaw."

a feature of American rather than British style.

- The overall arrangement on the page is based on a small left column for general headings and numbered tasks on the right, sometimes divided into sub-columns for vocabulary lists (bold), e.g.:

  check underline circle fill in cross out

  At one level this can be seen as relying on left-to-right, top-to-bottom arrangement, at another its lightness on the page, its use of photographs, its mixing of fonts, italics and bold face and its bitty layout, make it resemble a mail-order catalogue rather than a unified page of prose in a book. In a culture where education is presented as a serious matter, this light-hearted presentation can be considerably off-putting.

Spelling Syllabuses

Perhaps concentrating on coursebooks is unfair and writing systems have been thought about at greater length within the educational sphere. Let us take two examples of current curricula for modern languages, one set by a national body in the UK, the other by a cross-national body in Europe.

(1) *The Adult ESOL Core Curriculum in England* (DfES, 2001) is aimed at the million adults with literacy problems in the UK who do not have English as their first language, whether as ethnic minority communities, refugees, migrant workers or partners. It describes three levels – Entry (with 3 sub-levels) and Levels 1 & 2, all defined in terms of UK school curriculum equivalence; for example the end of the Entry level is the same as the UK National Curriculum Level 5. It is divided into the conventional teaching distinction of the four skills – speaking, listening, reading and writing. Here is the entire content of the section on 'Spelling and handwriting'.

Entry 1:	spell correctly some personal key words and familiar words write the letters of the alphabet using upper and lower case
Entry 2:	spell correctly the majority of personal details and familiar common words produce legible text

Entry 3: spell correctly common words and relevant key words for work and special interest
produce legible text

Level 1: spell correctly words used most often in work, studies and daily life
produce legible text

Level 2: spell correctly words used most often in work, studies and daily life, including familiar technical words
produce legible text

It is hard to see how this syllabus begins to engage with the aspects of the writing system described above. Its core is the spelling of words – 'common' words, 'key' words, 'technical' words, perhaps assuming that only the lexical meaning-based route is necessary for English (4). The description of the letter forms (2) is confined to ideas about 'legibility', hardly crucial given the illegibility of much native-produced hand-writing and that most written language is probably produced using a keyboard these days. The curriculum goes no further than a common-sense list, uninformed by any idea of writing system or of the problems inherent in switching from one writing system to another. It does not accommodate the fact that the students come with a variety of different L1 writing systems. Nor does it mention the everyday problem of EFL teachers in England that some students are not literate in their first language.

(2) *The European Framework* (Council of Europe, 2001) provides 'a common basis for the elaboration of language syllabuses, curriculum guidelines, examinations, textbooks etc. across Europe'. It lists ways in which learners can 'develop their ability to handle the writing system of a language':

(a) by simple transfer from L1;
(b) by exposure to authentic texts . . .;
(c) by memorisation of the alphabet concerned. . .;
(d) by practising cursive writing. . .;
(e) by memorising word-forms . . .;
(f) by the practice of dictation.

Unlike the UK ESOL curriculum, this seems clearly informed by a concept of what it means to teach writing systems across languages, balancing different routes and different scripts in a principled fashion, uncluttered by the long history of the teaching of English spelling. It covers aspects of (2) letter-formation, (4) the lexical route, and possibly other areas of 'transfer'; it does not need to mention others such as direction because of its limitation to languages used in Europe, which share a common left-to-right direction. But at least it is a step in the right direction.

Moral

To sum up, a systematic approach to teaching written language in the early stages of second language acquisition would:

(1) teach distinctive aspects of the written language, e.g. spelling, capital letters, punctuation, functions etc. The written language would be handled systematically, not simply as a spin-off from speech and its distinctive aspects would receive emphasis of their own.
(2) use the written language 'authentically' in the coursebook: newspapers, notices, road signs, headlines, advertisements etc. Students who attempted to get a picture of the current written language from current beginners coursebooks would get a very strange impression indeed.
(3) exploit the written language properly, i.e. employ tasks that are proper written language rather than lead-ins to writing.

References

Albrow, K.H. (1972) *The English Writing System: Notes towards a Description*. London: Longman.

Baines, P. and Haslam, A. (2002) *Type and Typography.* London: Laurence King.

Banathy, B.H. and Sawyer, J.O. (1969) The primacy of speech: An historical sketch. *Modern Language Journal* 53, 537–44.

Biber, D. (1995) *Dimensions of Register Variation*. Cambridge: Cambridge University Press.

Cook, V.J. (1970) Freedom and control in language teaching materials. In R.W. Rutherford (ed.) *BAAL Seminar Papers: Problems in the Preparation of Foreign Language Teaching Materials*. On-line at http://homepage@ntlworld.com/vivian.c/

Cook, V.J. (1980) *People and Places*. Oxford: Pergamon.

Cook, V.J. (1997) L2 users and English spelling. *Journal of Multilingual and Multicultural Development* 18 (6), 474–88.

Cook, V.J. (ed.) (2002) *Portraits of the L2 User.* Clevedon: Multilingual Matters.

Cook, V.J. (2003) Materials for adult beginners from an L2 user perspective. In B. Tomlinson (ed.) *Developing Materials for Language Teaching* (pp. 275–90). London: Continuum.

Cook, V.J. (2004) *The English Writing System*. London: Edward Arnold.

Council of Europe (2001) Common European Framework of Reference for Languages. Online at http://www.coe.int/T/E/Cultural_Co-operation/education/Languages/Language_Policy/Common_Framework_of_Reference/.

Courtillon, J. and de Salins, G.-D. (1995) *Libre Echange*. Paris: Hatier/Didier.

Derwing, B.L. (1992) Orthographic aspects of linguistic competence. In P. Downing, S.D. Lima, and M. Noonan (eds) *The Linguistics of Literacy* (pp. 193–210). Amsterdam: Benjamins.

DfES (Department for Education and Skills) (2001) Adult ESOL Core Curriculum in England. Online at http://www.dfes.gov.uk/curriculum_literacy/.

Goody, J. (2000) *The Power of the Written Tradition*. Washington: Smithsonian Institute.

Greenall, S. (1994) *Reward*. Oxford: Heinemann.

Guarnuccio, C. and Guarnuccio, E. (1997) *Ci siamo*. Victoria: CIS Heinemann.

Harmer, J. (1998) *How to Teach English*. Harlow: Longman.

Haynes, M. and Carr, T.H. (1990) Writing system background and second language reading: A component skills analysis of English reading by native speaker-readers of Chinese. In T.H. Carr and B.A. Levy (eds) *Reading and its Development: Component Skills Approaches* (pp. 375–421). San Diego: Academic Press.

Lado, R. (1964) *Language Teaching: A Scientific Approach*. New York: McGraw-Hill.

Luria, A.R. (1976) *Cognitive Development: Its Cultural and Social Foundations*. Boston: Harvard University Press.

Lyons, J. (1968) *Introduction to Theoretical Linguistics*. Cambridge: Cambridge University Press.

Nunan, D. (1995) *Atlas*. Boston: Heinle and Heinle.

Nunes, T., Bryant, P. and Bindham, M. (1997) Spelling and grammar – The NECSED Move. In C.A. Perfetti, L. Rieben and M. Fayol (eds) *Learning to Spell: Research, Theory and Practice across Languages* (pp. 151–70). Mahwah: Lawrence Erlbaum Associates.

Olson, D.R. (1996) Toward a psychology of literacy: On the relations between speech and writing. *Cognition* 60, 83–104.

Petersen, K.M., Reis, A., Askelöf, S., Castro-Caldas, A. and Ingvar, M. (2000) Language processing modulated by literacy: A network analysis of verbal repetition in literate and illiterate subjects. *Journal of Cognitive Neuroscience* 12 (3), 364–82.

Richards, J.C. (1998) *Changes*. Cambridge: Cambridge University Press.

Sassoon, R. (1995) *The Acquisition of a Second Writing System*. Exeter: Intellect.

Sassoon, R. (1999) *Handwriting of the Twentieth Century*. London: Routledge.

Seidenberg, M.S. (1992) Beyond orthographic depth in reading: Equitable division of labour. In R. Frost and L. Katz (eds) *Orthography, Phonology, Morphology, and Meaning* (pp. 85–118). Amsterdam: Elsevier.

Soars L. and Soars, J. (1993) *Headway Elementary.* Oxford: Oxford University Press.

Stern, H.H. (1983) *Fundamental Concepts of Language Teaching*. Oxford: Oxford University Press.

Vellaccio, L. and Elston, M. (1998) *Teach Yourself Italian*. London: Teach Yourself Books.

Treiman, R., Zukowski, A. and Richmond-Welty, E.D. (1995) What happened to the 'n' of 'sink'? Children's spelling of final consonant clusters. *Cognition* 55, 1–38.

Tseliga, T. (2003) *Computer-mediated Greeklish: Key Linguistic and Socio-cultural Issues*. Ph.D. dissertation, University of Brighton.

Unesco (2000) *UNESCO Statistical Yearbook*. Online at http://www.uis.unesco.org/en/stats/statistics/yearbook/YBIndexNew.htm.

Index